CITY OF GOD

POPULAR ABRIDGMENT

OF

THE DIVINE HISTORY AND LIFE

OF THE

VIRGIN MOTHER OF GOD

MANIFESTED TO MARY OF AGREDA
FOR THE ENCOURAGEMENT OF MEN

Translated from the Original Spanish

BY

FISCAR MARISON
(Rev. Geo. J. Blatter)

SIXTH PRINTING

TAN BOOKS AND PUBLISHERS, INC.
Rockford, Illinois 61105

The Mystical City of God in four volumes by Venerable Mary of Agreda was translated into English from the original Spanish by Fr. George J. Blatter (Fiscar Marison — his *nom de plume)* and published by him in 1912 with the imprint of the Theopolitan Company of Chicago, composed of Fr. Blatter, his brother, and some friends for purposes of disseminating the book. In 1929, Mr. Louis W. Bernicken assumed publication of the four volumes, and in 1949 this work was taken over by Mr. Harry D. Corcoran of Albuquerque, New Mexico under the name of the Corcoran Publishing Co. In 1971 rights to the book were purchased by Ave Maria Institute (the Blue Army) of Washington, New Jersey, the present publisher.

This popular abridgement of the four-volume work was compiled, it is believed, by Fr. Cassian Burgert, O.F.M. Cap. and was published by Mr. Bernicken. It had gone through five printings of about 1,000 copies each by the time of the printing of this paperbound edition.

IMPRIMATUR

Santa Fe, New Mexico, February 9, 1949.

I gladly give my "Imprimatur" as of today, to the new edition of the work, "The City of God" by Sister Mary of Jesus, to be reprinted from the original authorized Spanish Edition of the year 1902 without change, and already bearing the Imprimatur of His Excellency, Most Reverend H. J. Alerding, Bishop of Fort Wayne.

✠ Edwin V. Byrne, D.D.,
Archbishop of Santa Fe.

Library of Congress Catalog Card Number: 78-62255

ISBN: 0-89555-070-9

Copyright
By
Rev. Geo. J. Blatter
———
All Rights Reserved.

TAN BOOKS AND PUBLISHERS, INC.
P.O. Box 424
Rockford, Illinois 61106

CONTENTS

PART I. Books One and Two

THE CONCEPTION

BOOK ONE

BOOK TWO

1

PART II.

Books Three, Four, Five and Six

THE INCARNATION AND TRANSFIXION

BOOK THREE

BOOK FOUR

BOOK FIVE

CONTENTS 3

PART III. BOOKS SEVEN AND EIGHT

THE CORONATION

BOOK SEVEN

CONTENTS

4

BOOK EIGHT

What the Universities of Europe, the Religious Orders and Learned Men Say of the "Ciudad de Dios."

FORTY years after the first appearance of the "Ciudad de Dios" the great universities of Europe were called upon to give their opinion about this great work. All the faculties, except the Jansenistic members of the Sorbonne at Paris, published highest recommendations. At the same time the learned men and teachers of each religious order that maintained institutions of learning in Europe, were asked to contribute their opinions. The following religious orders complied: The Augustinians, Benedictines, Carmelites, Dominicans, Jesuits, Cistercians, Basilians, Trinitarians, Mercedarians, Minims, Hieronymites, Premonstratensians, Reformed Augustinians, Theatines, Minors of the Regular Clergy, all unanimously endorsing the favorable decision previously published by the University of Salamanca. To the approbation of nearly all the Universities and Religious Orders, were then added the high eulogiums of other learned men, great divines, bishops and princes of the Church and of the Popes and the Roman Congregations. As a sample of what these witnesses said concerning the wonderful "Ciudad de Dios," we here select the official approbation of the University of Louvain, one of the great Universities of Europe.

After pointing out that God's power of giving private revelations to whom He chooses, must not be circumscribed, and after referring to some general rules in regard to private revelations, the document proceeds to say:

"Now, while abiding the decision of the Church concerning the revelations, which are given us under the title of The City of God, we, having read the whole work, say and are of the opinion, that the faithful can read it without danger to their faith and without damage to the purity of morals; for there is not found anything within it, which could lead to relaxation or to indiscreet rigor; but on the contrary, we have come to the conclusion that it will be most useful for enlivening and augmenting the piety of the faithful, the veneration of the most holy Virgin, and the respect for the sacred mysteries."

"The strong and the weak, the wise and the ignorant, and in fine, all the world will gather richest fruit from the reading of these books: for they contain what is most sublime in theology and in a style so simple, easy and perspicuous that, in order to enter deeply into an understanding of the holy mysteries, no more is necessary than to read them with sound judgment."

"Combined with this simplicity are found many doctrines and valid proofs, free from contradictions and not easily found in other writings. This History explains more than a thousand difficulties in holy Scripture, in a manner equally natural and wonderful. At every step are encountered exquisite interpretations, until now unknown, and which had been hidden beneath the mere letter, but are laid open in these writings and brought to the light. In short, the whole work is a beautiful web of scripture passages which, though spun from its different books, are directly and specially woven into a whole for the purpose intended by the Venerable Mother."

"In addition thereto the instructions given by the most holy Virgin at the end of each chapter contain the purest morality, instruct, entertain, and at the same time sweetly inculcate the love of virtue and abhorrence of vice, painting them in the most vivid and natural colours. They do not only convince the intellect, but they contain such a special unction, that they enkindle a sacred ardor in the soul. In meditating upon them one certainly will experience a delight not met with in ordinary writings; and the more they are read the greater is the delight experienced. Finally, the whole work contains something so unwonted and attractive that, once begun, the reading of it can scarcely be relinquished."

"The novelty and variety found in these writings delight and recreate the reader beyond all that is pleasant in the world, at the same time instructing him and inspiring him with new fervor. All can easily persuade themselves that, if the interior life of Christ our Lord and of the most holy Virgin was not just as described in these books, it could certainly have been like it; and that it would have been well worthy of Them, if it was as it is there depicted. All that is there said is befitting the majesty and humility of Christ, and in correspondence with the holiness of the Virgin and the dignity of the Mother; since there is found nothing in the whole work which was not worthy of both one and the other.

"Notwithstanding all this, we should not at all won-

der if the book met with men who are disposed to be
critical; for what book is there which can hope to escape
the opposition of the people of our times? God has not
even provided that the sacred Scriptures should be free
from such attack among the greater part of the learned
of this world. The whole philosophy of the pagans
causes them to join the number of those who are opposed
to the cross of Christ crucified; and among that number
are also the libertines of our day."

"Of course there are certain points in this work which
might give rise to apparent difficulties, and some of them
occurred, and do occur, to us. But, in accordance with
what we have said of the excellence and usefulness of
this work, we have come to the conclusion that these few
passages must not hinder us from giving it the com-
mendation already given; besides, we must confess that
we might possibly be ourselves mistaken in making these
objections."

"This seemed to us the most reasonable course, since
in this book there is something more than human. Anything so excellent and sublime cannot be ascribed to an
over-excited imagination, since the whole work is con-
sistent throughout. Nor can it be believed to be the
work of a perverted mind, for, with a constant equanimity, it treats of the most deeply hidden and abstruse
matters without involving itself in any contradictions;
though often also it descends to innumerable minute and
particular circumstances."

"There are contained in this work such noble, such
devout circumstantial and pertinent discourses, as cannot
be the result of mere discursive thought. Nor can it be
attributed to the demon; for, from beginning to end, it

suggests and breathes nothing but humility, patience and endurance of hardships."

"Therefore, just as 'Ciudad' must without a doubt be attributed to the venerable Mother of Agreda, who is claimed as its author, so she cannot have composed it without particular help from on high. Our conclusive opinion is, that the City of God, for the good of the public, and for the advantages to be derived therefrom, should be brought forth to the light. This is our judgment, which we submit entirely to the supreme decision of the Holy See, to whom alone belongs the right of finally judging such writings."

Louvain, 20th of July 1715.

(Signed) HERMANN DAMEN,
Doctor, Professor Ordinary and Regent of the Theological Faculty, Don of Saint Peter, President of the College of Arras, Censor of Books, etc.

ANTON PARMENTIER,
Doctor, Professor Ordinary, Regent of the Theological Faculty, President of the Great College of Theologians, etc.

APPROBATIONS

THE first Pope officially to take notice of "Ciudad de Dios" was Pope Innocent XI, who, on July 3, 1686, in response to a series of virulent attacks and machinations of some members of the Sorbonne, known to be Jansenists, issued a breve permitting the publication and reading of the "Ciudad de Dios." Similar decrees were afterward issued by Popes Alexander VIII, Clement IX and Benedict XIII. These decrees were followed by two decrees of the Congregation of Rites, approved by Benedict XIV and Clement XIV, in which the authenticity of "Ciudad de Dios" as extant and written by the Venerable Servant of God, Mary of Jesus, is officially established. The great pope Benedict XIII, when he was archbishop of Benevent, used these revelations as material for a series of sermons on the Blessed Virgin. On Sept. 26, 1713, the bishop of Ceneda, Italy, objecting to the publication of the "City of God," was peremptorily ordered by the Holy Office to withdraw his objections as interfering with the decree of pope Innocent XI for the universal Church.

The process of canonization of Mary of Agreda was promoted by the Spanish bishops and other eminent men of the Church soon after her death in 1666. It has resulted so far in securing her the title of Venerabilis, thus clearing the way to her beatification, for which, let us hope, God will soon raise a promoter among the many pious and eminent men who hold in esteem her writings and have learned of her holy life and of the miracles wrought at her tomb.

The Redemptorist Fathers published a new German translation in 1885, which was approved and highly recommended by the Bishop of Ratisbon in the following terms:

"We take pleasure in giving our episcopal approbation to the annotated translation of the Spanish original "Ciudad de Dios" of Mary of Jesus and recommend this book, which will surely edify all readers and be the occasion of great spiritual blessings."

Ratisbon, September 29, 1885.

✠ IGNATIUS, Bishop of Ratisbon.

Notable is the high recommendation of the Prince-Archbishop of Salzburg, Apost. Legate, Primate of Germany, etc.

"According to the decrees of Pope Innocent XI and Clement XI the book known as 'Ciudad de Dios' written by the Venerable Servant of God, Maria de Jesus, may be read by all the faithful."

"A number of episcopal approbations, the recommendations of four renowned universities, namely, of Toulouse, Salamanca, Alcala and Louvain, and of prominent members of different orders, coincide in extolling the above-named work. The learned and pious Cardinal D'Aguirre says that he considers all the studies of fifty years of his previous life as of small consequence in comparison with the doctrines he found in this book, which in all things are in harmony with the Holy Scriptures, the Holy Fathers and Councils of the Church. The Venerable Superior-General of St. Sulpice, Abbé Emery, adds: "Only since I read the revelations of Mary of Agreda do I properly know Jesus and his Holy Mother."

"We therefore do not hesitate—in granting our episcopal approbation to—"Ciudad de Dios"—and wish to recommend it to the faithful and especially to our clergy."

✠Franz Albert,
Archbishop.

Archiepiscopal Chancery, Salzburg.
    September 12, 1885.

A more recent official approbation of "Ciudad de Dios" is from the Bishop of Tarazona, prefacing the new edition of 1911-1912.

"We, Dr. James Ozoidi y Udave, by the grace of God and of the Apostolic See, Bishop of Tarazona, Administrator Apostolic of the Diocese of Tudela, etc., etc.

Having charged the priest Don Eduardo Royo, chaplain and confessor at the convent of the Immaculate Conception of Agreda, carefully and exactly to compare the manuscript which is to serve as copy for the printing of the new edition of the "City of God" now about to be published by the religious of the above-named convent, with the authenticated autograph manuscript cf that work there preserved,—and having ascertained by a personal revision of a great part of the manuscript that the said priest has diligently and faithfully fulfilled this charge imposed upon him by us:

    We now therefore certify that this present edition of 'Ciudad de Dios,' with the exception of a few more orthographic modifications, is entirely conformable to the autograph of that work as composed and written by the Venerable Mother Mary of Jesus of Agreda.

    Tarazona, April 7, 1911.

[Diocesan Seal]   ✠James, Bishop of Tarazona.

Finally follows the official approbation of the **Right** Reverend Bishop of the Fort Wayne Diocese, where this English translation is published.

Rome City, Ind., Aug. 24, 1912.

The Rev. George J. Blatter,

Dear Rev. Father:—

My Imprimatur is herewith granted to your English translation of the work entitled 'Ciudad de Dios.' Wishing you every blessing, I remain,

Devotedly in Domino,

✠H. J. ALERDING, Bishop of Fort Wayne.

The author has made use of capital letters in the text slightly at variance with common usage, in order to avoid complication and secure greater clearness. The paragraph numbers are those of the newest Spanish edition of "Ciudad de Dios" in 1912. In the abridgment they vary slightly.

City of God is divided into three Parts and eight Books. Part I contains Books 1 and 2. Part II contains Books 3, 4, 5 and 6. Part III contains Books 7 and 8. As circumstances compel a serial publication of the four volumes, the author judged it best to head these divisions as follow:

THE CONCEPTION, Books 1 and 2.
THE INCARNATION, Books 3 and 4.
THE TRANSFIXION, Books 5 and 6.
THE CORONATION, Books 7 and 8.

PART FIRST

BOOKS I, II

THE CONCEPTION

BOOK ONE

Treats of the Divine Fore-Ordainment of Christ and His Mother as the
Highest Ideals of all Creation; of the Creation of the Angels and
Men as their Servants; of the Lineage of the Just Men,
Finally Resulting in the Immaculate Conception and
Birth of the Queen of Heaven; and of Her Life
up to Her Presentation in the Temple.

CHAPTER I.

WHY GOD REVEALED THE LIFE OF MARY IN THESE OUR TIMES.

The whole of this holy life of Mary is divided, for greater perspicuity, into three parts. The first treats of all that pertains to the first fifteen years of her life, from the moment of her most pure Conception until the moment when in her virginal womb the eternal Word assumed flesh, including all that the Most High performed for Mary during these years. The second part embraces the mystery of the Incarnation, the whole life of Christ our Lord, his Passion and Death and his Ascension into heaven, thus describing the life of our Queen in union with that of her divine Son and all that She did while living with Him. The third part contains the life of the Mother of grace during the time She lived alone, deprived of the companionship of Christ our Redeemer, until the happy hour of her transition, assumption and crowning as the Empress of heaven, where She is to live eternally as the Daughter of the Father, the Mother of the Son and the Spouse of the Holy Ghost. These three parts I subdivided into eight books, in order that they may be more convenient for use and always remain the subject of my thoughts, the spur of my will and my meditation day and night.

In order to say something of the time in which I wrote this heavenly history, it must be noticed that my father, brother Francis Coronel, and my mother, sister Catharine de Arana, my parents, founded in their own house this convent of the discalced nuns of the Immaculate Conception by the command and the will of God, which was declared to my mother, sister Catharine, in a special vision and revelation. This foundation took place on the octave of the Epiphany, January 13th, 1619. On the same day we took the habit, my mother and her two daughters; and my father took refuge in the order of our seraphic Father Saint Francis, in which two of his sons had already been living as religious. There he took the habit, made his profession, lived an exemplary life, and died a most holy death. My mother and myself received the veil on the day of the Purification of the Queen of heaven, on the second of February, 1620. On account of the youth of the other daughter her profession was delayed. The Almighty in his sheer goodness favored our family so much, that all of us were consecrated to Him in the religious state. In the eighth year of the foundation of this convent, in the twenty-fifth of my age, in the year of our Lord 1627, holy obedience imposed upon me the office of abbess, which to this day I unworthily hold. During the first ten years of the time in which I held this office, I received many commands from the Most High and from the Queen of heaven to write her holy life, and I continued in fear and doubt to resist these heavenly commands during all that time until the year 1637, when I began to write it the first time. On finishing it, being full of fears and tribulations, and being so counseled by a confessor (who directed **me** during the absence of my regular confessor), I burned all the writing containing not only this history, but many other grave and mysterious matters; for he told me, that women should not write in the Church. I obeyed his commands promptly; but I had to endure most severe reproaches on this account from my superiors and from the confessor, who knew my whole life. In order to force me to rewrite this history, they threatened me with censures. The Most High and the Queen of heaven also repeated their commands that I obey. By divine favor I begin re-writing this history on the eighth of December, 1655, on the day of the Immaculate Conception.

I confess to Thee (Matth. 11, 25) and magnify Thee, King Most High, that in thy exalted Majesty Thou hast hidden these high mysteries from the wise and from the teachers, and in thy condescension hast revealed them to me, the most insignificant and useless slave of thy Church, in order that Thou mayest be the more admired as the omnipotent Author of this history in proportion as its instrument is despicable and weak.

I saw a great and mysterious sign in heaven; I saw a Woman, a most beautiful Lady and Queen, crowned with the stars, clothed with the sun, and the moon was at her feet (Apoc. 12, 1). The holy angels spoke to me: "This is that blessed Woman, whom Saint John saw in the Apocalypse, and in whom are enclosed, deposited and sealed up the wonderful mysteries of the Redemption. So much has the most high and powerful God favored this Creature, that we, his angelic spirits, are full of astonishment. Contemplate and admire her prerogatives, record them in writing, because that is the purpose for which, according to the measure suitable to thy circumstances, they will be made manifest to thee." I was made to see such wonders, that the greatness of them took away my speech, and my admiration of them suspended my other faculties; nor do I think that all the created beings in this mortal life will ever comprehend them, as will appear in the sequel of my discourse. At another time I saw a most beautiful ladder with many rungs; around it were many angels, and a great number of them were ascending and descending upon it. His Majesty said to me: "This is the mysterious ladder of Jacob, the house of God and the portal of heaven (Gen. 28, 17); if thou wilt earnestly strive to live irreprehensible in my eyes, thou wilt ascend upon it to Me."

This promise incited my desires, set my will aflame and enraptured my spirit; with many tears I grieved, that I should be a burden to myself in my sinfulness (Job. 7, 20). I sighed for the end of my captivity and longed to arrive where there would be no obstacle to my love. In this anxiety I passed some days, trying to reform my life; I again made a general confession and corrected some of my imperfections. The vision of the ladder continued without intermission, but it was not explained to me. I made many promises to the Lord and proposed to free myself from all terrestrial things and to reserve the powers of my will entirely for his love, without allowing it to incline toward any creature, be it ever so small or unsuspicious; I repudiated all visible and sensible things. Having passed some days in these affections and sentiments, I was informed by the Most High, that the ladder signified the life of the most Holy Virgin, its virtues and sacraments. His Majesty said to me: "I desire, my spouse, that thou ascend this stair of Jacob and enter through this door of heaven to acquire the knowledge of my attributes and occupy thyself in the contemplation of my Divinity. Arise then and walk, ascend by it to Me. These angels, which surround it and accompany it, are those that I appointed as the guardians of Mary, as the defenders and sentinels of the citadel of Sion. Consider Her attentively, and, meditating on her virtues, seek to imitate them." It seemed to me then, that I ascended the ladder and that I recognized the great wonders and the ineffable prodigies of the Lord in a mere Creature and the greatest sanctity and perfection of virtue ever worked by the arm of the Almighty. At the top of the ladder I saw the Lord of hosts and the Queen of all creation. They commanded me to glorify, exalt and praise Him on account of these great mysteries and to write down so much of them, as I might bring myself to understand. The exalted and high Lord gave me a law, written not only on tablets, as He gave to Moses (Exod. 31, 18), but one wrought by his omnipotent finger in order that it might be studied and observed (Ps. 1, 2).

He moved my will so that in her presence I promised to overcome my repugnance and with her assistance to set about writing her history, paying attention to three things: First, to remember that the creature must ever seek to acknowledge the profound reverence due to God and to abase itself in proportion to the condescension of his Majesty toward men and that the effect of greater favors and benefits must be a greater fear, reverence, attention and humility; secondly, to be ever mindful of the obligation of all men, who are so forgetful of their own salvation, to consider and learn what they owe to the Queen and Mother of piety on account of the part assumed by Her in the Redemption, to think of the love and the reverence which She showed to God and the honor in which we are to hold this great Lady;

thirdly, to be willing to have my spiritual director, and if necessary the whole world, find out my littleness and vileness, and the small returns which I make for what I receive.

To these my protestations the most Holy Virgin answered: "My daughter, the world stands much in need of this doctrine, for it does not know, nor does it practice, the reverence due to the Lord omnipotent. On account of this ignorance his justice is provoked to afflict and humiliate men. They are sunken in their carelessness and filled with darkness, not knowing how to seek relief or attain to the light. This, however, is justly their lot, since they fail in the reverence and fear, which they ought to have."

Besides this the Most High and the Queen gave me many other instructions, in order to make clear to me their will in regard to this work. It seemed to me temerity and want of charity toward myself, to reject the instruction which She had promised me for narrating the course of her most holy life. It seemed equally improper to put off the writing of it, since the Most High had intimated this as the fitting and opportune time, saying to me in this regard: "My daughter, when I sent my Onlybegotten, the world, with the exception of the few souls that served Me, was in worse condition than it ever had been since its beginning; for human nature is so imperfect that if it does not subject itself to the interior guidance of my light and to the fulfillment of the precepts of my ministers by sacrificing its own judgment and following Me, who am the way, the truth and the life (John 14, 6), and by carefully observing my commandments in order not to lose my friendship, it will presently fall into the abyss of darkness and innumerable miseries, until it arrives at obstinacy in sin. From the creation and sin of the first man until I gave the law to Moses, men governed themselves according to their own inclinations and fell into many errors and sins (Rom. 5, 13). After having received the law, they again committed sin by not obeying it (John 7, 19) and thus they lived on, separating themselves more and more from truth and light and arriving at the state of complete forgetfulness. In fatherly love I sent them eternal salvation and a remedy for the incurable infirmities of human nature, thus justifying my cause. And just as I then chose the opportune time for the greater manifestation of my mercy, so I now select this time for showing toward them another very great favor. For now the hour has come and the opportune time to let men know the just cause of my anger, and they are now justly charged and convinced of their guilt. Now I will make manifest my indignation and exercise my justice and equity; I will show how well justified is my cause. In order that this may come to pass more speedily, and because it is now time that my mercy show itself more openly and because my love must not be idle, I will offer to them an opportune remedy, if they will but make use of it for returning again to my favor. Now, at this hour, when the world has arrived at so unfortunate a pass, and when, though the Word has become incarnate, mortals are more careless of their weal and seek it less; when the day of their transitory life passes swiftly at the setting of the sun of time; when the night of eternity is approaching closer and closer for the wicked and the day without a night is being born for the just; when the majority of mortals are sinking deeper and deeper into the darkness of their ignorance and guilt, oppressing the just and mocking the children of God; when my holy and divine law is despised in the management of the iniquitous affairs of state, which are as hostile as they are contrary to my Providence; when the wicked least deserve my mercy; in these predestined times, I wish to open a portal for the just ones through which they can find access to my mercy; I wish to give them a light by which they can dispel the gloom that envelops the eyes of their minds. I wish to furnish them a suitable remedy for restoring them to my grace. Happy they who find it, and blessed they who shall appreciate its value, rich they who shall come upon this treasure, and blessed and very wise those who shall search into and shall understand its marvels and hidden mysteries. I desire to make known to mortals how much intercession of Her is worth, who brought restoration of life by giving mortal existence to the immortal God. As recompense I desire that they look upon the wonders wrought by my mighty arm in that pure Creature, as upon a mirror by which they can estimate their own ingratitude. I wish to make known to them much of that, which according to my high judgment is still hidden concerning the Mother of the Word."

"I have not revealed these mysteries in the primitive Church, because they are so great, that the faithful would have been lost in the contemplation and admiration of them at a time when it was more necessary to establish firmly the law of grace and of the Gospel. Although all mysteries of religion are in perfect harmony with each other, yet human ignorance might have suffered recoil and doubt at their magnitude, when faith in the Incarnation and Redemption and the precepts of the new law of the Gospel were yet in their beginnings. On this same account the person of the incarnate Word said to his disciples at the last supper: "Many things have I to say to you; but you are not yet disposed to receive them" (John 16, 12). These words He addressed to all the world, for it was not yet capable of giving full obedience to the law of grace and full assent to the faith in the Son, much less was it prepared to be introduced into the mysteries of his Mother. But now mankind has greater need for this manifestation, and this necessity urges Me to disregard their evil disposition. And if men would now seek to please Me by reverencing, believing, and studying the wonders, which are intimately connected with this Mother of Piety, and if they would all begin to solicit her intercession from their whole heart, the world would find some relief. I will not longer withhold from men this mystical City of refuge; describe and delineate it to them, as far as thy shortcomings allow. I do not intend that thy descriptions and declarations of the life of the Blessed Virgin shall be mere opinions or contemplations, but reliable truth. They that have ears to hear, let them hear. Let those who thirst come to the living waters and leave the dried-out cisterns; let those that are seeking for the light, follow it to the end. Thus speaks the Lord, God Almighty!"

CHAPTER II.

O King, most high and most wise Lord: How incomprehensible are thy judgments, and inscrutable thy ways (Rom. 11, 24)! Invincible God, enduring forever and whose beginning is unknown (Eccli. 18, 1)! Who can understand thy greatness and who can be worthy of thy most magnificent works, or who can tell Thee why Thou hast created them (Rom. 9, 20)? For Thou art exalted above all of them and our vision cannot reach Thee and our understanding cannot comprehend Thee. Mayest Thou be blest, magnificent King, because Thou has deigned to show me, thy slave and a vile worm of the earth, great sacraments and most sublime mysteries.

I saw the Most High, at the same time understanding how his Majesty is in Himself; I received a clear intelligence and a true perception of what is meant by a God, infinite in his substance and attributes, eternal, exalted above all, being three in Person, and one true God. Three in Person, because of the three activities of knowing, comprehending and loving each other; one, so as to secure the boon of eternal unity. It is the Trinity of the Father, the Son and the Holy Ghost. The Father is not made, nor created, nor begotten, nor can He be generated or have a beginning. I perceived, that the Son derives his origin from the Father alone by eternal generation; and that They are equal in their duration from eternity; and that He is begotten by the fecundity of the intelligence of the Father. The Holy Ghost pro-

ceeds from the Father and the Son through love. In
their indivisible Trinity there is nothing which can be
called first or last, greater or smaller: all three Persons
are equally eternal and eternally equal; there is unity of
essence in a trinity of persons. Nor are the Persons
mingled in order to form one God, nor the divine substance separated or divided in order to form three Persons, being distinct as the Father, as the Son and as the
Holy Ghost. They are nevertheless one and the same
Divinity, equal in Each is the glory, and majesty, the
power, the eternity, the immensity, the wisdom and sanctity, and all the attributes. And though there are three
Persons, in whom these infinite perfections subsist, He
is the one and true God, the Holy, the Just, the Powerful, the Eternal and the Measureless.

I also obtained an understanding of the manner in
which this Trinity comprehends Itself by simple vision,
so that no new or distinct cognition is necessary: the
Father knows that, which is known to the Son, and the
Son and the Holy Ghost know that which is in the intelligence of the Father. I understood how they love
One another with one and the same immense and eternal
love; how there is a single, indivisible and equal oneness
of intelligence, love and action, how there is one simple,
incorporeal and indivisible nature, a divine essence of the
true God, in which are joined and united all the perfections in their highest and in an infinite degree.

I learnt also to understand the quality of these perfections of the highest Lord: that He is beautiful without a blemish, great without quantity, good without need
of qualification, eternal without the duration of time,
strong without any weakness, living without touch of
decay, true without deceit, present in all places, filling
them without occupying them, existing in all things with-

out occupying any space. There is no contradiction in his kindness, nor any defect in his wisdom. In his wisdom He is inscrutable, in his decrees He is terrible, in his judgments just, in his thoughts most hidden, in his words most true, in his works holy, in his riches affluent. To Him no space is too wide, no narrowness causes restraint, his will does not vary, the sorrowful does not cause Him pain, the past has not passed for Him, nor does the future happen in regard to Him. O eternal Immensity, what illimitable expansion have I seen in Thee? What vastness do I see in thy infinite Being? Vision does not terminate, nor ever exhaust itself in thy abyss of being. This is the unchangeable Essence, the Being above all other beings, the most perfect sanctity, the most constant truth; this is the infinite, the length, the breadth, the height and the depth, glory and its cause, rest without fatigue, goodness immeasurable.

I understood, that the Most High was in the quiescent state of his own being, when the three Persons (according to our way of understanding things), decreed to communicate his perfections as a free gift. For greater clearness, I must remark, that God comprehends in Himself all things by one indivisible, most simple and instantaneous act. He does not go on from the understanding of one thing to the understanding of another like we do, distinguishing and perceiving first one thing by an act of the understanding, and after that proceeding to the knowledge of others by their connection with those already known. God knows them conjointly all at once, without before or after, since all are together and at once contained in the divine and uncreated knowledge and science, just as they are comprehended and enclosed in his infinite Being, as in their first beginning.

Although this divine knowledge is one, most simple and indivisible, nevertheless, since the things which I see are many, and since there is a certain order, by which some are first and some come after, it is necessary to divide the knowledge of God's intelligence and the knowledge of his will into many instants, or into many different acts, according as they correspond to the diverse orders of created things. For as some of the creatures hold their existence because of others, there is a dependence of one upon the other. Accordingly we say that God intended and decreed this before that, the one on account of the other; and that if He had not desired or included in the science of vision the one, He would not have desired the other. But by this way of speaking, we must not try to convey the meaning that God placed many acts of intelligence, or of the will; rather we must intend merely to indicate, that the creatures are dependent on each other and that they succeed one another. In order to be able to comprehend the manner of creation more easily, we apply the order of things as we see them objectively, to the acts of the divine intelligence and will in creating them.

I understood, that this order comprises the following instants. The first instant is: God recognizing his infinite attributes and perfections together with the propensity and the ineffable inclination to communicate Himself outwardly. This knowledge of God as being communicative *ad extra* comes first. The Majesty of God, beholding the nature of his infinite perfections, their virtue and efficacy operating with magnificence, saw, that it was just and most proper, and, as it were, a duty and a necessity, to communicate Himself and to follow that inclination of imparting and exercising his liberality and mercy, by distributing outside of Himself with magnificence the plenitude of the infinite treasures, contained in the Divinity. For, being infinite in all things, it is much more natural that He communicate gifts and graces, than that fire should ascend, or the stone should gravitate toward its center, or that the sun should diffuse its light. This unfathomable depth of perfections, this affluence of treasures, this impetuous infinity of riches, is set in motion by its own inclinations to communicate itself. At the same time God is in Himself conscious that to distribute gifts and graces, is not to diminish his riches, but to increase them in the only possible way, by giving an outlet to the inexhaustible fountain of his riches.

In this enlightenment and knowledge which I possess, two things hold my lukewarm heart in wonder and inflame it unto annihilation. The first is the inclination and urgent desire, which I see in God, and the strong will, to communicate his Divinity and the treasures of his grace. The second is the unspeakable and incomprehensible immensity of the good gifts, which I see He wishes to distribute according to this degree, assigning them for this purpose and yet remaining infinite, as if He had yet given nothing. In this desire and inclination, which fills his Majesty I see Him prepared to sanctify, justify, overwhelm with gifts and perfections all creatures together and each one in particular for itself. He would be ready to give to each of the creatures more than what is held by all the angels and seraphim together; even if all the drops in the ocean and the grains of sand on their shores, all the stars, the planets and the elements, and all creatures were capable of reason and of his gifts, they would receive them without measure, provided they would dispose themselves and place no obstacle toward receiving them. O fearful malice of sin, which alone is capable of holding up the impetuous stream of such great and eternal gifts!

The second instant was to confirm and determine the object and intention of this communication of the Divinity *ad extra,* namely, that it should redound to his greater glory and to the exaltation of his Majesty and the manifestation of his greatness. This his own exaltation God saw as the end, for which He would communicate Himself, make Himself known by his liberality in the distribution of his attributes, and set in motion his Omnipotence in order that He might be known, praised and glorified.

The third instant consisted in selecting and determining the order and arrangement, or the mode of this communication, so as to realize in an adequate manner the most exalted ends. The order namely, which it is proper should be maintained in regard to the communications of the Godhead and its divine attributes; so that this activity of the Lord may have its proper reasons and objects, and so that it might proceed with the most beautiful and admirable sequence, harmony and subordination. In this instant was decreed first of all, that the divine Word should assume flesh and should become visible. The perfection and the composition of the most holy humanity of Christ our Lord was decreed and modeled in the divine intelligence. Secondarily, also were formed the ideals of the rest of men in imitation of the First. The divine mind prearranged the harmony and adornment of the human nature composed of an organic body and a vivifying soul, endowed with faculties to know and enjoy its Creator, to discern between good and evil, and with a free will to love that same Lord.

The fourth instant was to determine the gifts and

graces, which were to be conferred upon the humanity of Christ, our Lord, in union with the Divinity. Here the Most High opened the liberal hands of his Omnipotence and his other attributes, in order to enrich the most sacred humanity and the soul of Christ with the highest possible plenitude of his gifts and graces. Then was fulfilled what afterward David said: "The stream of the river maketh the city of God joyful" (Ps. 45, 5). When the stream of his gifts flowed toward the humanity of the Word, communicating to it all the infused science, the grace and goodness of which his blessed soul was capable, and which fitted that Being, which was to be God and true man, and at the same time, the Head of all creatures capable of grace and glory, in order that from this impetuous stream they might partake in the manner in which it afterwards really happened.

To this instant also, and, as it were, in natural sequence, pertain the decree and predestination of the Mother of the Divine Word incarnate; for here, I understand, was ordained that pure Creature before aught else whatever. Thus, before all other creatures, was She conceived in the divine mind, in such manner and such state as befitted and became the dignity, excellence and gifts of the humanity of her most holy Son. To Her flowed over, at once and immediately, the river of the Divinity and its attributes with all its impetuosity, in as far as a mere creature is capable and as is due to the dignity of the Mother of God.

In the knowledge of these exalted mysteries and decrees, I confess myself ravished in admiration and transported beyond my proper self. Perceiving this most holy and pure Creature formed and conceived in the divine mind from the beginning and before all the ages, I joyously and exultingly magnify the Omnipotent for the admirable and mysterious decree, by which He formed for us such a pure and grand, such a mysterious and godlike Creature, worthy rather to be admired and praised by all beings, than to be described by any one. In my admiration I can say with St. Dionysius the Areopagite: "If faith would not instruct me, and if the understanding of what I see would not teach me, that it is God, who has conceived Her in his mind, and who alone could and can in his Omnipotence form such an image of his Divinity, if this all were not present to my mind, I might begin to doubt, whether the Virgin Mother contain not in Herself Divinity."

O what tears flowed from my eyes, and what sorrowful astonishment possessed my soul, to see that divine prodigy not acknowledged and that wonder of the Most High not manifest to all the mortals. Much is known of it, but much more is unknown, as this sealed book has not been opened. I am ravished in the perception of this tabernacle of God, and I perceive that the Author of it is more admirable in her creation, than in that of all the rest of the world, although the diversity of the creatures manifests the wonderful power of their Creator. In this Queen alone are comprehended and contained more treasures than in all the rest of things joined together, and the variety and the preciousness of her riches honor the Lord above all the multitudes of the other creatures.

Here (according to our way of understanding) the promise and, as it were, the contract was made with the Word as to the degree of sanctity, and perfection and the gifts and graces, which were to be possessed by Mary his Mother. Also as to the protection, support and defense, which was to be provided for this true City of God, in which his Majesty contemplated the graces and merits, which She earned for Herself, as well as the fruits to be gathered for his people by the loving returns, which She was to make to his Majesty. In the same instant, and as it were in the third and last place, God determined to create a locality and an abode, where the incarnate Word and his Mother should converse and dwell. For Them primarily did He create the heaven and earth with its stars and elements and all that is contained in them. Secondarily the intention and decree included the creation of the members, of which Jesus was to be the Head, and of whom He would be the King; in order that with kingly providence, all the necessary and befitting arrangements might be made beforehand.

I pass over to the fifth instant, although in reality I have found that, which I sought. In this fifth decree the creation of the angelic nature which is more excellent and more like unto the spiritual being of the Divinity, was determined upon, and at the same time the division or arrangement of the angelic hosts into nine choirs and three hierarchies, was provided and decreed. As they are created first of all for the glory of God, to assist before his divine Majesty and to know and love Him, so secondarily they are ordained to assist, glorify and honor, reverence and serve the deified humanity of the eternal Word, recognizing Him as Head, and honoring Him also in his Mother, the most holy Mary, Queen of these same angels. Commission was given to these angels, "to bear them up in their hands" in all their ways (Ps. 90, 12). In this instant Christ our Lord earned for them by his infinite merits, present and foreseen, all the grace, which they were to receive. He was constituted as their Head, Exemplar and supreme King, of whom they should be subjects. Even if the number of angels had been infinite, the merits of Christ our highest Good, would be abundantly sufficient to supply them all with grace.

To this instant belongs also the predestination of the good, and the reprobation of the bad angels. God saw in it, by means of his infinite science, all the works of the former and of the latter and the propriety of predestinating, by his free will and by his merciful liberality, those that would obey and give honor, and of reprobating by his justice those who would rise up against his Majesty in pride and disobedience on account of their disordered selflove. In the same instant also was decreed the creation of the empyrean heaven, for the manifestation of his glory and the reward of the good; also the earth and other heavenly bodies for the other creatures; moreover also in the center or depth of the earth, hell, for the punishment of the bad angels.

In the sixth instant was decreed the creation of a people and congregation of men for Christ, who was already formed in the divine mind and will, and according to whose image and likeness man was to be made, in order, that the incarnate Word might find brethren, similar but inferior to Himself and a people of his own nature, of whom He might be the Head. In this instant was determined the order of the creation of the whole human race, which was to begin from one man and woman and propagate itself, until the Virgin and her Son should be born in the predestined order. On account of the merits of Christ, our Savior, the graces and gifts were prearranged, and also original justice, if they would only preserve it. The fall of Adam was foreseen and in him that of all others, except of the Queen, who did not enter into this decree. As a remedy, it was ordained that the most holy humanity should be capable of suffering. The predestined were chosen by free grace, and the foreknown were reprobated with exact justice. All that was convenient and necessary for the conservation of the human race and for obtaining the end of the Redemption and the Predestination, was preordained, without interfering with the free will of men; for such ordainment was more conformable to God's nature and to divine equity. There was no injustice done to them, for if with their free will they could sin, so also could they abstain from sin by means of grace and the light of reason. God violated the right of no one, since He forsook no one nor denied to any one that which is necessary. Since his law is written in the hearts of men, nobody is excused for not knowing and loving Him as the highest Good of all creation.

In the perception of these mysteries I saw with great clearness and force the high motives which caused God to manifest and magnify Himself and which should induce men to praise and adore the greatness of the Creator and Redeemer of all. I also saw how tardy they are in the acknowledgment of these obligations and in making return for these benefits; and I was made aware of the complaints and the indignation of the Most High on account of this forgetfulness. His Majesty commanded and exhorted me not to be guilty of such ingratitude, but to offer Him a sacrifice of praise, and a new song, and that I magnify Him in the name of all creatures.

O most high and incomprehensible Lord! Would that I had the love and the perfections of all the angels and the just in order to confess and praise worthily thy greatness! I acknowledge, great and mighty Lord, that such a vile creature as I cannot merit the memorable benefit of receiving this clear and exalted knowledge and light concerning thy exalted Majesty. At the sight of thy greatness I perceive my littleness, which before that happy hour was unknown to me; and I was ignorant of the greatness and excellence of the virtue of humility, which is learnt in this science. I do not wish to say that I now possess that virtue, but neither can I deny that I have been shown the certain path which leads to it. Thy light, O most high Lord, illumines me and thy lamp shows me the paths (Ps. 118, 105), so that I see what I have been and what I am, and fear what I may become to be. Thou hast lighted up, most high King, my understanding and inflamed my will with its most exalted object.

CHAPTER III.

CREATION OF THE ANGELS AND THE FALL OF LUCIFER.

The Cause of all causes is God, who created all things that have being. His powerful arm gave existence to all his wonderful works *ad extra* when and how He chose. The beginning and succession of the work of Creation is described by Moses in the opening chapter of Genesis. Since the Lord has given me an understanding thereof, I will mention what I think useful for elucidating the mysterious origin of the Incarnation of the Word and of our Redemption.

The words of the first chapter of Genesis are as follows:

1. "In the beginning God created heaven and earth.

2. "And the earth was void and empty, and darkness was upon the face of the deep; and the spirit of God moved over the waters.

3. "And God said: Be light made. And light was made.

4. "And God saw the light that it was good; and he divided the light from the darkness.

5. "And he called the light day, and the darkness night; and there was evening and morning one day," etc.

Of the first day Moses says that "In the beginning God created heaven and earth." He created heaven for angels and men; and the earth as a place of pilgrimage for mortals. These places are so adapted to their end and so perfect, that as David says of them, the heavens publish the glory of the Lord, the firmament and the earth announce the glory of the works of his hands (Ps. 18, 2).

The angels were created in the empyrean heavens and in the state of grace by which they might be first to merit the reward of glory. For although they were in the midst of glory, the Divinity itself was not to be made manifest to them face to face and unveiled, until they should have merited such a favor by obeying the divine will. The holy angels, as well as the bad ones, remained only a very short time in the state of probation; for their creation and probation with its result were three distinct instants or moments, separated by short intermissions. In the first instant they were all created and endowed with graces and gifts, coming into existence as most beautiful and perfect creatures. Then followed a short pause, during which the will of the Creator was propounded and intimated, and the law and command was given them, to acknowledge Him as their Maker and supreme Lord, and to fulfill the end for which they had been created. During this pause, instant or interval, Saint Michael and his angels fought that great battle with the dragon and his followers, which is described by the apostle Saint John in the twelfth chapter of the Apocalypse. The good angels, persevering in grace, merited eternal happiness and the disobedient ones, rebelling against God, merited the punishment, which they now suffer.

At first they received a more explicit intelligence of the being of God, one in substance, trine in person, and that they were commanded to adore and reverence Him as their Creator and highest Lord, infinite in his essence and attributes. All subjected themselves to this command and obeyed it, but with a certain difference; the good angels obeyed through love and on account of the justice of it, offering their love and good will, freely admitting and believing what was above their intelligence, and obeying with joy. Lucifer, on the other hand, submitted himself, because the opposite seemed to him impossible. He did not do it with perfect charity, for he, as it were, was divided in his will between himself and the infallible truth of the Lord. In consequence it happened that the precept appeared to him in a measure difficult and violent, and his fulfilling of it was wanting in love and in the desire to do justice. Thus he exposed himself beforehand to the danger of not persevering. Although grace did not leave him on account of this remissness and slowness in the accomplishment of these first acts, nevertheless his bad disposition began with them; for there remained with him a certain weakness and laxity of virtue and spirit, and the perfection of his nature did not shine forth as it should. It appears to me that the effect of this remissness in Lucifer, is similar to that which is caused in the soul by a deliberate venial sin. I do not say that he sinned mortally, nor even venially at that time, since he fulfilled the precept of God; but this fulfillment was remiss and imperfect, springing more from a sense of overwhelming compulsion, than from a loving willingness to obey. Thus he put himself in danger of falling.

In the second place, the angels were informed that God was to create a human nature and reasoning creatures lower than themselves, in order that they too should love, fear and reverence God, as their Author and eternal Good. They were informed that these were to stand in high favor, and that the second Person of the blessed Trinity was to become incarnate and assume their nature, raising it to the hypostatic union and to divine Personality; that therefore they were to acknowledge Him as their Head, not only as God, but as God and man, adoring Him and reverencing Him as God-man. Moreover, these same angels were to be his inferiors in dignity and grace and were to be his servants. God gave them an intelligence of the propriety and equity, of the justice and reasonableness of such a position. For the acceptation of the merits foreseen of this Mangod was exhibited to them as the source of the grace which they now possessed and of the glory which they were to obtain. They understood also that they themselves had been, and all the rest of the creatures should be created for his glory, and that He was to be their Head. All those that were capable of knowing and enjoying God, were to be the people of the Son of God, to know and reverence Him as their Chief. These commands were at once given to the angels.

To this command all the obedient and holy angels submitted themselves and they gave their full assent and acknowledgment with an humble and loving subjection of the will. But Lucifer, full of envy and pride, resisted and induced his followers to resist likewise, as they in reality did, preferring to follow him and disobey the divine command. This wicked prince persuaded them, that he would be their chief and that he would set up a government independent and separate from Christ. So great was the blindness which envy and pride could cause in an angel, and so pernicious was the infection that the contagion of sin spread among innumerable other angels.

Then happened that great battle in heaven, which St. John describes (Apoc. 12). For the obedient and holy angels, filled with an ardent desire of hastening the glory of the Most High and the honor of the incarnate Word, asked permission and, as it were, the consent of God, to resist and contradict the dragon, and the permission was granted. But also another mystery was concealed in all this: When it was revealed to the angels that they would have to obey the incarnate Word, another, a third precept was given them, namely, that they were to admit as a superior conjointly with Him, a Woman, in whose womb the Onlybegotten of the Father was to assume flesh and that this Woman was to be the Queen and Mistress of all the creatures. The good angels by obeying this command of the Lord, with still increasing and more alert humility, freely subjected themselves, praising the power and the mysteries of the Most High. Lucifer, however, and his confederates, rose to a higher pitch of pride and boastful insolence. In disorderly fury he aspired to be himself the head of all the human race and of the angelic orders, and if there was to be a hypostatic union, he demanded that it be consummated in him.

The decree constituting him inferior to the Mother of the Incarnate Word, our Mistress, he opposed with horrible blasphemies. Turning against the Author of these great wonders in unbridled indignation and calling upon the other angels, he exhorted them, saying: "Unjust are these commands and injury is done to my greatness; this human nature which Thou, Lord, lookest upon with so much love and which thou favorest so highly, I will persecute and destroy. To this end I will direct all my power and all my aspirations. And this Woman, Mother of the Word, I will hurl from the position in which Thou hast proposed to place Her, and at my hands, the plan, which Thou settest up, shall come to naught."

This proud boast so aroused the indignation of the Lord that in order to humble it, He spoke to Lucifer: "This Woman, whom thou refusest to honor, shall crush thy head and by Her shalt thou be vanquished and annihilated (Gen. 3, 15). And if, through thy pride, death enters into the world (Wis. 2, 24), life and salvation of mortals shall enter through the humility of this Woman. Those that are of the nature and likeness of that Man and Woman, shall enjoy the gifts and the crowns, which thou and thy followers have lost." To all this the dragon, filled with indignation against whatever he understood of the divine will and decrees, answered only with pride and by threatening destruction to the whole human race. The good angels saw the just indignation of the Most High against Lucifer and his apostates and they combated them with the arms of the understanding, reason and truth.

The Almighty at this conjuncture worked another wonderful mystery. Having given to all the angels a sufficiently clear intelligence of the great mystery of the hypostatic Union, He showed them the image of the most holy Virgin by means of an imaginary vision (I speak here according to our way of understanding such things). They were shown the perfection of the human nature in the revelation of an image representing a most perfect Woman, in whom the almighty arm of the Most High would work more wonderfully than in all the rest of the creatures. For therein He was to deposit the graces and gifts of his right hand in a higher and more eminent manner. This sign or vision of the Queen of heaven and of the Mother of the incarnate Word was made known and manifest to all the angels, good and bad. The good ones at the sign of it broke forth in admiration and in canticles of praise and from that time on began to defend the honor of the God incarnate and of his holy Mother, being armed with ardent zeal and with the invincible shield of that vision. The dragon and his allies on the contrary conceived implacable hatred and fury against Christ and his most holy Mother. Then happened all that which is described in the twelfth chapter of the Apocalypse, which I will explain, as far as it has been given me.

The literal version of that chapter of the Apocalypse is as follows:

1. "And a great sign appeared in heaven: A woman clothed with the sun and the moon under her feet, and on her head a crown of twelve stars:

2. And being with child, she cried travailing in birth, and was in pain to be delivered.

3. And there was seen another sign in heaven; and behold a great red dragon having seven heads and ten horns; and on his head seven diadems.

4. And his tail drew the third part of the stars of heaven and cast them to the earth and the dragon stood before the woman, who was ready to be delivered; that, when she should be delivered, he might devour her son.

5. And she brought forth a man-child, who was to rule all nations with an iron rod; and her son was taken up to God, and to his throne.

6. And the woman fled into the wilderness where she had a place prepared by God, that there they should feed her a thousand two hundred and sixty days.

7. And there was a great battle in heaven; Michael and his angels fought with the dragon and the dragon fought and his angels.

8. And they prevailed not, neither was their place found any more in heaven.

9. And the dragon was cast out, that old serpent, who is called the devil and satan, who seduceth the

whole world; and he was cast unto the earth, and his angels were thrown down with him.

10. And I heard a loud voice saying: Now is come salvation and strength, and the kingdom of our God and the power of his Christ; because the accuser of our brethren is cast forth, who accused them before our God day and night.

11. And they overcame him by the blood of the Lamb and by the word of the testimony, and they loved not their lives unto death.

12. Therefore rejoice, O heavens, and you that dwell therein. Woe to the earth and the sea, because the devil is come down unto you, having a great wrath and knowing that he hath but a short time.

13. And when the dragon saw that he was cast unto the earth he persecuted the woman, who brought forth the man-child:

14. And there were given to the woman two wings of a great eagle, that she might fly into the desert unto her place, where she is nourished for a time and times and half a time, from the face of the serpent.

15. And the serpent cast out of his mouth after the woman, water as if it were a river, that he might cause her to be carried away by the river.

16. And the earth helped the woman and the earth opened her mouth and swallowed the river, which the dragon cast out of his mouth.

17. And the dragon was angry against the woman and went to make war with the rest of her seed, who keep the commandments of God, and have the testimony of Jesus Christ.

18. And he stood upon the sands of the sea."

CHAPTER IV.

On the sixth day he formed and created Adam, as it were of the age of thirty-three years. This was the age in which Christ was to suffer death, and Adam in regard to his body was so like unto Christ, that scarcely any difference existed. Also according to the soul Adam was similar to Christ. From Adam God formed Eve so similar to the Blessed Virgin, that she was like unto Her in personal appearance and in figure. God looked upon these two images of the great Originals with the highest pleasure and benevolence, and on account of the Originals He heaped many blessings upon them, as if He wanted to entertain Himself with them and their descendants until the time should arrive for forming Christ and Mary.

But the happy state in which God had created the parents of the human race lasted only a very short while. The envy of the serpent was immediately aroused against them, for satan was impatiently awaiting their creation, and no sooner were they created, than his hatred became active against them. However, he was not permitted to witness the formation of Adam and Eve, as he had witnessed the creation of all other things: for the Lord did not choose to manifest to him the creation of man, nor the formation of Eve from a rib; all these things were concealed from him for a space of time until both of them were joined. But when the demon saw the admirable composition of the human nature, perfect beyond that of any other creature, the beauty of the souls and also of the bodies of Adam and Eve; when he saw the paternal love with which the Lord regarded them, and how He made them the lords of all creation, and that He gave them hope of eternal life: the wrath of the dragon was lashed to fury, and no tongue can describe the rage with which that beast was filled, nor how great was his envy and his desire to take the life of these two beings. Like an enraged lion he certainly would have done so, if he had not known, that a superior force would prevent him. Nevertheless he studied and plotted out some means, which would suffice to deprive them of the grace of the Most High and make them God's enemies.

Here Lucifer was deceived; for the Lord had from the beginning mysteriously manifested to him, that the Word was to assume human nature in the womb of the most holy Mary, but not how and when; and thus He had also concealed the creation of Adam and the formation of Eve, in order that Lucifer might from the beginning labor under his ignorance concerning the mystery and the time of the Incarnation. As his wrath and his watchfulness had thus been so signally forestalled in regard to Christ and Mary, he suspected that Adam had come forth from Eve, and that She was the Mother and Adam the incarnate Word. His suspicions grew, when he felt the divine power, which prevented him from harming the life of these creatures. On the other hand he soon became aware of the precepts of God, for these did not remain concealed from him, since he heard their conversation in regard to them. Being freed more and more from his doubt as he listened to the words of the first parents and sized up their natural gifts, he began to follow them like a roaring lion (I Pet. 5, 8), seeking an entrance through those inclinations, which he found in each of them. Nevertheless, until he was undeceived in the course of the Redemption, he continued to hesitate between his wrath against Christ and Mary and the dread of being overcome by Them. Most of all he dreaded the confusion of being conquered by the Queen of heaven, who was to be a mere creature and not God.

Taking courage therefore in the precept, which was given to Adam and Eve, and having prepared the snare, Lucifer entered with all his energy upon the work of entrapping them and of opposing and hindering the execution of the divine Will. He first approached the woman, and not the man, because he knew her to be by nature more frail and weak, and because in tempting her he would be more certain that it was not Christ whom he was encountering. Against her also he was more enraged ever since he had seen the sign in the heaven and since the threat, which God had made in it against him. On all these accounts his wrath was greater against Eve than against Adam. Before he showed himself to her, however, he aroused in her many disturbing thoughts or imaginations, in order to approach her in a state of excitement and pre-occupation. But because I have written about this in another place, I will not enlarge here upon the violence and inhumanity of this temptation; it is enough for my purpose to mention what Scripture says: that he took the form of a serpent (Gen. 2, 1), and thus speaking to Eve drew her into a conversation, which she should not have permitted. Listening to him and answering, she began to believe him; then she violated the command of God, and finally persuaded her husband likewise to transgress the precept. Thus ruin overtook them and all the rest: for themselves and for us they lost the happy position, in which God had placed them.

When Lucifer saw the two fallen and their interior beauty and grace and original justice changed into the ugliness of sin, he celebrated his triumph with incredible joy and vaunting in the company of his demons. But he soon fell from his proud boasting, when he saw, contrary to his expectations, how kindly the merciful love of God dealt with the delinquents, and how He offered them a chance of doing penance by giving them hope of pardon and return of grace. Moreover he saw how they were disposing themselves toward this forgiveness by sorrow and contrition, and how the beauty of grace was restored to them. When the demons perceived the effect of contrition, all hell was again in confusion. His consternation grew, when he heard the sentence, which God pronounced against the guilty ones, in which he himself was implicated. More especially and above all was he tormented by the repetition of that threat: The Woman shall crush thy head (Gen. 3, 15), which he had already heard in heaven.

The offspring of Eve multiplied after the fall and so arose the distinction and the multiplication of the good and the bad, the elect and the reprobate, the ones following Christ the Redeemer, and the others following satan. The elect cling to their Leader by faith, humility, charity, patience and all the virtues and in order to obtain victory, they are assisted, helped and beautified by the divine grace and the gifts, which the Redeemer and Lord of all merited for them. But the reprobate, without receiving any such benefits from their false leader, or earning any other reward than the eternal pain and the confusion of hell, follow him in pride, presumption, obscenity and wickedness, being led into these disorders by the father of lies and the originator of sin.

Notwithstanding all this the Most High, in his

ineffable kindness, gave our first parents his benediction, in order that the human race might grow and multiply (Gen. 4, 3). The most high Providence permitted, that Eve, in the unjust Cain, should bring forth a type of the evil fruits of sin, and in the innocent Abel, both in figure and in imitation, the type of Christ our Lord. For in the first just one the law and doctrine of Christ began to exert its effects. All the rest of the just were to follow it, suffering for justice sake (Matth. 10, 22), hated and persecuted by the sinners and the reprobate and by their own brothers. Accordingly, patience, humility and meekness began to appear in Abel, and in Cain, envy and all wickedness, for the benefit of the just and for his own perdition. The wicked triumph and the good suffer, exhibiting the spectacle, which the world in its progress shows to this day, namely, the Jerusalem of the godfearing and the Babylon of the godforsaken, each with its own leader and head.

The Most High also wished that the first Adam should be the type of the second in the manner of their creation; for, just as before the creation of the first, He created and ordered for him the republic of all the beings, of which he was to be the lord and head; so before the appearance of his Onlybegotten, He allowed many ages to pass by, in order that his Son might, in the multiplied numbers of the human race, find prepared for Himself a people, of which He was to be the Head, the Teacher, and the King. He was not to be even for a moment without a people and without followers: such is the wonderful harmony and order, in which the divine wisdom disposed all things, making that later in the execution, which was first in the intention.

As the world progressed in its course, in order that the Word might descend from the bosom of the

Father and clothe Itself in our mortality, God selected and prepared a chosen and most noble people, the most admirable of past and future times. Within it also He constituted a most illustrious and holy race, from which He was to descend according to the flesh. I will not linger in detailing the genealogy of Christ our Lord, for the account of the holy Evangelists has made that unnecessary. I will only say, in praise of the Most High, that He has shown to me many times the incomparable love, which He bore toward his people, the favors shown to it, and the mysteries and holy Sacraments, which He entrusted to it, as was afterwards made manifest through his holy Church. For at no time has slept nor slumbered He, who has constituted Himself the watcher of Israel (Ps. 120, 4).

He reared most holy Prophets and Patriarchs, who in figures and prophecies announced to us from far off, that, which we have now in possession. He wishes us to venerate them, knowing how they esteemed the law of grace and how earnestly they yearned and prayed for it. To this people God manifested his immutable Essence by many revelations, and they again transmitted these revelations to us by the holy Scriptures, containing immense mysteries, which we grasp and learn to know by faith. All of them, however, are brought to perfection and are made certain by the incarnate Word, who transmitted to us the secure rule of faith and the nourishment of the sacred Scriptures in his Church. Although the Prophets and the just ones of that people were not so far favored as to see Christ in his body, they nevertheless experienced the liberality of the Lord, who manifested Himself to them by prophecies and who moved their hearts to pray for his coming and for the Redemption of the whole human race. The consonance and harmony of all these prophecies, mysteries and aspirations of the ancient fathers, were a sweet music to the Most High, which resounded in the secret recesses of the Divinity and which regaled and shortened the time (to speak in a human manner) until He should descend to converse with man.

CHAPTER V.

The posterity and race of Adam spread out in
great numbers, for the just and the unjust were multiplied; likewise did increase the clamors of the just for
the Redeemer, and the transgressions of the wicked in
demerit of that benefit. The people of the Most High
and the plans for the triumph of the Lord in assuming
human nature, were already in the last stages of preparation for the advent of the Messias. The kingdom
of sin in the generation of the wicked had now spread
its dominion to the utmost limits and the opportune time
for the remedy had arrived.

When the ancient serpent had infected the whole
earth with its poisonous breath and apparently enjoyed
peaceful control over mortals who had become blind
to the light of reason (Rom. 1, 20) and to the precepts
contained in the ancient written law, when, instead of
seeking the true Divinity, men set up for themselves
many false laws and each one created a god for himself
according to his liking, without considering, that the confusion of so many gods was repugnant to all goodness,
order, and peace, when by these errors malice, ignorance and forgetfulness of the true God had become
naturalized; when, ignorant of its mortal disease and
lethargy, the world had grown mute in its prayer for
deliverance; when pride reigned supreme and fools had
become innumerable (Eccles. 9, 15); when Lucifer in

53

his arrogance was about to swallow the pure waters of the Jordan (Job 40, 18): when through these injuries God was more and more deeply offended and less and less beholden to man; when his justice had such an excellent cause for annihilating all creation and reducing it to its original nothingness:

At this juncture (according to our way of understanding), the Most High directed his attention to the attribute of his mercy, counterbalanced the weight of his incomprehensible justice with the law of clemency, and chose to yield more to his own goodness, to the clamors and faithful services of the just and the prophets of his people, than to his indignation at the wickedness and sins of all the rest of mankind. In this dark night of the ancient law, He resolved to give most certain pledges of the day of grace, sending into the world two most bright luminaries to announce the approaching dawn of the sun of Justice, Christ our Salvation. These were saint Joachim and Anne, prepared and created by especial decree according to his own heart. Saint Joachim had his home, his family and relations in Nazareth, a town of Galilee. He, always a just and holy man and illumined by especial grace and light from on high, had a knowledge of many mysteries of the holy Scriptures and of the olden Prophets. In continual and fervent prayer he asked of God the fulfillment of his promises, and his faith and charity penetrated the heavens. He was a man most humble and pure, leading a most holy and sincere life, yet he was most grave and earnest, and incomparably modest and honest.

The most fortunate Anne had a house in Bethlehem and was a most chaste, humble and beautiful maiden. From her childhood she led a most virtuous, holy and retired life, enjoying great and continual enlightenment in exalted contemplation. Withal she was most diligent and industrious, thus attaining perfection in both the active and the contemplative life. She had an infused knowledge of the divine Scriptures and a profound understanding of its hidden mysteries and sacraments. In the infused virtues of faith, hope and love she was unexcelled. Equipped with all these gifts, she continued to pray for the coming of the Messias. Her prayers were so acceptable to the Lord, that to her He could but answer with the words of the Spouse: "Thou hast wounded my heart with one of the hairs of thy neck" (Cant. 4, 9). Therefore, without doubt, saint Anne holds a high position among the saints of the old Testament, who by their merits hastened the coming of the Redeemer.

This woman also prayed most fervently, that the Almighty deign to procure for her in matrimony a husband, who should help her to observe the ancient law and testament, and to be perfect in the fulfillment of all its precepts. At the moment in which saint Anne thus prayed to the Lord, his Providence ordained, that saint Joachim made the same petition: both prayers were presented at the same time before the tribunal of the holy Trinity, where they were heard and fulfilled, it being then and there divinely disposed, that Joachim and Anne unite in marriage and become the parents of Her, who was to be the Mother of the incarnate God. In furtherance of this divine decree the archangel Gabriel was sent to announce it to them both. To saint Anne he appeared in visible form, while she was engaged in fervent prayer for the coming of the Savior and the Redeemer of men. When she saw the holy prince, most beautiful and refulgent, she was disturbed and frightened and yet at the same time interiorly rejoiced and enlightened.

The holy maiden prostrated herself in profound humility to reverence the messenger of heaven; but he prevented and encouraged her, as being destined to be the ark of the true manna, Mary most holy, Mother of the Word. For this holy angel had been informed of this sacramental mystery on being sent with this message. The other angels did not yet know of it, as this revelation or illumination had been given directly from God only to Gabriel. Nevertheless the angel did not then manifest this great sacrament to St. Anne; but he asked her to attend and said to her: "The Most High give thee his blessing, servant of God, and be thy salvation. His Majesty has heard thy petitions and He wishes thee to persevere therein and that thou continue to clamor for the coming of the Redeemer. It is his will, that thou accept Joachim as thy spouse, for he is a man of upright heart and acceptable to the Lord: in his company thou wilt be able to persevere in the observance of his law and in his service. Continue thy prayers and thy supplications and be not solicitous for anything else, for the Lord will see them fulfilled. Walk in the straight paths of justice and let thy soul's converse be in heaven. Continuing to pray for the Messias, be thou joyful in the Lord, who is thy salvation." With these words the angel disappeared, leaving her enlightened in many mysteries of holy Scriptures, and comforted and renewed in spirit.

To saint Joachim the archangel did not appear in a corporeal manner, but he spoke to the man of God in sleep as follows: "Joachim, be thou blessed by the right hand of the Most High! Persevere in thy desires and live according to rectitude and perfection. It is the will of the Almighty, that thou receive saint Anne as thy spouse, for her the Lord has visited with his blessing.

Take care of her and esteem her as a pledge of the most High and give thanks to his Majesty, because he has given her into thy charge." In consequence of this divine message saint Joachim immediately asked for the hand of the most chaste Anne and, in joint obedience to the divine ordainment, they espoused each other. But neither of them manifested to each other the secret of what had happened until several years afterwards, as I will relate in its place. The two holy spouses lived in Nazareth, continuing to walk in the justification of the Lord. In rectitude and sincerity they practiced all virtue in their works, making themselves very acceptable and pleasing to the Most High and avoiding all blemish in all their doings. The rents and incomes of their estate they divided each year into three parts. The first one they offered to the temple of Jerusalem for the worship of the Lord; the second they distributed to the poor, and the third they retained for the decent sustenance of themselves and family. God augmented their temporal goods on account of their generosity and charity.

They themselves lived with each other in undisturbed peace and union of heart, without quarrel or shadow of a grudge. The most humble Anne subjected herself and conformed herself in all things to the will of Joachim: and that man of God, with equal emulation of humility, sought to know the desires of holy Anne, confiding in her with his whole heart (Prov. 31, 11), and he was not deceived. Thus they lived together in such perfect charity, that during their whole life they never experienced a time, during which one ceased to seek the same thing as the other (Matth. 27, 20). But rather as being united in the Lord, they enjoyed his presence in holy fear. Saint Joachim, solicitous to obey the command of the angel, honored his spouse and lavished his attention upon her.

The Lord forestalled the holy Matron Anne with the blessings of his sweetness (Psalm 20, 4), communicating to her the most exalted graces and infused science, which prepared her for the happy destiny of becoming the mother of Her, who was to be the Mother of God himself. As the works of God are perfect and consummate, it was natural to expect, that He should make her a worthy mother of that most pure Creature, who should be superior in sanctity to all creatures and inferior only to God.

This fortunate couple passed twenty years of their married life without issue. In those times and among the people of the Jews this was held to be the greatest misfortune and disgrace. On this account they had to bear much reproach and insult from their neighbors and acquaintances, for all those that were childless, were considered as excluded from the benefits of the Messias. But the Most High wished to afflict them and dispose them for the grace which awaited them, in order that in patience and submission they might tearfully sow the glorious Fruit, which they were afterwards to bring forth. They continued in most fervent prayers from the bottom of their hearts, mindful of the command from on high. They made an express vow to the Lord, that if He should give them issue, they would consecrate It to his service in the temple of Jerusalem.

Having, at the command of the Lord, persevered a whole year in fervent petitions, it happened by divine inspiration and ordainment, that Joachim was in the temple of Jerusalem offering prayers and sacrifices for the coming of the Messias, and for the fruit, which he desired. Arriving with others of his town to offer the common gifts and contributions in the presence of the high priest, Isachar, an inferior priest, harshly reprehended the old and venerable Joachim, for presuming to come with the other people to make his offerings in spite of his being childless. Among other things he said to him: "Why dost thou, Joachim, come with thy offerings and sacrifices, which are not pleasing in the eyes of God, since thou art a useless man? Leave this company and depart; do not annoy God with thy offerings and sacrifices, which are not acceptable to Him." The holy man, full of shame and confusion, in humble love thus addressed the Lord: "Most high Lord and God, at thy command and desire I came to the temple; he that takes thy place, despises me; my sins merit this disgrace; but since I accept it according to thy will, do not cast away the creature of thy hands" (Ps. 275, 10). Joachim hastened away from the temple full of sorrow, though peaceful and contented, to a farm or storehouse, which he possessed, and there in solitude he called upon the Lord for some days, praying as follows:

"Most high and eternal God, on whom depends the whole existence and the reparation of the human race, prostrate in thy living presence, I supplicate thy infinite goodness to look upon the affliction of my soul and to hear my prayers and those of thy servant Anne. To thine eyes are manifest all our desires (Ps. 37, 10) and if I am not worthy to be heard, do not despise my humble spouse. Lord God of Abraham, Isaac and Jacob, our first forefathers, do not hide thy kindness from us, nor permit, since Thou art a Father, that I be numbered among the reprobate and the outcasts in my offerings, because Thou givest me no issue. Remember, O Lord, the sacrifices (Deut. 11, 27) and oblations of thy servants and prophets, my ancestors, and look upon their works, which were pleasing to thy divine eyes. Since Thou commandest me, my Lord to pray to Thee in confidence, grant me, according to the greatness of thy mercy and power, that which at thy wish I pray for. In beseeching Thee I fulfill thy will and render the obedience, in which Thou hast promised to grant my petition. If my sins hinder the exercise of thy mercies, take away what displeases and hinders Thee. Thou art mighty, Lord God of Israel, and all that Thou wishest, Thou canst accomplish without hindrance. Let my prayer reach thy ears, and if I am poor and insignificant, Thou art infinite and always ready to exercise mercy with the downcast. Whither shall I flee from Thee, who art the King of kings and the Lord of lords? Thou hast filled thy sons and servants with benedictions in their generations and Thou hast instructed me to expect and desire from thy bounty what Thou hast wrought in my brethren. If it is Thy pleasure to yield to my petition, and grant me issue I will offer it and consecrate it to thy holy temple in perpetual service. I have riveted my eyes and my will on thy holy Will and have always desired to keep them free from the vanishing things of this world. Fulfill in regard to me, what is according to thy pleasure, and rejoice our spirit with the accomplishment of our hopes. Look down from thy throne upon this vile dust, and raise it up, in order that it may magnify Thee and adore Thee, and let in all things be fulfilled thy will, and not mine."

While Joachim was making these petitions in his retirement, the holy angel manifested to holy Anne, that her prayer for an issue, accompanied by such holy desires and intentions, was pleasing to the Almighty. Having thus recognized the will of God and of her husband Joachim, she prayed with humble subjection and confidence, that it be fulfilled. "Most high God, my Lord, Creator and Preserver of the universe, whom my soul reveres as the true God, infinite, holy and eternal! Prostrate in thy real presence I will speak, though I am but dust and ashes (Esther 13, 9) proclaiming my need and my affliction. Lord God uncreated, make us worthy of thy benediction, and give us holy fruit of the womb, in order that we may offer it to thy service in the temple (Gen. 18, 27). Remember, O Lord, that Anne, thy servant, the mother of Samuel, was sterile and that by thy generous mercy she received the fulfillment of her desires. I feel within me a courage which incites and animates me to ask Thee to show me the same mercy. Hear then, O sweetest Lord and Master, my humble petition: remember the sacrifices, offerings and services of my ancestors and the favors, which thy almighty arm wrought in them. I wish to offer to Thee, O Lord, an oblation pleasing and acceptable in thy eyes: but the greatest in my power, is my soul, my faculties and inclinations given to Thee, and my whole being. If Thou look upon me from thy throne giving me issue, I will from this moment sanctify and offer it for thy service in the temple. Lord God of Israel, if it should be thy pleasure and good will to look upon this lowly and impoverished creature, and to console thy servant Joachim, grant me my prayer and may in all things be fulfilled thy holy and eternal will."

These were the prayers, which saint Joachim and Anne offered. On account of my great shortcoming and insufficiency I cannot fully describe what I was made to understand concerning the holiness of these prayers and of these saintly parents. It is impossible to tell all; nor is it necessary, since what I have said is sufficient for my purpose. In order to obtain a befitting idea of these saints, it is necessary to estimate and judge them in connection with the most high end and ministry, for which they were chosen by God; for they were the immediate grandparents of Christ our Lord, and parents of his most holy Mother.

The petitions of the holy Joachim and Anne reached the throne of the holy Trinity, where they were accepted and the will of God was made known to the holy angels. The three divine Persons, according to our way of expressing such things, spoke to them as follows: "We have in our condescension resolved, that the Person of the Word shall assume human flesh and that through Him all the race of mortals shall find a remedy. We have already manifested and promised this to our servants, the Prophets, in order that they might announce it to the world. The sins of the living, and their malice are so great, that We are much constrained by the rigor of justice. But our goodness and mercy is greater than all their evil-doing, nor can it extinguish our love toward men. We will look with mercy upon the works of our hands, which We have created according to our image and likeness, so as to enable them to become inheritors and participators of our eternal glory (I Pet. 3, 22). We will consider the services and the pleasure derived from our servants and friends and regard the multitude of those, who shall distinguish themselves in our praise and friendship. And above all have We before our eyes Her, who is to be the chosen One, who is to be acceptable above all creatures and singled out for our delight and pleasure; because She is to conceive the person of the Word in her womb and clothe Him with human flesh. Since there must be a beginning of this work, by which We shall manifest to the world the treasures of the Divinity, this shall be the acceptable and opportune time for its execution. Joachim and Anne have found grace in our eyes; We look upon them with pleasure and shall enrich them with choicest gifts and graces. They have been faithful and constant in their trials and in simplicity and uprightness their souls have become acceptable and pleasing before Us. Let Gabriel as our ambassador bring tidings of joy for them and for the whole human race; let him announce to them, that in our condescension We have looked upon them and chosen them."

Thus the celestial spirits were instructed in regard to the will and the decree of the Almighty. The holy archangel Gabriel humbled himself before the throne of the most blessed Trinity, adoring and revering the divine Majesty in the manner which befits these most pure and spiritual substances. From the throne an intellectual voice proceeded, saying: "Gabriel, enlighten, vivify and console Joachim and Anne, our servants, and tell them, that their prayers have come to our presence and their petitions are heard in clemency. Promise them, that by the favor of our right hand they will receive the Fruit of benediction, and that Anne shall conceive a Daughter, to whom We give the name of MARY."

Together with this mandate of the Most High many mysteries and sacraments pertaining to this message were revealed to saint Gabriel. With it he descended from the vault of the empyrean heaven and appeared to holy Joachim, while he was in prayer, saying to him: "Just and upright man, the Almighty from his sovereign throne has taken notice of thy desires and has heard thy sighs and prayers, and has made thee fortunate on earth. Thy spouse Anne shall conceive and bear a Daughter, who shall be blessed among women (Luc. 42, 48). The nations shall know Her as the

Blessed. He who is the eternal God, increate, and the Creator of all, most upright in his judgments, powerful and strong, sends me to thee, because thy works and alms have been acceptable. Love has softened the heart of the Almighty, and has hastened his mercies, and in his liberality He wishes to enrich thy house and thy family with a Daughter, whom Anne shall conceive; the Lord himself has chosen for Her the name of MARY. From her childhood let Her be consecrated to the temple, and in it to God, as thou hast promised. She shall be elect, exalted, powerful and full of the Holy Ghost; on account of the sterility of Anne her conception shall be miraculous; She shall be a Daughter wonderful in all her doings and in all her life. Praise the Lord, Joachim, for this benefit and magnify Him, for in no other nation has He wrought the like. Thou shalt go to give thanks in the temple of Jerusalem and in testimony of the truth of this joyful message, thou shalt meet, in the Golden Gate, thy sister Anne, who is coming to the temple for the same purpose. Remember that marvelous is this message, for the Conception of this Child shall rejoice heaven and earth."

In the meanwhile the thrice blessed Anne was exalted in prayer and divine contemplation and totally wrapped up in the mystery of the Incarnation, which, after having been previously filled with a most high understanding and a specially infused light, she solicited from the eternal Word. With the profoundest humility and lively faith she was praying for the hastening of the coming of the Redeemer of the human race in the following words: "Most high King and Lord of all creation, I, a most vile and despicable creature, and yet the work of thy hands, desire at the price of the life which Thou hast given me, to urge Thee to hasten in thy mercy the time of our salvation. O may thy infinite kindness incline toward our need! O that our eyes might look upon the Restorer and the Redeemer of men! Remember, O Lord, the mercies of old shown to thy people, wherein Thou hast promised thy Onlybegotten, and may this promise of infinite kindness unbend Thee! May it come now, that day so much longed for! Is it possible, that the Most High should descend from his holy heaven? Is it possible, that He is to have a terrestrial Mother? What woman shall She be, that is so fortunate and blessed? O who shall be so favored as to look upon Her? Who shall be worthy to be the servant of her servants? Blessed the race, that shall be able to see Her and prostrate themselves at her feet to reverence Her! How sweet shall be the sight of Her and her company! Blessed the eyes, that shall see Her and the ears, that shall listen to her words, and the family, from whom the Most High shall select his Mother! Execute, O Lord, this decree: fulfill thy divine benevolence!"

"The humility, faith and the alms of Joachim and of thyself have come before the throne of the Most High and now He sends me, his angel, in order to give thee news full of joy for thy heart: His Majesty wishes, that thou be most fortunate and blessed. He chooses thee to be the mother of Her who is to conceive and bring forth the Onlybegotten of the Father. Thou shalt bring forth a Daughter, who by divine disposition shall be called MARY. She shall be blessed among women and full of the Holy Ghost. She shall be the cloud that shall drop the dew of heaven for the refreshment of mortals (III Kings 18, 44): and in Her shall be fulfilled the prophecies of thy ancestors. She shall be the portal of life and salvation for the sons of Adam. Know also that I have announced to Joachim,

that he shall have a Daughter who shall be blessed and
fortunate: but the full knowledge of the mystery is not
given him by the Lord, for he does not know, that She
is to be the Mother of the Messias. Therefore thou
must guard this secret; and go now to the temple to
give thanks to the Most High for having been so highly
favored by his powerful right hand. In the Golden Gate
thou shalt meet Joachim, where thou wilt confer with
him about this tiding. Thou art the one, who art especially blessed of the Lord and whom He wishes to visit and
enrich with more singular blessings. In solitude He will
speak to thy heart and there give a beginning to the law
of grace, since in thy womb He will give being to Her,
who is to vest the Immortal with mortal flesh and human form. In this humanity, united with the Word, will
be written, as with his own blood, the true law of Mercy."

In order that the humble heart of the holy Anne
might not faint away with admiration and joy at these
tidings of the holy angel, she was strengthened by the
holy Spirit and thus she heard it and received it with
magnanimity and incomparable joy. Immediately arising
she hastened to the temple of Jerusalem, and there found
saint Joachim, as the angel had foretold to them both.
Together they gave thanks to the Almighty for this wonderful blessing and offered special gifts and sacrifices.
They were enlightened anew by the grace of the holy
Spirit, and, full of divine consolation, they returned to
their home. Joyfully they conversed about the favors,
which they had received from the Almighty, especially
concerning each one's message of the archangel Gabriel,
whereby, on behalf of the Lord, they had been promised
a Daughter who should be most blessed and fortunate.
On this occasion they also told each other, how the same
angel, before their espousal, had commanded each to ac-

cept the other, in order that together they might serve God according to his divine will. This secret they had kept from each other for twenty years, without communicating it, until the same angel had promised them the issue of such a Daughter. Anew they made the vow to offer Her to the temple and that each year on this day they would come to the temple to offer special gifts, spend the day in praise and thanksgiving, and give many alms. This vow they fulfilled to the end of their lives, spending this day in great praise and exaltation of the Most High.

The prudent matron Anne never disclosed the secret, that her Daughter was to be the Mother of the Messias, either to Joachim or to any other creature. Nor did that holy parent in the course of his life know any more than that She was to be a grand and mysterious woman. However, in the last moments of his life the Almighty made the secret known to him, as I will relate in its place.

CHAPTER VI.

THE IMMACULATE CONCEPTION.

In the tribunal of the divine will, as the inevitable source and universal cause of the whole creation, all things with their conditions and circumstances, are decreed and determined, so that nothing is forgotten and no created power can in the least impede the fulfillment of the decree. All the spheres and the inhabitants contained in them are dependent on this ineffable government that rules them and coöperates with the natural causes unfailingly and unerringly in all that must be done. God works in all and sustains all by his sole will; in Him lies the preservation of all things or their annihilation, for without Him they would return to the non-existence, from which they were drawn. But since He has created the universe for his glory and for the glory of the incarnate Word, therefore He has from the beginning opened the paths and prearranged the ways by which the same Word should lower Himself to assume human flesh and to live among men, and by which they might ascend toward God, know Him, fear Him, seek Him, serve Him, love Him, praise Him and enjoy Him eternally. As the opportune and pre-ordained time had arrived, the three divine Persons conferred with each other saying: "Now is the time to begin the work of our pleasure and to call into existence that pure Creature and that soul, which is to find grace in our eyes above all the rest. Let Us furnish Her with the richest gifts and let Us deposit in Her the great treasures of our grace. Since all others, whom We called into existence, have turned out ungrateful and rebellious to our wishes, frustrating our intention and impeding by their own fault our purpose, namely, that they conserve themselves in the happy state of their first parents, and since it is not proper, that our will should be entirely frustrated, let Us therefore create this being in entire sanctity and perfection, so that the disorder of the first sin shall have no part in Her. Let Us create a soul according to our pleasure, a fruit of our attributes, a marvel of our infinite power, without touch or blemish of the sin of Adam. Let Us perfect a work which is the object of our Omnipotence and a pattern of the perfection intended for our children, and the finishing crown of creation. All have sinned in the free will and resolve of the first man (Rom. 5, 12); let Her be the sole creature in whom We restore and execute that which they in their aberration have lost. Let Her be a most special image and likeness of our Divinity and let Her be in our presence for all eternity the culmination of our good will and pleasure. In Her We deposit all the prerogatives and graces which in our first and conditional resolve We had destined for the angels and men, if they had remained in their first estate. What they have lost We renew in that Creature and We will add to these gifts many others. Thus our first decree shall not be frustrated, but it shall be fulfilled in a higher manner through this our chosen and only One (Cant. 6, 8). And since We assigned and prepared the most perfect and estimable of our gifts for the creatures who have lost them, We will divert the stream of our bounty to our Well-beloved. We will set Her apart from the ordinary law, by which the rest of the mortals are brought into existence, for in Her the seed of the serpent shall have no part. I will descend from heaven into her womb and in it vest Myself from her substance with human nature."

"It is befitting and due to the infinite goodness of our Divinity, that It be founded and enclosed in the most pure matter, untouched and unstained by fault. Nor is it proper that our equity and providence overlook what is most apt, perfect and holy, and choose that which is inferior, since nothing can resist our will (Esther 13, 9). The Word, which is to become man, being the Redeemer and Teacher of men, must lay the foundation of the most perfect law of grace, and must teach through it, that the father and mother are to be obeyed and honored as the secondary causes of the natural existence of man. The law is first to be fulfilled by the divine Word by honoring Her as his chosen Mother, by exalting Her with a powerful arm, and lavishing upon Her the most admirable, most holy and most excellent of all graces and gifts. Among these shall be that most singular honor and blessing of not subjecting Her to our enemy, nor to his malice; and therefore She shall be free from the death of sin."

"On earth the Word shall have a Mother without a father, as in heaven He has a Father without a mother. And in order that there may be the proper correspondence, proportion and consonance in calling God his Father and this Woman his Mother, We desire that the highest correspondence and approach possible between a creature and its God be established. Therefore at no time shall the dragon boast of being superior to the Woman, whom God will obey as his true Mother. This dignity of being free from sin is due and corresponds to that of being Mother of the Word, and it is in itself even more estimable and useful. It is a greater good to be holy than to be only mother; but all sanctity and perfection is nevertheless due to the motherhood of God. The human flesh, from which He is to assume form, must be free from sin. Since He is to redeem in it the sinners, He must not be under the necessity of redeeming his own flesh, like that of sinners. Being united to the Divinity his humanity is to be the price of Redemption, wherefore it must before all be preserved from sin, and We have already foreseen and accepted the merits of the Word in this very flesh and human nature. We wish that for all eternities the Word should be glorified through this tabernacle and habitation of the human nature."

"She is to be a daughter of the first man; but in the order of grace She is to be singularly free and exempt from fault; and in the order of nature She is to be most perfect, and to be formed according to a special providence. And since the incarnate Word is to be the Teacher of humility and holiness and for this end is to endure labors, confounding the vanity and deceitful fallacies of mortals by choosing for Himself sufferings as the treasure most estimable in our eyes, We wish that She, who is to be his Mother, experience the same labors and difficulties, that She be singularly distinguished in patience, admirable in sufferings, and that She, in union with the Onlybegotten, offer the acceptable sacrifices of sorrow to Us for her greater glory."

"Now the time has arrived," added his Majesty, "which was resolved upon by our Providence for bringing to light the Creature most pleasing and acceptable to our eyes. That Creature, in whom the human nature is freed from its first sin, who is to crush the head of the dragon, who was typified by that singular sign, the Woman that appeared in the heavens in our presence, and who is to clothe the eternal Word with human flesh. The hour is at hand, so blessed for mortals, in which the treasures of our Divinity are to be opened and the gates of heaven to be unlocked. Let the rigor of our justice be softened by the chastisements, which we have until now executed upon the mortals; let the attribute of our mercy become manifest; let the creatures be enriched, and let the divine Word merit for them the treasures of grace and of eternal glory."

"Now let the human race receive the Repairer, the Teacher, the Brother and Friend, to be life for mortals, a medicine for the sick, a consoler for the sorrowful, a balsam for the wounded, a guide and companion for those in difficulties. Let now the prophecies of our servants and the promises made to them, that We would send a Savior to redeem them, be fulfilled. And in order that all may be executed according to our good pleasure, and that We may give a beginning to the mystery hidden since the constitution of the world, We select for the formation of our beloved Mary the womb of our servant Anne; in her be She conceived and in her let that most blessed Soul be created. Although her generation and formation shall proceed according to the usual order of natural propagation, it shall be different in the order of grace, according to the ordainment of our Almighty power."

"You do already know how the ancient serpent, since he saw the sign of this marvelous Woman, attempts to circumvent all women, and how, from the first one created, he persecutes all those, whom he sees excelling in the perfection of their works and life, expecting to find among them the One, who is to crush his head (Gen. 3, 15). When he shall encounter this most pure and spotless Creature, he shall find Her so holy that he will exert all his powers to persecute Her in pursuance of the concept which he forms of Her. But the arrogance of this dragon shall be greater than his powers (Is. 12, 7); and it is our will that you have particular charge of this our holy City and tabernacle of the incarnate Word, protecting, guarding, assisting and defending Her against our enemies, and that you enlighten, strengthen and console Her with all due solicitude and reverence, as long as She shall be a wayfarer among the mortals."

At this proposal of the Most High all the holy angels, prostrate before the royal throne of the most holy Trinity, avowed their promptitude and eagerness to obey the divine mandate. Each one desired in holy emulation to be appointed, and offered himself for such a happy service; all of them gave to the Almighty praise and thanksgiving in new songs, because the hour had arrived for the fulfillment of that for which they had, with the most ardent desires, prayed through many ages. I perceived on this occasion that from the time of that great battle of saint Michael with the dragon and his allies, in which they were hurled into everlasting darkness while the hosts of Michael remained victorious and confirmed in grace and glory, these holy spirits commenced immediately to pray for the fulfillment of the mysteries of the Incarnation of the Word, of which they became cognizant at that time. And they persevered in these oft repeated prayers up to the hour in which God manifested to them the fulfillment of their desires and petitions.

On this account the celestial spirits at this new revelation conceived an additional joy and obtained new accidental glory, and they spoke to the Lord: "Most High and incomprehensible God and Lord, Thou art worthy of all reverence, praise and eternal glory; and we are thy creatures and made according to thy divine will. Send us, most powerful Lord, to execute thy most wonderful works and mysteries, in order that in all things thy most just pleasure may be fulfilled." In such terms of affection the heavenly princes acknowledged themselves as subjects; and if it had been possible, they desired to increase in purity and perfection in order to be more worthy guardians and servants of Mary.

Then the Most High chose and appointed those who were to be occupied in this exalted service (the guardianship of Mary) from each of the nine choirs of angels. He selected one hundred, being nine hundred in all. Moreover he assigned twelve others who should in a special manner assist Mary in corporeal and visible forms; and they were to bear the emblems or escutcheons of the Redemption. These are the twelve which are mentioned in the twenty-first chapter of the Apocalypse as guarding the portals of the city; of them I will speak in the explanation of that chapter later on. Besides these the Lord assigned eighteen other angels, selected from the highest ranks, who were to ascend and descend by that mystical stairs of Jacob with the message of the Queen to his Majesty and those of the Lord to Her.

In addition to all these holy angels the Almighty assigned and appointed seventy seraphim, choosing them from the highest ranks and from those nearest to the Divinity, in order that they might communicate and converse with this Princess of heaven in the same way as they themselves have intercourse with each other, and as the higher communicate with the lower ones.

In order that this invincible warrior-troop might be well appointed, saint Michael, the prince of the heavenly militia was placed at their head, and although not always in the company of the Queen, he was nevertheless often near Her and often showed himself to Her. The Almighty destined him as a special ambassador of Christ our Lord and to act in some of the mysteries as the defender of his most holy Mother. In a like manner the holy prince Gabriel was appointed to act as legate and minister of the eternal Father in the affairs of the Princess of heaven. Thus did the most holy Trinity provide for the custody and the defense of the Mother of God.

The divine wisdom had now prepared all things for drawing forth the spotless image of the Mother of grace from the corruption of nature. The number and congregation of ancient Patriarchs and Prophets had been completed and gathered, and the mountains had been raised, on which this mystical City of God was to be built (Ps. 86, 2). By the power of his right hand He had already selected incomparable treasures of the Divinity to enrich and endow Her. A thousand angels were equipped for her guard and custody, that they might serve as most faithful vassals of their Queen and Lady. He had provided a noble and kingly ancestry from whom She should descend and had selected for Her most holy and perfect parents, than whom none holier or more perfect could be found in the world. For there is no doubt that if better and more apt parents existed, the Almighty would have selected them for Her, who was to be chosen by God as his Mother.

In the formation of the body of the most holy Mary the wisdom and power of the Almighty proceeded so cautiously that the quantities and qualities of the four natural elements of the human body, the sanguine, melancholic, phlegmatic and choleric, were compounded in exact proportion and measure; in order that by this most perfect proportion in its mixture and composition it might assist the operations of that holy Soul with which it was to be endowed and animated. This wonderfully composed temperament was afterwards the source and the cause, which in its own way made possible the serenity and peace that reigned in the powers and faculties of the Queen of heaven during all her life. Never did any of these elements oppose or contradict nor seek to predominate over the others, but each one of them supplemented and served the others, continuing in this well-ordered fabric without corruption or decay. Never did the body of the most Holy Mary suffer from the taint of corruption, nor was there anything wanting or anything excessive found in it; but all the conditions and proportions of the different elements were continuously adjusted, without any want or excess in what was necessary for her perfect existence and without excess or default in dryness or moisture. Neither was there more warmth than was necessary for maintenance of life or digestion; nor more cold than was necessary for the right temperature and for the maintenance of the bodily humors.

On the Saturday next following, the Almighty created the soul of his Mother and infused it into the body; and thus entered into the world that pure Creature, more holy, perfect and agreeable to His eyes than all those He had created, or will create to the end of the world, or through the eternities. God maintained a mysterious correspondence in the execution of this work with that of creating all the rest of the world in seven days, as is related in the book of Genesis. Then no doubt He rested in truth, according to the figurative language of Scripture, since He has now created the most perfect Creature of all, giving through it a beginning to the work of the divine Word and to the Redemption of the human race. Thus was this day a paschal feast for God and also for all creatures.

By the force of this divine pronouncement and through the love with which it issued from the mouth of Almighty, was created and infused into the body of most holy Mary her most blessed Soul. At the same time She was filled with grace and gifts above those of the highest seraphim of heaven, and there was not a single instant in which She was found wanting or deprived of the light, the friendship and love of the Creator, or in which She was touched by the stain or darkness of original sin. On the contrary She was possessed of the most perfect justice, superior to that of Adam and Eve in their first formation. To Her was also conceded the most perfect use of the light of reason, corresponding to the gifts of grace, which She had received. Not for one instant was She to remain idle, but to engage in works most admirable and pleasing to her Maker.

Although She was adorned as the Bride, descending from heaven, endowed with all perfections and with the whole range of infused virtues, it was not necessary that She should exercise all of them at once, it being sufficient that She exercise those, which were befitting her state in the womb of her mother. Among the first thus exercised were the three theological virtues, faith, hope and charity, which relate immediately to God. These She at once practiced in the most exalted manner recognizing by a most sublime faith the Divinity with all its perfections and its infinite attributes, and the Trinity with its distinction of Persons. This knowledge by faith was not impeded by the higher knowledge which God gave her, as I will soon demonstrate. She exercised also the virtue of hope, seeing in God the object of her happiness and her ultimate end. Toward this her sanctified Soul at once hastened and aspired with the most intense desires of uniting Herself with God and without having for one moment turned to any other object or tarried one moment in her upward flight. At the same instant also She put into action the virtue of charity, seeing in God the infinite and highest Good, and conceiving such an intense appreciation of the Divinity, that not all the seraphim could ever reach such an eminent degree of fervor and virtue.

The other virtues which adorn and perfect the rational part of the creature, She possessed in a proportion corresponding to the theological virtues. The moral and natural virtues were hers in a miraculous and supernatural measure, and in a still more exalted manner was She possessed of the gifts and fruits of the Holy Ghost in the order of grace. She had an infused knowledge and habit of all these virtues and of all the natural arts, so that She knew and was conversant with the whole natural and supernatural order of things, in accordance with the grandeur of God. Hence from her first instant in the womb of her mother, She was wiser, more prudent, more enlightened, and more capable of comprehending God and all his works, than all the creatures have been or ever will be in eternity, excepting of course her most holy Son.

In correspondence with this wonderful knowledge of her most holy soul at the instant of its union with the body, Mary exerted Herself by eliciting heroic acts of virtue, of incomparable admiration, praise, glorification, adoration, humility, love of God and sorrow for the sins committed against Him, whom She recognized as the Autnor and end of these admirable works. She hastened to offer Herself as an acceptable sacrifice to the Most High, beginning from that instant with fervent desire to bless Him, love Him and honor Him, because She perceived that the bad angels and men failed to know and love Him. She requested the holy angels whose Queen She already was, to help Her to glorify the Creator and Lord of all, and to pray also for Her.

The Lord in this instant showed Her also her guardian angels, whom she recognized and accepted with joyful submission, inviting them to sing canticles of praise to the Most High alternately with Her. She announced to them beforehand that this was to be the service which they were to render Her during the whole time of her mortal life, in which they were to act as her assistants and guards. She was informed moreover of her whole genealogy, and the genealogy of all of the rest of the holy people chosen by God, the Patriarchs and Prophets, and how admirable his Majesty was in the gifts, graces and favors wrought in them. It is worthy of admiration, that, although the exterior faculties of her body at the creation of her most holy Soul were hardly large enough to be distinguished, nevertheless, in order that none of the miraculous excellence with which God could endow his Mother might be wanting, He ordained by the power of his right hand, that in perceiving the fall of man She shed tears of sorrow in the womb of her mother at the gravity of the offense against the highest Good.

In this wonderful sorrow at the instant of her coming into existence, She began to seek a remedy for mankind and commenced the work of mediation, intercession and reparation. She offered to God the clamors of her ancestors and of the just of the earth, that his mercy might not delay the salvation of mortals, whom she even then looked upon as her brethren. Before She ever conversed with them She loved them with the most ardent charity and with the very beginning of her existence She assumed the office of Benefactress of men and exercised the divine and fraternal love enkindled in her heart. These petitions the Most High accepted with greater pleasure than the prayers of all the saints and angels and this pleasure of God was also made known to Her, who was created to be the Mother of God. She perceived the love of God and his desire to descend from heaven in order to redeem men, though She knew not how it should be consummated. It was befitting that God should feel Himself impelled to hasten his coming on account of the prayers and petitions of this Creature; since it was principally for the love of Her that He came, and since in Her body He was to assume human flesh, accomplish the most admirable of all his works, and fulfill the end of all other creatures.

In writing of these sacraments of the King, howsoever honorable it is to reveal his works, I confess my inaptitude and incapacity, being only a woman, and I am afflicted, because I am speaking in such common and vague terms, which fall entirely short of that, which I perceive in the light given to my soul for the understanding of these mysteries. In order to do justice to such sublimity, there were need of other words, more particular and especially adapted terms and expressions, which are beyond my ignorance. And even if they were at my service, they would be weighed down and made insipid by human weakness. Let therefore this human imbecility acknowledge itself unequal and incapable of fixing its eyes on this heavenly sun, with which the rays of the Divinity break upon the world, although yet beclouded in the maternal womb of holy Anne. If we seek permission to approach this wonderful sight, let us come near free and unshackled. Let us not allow ourselves to be detained, neither by our natural cowardice nor by a base fear and hesitation, even though it be under the cloak of humility. Let us all approach with the greatest devotion and piety, free from the spirit of contention (Rom. 13, 12); then we will be permitted to examine with our own eyes the fire of the Divinity burning in the bush without consuming it (Exodus 2, 2).

WORDS OF THE QUEEN.

It is an act of justice due to the eternal God that the creature coming to the use of reason, direct its very first movement toward God. By knowing, it should begin to love Him, reverence Him and adore Him as its Creator and only true Lord. The parents are naturally bound to instruct their children from their infancy in this knowledge of God and to direct them with solicitous care, so that they may at once see their ultimate end and seek it in their first acts of the intellect and will. They should with great watchfulness withdraw them from the childishness and puerile trickishness to which depraved nature will incline them if left without direction. If the fathers and mothers would be solicitous to prevent these vanities and perverted habits of their children and would instruct them from their infancy in the knowledge of their God and Creator, then they would afterwards easily accustom them to know and adore Him. My holy mother, who knew not of my wisdom and real condition, was most solicitously beforehand in this matter, for when She bore me in her womb, she adored in my name the Creator and offered worship

and thanks for his having created me, beseeching Him
to defend me and bring me forth to the light of day
from the condition in which I then was. So also parents
should pray with fervor to God, that the souls of their
children, through his Providence, may obtain Baptism
and be freed from the servitude of original sin.

And if the rational creature has not known and
adored the Creator from the first dawn of reason, it
should do this as soon as it obtains knowledge of the
essential God by the light of faith. From that very moment the soul must exert itself never to lose Him from
her sight, always fearing Him, loving Him, and reverencing Him.

CHAPTER VII.

The most holy Mary, being conceived without sin as described above, was entirely absorbed in spirit and entranced by her first vision of the Divinity. At the first instant, and in the narrow dwelling of the maternal womb, began the love of God in her most blessed soul, never to be interrupted, but to continue through all the eternities of that high glory, which She now enjoys at the right hand of her divine Son.

The most happy mother, holy Anne, passed the days of her pregnancy altogether spiritualized by the divine operations and by the sweet workings of the Holy Ghost in all her faculties. Divine Providence, however, in order to direct her course to greater merit and reward, ordained, that the ballast of trouble be not wanting, for without it the cargo of grace and love is scarcely ever secure. In order to understand better, what happened to this holy woman, it must be remembered, that satan, after he was hurled with the other bad angels from heaven into the infernal torments, never ceased, during the reign of the old Law, to search through the earth hovering with lurking vigilance above the women of distinguished holiness, in order to find Her, whose sign he had seen (Gen. 3, 15) and whose heel was to bruise and crush his head. Lucifer's wrath against men was so fierce, that he would not trust this investigation to his inferiors alone; but leaving them to operate against the virtuous women in general, he himself attended to this matter and assiduously hovered around those, who signalized themselves more particularly in the exercise of virtue and in the grace of the Most High.

Filled with malice and astuteness, he observed closely the exceeding great holiness of the excellent matron Anne and all the events of her life: and although he could not estimate the richness of the Treasure, which was enclosed in her blessed womb (since the Lord concealed this as well as many other mysteries from him), yet he felt a powerful influence proceeding from saint Anne. The fact that he could not penetrate into the source of this activity, threw him at times into great fury and rage. At other times he quieted himself with the thought, that this pregnancy arose from the same causes as others in the course of nature and that there was no special cause for alarm; for the Lord left him to his own hallucinations and to the vagaries of his own fury. Nevertheless the whole event was a source of great misgiving to this perverse spirit, when he saw how quietly her pregnancy took its course and especially, when he saw, that many angels stood in attendance. Above all he was enraged at his weakness in resisting the force, which proceeded from the blessed Anne and he suspected that it was not she alone, who was the cause of it.

Filled with this mistrust, the dragon determined, if possible, to take the life of the most felicitous Anne; or, if that was impossible, to see that she should obtain little satisfaction from her pregnancy. For the pride of Lucifer was so boundless as to persuade him of his ability to overcome or take away the life of Her, who was to be the Mother of the incarnate Word, or even the life of the Messias and Redeemer of the world, if only he could obtain knowledge of their whereabouts. His arrogance was founded upon the superiority of his angelic nature to the condition and power of mere human nature: as if both were not subject to grace and entirely dependent upon the will of their Creator. Audaciously therefore he set himself to tempt holy Anne, with many suggestions, misgivings, doubts and diffidences about the truth of her pregnancy, alleging her protracted years. All this the demon attempted in order to test the virtue of the saint, and to see, whether these temptations would not afford some opening for the perversion of her will.

But the invincible matron resisted these onslaughts with humble fortitude, patience, continued prayer and vivid faith in the Lord. She brought to naught the perplexing lies of the dragon and on account of them gained only additional grace and protection from on high. For besides the protection abundantly merited by her past life She was defended and freed from the demons by the great princes, who were guarding her most holy Daughter. Nevertheless in his insatiable malice the enemy did not desist on that account; and since his arrogance and pride far exceeds his powers, he sought human aid; for with such help he always promises himself greater ease of victory. Having at first tried to overthrow the dwelling of saint Joachim and Anne, in order that she might be frightened and excited by the shock of its fall, but not being able to succeed on account of the resistance of the holy angels, he incited against saint Anne one of the foolish women of her acquaintance to quarrel with her. This the woman did with great fury, insolently attacking saint Anne with reproach and scorn; she did not hesitate to make mockery of her pregnancy, saying, that she was the sport of the demon in being thus found pregnant at the end of so many years and at so great an age.

The blessed Anne did not permit herself to be disturbed by this attack, but in all meekness and humility bore the injuries and treated her assailants with kindness. From that time on she looked with greater love upon these women and lavished upon them so much the greater benefits. But their wrath was not immediately pacified, for the demon had taken possession of them, filling them with hate against the saint; and, as any concession to this cruel tyrant always increases his power over his victims, he incited these miserable dupes to plot even against the person and life of saint Anne. But they could not put their plots into execution, because divine power interfered to foil their natural womanly weakness. They were not only powerless against the saint, but they were overcome by her admonitions and brought to the knowledge and amendment of their evil course by her prayers.

The dragon was repulsed, but not vanquished; for he immediately availed himself of a servant, who lived in the house with Joachim and Anne, and exasperated her against the holy matron. Through her he created even a greater annoyance than through the other women, for she was a domestic enemy and more stubborn and dangerous than the others. I will not stay to describe, what the enemy attempted through this servant, since it was similar to that of the other woman, only more annoying and malicious. But with the help of God saint Anne won a more glorious victory than before; for the watcher of Israel slumbered not, but guarded his holy City (Ps. 120, 4) and furnished it so well with sentinels, chosen from the strongest of his hosts, that they put to ignominious flight Lucifer and his followers. No more were they allowed to molest the fortunate mother, who was already expecting the birth of the most blessed Princess of heaven, and who, enriched by heroic acts of virtue and many merits in these conflicts, had now arrived at the fulfillment of all her highest wishes.

The day destined for the parturition of saint Anne and for the birth of Her, who was consecrated and sanctified to be the Mother of God, had arrived: a day most fortunate for the world. This birth happened on the eighth day of September, fully nine months having elapsed since the Conception of the soul of our most holy Queen and Lady. Saint Anne was prepared by an interior voice of the Lord, informing Her, that the hour of her parturition had come. Full of the joy of the holy Spirit at this information, she prostrated herself before the Lord and besought the assistance of his grace and his protection for a happy deliverance. The most blessed child Mary was at the same time by divine providence and power ravished into a most high ecstasy. Hence Mary was born into the world without perceiving it by her senses, for their operations and faculties were held in suspense.

She was born pure and stainless, beautiful and full of grace, thereby demonstrating, that She was free from the law and the tribute of sin. Although She was born substantially like other daughters of Adam, yet her birth was accompanied by such circumstances and conditions of grace, that it was the most wonderful and miraculous birth in all creation and will eternally redound to the praise of her Maker. At twelve o'clock in the night this divine Luminary issued forth, dividing the night of the ancient Law and its pristine darknesses from the new day of grace, which now was about to break into dawn. She was clothed, handled and dressed like other infants, though her soul dwelt in the Divinity; and She was treated as an infant, though She excelled all mortals and even all the angels in wisdom. Her mother did not allow Her to be touched by other hands than her own, but she herself wrapped Her in swaddling clothes: and in this Saint Anne was not hindered by her present state of childbirth; for she was free from the toils and labors, which other mothers usually endure in such circumstances.

So then saint Anne received in her arms Her, who was her Daughter, but at the same time the most exquisite Treasure of all the universe, inferior only to God and superior to all other creatures. With fervent tears of joy she offered this Treasure to his Majesty, saying interiorly: "Lord of infinite wisdom and power, Creator of all that exists, this Fruit of my womb, which I have received of thy bounty, I offer to Thee with eternal thanks, for without any merit of mine Thou hast vouchsafed it to me. Dispose Thou of the mother and Child according to thy most holy will and look propitiously down upon our lowliness from thy exalted throne. Be Thou eternally blessed, because Thou hast enriched the world with a Creature so pleasing to thy bounty and because in Her Thou hast prepared a dwelling-place and a tabernacle for the eternal Word (Sap. 9, 8). I tender my congratulations to my holy forefathers and to the holy Prophets, and in them to the whole human race, for this sure pledge of Redemption, which Thou hast given them. But how shall I be able worthily to treat Her, whom Thou hast given me as a Daughter? I that am not worthy to be her servant? How shall I handle the true ark of the Testament? Give me, O my Lord and King, the necessary enlightenment to know thy will and to execute it according to thy pleasure in the service of my Daughter."

The Lord answered the holy matron interiorly, that she was to treat her heavenly Child outwardly as mothers treat their daughters, without any demonstration of reverence; but to retain this reverence inwardly, fulfilling the laws of a true mother toward Her, and rearing Her up with all motherly love and solicitude. All this the happy mother complied with; making use of this permission and her mother's rights without losing her reverence, she regaled herself with her most holy Daughter, embracing and caressing Her in the same way as other mothers do with their daughters. But it was always done with a proper reverence and consciousness of the hidden and divine sacrament known only to the mother and Daughter. The guardian angels of the sweet Child with others in great multitudes showed their veneration and worship to Mary as She rested in the arms of her mother; they joined in heavenly music, some of which was audible also to blessed Anne. The thousand angels appointed as guardians of the great Queen offered themselves and dedicated themselves to her service. This was also the first time, in which the heavenly Mistress saw them in a corporeal form with their devises and habiliments, as I shall describe in another chapter and the Child asked them to join with Her in the praise of the Most High and to exalt Him in her name.

At the moment of the birth of our Princess Mary the Most High sent the archangel Gabriel as an envoy to bring this joyful news to the holy Fathers in limbo. Immediately the heavenly ambassador descended, illumining that deep cavern and rejoicing the just who were detained therein. He told them that already the dawn of eternal felicity had commenced and that the reparation of man, which was so earnestly desired and expected by the holy Patriarchs and foretold by the Prophets, had been begun, since She, who was to be the Mother of the Messias, had now been born; soon would they now see the salvation and the glory of the Most High. The holy prince gave them an understanding of the excellence of the most holy Mary and of what the Omnipotent had begun to work in Her, in order that they might better comprehend the happy beginning of the mystery, which was to end their prolonged imprisonment. Then all the holy Patriarchs and Prophets and the rest of the just in limbo rejoiced in spirit and in new canticles praised the Lord for this benefit.

All these happenings at the birth of our Queen succeeded each other in a short space of time. The first exercise of her senses in the light of the material sun, was to recognize her parents and other creatures. The arms of the Most High began to work new wonders in Her far above all conceptions of men, and the first and most stupendous one was to send innumerable angels to bring the Mother of the eternal Word body and soul into the empyrean heaven for the fulfilling of his further intentions regarding Her. The holy princes obeyed the divine mandate and receiving the child Mary from the arms of her holy Mother Anne, they arranged a new and solemn procession bearing heavenward with incomparable songs of joy the true Ark of the covenant, in order that for a short time it might rest, not in the house of Obededon, but in the temple of the King of kings and of the Lord of lords, where later on it was to be placed for all eternity. This was the second step, which most holy Mary made in her life, namely, from this earth to the highest heaven.

Who can worthily extol this wonderful prodigy of the right hand of the Almighty? Who can describe the joy and the admiration of the celestial spirits, when they beheld this new and wonderful work of the Most High, and when they gathered to celebrate it in their songs? In these songs they acknowledged and reverenced as their Queen and Mistress, Her, who was to be the Mother of their Lord, and the source of the grace and glory, which they possessed; for it was through his fore-seen merits, that they had been made the recipients of the divine bounty. But above all, what human tongue, or what mortal could ever describe or comprehend the heart-secrets of that tender Child during these events? I leave the imagination of all this to Catholic piety, and still more to those who in the Lord are favored with an un-derstanding of it, but most of all to those who, by di-vine bounty shall have arrived at the beatific vision face to face.

Borne by the hands of the angels the child Mary entered the empyrean heaven where She prostrated Herself full of love before the royal throne in the pres-ence of the Most High. Then (according to our way of understanding), was verified what long before had hap-pened in figure, when Bethsabee entered into the presence of her son Solomon, who, while presiding over his people of Israel, arose from his throne, received her with honor and reverence, and seated her at his side as queen. Sim-ilarly, but in a more glorious and admirable manner, the person of the divine Word now received the child Mary, whom He had chosen as Mother, as Queen of the uni-verse. Although her real dignity and the purpose of these ineffable mysteries were unknown to Mary, yet her infant faculties were strengthened by divine power for the proper reception of these favors. New graces and gifts were bestowed upon Her, by which her faculties were correspondingly elevated. Her powers of mind, besides being illumined and prepared by new grace and

light, were raised and proportioned to the divine manifestation, and the Divinity displayed Itself in the new light
vouchsafed, revealing Itself to Her intuitively and clearly
in a most exalted manner. This was the first time in
which the most holy soul of Mary saw the blessed Trinity
in unveiled beatific vision.

The sole witnesses of the glory of Mary in this
beatific vision, of the sacraments then again revealed to
Her, of the divine effect that overflowed into her most
pure soul, was God the Author of this unheard of wonder, and the astounded angels, who in some measure perceived these mysteries in God Himself. The Queen seated at the side of the Lord, who was to be her Son, and
seeing Him face to face, was more successful in her
prayer than Bethsabee (III Kings, 2, 21). For She prayed
that He bestow the untouched Sunamite Abisag, his inaccessible Divinity, upon his sister, human nature; She
prayed that his promised coming from heaven to the
earth and his marriage with human nature by the hypostatic union be fulfilled in the person of the Word. Many
times had He pledged Himself to it among men through
the ancient Patriarchs and Prophets and now Mary besought Him to accelerate the reparation of the human
race, expected for so many ages amid the multiplied
iniquity and the ruin of souls. The Most High heard
this most pleasing petition of his Mother, and acting
more graciously than Solomon of old toward his mother,
He assured Her that soon his promises should be fulfilled, and that He should descend to the world in order
to assume and redeem human nature.

In this divine consistory and tribunal of the most
holy Trinity it was determined to give a name to the
Child Queen. As there is no proper and legitimate name,
except it be found in the immutable being of God himself

(for from it are participated and determined according to their right weight and measure all things in infinite wisdom) his Majesty wished himself to give and impose that name in heaven. He thereby made known to the angelic spirits, that the three divine Persons, had decreed and formed the sweet names of Jesus and Mary for the Son and Mother from the beginning before the ages, and that they had been delighted with them and had engraved them on their eternal memories to be as it were the Objects for whose service They should create all things. Being informed of these and many other mysteries, the holy angels heard a voice from the throne speaking in the person of the Father: "Our chosen One shall be called MARY, and this name is to be powerful and magnificent. Those that shall invoke it with devout affection shall receive most abundant graces; those that shall honor it and pronounce it with reverence shall be consoled and vivified, and will find in it the remedy of their evils, the treasures for their enrichment, the light which shall guide them to heaven. It shall be terrible against the power of hell, it shall crush the head of the serpent and it shall win glorious victories over the princes of hell." The Lord commanded the angelic spirits to announce this glorious name to saint Anne, so that what was decreed in heaven might be executed on earth. The heavenly Child, lovingly prostrate before the throne, rendered most acceptable and human thanks to the eternal Being; and She received the name with most admirable and sweet jubliation. If the prerogatives and graces, which She then was favored with, were to be described, it would necessitate an extra book of many volumes. The holy angels honored and acknowledged most holy Mary as the future Mother of the Word and as their Queen and Mistress enthroned at the right hand of her Son; they showed their veneration of her holy name, prostrating themselves as it proceeded from the throne in the voice of the eternal Father, especially those, who had it written on the devises over their breast. All of them gave forth canticles of praise for these great and hidden mysteries. In the meanwhile the infant Queen remained ignorant of the real cause of all that She thus experienced, for her dignity of Mother of the incarnate Word was not revealed to Her till the time of the Incarnation. With the same reverential jubilee did the angels return in order to replace Her into the arms of holy Anne, to whom this event remained a secret, as was also the absence of her Daughter; for a guardian angel, assuming an aerial body, supplied her place for this very purpose. More than that, during a great part of the time in which the heavenly Child remained in the empyrean heaven, her mother was wrapped in an ecstasy of highest contemplation, and in it, although she did not know what was happening to the Child, exalted mysteries concerning the dignity of Mother of God, to which She was to be chosen, were revealed to her. The prudent matron kept them enshrined within her breast, conferring them in her thoughts with the duties she owed to her Child.

On the eighth day after the birth of the great Queen multitudes of most beautiful angels in splendid array descended from on high bearing an escutcheon on which the name of MARY was engraved and shone forth in great brilliancy. Appearing to the blessed mother Anne, they told her, that the name of her daughter was to be MARY, which name they had brought from heaven, and which divine Providence had selected and now ordained to be given to their child by Joachim and herself. The saint called for her husband and they conferred with each other about this disposition of God in regard to the name of their Daughter. The more than happy father accepted the name with joy and devout affection. They decided to call their relatives and a priest and then, with much solemnity and festivity, they imposed the name of MARY on their Child. The angels also celebrated this event with most sweet and ravishing music, which, however, was heard only by the mother and her most holy Daughter.

WORDS OF THE QUEEN.

My admonition to thee, whom in spite of thy weakness and poverty I have chosen with such generous kindness as my disciple and companion, is this: that thou strive with all thy powers to imitate me in an exercise, in which I persevered during my whole life from the very first moment of my birth, omitting it on not a single day, however full of cares and labors it might have been. This exercise was the following: every day at beginning of dawn, I prostrated myself in the presence of the Most High and gave Him thanks and praise for his immutable Being, his infinite perfections, and for having created me out of nothing; acknowledging myself as his creature and the work of his hands, I blessed Him and adored Him, giving Him honor, magnificence and Divinity, as the supreme Lord and Creator of myself and of all that exists. I raised up my spirit to place it into his hands, offering myself with profound humility and resignation to Him and asking Him to dispose of me according to his will during that day and during all the days of my life, and to teach me to fulfill whatever would be to his greater pleasure. This I repeated many times during the external works of the day, and in the internal ones I first consulted his Majesty, asking his advice, permission and benediction for all my actions.

Be very devout toward my most sweet name. I wish that thou be convinced of the great prerogatives and privileges, which the Almighty concedes to it, so that I myself, when I saw them in the Divinity, felt most deeply obliged and solicitous to make a proper return; and whenever the name MARY occurred to my mind (which happened often) and whenever I heard myself called by that name, I was aroused to thankfulness and urged to new fervor in the service of the Lord, who gave it to me. Thou hast the same name and I wish, that in proportion it should cause the same effects in thee and that thou imitate me faithfully by following the lesson given thee in this chapter, without failing in the least point from this day onward. And if in thy weakness thou shouldst fail, rouse thyself immediately, and in the presence of thy Lord and mine, acknowledge thy fault, confessing it in sorrow. Repeating these holy exercises over and again with solicitous care, thou shalt find forgiveness for imperfections and grow accustomed to strive after what is highest in all virtues and most pleasing to the Lord. Then, following the light which He gives and in pursuance of that which is most pleasing and agreeable to thy own tastes and mine, thou shalt not be denied the grace of employing thyself entirely in listening, attending to and obeying in all things thy Spouse and Lord, who seeks in thee only what is most pure, most holy and perfect, and a will prompt and eager to put the same into practice.

CHAPTER VIII.

The sovereign Child was treated like other children of her age. Her nourishment was of the usual kind, though less in quantity; and so was her sleep, although her parents were solicitous that She take more sleep. She was not troublesome, nor did She ever cry for mere annoyance, as is done by other children, but She was most amiable and caused no trouble to anybody. That She did not act in this regard as other children caused no wonder; for She often wept and sighed (as far as her age and her dignity of Queen and Mistress would permit) for the sins of the world and for its Redemption through the coming of the Savior. Ordinarily She maintained, even in her infancy, a pleasant countenance, yet mixed with gravity and a peculiar Majesty, never showing any childishness. She sometimes permitted Herself to be caressed, though, by a secret influence and a certain outward austerity, She knew how to repress the imperfections connected with such endearments. Her prudent mother Anne treated her Child with incomparable solicitude and caressing tenderness; also her father Joachim loved Her as a father and as a saint, although he was ignorant of the mystery at that time. The Child on its part showed a special love toward him, as one whom She knew for her father and one much beloved of God. Although She permitted more tender caresses from her father than from others, yet God inspired the father as well as all others, with such an extraordinary reverence and modesty towards Her whom He had chosen for his Mother, that even his pure and fatherly affection was outwardly manifested only with the greatest moderation and reserve.

In all things the infant Queen was most gracious, perfect and admirable. Though She passed her infancy subject to the common laws of nature, yet this did not hinder the influx of grace. During her sleep her interior acts of love, and all other exercises of her faculties which were not dependent on the exterior senses, were never interrupted. This special privilege is possible also in other creatures, if the divine power confers it on them; but it is certain that in regard to Her whom He had chosen as his Mother and the Queen of all creation, He extended this special favor beyond all previous or subsequent measure in other creatures and beyond the conception of any created mind.

The enforced silence of other children in their first years, and the slow evolution of their intellect and of their power of speech arising from natural weakness, was heroic virtue in the infant Queen. For if speech is the product of the intellect and as it were the result of its activity, and if She was in perfect possession of all her faculties since her Conception, then the fact of her not speaking as soon as She was born, did not arise from the want of ability, but because She did not wish to make use of her power. Other children are not furnished with the natural forces, which are required to open their mouth and move their tender tongue as required for speech, but in the child Mary there was no such defect; for as far as her natural powers were concerned She was stronger than other children, and as She exercised sovereignty and dominion over all creation, She certainly could exercise it in regard to her own powers and faculties, if She had chosen to do so. Her not speaking therefore was virtue and great perfection, which opportunely concealed her science and grace, and evaded the astonishment naturally caused by one speaking in infancy. Besides, if it is wonderful that one should speak, who according to the natural course ought to be incapable of speech, I do not know, whether it is not more wonderful, that one, who is able to speak from her birth should be silent for one year and a half.

It was ordained therefore by the Most High, that the sovereign Child should voluntarily keep this silence during the time in which ordinarily other children are unable to speak. The only exception made was in regard to the conversation held with the angels of her guard, or when She addressed Herself in vocal prayer to the Lord. For in regard to intercourse with God, the Author of speech, and with the holy angels, his messengers, when they treated in a visible manner with Her, this reason for maintaining silence did not hold good: on the contrary it was befitting, that, since there was no impediment, She should pray with her lips and her tongue; for it would not be proper to keep them unemployed for so long a time. But her mother never heard Her, nor did she know of her being able to speak during that period; and from this it can be better seen, what perfection it required in Her to pass that year and a half of her infancy in total silence. But during that time, whenever her mother freed her arms and hands, the child Mary immediately grasped the hands of her parents and kissed them with great submission and reverent humility, and in this practice She continued as long as her parents lived. She also sought to make them understand during that period of her age, that She desired their blessing, speaking more by the affection of her heart than by word of mouth. So great was her reverence for them, that never did She fail in the least point concerning the honor and obedience due to them. Nor did She cause them any trouble or annoyance, since She knew beforehand all their thoughts and was anxious to fulfill them before they were made manifest.

When She reached the age of two years She began to exercise her special pity and charity toward the poor. She solicited alms for them of saint Anne, and the kind-hearted mother readily granted her petitions, both for the sake of the poor and to satisfy the tender charity of her most holy Daughter, at the same time encouraging Her who was the Mistress of mercy and charity, to love and esteem the poor. Besides giving what She obtained expressly for distribution among the poor, She reserved part of her meals for the same purpose, in order that from her infancy it might be said of Her more truly than of Job: from my infancy compassion grew with me (Job 31, 18). She gave to the poor not as if conferring a benefit upon them, but as paying a debt due in justice, saying in her heart: this my brother and master deserves what he needs and what I possess without desert. In giving alms She kissed the hands of the poor, and whenever She was alone, She kissed their feet, or, if this was impossible, She would kiss the ground over which they had passed. Never did She give an alms to the poor without conferring still greater favors on their souls by interceding for them and thus dismissing them relieved in body and soul.

Not less admirable were the humility and obedience of the most holy Child in permitting Herself to be taught to read and to do other things as other children in that time of life. She was instructed in reading and other arts by her parents and She submitted, though

She had infused knowledge of all things created. The angels were filled with admiration at the unparalleled wisdom of this Child, who willingly listened to the teaching of all. Her holy mother Anne, as far as her intuition and love permitted, observed with rapture the heavenly Princess and blessed the Most High in Her. But with her love, as the time for presenting Her in the temple approached, grew also the dread of the approaching end of the three years set by the Almighty and the consciousness, that the terms of her vow must punctually be fulfilled. Therefore the child Mary began to prepare and dispose her mother, manifesting to her, six months before, her ardent desire of living in the temple. She recounted the benefits, which they had received at the hands of the Lord, how much they were obliged to seek his greater pleasure, and how, when She should be dedicated to God in the temple, She would be more her Daughter than in their own house.

The holy Anne heard the discreet arguments of her child Mary; but, though She was resigned to the divine will and wished to fulfill her promise of offering up her beloved Daughter, yet the natural force of her love toward such an unequalled and beloved Treasure, joined with the full understanding of its inestimable value, caused a mortal strife in her most faithful heart at the mere thought of her departure, which was closely at hand. There is no doubt, that she would have lost her life in this fierce and vivid sorrow, if the hand of the Almighty had not comforted her: for the grace and dignity of her heavenly Daughter was fully known to her and had entirely ravished her heart, making the presence of Mary more dear to her than life. Full of this grief she said to the Child: "My beloved Daughter, for many years I have longed for Thee and only for a

few years do I merit to have thy company; but thus let the will of God be fulfilled; I do not wish to be unfaithful to my promise of sending Thee to the temple, but there is yet time left for fulfilling it: have patience until the day arrives for the accomplishment of thy wishes."

A few days before most holy Mary reached the age of three years, She was favored with an abstract vision of the Divinity, in which it was made known to Her that the time of her departure for the temple ordained by God, had arrived, and that there She was to live dedicated and consecrated to his service. Her most pure soul was filled with new joy and gratitude at this prospect and speaking with the Lord, She gave Him thanks saying: "Most high God of Abraham, Isaac and Jacob, my eternal and highest Good, since I cannot praise Thee worthily, let it be done in the name of this humble slave by the angelic spirits; since Thou, immense Lord, who hast need of none, dost look upon this lowly wormlet of the earth in thy unbounded mercy. Whence this great benefit to me, that Thou shouldst receive me into thy house and service, since I do not even merit the most abject spot of the earth for my place of habitation? But as Thou art urged thereto by thy own greatness, I beseech Thee to inspire the hearts of my parents to fulfill thy holy will."

At the same time saint Anne had a vision, in which the Lord enjoined her to fulfill her promise by presenting her Daughter in the temple on the very day, on which the third year of her age should be complete. There is no doubt that this command caused more grief in saint Anne, than that given to Abraham to sacrifice his son Isaac. But the Lord consoled and comforted Her, promising his grace and assistance in her loneliness during the absence of her beloved Daughter.

Saint Joachim also had a visitation or vision of the Lord at this time, receiving the same command as Anne. Having conferred with each other and taking account of the will of the Lord, they resolved to fulfill it with humble submission and appointed the day on which the Child was to be brought to the temple. Great was also the grief of this holy old man, though not quite so great as that of saint Anne, for the high mystery of her being the future Mother of God was yet concealed from him.

WORDS OF THE QUEEN.

My dearest daughter, keep in mind, that all the living are born destined for death, but ignorant of the time allowed them; this they know for certain however, that the term of life is short, that eternity is without end, and that in this life only they can harvest what will yield life or death eternal. In this dangerous pilgrimage of life God has ordained, that no one shall know for certain, whether he is worthy (Eccles. 9, 1) of his love or hate; for if he uses his reason rightly, this uncertainty will urge him to seek with all his powers the friendship of that same Lord. God justifies his cause as soon as the soul acquires the use of reason; for from that time onward He enlightens and urges and guides man toward virtue and draws him away from sin, teaching him to distinguish between water and fire, to approve of the good and reject evil, to choose virtue and repel vice. Moreover, God calls and rouses the soul by his holy inspirations and continual promptings, provides the help of the Sacraments, doctrines and commandments, urges man onward through his angels, preachers, confessors, ministers and teachers, by special tribulations and favors, by the example of strangers, by trials, deaths and other

happenings and dispositions of his Providence; He disposes the things of life so as to draw toward Him all
men, for He wishes all to be saved. Thus He places at
the disposal of the creature a vast field of benevolent
help and assistance, which it can and should use for its
own advancement. Opposing all this are the tendencies
of the inferior and sensitive nature, infected with the
fomes peccati, the foment of sin, tending toward sensible
objects and by the lower appetites and repugnances, disturbing the reason and enthralling the will in the false
liberty of ungoverned desires. The demon also, by his
fascinations and his deceitful and iniquitous suggestions
obscures the interior light, and hides the deathly poison
beneath the pleasant exterior. But the Most High does
not immediately forsake his creatures; He renews his
mercy and his assistance, recalling them again and again,
and if they respond to his first call, He adds others according to his equity, increasing and multiplying them
in proportion as the soul corresponds. As a reward of
the victory, which the soul wins over itself, the force
of his passions and concupiscences is diminished, the
spirit is made free to soar higher and rise above its own
inclinations and above the demons.

But if man neglects to rise above his low desires
and his forgetfulness, he yields to the enemy of God
and man. The more he alienates himself from the goodness of God, so much the more unworthy does he become of the secret callings of the Most High, and so
much the less does he appreciate his assistance, though
it be great. For the demon and the passions have obtained a greater dominion and power over his intellect
and have made him more unfit and more incapable of the
grace of the Almighty. Thereon, my dear daughter,
rests the whole salvation or condemnation of souls, that

is, in commencing to admit or resist the advances of the Lord. I desire thee not to forget this doctrine, so that thou mayest respond to the many calls which thou receivest of the Most High. See thou be strong in resisting his enemies and punctually solicitous in fulfilling the pleasure of thy Lord, for thereby thou wilt gratify Him and attend to the commands made known to thee by divine light. I loved my parents dearly, and the tender words of my mother wounded my heart; but as I knew it to be the will of the Lord to leave them, I forgot her house and my people in order to follow my Spouse. The proper education and instruction of children will do much toward making them more free and habituated to the practice of virtue, since thus they will be accustomed to follow the sure and safe guiding star of reason from its first dawn.

BOOK TWO

Treats of the Presentation of the Princess of Heaven in the Temple, the
Favors She Received at the Hand of God, the Sublime Perfection
with which She Observed the Rules of the Temple,
the Heavenly Excellence of Her Heroic Virtues
and Visions, Her Most Holy Espousal and
other Events up to the Incarnation
of the Son of God.

CHAPTER I.

HER PRESENTATION IN THE TEMPLE.

The three years' time decreed by the Lord having been completed, Joachim and Anne set out from Nazareth, accompanied by a few of their kindred and bringing with them the true living Ark of the covenant, the most holy Mary, borne on the arms of her mother in order to be deposited in the holy temple of Jerusalem. The beautiful Child, by her fervent and loving aspirations, hastened after the ointments of her Beloved, seeking in the temple Him, whom She bore in her heart. This humble procession was scarcely noticed by earthly creatures, but it was invisibly accompanied by the angelic spirits, who, in order to celebrate this event, had hastened from heaven in greater numbers than ordinary as her bodyguard, and were singing in heavenly strains the glory and praise of the Most High. The Princess of heaven heard and saw them as She hastened her beautiful steps along in the sight of the highest and the true Solomon. Thus they pursued their journey from Nazareth to the holy city of Jerusalem, and also the parents of the holy child Mary felt in their hearts great joy and consolation of spirit.

They arrived at the holy temple, and the blessed Anne on entering took her Daughter and Mistress by the hand, accompanied and assisted by saint Joachim. All three offered a devout and fervent prayer to the Lord; the parents offering to God their Daughter, and the most holy Child, in profound humility, adoration and worship, offering up Herself. She alone perceived that the Most High received and accepted Her, and, amid divine splendor which filled the temple, She heard a voice saying to Her: "Come, my Beloved, my Spouse, come to my temple, where I wish to hear thy voice of praise and worship." Having offered their prayers, they rose and betook themselves to the priest. The parents consigned their Child into his hands and he gave them his blessing. Together they conducted Her to the portion of the temple buildings, where many young girls lived to be brought up in retirement and in virtuous habits, until old enough to assume the state of matrimony. It was a place of retirement especially selected for the first-born daughters of the royal tribe of Juda and the sacerdotal tribe of Levi.

Fifteen stairs led up to the entrance of these apartments. Other priests came down these stairs in order to welcome the blessed child Mary. The one that had received them, being according to the law one of a minor order, placed Her on the first step. Mary, with his permission, turned and kneeling down before Joachim and Anne, asked their blessing and kissed their hands, recommending herself to their prayers before God. The holy parents in tenderest tears gave Her their blessing; whereupon She ascended the fifteen stairs without any assistance. She hastened upward with incomparable fervor and joy, neither turning back, nor shedding tears, nor showing any childish regret at parting from her parents. To see Her, in so tender an age, so full of strange majesty and firmness of mind, excited the admiration of all those present.   The priests received Her among the rest of the maidens, and saint Simeon consigned Her to the teachers, one of whom was the prophetess Anne. This holy matron had been prepared by the Lord by especial grace and enlightenment, so that She joyfully took charge of this Child of Joachim and Anne.   She considered the charge a special favor of divine Providence and merited by her holiness and virtue to have Her as a disciple, who was to be the Mother of God and Mistress of all the creatures.

Sorrowfully her parents Joachim and Anne retraced their journey to Nazareth, now poor as deprived of the rich Treasure of their house.   But the Most High consoled and comforted them in their affliction.   The holy priest Simeon, although he did not at this time know of the mystery enshrined in the child Mary, obtained great light as to her sanctity and her special selection by the Lord; also the other priests looked upon Her with great reverence and esteem.   In ascending the fifteen stairs the Child brought to fulfillment, that, which Jacob saw happening in sleep; for here too were angels ascending and descending: the ones accompanying, the others meeting their Queen as She hastened up; whereas at the top God was waiting in order to welcome Her as his Daughter and Spouse.   She also felt by the effects of the overflowing love, that this truly was the house of God and the portal of heaven.

The child Mary, when brought to her teacher, knelt in profound humility before her and asked her blessing.   She begged to be admitted among those under her direction, obedience and counsel, and asked her kind forbearance in the labor and trouble, which She would occasion.   The prophetess Anne, her teacher, received

Her with pleasure, and said to Her: "My Daughter, Thou shalt find in me a helpful mother and I will take care of Thee and of thy education with all possible solicitude." Then the holy Child proceeded to address Herself with the same humility to all the maidens which were then present; each one She greeted and embraced, offering Herself as their servant and requesting them, as older and more advanced than She in the duties of their position, to instruct and command Her. She also gave them thanks, that without her merit they admitted Her to their company.

When the heavenly child Mary had dismissed her parents and entered upon her life in the temple, her teacher assigned to Her a place among the rest of the maidens, each of whom occupied a large alcove or little room. The Princess of heaven prostrated Herself on the pavement, and, remembering that it was holy ground and part of the temple, She kissed it. In humble adoration She gave thanks to the Lord for this new benefit, and She thanked even the earth for supporting Her and allowing Her to stand in this holy place; for She held Herself unworthy of treading and remaining upon it. Then She turned toward her holy angels and said to them: "Celestial princes, messengers of the Almighty, most faithful friends and companions, I beseech you with all the powers of my soul to remain with me in this holy temple of my Lord and as my vigilant sentinels, reminding me of all that I should do; instructing me and directing me as the teachers and guides of my actions, so that I may fulfill in all things the perfect will of the Most High, give pleasure to the holy priests and obey my teacher and my companions." And addressing in particular those whom I mentioned above as the twelve angels of the Apocalypse, She said: "And I beseech you, my ambassadors, if the Almighty permit you, go and console my holy parents in their affliction and solitude."

While the twelve angels executed her command, Mary remained with the others in heavenly conversation. She began to feel a supernal influence of great power and sweetness, spiritualizing Her and elevating Her in burning ecstasy, and immediately the Most High commanded the seraphim to assist in illumining and preparing her most holy soul. Instantly She was filled with a divine light and force, which perfected and proportioned her faculties in accordance with the mysteries now to be manifested to Her. Thus prepared and accompanied by her holy angels and many others, in the midst of a refulgent host, the celestial Child was raised body and soul to the empyrean heaven, where She was received by the holy Trinity with befitting benevolence and pleasure. She prostrated Herself in the presence of the most mighty and high Lord, as She was wont to do in all her visions, and adored Him in profound reverence and humility. Then She was further transformed by new workings of divine light, so that She saw, intuitively and face to face, the Divinity itself. This was the second time that It manifested Itself to Her in this intuitive manner during the first three years of her life.

By no human tongue or any sensible faculty could the effects of this vision and participation of the divine Essence ever be described. The Person of the Father spoke to the future Mother of his Son, and said: "My Dove, my beloved One, I desire thee to see the treasures of my immutable being and of my infinite perfections, and also to perceive the hidden gifts destined for the souls, whom I have chosen as heirs of my glory and who are rescued by the life-blood of the Lamb. Behold, my

Daughter, how liberal I am toward my creatures, that know and love Me; how true in my words, how faithful in my promises, how powerful and admirable in my works. Take notice, my Spouse, how ineffably true it is, that he who follows Me does not walk in darkness. I desire that thou, as my chosen One, be an eye-witness of the treasures which I hold in reserve for raising up the humble, enriching the poor, exalting the downtrodden, and for rewarding all that the mortals shall do and suffer for my name."

Other great mysteries were shown to the holy Child in this vision of the Divinity, for, as the object presented to the soul in such repeated intuitive visions is infinite, that which remains to be seen will always remain infinite and will excite greater and greater wonder and love in the one thus favored. The most holy Mary answered the Lord and said: "Most high, supreme and eternal God, incomprehensible Thou art in thy magnificence, overflowing in thy riches, unspeakable in thy mysteries, most faithful in thy promises, true in thy words, most perfect in thy works, for Thou art the Lord, infinite and eternal in thy essence and perfections. But, most high Lord, what shall my littleness begin to do at the sight of thy magnificence? I acknowledge myself unworthy to look upon thy greatness, yet I am in great need of being regarded by it. In thy presence, Lord, all creation is as nothing. What shall I thy servant do, who am but dust? Fulfill in me all thy desire and thy pleasure; and if trouble and persecutions suffered by mortals in patience, if humility and meekness are so precious in thy eyes, do not consent, O my Beloved, that I be deprived of such a rich treasure and pledge of thy love. But as for the rewards of these tribulations, give them to thy servants and friends, who deserve them better than I, for I have not yet labored in thy service and pleasure."

The Most High was much pleased with the petition of the heavenly Child and He gave Her to understand that He would admit Her to suffering and labor for his love in the course of her life, without at the time revealing to Her the order and the manner in which He was to dispense them. The Princess of heaven gave thanks for this blessing and favor of being chosen to labor and suffer for the glory of God's name. Burning with desire of securing such favor, She asked of his Majesty to be allowed to make four vows in his presence: of chastity, of poverty, of obedience, and of perpetual enclosure in the temple whither He had called Her. To this petition the Lord answered and said to Her: "My Spouse, my thoughts rise above all that is created, and thou, my chosen one, dost not yet know what is to happen to thee in the course of thy life, and thou dost not yet understand why it is impossible to fulfill thy fervent desires altogether in the manner in which thou now dost imagine. The vow of chastity I permit and I desire that thou make it; I wish that from this moment thou renounce earthly riches. It is also my will that as far as possible, thou observe whatever pertains to the other vows, just as if thou hadst made them all. Thy desire shall be fulfilled through many other virgins in the coming law of grace; for, in order to imitate thee and to serve Me, they will make these same vows and live together in community and thou shalt be the Mother of many daughters."

The most holy Child then, in the presence of the Lord, made the vow of chastity and as for the rest without binding Herself, She renounced all affection for terrestrial and created things. She moreover resolved to obey all creatures for the sake of God. In the fulfillment of these promises She was more punctual, fervent and faithful than any who have ever made these vows or ever will make them. Forthwith the clear and intuitive vision of the Divinity ceased, but She was not immediately restored to the earth. For, remaining in the empyrean heaven, She enjoyed another, an imaginary vision of the Lord in a lower state of ecstasy, so that in connection with it, She saw other mysteries.

In this secondary and imaginary vision some of the seraphim closest to the Lord approached Her and by his command adorned and clothed Her in the following manner. First all her senses were illumined with an effulgent light, which filled them with grace and beauty. Then they robed Her in a mantle or tunic of most exquisite splendor, and girded Her with a cincture of vary-colored and transparent stones, of flashing brilliancy, which adorned Her beyond human comprehension. They signified the immaculate purity and the various heroic virtues of her soul. They placed on Her also a necklace or collar of inestimable and entrancing beauty, which contained three large stones, symbolic of the three great virtues of faith, hope and charity; this they hung around her neck letting it fall to her breast as if indicating the seat of these precious virtues. They also adorned her hands with seven rings of rare beauty whereby the Holy Ghost wished to proclaim that He had enriched Her with his holy gifts in a most eminent degree. In addition to all this the most holy Trinity crowned her head with an imperial diadem, made of inestimable material and set with most precious stones, constituting Her thereby as his Spouse and as the Empress of heaven. In testimony whereof the white and refulgent vestments were emblazoned with letters or figures of the finest and the most shining gold, proclaiming: Mary, Daughter of the eternal Father, Spouse of the Holy Ghost and Mother of the true Light. This last name or title the heavenly Mistress did not understand; but the angels understood it, who, lost in wonder and praise of the Author, were assisting at this new and strange ceremony. Finally the attention of all the angelic spirits was drawn toward the Most High and a voice proceeded from the throne of the blessed Trinity, which, addressing the most holy Mary, spoke to Her: "Thou shalt be our Spouse, our beloved and chosen One among all creatures for all eternity; the angels shall serve thee and all the nations and generations shall call thee blessed" (Luc. 1, 48).

The sovereign Child being thus attired in the court dress of the Divinity, then celebrated a more glorious and marvelous espousal than ever could enter the mind of the highest cherubim and seraphim. For the Most High accepted Her as his sole and only Spouse and conferred upon Her the highest dignity which can befall a creature; He deposited within Her his own Divinity in the person of the Word and with it all the treasures of grace befitting such eminence. Meanwhile the most Humble among the humble was lost in the abyss of love and wonder which these benefits and favors caused in Her, and in the presence of the Lord She spoke: "Most high King and incomprehensible God, who art Thou and who am I, that thy condescension should look upon me who am dust, unworthy of such mercy? In Thee, my Lord, as in a clear mirror seeing thy immutable being, I behold and understand without error my lowliness and vileness, I admire thy immensity and deprecate my nothingness. At the sight of Thee I am annihilated and lost in astonishment, that the infinite Majesty should stoop to so lowly a worm, who can merit only oblivion and contempt of all the creatures. O Lord, my only Good, how art Thou magnified and exalted in this deed! What marvel dost Thou cause through me in thy angelic spirits, who understand thy infinite bounty, magnificence and mercy in raising up from the dust her who in it is poor, and placing her among the princes (Ps. 112, 7)! I accept Thee, O my King and my Lord, as my Spouse and I offer myself as thy slave. Let not my understanding attend to any other object, nor my memory hold any other image, nor my will seek other object or pleasure than Thee, my highest Good, my true and only Love. Let not my eyes look upon human creature, nor my faculties and senses attend upon anything beside Thee and whatever thy Majesty shall direct. Thou alone for thy spouse, my Beloved, and she for Thee only, who art the immutable and eternal Good."

The Most High received with ineffable pleasure this consent of the sovereign Princess to enter into the new espousal with her most holy soul. As upon his True Spouse and as Mistress of all creation, He now lavished upon Her all the treasures of his grace and power, instructing Her to ask for whatever She desired and assuring Her that nothing would ever be denied Her. The most humble Dove at once proceeded to beseech the Lord with the most burning charity, to send his Onlybegotten to the world as a remedy for mortals; that all men be called to the true knowledge of his Divinity; that her natural parents, Joachim and Anne, receive an increase of the loving gifts of his right hand; that the poor and afflicted be consoled and comforted in their troubles; and that in Herself be fulfilled the pleasure of the divine will. These were some of the more express petitions addressed by the new Spouse on this occasion to the blessed Trinity. And all the angelic host sang new songs of admiration in praise of the Most High, while those appointed by his Majesty, midst heavenly music, bore back the holy Child from the empyrean heaven to the place in the temple, from which they had brought Her.

In order to commence at once to put in practice what She had promised in the presence of the Lord, She betook Herself to her instructress and offered her all that her mother, saint Anne, had left for her comfort and sustenance, with the exception of a few books and clothes. She requested Her to give it to the poor or use it for any other purpose according to her pleasure, and that She command and direct Her what She was to do. The discreet matron, (who was, as I have already said, the prophetess Anne) by divine impulse accepted and approved of the offering of the beautiful Child and dismissed Her entirely poor and stripped of everything except the garments which She wore. She resolved to take care of Her in a special manner as one destitute and poor; for the other maidens each possessed their spending money and a certain sum assigned and destined for their wearing apparel and for other necessities according to their inclinations.

The holy matron, having first consulted the high priest, also gave to the sweetest Child a rule of life. By thus despoiling and resigning Herself the Queen and Mistress of creation obtained a complete freedom and detachment from all creatures and from her own Self, neither possessing nor desiring anything except only the most ardent love of God and her own abasement and humiliation.

WORDS OF THE QUEEN.

My daughter, among the great and ineffable favors of the Omnipotent in the course of my life, was the one which thou has just learned and described; for by this clear vision of the Divinity and of the incomprehensible essence I acquired knowledge of the most hidden sacraments and mysteries, and in this adornment and espousal I received incomparable blessings and felt the sweetest workings of the Divinity in my spirit. My desire to take the four vows of poverty, obedience, chastity and enclosure pleased the Lord very much, and I merited thereby that the Godfearing in the Church and in the law of grace are drawn to live under these vows, as is the custom in the present time. This was the beginning of that which you religious practice now, fulfilling the words of David in the forty-fourth psalm: "After Her shall virgins be brought to the King;" for the Lord ordained that my aspirations be the foundation of religious life and of the evangelical law. I fulfilled entirely and perfectly all that I proposed to the Lord, as far as was possible in my state of life; never did I look upon the face of a man, not even on that of my husband Joseph, nor on that of the angels, when they appeared to me in human form, though I saw and knew them all in God. Never did I incline toward any creature, rational or irrational, nor toward any human operation or tendency. But in all things I was governed by the Most High, either directly by Himself or indirectly through the obedience, to which I freely subjected myself.

Be careful therefore, my daughter, and fear so dreadful a danger; by divine assistance of grace raise thyself above thyself, never permitting thy will to consent to any disorderly affection or movement. I wish thee to consume thyself in dying to thy passions and in becoming entirely spiritualized, so that having extinguished within thee all that is of earth, thou mayest come to lead an angelic life and conversation. In order to deserve the name of spouse of Christ, thou must pass beyond the limits and the sphere of a human being and ascend to another state and divine existence. Although thou art earth, thou must be a blessed earth, without the thorns of passion, one whose fruit is all for the Lord, its Master. If thou hast for thy Spouse that supreme and mighty Lord, who is the King of kings and the Lord of lords, consider it beneath thy dignity to turn thy eyes, and much more thy heart, toward such vile slaves, as are the human creatures, for even the angels love and respect thee for thy dignity as spouse of the Most High. If even among men it is held to be a daring and boundless insolence in a plebeian to cast longing eyes upon the spouse of a prince, what a crime would it be to cast them on the spouse of the heavenly and omnipotent King? And it would not be a smaller crime if she herself would receive and consent to such familiarity. Consider and assure thyself that the punishment reserved for this sin is inconceivably terrible and I do not show it to thee visibly, lest thou perish in thy weakness. I wish that for thee my instructions suffice to urge thee to the fulfillment of all I admonish and to imitate me as my disciple, as far as thy powers go. Be also solicitous in recalling this instruction to the mind of thy nuns and in seeing that they live up to it.

My daughter, the greatest happiness, which can befall any soul in this mortal life, is that the Almighty call her to his house consecrated to his service. For by this benefit He rescues the soul from a dangerous slavery and relieves her of the vile servitude of the world, where, deprived of true liberty, she eats her bread in the sweat of her brow. Who is so dull and insipid as not to know the dangers of the worldly life, which is hampered by all the abominable and most wicked laws and customs introduced by the astuteness of the devil and the perversity of men? The better part is religious life and retirement; in it is found security, outside is a torment and a stormy sea, full of sorrow and unhappiness. Through the hardness of their heart and the total forgetfulness of themselves men do not know this truth and are not attracted by its blessings. But thou, O soul, be not deaf to the voice of the Most High, attend and correspond to it in thy actions: I wish to remind thee, that one of the greatest snares of the demon is to counteract the call of the Lord, whenever he seeks to attract and incline the soul to a life of perfection in his service.

Even by itself, the public and sacred act of receiving the habit and entering religion, although it is not always performed with proper fervor and purity of intention, is enough to rouse the wrath and fury of the infernal dragon and his demons; for they know that this act tends not only to the glory of the Lord and the joy of the holy angels, but that religious life will bring the soul to holiness and perfection. It very often happens, that they who have received the habit with earthly and human motives, are afterwards visited by divine grace, which perfects them and sets all things aright. If this is possible even when the beginning was without a good intention, how much more powerful and efficacious will be the light and influence of grace and the discipline of religious life, when the soul enters under the influence of divine love and with a sincere and earnest desire of finding God, and of serving and loving Him?

CHAPTER II.

INSTRUCTION GIVEN BY THE QUEEN CONCERNING RELIG-
IOUS VOWS.   HER FIRST YEARS IN THE TEMPLE.

My dear daughter, I will not deny thee the instruction thou askest of me with the desire of putting it into practice; but do thou receive it with an appreciative and devout mind, ready to follow it in deed.   The wise man says: "My son, if thou be surety for thy friend, thou hast engaged fast thy hand to a stranger, thou art ensnared with the words of thy mouth, and caught with thy own words" (Prov. 6, 12).   Accordingly he who has made vows to God has bound his own will; so that he has no freedom of acting except according to the will and direction of Him to whom he has bound himself; for he is chained down by the words of his own mouth uttered in the profession of his vows.   Before taking his vows, the choice of his ways was in his own hands; but having once bound and obliged himself, let him know that he has entirely lost his liberty and had delivered himself up to God in his superiors. The whole ruin or salvation of souls depends upon the use of their free will; but since most men use it ill and damn themselves, the Most High has established religious life under the sacred vows. Thus the creature, by once using its liberty to make a perfect and prudent choice, can deliver up to his Majesty that very liberty, which so many pervert, if it remains free and unhampered in its choice.

By these vows the liberty to do evil is happily lost, and the liberty for doing good is assured.   It is like

120

a bridle, which leads away from danger and directs into the smooth and sure road. The soul is freed from the slavery and subjection of the passions, and acquires a new power over them, resuming her place as mistress and queen in the government of her kingdom and remaining subject only to the law of grace and the inspirations of the Holy Ghost. If she thus applies her whole will solely to the fulfillment of all that she has promised to God, the holy Spirit will govern and direct all her operations. The creature thereby passes from the condition and state of a slave to that of a child of the Most High, from an earthly to an angelic life, while the corruption and evil effects of sin cannot exert their full power. It is impossible that thou ever be able in this earthly life to calculate or comprehend, what and how many are the blessings and treasures those souls gather for themselves, who with all their powers and affection strive to fulfill perfectly the vows of their profession. For I assure thee, my dearest, that those who are perfect and punctual in their religious obligations can equal and even surpass the martyrs in merit.

The order which religious souls should maintain in their desires should be: that they strive to be punctual in fulfilling the obligations of their vows and all the virtues, which are connected with them. Afterwards and secondarily they may engage in voluntary practices, such as are called supererogatory. This order some of the souls, who are misled by the devil to entertain an indiscreet zeal for perfection, are wont to invert; thus, while they fail seriously in the obligations of their state, they are eager to add other voluntary exercises and practices, which are usually of small use or benefit, or arise from a spirit of presumption and singularity. They secretly desire to be looked upon as distinguished in zeal and perfection, while in truth they are very far even from the beginning of perfection. I do not wish to see in thee a fault so reprehensible: but first fulfill all the duties of thy vows and of community life, and then thou mayest add what thou canst, according to thy ability and the inspiration of divine grace. This together will beautify thy soul and will make it perfect and agreeable in the eyes of God.

The vow of obedience is the principal one in religion; for it implies a total renunciation and denial of one's will. By it the religious renounces all jurisdiction or right to say for himself: I will or I will not, I shall or I shall not act: all this he throws aside and renounces by obedience, delivering himself into the hands of his superior. In order to fulfill this obligation it is necessary for thee not to be wise in thy own conceit, not to imagine thyself still mistress of thy likings, thy desires, or thy opinion; for true obedience must be of the quality of faith, so that the commands of the superior are esteemed, reverenced and put into execution, without any pretense of examination or criticism. Accordingly, in order to obey, thou must consider thyself without opinion, without life of thy own, without right of speech; but thou must allow thyself to be moved and governed like a corpse, alive only in order to execute devotedly all that the superior desires. Never discuss within thyself whether thou shouldst fulfill his commands or not, but only consider how thou canst best execute that which is commanded.

Remember that the most perfect manner of obeying is to avoid offending the superior by showing that you disagree with him. He should find a willing obedience, convincing him that his commands are obeyed promptly, without objection or murmur, either in words or by any other signs. The superiors take the place of God, and he who obeys his superiors, obeys the Lord himself, who is in them and governs them and enlightens them, so that their commands will be for the salvation of souls. The contempt shown to superiors passes on to God himself, who through them manifests and makes known his will (Luke 10, 16). Thou must persuade thyself, that the Lord moves them to speak, and that it is the word of the Omnipotent himself. My daughter, strive to be obedient in order that thou mayest speak of victories (Prov. 21, 28); do not fear to obey, for that is the secure path; so secure, that God will not bring to account the errors of the obedient on the day of judgment, but He will rather blot out other sins in consideration of the sacrifice made in obedience. My most holy Son offered his precious sufferings and death in special love for the obedient, and procured for them special rights in regard to mercy and grace, and special privileges toward the success and perfection of all that is due under obedience. Even now, in order to appease Him, He reminds the eternal Father of his obedience unto death and unto the cross (Phil. 2, 8), and so the Father is placated toward men.

The vow of poverty is a generous renunciation and detachment from the heavy burden of temporal things. It is an alleviation of the spirit, it is a relief afforded to human infirmity, the liberty of a noble heart to strive after eternal and spiritual blessings. It is a satiety and abundance, in which the thirst after earthly treasures is allayed, and a sovereignty and ownership, in which a most noble enjoyment of all riches is established. All this, my daughter, and many other blessings are contained in voluntary poverty, and all this the sons of the world are ignorant and deprived of, precisely because they are lovers of earthly riches and enemies of this holy and opulent poverty. They do not consider, although they feel and suffer, the heavy weight of riches, which pins them to the earth and drives them into its very bowels to seek gold and silver in great anxiety, sleeplessness, labors and sweat, as if they were not men, but wild beasts that know not what they are suffering and doing. And if they are thus weighed down before acquiring riches, how much more when they have come into their possession? Let the countless hosts that have fallen into hell with their burden, proclaim it; let their incalculable anxieties of preserving their riches, and much more, let the intolerable laws, which riches and those that possess them have foisted upon the world, testify what is required to retain them!

If, on the one hand, possessions throttle the spirit and tyrannically oppress it in its weakness, if they suppress the soul's most noble privilege of following eternal goods and God himself: it is certain on the other hand, that voluntary poverty restores to man the nobility of his condition and, liberating him from vile servitude and reinstating him his noble freedom and mastery of all things. The soul is never more a mistress than when she despises them, and only then has she the more firm possession and makes the more excellent use of riches, when she gives them away or leaves them of her own free will; only then her appetite for them is best satiated, when she does not care to possess them. Then above all is the heart set free and made capable of the treasures of the Divinity, for which it is furnished by the Creator with almost infinite capacity.

The temporal goods are created by the Most High for the sole purpose of sustaining life; having attained this end, the need of them ceases. And as this need is limited, soon and easily satisfied, there is no reason that the care for the immortal soul should be only fitful and temporary, while the hunger after riches should be so perpetual and unintermitting, as it has come to be among men.

It is the height of perverseness for man to mix up the end and the means in an affair so important and urgent, that he devote all his time, all his care, all the exertion of his powers and all the alertness of his mind to the life of his body, of which he knows not the duration nor the end, and that on the other hand, in many years of his existence he spare for his poor soul only one hour, and that very often the last and the worst one of his whole life.

The vow of chastity includes purity of body and soul; this is easily lost, and it is difficult, sometimes, according to the manner of losing it, even impossible to repair. This great treasure is deposited in a castle, which has many portals and openings, and if these are not all well guarded and defended, the treasure is without security. My daughter, in order to preserve perfectly this vow, it is necessary to make an inviolable pact with thy senses, not to use them, except for what is according to the dictates of reason and for the glory of the Creator. After once the senses are mortified, it will be easy to overcome thy enemies, for only through them can they conquer thee; for no thoughts can recur, or be awakened to activity, unless fomented and excited by the images and impressions admitted through the exterior senses.

Although no virtue should be wanting in her, who professes herself, and is entitled to call herself, a spouse of Christ; yet it is the virtue of chastity which makes her most worthy and like to her Spouse. For it is chastity, which makes her spiritual and withdraws her from earthly corruption, elevating her to angelic life and to a certain resemblance of God himself. This virtue beautifies and adorns all the rest, raises the body to a higher existence, enlightens the mind and preserves in the soul a nobility above all that is corruptible. Because this virtue was in an especial fruit of the Redemption, merited by my Son on the Cross, where He paid for the sins of the world, therefore holy Scripture expressly mentions that virgins accompany and follow the Lamb (Apoc. 14, 4).

The vow of enclosure is the wall of chastity and of all virtues, the preserve where they are nourished and expanded: it is a privilege granted by heaven to the spouses of Christ in religion, dispensing them from the burdensome and dangerous tribute, which the freedom of the world pays to the ruler of its vanities. By this vow the religious live as in a secure port, while other souls navigate and are tossed about in the storms of a dangerous sea. With so many advantages enclosure cannot be considered as a confinement in a narrow space, for in it are offered to the religious the spacious fields of virtue, of the knowledge of God, of his infinite perfections, of his mysteries, and of his benefits conferred on man. On such spacious grounds can a nun, recreate and enjoy herself; and only when she fails in this enjoyment, does she begin to feel narrow confinement in this, the greatest freedom. For thee, my daughter, let there be no other playground, nor do I wish to see thee confine thyself to so narrow limits as even the whole visible world. Rise up to the height of the knowledge and love of God, where there are no limits or confines to hold thee, and where thou canst live in unbounded liberty. From that eminence thou wilt see how small, vile and despicable is all that is created, and how much too narrow it is to hold thy soul.

I will relate that, which the Most High explained to me on one occasion in his own words:

"The works of Her, who was to be the Mother of the Godman, were altogether and in every way most perfect, and even to understand them exceeds the capacity of all human creatures and of the angels. Her interior acts of the virtues were so precious and of such great merit and favor, that they surpass all that the seraphim can do; and thou, my soul, wilt much better understand, than be able to explain them with words of thy tongue. But it is my will, that during thy pilgrimage in thy mortal body thou place most holy Mary as the beginning of thy joy, and that thou follow Her through the desert of renunciation and abnegation of all that is human and visible. Follow Her by a perfect imitation according to the measure of thy strength and of the light which thou receivest. Let Her be thy guiding star and thy Directress: She will manifest to thee my will and will let thee find my holy law which is written in Her by the power of my right hand: meditate upon it day and night. She by her intercession will strike the rock of Christ's humanity (Num. 220, 11), in order that in this desert may abound the waters of divine grace and light, so that thy thirst may be quenched, thy understanding enlightened, and thy will inflamed. She will be a pillar of light to illuminate thy path (Exod. 12, 21) and a cloud to afford thee shade and refreshment against the ardors of thy passions and the fierceness of thy enemies."

"Thou wilt have in Her an angel, who will guard and guide thee, and (Exod. 13, 21) lead thee away from the dangers of Babylon and of Sodom, so that my punishment shall not reach thee. Thou wilt have in Her a Mother to love thee, a Friend to counsel thee, a Mistress to direct thee, a Protectress to shield thee and a Queen whom thou canst serve and obey as a handmaid. In the virtues, which this Mother of the Onlybegotten exercised in the temple, thou wilt find a summary of all the highest perfections according to which thou shouldst arrange thy life; an exact and reliable copy of all her sanctity; the beauty of virginity, the loveliness of humility, the utmost promptness in devotion and obedience, the steadfastness of faith, the certitude of hope, the fire of love and the most complete outline map of all the wonders of my right hand. According to this rule thou must regulate thy life, by this mirror thou must arrange and adorn it, adding to the beauty and grace of a bride that wishes to enter into the chamber of her Spouse and Lord."

"If the nobility and condition of the teacher are a spur to the disciple and make his doctrine more amiable acceptable, who can attract thee more powerfully than thy Instructress, who is the Mother of thy Spouse, chosen as the most pure and holy among women, and without blemish of sin, being at the same time a Virgin and the Mother of the Onlybegotten of the eternal Father, the splendor of his Divinity in his own essence? Hear then this sovereign Mistress; follow Her in close imitation, and meditate without ceasing upon her admirable excellence and virtues. Remember, that the life and conversation She led in the temple is the original, which all the souls, that consecrate themselves after Her as spouses of Christ, must copy within themselves." The above is the explanation and instruction, which the Most High gave me in outline concerning the life and conduct of the most holy Mary in the temple.

But let us proceed now to a more particular description of her actions. After the vision of the Divinity, described in the second chapter, after She had offered Herself entirely to the Lord and delivered up to her instructress all that She possessed, being thus deprived of all, entirely bound over to obedience, and hiding, beneath the veil of these virtues, treasures of grace and wisdom greater than that of the seraphim, She requested the priest and her teacher to prescribe for Her an order of life and to direct Her in the occupations, which She was to assume. The priest and her instructress, having together considered her petition with the aid of a special enlightenment from on high and desiring to regulate from now on the exercises of this heavenly Child of only three years, called Her to their presence. The Princess of heaven remained kneeling before them during this interview and, although they bade Her rise, She begged most humbly to be allowed to remain in this reverent position in the presence of the minister and priest of the Most High and of her teacher, on account of their office and dignity.

The priest spoke to Her and said: "My Daughter, as a very young Child the Lord has drawn Thee to his house and holy temple; be thankful for this favor and seek to profit by it by striving hard to serve Him in truth and with an upright heart. Acquire all the virtues, in order that thou mayest return from this holy place prepared and fortified against the troubles and the dangers of this world. Obey thy Mistress Anne and commence early to bear the sweet yoke of virtue, in order that thou mayest find it more easy to bear during the rest of thy life" (Thren. 3, 27). The sovereign Child answered: "Do thou, my master, who art the minister and priest of God and holdest his place, and thou my Mistress together with him, command and instruct me in whatever I am to do so that I may not commit any fault: this I beg of you, wishing to obey you in all things."

The priest and her teacher Anne felt within themselves a great enlightenment and a divine impulse to attend especially to this heavenly Child and to care for Her more than the other maidens. Conferring with themselves about this great esteem, with which they had been inspired, though ignorant of the mystery by which it came to them, they resolved to devote particular attention to her guidance and assistance. But as their care could extend only to the exterior and visible actions, they were far from suspecting the interior acts and inspirations of her heart, for over these the Most High watched with singular protection and favor. Thus the pure heart of the Princess of heaven remained free to advance and grow in interior vision, without losing one instant, in which She did not reach what is highest and most excellent in virtue.

The priest also gave Her a rule for her occupations and said: "My Daughter thou wilt assist at the exercises of divine praise and song in honor of the Lord with all reverence and devotion, and always pray to the Most High for the necessities of his holy temple and of his people, and for the coming of the Messias. At eight o'clock thou wilt retire for sleep and at the beginning of dawn thou wilt arise in order to praise the Lord until the third hour (this hour corresponds to our nine o'clock in the morning). From the third hour until evening thou wilt occupy thyself in some manual works, in order that thou mayest be instructed in all things. At meals, of which thou wilt partake after thy exercise, observe befitting moderation. Then thou wilt go to hear the instructions of thy teacher; the rest of the day thou wilt engage thyself in the reading of holy Scriptures, and in all things be humble, affable, and obedient to the commands of thy instructress."

The most holy Child remained on her knees, while She listened to the words of the priest and then asked his blessing; having kissed his hand and the hand of her mistress, She proposed in her heart to observe the order of life assigned Her during her stay in the temple and as long as they should not command her otherwise. And She, who was the Mistress of sanctity, fulfilled their orders as if She were the least of all the scholars. Her desires and her most ardent love impelled Her to many other external exercises, which they had not included in their orders; but with regard to these She subjected Herself to the minister of the Lord, preferring the sacrifice of a perfect and holy obedience to the high dictates of her own fervor. She knew, as Mistress of all perfection, that the divine will is more surely fulfilled by the humble acquiescence of obedience, than in following the highest aspirations to other virtues. By this rare example let souls, and especially those in the religious state, learn not to follow their own effervescences and whims contrary to obedience and the will of their superiors; for in the latter God makes known to us his desire and pleasure, whereas in the former we seek only our own fancies; in the superiors God himself operates, in ourselves (if we work contrary to their orders), temptations, blind passion and deceit is active.

In the performance of works not commanded Her our Queen and Lady distinguished Herself from other maidens by asking her teacher to be allowed to serve them all and be engaged in the humble occupation of scrubbing and cleaning the rooms and of washing the dishes. Although this seemed extraordinary, especially in one of the firstborn children, who were treated with greater consideration and respect, yet the incomparable humility of the heavenly Princess could not be restrained or confined by any consideration of what was due to her position, but reached out for the most humble occupations. With such an eager humility She knew how to gain time and opportunity for doing such work, that She was beforehand in assuming the tasks of others. By means of her infused science She understood all the mysteries and ceremonies of the temple; but She was anxious to learn them also by study and practice, as if She were ignorant of them, nor did She ever fail in any ceremony or duty, no matter how small. She was most eager for humiliation and most submissive in her selfcontempt; every morning and evening She asked the blessing of her teacher and kissed her hand, and the same She did whenever She was ordered or was permitted to perform works of humility. Sometimes, when it was allowed Her, She kissed her feet with profound humility.

The sovereign Princess was so docile, so sweet and friendly in her actions, so ready to serve and so eager and diligent in humbling Herself, so anxious to show kindness and esteem toward all the maidens in the temple, obeying them as if each had been Her Mistress, that She ravished all the hearts. By Her ineffable and heavenly prudence She proceeded in all her actions in such a manner, that She never lost an occasion for engaging in lowly work, in humble service of her companions, and in the fulfillment of the divine pleasure.

But what shall I, most vile creature, and what shall all faithful children of the Catholic Church think, when describing and considering such a vivid example of humility? It seems to us great virtue, when the inferior obeys the superior, the lowly yields to the exalted; and we esteem it a great humility, that the equal submit to his equal. But when the inferior commands and the superior obeys, when the Queen humbles Herself before her slave, when the most holy and the most perfect of all creatures submits to a mere wormlet, the Queen of heaven and earth to the least of women, and when this is done with all her heart and in all sincerity: who is not astonished and confounded in his vapid pride? Who will not see, as in a clear mirror, his unhappy presumption? Who can convince himself, that he knows what true humility is, much less exercise it, when he sees it exhibited, in its reality and in its own element, the most holy Mary? Let us souls, who live under the vow of obedience, approach this light in order to perceive and correct the disorders, which show themselves, whenever obedience to our god-given superiors requires renouncement of our whims and therefore becomes hard and troublesome. Here let our hardness be crushed, let the proudest humiliate herself and be confounded in her shameful pride; let her banish all presumption and let her not account herself obedient and humble, because on certain occasions she has yielded to the superiors, for she is yet far from thinking herself inferior and beneath her companion, as Mary did, who is superior to all.

The beauty, grace, elegance and courteousness of our Queen were incomparable; for all the natural graces and gifts, which were hers in a most perfect degree, were re-enforced by the splendor of supernatural or divine grace, and effected a marvelous union of grace and beauty in all her being and activity, enthralling all in love and admiration of Her. Divine Providence moderated the outward demonstrations of this affection, which those who conversed with Her, would have shown, if they had been left to the natural force of their spontaneous love of the Queen. In eating and in sleep, as in all other virtues, She was most perfect: She observed the measure dictated by temperance; never did She exceed, nor could She, rather She deducted from the necessary. Although her curtailed sleep did not interrupt her high contemplation, as I have said before, yet She would have gladly omitted it altogether; in virtue of obedience however, She retired to rest at the time appointed, and on her humble and poor couch, strewn with the flowers of virtue (Cant. 1, 15) and surrounded by the seraphim and the angelic host who guarded and assisted Her, She enjoyed more exalted contemplation (outside of beatific vision), and more ardent ecstasies of love, than all of them together.

She divided her time and applied it with rare prudence so as to give to each of her actions and occupations its proper share. She read much in the sacred writings of the ancients and, by means of her infused science, She was so well versed in them and in all their profound mysteries, that none of them was unfamiliar to Her; for the Most High made known to Her all their mysteries and sacraments; She treated and conversed about them in her conferences with the holy angels of her guard, familiarizing Herself with them and asking about them with incomparable intelligence and great acuteness. If this sovereign Mistress had written what She understood, we would have many other additions to the sacred Scriptures; and we would be able to draw out of them a perfect understanding of those writings and the deep meanings and mysteries of all those preserved in the Church.

WORDS OF THE QUEEN.

My daughter, human nature is imperfect and remiss in practicing virtue, and easily weakens in its exercise; for it continually seeks rest and evades labor with all its might. When the soul listens to and extemporizes with the animal and carnal part of its nature this latter will engross and overcome the forces of reason and of the spirit, and will reduce them to a dangerous and shameful slavery. This disorder is abominable and much to be feared by all; but God abhors it without comparison more in his ministers and in religious: they, as a matter of course, are supposed to be perfect, and therefore are injured so much the more seriously, if they do not come out victorious in the conflict of the passions. By remissness in battle and by their frequent defeats they live themselves into a paralyzing and self-satisfied conviction of false security, content with the performance of certain easy outward practices of virtue, at the same time imagining (without the least real advancement) that they are moving mountains. The demon then introduces other distractions and temptations, and on account of their small appreciation of the rules and practices of religion, they begin to weaken in all of them, esteem them as light and unimportant matter, and, living on in their false security, come to lose the very perception of true virtue.

I desire that thou, my daughter, guard against this error. Remember, that a voluntary remissness in regard to one imperfection prepares and opens the way for others: these facilitate the commission of venial sins, these again of mortal sins. Thus the descent is from one abyss to another, until the bottom is found in the disregard of all evil. In order to prevent such a misfortune it is necessary to intercept from afar the current of sin, for the practice or ceremony, which seems but small, is an outwork which keeps the enemy at a distance, while the precepts and laws concerning more important matters are the fortress walls of conscience. If the demon can break through and gain the outer defenses, he is in better position to gain the inner ones. If then an opening is made in the bulwarks by the commission of sin, although it may not be a very grievous one, he already has a better opportunity to make an assault on the interior reign of a soul. As the soul finds herself weakened by vicious acts and habits and without strength of grace, she does not resist the attack with fortitude, and the devil, acquiring more and more power over her, begins to subject and oppress her without opposition.

CHAPTER III.

On account of this beauty and harmony regarding the habits of virtue, the soul of the most holy Mary was so enlightened, ennobled and entirely bent on the highest Good and last End of all creation; so alert, prompt, efficient and joyful in the practice of virtue, that, if it were possible for our weak insight to penetrate into the interior of her sacred soul, we would there find a more wonderful beauty than that of all creatures combined and inferior only to that of God himself. All the perfection of creatures were in purest Mary as if in their own sphere and center, and all virtues reached in Her the highest perfection, so that in no manner could it ever be said of Her: this or that is wanting in order to make Her altogether beautiful and perfect. Besides the infused virtues, She possessed all the acquired ones, which She augmented by practice and exercise. In other souls, one single act cannot be called virtue, because many repeated acts are necessary to constitute virtue; but in the most holy Mary each act was so efficacious, intense and consummate, that each one was superior to the virtues of all the other creatures. Accordingly, as her acts of virtue were so frequent and did not fall short in the least point of the highest degree of perfection, how incomparably excellent were not the habits of virtue, which the heavenly Mistress attained by her personal exertion? The end for which something is done is that which makes an act virtuous as being well done. In Mary, our Mistress, this end was God himself, highest possible end of all activity; for She did nothing through which She was not certain to advance the greater glory and pleasure of the Lord and She looked upon this as the motive and ultimate end of all her actions.

The infused virtues are divided into two classes. To the first belong only those, that have God himself for their immediate object; therefore they are called theological virtues, being faith, hope, and charity. To the second class belong all those other virtues, which have as their proximate object some means or some honorable good, which advances the soul toward its last end, namely God. These are called the moral virtues, because they are intimately connected with established customs, and, although they are many in number, they can be reduced to four, which are called the cardinal virtues: prudence, justice, fortitude and temperance. Of all these virtues and their different species I will say farther on as much as I can in order that I may make clear, how all of them and each one in particular adorned the faculties of the most holy Mary. At present I only mention in general, that none of them was wanting in Her, and that all were possessed by Her in the most perfect manner; moreover they were supplemented by the gifts of the Holy Ghost, the fruits of the Spirit, and the Beatitudes. God did not fail to infuse into Her from the first moment of her Conception, all of the graces and gifts conducive to the highest beauty of the human soul and faculties; and this was true of the will as well as of the understanding, so that She had as well the knowledge as the habit of the sciences. In order to say it all in one word: all the good, which the Most High could give Her as the Mother of his Son and as a mere creature, He conferred upon Her in the most exalted degree. In addition to all this her virtues continually augmented: the infused virtues, because She added to them by her own merits, and the acquired virtues, because She nurtured and multiplied them by the intensity of her meritorious acts.

In few words the holy Elizabeth described the greatness of the faith of most holy Mary, when, as reported to us by the evangelist Luke, She exclaimed: "Blessed art thou for having believed, because the words and promises of the Lord shall be fulfilled in Thee" (Luke 1, 45). The faith of this great Lady must be estimated from the greatness of her good fortune and beatitude, and from her ineffable dignity.

The faith of the most holy Mary was an image of the whole creation and an open prodigy of the divine power, for in Her the virtue of faith existed in the highest and the most perfect degree possible; in a certain manner and to a great extent, it made up for the want of faith in men. The Most High has given this excellent virtue to mortals so that, in spite of the carnal and mortal nature, they might have the knowledge of the Divinity and of his mysteries and admirable works: a knowledge so certain and infallibly secure, that it is like seeing Him face to face, and like the vision of the blessed angels in heaven. The same object and the same truth, which they see openly, we perceive obscured under the veil of faith.

One glance at the world will make us understand, how many nations, reigns and provinces, since the beginning of the world, have lost their claims to this great blessing of the faith, so little understood by the thankless mortals: how many have unhappily flung it aside, after the Lord had conferred it on them in his generous mercy, and how many of the faithful, having without their merit received the gift of faith, neglect and despise it, letting it lie idle and unproductive for the last end to which it is to direct and guide them. It was befitting therefore, that the divine equity should have some recompense for such lamentable loss, and that such an incomparable benefit should find an adequate and proportionate return, as far as is possible from creatures; it was befitting that there should be found at least one Creature, in whom the virtue of faith should come to its fullest perfection, as an example and rule for the rest.

All this was found in the great faith of the most holy Mary and on account of Her and for Her alone, if there had been no other creature in the world, it would have been most proper, that God should contrive and create the excellent virtue of faith; for according to our way of understanding, Mary by Herself was a sufficient pledge to the divine Providence, that He would find a proper return on the part of man, and that the object of this faith would not be frustrated by the want of correspondence among mortals. The faith of this sovereign Queen was to make recompense for their default and She was to copy the divine prototype of this virtue in its highest perfection. All the other faithful can measure and gage themselves by the faith of this Mistress; for they will be more or less faithful, the more or less they approach the perfection of her incomparable faith. Therefore She was set as Teacher and example of all the believing, including the Patriarchs, Prophets, Apostles and Martyrs and all that have believed or will believe in the Christian doctrines to the end of the world.

The intelligent love, with which She explicitly believed all the divine truths, cannot be expressed in words, without misrepresenting its intensity. The most holy Mary knew all that She believed and believed all that She knew; for the infused theological knowledge of the credibility of faith's mysteries, and the understanding of this credibility, existed in the wisest Virgin Mother in the highest degree possible in a mere creature. Her knowledge was kept in a constant actuality, and by means of her memory, like that of an angel, She never forgot, that which once She had learnt. This gift and faculty of the understanding She kept in constant operation in order to exercise her deep faith; only at times, as already said, God suspended faith by other acts of the mind. Except that She was not yet a comprehensor, nothing was wanting in regard to her intelligence of the matters of faith and in regard to the clear knowledge of the Divinity. In this regard She held a position far above that of all the wayfarers and She by Herself constituted a class of such high degrees, as cannot be attained by any other wayfarer to heaven.

And if the most holy Mary, while She exercised the acts of faith and hope, was in what might be called her most ordinary and therefore the lowest degree of activity, and if in that state She excelled all the angels and saints in merits by her faith and love, what must we say of the excellence of her acts, her merits and her affections, during the time in which She was exalted by the divine power to the blessed state of highest intuitive vision and clear knowledge of the Divinity? If this is beyond the comprehension of the angelic mind, how can an earthly creature ever hope to find words to describe it? I therefore can only express the mere wish, that all mortals might come to a knowledge of the precious value of faith, by learning it from this heavenly Original, in whom faith attained its ultimate perfection and where it completely fulfilled the end for which it was created. Let the infidels, the heretics, the pagans and idolaters approach this Mistress of faith, most holy Mary, in order to be enlightened in their falsehoods and darksome errors and in order to find the sure way toward the last end of their being. Let also Catholics approach and learn to understand the copious rewards of this virtue; let them ask the Lord with the Apostles to increase their faith (Luke 7, 5). Not that they ever can reach the faith of most holy Mary, but let them ask for the desire to imitate Her and follow Her, for by her faith She teaches us, and by her merits She helps us to obtain this virtue.

Saint Paul calls the patriarch Abraham the father of all the faithful (Rom. 6, 11), because he first received the promise, hoping against hope (Rom. 4, 18); He wishes to extol the excellence of the Patriarch's faith, because he believed the promise of the Lord, that Sarah, his wife, would bear him a son though she was sterile, and, according to the laws of nature, incapable of conception; moreover, in offering his son as a sacrifice at God's command, he relinquished at the same time the prospect of the countless offspring, which the Lord had promised to Him. This all, and many other sayings and promises of the Lord were made impossible of fulfillment according to the laws of nature, yet Abraham believed, that the divine power could execute them in a supernatural manner. Therefore he merited to be called the Father of all the believers and to receive the seal of his faith which justified him, namely circumcision.

But our supereminent Lady, Mary, possesses much greater rights and titles to be called the Mother of faith and of all the faithful. In her hand is hoisted the standard and ensign of faith for all the believers in the law of grace. First indeed, according to the order of time, was the Patriarch and consequently he was ordained to be the father and head of the Hebrew people: great was his belief in the promises concerning Christ our Lord, and in the works of the Most High. Nevertheless incomparably more admirable was the faith of Mary in all these regards and She excels him in dignity. Greater difficulty and incongruity was there that a virgin should conceive and bring forth, than that an aged and sterile woman should bear fruit; and the patriarch Abraham was not so certain of the sacrifice of Isaac, as Mary was of the inevitable sacrifice of her most holy Son. She is the One, who perfectly believed and hoped in all the mysteries, and She shows to the whole Church, how it must believe in the Most High and in the works of his Redemption. Having thus understood the faith of Mary our Queen, we must admit Her to be the Mother of the faithful and the prototype of the Catholic faith and of holy hope. And in order to conclude this chapter, I will add, that Christ, our Redeemer and Teacher, as He was a comprehensor and as his most holy soul enjoyed the highest glory and the beatific vision, had no necessity or occasion for faith, nor could He in his own actions give us an example of this virtue. But what the Lord could not do in his own Person, He did in the person of his most holy Mother, constituting Her as the Foundress, the Mother and the example of faith in his evangelical Church. And thus on the day of universal accounting this sovereign Mistress and Queen shall in an especial manner assist her most holy Son in the judgment of those, who, in spite of such an example, have not believed during their stay on earth.

WORDS OF THE QUEEN.

My daughter, the inestimable treasure of the virtue of divine faith is hidden to those mortals who have only carnal and earthly eyes; for they do not know how to appreciate and esteem a gift and blessing of such incomparable value. Consider, my dearest, what the world was without faith and what it would be today if my Son and Lord would not preserve faith. How many men whom the world has celebrated as great, powerful and wise have precipitated themselves, on account of the want of light of faith, from the darkness of their unbelief into most abominable sins, and thence into the eternal darkness of hell! How many kingdoms and provinces, being blind themselves, follow these still more blind leaders until they together fall into the abyss of eternal pains! And they are followed by the bad Christians, who having received the grace and blessing of faith, live as if they had it not in their hearts.

Do not forget, my dear friend, to be thankful for this precious jewel which the Lord has given thee as a dower and a wedding gift of thy espousal with Him, in order to draw thee to the bridal chamber of his holy Church and afterwards to have intercourse with Him in the eternal beatitude. Continually exercise this virtue of faith, for it places thee near to thy last end, after which thou strivest, and brings thee near to the object of thy desires and thy love. Faith teaches the sure way of eternal salvation, faith is the light that shines in the darkness of this mortal life and pilgrimage; it leads men securely to the possession of the fatherland to which they are wayfaring, if they do not allow it to die out by infidelity and sinfulness. Faith enlivens the other virtues and serves as a nourishment of the just man and a support in his labors. Faith confounds and fills with fear the infidels and the lax Christians in their negligence; for it convinces them in this world of their sin and threatens punishment in the life to come. Faith is powerful to do all things, for nothing is impossible to the believer; faith makes all things attainable and possible. Faith illumines and ennobles the understanding of man, since it directs him in the darkness of his natural ignorance, not to stray from the way, and it elevates him above himself so that he sees and understands with infallible certainty what is far above his powers and assures him of it no less than if he saw it clearly before him. He is thus freed from the gross and vile narrow-mindedness of those who will believe only what they can experience by their own limited natural powers, not considering that the soul, as long as it lives in the prison of this corruptible body, is very much circumscribed and limited in its sphere of action by the knowledge drawn from the coarse activity of the senses. Appreciate, therefore, my daughter, this priceless treasure of the Catholic faith given thee by God, watch over it and practice it in great esteem and reverence.

CHAPTER IV.

The virtue of hope naturally follows upon that of
faith, since it is ordained as its complement. For if the
Most High instills in us the divine light of faith, and if
He wishes us, without regard to differences of position
and of age, to come into the infallible knowledge of the
Godhead and of his mysteries and promises, it is for no
other reason than that each one of us, knowing Him as
our last end and object, and learning of the means of
arriving at it, may engender within himself the vehement
desire to reach that goal. This desire, which naturally
carries with it the inclination to attain this highest Good,
is called hope and is infused into our will or natural appetite in Baptism. For it belongs to the proper activity
of the will to strive after eternal felicity as its greatest
good and blessing, to make use of divine grace for obtaining it and for overcoming the difficulties which will
occur in its pursuit.

How excellent the virtue of hope is, may be learned
from the fact that its ultimate object is God himself, our highest Good. Although it perceives and seeks
Him as something that is absent, yet at the same time it
seeks Him also as something that is attainable through
the merits of Christ and through the proper activity of
the one that hopes for it. The acts and operations of this
virtue are regulated by the light of divine faith and by
the prudent reliance on the infallible promise of the Lord.

Thus hope, by means of the reasoning powers, maintains the middle road between despair and presumption, not permitting man to presume on his own powers for the attainment of eternal glory or to set aside meritorious activity on his own part, nor allowing fear or despondency to hinder Him from exerting himself toward it on account of the Lord's promises and assurances of final success. In this security, guaranteed by divine faith in all that pertains to these things and applied in prudent and sound reasoning, man hopes without fear of being deceived and yet also without presumption.

From this it can be seen that despair may arise both from a want of believing what faith promises and also from a failure to apply to one's own self the security of the divine promises, in which one believes, but which one falsely supposes unattainable in one's own regard. Between these two dangerous extremes hope directs us in the safe way, maintaining us in the confident belief on the one hand that God will not deny to ourselves what He has promised to all, and on the other, that the promise was not made unconditionally and absolutely, but requires our exertion and effort to merit its fulfillment as far as it is possible with the help of divine grace. For if God has made man capable of the vision of eternal glory, it was not just that any one should attain to such felicity by sinful abuse of the very faculties with which he is to enjoy it; but that he use them in such a way as to befit the end for which he received them. This proper use of the faculties consists in the exercise of the virtues, which prepare man for the enjoyment of his highest good, and in seeking it already in this life by the knowledge and love of God.

Now, in most holy Mary this virtue of hope reached the highest degree possible both in regard to itself and in regard to all its effects, circumstances and qualities; for the desire and the striving after the last end, which is the vision and the fruition of God, was in Her more active than in all other creatures; moreover this most faithful and prudent Lady did nothing to impede these aspirations, but followed them up with all the perfection possible in a creature. Not only did She possess the infused virtue of faith in the promises of our Lord and its concomitant intensity of hope; but over and above all this She enjoyed beatific vision, in which She learnt to know by experience the infinite truth and fidelity of the Most High. And although She did not have occasion to make use of hope, while enjoying the vision and possession of the Divinity; nevertheless, after again resuming Her ordinary state, She was impelled by the memory of what She had enjoyed, to hope and strive after it with so much the greater force and avidity. Thus the longings of the Queen of all virtues constituted a certain kind of new and particular kind of hope.

There was another reason why the hope of the most holy Mary excelled the hope of all the other faithful joined together: namely the greatness of the prospective reward and glory due to this sovereign Queen, for reward is after all the real object of hope and in Her it was to be far above all the glory of the angels and saints; that is, proportionate to the knowledge of this glory assured to Her in God was also her expectation and desire to acquire it. Moreover in order that She might attain the highest summit of this virtue, and that She might worthily hope for all that the powerful arm of God would work in Her, She was befittingly furnished with the light of a supreme faith and all the helps and gifts pertaining thereto, and with an especial assistance of the Holy Ghost. What we have said of the virtue of

hope in the blessed Virgin in regard to its principal object must also be affirmed in regard to its secondary objects, for the gifts and mysterious blessings enjoyed by
this Queen of Heaven were so great that they could not
be amplified even by the arm of the Almighty God in a
mere creature. Now as the great Lady was to receive
these favors through the medium of faith and hope, these
virtues were proportionately great, and therefore the
greatest that could possibly fall to the lot of a handiwork
of God.

Moreover if, as has already been said of the virtue
of faith, the Queen of heaven was endowed with
an explicit knowledge and faith of all the revealed truths
and of all the mysteries and operations of the Most High,
and if the acts of hope corresponded to these acts of
faith, who, except the Lord himself could ever comprehend how many and how excellent were the acts of hope,
which the Mistress of virtues elicited, since She was aware
of her own eternal glory and felicity and of that, which
was to be wrought in the rest of the evangelical Church
by the merits of her most holy Son? For the sole sake of
Mary, as we have before said of her faith, God would
have created this virtue, and for her sake He would have
conferred it, as He really did, on the whole human race.

On this account the holy Spirit calls Her the
Mother of beautiful love and holy hope (Eccli. 25, 24);
for just as She became the Mother of Christ because She
furnished Him with the flesh of his body, so the holy
Spirit made Her the Mother of hope, because by her especial concurrence and coöperation She conceived and
brought forth this virtue for the faithful of the Church.
Her prerogative of being the Mother of holy hope was
connected with and consequent upon Her being the
Mother of Jesus Christ our Lord, for She knew that in

her Son She would lay the foundation of all the security of our hope. On account of these conceptions and births of the most holy Queen, She obtained a certain dominion and sovereignty over those graces and the promises of the Most High, which depended upon the death of Christ, her Son, for their fulfillment. When She of her own free will gave conception and birth to the incarnate Word She turned them all over to us and thereby gave birth to our hope. Thus was accomplished in its legitimate sense that which the Holy Ghost said to Her: "Thy plants are a paradise" (Cant. 4, 13); for all that came forth from Mary, the Mother of grace, was to constitute our happiness, our paradise, and our certain hope of being able to attain them.

The Church has a celestial and true father in Jesus Christ, for He engendered and founded it by his merits and labors, and enriched it with his graces, his example and his doctrines, as was to be expected from the Father and Author of such an admirable work. Therefore it was befitting that the Church should have also a loving and kind Mother, who with sweet regalement and caresses, and with maternal solicitude and assistance, should nurse the little children at her breast (I. Cor. 3, 12), nourish them with tender and delicious food as long as they cannot in their infancy bear the food of the robust and strong. This sweet Mother was most holy Mary, who since the beginning of the Church, when the law of grace was born in her yet tender children, began to give forth the sweet milk of her enlightened teaching as a merciful Mother; and who will continue to the end of the world thus to assist and intercede for the new children, which Christ our Lord engenders every day by his merits and at the petitions of this Mother of mercy. She it is for whom they are born, who raises and nourishes them. She is our sweet Mother, our life and our hope, the original of the blessings, which are ours, She is the example which we are to imitate, She is our assurance in the pursuit of the eternal happiness, merited by her most holy Son, She furnishes the assistance necessary for its final attainment.

WORDS OF THE QUEEN.

Thou, my dearest, having received such great enlightenment concerning the excellence of this virtue and the works which I practiced by its help, shouldst work without ceasing to imitate me according to the assistance of divine grace. Renew continually and confer within thyself the promises of the Most High and, with unshaken confidence in their divine truthfulness, raise thy heart to ardent desires and longings for their attainment. In this firm hope thou canst assure thyself of arriving through the merits of my most holy Son, at the blessed cohabitation in the celestial fatherland and at the companionship of all those who there see in immortal glory the face of the Most High. With its help thou canst raise thy heart above earthly things and fix thy mind upon the immutable Good, to which thou aspirest; all visible things will appear to thee burdensome and disagreeable, and thou wilt esteem them as vile and contemptible; nothing wilt thou strive after except that most lovable and delightful object of thy desires. In my soul there was an ardor of hope, such as is possible only to those who have apprehended its object in faith and tasted it by experience; no tongue and no words can describe or express its intensity.

Besides, in order to spur thee on still more, consider and deplore with heartfelt sorrow the unhappiness of so many souls who are images of God and capable of his glory, and who through their own fault are deprived of the true hope of enjoying it. If the children of the holy Church would pause in their vain occupations and would take time to consider and weigh the blessings of unerring faith and hope, which separates them from darkness and which, without their merit, distinguishes them from the followers of blind unbelief, they would without doubt be ashamed of their torpid forgetfulness and repudiate their vile ingratitude. But let them be undeceived, for most terrible punishments await them; they are most detestable in the sight of God and the saints, because they despise the blood shed by Christ for the very purpose of gaining them these blessings. As if all were only a fiction they treat with contempt the blessings of truth, hastening about during their whole life without spending even one day, and many of them not even an hour, in the consideration of their duties and of their danger. Weep, O soul, over this lamentable evil, and according to thy power work and pray for its extirpation through my most holy Son. Believe me that whatever exertion and attempt thou makest toward this purpose shall be rewarded by his Majesty.

CHAPTER V.

The most excellent virtue of charity is the mistress, the queen, the mother, the life and beauty of all the other virtues; charity governs, moves and directs them to their ultimate and true end, charity leads them on to their ultimate perfection, preserves them and makes them grow, enlightens them and beautifies them, gives them life and efficacy. If the other virtues confer each their measure of perfection on creatures, charity gives them perfection itself and brings them to their full complement. Without charity all is of small value, obscure, languid, lifeless and unprofitable, not being endowed either with the essence or the appurtenances of true vitality. Charity is kind, patient, meek, without emulation, without envy, without offensiveness, desires not to acquire, but readily distributes all, is the cause of all good and consents not to evil; as far as it is concerned (I Cor. 13, 4) it is the fullest participation in the true and ultimate Good. O Virtue of virtues and greatest treasure of heaven! Thou alone hast the key of paradise! Thou art the dawn of eternal light, the sun of eternity's day, the fire which purifies, the wine which inebriates with new delights, the nectar which rejoices, the sweetness which satiates without surceasing, the chamber of rest for the soul, a bond so intimate that it makes us one with God (Joan 17, 21), with the same bond that unites the eternal Father to the Son, and Both to the holy Spirit.

On account of the nobility of this most excellent of all virtues, our God and Lord, according to the Gospel of St. John, wished to honor Himself or wished to honor it, by calling Himself Charity (I John 4, 16). There are many reasons why the Catholic Church attributes the divine perfections of omnipotence to the Father, of wisdom to the Son, and of love to the Holy Ghost. For the Father is the beginning, the Son is engendered of the Father through the divine intelligence, and the Holy Ghost proceeds from Both through the will. But the name of Charity and the perfection which it implies is attributed to the Lord himself without distinction of Persons, since the Evangelist says indiscriminately: "God is charity." This virtue in the Lord has the distinction of being the terminus or end of all his operations *ad intra* and *ad extra*. For on the one hand all the divine processions (which are the operations of the Godhead with Himself or *ad intra*), terminate in the reciprocal union and love of the three divine Persons, and thus they constitute an indissoluble bond of unity over and above the indivisibility of the divine Essence, proper to it as being one and the same God. On the other hand the works *ad extra,* namely the creatures, are an offspring of divine charity and are ordained towards it, so that, issuing from that immense sea of divine bounty, they also return by charity and love to the source from whence they sprang. It is peculiar to the virtue of charity in opposition to all the other virtues and gifts, that it is a perfect participation of a divine virtue; it is born of one source, is directed back to the same, and is more adapted to that eternal source than all other virtues. If we call God our hope, our patience, or our wisdom, it is because we receive them from his hand, and not because these perfections are in God as they exist in ourselves.

But we call God our charity, not only because we receive it from the Lord, and because He communicates it to us, but because He himself is essential charity, and the overflow of this divine perfection, which we represent to ourselves as a form and attribute of his Divinity, redounds in our souls, transforming it more perfectly and abundantly than any other virtue.

This is in part the nature of Charity in its divine original, God. Outside of God himself, however, we will find it in the fullest perfection possible to a mere creature in none other than most holy Mary, and in Her we find the model after which we are more immediately to copy our own charity. It is evident that the light proceeding from the uncreated Sun of charity, where it is contained without limit or circumscription, communicates itself to all creatures even the most remote according to an order and measurement adjusted in proportion to the proximity or distance of each from the divine source. And this order manifests the fullness and perfection of the divine Providence; for without it, this Providence would show a certain defect, confusedness and discord in the creatures as far as the participation of his goodness and love is concerned. The first place after God himself, in the distribution of divine Charity, was due to that Soul and that Person, who was at the same time uncreated God and created man; for the highest grace and participation of love naturally was to be found where existed the closest and most intimate union with God, as it existed and as it will exist forever in Christ our Lord.

The second place is due to his most holy Mother Mary, in whom charity and divine love found its resting place in an especial manner. For, according to our way of apprehending, the uncreated Charity could not be quieted until It should find a creature to which It could communicate Itself in such great plenitude, that the love and affection of the whole human race should in its entirety be reproduced in that Creature alone. It was intended that this chosen Creature should in Herself be endowed with the gifts of charity, without the shortcomings and defects common to the rest of mortals infected with sin, so that She by Herself would be able to supply the balance of creation and make for it the greatest possible return of love. Mary alone was chosen among all creatures to imitate the Sun of justice in charity (I Cant. 4, 9), and faithfully to copy this virtue from its Original. She by Herself knew how to love more ardently and perfectly than all the rest of creatures combined, to love God entirely for his own sake, purely, intensely and without defect, and also loving creatures for God's sake and in a manner similar to Him. She alone adequately followed the impulse of charity and her generous inclination of loving the highest Good as highest Good, without any side intentions; and of loving the creatures on account of their participation in God, without the thought of a return or reward of her love. And in perfect imitation of the uncreated Charity, Mary by her charity was able and knew how to love in such a way as to make better that which is loved; for by her love She made better heaven and earth and all things that exist outside of God.

If the charity of this great Lady were put in the balance with that of all the men and angels, hers would outweigh theirs by far; for She by Herself exceeded them all in her knowledge of the essence and qualities of the divine Charity and consequently only Mary knew how to imitate It with adequate perfection and above all the powers of intellectual creatures. In this excess of love and charity She repaid and satisfied the debt of infinite love due to the Lord from creatures, as far as He could demand a return of them, for their return was not to be infinite in value, that being impossible. Just as the love and the charity of the most holy soul of Jesus Christ was in its greatness proportionate to the hypostatic union, so the love of Mary was great in proportion to the excellence conferred upon Her by the eternal Father, when He appointed Her as the one, who as Mother was to conceive and bear his Son for the salvation of the world.

Thence we understand that all the gifts and the blessings of creatures depend in some manner on the love and charity of the blessed Virgin toward God. In Her alone it was possible that divine Charity could exist in this world in its highest and ultimate perfection. She paid the whole debt of charity at a time when all men were unable to pay or even to understand the greatness of their debt. She, by her most perfect charity, obliged the eternal Father to sacrifice his most holy Son for Herself and in Redemption of the whole world; for if Mary had loved less and if her charity had been defective, the proper preparation for his Incarnation would have been wanting. But as soon as any creature was found, which resembled God so closely as She, it was, so to say, but a natural consequence that He should descend to Her as He did.

All this is the meaning of the words of the Holy Ghost when He calls Mary the mother of beautiful love (Eccli. 24, 24), as has already been explained correspondingly in regard to hope. These words to Mary signify: Mary is the Mother of Him, who is our sweetest love, Jesus, our Lord and Redeemer, who became the most beautiful among men by a divine, infinite and uncreated beauty, and by a human nature which was to be without guilt or blemish and to which no beauty of grace that could be communicated by the Divinity, was wanting (I

Pet. 2, 22). She is also the Mother of beautiful love, for She alone engendered in her soul the perfect love and charity and the most beautiful affection. All the rest of the creatures combined could not attain the beauty and faultlessness of her Charity for theirs was not worthy to be called absolutely beautiful. She is the Mother of our love; for She drew it toward the earth for us; She cultivated it for us; She taught us to know and practice it; there is no other creature in heaven or on earth that could be such a teacher of this beautiful love for men or angels. Therefore all the saints are but rays of this sun, and streamlets flowing from this ocean; so much the better will they know how to love, the more they participate in this love and charity of most holy Mary, and in as far as they succeed in imitating and copying it more exactly.

The sources of this charity and love of our princess Mary were her profound knowledge and wisdom, derived as well from her infused faith and hope, as also from the gifts of science, intellect and wisdom given to Her by the Holy Ghost; but the greatest of all the sources of her love were the intuitive and abstractive visions of the Divinity. Through all these mediums She reached the highest knowledge of the uncreated Charity and drank of it at its very fountain, and as She thus learned, how God was to be loved for his own sake and the creature for the sake of God, also how to practice and execute this love with the most intense and fervent desire. Moreover, as the power of God found no impediment or hindrance, no inadvertence, ignorance or imperfection, nor any tardiness of the will in this Queen, it could operate in Her according to his pleasure. This was not possible in other creatures, since in none of them it found the same disposition as in most holy Mary.

In Her was the fulfillment of that great natural

and divine precept: "Thou shalt love thy God with thy whole heart, and with thy whole soul, and with thy whole strength." Mary alone satisfied this obligation and debt for all men, which in this life and before seeing God they neither knew nor could ever fulfill entirely. This Lady fulfilled it more perfectly during her pilgrimage than the saints even in the state of beatitude. Moreover She also satisfied the intentions of God in regard to this precept, namely that it remain not unfruitful and as it were frustrated on the part of wayfaring men; for most holy Mary by Herself sanctified and fulfilled it entirely for all of them, supplying by her charity all that was wanting in the fulfillment of this precept among men. And probably if God had not foreknown that Mary our Queen would be among the number of the mortals, He would not have given this command in this form. But on Her account He was pleased to give it; to Her we owe not only this command of perfect charity, but also the adequate fulfillment of it among men.

O most sweet and most beautiful Mother of beautiful love and charity! Let all the nations know Thee, let all generations bless Thee, and let all the creatures magnify and praise Thee! Thou alone art the perfect One, the beloved One, the chosen Mother of uncreated Charity. It formed Thee and selected Thee to shine like the sun in thy most beautiful and most perfect love (Cant. 6, 9)! Let all us miserable children of Eve approach this sun in order to be enlightened and inflamed. Let us approach this Mother in order to be born again in love. Let us approach this Teacher in order to be taught the love, affection and charity which is without defect. Love is a disposition which is pleased and satisfied with the thing loved. Affection is a selection and separation of the beloved from other of the same kind, and charity implied in addition to these, a high appreciation and esteem for the goodness of the beloved. All this we will learn from the Mother of true love, who is called by that name precisely because her love possesses all these qualities. In Her we learn to love God for his own sake, resting satisfied in Him with all our heart; to give Him a separate place in all our love from all that is not God, for loving Him, together with other things, only diminishes our love of God. We learn to appreciate Him and esteem Him above gold and above all precious things, for in comparison with Him all precious things are of no value, all beauty is ugliness, and all that is great and estimable in carnal eyes, becomes contemptible and valueless. Of the effects of this love of the most holy Mary, this whole history treats and of them heaven and earth are full. Therefore I will not stay to describe more particularly what no human tongue, nor words of men or angels can convey.

WORDS OF THE QUEEN.

My daughter, if I desire in maternal affection, that thou follow me and imitate me in all the other virtues, then more especially do I make known and declare to thee my desire to see thee follow me in the virtue of charity, for this is the end and the crowning glory of all other virtues. I desire that thou exert thy utmost powers to copy in thy soul, with the greatest perfection, all that thou hast learnt of my charity. Light up the lamp of thy faith and reason in order to find this drachm of infinite value, and after thou hast (Luke 15, 8) found it, forget and despise all that is earthly and corruptible. In thy own mind consider again and again, ponder and take heed of the infinite reasons and causes that make God lovable above all other things. In order that thou mayest be sure that thou lovest Him perfectly and truly, search within thyself for the following signs and effects of that love; whether thy thought and meditation dwell continually on God, whether his commands and counsel find in thee no repugnance or remissness, whether thou fearest to offend Him, whether thou seekest immediately to appease Him after having offended Him, whether thou grievest to see Him offended and rejoicest to see Him served by all creatures, whether thou desirest and art delighted to speak continually of his love; see whether thou delightest in the memory of his presence, whether thou grievest at thy forgetfulness of Him and at his absence from thee, whether thou lovest what He loves, and abhorrest what He abhors, whether thou seekest to draw all men towards his friendship and grace, whether thou prayest with confidence; see whether thou receivest with gratitude his benefits, whether thou dost not waste them but rather turnst them to good account for his honor and glory, whether thou strivest to extinguish in thyself all the movements of the passions, which retard thee or hinder thee in thy loving aspirations and in thy works of virtue.

The right order of this virtue is to love God above all the creatures, then to love oneself, and him who is nearest to oneself, namely, our neighbor. God must be loved with the whole understanding, without deceit, with the whole will, without reserve or division, with the whole mind, without forgetfulness, without diminution, without negligence or remissness. The motive of charity in loving God is none else than God Himself; for He must be loved for his own sake, being the highest Good and most perfect goodness and holiness. Loving God for such motives causes the creature to love itself and the neighbor and itself; for both belong to one and the same

God, from whom they derive their origin, their life and activity. He that loves God truly for Himself will also love all that is of God and all that in some way participates in his goodness. Therefore charity looks upon the neighbor as a work and a participation of God and makes no distinction between friend or enemy. Charity looks only upon that which is of God and which pertains to Him in others, no matter whether the neighbor is friendly or hostile, a benefactor or a persecutor. It attends only to the difference in the participation of the divine and infinite goodness and according to this standard it loves all in God and for God.

CHAPTER VI.

THE TRIALS OF THE QUEEN IN THE TEMPLE AND THE DEATH OF HER PARENTS.

We left our sovereign Princess, most holy Mary, passing the years of her childhood in the temple, while we made a diversion to speak of the virtues, gifts and divine revelations, which She, a child in years but an adult in supreme wisdom, received from the hand of the Most High and which She put to practical use in her life. The most holy Child grew in age and grace before God and men: but always in such a proportion, that zeal exceeded the powers of nature, and that grace was measured not by her age, but by the beneficent designs and high purposes of the Divinity, whose impetuous currents sought their gathering-place and resting-place in this City of God. The Most High continued his gifts and favors, renewing every hour the marvels of his powerful arm, as if all its activity were reserved solely for most holy Mary. And so well did her Majesty correspond in her tender age to this divine influx, that She filled the heart of the Lord with a perfect and adequate complacency, and all the angels of heaven with admiration. The celestial spirits were witnesses of something like a wonderful strife and competition between the Most High and the child Princess: the divine power, in order to enrich Her, daily drawing from his treasures new and old blessings reserved solely for the purest Mary, and She, as blessed earth, not only causing the seed of the divine word to sprout and God's gifts and favors to yield fruit a hundredfold, as

was the case with the saints; but exciting the admiration
of all the heavens that She, a tender child, should exceed
in love, thanksgiving, in praise and all virtues, the highest
and most ardent seraphim, without losing time, place,
occasion, or any service, in which She did not practice
the highest possible perfection.

Even in the years of her tender infancy it was
noticeable that She understood the Scriptures and She
spent much time in reading them.   As She was full of
wisdom She conferred in her heart what She knew from
the divine revelations made to her own self, with what is
revealed to all men in the holy Scriptures; and therefore
in her reading and private meditation She sent up continual and fervent prayers and petitions for the Redemption
of the human race and for the incarnation of the Word.
She read more ordinarily from the prophets Isaias and
Jeremias and from the Psalms, because the mysteries of the
Messias and the law of grace are more plainly expressed
and repeated in these writings.   In addition to what She
herself understood and comprehended, She extended her
knowledge by asking deep and wonderful questions, and
proposing difficulties to the angels, and many times She
spoke of the mystery of the humanity of the Word with
incomparable tenderness, lovingly wondering, that He
was to become an infant, that He was to be born of a
Virgin Mother, come to manhood, as other men, suffer,
and die for all the children of Adam.

In these conferences and questionings the holy
angels and seraphim gave their answers, illuminating
Her, confirming and inflaming Her virginal heart with
new ardors of divine love.   But they always concealed
from Her her own most high dignity, although She
many times offered Herself in profoundest humility as
a slave to the Lord and to the happy Mother, whom He
was to select for his birth into the world.

The Most High resolved, that the plenitude of the graces and virtues of the princess Mary should, as it were, anticipate the time set for reaching the apex of her merits, and that they should extend to the most difficult and magnanimous undertakings, as much as possible, even in her most tender years. In one of the visions in which the Majesty of God manifested Itself to Her, He said: "My Spouse and my Dove, I love thee with an infinite love and I desire of thee what is most pleasing in my eyes and the fulfillment of all my desires. Thou art not unaware, my Daughter, of the hidden treasure, which is contained in hardships and tribulations, so much dreaded by the blind ignorance of mortals, nor is it unknown to thee that my Onlybegotten, when He shall clothe Himself in human nature, shall teach the way of the cross as well in words as in deeds; that He shall leave it as a heritage to my chosen ones; and that He shall choose it for Himself and establish upon it the law of grace, making humility and patience in suffering the foundation of the firmness and excellence of that law. For this is best suited to the present condition of human nature, and much more so, after it has been depraved and evilly inclined by so many sins. It is also conformable to my equity and providence, that the mortals should attain and merit for themselves the crown of glory through hardships and the cross, since my onlybegotten Son is to merit it by the same means in human flesh. Therefore, my Spouse, thou wilt understand, that, having chosen thee by my right hand for my delight, and having enriched thee with my gifts, it would not be just, that my grace should be idle in thy heart, nor that thy love should want its fruit, nor that thou shouldst be excluded from the inheritance of my elect. Hence I wish that thou dispose thyself for tribulations and sorrows for love of Me."

To this proposal of the Most High the invincible Princess Mary answered with a more courageous heart than all the saints and martyrs have ever shown in the world; and She said: "Lord God and my highest King, all my faculties and their operations, and my being itself, which I have received of thy infinite bounty, I hold in readiness as a sacrifice to thy divine pleasure, wishing that it be fulfilled entirely according to the desires of thy infinite wisdom and goodness. And if Thou give me any freedom of choice in regard to anything, I wish only to chose suffering unto death in love for Thee; and I beseech Thee, my only Good, that Thou make of thy slave a sacrifice and holocaust of suffering acceptable in thy eyes. I acknowledge, Lord, powerful and most liberal God, my debt, and that no creature owes to Thee so great a return, nor are all of them together so much indebted to Thee as I alone, who am so entirely unequal to the task of discharging this indebtedness to thy magnificence. But if Thou wilt admit suffering as a sort of return, let all the sorrows and tribulations of death come over me. I will only ask for thy divine protection, and, prostrate before the throne of thy infinite Majesty, I supplicate Thee not to forsake me. Remember, O my Lord, the faithful promises, which Thou hast made to our Ancestors and Prophets, that Thou wilt favor the just, stand by those who are in tribulation, console the afflicted, be a protection and a defense to them in their tribulations. True are thy words, infallible and certain are thy promises; the heavens and the earth shall sooner fall to pieces than that thy words should ever fail. The malice of the creature cannot extinguish thy charity toward those that hope in thy mercy; fulfill in me thy holy and perfect will."

The Most High accepted this morning offering from his tender Spouse and holy child Mary, and with a most benign countenance He said to Her: "Beautiful art thou in thy thoughts, Daughter of the Prince, my Dove, my beloved and chosen One. I accept thy desires as highly pleasing to me and I wish that as a beginning of their fulfillment thou take notice, that according to my divine ordainment, thy father Joachim must pass from this mortal to the eternal and immortal life. His death will happen shortly and He will pass in peace and shall be placed among the saints in limbo, to await the Redemption of the human race." This announcement did not disturb the royal heart of the Princess of heaven, the blessed Mary; but as the love of children for their parents is a just debt of nature, and as in this most holy Child this love had attained its highest perfection, the natural sorrow for the loss of her father Joachim could not be wanting, for She loved him with a holy love. The tender and sweet Child therefore felt, that this sorrowful compassion was perfectly compatible with the serenity of her magnanimous heart, and, working in all things with grandeur, giving nature and grace each their due, She offered an ardent prayer for her father saint Joachim. She besought the Lord to give him grace to depend upon Him as his powerful and true God in his transit through a blessed death; and asked Him to defend Joachim against the demon especially in that hour, preserve him for and constitute him among the number of the elect, since during his life He had confessed and magnified his admirable and holy name. And in order to oblige his Majesty the more, the most faithful Daughter offered to suffer all that the Lord might ordain.

The Lord accepted this petition and consoled the heavenly Child by assuring Her, that He would assist her father as a most merciful and kind Rewarder of those that love and serve Him, and that He would place him among the Patriarchs Abraham, Isaac and Jacob. At the same time He prepared Her anew for the acceptance and endurance of troubles. Eight days before the death of the patriarch Joachim the most holy Mary received another notice from the Lord, advising Her of the day and hour in which He was to die. His death took place only six months after Her entrance into the temple. Having received this notice from the Lord, She requested the twelve angels, mentioned by saint John in the Apocalypse, to assist her father Joachim and to comfort and console Him in his sickness, which they did. For the last hours of his life She sent all the angels of her guard asking the Lord, to make them visible to him for his greater consolation. God conceded this favor and confirmed all the wishes of his chosen and only One; and the great patriarch, most happy Joachim, saw the thousand angels which guarded Mary. In response to her prayer and wishes the Almighty allowed his graces to overflow, commanding the angels to address Joachim as follows:

"Man of God, may the Most High and powerful Lord be thy eternal salvation and may He send thee from his holy place the necessary and opportune help for thy soul. Mary thy Daughter has sent us in order to assist thee in this hour, in which thou must pay the debt of mortality to thy Creator. She is a most faithful and powerful Intercessor before the Almighty, in whose name and peace thou wilt now pass consoled and joyous from this world, because He has made thee the father of such a blessed Daughter. Although his incomprehensible Majesty, on account of his hidden decrees, has not as yet revealed the sacraments and dignity, in which He shall invest thy Daughter, He wishes thee to know it now in order that thou mayest magnify and praise Him, and in order that the pain and sorrow of natural death may be

relieved by the joy of thy spirit at this news. Mary, thy
Daughter, is chosen and ordained by the Almighty as
the One, in whom the divine Word shall vest Himself
with human flesh and form. She is to be the happy Mother
of the Messias and the Blessed among women, the most
exalted among all creatures, and only inferior to God
himself. Thy most fortunate Daughter is to restore what
the human race lost by the first sin, and She is the high
mountain on which is to be established and constructed
the new law of grace. Since thou leavest to the world
a Daughter, through whom God will restore it and prepare a full remedy, do thou part from it in the joy of thy
soul, and may the Lord bless thee from Sion (Psalm 127,
5) and constitute thee in the inheritance of the saints and
bring thee to the vision and enjoyment of the blessed
Jerusalem."

During these words of the holy angels to Joachim,
his spouse, holy Anne, stood at the head of his bed
and by divine disposition She heard and understood
what they said. In the same moment the holy patriarch lost the use of speech and, treading into the path
common to all flesh, he commenced his agony in a marvelous struggle between his joy at this message and the pain
of death. In this conflict of the interior powers of his
soul he made many fervent acts of divine love, of faith, of
admiration, of praise, of thanksgiving, of humility and
heroic acts of many other virtues. Thus absorbed in
the knowledge of so divine a mystery, he arrived at
the term of his natural life and died the precious death of
the saints (Psalm 115, 15). His holy soul was carried by
the angels to the limbo of the Patriarchs and just souls;
and, for a new consolation and light in the protracted
night in which they lived, the Most High sent the soul of
Joachim as the last messenger and legate of the Lord to

announce to the whole congregation of the just: that the dawn of the eternal day was at hand; that the morning light was breaking upon the world in most holy Mary, the Daughter of Joachim and Anne; that from Her was to be brought forth the Sun of the Divinity, Christ, the Redeemer of all the human race. This great news the holy fathers and the just in limbo heard and received with jubilee and in their exultation they sang many hymns of thanksgiving to the Most High.

The first affliction, which our Princess suffered, was that the Lord suspended the continual visions, which He had so far vouchsafed Her. So much the greater was the sorrow occasioned Her thereby, in proportion as it was a new and unaccustomed experience and in proportion as the treasure thus withdrawn was high and precious. Also the holy angels concealed themselves from Her, and at the withdrawal from her sight of so many, so excellent and heavenly beings, which took place all at once (although they did not cease to surround Her invisibly for her protection), that most pure Soul seemed to Herself entirely forsaken and left alone in the dark night occasioned by the absence of her Beloved.

It was a great surprise to our little Queen; for the Lord, though He had in general prepared Her for the coming of tribulations, had not specified their nature. And as the innocent heart of the most simple Dove harbored no thoughts, and entertained no practical conclusions except such as were conformable to her humility and incomparable love, She explained all according to this same light. In her humility She began to think, that She had not merited the further presence and possession of the lost Good on account of her ingratitude; and in her inflamed love She sighed and yearned after It with such great and loving affection and sorrow, that there are no words to express them. She turned with her whole soul to the Lord in this new state and said to Him:

"Highest God and Lord of all creation, infinite in bounty and rich in mercies, I confess, my Lord, that such a vile creature cannot merit thy favors and my soul in utmost sorrow reproaches itself with its own ingratitude and with the loss of thy friendship. If my ingratitude has eclipsed the Sun, which vivified, animated and illumined me, and if I have been remiss in giving thanks for the great benefits, I acknowledge, my Lord and Shepherd, the sin of my great negligence. If, like an ignorant and simple little sheep, I did not know how to be thankful and do what is most acceptable in thy eyes, see me prostrate on the earth, adhering to the dust, in order to be raised from my poverty and destitution by Thee, my God, who dwellest on high. Thy powerful hands have formed me (Job 10, 8), and Thou canst not be ignorant of our composition (Psalm 102, 14) and in what kind of a vase Thou has placed thy treasures. My soul wastes away in bitterness (Psalm 30, 11); and in thy absence, since Thou art its sweetest life, none but Thou can restore its drooping life. To whom shall I go in thy absence? Whither shall I turn my eyes without having light to direct them? Who shall console me when all is affliction? Who shall preserve me from death, when there is no life left?"

She also turned toward the angels and continued without ceasing in her loving complaints, saying to them: "Celestial Princes, ambassadors of the great and highest King and most faithful friends of my soul: why have you also left me? Why do also you deprive me of your sweet countenances and deny me your intercourse? But I do not wonder, my lords, at your displeasure, if through my unthankfulness I have merited to fall into the disgrace of your and my Creator. Lights of the heavens, enlighten

me in my ignorance in this matter, and if I have been at
fault, correct me and obtain again for me the pardon of
my Lord. Most noble courtiers of the celestial Jerusalem,
have pity on my sorrow and dereliction: tell me where is
my Beloved; tell me where He has hidden Himself (Cant.
3, 3). Tell me where I can find Him without wandering
about, (Cant. 1, 6) and without going through the gather-
ings of all the creatures. But woe to me, for you do not
answer, though you are so courteous and well know the
hiding-place of my Spouse, since He never withdraws his
face and his beauty from your sight!"

Thereupon She turned toward all the rest of creation and in continual anxieties of her love She spoke to
them and said: "Without doubt you also, being thankful,
and being armed against all the ungrateful, are exasperated against her, who was ungrateful. But even if
by the goodness of the Lord you permit me to remain in
your midst, although I am so vile, you cannot thereby
satisfy my longings. Very beautiful and extensive are ye,
O heavens; beautiful and refulgent are the planets and all
the stars; great and mighty are the elements, the earth is
adorned and clothed in the perfumed plants and herbs,
innumerable are the fishes of the waters, admirable are the
elevations of the sea, (Psalm 92, 4), swift are the birds
in their feathery weight, hidden are the minerals, courageous are the animals in their strength, and all of these
together serve as a gradual ascent and in a sweet harmony
teach the way to my Beloved; yet they are but circuitous
paths for one that loves Him, and if I course swiftly over
them I find myself at the end absent from my blessedness.
For with the measured approach of these creatures to his
unmeasurable bounty, my flight is not content, my sorrow
is not allayed, my pains are unrelieved, my anguish increases, my desires are augmented, my heart is more in-

flamed and faints away in the unsatiating love of mere earthly things."

The dragon, though seeing her courage and constancy, and though feeling the force of the divine assistance, knew nothing of the hidden wisdom and prudence of our sovereign Queen. Nevertheless he persisted in his pride and besieged the City of God in diverse ways and several kinds of warfare. The astute enemy during this warfare often changed his engines of war, but his machinery was like the sting of a weak hornet against a diamond, or adamantine wall. Our Princess was that strong woman (Prov. 31, 11) on whom the heart of her husband confidently relied, without the least anxiety lest his desires should be frustrated in Her. Her adornments were fortitude (Prov. 31, 25) which filled Her with beauty, and her vestments were purity and charity, which served Her as a helmet. The unclean and proud serpent could not look upon this Creature without being blinded anew in the fury of his confusion; therefore he resolved to take away her life, and the horde of malignant spirits began to exert their utmost powers toward this end. In this attempt they spent some time, but with just as little success.

The knowledge of this hidden mystery caused in me great wonder, especially when I considered the extremes, to which the fury of Lucifer was allowed to proceed against the most holy Mary in her tender years and when I beheld the hidden and vigilant defense and protection of the Most High. I saw how attentive the Lord was toward his chosen and only One among creatures; and I saw at the same time all hell lashed into fury against Her and exerting against Her in fullest indignation such a wrath as had never till then been exerted against any other creature; and I saw the facility with which God neutralizes the infernal power and astuteness. O more than unhappy Lucifer! How much greater is thy pride and arrogance than thy strength! (Isaias 16, 6).

After the most holy Virgin had successfully fought these secret temptations and battles, the serpent instituted a new conflict by means of creatures. For this purpose he secretly kindled the sparks of envy and emulation against the most holy Mary in the hearts of her maiden companions of the temple. This contagion was much the harder to counteract, as it arose from the punctuality with which our heavenly Princess distinguished Herself in the practice of all virtues, growing in wisdom and grace before God and man. For where the prodding of ambition is, the very light of virtue darkens and blinds the judgment, and at last enkindles the flames of envy. The dragon through his secret suggestions persuaded these simple maidens, that the light of this sun, most holy Mary, would obscure them and cause them to be little noticed; that on her account their own negligences were more clearly apparent to the priests and their teacher; and that Mary alone was preferred in the estimation and judgment of all.

The companions of our Queen allowed the devil to sow this bad seed in their bosoms; for they were heedless and little experienced in spiritual ways. They allowed it to increase until it grew into a sort of interior abhorrence of the most pure Mary, and this into anger. Filled with this anger, they began to look upon and treat Her with hatred, not being able to endure the modesty of that most innocent Dove. For the dragon had incited them and had already imbued the incautious girls with some of his own wrath. The temptation continuing, its effects became manifest and the temple maidens began to plot among themselves, ignorant of the spirit that moved them. They agreed among themselves to molest and persecute the unknown Princess of the world, until She should be forced to leave the temple. Accordingly they called Her aside and spoke to Her very sharp words, treating Her at the same time very haughtily. They called Her a hypocrite and reproached Her with scheming to obtain the favor of the priests and of their teacher, while seeking to discredit all the other girls by her complaints and her exaggerations of their faults, whereas She was the most useless of them all and therefore deserved their hatred as an enemy.

These contumelies and many other accusations the most prudent Virgin bore without disturbance and with equable humility. She answered: "My friends and my mistresses, you are right no doubt in saying, that I am the least and the most imperfect among you; but then you, my sisters, being better informed, must pardon me my faults and must teach me in my ignorance. Direct me therefore, that I may succeed in doing better and act according to your pleasure. I beseech you, my friends, not to deny me your good will, which, though I am so imperfect, I sincerely wish to merit; for I love you and reverence you as a servant, and I will obey you in all things, in which you desire to make a trial of my good will. Command me then, and tell me what you wish of me."

These humble and sweet reasonings of the most humble Mary did not soften the hardened hearts of her associates and companions, for they were infected by the poisonous fury of the dragon against Her. Precisely on account of her sweet humility he became so much the more infuriated, and thus turned this sweet antidote against the poisonous bite into a means of inflaming them with open wrath against Her who was the great sign in heaven (Apoc. 13, 15). For many days this persecution continued, during which the heavenly Lady sought in vain to appease the hate of her companions by her humility, patience, modesty and tolerance. On the contrary the demon was emboldened to inspire them with many thoughts full of temerity, urging them to lay violent hands on the most humble lamb and maltreat Her, even so far as to take away her life. But the Lord did not permit the execution of such sacrilegious suggestions; and the farthest which they were allowed to proceed, was to insult Her by words or to inflict some blows. This quarreling remained concealed from the teacher of the maidens and from the priests, and during this time most holy Mary gained incomparable merits in the sight of the Almighty, because She took occasion to exercise all the virtues, as well in regard to God as also in regard to the creatures, which were persecuting and hating Her. She performed heroic acts of charity and humility, yielding good for evil, blessings for curses, prayers for blasphemies (I Cor. 4, 13), fulfilling in all things the most perfect and the highest requirements of the divine law. Before the Lord She exercised the most exalted virtues, by praying for his creatures who were persecuting Her; and She excited the admiration of the angels, by humiliating Herself as if She were the vilest of mortals deservedly treated in that way. In all these things She surpassed the conceptions of men and the highest merits of the seraphim.

It happened one day, that, impelled by the diabolical suggestions, these girls brought Mary to a retired room, where they could act with more safety. Here they began to heap unmeasured injuries and insults upon Her, in order to excite Her to weakness or anger and to entrap Her imperturbable modesty into some hasty action. But as the Queen of virtues could not even for a moment be subject to vice, She showed Herself immovable, and She answered them with great kindness and sweetness. Being enraged beyond bounds on account of not succeeding in their purpose, her companions raised their voices in discordant strife, so that they were heard in the temple and by such unwonted noise caused great astonishment and confusion. The priests and the teacher hastened to the place whence the noise proceeded, and the Lord permitted a new humiliation of his Spouse, for they asked with severity, what was the cause of this strife. While the most meek Dove remained silent, the other maidens angrily answered and said: "Mary of Nazareth brings us all into strife and quarreling by her horrid conduct: for in your absence, She irritates and provokes us in such a manner, that if She does not leave the temple, it will be impossible to keep any peace with Her. When we allow Her her own way, She becomes overbearing; if we reprehend Her, She makes fun of all of us by prostrating Herself at our feet with feigned humility, and afterwards She quarrels anew and throws all into uproar."

The priests and the instructress brought the Mistress of the world into another room, and there they severely reprehended Her, giving full credit at that time to all the accusations of her companions, and, having exhorted Her to reform and behave as one living in the house of God, they threatened to expel Her from the temple, if She would not mend Her conduct. This threat was the most severe punishment, which they could have given Her, even if She had been guilty; so much the more severe was it, when She was altogether innocent of any of the faults imputed to Her.

Our Queen added other words full of sweetest

innocence and modesty; and therewith the instructress and the priests dismissed Her, enjoining anew upon Her that doctrine, of which She herself was the most wise Teacher. Immediately She betook Herself to her companions, and prostrating Herself at their feet, She asked them pardon, as if the faults, with which they had charged Her, could ever have been shared by the Mother of all innocence. They received Her this time with more good will, because they thought that her tears were the effect of the punishment and the warning of the priests and the instructress, whom they had induced to act thus in pursuance of their badly governed passions. The dragon, who was secretly contriving this entanglement, urged the incautious hearts of all these girls to still greater haughtiness and presumption, and as they had now made headway in the estimation of the priests themselves, they proceeded to greater audacity in discrediting and lowering the good name of the most pure Virgin. Accordingly by instigation of the devil, they fabricated new accusations and lies; but the Most High never permitted them to say anything very grave and dishonorable of Her, whom He had chosen as the most holy Mother of his Onlybegotten. He merely allowed the indignation and deceit of the maidens to go so far as to exaggerate very much some small faults, which were even in themselves altogether fictitious, but which they accused Her of. Moreover they were permitted to practice many feminine intrigues, to which their own restlessness drove them. In these different ways and in the reprehensions of her instructress and of the priests our most humble Lady Mary found many occasions of exercising virtues, of increasing the gifts of the Most High, and of exalting Her merit.

The Lord did not sleep, nor did He slumber (Psalm 120, 4) during the clamors of his beloved spouse

Mary, although He pretended not to hear them, delighting in the prolonged exercise of her sufferings, which occasioned so many glorious triumphs and the admirations and praises of the supernal spirits. The smouldering fire of the persecution already mentioned continued unabated, in order that the Phenix, Mary, might many times renew Herself from the ashes of her humility, and in order that her most pure heart be regenerated over and over again to new estates and conditions of divine grace. But when the opportune time arrived for putting an end to the blind envy and jealousy of those ensnared maidens, and in order that their petulance might not altogether discredit Her who was to be the excellence of nature and grace itself, the Lord spoke to the priest in his sleep and said to Him: "My servant Mary is pleasing in my eyes, and She is my perfect and my chosen One: She is entirely innocent of anything of which She is accused." The same revelation was given to Anne, the instructress of the maidens. That morning the priest and the instructress conferred with each other about the message, which both had received. Being now certain, they repented of the deceit, into which they had been led, and called the Princess Mary, asking her pardon for having given credit to the false report of the girls and offering Her all the reparation necessary to defend Her from the persecution and the sufferings consequent upon it.

She that was the Mother and origin of humility, after listening to their words, answered the priest and the instructress: "My superiors, I am the one that deserves your reprehensions and I beseech you do not hold me unworthy of undergoing them, since I ask for them as most necessary to me. The intercourse with my sisters, the other maidens, is most highly prized by me, and I do not wish to be deprived of it through my fault, since I owe them so much for having borne with me; and as a return for that benefit, I desire to serve them more faithfully; nevertheless if you command me anything else, I stand prepared to obey your will." This answer of the most holy Mary still more comforted and consoled the priest and the instructress; and they approved of her humble petition, but from that time on they attended to Her and observed Her with new reverence and affection. The most humble Maiden begged to kiss the hand of the priest and of the matron, asking for their blessing according to her custom; with this they dismissed Her. Just as the parched desire of the thirsty for drink is increased at the sight of clear water withdrawn beyond their reach, so was the heart of Mary our Mistress filled with yearning regret for the exercise of suffering. Thirsting and burning for the divine love She feared lest through the watchful care of the priest and of the instructress, She should from thenceforward be deprived of the treasure of affliction.

The enlightenment of the priests and the instructress concerning Mary abated the persecutions of the maidens. The Lord also restrained them and prevented the demon from inciting them thereafter. But the time, during which He absented Himself and during which He hid Himself from this heavenly spouse, lasted (wonderful to relate!) ten years; although the Most High interrupted this absence a few times by allowing the veil to fall from his face for the relief of his Beloved; but it was not often that He dispensed this favor during that time, and He did it with less lavishness and tenderness than in the first years of her childhood. This absence of the Lord was ordained for our Queen in order that She might, by actual exercise of all perfection, be made worthy for the dignity to which She was destined by the Most High. For if She had continually enjoyed the vision of his Majesty in the manner described by us in the fourteenth chapter of this book, She could not have suffered according to the common order of a mere creature.

But during this retirement and absence of the Lord, although most holy Mary missed the intuitive and abstractive visions of the divine Essence and of the angels as mentioned above, her most holy soul and her faculties enjoyed more gifts of grace and more supernatural enlightenment, than all the saints ever attained or received. For in regard to this the hand of God never withdrew from Her. But in comparison with the frequent visitations of the Lord in her first years, I call the state of her privation of his presence for such a long time, an absence and withdrawal of the Lord. It commenced eight days before the death of her father, saint Joachim, and afterwards the persecution of hell began, followed by the persecutions on the part of creatures. They lasted until our Princess reached the age of twelve years. Having passed this age, the holy angels on a certain day, without manifesting themselves, spoke to Her as follows: "Mary, the end of the life of thy holy mother Anne as ordained by the Most High, is now about to arrive, and his Majesty has resolved to free her from the prison of her mortal body and bring her labors to a happy fulfillment."

At this unexpected and sorrowful message the heart of the affectionate Daughter was filled with compassion. Prostrating Herself in the presence of the Most High, She poured forth a fervent prayer for the happy death of her mother saint Anne in the following words: "King of the ages, invisible and eternal Lord, immortal and almighty Creator of the universe, although I am but dust and ashes and although I must confess, that I am in debt to thy greatness, I will not on that account be prevented from speaking to my Lord (Gen. 18, 17), and I pour out before thee my heart, hoping, O my God, that Thou wilt not despise her, who has always confessed thy holy name. Dismiss, O Lord, in peace thy servant, who has with invincible faith and confidence desired to fulfill thy divine pleasure. Let her issue victoriously and triumphantly from the hostile combat and enter the portal of thy holy chosen ones; let thy powerful arm strengthen her; at the close of her mortal career, let that same right hand, which has helped her to walk in the path of perfection, assist her, and let her enter, O my Father, into the peace of thy friendship and grace, since she has always sought after it with an upright heart."

The Lord did not respond expressly in words to this petition of his Beloved; but his answer was a marvelous favor, shown to Her and to her mother, saint Anne. During that night his Majesty commanded the guardian angels of the most holy Mary to carry Her bodily to the sickbed of her mother and one of them to remain in her stead, assuming for this purpose an aerial body as a substitute for hers. The holy angels obeyed the mandate of God and they carried their and our Queen to the house and to the room of her holy mother Anne. Being thus brought to the presence of her mother, the heavenly Lady kissed her hand and said to her: "My mother and mistress, may the Most High be thy light and thy strength, and may He be blessed, since He has in his condescension not permitted me in my necessity to remain without the benefit of thy last blessing; may I then receive it, my mother, from thy hand." Holy Anne gave her last blessing to Mary and with overflowing heart also thanked the Lord for the great favor thus conferred upon Herself. For She knew the sacrament of her Daughter and Queen, and she did not forget to express her gratitude for the love, which Mary had shown her on this occasion.

In the midst of such exalted and heavenly collo-quies the blessed mother saint Anne felt the throes of death approaching and, reclining upon the throne of grace, that is, in the arms of her most holy Daughter Mary, she rendered her most pure soul to her Creator. Having closed the eyes of her mother, as saint Anne had requested, and leaving the sacred body in position for burial, the Queen Mary was again taken up by the holy angels and restored to her place in the temple. The Most High did not impede the force of her filial love, which naturally would cause a great and tender sorrow at the death of her mother and a sense of loneliness at being deprived of her assistance. But these sorrows were most holy and perfect in our Queen, governed by the graces of her most prudent innocence and purity. In the midst of them She gave praise to the Most High for the infinite mercies, which He had shown to her mother both in life and in death, while her sweet and loving complaints on account of the absence of the Lord continued unabated.

Already our heavenly Princess felt that the day of the clear vision of the Divinity was approaching and that like the harbingers of early dawn, the rays of the divine light were breaking upon her soul. Her heart began to be inflamed by the nearness of the invisible fire, which illumines but does not consume; and made atten-tive by this new clearness, She questioned her angels and said to them: "My friends and lords, my most faith-ful and vigilant sentinels, tell me: what hour is it of my night? And when will the bright light of the day arise, in which my eyes shall see the Sun of justice which illumines them and gives life to my affections and my soul?" The holy Princess answered her and said: "Spouse of the Most High, thy wished-for light and truth is near; it will not tarry long, for already it approaches." At these words the veil which hid the view of these spiritual substances was slightly lifted; and the holy angels became visible, showing themselves as during her first years in their own essence, without hindrance or dependence of the bodily senses.

They transmitted to Her that light, of which I have spoken, in order to purify her faculties; not because there were any defects to be remedied, for She could not be guilty of any defects. On the contrary all her actions and operations during the absence of the Lord had been meritorious and holy. Nevertheless it was necessary that She be endowed with new gifts, in order to tranquilize her spirit and her faculties, which had been moved by affectionate labors and anxieties during the absence of the Lord, and also in order to withdraw Her from her present state and raise Her to a position, where She could enjoy new and different favors, for in order that her faculties might again be proportioned to the high Object and to the manner of enjoying It, they must necessarily be renewed and redisposed. All this the holy seraphim proceeded to do with Her in the manner already described in book second, chapter fourteenth. When the Lord conferred upon Her the final adornment and the quality necessary for the immediate vision about to take place.

As far as I can explain, this successive elevation of the faculties of the heavenly Queen engendered those particular affections and sentiments of love and virtues

which the Lord desired, and in the midst of these elevations his Majesty withdrew the veil. Then after his
long concealment He manifested Himself to his only
Spouse, his beloved and most holy Mary, by an abstractive vision of the Divinity. Although this vision was
given through abstractive images and not intuitive, yet it
was most clear and exalted in its kind. By it the Lord
dried the continual tears of our Queen, rewarded her
affection and her loving anxiety, satisfied all her desires
and overwhelmed Her with delight as She reclined in the
arms of her Beloved (Cant. 8, 5). Then was renewed the
youth of that aspiring Eagle, winging its flight into the
impenetrable regions of the Divinity (Psalm 102, 5), and
by the after-effects of this vision She ascended whither no
other creature can ascend, or no other intellect can reach
outside of God's.

Our Princess issued from this vision altogether
renovated and made godlike; full of the new science of
the Divinity and of the hidden sacraments of the King,
confessing Him, adoring Him, and praising Him with
incessant canticles and by the flights of her pacified and
tranquilized spirit. In like proportion also was the increase of her humility and of all the other virtues. Her
most ardent prayer was to penetrate more and more
deeply into that which is most perfect and most pleasing to the will of the Most High, and to fulfill and execute it in her actions. Thus passed a number of days,
until that happened, which is to be related in the next
chapter.

CHAPTER VII.

At the age of thirteen and a half years, having grown considerably for her age, our most charming Princess, most pure Mary, had another abstractive vision of the Divinity of the same order and kind as those already described. In this vision, we might say, happened something similar to that which the holy Scriptures relate of Abraham, when God commanded him to sacrifice his beloved son Isaac, the only pledge of all his hopes. God tempted Abraham, says Moses (Gen. 12, 12), trying and probing the promptness of his obedience in order to reward it. We can say the same thing of our great Lady, that God tried Her in this vision, by commanding Her to enter the state of matrimony. Thence we can also understand the truth of the words: How inscrutable are the judgments of the Lord and how exalted are his ways and thoughts above our own (Rom. 11, 33)! As distant as heaven is from earth, were the thoughts of most holy Mary from the plans which the Most High now made known to Her, by commanding Her to accept a husband for her protection and company; for as far as depended upon her will She had desired and resolved during all her life not to have a husband and She had often repeated and renewed the vow of chastity, which She had taken at such a premature age.

Nevertheless at this unexpected command the most prudent Virgin suspended her judgment, and preserved the calmness of her hope and belief more perfectly than Abraham. Hoping against hope (Rom. 4, 18), She made answer to the Lord saying: "Eternal God and incomprehensible Majesty, Creator of heaven and earth, and of all things contained therein, Thou, O Lord, who weighest the winds (Job 28, 25), and by thy commands settest bounds to the sea and subjectest all creation to thy will, canst dispose of me, thy worthless wormlet, according to thy pleasure, without making me fail in that which I have promised to Thee; and if it be not displeasing to Thee, my good Lord, I confirm and ratify anew my desire to remain chaste during all my life and to have Thee for my Lord and Spouse; and since my only duty as a creature is to obey Thee, see Thou to it, my Spouse, that according to thy Providence I may escape from this predicament in which thy holy love places me." There was, however, some uneasiness in the most chaste maiden Mary, as far as her inferior nature was concerned, just as happened afterwards at the message of the archangel Gabriel (Luke 1, 8); yet, though She felt some sadness, it did not hinder Her from practicing the most heroic obedience which until then had fallen to her lot, and She resigned Herself entirely into the hand of the Lord. His Majesty answered her: "Mary, let not thy heart be disturbed, for thy resignation is acceptable to Me and my powerful arm is not subject to laws; by my disposition that will happen, which is most proper for Thee."

Consoled only by this vague promise of the Lord, most holy Mary recovered from her vision and returned to her ordinary state. Left between doubt and hope by the divine command and promise, She was full of solicitude, for the Lord intended that She should multiply Her tearful sentiments of love and confidence, of faith, humility, of obedience, of purest chastity and of other virtues, impossible to enumerate. In the meanwhile, while our great Lady applied Herself to vigilant prayer, and to her resigned and prudent sighs and solicitude, God spoke in sleep to the high priest, saint Simeon, and commanded him to arrange for the marriage of Mary, the daughter of Joachim and Anne of Nazareth; since He regarded Her with special care and love. The holy priest answered, asking what was his will in regard to the person, whom the maiden Mary was to marry and to whom She was to give Herself as Spouse. The Lord instructed Him to call together the other priests and learned persons and to tell them that this Maiden was left alone and an orphan and that She did not desire to be married; but that, as it was a custom for the firstborn maidens not to leave the temple without being provided for, it was proper She should be married to whomever it seemed good to them.

The most prudent Virgin, with a countenance betokening virginal modesty, answered the priest with great composure and humility: "Sir, as far as my inclinations are concerned, I desire to preserve perpetual chastity during all my life; for I wished to dedicate myself to God in the service of this holy temple in return for the great blessings which I have received in it; I never had the intention or the desire to enter the state of matrimony, since I consider myself incapable of fulfilling the duties connected with it. This was my inclination, but thou, my master, who art to me in place of God, wilt teach me what is according to his holy Will." "My Daughter," answered the priest, "thy holy desires are acceptable to the Lord; but remember, that no maiden of Israel abstains from marriage as long as we expect the coming of the Messias conformably to the divine prophecies. Therefore all who obtain issue of children among our people, esteem themselves happy and blessed. In the matrimonial state Thou canst serve God truly and in great perfection; and in order that Thou mayest obtain a companion according to the heart of God and who will be conformable to thy wishes, we will pray to the Lord, as I have told Thee, asking Him to single out a husband for Thee, who shall be pleasing to Him and of the line of David; do Thou also pray continually for the same favor, in order that the Most High may favor Thee and may direct us all."

This happened nine days before the one appointed for the execution and realization of their resolve. During this time the most holy Virgin multiplied her prayers, beseeching the Lord with incessant tears and sighs, to fulfill his divine pleasure in that which She had so much at heart. On one of those nine days the Lord appeared to Her and said to Her: "My Spouse and my Dove, let thy afflicted heart expand and let it not be disturbed or sad; I will attend to thy yearnings and to thy requests, I will direct all things, and will govern the priests by my enlightenment; I will give Thee a spouse selected by Myself, and one who will put no hindrance to thy holy desires, but who, by my grace will prosper Thee in them. I will find for Thee a perfect man conformable to my heart and I will choose him from the number of my servants; my power is infinite, and my protection and aid shall never fail Thee."

The most holy Mary answering said: "Highest Good and Love of my soul, Thou well knowest the secret of my bosom and my desires, which Thou hast excited in me from the first moment of the existence received from Thee; preserve me, then, my Spouse, pure and chaste, as I have desired for Thee and through Thee.

Do not despise my sighs and deprive me not of thy countenance. Remember, my Lord and God, that I am but a useless wormlet, weak and despicable on account of my insignificance; and if I should fall away from virtue in the state of matrimony, I shall disappoint Thee and my desires; provide Thou for my security and be not deterred by my demerits. Although I am but useless dust (Gen. 18, 27), I will call on thy greatness, O Lord, trusting in thy infinite mercies."

On the day on which, as we have said in the preceding chapter, our Princess Mary completed the fourteenth year of her life, the men, who at that time in the city of Jerusalem were descendants of the tribe of Juda and of the race of David, gathered together in the temple. The sovereign Lady was also of that lineage. Among the number was Joseph, a native of Nazareth, and then living in Jerusalem; for he was one of the descendants of the royal race of David. He was then thirty-three years of age, of handsome person and pleasing countenance, but also of incomparable modesty and gravity; above all he was most chaste in thought and conduct, and most saintly in all his inclinations. From his twelfth year he had made and kept the vow of chastity. He was related to the Virgin Mary in the third degree, and was known for the utmost purity of his life, holy and irreprehensible in the eyes of God and of men.

All these unmarried men gathered in the temple and prayed to the Lord conjointly with the priests, in order to be governed by the holy Spirit in what they were about to do. The Most High spoke to the heart of the highpriest, inspiring him to place into the hands of each one of the young men a dry stick, with the command that each ask his Majesty with a lively faith, to single out the one whom He had chosen as the spouse

of Mary. And as the sweet odor of her virtue and nobility, the fame of her beauty, her possessions and her
modesty, and her position as being the firstborn in her
family was known to all of them, each one coveted the
happiness of meriting Her as a spouse. Among them
all only the humble and most upright Joseph thought
himself unworthy of such a great blessing; and remembering the vow of chastity which he had made and resolving anew its perpetual observance, he resigned himself to God's will, leaving it all to his disposal and being
filled at the same time with a veneration and esteem
greater than that of any of the others for the most noble
maiden Mary.

While they were thus engaged in prayer the staff
which Joseph held was seen to blossom and at the same
time a dove of purest white and resplendent with admirable light, was seen to descend and rest upon the
head of the saint, while in the interior of his heart God
spoke: "Joseph, my servant, Mary shall be thy Spouse;
accept Her with attentive reverence, for She is acceptable in my eyes, just and most pure in soul and body,
and thou shalt do all that She shall say to Thee." At
this manifestation and token from heaven the priests declared saint Joseph as the spouse selected by God himself for the maiden Mary. Calling Her forth for her
espousal, the Chosen one issued forth like the sun, more
resplendent than the moon, and She entered into the
presence of all with a countenance more beautiful than
that of an angel, incomparable in the charm of her
beauty, nobility and grace; and the priests espoused Her
to the most chaste and holy of men, saint Joseph.

The heavenly Princess, more pure than the stars
of the firmament, with tearful and sorrowful countenance and as the Queen of majesty, most humble yet

uniting all perfections within Herself, took leave of the priests, asking their blessing, and of her instructress and her companions, begging their pardon. She gave thanks to all of them for the favors received at their hands during her stay in the temple. The humility of her behavior enhanced the prudence and aptness of her words for the performance of these last duties in the temple; for on all occasions She spoke in few and weighty words. She took leave of the temple not without great grief on account of the sacrifice of her inclinations and desires. In the company of attendants who were some of the more distinguished laymen in the service of the temple, She betook Herself with her spouse Joseph to Nazareth, the native city of this most fortunate married couple. Joseph, although he had been born in that place, had, by the providential disposition of circumstances, decided to live for some time in Jerusalem. Thus it happened that he so improved his fortune as to become the spouse of Her, whom God had chosen to be his own Mother.

Having arrived at their home in Nazareth, where the Princess of heaven had inherited the possessions and estates of her blessed parents, they were welcomed and visited by their friends and relatives with the joyful congratulations customary on such occasions. After they had in a most holy manner complied with the natural duties of friendship and politeness, and satisfied the worldly obligations connected with the conversation and intercourse of their fellowmen, the two most holy spouses, Joseph and Mary, were left at leisure and to their own counsel in their house. Custom had introduced the practice among the Hebrews, that for the first few days of their married state the husband and wife should enter upon a sort of study or trial of each others' habits and temperament, in order that afterwards they might be able to make reciprocal allowance in their conduct one toward the other.

During this time saint Joseph said to his spouse Mary: "My spouse and Lady, I give thanks to the Lord most high God for the favor of having designed me as your husband without my merits, though I judged myself unworthy even of thy company; but his Majesty, who can raise up the lowly whenever He wishes, showed this mercy to me, and I desire and hope, relying on thy discretion and virtue, that Thou help me to make a proper return in serving Him with an upright heart. Hold me, therefore, as thy servant, and by the true love which I have for thee, I beg of thee to supply my deficiencies in the fulfillment of the domestic duties and of other things, which as a worthy husband, I should know how to perform; tell me, Lady, what is thy pleasure, in order that I may fulfill it."

The heavenly Spouse heard these words with an humble heart, and yet also with a serene earnestness, and She answered the saint: "My master, I am fortunate, that the Most High, in order to place me in this state of life, has chosen thee for my husband and that He has given me such evident manifestation of his will, that I serve thee; but if thou givest me leave I will speak of my thoughts and intentions, which I wish to manifest to thee for this purpose." The Most High forestalled the sincere and upright heart of saint Joseph with his grace and inflamed it anew with divine love through the word of most holy Mary, and he answered Her, saying: "Speak, Lady, thy servant hears." On this occasion the Mistress of the world was surrounded by the thousand angels of her guard, in visible form. She had asked them to be present in that manner, because the Lord, in order that the most pure Virgin might act with greater grace and merit, had permitted her to feel the respect and reverence, with which She was bound to speak to her husband and left her to the natural shyness and dread, which She always felt in speaking to men alone; for She had never done this, except perhaps by accident with the highpriest.

The holy angels obeyed their Queen and, visible only to Her, stood in attendance. In this glorious company She spoke to her spouse saint Joseph, and said to him: "My lord and spouse, it is just that we give praise and glory with all reverence to our God and Creator, who is infinite in goodness and incomprehensible in his judgments. To us, who are so needy, He has manifested his greatness and mercy in choosing us for his service. I acknowledge myself among all creatures as more beholden and indebted to Him than all others, and more than all of them together; for, meriting less, I have received from his liberal hand more than they. At a tender age, being compelled thereto by the force of this truth, which, with the knowledge of the deceitfulness of visible things, his divine light made known to me, I consecrated myself to God by a perpetual vow of chastity in body and soul; his I am and Him I acknowledge as my Spouse and Lord, with fixed resolve to preserve for Him my chastity. I beseech thee, my master, to help me in fulfilling this vow, while in all other things I will be thy servant, willing to work for the comfort of thy life as long as mine shall last. Yield, my spouse, to this resolve and make a like resolve, in order that, offering ourselves as an acceptable sacrifice to our eternal God, He may receive us in the odor of sweetness and bestow on us the eternal goods for which we hope."

The most chaste spouse Joseph, full of interior

joy at the words of his heavenly Spouse, answered Her:
"My Mistress, in making known to me thy chaste and
welcome sentiments, thou hast penetrated and dilated
my heart. I have not opened my thoughts to Thee before knowing thy own. I also acknowledge myself under greater obligation to the Lord of creation than other
men; for very early He has called me by his true enlightenment to love Him with an upright heart; and I
desire Thee to know, Lady, that at the age of twelve
years I also made a promise to serve the Most High
in perpetual chastity. On this account I now gladly
ratify this vow in order not to impede thy own; in the
presence of his Majesty I promise to aid Thee, as far
as in me lies, in serving Him and loving Him according
to thy full desires. I will be, with the divine grace, thy
most faithful servant and companion, and I pray Thee
accept my chaste love and hold me as thy brother, without ever entertaining any other kind of love, outside the
one which Thou owest to God and after God to me."
In this conversation the Most High confirmed anew the
virtue of chastity in the heart of saint Joseph, and the
pure and holy love due to his most holy spouse Mary.
This love the saint already had in an eminent degree,
and the Lady herself augmented it sweetly, dilating his
heart by her most prudent discourse.

By divine operation the two most holy and
chaste Spouses felt an incomparable joy and consolation.
The heavenly Princess, as one who is the Mistress of all
virtues and who in all things pursued the highest perfection of all virtues, lovingly corresponded to the desires of saint Joseph. The Most High also gave to saint
Joseph new purity and complete command over his natural inclinations, so that without hindrance or any trace
of sensual desires, but with admirable and new grace,

he might serve his spouse Mary, and in Her, execute his will and pleasure. They immediately set about dividing the property inherited from saint Joachim and Anne, the parents of the most holy Virgin; one part they offered to the temple, where She had stayed, another they destined for the poor, and the third was left in the hands of the holy spouse saint Joseph to be disposed of according to his judgment. Our Queen reserved for Herself only the privilege of serving Him and of attending to the household duties. For from intercourse with outsiders and from the management of property, buying or selling, the most prudent Virgin always kept aloof, as I will mention farther on.

In his former life saint Joseph had learnt the trade of carpentering as being a respectable and proper way of earning the sustenance in life. He was poor in earthly possessions, as I have said above. He therefore asked his most holy Spouse, whether it was agreeable to Her, that he should exercise his trade in order to be able to serve Her and to gain something for distribution among the poor; since it was necessary to do some work and not to remain idle. The most prudent Virgin approved of this resolve, saying that the Lord did not wish them to be rich, but poor and lovers of the poor, desirous of helping them in as far as their means would allow. Then arose between the two Spouses a holy contest, who should obey the other as superior. But She, who among the humble was the most humble, won in this contest of humility; for as the man is the head of the family, She would not permit this natural order to be inverted. She desired in all things to obey her spouse saint Joseph, asking him solely for permission to help the poor, which the saint gladly gave.

As saint Joseph during these days by divine en-

lightenment learnt to know more and more the qualities
of his spouse Mary, her rare prudence, humility, purity
and all her other virtues exceeding by far his thoughts
and estimates, he was seized with ever new admiration
and, in great joy of spirit, continued to praise and thank
the Lord again and again for having given him a Companion and Spouse so far above his merits. And in
order that this work of the Most High might be entirely
perfect (for it was the beginning of the greatest, which
He was to execute by his Omnipotence) He ordained
that the Princess of heaven, by her mere presence and
intercourse, should infuse into the heart of her spouse a
holy fear and reverence greater than words could ever
suffice to describe. This effect was wrought upon saint
Joseph by an effulgence or reflection of the divine light,
which shone from the face of our Queen and which was
mingled with an ineffable and always visible majesty.
So much the more was this due to Her than to Moses
descending from the mountain, (Exod. 24, 30) as her
intercourse and conversation with God had been more
extended and intimate.

WORDS OF THE QUEEN.

My daughter, in the example of the matrimonial
life wherein the Most High placed me, thou findest a
reproof for those souls, who allege their life in the world
as an excuse for not following perfection. To God
nothing is impossible, and nothing is likewise impossible
to those, who with a lively faith, hope in Him, and resign themselves entirely to his divine Providence. I
lived in the house of my spouse with the same perfection as in the temple; for in changing my state of life I
altered neither my sentiments nor the desire and anxiety

to love and serve God; on the contrary I added to my solicitude lest the obligations of a spouse should hinder me in God's service. On this account God favored me and disposed and accommodated powerfully all things in conformity to my desires. The Lord will do the same for all men, if on their part they correspond. They however blame the state of matrimony, deceiving themselves; for the hindrance to a holy and perfect life, is not the state, but the vain and superfluous cares and anxieties, in which they involve themselves forgetting the sweetness of the Lord and seeking and preferring their own.

PART SECOND

BOOKS III, IV, V, VI

THE INCARNATION AND TRANSFIXION

PART SECOND

BOOK III, IV, V

THE INCARNATION AND
TRANSFIXION

BOOK THREE

Contains the most Exquisite Preparations of the Almighty for the Incarnation of the Word in Mary most Holy; the Circumstances Accompanying this Mystery; the Exalted State, in which the Blessed Mother was placed; her Visit to Saint Elisabeth and the Sanctification of the Baptist: Her Return to Nazareth and a Memorable Battle of the Virgin with Lucifer

---

CHAPTER I.

THE NOVENA BEFORE THE INCARNATION.

In order that her most faultless life might be to all an example of the highest holiness, the Most High had placed upon our Queen and Mistress the duties of a spouse of saint Joseph which was a position requiring more intercourse with her neighbors. The heavenly Mistress, finding Herself in this new estate, was filled with such exalted thoughts and sentiments in the fulfillment of her duties, and ordered all the activities of her life with such wisdom, that She was an object of admirable emulation to the angelic spirits and an unparalleled example for men. Few knew Her and still fewer had intercourse with Her: but these happy ones were so filled with that celestial influence of Mary, that with a wonderful joy and with unwonted flights of spirit they sought to express and manifest the light, which illumined their hearts and which they knew came from Her. The most prudent Queen was not unaware of these operations of the Most High; but neither was it yet time, nor would her most profound humility as yet consent to their becoming known to the world. She continually besought the Lord to hide them from men, to make all the favors of his right hand redound solely to his praise, and to permit Her to be ignored and despised by all the mortals, in as far as his infinite goodness would not be offended thereby.

In such fruitful occupations and in augmenting the gifts and graces from which all this good proceeded, our Queen, the Spouse of Joseph, busied Herself during the six months and seventeen days, which intervened between her espousal and the Incarnation of the Word.   I cannot pretend to refer even briefly to her great heroic acts of all the virtues, interior and exterior, to all her deeds of charity, humility, religion, and all her works of mercy, the alms and benefactions; for this exceeds the power of the pen.   The best I can do is to sum up and say: that the Most High found in most holy Mary the fulfillment of all his pleasure and of his wishes, as far as is possible in the correspondence of a creature with its Creator.   By her sanctity and merits God felt Himself as it were obliged, and, (according to our way of speaking), compelled, to hasten his steps and extend the arms of his Omnipotence to bring about the greatest of wonders conceivable in the world before or after: namely the Incarnation of the Onlybegotten of the Father in the virginal womb of this Lady.

In order to proceed with a dignity befitting Himself, God prepared most holy Mary in a singular manner during the nine days immediately preceding this mystery, and allowed the river of his Divinity to rush impetuously forth (Psalm 45, 5) to inundate this City of God with its floods.   He communicated such great graces and gifts and favors, that I am struck dumb by the perception of what has been made known to me concerning this miracle, and my lowliness is filled with dread at even the mention of what I understood.   For the tongue, the pen, and all the faculties of a creature fall far below any possibility of revealing such incomprehensible sacraments. Therefore I wish it to be understood, that all I say here is only an insignificant shadow of the smallest part of these wonders and ineffable prodigies, which are not at all to be encompassed by our limited words, but only by the power divine, which I do not possess.

On the first day of this most blessed novena the heavenly Princess Mary, after a slight rest, according to the example of her father David and according to the diurnal order and arrangement laid out for Her by the Lord, left her couch at midnight (Psalm 118, 62), and, prostrate in the presence of the Most High, commenced her accustomed prayer and holy exercises.

In this vision our Princess Mary learned most high secrets of the Divinity and of its perfections, and especially of God's communications *ad extra* in the work of creation. She saw that it originated in the goodness and liberality of God, that creatures were not necessary for supplementing his Divine existence, nor for his infinite glory, since without them He was glorious through the interminable eternities before the creation of the world. Many sacraments and secrets were manifested to our Queen, which neither can nor should be made known to all; for She alone was the only One (Cant. 6, 8; 7, 6), the chosen One, selected by the highest King and Lord of creation for these delights. But as her Highness in this vision perceived this impulse and inclination of the Divinity to communicate Itself *ad extra* with a force greater than that which makes all the elements tend toward their center, and as She was drawn within the sphere of this divine love, She besought the eternal Father with heart aflame, that He send his Onlybegotten into the world and give salvation to men, since in this manner He should satisfy, and, (speaking humanly), execute the promptings of his Divinity and its perfections.

These petitions of his Spouse were very sweet to the Lord; they were the scarlet lace, with which She bound and secured his love. And in order to put his desires into execution He sought first to prepare the tabernacle or temple, whither He was to descend from the bosom of the eternal Father. He resolved to furnish his beloved and chosen Mother with a clear knowledge of all his works *ad extra,* just as his Omnipotence had made them. On the first day therefore, and in this same vision, He manifested to Her all that He had made on the first day of the creation of the world, as it is recorded in Genesis, and She perceived all with greater clearness and comprehension, than if She had been an eye-witness; for She knew them first as they are in God, and then as they are in themselves.

She perceived and understood, how the Lord in the beginning (Gen. 1; 1, 5), created heaven and earth; in how far and in what way it was void, and how the darkness was over the face of the abyss; how the spirit of the Lord hovered over the waters and how, at the divine command, light was made, and what was its nature; how, after the darkness was divided, it was called night and the light day, and how thus the first day was made. She knew the size of the earth, its longitude, latitude and depth, its caverns, hell, limbo and purgatory with their inhabitants; the countries, climes, the meridians and divisions of the world, and all its inhabitants and occupants. With the same clearness She knew the inferior orbs and the empyrean heaven; how the angels were made on the first day; She was informed of their nature, conditions, diversity, hierarchies, offices, grades and virtues. The rebellion of the bad angels was revealed to Her, their fall and the occasion and the cause of that fall, though the Lord always concealed from Her that which concerned Herself. She understood the punishment and the effects of sin in the demons, beholding them as they are in themselves; and at the conclusion of the first day, the Lord showed to Her, how She too was formed of this lowly earthly material and endowed with the same nature as all those, who return to the dust; He did not however say, that She would again return to it; yet He gave Her such a profound knowledge of the earthly existence, that the great Queen humiliated Herself to the abyss of nothingness; being without fault, She debased Herself more than all the children of Adam with all their miseries.

This whole vision and all its effects the Most High arranged in such a way as to open up in the heart of Mary the deep trenches that were required for the foundations of the edifice, which He wished to erect in Her: namely so high a one, that it would reach up to the substantial and hypostatic union of the human and divine nature. And as the dignity of Mother of God was without limits and to a certain extent infinite, it was becoming that She should be grounded in a proportionate humility, such as would be without limits though still within the bounds of reason itself. Attaining the summit of virtue, this blessed One among women humiliated Herself to such an extent, that the most holy Trinity was, as it were, fully paid and satisfied, and (according to our mode of understanding) constrained to raise Her to the highest position and dignity possible among creatures and nearest to the Divinity itself. In this highest benevolence his Majesty spoke and said to Her:

"My Spouse and Dove, great is my desire of redeeming man from sin and my immense kindness is as it were strained in waiting for the time, in which I shall descend in order to repair the world; ask Me con-

tinually during these days and with great affection for
the fulfillment of this desire.   Prostrate in my royal
presence let not thy petitions and clamors cease, asking
Me that the Onlybegotten of the Father descend in
reality to unite Himself with the human nature." Whereupon the heavenly Princess responded and said: "Lord
and God eternal, whose is all the power and wisdom,
whose wish none can resist (Esther 13, 9), who shall
hinder thy Omnipotence? Who shall detain the impetuous current of thy Divinity, so that thy pleasure
in conferring this benefit upon the whole human race
remain unfulfilled? If perhaps, O my Beloved, I am a
hindrance to such an immeasurable benefit, let me perish
before I impede thy pleasure; this blessing cannot depend
upon the merits of any creature; therefore, my Lord and
Master, do not wait, as we might later on merit it so
much the less.   The sins of men increase and the offenses
against Thee are multiplied; how shall we merit the very
blessing, of which we become daily more unworthy?   In
Thee thyself, my Lord, exists the last cause and motive
of our salvation; thy infinite bounty, thy numberless
mercies incite Thee, the groans of thy Prophets and of
the Fathers of thy people solicit Thee, the saints sigh
after Thee, the sinners look for Thee and all of them
together call out to Thee; and if I, insignificant wormlet,
on account of my ingratitude, am not unworthy of thy
merciful condescension, I venture to beseech Thee, from
the bottom of my heart, to speed thy coming and to
hasten thy Redemption for thy greater glory."

When the Princess of heaven had finished this
prayer, She returned to her ordinary and more natural
state; but anxious to fulfill the mandate of the Lord, She
continued during that whole day her petitions for the
Incarnation of the Word and with the deepest humility

She repeated the exercises of prostrating Herself to the ground and praying in the form of a cross. For the Holy Ghost, who governed Her, had taught Her this posture, by which She so highly pleased the most blessed Trinity. God saw, in the body of the future Mother of the Word, as it were the crucified person of Christ and therefore He received this morning sacrifice of the most pure Virgin as an advance offering of that of his most holy Son.

On the second day, at the same hour of midnight, the Virgin Mary was visited in the same way as described in the last chapter. The divine power raised Her up by the same elevations and illuminings to prepare Her for the visions of the Divinity. He manifested Himself again in an abstractive manner as on the first day, and She was shown the works performed on the second day of the creation. She learnt how and when God divided the waters (Gen. 1, 6), some above and others below, establishing the firmament, and above it the crystal, known also as the watery heaven. Her insight penetrated into the greatness, order, conditions, movements and all the other qualities and conditions of the heavens.

And in the most prudent Virgin this knowledge did not lay idle, nor remain sterile; for immediately the most clear light of the Divinity overflowed in Her, and inflamed and emblazoned Her with admiration, praise and love of the goodness and power of God. Being transformed as it were with a godlike excellence, She produced heroic acts of all the virtues, entirely pleasing to his divine Majesty. And as in the preceding first day God had made Her a participant of his wisdom, so on this second day, He made Her in corresponding measure a participant in the divine Omnipotence, and gave Her power over the influences of the heavens, of the planets and elements, commanding them all to obey Her. Thus was this great Queen raised to Sovereignty over the sea, the earth, the elements and the celestial orbs, with all the creatures, which are contained therein.

More and more the Queen of heaven reflected his infinite attributes and virtues; more and more brilliantly shone forth her beauty under the touch of the pencil of the divine Wisdom and under the colors and lights added to it from on high. On the third day She was informed of the works of creation as they happened on the third day. She learned when and how the waters, which were beneath the firmament, flowed together in one place, (Gen. 1, 9), disclosing the dry land, which the Lord called earth, while He called the waters the sea. She learned in what way the earth brought forth the fresh herbs, and all plants and fructiferous trees with their seeds, each one according to its kind. She was taught and She comprehended the greatness of the sea, its depth and its divisions, its correspondence with the streams and the fountains, that take their rise from it and flow back into it; the different plants and herbs, the flowers, trees, roots, fruits and seeds; She perceived how all and each one of them serve for the use of man. All this our Queen understood and penetrated with the keenest insight more clearly, distinctly and comprehensibly than Adam or Solomon. In comparison with Her all those skilled in medicine in the world would appear but ignorant even after the most thorough studies and largest experience. The most holy Mary knew all that was hidden from sight, as Wisdom says (Wis. 7, 21); and just as She learned it without any fiction, She also communicates it without envy. Whatever Solomon says there in the book of Wisdom was realized in Her with incomparable and eminent perfection.

There is another special favor, which the most holy Mary received for the benefit of the mortals on the third day and in that vision of the Divinity; for during this vision God manifested to Her in a special way the desire of his divine love to come to the aid of men and to raise them up from all their miseries. In accordance with the knowledge of his infinite mercy and the object for which it was conceded, the Most High gave to Mary a certain kind of participation of his own attributes, in order that afterwards, as the Mother and Advocate of sinners, She might intercede for them. This participation of the most holy Mary in the love of God and in his inclination to help her, was so heavenly and powerful that if from that time on the strength of the Lord had not come to her aid, She would not have been able to bear the impetuosity of her desire to assist and save mankind. Filled with this love and charity, She would, if necessary or feasible, have delivered Herself an infinite number of times to the flames, to the sword and to the most exquisite torments of death for their salvation. All the torments, sorrows, tribulations, pains, infirmities She would have accepted and suffered; and She would have considered them a great delight for the salvation of sinners. Whatever all men have suffered from the beginning of the world till this hour, and whatever they will suffer till the end, would have been a small matter for the love of this most merciful Mother. Let therefore mortals and sinners understand what they owe to most holy Mary.

From that day on, we can say, the heavenly Lady continued to be the Mother of kindness and great mercy, and for two reasons: first, because from that moment She sought with an especial and anxious desire to communicate without envy the treasures of grace, which She had comprehended and received; and therefore such an admirable sweetness grew up in her heart, that She was ready to communicate it to all men and to shelter them in her heart in order to make them participants of the divine love, which there was enkindled. Secondly, because this love of most holy Mary for the salvation of men was one of the principal dispositions required for conceiving the eternal Word in her virginal womb. It was eminently befitting that She should be all mercy, kindness, piety and clemency, who was Herself to conceive and give birth to the Word made man, since He in his mercy, clemency and love desired to humiliate Himself to the lowliness of our nature, and wished to be born of Her in order to suffer for men. It is said: like begets like: just as the water partakes of the qualities of the minerals through which it flows; and although the birth of Christ originated in the Divinity, yet it also partook of the conditions of the Mother as far as was possible. She therefore would not have been suitable for concurrence with the Holy Ghost in this conception, in which only the activity of the man was wanting, if She had not been endowed with perfections corresponding to those of the humanity of Christ.

The Most High manifested to Her in this vision, by most special enlightenments, the new Law of grace which the Redeemer of the world was to establish, the Sacraments contained in it, the end for which He would leave them in his new Church of the Gospel, the gifts and blessings prepared for men, and his desire, that all should be saved and that all should reap the fruit of the Redemption. And so great was the wisdom, which the most holy Mary drew from these visions, wherein She was taught by the highest Teacher and the Corrector of the wise (Wis. 7, 15), that, if by any means man or angel could describe it, more books would have to be written of this science of our Lady than all those which have been composed in this world concerning all the arts and sciences, and all the inventions of men. And no wonder her science was greater than that of all other men: for into the heart and mind of our Princess was emptied and exhausted the ocean of the Divinity, which the sins and the evil disposition of the creatures had confined, repressed and circumscribed. It was concealed within its own source until the proper time, which was no other than the hour in which She was chosen as Mother of the Onlybegotten of the Father.

Joined with the sweetness of this divine science, our Queen felt a loving, yet piercing sorrow, which this very science continued to renew. She perceived in the Most High the ineffable treasures of grace and blessings, which He had prepared for mortals and She saw the weight of the Divinity as it were inclined toward the desire of seeing all men enjoy them eternally. At the same time She saw and considered the wicked disposition of the world, and how blindly mortals impeded the flow of these treasures and deprived themselves of participation of the Divinity. From this resulted a new kind of martyrdom full of grief for the perdition of men and of the desire of remedying such lamentable loss. This caused Her to offer up the most exalted prayers, petitions, sacrifices, humiliations and heroic acts of love of God and of men, in order that no one, if possible, should henceforth damn himself, and that all should recognize their Creator, and Redeemer, confess Him, adore and love Him. All this took place in this very vision; but as these petitions were of the same kind as those already described, I do not expatiate on them here.

In conjunction therewith the Lord showed Her

also the works of creation performed on the fourth day
(Gen. 1, 14-17). The heavenly Princess Mary learned
how and when the luminaries of heaven were formed in
the firmament for dividing day and night and for indicating the seasons, the days and the years; how for this
purpose was created the great light of heaven, the sun,
presiding as the Lord of the day, and joined with it, the
moon, the lesser light, which reigns over the darkness
of the night. In like manner were formed the stars of
the eighth heaven, in order that they might gladden the
night with their brilliance and preside with their various
influences over both the day and the night. She understood what was the material substance of these luminous
orbs, their form, their size, their properties, their various
movements and the uniformity as well as the inequality
of the planets. She knew the number of the stars, and
all their influences exerted upon the earth, both in regard
to the living and the lifeless creatures; the effects and
changes, which they cause in them by these influences.

The fifth day of the novena, which the most blessed
Trinity celebrated in the temple of most holy Mary, in
order that the eternal Word might assume human shape
in Her, had arrived. Just as in the preceding days She
was elevated to an abstractive vision of the Divinity,
and, as the veil fell more and more from the secrets of
the infinite wisdom, She discovered new mysteries also
during this day. For the preparations and enlightenments emitted ever stronger rays of light and divine
graces, which flashed into her most holy soul and emptied
the treasures of infinity into her faculties, assimilating
and transforming the heavenly Lady more and more to
a likeness of her God in order to make Her worthy of
being his Mother.

The Princess Mary, through these words of the

Most High, was instructed in the great mysteries regarding the number of the predestined and the reprobate; and also regarding the hindrances and impediments by which sinful men delayed the coming of the eternal Word as man into the world. Having present before Herself the vision both of the infinite bounty and equity of the Creator and of the measureless iniquity and malice of men, the most prudent Mistress, inflamed by the fire of divine love, spoke to his Majesty and said:

"My Lord and infinite God of wisdom and incomprehensible sanctity, what mystery is this, which Thou hast manifested to me? Without measure are the misdeeds of men, so that only thy wisdom can comprehend them. But can all these and many more, perhaps, extinguish thy bounty and love, or vie with them? No, my Lord and Master, it must not be so; the malice of men must not detain thy mercy. I am the most useless of all the human race; yet on its behalf I remind Thee of thy fidelity. Infallibly true it is, that heaven and earth will come to naught, before thy word can fail (Is. 51, 6), and it is also true, that Thou hast many times given thy word through the holy Prophets; and Thou hast promised them by word of mouth, a Redeemer and our salvation. How then, my God, can these promises fail of fulfillment without conflicting with thy infinite wisdom; or how can man be deceived without conflicting with thy goodness? In order to induce Thee to fulfill thy promise and to secure them eternal felicity through thy incarnate Word, I have nothing to offer on the part of mortals nor can any creature oblige Thee; and if this blessing could be merited, then thy infinite and bounteous clemency would not thereby be glorified. Only through thy own Self can this obligation be imposed upon Thee, for only in God can a sufficient reason be found for his becoming man: in Thee alone was the reason and the motive for our creation, and therefore in Thee alone also the reason for our reparation after our fall. Do not seek, my God and most high King, for merits, nor for a greater motive, than thy own mercy and the exaltation of thy holy name."

"It is true, my Spouse," answered the Most High, "that on account of my goodness I bound Myself to the promise of vesting Myself in human nature and of dwelling among them, and that no one could merit in my sight such a promise; but the ungrateful behavior of men, so abominable in my sight and in my justice, does not merit the execution of this promise.

It is impossible to describe the hidden secrets, which most holy Mary then saw in the Lord; for She perceived in Him all the creatures of the past, present and the future, and the position of each one in creation, the good and bad actions and the final ending of each one. If She had not been strengthened, She could not have preserved her life under the effects and feelings caused by the knowledge and insight into these hidden sacraments and mysteries. But as his Majesty, in these new miracles and blessings had such high ends in view, He was not sparing but most liberal with the beloved One, whom He had chosen as his Mother. And as our Queen derived this science from the bosom of God itself, She participated also in the fire of his eternal Charity, which inflamed Her with the love of God and the neighbor. Therefore, continuing her intercession, She said:

"Lord and eternal God, invisible and immortal, I confess thy justice, I magnify thy works, I adore thy infinite Essence and hold in reverence thy judgments. My heart melts within me with tenderest affection, when I perceive thy unlimited bounty toward men and their dark ingratitude and grossness toward Thee. For all of them, O my God, Thou seekest eternal life; but there are few who are thankful for this inestimable benefit, and many who will perish by their malice. If on this account, O my eternal Good, Thou relinquishest thy undertaking, we mortals are lost; but while Thou, in thy divine fore-knowledge, perceivest the sins and the malice of men who offend Thee so much, Thou also foreseest thy Onlybegotten made man and his works of infinite price and value in thy sight; and these will counterbalance and exceed the malice of sin beyond all comparison."

At this prayer of most pure Mary, the eternal Father (in our way of speaking) represented to Himself his Onlybegotten as borne in the virginal womb of this great Queen; and He was moved by her humble and loving petitions. His apparent hesitation was merely a device of his tender love in order to enjoy so much the longer the voice of his Beloved, causing her sweet lips to distil most sweet honey (Cant. 4, 11) and her emissions to be like those of paradise (Cant. 4, 13). And to draw out still more this loving contention, the Lord answered Her: "My sweetest Spouse and chosen Dove, great is that which thou askest of Me and little is that which obliges Me on the part of men; how then shall such a singular blessing be conferred on those unworthy ones? Leave Me, my friend, to treat them according to their evil deserts." Our powerful and kind Advocate responded: "No, my Master, I will not desist from my importunity; if much I ask, I ask it of Thee, who are rich in mercies, powerful in action, true in thy words. My father David said of Thee and of the eternal Word: "The Lord hath sworn, and He will not repent: Thou art a priest forever according to the order of Melchisedech" (Ps. 109, 4). Let then that Priest come, who is at the same time to be the sacrifice for our rescue; let Him come, since Thou canst not repent of thy promise; for Thou dost not promise in ignorance. Let me be clothed.

In this contest (just as it once happened to Jacob) our Lady and Queen was asked, what was her name; and She said: "I am a daughter of Adam, formed by thy hands from the insignificant dust." And the Most High answered: "Henceforth Thou shalt be called: Chosen for the Mother of the Onlybegotten." But the latter part of this name was heard only by the courtiers of heaven, while to Her it was as yet hidden until the proper time. She therefore heard only the word "Chosen." Having thus protracted this amorous contention according to the disposition of his divine wisdom and as far as served to inflame the heart of this elected One, the whole blessed Trinity gave to Mary, our most pure Queen, the explicit promise, that They would now send into the world the eternal Word made man. Filled with incomparable joy and exultation by this fiat, She asked and received the benediction of the Most High. Thus this strong Woman issued forth from the contest with God more victorious than Jacob; for She came out rich, strong and laden with spoils, and the One that was wounded and weakened (to speak in our way) was God himself; for He was drawn by the love of this Lady to clothe Himself in that sacred bridal chamber of her womb with the weakness of our passible nature. He disguised and enveloped the strength of his Divinity, so as to conquer in allowing Himself to be conquered, and in order to give us life by his death. Let the mortals see and acknowledge, how most holy Mary, next to her most blessed Son, is the cause of their salvation.

During this vision were also revealed to this great

Queen the works of the fifth day of the creation in the
manner in which they happened; She saw how, by the
force of the divine command, were engendered and produced in the waters beneath the firmament, the imperfect
reptiles, which creep upon the earth, the winged animals
that course through the air, and the finny tribes that glide
through the watery regions. Of all these creatures She
knew the beginnings, the substance, the form and figure
according to their kinds; She knew all the species of the
animals that inhabit the fields and woods, their conditions, peculiarities, their uses and connections; She knew
the birds of heaven (for so we call the atmosphere),
with the varied forms of each kind, their ornaments,
feathers, their lightness; the innumerable fishes of the
seas and the rivers, the differences between the whales,
their forms, composition and qualities, their caverns and
the foods furnished them by the sea, the ends which they
serve, the use to which they can be put in the world.
And his Majesty especially commanded all these hosts of
creatures to recognize and obey most holy Mary, giving
Her the power to command all of them, as it happened
on many occasions to be mentioned later on. Therewith She issued from the trance of this day and She
occupied Herself during the rest of it in the exercises
and petitions, which the Most High had pointed out
to Her.

Having seen God in this vision She was immediately shown the works on the sixth day of the creation of
the world. She witnessed, as if She Herself had been
present, how at the command of the Lord the earth
brought forth the living beings according to their kinds,
as Moses says (Gen. 1, 24). Holy Scripture here refers
to the terrestrial animals, which being more perfect than
the fishes and birds in life and activity, are called by a

name signifying the more important part of their nature. She saw and understood all the kinds and species of animals, which were created on this sixth day, and by what name they were called: some, beasts of burden, because they serve and assist man, others, wild beasts, as being more fierce and untamed; others, reptiles, because they do not raise themselves or very little from the earth. She knew and comprehended the qualities of all of them: their fury, their strength, the useful purposes which they serve, and all their distinctions and singularities. Over all these She was invested with dominion and they were commanded to obey Her. She could without opposition on their part have trodden upon asps and basilisks, for all would have meekly borne her heel. Many times did some of these animals show their subjection to her commands, as when, at the birth of her most Holy Son, the ox and the ass prostrated themselves and by their breaths warmed the infant God at the command of his blessed Mother.

After seeing the creation of all the irrational creatures, She became aware, how the most blessed Trinity, in order to complete and perfect the world, said: "Let us make man to our image and likeness" (Gen. 1, 26), and how by virtue of this divine decree the first man was formed of the earth as the first parent of all the rest. She had a profound insight into the harmonious composition of the human body and soul and of their faculties, of the creation and infusion of the soul into the body and of its intimate union with the body. Of the structure of the human body and all its parts, She obtained a deep knowledge: She was informed of the number of the bones, veins, arteries, nerves and ligatures; of the concourse of humors to compose the befitting temperaments, the faculties of nutrition, growth and loco-

motion; She learned in what manner the disturbances or
changes in this harmony caused the sicknesses, and how
these can be cured.   All this the most prudent Virgin
understood and comprehended without the least error,
better than all the wise men of the world and better than
even the angels.

The Lord manifested to Her also the happy state
of original justice, in which He placed the first parents
Adam and Eve; She understood their condition, beauty
and perfection of innocence and grace, and for how short
a time they persevered in it.   She perceived how they
were tempted and overcome by the astuteness of the
serpent (Gen. 2, 51), and what were the consequences
of their sin; and how great were the fury and hate of the
demon against the human race.   At the vision of all
these things our Queen made great and heroic acts of
virtue, highly pleasing to God.   She understood, that
She was a daughter of these first parents and that She
descended from a nature so thankless to its Creator.   In
the remembrance of this She humiliated Herself in his
divine presence, thereby wounding the heart of God and
obliging Him to raise Her above all that is created.   She
took it upon Herself to weep for the first sin and for all
the rest, that followed from it, as if She Herself had been
guilty of them all.   Hence, even at that time, that first
sin might have been called a fortunate fault, which caused
tears so precious in the eyes of the Lord, and which
earned us such sureties and pledges of our Redemption.

The seventh day of this mysterious preparation
for the approaching sacrament arrived, and in the same
hour as already mentioned, the heavenly Lady was called
and elevated in spirit, but with this difference, that She
was bodily raised by her holy angels to the empyrean
heaven, while in her stead one of them remained to rep-

resent Her in corporeal appearance. Placed into this highest heaven, She saw the Divinity by abstract vision as in other days; but always with new and more penetrating light, piercing to new and more profound mysteries, which God according to his free will can conceal or reveal. Presently She heard a voice proceeding from the royal throne, which said: "Our Spouse and chosen Dove, our gracious Friend, who hast been found pleasing in our eyes and hast been chosen among thousands: We wish to accept thee anew as our Bride, and therefore We wish to adorn and beautify thee in a manner worthy of our design."

On hearing these words the most Humble among the humble abased and annihilated Herself in the presence of the Most High more than can be comprehended by human power. Entirely submissive to the divine pleasure and with entrancing modesty, She responded: "At thy feet, O Lord, lies the dust and abject worm, ready is thy poor slave for the fulfillment of all thy pleasure in her. Make use, O eternal Good, of this thy insignificant instrument according to thy desire, and dispose of it with thy right hand." Presently the Most High commanded two seraphim, of those nearest to his throne and highest in dignity to attend on this heavenly Virgin. Accompanied by others, they presented themselves in visible form before the throne, and there surrounded the most holy Mary, who was more inflamed with divine love than they.

The heavenly Princess, most holy Mary, had now attained such fullness of grace and beauty and the heart of God was so wounded by her tender affections and desires (Cant. 4, 9), that He was so to say irresistibly drawn to begin his flight from the bosom of the eternal Father to the bridal-chamber of her virginal womb and end the long delay of more than five thousand years. Nevertheless, since this new wonder was to be executed in the plenitude of his wisdom and equity, the Lord arranged this event in such a way, that the Princess of the heavens Herself, being the worthy Mother of the incarnate Word, should at the same time be also the most powerful Mediatrix of his coming and the Redeemer of his people much more than Esther was of Israel (Esther ch. 7 and 8). In the heart of most holy Mary burned the flame, which God himself had enkindled, and without intermission She prayed for the salvation of the human race. However, as yet the most humble Lady restrained Herself in modesty, knowing that on account of the sin of Adam, the sentence of death and of eternal privation from the vision of God had been promulgated (Gen. 3, 9).

The Most High received his holy and chosen Bride, most holy Mary, into his presence. Although this happened not in an intuitive, but in an abstractive vision of the Divinity, it was accompanied with incomparable favors of light and purification proceeding from the Lord himself, such as were specially reserved for this day. For they were so divine, that, in our way of speaking, God himself who wrought them, was astonished and was charmed with the work of his hand. As if entranced with love, He spoke to Her and said: "Revertere, revertere, Sulamitis, ut intueamur te" (Return, return, O Sulamitess, that We may behold thee). "My Spouse, my most perfect and beloved Dove, pleasing in my sight, turn and advance toward Us, that We may behold thee and be charmed by thy beauty. I do not regret to have created man and I delight in his formation, since thou hast been born of him. Let my celestial spirits see how justly I have desired and do desire to choose thee as my Spouse and the Queen of all the creatures. Let them see what good reason I have to rejoice in this my bridal chamber, from whence my Onlybegotten, next to that of my own bosom, shall derive the greatest glory. Let all understand, that if I justly repudiated Eve, the first queen of the earth, on account of her disobedience, I now place thee and establish thee in the highest dignity, showing my magnificence and power in dealing with thy purest humility and self-abasement."

In order to put the last touch to this prodigious work of preparing the most holy Mary, the Lord extended his powerful arm and expressly renewed the spirit and the faculties of the great Lady, giving Her new inclinations, habits and qualities, the greatness and excellence of which are inexpressible in terrestrial terms. It was the finishing act and the final retouching of the living image of God, in order to form, in it and of it, the very shape, into which the eternal Word, the essential image of the eternal Father (II Cor. 4, 4) and the figure of his substance (Heb. 1, 3), was to be cast. Thus the whole temple of most holy Mary, more so than that of Solomon, was covered with the purest gold of the Divinity inside and out, (III Kings, 6, 30), so that nowhere could be seen in Her any grossness of an earthly daughter of Adam. Her entire being was made to shine forth the Divinity; for since the divine Word was to issue from the bosom of the eternal Father to descend to that of Mary, He provided for the greatest possible similarity between the Mother and the Father.

No words at my disposal could ever suffice to describe as I would wish, the effects of these favors in the heart of our great Queen and Mistress. Human thought cannot conceive them, how then can human words express them? But what has caused the greatest wonder in me, when I considered these things in the light given to me, is the humility of this heavenly Woman and the mutual contest between her humility and the divine power.   Rare and astonishing prodigy of humility, to see this Maiden, most holy Mary, though raised to the supremest dignity and holiness next to God, yet humiliating Herself and debasing Herself below the meanest of the creatures; so that, by the force of this humility, no thought of her being destined for the Mothership of the Messias could find entrance into her mind! And not only this: She did not even have a suspicion of anything great or admirable in Herself (Ps. 130, 1). Her eyes and heart were not elated; on the contrary the higher She ascended by the operation of the right hand of her God, so much the more lowly were her thoughts concerning Herself.   It was therefore just, that the Almighty should look upon her humility (Luke 1, 48), and that therefore all generations should call her fortunate and blessed.

WORDS OF THE QUEEN.

My daughter, whoever has only a selfish and servile love is not a worthy spouse of the Most High, for she must not love or fear like a slave, nor is she supposed to serve for her daily wages.   Yet although her heart must be a filial and generous love on account of the excellence and immense goodness of her Spouse, she must nevertheless also feel herself much bounden to Him, when she considers how rich and liberal He is; how, on account of his love for souls, He has created such a variety of visible goods in order that they might serve those who serve Him; and especially, when she considers how many hidden treasures He has in readiness in the abundance of his sweetness (Ps. 30, 20) for those that fear Him as his true children.   I wish that thou feel deeply obliged to thy Lord and Father, thy Spouse and Friend, at the thought of the riches given to those souls, who become his dearest children. For, as a powerful Father, He holds in readiness these great and manifold gifts for his children, and if necessary, all of his gifts for each one of them in particular. In the midst of such motives and incentives of love the disaffection of men is inexcusable, and at the sight of so many blessings, given without measure, their ingratitude is unpardonable.

Remember, also, my dearest, that thou wast no foreigner, or stranger in this house of the Lord, his holy Church (Ephes. 2, 19) ; but thou wast made a domestic and a spouse of Christ among the saints, favored by his gifts and by the dowry of a bride. Since all the treasures and riches of the bridegroom belong to the legitimate spouse, consider of how great possessions He makes thee participant and mistress. Enjoy them all, then, as his domestic, and be zealous for his honor as a much-favored daughter and spouse; thank Him for all these works and benefits, as if they had all been prepared for thee alone by the Lord. Love and reverence Him for thyself and for all thy neighbors, to whom God has been so liberal. In all this imitate, with thy weak faculties, that which thou hast understood of what I have done. I assure thee also, daughter, that it will be very pleasing to me, if thou magnify and praise the Omnipotent with fervent affection, for the favors and riches which, beyond all human conception, the divine right hand showered upon me.

CHAPTER II.

Thereupon his Majesty announced to all the other angels that the time of the Redemption had come and that He had commanded it to be brought to the world without delay; for already, in their own presence, the most holy Mary had been prepared and adorned to be his Mother, and had been exalted to the supreme dignity. The heavenly spirits heard the voice of their Creator, and with incomparable joy and thanksgiving for the fulfillment of his eternal and perfect will, they intoned new canticles of praise, repeating therein that hymn of Sion: "Holy, holy, holy art thou, God and Lord Sabaoth (Is. 6, 3). Just and powerful art Thou, Lord our God, who livest in the highest (Ps. 112, 5) and lookest upon the lowly of the earth. Admirable are all thy works, most high and exalted in thy designs."

The supernal prince Gabriel, obeying with singular delight the divine command and accompanied by many thousands of most beautiful angels in visible forms, descended from the highest heaven. The appearance of the great prince and legate was that of a most handsome youth of rarest beauty; his face emitted resplendent rays of light, his bearing was grave and majestic, his advance measured, his motions composed, his words weighty and powerful, his whole presence displayed a pleasing, kindly gravity and more of godlike qualities than all the other angels until then seen in visible form by the heavenly Mistress. He wore a diadem of exqui-

site splendor and his vestments glowed in various colors
full of refulgent beauty. Enchased on his breast, he
bore a most beautiful cross, disclosing the mystery of
the Incarnation, which He had come to announce. All
these circumstances were calculated to rivet the affectionate attention of the most prudent Queen.

The whole of this celestial army with their
princely leader holy Gabriel directed their flight to Nazareth, a town of the province of Galilee, to the dwelling
place of most holy Mary. This was an humble cottage
and her chamber was a narrow room, bare of all those
furnishings which are wont to be used by the world in
order to hide its own meanness and want of all higher
goods. The heavenly Mistress was at this time fourteen
years, six months and seventeen days of age; for her
birthday anniversary fell on the eighth of September and
six months seventeen days had passed since that date,
when this greatest of all mysteries ever performed
by God in this world, was enacted in Her.

The bodily shape of the heavenly Queen was
well proportioned and taller than is usual with other
maidens of her age; yet extremely elegant and perfect in
all its parts. Her face was rather more oblong than
round, gracious and beautiful, without leanness or grossness; its complexion clear, yet of a slightly brownish
hue; her forehead spacious yet symmetrical; her eye-
brows perfectly arched; her eyes large and serious, of
incredible and ineffable beauty and dovelike sweetness,
dark in color with a mixture tending toward green; her
nose straight and well shaped; her mouth small, with
red-colored lips, neither too thin nor too thick. All the
gifts of nature in Her were so symmetrical and beautiful,
that no other human being ever had the like. To look
upon Her caused feelings at the same time of joy and

seriousness, love and reverential fear. She attracted the heart and yet restrained it in sweet reverence; her beauty impelled the tongue to sound her praise, and yet her grandeur and her overwhelming perfections and graces hushed it to silence. In all that approached Her, She caused divine effects not easily explained; She filled the heart with heavenly influences and divine operations, tending toward the Divinity.

Her garments were humble and poor, yet clean, of a dark silvery hue, somewhat like the color of ashes, and they were arranged and worn without pretense, but with the greatest modesty and propriety. At the time when, without her noticing it, the embassy of heaven drew nigh unto Her, She was engaged in the highest contemplation concerning the mysteries which the Lord had renewed in Her by so many favors during the nine preceding days. And since, as we have said above, the Lord himself had assured Her that his Onlybegotten would soon descend to assume human form, this great Queen was full of fervent and joyful affection in the expectation of its execution and inflamed with humble love, She spoke in her heart: "Is it possible that the blessed time has arrived, in which the Word of the eternal Father is to be born and to converse with men? (Brauch 10, 38). That the world should possess Him? That men are to see Him in the flesh? (Is. 40. 5). That his inaccessible light is to shine forth to illumine those who sit in darkness? (Is. 9, 2). O, who shall be worthy to see and know Him! O, who shall be allowed to kiss the earth touched by his feet!"

"Rejoice, ye heavens, and console thyself, O earth (Ps. 95, 11); let all things bless and extol Him, since already his eternal happiness is nigh! O children of Adam, afflicted with sin, and yet creatures of my Be-

loved, now shall you raise your heads and throw off the
yoke of your ancient servitude! (Is. 14, 25).   O, ye ancient Forefathers and Prophets, and all ye just, that are
detained in limbo and are waiting in the bosom of Abraham, now shall you be consoled and your much desired
and long promised Redeemer shall tarry no longer! (Agg.
2, 8).   Let us all magnify Him and sing to Him hymns
of praise!   O who shall be the slave of Her, whom
Isaias points out as his Mother (Is. 7, 4) ; O Emmanuel,
true God and Man!   O key of David, who art to unlock
heaven! (Is. 22, 22).   O eternal Wisdom!   O Lawgiver
of the new Church! Come, come to us, O Lord, and end
the captivity of thy people; let all flesh see thy salvation!" (Is. 40, 5).

In order that the mystery of the Most High
might be fulfilled, the holy archangel Gabriel, in the
shape described in the preceding chapter and accompanied by innumerable angels in visible human forms
and resplendent with incomparable beauty, entered into
the chamber, where most holy Mary was praying.   It
was on a Thursday at six o'clock in the evening and at
the approach of night.   The great modesty and restraint
of the Princess of heaven did not permit Her to look at
him more than was necessary to recognize him as an
angel of the Lord.   Recognizing him as such, She, in
her usual humility, wished to do him reverence; the holy
princes would not allow it; on the contrary he himself
bowed profoundly as before his Queen and Mistress, in
whom he adored the heavenly mysteries of his Creator.
At the same time he understood that from that day on
the ancient times and the custom of old whereby men
should worship angels, as Abraham had done (Gen. 38,
2), were changed.   For as human nature was raised to
the dignity of God himself in the person of the Word,

men now held the position of adopted children, of companions and brethren of the angels, as the angel said to Evangelist Saint John, when he refused to be worshipped (Apoc. 19, 10).

The holy archangel saluted our and his Queen and said: "Ave gratia plena, Dominus tecum, benedicta tu in mulieribus" (Luke 1, 28). Hearing this new salutation of the angel, this most humble of all creatures was disturbed, but not confused in mind (Luke 1, 29). This disturbance arose from two causes: first, from her humility, for She thought Herself the lowest of the creatures and thus in her humility, was taken unawares at hearing Herself saluted and called the "Blessed among women;" secondly, when She heard this salute and began to consider within Herself how She should receive it, She was interiorly made to understand by the Lord, that He chose Her for his Mother, and this caused a still greater perturbance, having such an humble opinion of Herself. On account of this perturbance the angel proceeded to explain to Her the decree of the Lord, saying: "Do not fear, Mary, for thou hast found grace before the Lord (Luke 1, 30); behold thou shalt conceive a Son in thy womb, and thou shalt give birth to Him, and thou shalt name Him Jesus; He shall be great, and He shall be called Son of the Most High," and the rest as recorded of the holy archangel.

Our most prudent and humble Queen alone, among all the creatures, was sufficiently intelligent and magnanimous to estimate at its true value such a new and unheard of sacrament; and in proportion as She realized its greatness, so She was also moved with admiration. But She raised her humble heart to the Lord, who could not refuse Her any petition, and in the secret of her spirit She asked new light and assistance by which to govern Herself in such an arduous transaction; for, as we have said in the preceding chapter, the Most High, in order to permit Her to act in this mystery solely in faith, hope and charity, left Her in the common state and suspended all other kinds of favors and interior elevations, which She so frequently or continually enjoyed. In this disposition She replied and said to holy Gabriel, what is written in saint Luke: "How shall this happen, that I conceive and bear; since I know not, nor can know, man?" At the same time She interiorly represented to the Lord the vow of chastity, which She had made and the espousal, which his Majesty had celebrated with Her.

The holy prince Gabriel replied (Luke 1, 24): "Lady, it is easy for the divine power to make Thee a Mother without the co-operation of man; the Holy Spirit shall remain with Thee by a new presence and the virtue of the Most High shall overshadow Thee, so that the Holy of holies can be born of Thee, who shall himself be called the Son of God. And behold, thy cousin Elisabeth has likewise conceived a son in her sterile years and this is the sixth month of her conception; for nothing is impossible with God. He that can make her conceive, who was sterile, can bring it about, that Thou, Lady, be his Mother, still preserving thy virginity and enhancing thy purity.

With these and many other words the ambassador of heaven instructed the most holy Mary, in order that, by the remembrance of the ancient promises and prophecies of holy Writ, by the reliance and trust in them and in the infinite power of the Most High, She might overcome her hesitancy at the heavenly message. But as the Lady herself exceeded the angels in wisdom, prudence and in all sanctity, She withheld her answer, in order to be able to give it in accordance with the divine will and that it might be worthy of the greatest of all the mysteries and sacraments of the divine power. She reflected that upon her answer depended the pledge of the most blessed Trinity, the fulfillment of his promises and prophecies, the most pleasing and acceptable of all sacrifices, the opening of the gates of paradise, the victory and triumph over hell, the Redemption of all the human race, the satisfaction of the divine justice, the foundation of the new law of grace, the glorification of men, the rejoicing of the angels, and whatever was connected with the Incarnation of the Onlybegotten of the Father and his assuming the form of servant in her virginal womb (Philip 2, 7).

A great wonder, indeed, and worthy of our admiration, that all these mysteries and whatever others they included, should be intrusted by the Almighty to an humble Maiden and made dependent upon her fiat. But befittingly and securely He left them to the wise and strong decision of this courageous Woman (Prov. 31, 11), since She would consider them with such magnanimity and nobility, that perforce his confidence in Her was not misplaced. The operations, which proceed within the divine Essence, depend not on the co-operation of creatures, for they have no part in them and God could not expect such co-operations for executing the works *ad intra;* but in the works *ad extra* and such as were contingent, among which that of becoming man was the most exalted, He could not proceed without the co-operation of most holy Mary and without her free consent. For He wished to reach this acme of all the works outside Himself in Her and through Her and He wished that we should owe this benefit to this Mother of wisdom and our Reparatrix.

Therefore this great Lady considered and inspected profoundly this spacious field of the dignity of Mother of God (Prov. 21, 16) in order to purchase it by her *fiat;* She clothed Herself in fortitude more than human, and She tasted and saw how profitable was this enterprise and commerce with the Divinity. She comprehended the ways of his hidden benevolence and adorned Herself with fortitude and beauty. And having conferred with Herself and with the heavenly messenger Gabriel about the grandeur of these high and divine sacraments, and finding Herself in excellent condition to receive the message sent to Her, her purest soul was absorbed and elevated in admiration, reverence and highest intensity of divine love. By the intensity of these movements and supernal affections, her most pure heart, as it were by natural consequence, was contracted and compressed with such force, that it distilled three drops of her most pure blood, and these, finding their way to the natural place for the act of conception, were formed by the power of the divine and holy Spirit, into the body of Christ our Lord. Thus the matter, from which the most holy humanity of the Word for our Redemption is composed, was furnished and administered by the most pure heart of Mary and through the sheer force of her true love. At the same moment, with a humility never sufficiently to be extolled, inclining slightly her head and joining her hands, She pronounced these words, which were the beginning of our salvation: "Fiat mihi secundum verbum tuum" (Luke 1, 31).

At the pronouncing of this "fiat," so sweet to the hearing of God and so fortunate for us, in one instant, four things happened. First, the most holy body of Christ our Lord was formed from the three drops of blood furnished by the heart of most holy Mary. Secondly, the most holy soul of the same Lord was created, just as the other souls. Thirdly, the soul and the body united in order to compose his perfect humanity. Fourthly, the Divinity united Itself in the Person of the Word with the humanity, which together became one composite being in hypostatical union; and thus was formed Christ true God and Man, our Lord and Redeemer. This happened in springtime on the twenty-fifth of March, at break or dawning of the day, in the same hour, in which our first father Adam was made and in the year of the creation of the world 5199, which agrees also with the count of the Roman Church in her Martyrology under the guidance of the Holy Ghost. This reckoning is the true and certain one, as was told me, when I inquired at command of my superiors. Conformable to this the world was created in the month of March, which corresponds to the beginning of creation. And as the works of the Most High are perfect and complete (Deut. 32, 4), the plants and trees come forth from the hands of his Majesty bearing fruit, and they would have borne them continually without intermission, if sin had not changed the whole nature. The divine Child began to grow in the natural manner in the recess of the womb, being nourished by the substance and the blood of its most holy Mother, just as other men; yet it was more free and exempt from the imperfections, to which other children of Adam are subject in that place and period. For from some of these, namely those that are accidental and unnecessary to the substance of the act of generation, being merely effects of sin, the Empress of heaven was free. She was also free from the superfluities caused by sin, which in other women are common and happen naturally in the formation, sustenance and growth of their children. For the necessary matter, which is proper to the infected nature of the descendants of Eve and which was wanting in Her, was supplied and administered in Her by the exercise of heroic acts of virtue and especially by charity. By the fervor of her soul and her loving affections the blood and humors of her body were changed and thereby divine Providence provided for the sustenance of the divine Child. Thus in a natural manner the humanity of our Redeemer was nourished, while his Divinity was recreated and pleased with her heroic virtues. Most holy Mary furnished to the Holy Ghost, for the formation of this body, pure and limpid blood, free from sin and all its tendencies. And whatever impure and imperfect matter is supplied by other mothers for the growth of their children was administered by the Queen of heaven most pure and delicate in substance. For it was built up and supplied by the power of her loving affections and her other virtues. In a like manner was purified whatever served as food for the heavenly Queen. For, as She knew that her nourishment was at the same time to sustain and nourish the Son of God, She partook of it with such heroic acts of virtue, that the angelic spirits wondered how such common human actions could be connected with such supernal heights of merit and perfection in the sight of God.

Thus adorned and deified by the Divinity and its gifts, the most holy soul of Christ our Lord proceeded in its operations in the following order: immediately it began to see and know the Divinity intuitively as It is in Itself and as It is united to his most holy humanity, loving It with the highest beatific love and perceiving the inferiority of the human nature in comparison with the essence of God. The soul of Christ humiliated itself profoundly, and in this humility it gave thanks to the immutable being of God for having created it and for the benefit of the hypostatic union, by which, though remaining human, it was raised to the essence of God. It also recognized that his most holy humanity was made capable of suffering, and was adapted for attaining the end of the Redemption. In this knowledge it offered itself as the Redeemer in sacrifice for the human race (Ps. 39, 8), accepting the state of suffering and giving thanks in his own name and in the name of mankind to the eternal Father. He recognized the composition of his most holy humanity, the substance of which it was made, and how most holy Mary by the force of her charity and of her heroic virtues, furnished its substance. He took possession of this holy tabernacle and dwelling; rejoicing in its most exquisite beauty, and, well pleased, reserved as his own property the soul of this most perfect and most pure Creature for all eternity. He praised the eternal Father for having created Her and endowed Her with such vast graces and gifts; for having exempted Her and freed Her from the common law of sin, as his Daughter, while all the other descendants of Adam have incurred its guilt (Rom. 5, 18). He prayed for the most pure Lady and for saint Joseph, asking eternal salvation for them. All these acts, and many others, were most exalted and proceeded from Him as true God and Man. Not taking into account those that pertain to the beatific vision and love, these acts and each one by itself, were of such merit that they alone would have sufficed to redeem infinite worlds, if such could exist.

Even the act of obedience alone, by which the most holy humanity of the Word subjected itself to suffering and prevented the glory of his soul from being communicated to his body, was abundantly sufficient for our salvation. But although this sufficed for our salvation, nothing would satisfy his immense love for men except the full limit of effective love (John 13, 1); for this was the purpose of his life, that He should consume it in demonstrations and tokens of such intense love, that neither the understanding of men nor of angels was able to comprehend it. And if in the first instant of his entrance into the world He enriched it so immeasurably, what treasures, what riches of merits must He have stored up for it, when He left it by his Passion and Death on the cross after thirty-three years of labor and activity all divine! O immense love! O charity without limit! O mercy without measure! O most generous kindness! and, on the other hand, O ingratitude and base forgetfulness of mortals in the face of such unheard of and such vast benefaction! What would have become of us without Him? How much less could we do for this our Redeemer and Lord, even if He had conferred on us but small favors, while now we are scarcely moved and obliged by his doing for us all that He could? If we do not wish to treat as a Redeemer Him, who has given us eternal life and liberty, let us at least hear Him as our Teacher, let us follow Him as our Leader, as our guiding light, which shows us the way to our true happiness.

These operations of Christ our Lord in the first instant of his conception were followed, in another essential instant, by the beatific vision of the Divinity, which we have mentioned in the preceding chapter (No. 139); for in one instant of time many instants of essence can take place. In this vision the heavenly Lady perceived with clearness and distinction the mystery of the hypostatic union of the divine and the human natures in the person of the eternal Word, and the most holy Trinity confirmed Her in the title and the rights of Mother of God. This in all rigor of truth She was, since She was the natural Mother of a Son, who was eternal God with the same certainty and truth as He was man. Although this great Lady did not directly co-operate in the union of the Divinity with the humanity, She did not on this account lose her right to be called the Mother of the true God; for She concurred by administering the material and by exerting her faculties, as far as it pertained to a true Mother; and to a greater extent than to ordinary mothers, since in Her the conception and the generation took place without the aid of a man. Just as in other generations the agents, which bring them about in the natural course, are called father and mother, each furnishing that which is necessary, without however concurring directly in the creation of the soul, nor in its infusion into the body of the child; so also, and with greater reason, most holy Mary must be called, and did call Herself, Mother of God; for She alone concurred in the generation of Christ, true God and Man, as a Mother, to the exclusion of any other natural cause; and only through this concurrence of Mary in the generation, Christ, the Man-God, was born.

But She was especially persistent and fervent in her prayer to obtain guidance of the Almighty for the worthy fulfillment of her office as Mother of the Onlybegotten of the Father. For this, before all other graces, Her humble heart urged Her to desire, and this was especially the subject of her solicitude, that She might be guided in all her actions as becomes the Mother of God. The Almighty answered Her: "My Dove, do not fear, for I will assist thee and guide thee, directing

thee in all things necessary for the service of my onlybegotten Son." With this promise She came to Herself
and issued from her ecstasy, in which all that I have
said had happened, and which was the most wonderful
She ever had. Restored to her faculties, her first action
was to prostrate Herself on the earth and adore her
holiest Son, God and Man, conceived in her virginal
womb; for this She had not yet done with her external
and bodily senses and faculties. Nothing that She could
do in the service of her Creator, did this most prudent
Mother leave undone. From that time on She was conscious of feeling new and divine effects in her holiest
soul and in her exterior and interior faculties. And
although the whole tenor of her life had been most
noble both as regards her body as her soul; yet on this
day of the incarnation of the Word it rose to still greater
nobility of spirit and was made more godlike by still
higher reaches of grace and indescribable gifts.

WORDS OF THE QUEEN.

My dearest daughter, many times I have confided
and manifested to thee the love burning within my
bosom: for I wish that it should be ardently re-enkindled
within thy own, and that thou profit from the instruction,
which I give thee. Happy is the soul, to which the Most
High manifests his holy and perfect will; but more happy
and blessed is he, who puts into execution, what he has
learned. In many ways God shows to mortals the high-
ways and pathways of eternal life: by the Gospels and
the holy Scriptures, by the Sacraments and the laws of
the holy Church, by the writings and examples of the
saints, and especially, by the obedience due to the guid-
ings of its ministers, of whom his Majesty said: "Whoever hears you, hears Me;" for obeying them is the

same as obeying the Lord himself. Whenever by any of these means thou hast come to the knowledge of the will of God, I desire thee to assume the wings of humility and obedience, and, as if in ethereal flight or like the quickest sunbeam, hasten to execute it and thereby fulfill the divine pleasure.

Besides these means of instruction, the Most High has still others in order to direct the soul; namely, He intimates his perfect will to them in a supernatural manner, and reveals to them many sacraments. This kind of instruction is of many and different degrees; not all of them are common or ordinary to all souls; for the Lord dispenses his light in measure and weight (Wis. 11, 21). Sometimes He speaks to the heart and the interior feelings in commands; at others, in correction, advising or instructing: sometimes He moves the heart to ask Him; at other times He proposes clearly what He desires, in order that the soul may be moved to fulfill it; again He manifests, as in a clear mirror, great mysteries, in order that they may be seen and recognized by the intellect and loved by the will. But this great and infinite Good is always sweet in commanding, powerful in giving the necessary help for obedience, just in his commands, quick in disposing circumstances so that He can be obeyed, notwithstanding all the impediments which hinder the fulfillment of his most holy will.

In receiving this divine light, my daughter, I wish to see thee very attentive, and very quick and diligent in following it up in deed. In order to hear this most delicate and spiritual voice of the Lord it is necessary, that the faculties of the soul be purged from earthly grossness and that the creature live entirely according to the spirit; for the animal man does not perceive the elevated things of the Divinity (I Cor. 2, 14). Be attentive then to his secrets (Is. 34, 16) and forget all that is of the outside; listen, my daughter, and incline thy ear; free thyself from all visible things (Ps. 44, 11). And in order that thou mayest be diligent, cultivate love; for love is a fire, which does not have its effect until the material is prepared; therefore let thy heart always be disposed and prepared. Whenever the Most High bids thee or communicates to thee anything for the welfare of souls, or especially for their eternal salvation, devote thyself to it entirely; for they are bought at the inestimable price of the blood of the Lamb and of divine love. Do not allow thyself to be hindered in this matter by thy own lowliness and bashfulness; but overcome the fear which restrains thee, for if thou thyself art of small value and usefulness, the Most High is rich (I Pet. 1, 18), powerful, great, and by Himself performs all things (Rom. 10, 12). Thy promptness and affection will not go without its reward, although I wish thee rather to be moved entirely by the pleasure of thy Lord.

CHAPTER III.

"And Mary rising up in those days," says the sacred text, "went into the hill country with haste, into a city of Jude" (Luke 1, 39). This rising up of our heavenly Queen signified not only her exterior preparations and setting out from Nazareth on her journey, but it referred to the movement of her spirit and to the divine impulse and command which directed Her to arise interiorly from the humble retirement, which She had chosen in her humility. She arose as it were from the feet of the Most High, whose will and pleasure She eagerly sought to fulfill, like the lowliest handmaid, who according to the word of David (Ps. 122, 2) keeps her eyes fixed upon the hands of her Mistress, awaiting her commands. Arising at the bidding of the Lord She lovingly hastened to accomplish his most holy will, in procuring without delay the sanctification of the Precursor of the incarnate Word, who was yet held prisoner in the womb of Elisabeth by the bonds of original sin. This was the purpose and object of this journey. Therefore the Princess of heaven arose and proceeded in diligent haste, as mentioned by the Evangelist saint Luke.

Leaving behind then the house of her father and forgetting her people (Ps. 44, 11), the most chaste spouses, Mary and Joseph, pursued their way to the house of Zacharias in mountainous Judea. It was twenty-six leagues distant from Nazareth, and the greater part of the way was very rough and broken, unfit for such a delicate and tender Maiden.   All the convenience at their disposal for the arduous undertaking was an humble beast, on which She began and pursued her journey. Although it was intended solely for her comfort and service, yet Mary, the most humble and unpretentious of all creatures, many times dismounted and asked her spouse saint Joseph to share with Her this commodity and to lighten the difficulties of the way by making use of the beast.   Her discreet spouse never accepted this offer; and in order to yield somewhat to the solicitations of the heavenly Lady, he permitted her now and then to walk with him part of the way, whenever it seemed to him that her delicate strength could sustain the exertion without too great fatigue.   But soon he would again ask Her, with great modesty and reverence, to accept of this slight alleviation and the celestial Queen would they obey and again proceed on her way seated in the saddle.

Thus alleviating their fatigue by humble and courteous contentions, the most holy Mary and saint Joseph continued on their journey, making good use of each single moment.   They proceeded alone, without accompaniment of any human creatures; but all the thousand angels, which were set to guard the couch of Solomon, the most holy Mary, attended upon them (Cant. 3, 7).   Although the angels accompanied them in corporeal form, serving their great Queen and her most holy Son in her womb, they were visible only to Mary. In the company of the angels and of saint Joseph, the Mother of grace journeyed along, filling the fields and the mountains with the sweetest fragrance of her presence and with the divine praises, in which She unceasingly occupied Herself.   Sometimes She conversed with the angels and, alternately with them, sang divine canticles concerning the different mysteries of the Divinity and the works of Creation and of the Incarnation. Thus ever anew the pure heart of the immaculate Lady was inflamed by the ardors of divine love. In all this her spouse saint Joseph contributed his share by maintaining a discreet silence, and by allowing his beloved Spouse to pursue the flights of her spirit; for, lost in highest contemplation, he was favored with some understanding of what was passing within her soul.

At other times the two would converse with each other and speak about the salvation of souls and the mercies of the Lord, of the coming of the Redeemer, of the prophecies given to the ancient Fathers concerning Him, and of other mysteries and sacraments of the Most High. Something happened on the way, which caused great wonder in her holy spouse Joseph: he loved his Spouse most tenderly with a chaste and holy love, such as had been ordained in Him by the special grace and dispensation of the divine love itself (Cant. 2, 4); in addition to this privilege (which was certainly not a small one) the saint was naturally of a most noble and courteous disposition, and his manners were most pleasing and charming; all this produced in him a most discreet and loving solicitude, which was yet increased by the great holiness, which he had seen from the beginning in his Spouse and which was ordained by heaven as the immediate object of all his privileges. Therefore the saint anxiously attended upon most holy Mary and asked her many times, whether She was tired or fatigued, and in what He could serve Her on the journey. But as the Queen of heaven already carried within the virginal chamber the divine fire of the incarnate Word, holy Joseph, without fathoming the real cause, experienced in his soul new reactions, proceeding from the words and conversations of his beloved Spouse. He felt himself so inflamed by divine love and imbued with such exalted knowledge of the mysteries touched upon in their conversations, that he was entirely renewed and spiritualized by this burning interior light. The farther they proceeded and the more they conversed about these heavenly things, so much the stronger these affections grew, and he became aware, that it was the words of his Spouse, which thus filled his heart with love and inflamed his will with divine ardor.

Having pursued their journey four days, the most holy Mary and her spouse arrived at the town of Juda, where Zachary and Elisabeth then lived. This was the special and proper name of the place, where the parents of saint John lived for a while, and therefore the Evangelist saint Luke specifies it, calling it Juda, although the commentators have commonly believed that this was not the name of the town in which Elisabeth and Zacharias lived, but simply the name of the province, which was called Juda or Judea; just as for the same reason the mountains south of Jerusalem were called the mountains of Judea. But it was expressly revealed to me that the town was called Juda and that the Evangelist calls it by its proper name; although the learned expositors have understood by this name of Juda the province, in which that town was situated. This confusion arose from the fact that some years after the death of Christ the town Juda was destroyed, and, as the commentators found no trace of such a town, they inferred that saint Luke meant the province and not a town; thus the great differences of opinion in regard to the place, where most holy Mary visited Elisabeth, are easily explained.

It was at this city of Juda and at the house of Zacharias that most holy Mary and Joseph arrived. In

order to announce their visit, saint Joseph hastened
ahead of Mary and calling out saluted the inmates of
the house, saying: "The Lord be with you and fill your
souls with divine grace." Elisabeth was already forewarned, for the Lord himself had informed her in a
vision that Mary of Nazareth had departed to visit her.
She had also in this vision been made aware that the
heavenly Lady was most pleasing in the eyes of the Most
High; while the mystery of her being the Mother of
God was not revealed to her until the moment, when
they both saluted each other in private. But saint Elisabeth immediately issued forth with a few of her family,
in order to welcome most holy Mary, who, as the more
humble and younger in years, hastened to salute her
cousin, saying: "The Lord be with you, my dearest
cousin," and Elisabeth answered: "The same Lord reward you for having come in order to afford me this
pleasure." With these words they entered the house of
Zacharias and what happened I will relate in the following chapter.

After the first salutation of Elisabeth by the
most holy Mary, the two cousins retired, as I have said
at the end of the preceding chapter. And immediately
the Mother of grace saluted anew her cousin saying:
"May God save thee, my dearest cousin, and may his
divine light communicate to thee grace and life" (Luke
1, 40). At the sound of most holy Mary's voice, saint
Elisabeth was filled by the Holy Ghost and so enlightened interiorly, that in one instant she perceived the
most exalted mysteries and sacraments. These emotions, and those that at the same time were felt by the
child John in the womb of his mother, were caused by
the presence of the Word made flesh in the bridal chamber of Mary's womb, for, making use of the voice of

Mary as his instrument, He, as Redeemer, began from that place to use the power given to Him by the eternal Father for the salvation and justification of the souls. And since He now operated as man, though as yet of the diminutive size of one conceived eight days before, He assumed, in admirable humility, the form and posture of one praying and beseeching the Father. He asked in earnest prayer for the justification of his future Precursor and obtained it at the hands of the blessed Trinity.

This happened before the most holy Mary had put her salutation into words. At the pronunciation of the words mentioned above, God looked upon the child in the womb of saint Elisabeth, and gave it perfect use of reason, enlightening it with his divine light, in order that he might prepare himself by foreknowledge for the blessings which he was to receive. Together with this preparation he was sanctified from original sin, made an adopted son of God, and filled with the most abundant graces of the Holy Ghost and with the plenitude of all his gifts; his faculties were sanctified, subjected and subordinated to reason, thus verifying in himself what the archangel Gabriel had said to Zacharias; that His son would be filled with the Holy Ghost from the womb of his mother (Luke 1, 17). At the same time the fortunate child, looking through the walls of the maternal womb as through clear glass upon the incarnate Word, and assuming a kneeling posture, adored his Redeemer and Creator, whom he beheld in most holy Mary as if enclosed in a chamber made of the purest crystal. This was the movement of jubilation, which was felt by his mother Elisabeth as coming from the infant in her womb (Luke 1, 44). Many other acts of virtue the child John performed during this interview, exercising faith, hope, charity, worship, gratitude, humility, devotion and all the other virtues possible to him there. From that moment he began to merit and grow in sanctity, without ever losing it and without ever ceasing to exercise it with all the vigor of grace.

Saint Elisabeth was instructed at the same time in the mystery of the Incarnation, the sanctification of her own son and the sacramental purpose of this new wonder. She also became aware of the virginal purity and of the dignity of the most holy Mary. On this occasion, the heavenly Queen, being absorbed in the vision of the Divinity and of the mysteries operated by it through her most holy Son, became entirely godlike, filled with the clear light of the divine gifts which She participated; and thus filled with majesty saint Elisabeth saw Her.

Filled with admiration at what She saw and heard in regard to these divine mysteries, saint Elisabeth was wrapt in the joy of the Holy Ghost; and, looking upon the Queen of the world and what was contained in Her, she burst forth in loud voice of praise, pronouncing the words reported to us by saint Luke: "Blessed are Thou among women and blessed is the fruit of thy womb. And whence is this to me, that the Mother of my Lord should come to me? For behold as soon as the voice of thy salutation sounded in my ears, the infant in my womb leaped for joy, and blessed art Thou, that has believed, because those things shall be accomplished, that were spoken to Thee by the Lord." In these prophetic words saint Elisabeth rehearsed the noble privileges of most holy Mary, perceiving by the divine light what the power of the Lord had done in Her, what He now performed, and what He was to accomplish through Her in time to come. All this also the child John perceived and understood, while listening to the words of his mother; for she was enlightened for the purpose of his sanctification, and since he could not from his place in the womb bless and thank her by word of mouth, She, both for herself and for her son, extolled the most holy Mary as being the instrument of their good fortune.

These words of praise, pronounced by saint Elisabeth were referred by the Mother of wisdom and humility to the Creator; and in the sweetest and softest voice She intoned the Magnificat as recorded by saint Luke (Ch. 1, 46-55).

46. My soul doth magnify the Lord;

47. And my spirit hath rejoiced in God my Saviour.

48. Because He hath regarded the humility of his handmaid; for behold from henceforth all generations shall call me blessed.

49. Because He that is mighty hath done great things to me; and holy is his name.

50. And his mercy is from generation unto generation to them that fear Him.

51. He hath showed might in his arm; He hath scattered the proud in the conceit of their heart.

52. He hath put down the mighty from their seat and hath exalted the humble.

53. He hath filled the hungry with good things; and the rich He hath sent empty away.

54. He hath received Israel, his servant, being mindful of his mercy;

55. As He spoke to our fathers, to Abraham and his seed forever."

Just as saint Elisabeth was the first one who heard this sweet canticle from the mouth of most holy Mary, so she was also the first one who understood it and, by means of her infused knowledge, commented upon it. She penetrated some of the great mysteries, which its Authoress expressed therein in so few sentences. The soul of most holy Mary magnified the Lord for the excellence of his infinite Essence; to Him She referred and yielded all glory and praise (I Tim. 1, 17), both for the beginning and the accomplishment of her works. She knew and confessed that in God alone every creature should glory and rejoice, since He alone is their entire happiness and salvation (II Cor. 10, 17). She confessed also the equity and magnificence of the Most High in attending to the humble and in conferring upon them his abundant spirit of divine love (Ps. 137, 6). She saw how worthy of mortals it is to perceive, understand and ponder the gifts that were conferred on the humility of Her, whom all nations were to call blessed, and how all the humble ones, each one according to his degree, could share the same good fortune. By one word also She expressed all the mercies, benefits and blessings, which the Almighty showered upon Her in his holy and wonderful name; for She calls them altogether "great things" since there was nothing small about anything that referred to this great Queen and Lady.

And as the mercies of the Most High overflowed from Mary's plenitude to the whole human race, and as She was the portal of heaven, through which they issued and continue to issue, and through which we are to enter into the participation of the Divinity; therefore She confessed, that the mercy of the Lord in regard to Her is spread out over all the generations, communicating itself to them that fear Him. And just as the infinite mercies raise up the humble and seek out those that fear God; so also the powerful arm of divine justice scatters and destroys those who are proud in the mind of their heart, and hurls them from their thrones in order to set in their place the poor and lowly. This justice of the Lord was exercised in wonderful splendor and glory upon the chief of all the proud, Lucifer and his followers, when the almighty arm of God scattered and hurled them (because they themselves precipitated themselves) from their exalted seats which befitted their angelic natures and their graces, and which they occupied according to the original (Isaias 14; Apoc. 12) decree of the divine love. For by it He intended that all should be blessed (I Tim. 2, 4) while they, in trying to ascend in their vain pride to positions, which they neither could attain nor should aspire to, on the contrary cast themselves from those which they occupied (Isaias 14, 13).

When it was time to come forth from their retirement, saint Elisabeth offered herself and her whole family and all her house for the service of the Queen of heaven. She asked Her to accept, as a quiet retreat, the room which she herself was accustomed to use for her prayers, and which was much retired and accommodated to that purpose. The heavenly Princess accepted the chamber with humble thanks, and made use of it for recollecting Herself and sleeping therein, and no one ever entered it, except the two cousins. As for the rest She offered to serve and assist Elisabeth as a handmaid, for She said, that this was the purpose of visiting her and consoling her. O what friendship is so true, so sweet and inseparable, as that which is formed by the great bond of the divine love! How admirable is the Lord in manifesting this great sacrament of the Incarnation to three women before He would make it known to any one else in the human race! For the first was saint Anne, as I have said in its place; the second one was her Daughter and the Mother of the Word, most holy Mary; the third one was saint Elisabeth, and conjointly with Her, her son, for he being yet in the womb of his mother, cannot be considered as distinct from her. Thus "the foolishness of God is wiser than men," as saint Paul says.

The most holy Mary and Elisabeth came forth from their retirement at nightfall, having passed a long time together; and the Queen saw Zacharias standing before her in his muteness, and She asked him for his blessing as from a priest of the Lord, which the saint also gave to Her. Yet, although She tenderly pitied him for his affliction, She did not exert her power to cure him, because She knew the mysterious occasion of his dumbness; yet She offered a prayer for him. Saint Elisabeth, who already knew the good fortune of the most chaste spouse Joseph, although he himself as yet was not aware of it, entertained and served him with great reverence and highest esteem. After staying three days in the house of Zacharias, however, he asked permission of his heavenly Spouse Mary to return to Nazareth and leave Her in the company of saint Elisabeth in order to assist her in her pregnancy. The holy husband left them with the understanding that he was to return in order to accompany the Queen home as soon as they should give him notice; saint Elisabeth offered him some presents to take home with him; but he would take only a small part of them, yielding only to their earnest solicitations, for this man of God was not only a lover of poverty, but was possessed of a magnanimous and noble heart. Therewith he pursued his way back to Nazareth, taking along with him the little beast of burden, which they had brought with them. At home, in the absence of his Spouse, he was served by a neighboring woman and cousin of his, who, also when most holy Mary was at home, was wont to come and go on the necessary errands outside of the house.

In conformity with this instruction and new mandate of the Most High, the Princess of heaven ordered all her occupations in the house of her cousin Elisabeth. She rose up at midnight in accordance with her former custom, spending the hours in the continued contemplation of the divine mysteries and giving to waking and sleep the time, which most perfectly and exactly agreed with the natural state and conditions of her body. In labor and repose She continued to receive new favors, illuminations, exaltation and caresses of the Lord. During these three months She had many visions of the Divinity, mostly abstractive in kind. More frequent still were the visions of the most holy humanity of the Word in its hypostatic union; for her virginal womb, in which She bore Him, served Her as her continual altar and sanctuary. She beheld the daily growth of that sacred body. By this experience and by the sacraments, which every day were made manifest to Her in the boundless fields of the divine power and essence, the spirit of this exalted Lady expanded to vast proportions. Many times would She have been consumed and have died by the violence of her affections, if She had not been strengthened by the power of the Lord. To these occupations, which were concealed from all, She added those, which the service and consolation of her cousin Elisabeth demanded, although She did not apply one moment more to them, than charity required. These fulfilled, She turned immediately to her solitude and recollection, where she could pour out the more freely her spirit before the Lord.

Not less solicitous was She to occupy Herself interiorly, while She was engaged for many hours in manual occupations. And in all this the Precursor was so fortunate that the great Queen, with her own hands, sewed and prepared the swaddling clothes and coverlets in which he was to be wrapped and reared; for his mother Elisabeth, in her maternal solicitude and attention, had secured for saint John this good fortune, humbly asking this favor of the heavenly Queen. Mary with incredible love and subjection complied with her request in order to exercise Herself in obedience to her cousin, whom She wished to serve as the lowest handmaid; for in humility and obedience most holy Mary always surpassed all men. Although saint Elisabeth sought to anticipate Her in much that belonged to her service, yet, in her rare prudence and wisdom, Mary knew how to forestall her cousin, always gaining the triumph of humility.

In this way most holy Mary put into practice the doctrine of the eternal Word who humiliated Himself so far, that, being the form of the eternal Father, the figure of his substance, true God of the true God, He nevertheless assumed the form and condition of a servant (Heb. 1, 3, Philip 2, 6, 7). This Lady was the Mother of God, Queen of all creation, superior in excellence and dignity to all creatures, and yet She remained the humble servant of the least of them; and never would She accept homage and service as if due to Her, nor did She ever exalt Herself, or fail to judge of Herself in the most humble manner. What shall we now say of our most execrable presumption and pride? Since, full of the abomination of sin, we are so senseless as to claim for ourselves with dreadful insanity the homage and veneration of all the world? And if this is denied us, we quickly lose the little sense which our passions have left us. This whole heavenly history bears the stamp of humility, and is a condemnation of our pride. And since it is not my office to teach or correct, but to be taught and to be corrected, I beseech and pray all the faithful children of light to place this example before their eyes for our humiliation.

It would not have been difficult for the Lord to preserve his most holy Mother from such extreme lowliness and from the occasions in which She embraced it; He could have exalted Her before creatures, ordaining that She be renowned, honored and respected by all; just as He knew how to procure homage and renown for others as Assuerus did for Mardocheus. Perhaps, if this had been left to the judgment of men, they would have so managed that a Woman more holy than all the hierarchies of heaven, and who bore in her womb the Creator of the angels and of the heavens, should be surrounded by a continual guard of honor, withdrawn from the gaze of men and receiving the homage of all the world; it would have seemed to them unworthy of Her to engage in humble and servile occupations, or not to have all things done only at her command, or to refuse homage, or not to exercise fullest authority. So narrow is human wisdom, if that can be called wisdom, which is so limited. But such fallacy cannot creep into the true science of the saints, which is communicated to them by the infinite wisdom of the Creator, and which esteems at their just weight and price these honors without confounding the values of the creatures. The Most High would have denied his beloved Mother much and benefited Her little, if He had deprived and withdrawn from Her the occasion of exercising the profoundest humility and had instead exposed Her to the exterior applause of men. It would also be a great loss to the world to be without this school of humility and this example for the humiliation and confusion of its pride.

The hour for the rising of the morning star, which was to precede the clear Sun of justice and announce the wished-for day of the law of grace, had arrived (John 5, 35). The time was suitable to the Most High for the appearance of his Prophet in the world; and greater than a prophet was John, who pointing out with his finger the Lamb (John 1, 29), was to prepare mankind for the salvation and sanctification of the world. Before issuing from the maternal womb the Lord revealed to the blessed child the hour in which he was to commence his mortal career among men. The child had the perfect use of his reason, and of the divine science infused by the presence of the incarnate Word. He therefore knew that he was to arrive at the port of a cursed and dangerous land, and to walk upon a world full of evils and snares, where many are overtaken by ruin and perdition.

At the request of his mother the Queen received in her arms the new-born child and offered him as a new oblation to the eternal Father, and his Majesty, well pleased, accepted it as the first-fruits of the Incarnation and of the divine decrees. The most blessed child, full of the Holy Ghost, acknowledged his sovereign Queen, showing Her not only interior, but outward reverence by a secret inclination of his head, and again he adored the divine Word, which was manifested to him in her womb by an especial light. And as he also was aware, that he was privileged before all men, the grateful child performed acts of fervent thanksgiving, humility, love and reverence of God and of his Virgin Mother. The heavenly Queen, in offering him to the eternal Father, pronounced this prayer for him: "Highest Lord and Father, all holy and powerful, accept in thy honor this offering and seasonable fruit of thy most holy Son and my Lord. He is sanctified by the Onlybegotten and rescued from the effects of sin and from the power of thy ancient enemies. Receive this morning's sacrifice, and infuse into this child the blessings of thy holy Spirit, in order that he may be a faithful minister to Thee and to thy Onlybegotten." This prayer of our Queen was efficacious in all respects, and She perceived how the Lord enriched this child, chosen as his Precursor; and She also felt within Herself the effects of these admirable blessings.

Then they bespoke the arrangements for the circumcision of the child, for the time appointed by the law was approaching. Complying with the custom observed among the Jews, especially among the more distinguished, many relatives and other acquaintances of the house of Zacharias began to gather, in order to resolve upon the name to be given to the child; for, in addition to the ordinary preparations and consultations concerning the name to be given to a son, the high position of Zacharias and Elisabeth and the news of the miraculous fecundity of the mother naturally suggested the existence of some great mystery to the minds of all their relations. Zacharias was still dumb, and therefore it was necessary that saint Elisabeth should preside at this meeting. Over and above the high esteem which she inspired, she now exhibited such evident signs of the exalted renewal and sanctification of her soul, which resulted from the knowledge of the mysteries and from the intercourse with the Queen of heaven, that all her relatives and friends noticed the change. For even in her countenance she exhibited a kind of effulgence which made her mysteriously attractive and was the reflection of the Divinity, in whose presence she lived.

The relatives then appealed by signs to Zacharias, who, being unable to speak, asked for a pen and declared his will by writing upon the tablet: "Johannes est nomen ejus." "John is his name." At the same time most holy Mary, making use of her power over all nature, commanded the dumbness to leave him, his tongue to be loosened, as the moment had arrived when it should bless the Lord. At this heavenly command he found himself freed from his affliction, and, to the astonishment and fear of all present, he began to speak, as narrated by the Evangelist. What I say here is not adverse to the Gospel narrative; for, although it is there related, that the angel foretold Zacharias that he should remain mute until his message should be fulfilled, yet God, when He reveals any decree of his will, absolutely unfailing as they are, does not always reveal the means or the manner of their fulfillment, foreseen by Him in his infinite foreknowledge. Thus the archangel announced to Zacharias the punishment of his unbelief, but he did not tell him that he should be freed from it by the intercession of most holy Mary, although this also had been foreseen and decreed.

Therefore, just as the voice of our Lady Mary was the instrument for the sanctification of the child John and his mother, so her secret mandate and her intercession had the effect of loosening the tongue of Zacharias, filling him with the holy Spirit and the gift of prophecy. Hence he broke forth in the words (Luke 1, 68-79):

68. "Blessed be the Lord God of Israel; because He hath visited and wrought the redemption of his people:

69. And hath raised up an horn of salvation to us, in the house of David his servant:

70. And he hath spoken by the mouth of his holy prophets, who are from the beginning;

71. Salvation from our enemies, and from the hands of all that hate us:

72. To perform mercy to our fathers, and to remember his holy testament,

73. The oath, which he swore to Abraham our father, that he would grant to us,

74. That being delivered from the hand of our enemies, we may serve him without fear,

75. In holiness and justice before him, all our days.

76. And thou, child, shalt be called the prophet of the Highest: for thou shalt go before the face of the Lord to prepare his ways:

77. To give knowledge of salvation to his people: unto the remission of their sins:

78. Through the bowels of the mercy of our God, in which the Orient from on high hath visited us:

79. To enlighten them that sit in darkness, and in the shadow of death: to direct our feet into the way of peace."

In the divine canticle of the Benedictus Zacharias embodied all of the highest mysteries, which the ancient prophets had foretold in a more profuse manner concerning the Divinity, Humanity and the Redemption of Christ, and in these few words he embraces many great sacraments. He also understood them by the grace and light, which filled his spirit, and which raised him up in the sight of all that had come to attend the circumcision of his son; for all of them were witnesses to the solving of his tongue and to his divine prophecies. I will hardly be able to give an explanation of the deep meaning of these prophecies, such as they had in the mind of that holy priest.

At the call of Elisabeth, the most fortunate of husbands, saint Joseph, had come in order to attend most holy Mary on her return to her home in Nazareth. On arriving at the house of Zacharias he had been welcomed with indescribable reverence and devotion by saint Elisabeth and Zacharias; for now also the holy priest knew that he was the guardian of the sacramental treasures of heaven, though this was yet unknown to the great patriarch saint Joseph himself. His heavenly Spouse received him in modest and discreet jubilation, and, kneeling before him, She, as usual, besought his blessing, and also his pardon, for having failed to serve him for nearly three months during her attendance upon her cousin Elisabeth. Though She had been guilty of no fault, nor even of an imperfection in thus devotedly fulfilling the will of God in conformity with the wishes of her spouse, yet, by this courteous and endearing act of humility, She wanted to repay her husband for the want of her consoling companionship. The holy Joseph answered that as he now again saw Her, and again enjoyed her delightful presence, he was relieved of the pain caused by her absence. In the course of a few days they announced the day of their departure. Thereupon the princess Mary took leave of the priest Zacharias. As he had already been enlightened by the Lord concerning the dignity of the Virgin Mother, he addressed Her with the greatest reverence as the living sanctuary of the Divinity and humanity of the eternal Word. "My Mistress," he said, "praise and bless eternally thy Maker, who in his infinite mercy has chosen Thee among all his creatures as his Mother, as the sole Keeper of all his great blessings and sacraments. Be mindful of me, thy servant, before thy Lord and God, that He may lead me in peace through this exile to the security of the eternal peace which we hope for, and that through thee I may merit the vision of his Divinity, which is the glory of the saints. Remember also, O Lady, my house and family, and especially my Son John, and pray to the Most High for thy people."

The whole household of Zacharias had been sanctified by the presence of most holy Mary and of the incarnate Word in her womb; all its inmates had been edified by her example, instructed by her conversations and teachings, and sweetly affected by her intercourse and modest behavior. While She had drawn toward Herself all the hearts of that happy family, She also merited and obtained for them from her most holy Son the plenitude of celestial gifts. Holy Joseph was held in high veneration by Zacharias, Elisabeth and John; for they had come to know his high dignity before he himself was yet aware of it. The blessed Patriarch, happy in his Treasure, the full value of which as yet he did not know, took leave of all and departed for Nazareth: what happened on the way I will narrate in the following chapter. But before they began their journey most holy Mary, on bended knees, besought saint Joseph to bless Her, as She was accustomed to do on such occasions, and after She had received his blessing, they betook themselves on their journey.

WORDS OF THE QUEEN.

For two reasons, my daughter, the divine effects wrought through me by my Son in saint John and Elisabeth were concealed, while those in Zacharias were manifest. First, because Elisabeth spoke out clearly in praise of the incarnate Word and of me; yet at the time it was not proper that either this mystery or my dignity should be openly known; the coming of the Messias was to be manifested by other more appropriate means. Secondly, not all hearts were so well prepared as that of Elisabeth for receiving such precious and unprecedented seed of divine knowledge, nor would they have welcomed such sacramental revelation with due reverence. On the other hand it was more becoming that Zacharias in his priestly dignity should proclaim what was then to be made known; for the beginnings of the heavenly light would be accepted more readily from him than from saint Elisabeth, especially while he was present. That which she said, was reserved to bring forth its effects in due time. Although the words of God have their own inherent force; yet the more sweet and acceptable manner of communicating with the ignorant and the unskilled in divine mysteries is by means of the priest.

Likewise it was proper that the dignity and honor of the priesthood should receive its due; for the Most High holds the priests in such esteem, that if He finds them in the right disposition, He exalts them and fills them with his Spirit in order that the world may venerate them as his chosen and anointed ones. Moreover the wonders of the Lord run less risk in priests, even when they are more openly revealed to them. If they live up to their dignity, their works in comparison with those of the other creatures, are like those of the angels and of the seraphim. Their countenance should be resplendent, like that of Moses, when he came forth from converse with the Lord (Exod. 34, 29). At least they should deal with the rest of men in such a manner that they be honored and revered as next to God. I desire that thou understand, my dearest, that the Most High is greatly incensed against the world in this matter: as well against the priests as against laymen. Against the priests because, forgetting their exalted dignity, they debase themselves by a contemptible, degraded and scandalous life, giving bad example to the world by mixing up with it to the neglect of their sanctification. And against the laymen, because they act with a foolhardy presumption toward the anointed of the Lord, whom, though imperfect and blameless in their lives, they ought to honor and revere as taking the place of Christ, my most holy Son, on earth.

On account of this reverence due to the priesthood my behavior toward saint Zacharias was different from that toward Elisabeth. For, although the Lord wished, that I should be the instrument, by which the gifts of the holy Spirit should be communicated to both; yet I saluted Elisabeth in such a manner, that I at the same time showed a certain authority, exerting my power over the original sin of her son; for at my words this sin was forgiven him, and both mother and son were filled with the Holy Ghost. As I had not contracted original sin and was exempt from it, I possessed dominion over it on this occasion: I commanded as the Mistress, who had triumphed over it by the help of the Lord (Gen. 3, 5), and who was no slave of it, as all the sons of Adam, who sinned in him (Rom. 5, 12). Therefore the Lord desires that, in order to free John from the slavery and chains of sin, I should command over it as one who never was subject to its bondage. I did not salute Zacharias in this authoritative way, but I prayed for him, observing the reverence and decorum due to his dignity and my modesty. I would not have commanded the tongue of the priest to be loosened, not even mentally and secretly, if the Most High had not enjoined it upon me, intimating at the same time, that the defect of speech hardly suited his office, for a priest should stand ready to serve and praise the Almighty with all his powers. In regard to the respect due to priests I will tell thee more on another occasion; let this suffice at present for the solution of thy doubt.

But from my instruction today learn especially to seek direction in the way of virtue and of eternal life in all thy intercourse with men, be they above or below thee in dignity. Imitate therein me and my cousin Elisabeth, with due discretion asking all to direct thee and guide thee; for in return for such humility the Lord will provide thee with secure counsel and divine light for exercising thy discreet and sincere love of virtue. Drive away, or do not allow thyself to be influenced by even the least breath of flattery and avoid the conversations which expose thee to it; for such deceitful pleasure darkens the light and perverts the unsuspecting mind. The Lord is so jealous of the souls especially beloved by Him, that He will immediately turn away from them if they find pleasure in the praises of men and seek to recompense themselves by their flatteries; since by this levity they become unworthy of his favors. It is not possible to unite in a soul the adulations of the world and the caresses of the Most High. For these latter are sincere, holy, pure, and lasting: they humiliate, cleanse, pacify and illumine the heart; while on the other hand the flatteries of creatures are vain, fleeting, deceitful, impure and false, issuing from the mouths of those who are all liars (Ps. 115, 11); and whatever is deceitful is a work of the enemy.

BOOK FOUR

Describing the Anxieties of Saint Joseph on Account of the Pregnancy of Most Holy Mary, the Birth of Christ our Lord, His Circumcision, the Adoration of the Kings, the Presentation of the Infant Jesus In the Temple, the Flight into Egypt, the Death of the Holy Innocents, and the Return to Nazareth.

CHAPTER I.

ST. JOSEPH RESOLVES TO LEAVE HIS SPOUSE.

The divine pregnancy of the Princess of heaven had advanced to its fifth month when the most chaste Joseph, her husband, commenced to notice the condition of the Virgin; for on account of the natural elegance and perfection of her virginal body, as I have already remarked, any change could not long remain concealed and would so much the sooner be discovered. One day, when saint Joseph was full of anxious doubts and saw Her coming out of her oratory, he noticed more particularly this evident change, without being able to explain away what he saw so clearly with his eyes. The man of God was wounded to his inmost heart by an arrow of grief, unable to ward off the force of evidence, which at the same time wounded his soul. The principal cause of his grief was the most chaste, and therefore the most intense love with which he cherished his most faithful Spouse, and in which he had from the beginning given over to Her his whole heart. Moreover, her charming graces and incomparable holiness had captured and bound to Her his inmost soul. As She was so perfect and accomplished in her modesty and humble reticence, saint Joseph, besides his anxious solicitude to serve Her, naturally entertained the loving desire of meeting a response of his love from his Spouse. This was so ordained by the Lord, in order that by the desire for this interchange of affection he might be incited to love and serve Her more faithfully.

Besides all this was the certainty of his not having any part in this pregnancy, the effects of which were before his eyes; and there was the inevitable dishonor which would follow as soon as it would become public. This thought caused so much the greater anxiety in him, as he was of a most noble and honorable disposition, and in his great foresight he knew how to weigh the disgrace and shame of himself and his Spouse in each circumstances. The third and most intimate cause of his sorrow, and which gave him the deepest pain, was the dread of being obliged to deliver over his Spouse to the authorities to be stoned (Lev. 20, 10), for this was the punishment of an adulteress convicted of the crime. The heart of saint Joseph, filled with these painful considerations, found itself as it were exposed to the thrusts of many sharp-edged swords, without any other refuge than the full confidence which he had in his Spouse. But as all outward signs confirmed the correctness of his observations, there was no escape from these tormenting thoughts, and as he did not dare to communicate about his grievous affliction with anybody, he found himself surrounded by the sorrows of death (Ps. 17, 5), and he experienced in himself the saying of the Scriptures, that: "Jealousy is hard as hell" (Cant. 8, 6).

In the midst of these tormenting anxieties the holy Spouse Joseph appealed to the tribunal of the Lord in prayer and placing himself in her presence, he said: "Most high Lord and God, my desires and sighs are not unknown to Thee. I find myself cast about by the violent waves of sorrow (Ps. 31. 10) which through my senses have come to afflict my heart. I have given myself over with entire confidence to the Spouse whom thou hast given me. I have confided entirely in her holiness; and the signs of this unexpected change in Her are giving rise to tormenting and fearful doubts lest my confidence be misplaced. Nothing have I until now seen in Her which could give occasion for any doubt in her modesty and her extraordinary virtue; yet at the same time I cannot deny that She is pregnant. To think that She has been unfaithful to me, and has offended Thee, would be temerity in view of such rare purity and holiness: to deny what my own eyes perceive is impossible. But it is not impossible that I die of grief, unless there is some mystery hidden beneath it which I cannot yet fathom. Reason proclaims Her as blameless, while the senses accuse Her. She conceals from me the cause of her pregnancy, while I have it before my eyes. What shall I do? We both have come to an agreement concerning our vows of chastity, and we have both promised to keep them for thy glory; if it could be possible that She has violated her fidelity toward Thee and toward me, I would defend thy honor and would forget mine for love of Thee. Yet how could She preserve such purity and holiness in all other things if She had committed so grave a crime in this? And on the other hand, why does She, who is so holy and prudent, conceal this matter from me? I withhold and defer my judgment. Not being able to penetrate to the cause of what I see, I pour out in thy presence my afflicted soul (Ps. 141, 3), God of Abraham, Isaac and Jacob. Receive my tears as an acceptable sacrifice; and if my sins merit thy indignation, let thy own clemency and kindness move Thee not to despise my excruciating sorrow. I do not believe that Mary has offended Thee; yet much less can I presume that there is a mystery of which I, as her Spouse, am not to be informed. Govern Thou my mind and heart by thy divine light, in order that I may know and fulfill that which is most pleasing to Thee."

Saint Joseph persevered in this kind of prayer, adding many more affectionate petitions; for even though he conjectured that there must be some mystery in the pregnancy of the most holy Mary hidden from him, he could not find assurance therein. This thought had no greater force to exculpate most holy Mary than the other reasons founded upon her holiness; and therefore the idea that the most holy Queen might be the Mother of the Messias did not come to his mind. If at times he drove away his conjectures, they would return in greater number and with more urgent force of evidence. Thus he was cast about on the turbulent waves of doubt. From sheer exhaustion he would at times fall into a condition of mind wherein he could find neither an anchor of certainty for his doubts, nor tranquillity for his heart, nor any standard by which he could direct his course. Yet his forebearance under this torment was so great that it is an evident proof of his great discretion and holiness, and that it made him worthy of the singular blessing which awaited him.

All that passed in the heart of saint Joseph was known to the Princess of heaven, who penetrated into its interior by the light of her divine science. Although her soul was full of tenderness and compassion for the sufferings of her spouse, She said not a word in the matter; but She continued to serve him with all devotion and solicitude. The man of God watched Her without outward demonstration, yet with a greater anxiety than that of any man that ever lived. The pregnancy of most holy Mary was not burdensome or painful to Her; but as the great Lady in serving him at table or any other domestic occupations, necessarily disclosed her state more and more openly, saint Joseph noticed all these actions and movements and with deep affliction of soul verified all his observations. Notwithstanding his being a holy and just man, he permitted himself to be respected and served by the most holy Virgin after their espousal, claiming in all things the position of head and husband of the family, though with rare humility and prudence. As long as he was ignorant of the mystery of his Spouse he judged it right, within befitting limits, to show his authority in imitation of the ancient Fathers and Patriarchs. For he knew that they demanded subjection and prompt obedience of their wives, and he did not wish to recede from their example. He would have been right in this course if most holy Mary, our Lady, had been no more than other women. Yet although there was such a great difference, no woman ever existed or will exist who was or will be so obedient, humble and devoted to her husband as the most exalted Queen was toward her spouse. She served him with incomparable respect and promptitude; although She knew his troubled thoughts and observations concerning her pregnancy, She omitted no service due to him, nor did She try to conceal or palliate her state. For such evasion or duplicity would not have consorted with the angelic truthfulness and openness, nor with the nobility and magnanimity of her generous heart.

The great Lady could easily have asserted her entire innocence and referred to the testimony of saint Elisabeth and Zacharias; for, if saint Joseph had any suspicion of guilt in Her, he could naturally have supposed

it to have been incurred during her stay with them.
Hence, through them and by other references, She could
have justified Herself and quieted the anxieties of saint
Joseph without disclosing the mystery.   The Mistress of
prudence and humility did nothing of the kind; for these
virtues did not allow Her to think of Herself, nor to
trust the justification of her mysterious condition to her
own explanation.   With great wisdom She resigned the
whole matter into the hands of divine Providence.   Although her compassion for her spouse and her love for
him made Her anxious to console and comfort him, She
would not do it by clearing Herself or by concealing her
pregnancy, but rather by serving him with more devoted
demonstrations of love, and by trying to cheer him up,
asking him what She could do for him and lovingly showing her devoted and submissive affection.   Many times
She served him on her knees, and although this somewhat
consoled saint Joseph, yet on the other hand, it was also
a cause for new grief.   For thus he only saw the motives
of love and esteem multiplied and still remained uncer-
tain whether She had been untrue or not.   The heavenly
Lady offered up continual prayers for him and besought
the Most High to look upon him and console him; as for
the rest She submitted all to the will of his Majesty.

Saint Joseph could not entirely conceal his cruel
sorrow, and therefore he often appeared to be in doubt
and sad suspense.   Sometimes, carried away by his grief,
he spoke to his heavenly Spouse with some degree of
severity, such as he had not shown before.   This was
the natural effect of the affliction of his heart, not of
anger or vengeful feelings; for these never entered his
thoughts, as we shall see later.   The most prudent Lady,
however, never lost the sweetness of her countenance, nor
showed any feeling; but merely redoubled her efforts to

relieve her husband. She served at table, offered him a seat, administered food and drink, and if, after all these services, which She performed with incomparable grace, saint Joseph urged Her to sit down, he could convince himself more and more of her pregnancy.

Yet although her sorrow exceeded all bounds, the capacity of her generous and magnanimous soul was much greater and therefore She could conceal her grief more completely, and occupy her faculties in the loving care of saint Joseph, her spouse. Her sorrow therefore only incited Her to attend so much the more devotedly to his health and comfort. Nevertheless, as the inviolable rule of the actions of the most prudent Queen was to perform all in the fullness of wisdom and perfection, She continued to conceal the mystery about the disclosure of which She had received no command. Though She alone could relieve her spouse by an explanation, She withheld it in reverence and faithfulness due to the sacrament of the heavenly King (Tob. 13, 7). As far as She herself was concerned, She exerted her utmost powers; She spoke to him about his health, She asked what She could do to serve him and afford him help in the weakness which so mastered him. She urged him to take some rest and recreation, since it was a duty to yield to necessity and repair the weakened strength, in order to be able to work for the Lord afterward.

The Princess of heaven, becoming aware of the resolve of her spouse saint Joseph to leave Her and absent himself, turned in great sorrow to her holy angels and said to them: "Blessed spirits and ministers of the highest King, who raised you to felicity which you enjoy, and by his kind Providence accompany me as his faithful servants and as my guardians, I beseech you, my friends, to present before God's clemency the afflictions of my spouse Joseph. Beseech the Lord to look upon him and console him as a true Father. And you also, who so devotedly obey his words, hear likewise my prayers; in the name of Him who is infinite, and to whom I am to give human shape in my womb, I pray, beseech and supplicate you, that without delay you assist and relieve my most faithful spouse in the affliction of his heart and drive from his mind and heart his resolve of leaving me." The angels which the Queen selected for this purpose obeyed immediately and instilled into the heart of saint Joseph many holy thoughts, persuading him anew that his Spouse Mary was holy and most perfect, and that he could not believe anything wrong of Her; that God was incomprehensible in his works, and most hidden in his judgments (Ps. 33, 19); that He was always most faithful to those who confide in Him, and that He would never despise or forsake them in tribulation.

By these and other holy inspirations the troubled spirit of saint Joseph was somewhat quieted, although he did not know whence they came; but as the cause of his sorrow was not removed, he soon relapsed, not finding anything to assure and soothe his soul, and he returned to his resolve of withdrawing and leaving his Spouse. The heavenly Queen was aware of this and She concluded that it was necessary to avert this danger and to insist in earnest prayer on a remedy. She addressed Herself entirely to her most holy Son in her womb, and with most ardent affection of her soul She prayed: "Lord and God of my soul, with thy permission, although I am but dust and ashes (Gen. 8, 27), I will speak in thy kingly presence and manifest to Thee my sighs, that cannot be hidden from Thee (Ps. 37, 19). It is my duty not to be remiss in assisting the spouse whom I have received from thy hand. I see him overwhelmed by the tribulation, which Thou hast sent him, and it would not be kind in me to forsake him therein. If I have found grace in thy eyes, I beseech Thee, Lord and eternal God, by the love which obliged Thee to enter into the womb of thy servant for the salvation of mankind, to be pleased to console thy servant Joseph and dispose him to assist me in the fulfillment of thy great works. It would not be well that I, thy servant, be left without a husband for a protection and guardian. Do not permit, my Lord and God, that he execute his resolve and withdraw from me."

The Most High answered Her: "My dearest Dove, I shall presently visit my servant Joseph with consolation; and after I shall have manifested to him by my angel the sacrament, which is unknown to him, thou mayest speak openly about all that I have done with thee, without the necessity of keeping silent thenceforward in these matters. I will fill him with my spirit and make him apt to perform his share in these mysteries. He will assist Thee in them and aid Thee in all that will happen." With this promise of the Lord, most holy Mary was comforted and consoled, and She gave most fervent thanks to the same Lord, who disposes all things in admirable order, measure and weight. For besides the consolation, which the relief from this anxiety afforded Her, She also knew well how proper it was that the spirit of saint Joseph be tried and dilated by this tribulation before the great mysteries should be entrusted to his care.

In the meanwhile saint Joseph was anxiously debating within himself concerning the proper course of action, for he had borne his tribulation already for two months; and now, overcome by the greatness of it, he argued with himself: I do not find a better way out of these difficulties than to absent myself. I confess that my Spouse is most perfect and exhibits nothing but what shows Her a saint; but after all She is pregnant and of it I cannot fathom the mystery. I do not wish to injure Her reputation of holiness by involving Her in the punishment of the law; yet at the same time I cannot stand by and witness the consequences of her pregnancy. I will leave her now, and commit myself to the providence of the Lord, who governs me." He then resolved to depart during that night, and in order to prepare for his journey he packed some clothes and other trifles into a small bundle. Having also claimed some wages due to him for his work, he retired to rest with the intention of leaving at midnight. But on account of the strangeness of his undertaking, and because he was in the habit of commending his intentions to God in prayer, after he had come to this resolve he spoke to the Lord: "Highest and eternal God of our fathers Abraham, Isaac and Jacob, Thou true and only refuge of the poor and afflicted, the grief and tribulation of my heart are well known to thy clemency. Thou knowest also, O Lord (although I am unworthy), that I am innocent of that which causes my sorrow, and Thou likewise art aware of the infamy and danger consequent upon the condition of my Spouse. I do not believe Her an adulteress, because I see in Her great virtue and perfection; yet I certainly see Her pregnant. I do not know by whom or how it was caused; and therefore I find no way to restore my peace. In order to choose the least evil I will withdraw from Her and seek a place where no one knows me and, resigning myself to thy Providence, I will pass my life in a desert. Do not forsake me, my Lord and eternal God, since I desire solely thy honor and service."

Saint Joseph prostrated himself on the ground and made a vow to go to the temple of Jerusalem and offer up a part of the small sum of money which he had provided for his journey, in order that God might help and protect Mary his Spouse from the calamities of men and free Her from all misfortune; for great was the uprightness of that man of God, and the esteem in which he held the heavenly Lady. After this prayer he composed himself for a short sleep with the intention of departing in secret and at midnight from his Spouse. During this sleep, however, happened what I will relate in the next chapter. The great Princess of heaven, (assured by the divine promise), observed from her retirement all that saint Joseph was preparing to do; for the Almighty showed it to Her. And hearing the vow, which he made for her welfare, and seeing the small bundle and the poor provision he prepared for his journey, She was filled with tender compassion and prayed anew for him, giving praise and thanks to the Lord for his Providence in guiding the actions of men beyond all human power of comprehension. His Majesty so ordained events, that both most holy Mary and saint Joseph should be brought to the utmost reach of interior sorrow.

In these operations of course, the last reason is always the divine will itself, just, holy and perfect. However, as far as I have understood, I will partly mention some other reasons in explanation. The first reason is, that saint Joseph was so prudent, filled with such heavenly light, and had such high conception of our most holy Lady, the blessed Mary, that it was not necessary to convince him by strong evidence, in order to assure him of her dignity and of the mysteries of the Incarnation; for in hearts well-disposed the divine inspirations find easy entrance. The second reason is, because his trouble had its beginning in the senses, namely in seeing with his eyes the pregnancy of his Spouse; hence it was a just retribution, that they, having given occasion for deception or suspicion, should as it were be deadened or repressed by the privation of the angelic vision. The third reason is as it were a sequence of this last one: saint Joseph, although he was guilty of no fault, was under the influence of his affliction and his senses were so to say deadened and incapacitated for the sensible perception and intercourse of the angel. Therefore it was befitting, that the angel deliver this message to him at a time, when the senses, which had been scandalized, were inactive and suspended in their operations. Thus the holy man might afterwards, regaining their full use, purify and dispose himself by many acts of virtue for entertaining the operation of the holy Spirit, which had been entirely interrupted by his troubles.

Saint Joseph awoke with the full consciousness, that his Spouse was the true Mother of God. Full of joy on account of his good fortune and of his inconceivable happiness, and at the same time deeply moved by sudden sorrow for what he had done, he prostrated himself to the earth and with many other humble, reverential and joyful tokens of his feelings he performed heroic acts of humiliation and of thanksgiving. He gave thanks to the Lord for having revealed to him this mystery and for having made him the husband of Her, whom God had chosen for his Mother, notwithstanding that he was not worthy to be even her slave. Amid these recognitions and these acts of virtue, the spirit of saint Joseph remained tranquil and apt for the reception of new influences of the holy Spirit. His doubts and anxieties of the past few months had laid in him those deep foundations of humility, which were necessary for one who should be entrusted with the highest mysteries of the Lord; and the remembrance of his experiences was to him a lesson which lasted all his life. The holy man began to blame himself alone for all that had happened and broke forth in the following prayer: "O my heavenly Spouse and meekest Dove, chosen by the Most High for his dwelling-place and for his Mother: how could thy unworthy slave have dared to doubt thy fidelity? How could dust and ashes ever permit itself to be served by Her, who is the Queen of heaven and earth and the Mistress of the universe? How is it, that I have not kissed the ground which was touched by thy feet? Why have I not made it my most solicitous care to serve Thee on my knees? How will I ever raise my eyes in thy presence and dare to remain in thy company or open my lips to speak to Thee? O my Lord and God, give me grace and strength to ask her forgiveness; and move her heart to mercy, that She do not despise her sorrowful servant according to his guilt.

The holy spouse now left his little room, finding himself so happily changed in sentiments since the time he had composed himself for sleep. As the Queen of heaven always had kept herself in retirement, he did not wish to disturb her sweet contemplation, until She herself desired. In the meantime the man of God unwrapped the small bundle, which he had prepared, shedding many tears with feelings quite different from those with which he had made it up. Weeping, he began to show his reverence for his heavenly Spouse, by setting the rooms in order, scrubbing the floors, which were to be touched by the sacred feet of most holy Mary. He also performed other chores which he had been accustomed to leave to the heavenly Lady before he knew her dignity. He resolved to change entirely his relation toward Her, assume for himself the position of servant and leave to Her the dignity of Mistress. From that day on arose a wonderful contention between the two, which of them should be allowed to show most eagerness to serve and most humility. All that happened with saint Joseph the Queen of heaven saw, and not a thought or movement escaped her attention. When the time arrived, the saint approached the oratory of her Highness, and She awaited him with sweetest kindness and mildness.

The husband of Mary, saint Joseph, now better informed, waited until his most holy Spouse had finished her contemplation, and at the hour known to him he opened the door of the humble apartment which the Mother of the heavenly king occupied. Immediately upon entering the holy man threw himself on his knees, saying with the deepest reverence and veneration: "My Mistress and Spouse, true Mother of the eternal Word, here am I thy servant prostrate at the feet of thy clemency. For the sake of thy God and Lord, whom Thou bearest in thy virginal womb, I beseech Thee to pardon my audacity. I am certain, O Lady, that none of my thoughts is hidden to thy wisdom and to thy heavenly insight. Great was my presumption in resolving to leave Thee and not less great was my rudeness in treating Thee until now as my inferior, instead of serving Thee as the Mother of my Lord and God. But Thou also knowest that I have done all in ignorance, because I knew not the sacrament of the heavenly King and the greatness of thy dignity, although I revered in Thee other gifts of the Most High. Do not reflect, my Mistress, upon the ignorance of such a lowly creature, who, now better instructed, consecrates his heart and his whole life to thy service and attendance. I will not rise from my knees, before being assured of thy favor, nor until I have obtained thy pardon, thy good will and thy blessing."

The most holy Mary, hearing the humble words of saint Joseph, experienced diverse feelings. For with tender joy in the Lord She saw how apt he was to be entrusted with the sacraments of the Lord, since he acknowledged and venerated them with such deep faith and humility. But She was somewhat troubled by his resolve of treating Her henceforth with the respect and self abasement alluded to in his words; for the humble Lady feared by this innovation to lose the occasions of obeying and humiliating Herself as a servant of her spouse. Like one, who suddenly finds herself in danger of being deprived of some jewel or treasure highly valued, most holy Mary was saddened by the thought that saint Joseph would no longer treat Her as an inferior and as subject to him in all things, having now recognized in Her the Mother of the Lord. She raised her holy spouse from his knees and threw Herself at his feet (although he tried to hinder it), and said: "I myself, my master and spouse, should ask thee to forgive me and thou art the one who must pardon me the sorrows and the bitterness, which I have caused thee; and therefore I ask this forgiveness of thee on my knees, and that thou forget thy anxieties, since the Most High has looked upon my desires and afflictions in divine pleasure."

It seemed good to the heavenly Lady to console her spouse, and therefore, not in order to excuse Herself, She added: "As much as I desired, I could not on my own account give thee any information regarding the sacrament hidden within me by the power of the Almighty; since, as his slave, it was my duty to await the manifestation of his holy and perfect will. Not because I failed to esteem thee as my lord and spouse did I remain silent: for I was and always will be thy faithful servant, eager to correspond to thy holy wishes and affection. From my inmost heart and in the name of the Lord, whom I bear within me, I beseech thee not to change the manner of thy conversation and intercourse with me. The Lord has not made me his Mother in order to be served and to command in this life, but in order to be the servant of all and thy slave, obeying thy will in all things. This is my duty, my master, and outside of it I would lead a life without joy and full of sorrow. It is just that thou afford me the opportunity of fulfilling it, since so it was ordained by the Most High. He has furnished me with thy protection and devoted assistance, in order that I may live securely in the shade of thy provident solicitude and with thy aid rear the Fruit of my womb, my God and my Lord." With these words and others most sweet and persuasive most holy Mary consoled and quieted saint Joseph, and he raised Her from her knees in order to confer with Her upon all that would be necessary for this purpose. Since on this occasion the heavenly Lady was full of the Holy Ghost and moreover bore within Her, as his Mother, the divine Word, who proceeds from the Father and the Holy Ghost, saint Joseph received special enlightenment and the plenitude of divine graces. Altogether renewed in fervor of spirit he said:

"Blessed art thou, Lady, among all women, fortunate and preferred before all nations and generations. May the Creator of heaven and earth be extolled with eternal praise, since from his exalted kingly throne He has looked upon Thee and chosen Thee for his dwelling-place and in Thee alone has fulfilled the ancient promises made to the Patriarchs and Prophets. Let all generations bless Him: for in no one has He magnified his name as He has done in thy humility; and me, the most insignificant of the living, He has in his divine condescension selected for thy servant." In these words of praise and benediction saint Joseph was enlightened by the Holy Ghost, in the same manner as saint Elisabeth, when she responded to the salutation of our Queen and Mistress. The light and inspiration, received by the most holy spouse was wonderfully adapted to his dignity and office. The heavenly Lady, upon hearing the words of the holy man, answered in the words of the Magnificat, as She had done on her visit to saint Elisabeth, and She added other canticles. She was all aflame in ecstasy and was raised from the earth in a globe of light, which surrounded Her and transfigured Her with the gifts of glory.

At this heavenly vision saint Joseph was filled with admiration and unspeakable delight; for never had he seen his most blessed Spouse in such eminence of glory and perfection. Now he beheld Her with a full and clear understanding, since all the integrity and purity of the Princess of heaven and mystery of her dignity manifested themselves to him. He saw and recognized in her virginal womb the humanity of the infant God and the union of the two natures of the Word. With profound humility and reverence he adored Him and recognized Him as his Redeemer, offering himself to his Majesty. The Lord looked upon him in benevolence and kindness as upon no other man, for He accepted him as his foster-father and conferred upon him that title. In accordance with this dignity, He gifted him with that plenitude of science and heavenly gifts which Christian piety can and must acknowledge. I do not dilate upon this vast excellence of saint Joseph made known to me, because I would extend this history beyond the prescribed bounds.

However, if it was a proof of the magnanimity of the glorious saint Joseph and a clear evidence of his great sanctity, that he did not wear away and die of the grief sustained at the thought of the loss of his beloved Spouse, it is yet more astonishing, that he was not overwhelmed by the unexpected joy of this revelation of the true mystery connected with his Spouse. In the former he proved his high sanctity; but in the latter he showed himself worthy of gifts, such which, if the Lord had not expanded his heart, he could neither have been capable of receiving nor could he have outlived to bear in the joy of his spirit. In all things he was renewed and elevated, so as to be able to treat worthily Her, who was the Mother of God himself and his Spouse, and to co-operate with Her in the mystery of the Incarnation and in taking care of the Word made man, as I shall relate farther on. In order that he might be still more apt and so much the more recognize his obligation to serve his heavenly Spouse, it was also made known to him, that all the gifts and blessings came to him because of Her: those before his espousal, because he had been selected for her husband, and those afterward, because he had won and merited this distinction. He also perceived with what prudence the great Lady had acted toward him, not only in serving him with such inviolate obedience and profound humility, but also in consoling him in his affliction, soliciting for him the grace and assistance of the Holy Ghost, hiding her feelings with such discretion, tranquilizing and soothing his sorrow, thus fittingly disposing him for the influence of the divine Spirit. Just as the Princess of heaven had been the instrument for the sanctification of saint John the Baptist and his mother, so She also was instrumental in procuring for saint Joseph the plenitude of graces in still greater abundance. All this the most faithful and fortunate man understood and for it, as a most faithful servant, was proportionately thankful.

WORDS OF THE QUEEN.

My daughter, my object in revealing to thee in this history so many sacraments and secrets, both those which thou hast written and many others, which thou art unable to manifest, is, that thou use them as a mirror of my life and as an inviolable rule of action for thy own. All of them should be engraven in the tablets of thy heart and I recall to thy mind the teachings of eternal life, thereby complying with my duty as thy Teacher. Be ready to obey and fulfill all commands as a willing and careful pupil; let the humble care and watchfulness of my spouse saint Joseph, his submission to divine direction and his esteem for heavenly enlightenment, serve thee as an example. For only because his heart had been well disposed and prepared for the execution of the divine will, was he entirely changed and remodeled by the plenitude of grace for the ministry assigned to him by the Most High. Let therefore the consciousness of thy faults serve thee as a motive to submit in all humility to the work of God, not as a pretext to withdraw from the performance of that which the Lord desires of thee.

However, I wish on this occasion to reveal to thee the just reproach and indignation of the Most High against mortals; so that, comparing the conduct of other men with the humility and meekness, which I exercised toward my spouse saint Joseph, thou mayest understand it better in divine enlightenment. The cause of this reproach, which the Lord and I have to make against men, is the inhuman perversity of men in persisting to treat each other with so much want of humility and love.

In this they commit three faults, which displease the Most High very much and which cause the Almighty and me to withhold many mercies. The first is, that men, knowing that they are all children of the same Father in heaven (Is. 64, 8), works of his hands, formed of the same nature, graciously nourished and kept alive by his Providence, reared at the same table of divine mysteries and Sacraments, especially of his own body and blood, nevertheless forget and despise all these advantages, concentrating all their interest upon earthly and trivial affairs, exciting themselves without reason, swelling with indignation, creating discords, quarrels, indulging in detractions and harsh words, sometimes rising up to most wicked and inhuman vengeance or mortal hate of one another. The second is, that, when through human frailty and want of mortification, incited by the temptation of the devil, they happen to fall into one of these faults, they do not at once seek to rid themselves of it nor strive to be again reconciled, as should be done by brothers in the presence of a just judge. Thus they deny Him as their merciful Father and force Him to become the severe and rigid Judge of their sins; for no faults excite Him sooner to exercise his severity than the sins of revenge and hate. The third offense, which causes his great indignation, is, that sometimes, when a brother comes in order to be reconciled, he that deems himself offended will not receive him and asks a greater satisfaction than that which he knows would be accepted by the Lord, and which he himself offers as satisfaction to God's Majesty. For all of them wish that God, who is most grievously offended, should receive and pardon them, whenever they approach Him with humility and contrition; while those that are but dust and ashes, ask to be revenged upon their brothers and will not content themselves with the satisfaction, which the Most High himself readily accepts for their own sins.

Of all the sins, which the sons of the Church commit, none is more horrible than these in the eyes of the Most High. This thou wilt readily understand by the divine light and in the vigor of God's law, which commands men to pardon their brethren, although they may have offended seventy times seven. And if a brother offend many times every day, as soon as he says that he is sorry for it, the Lord commands us to forgive the offending brother as many times without counting the number. And those that are not willing to forgive, He threatens with severest punishment on account of the scandal, which they cause. This can be gathered from the threatening words of God himself: Woe to him from whom scandal comes and through whom scandal is caused! It were better for him, if he fell into the depths of the sea with a heavy millstone around his neck. This was said in order to indicate the danger of this sin and the difficulty of obtaining deliverance therefrom, which must be compared to that of a man dropping into the sea with a grinding-stone around his neck. It also points out that the punishment is the abyss of eternal pains (Matth. 8, 9). Therefore the command of my most holy Son is good advice to the faithful, that they rather permit their eyes to be torn out and their hands chopped off, than allow themselves to fall into this crime of scandalizing the little ones.

CHAPTER II.

THE AMIABLE HUMILITY OF MARY TOWARD HER SPOUSE.

The most faithful Joseph, after being informed of the mystery and sacrament of the Incarnation, was filled with such high and befitting sentiments concerning his Spouse, that, although he had always been holy and perfect, he was changed into a new man. He resolved to act toward the heavenly Lady according to a new rule and with much greater reverence, as I will relate farther on. This was conformable to the wisdom of the saint and due to the excellence of his Spouse; for saint Joseph by heavenly enlightenment saw well that he was the servant and She the Mistress of heaven and earth. In order to satisfy his desire for honoring and reverencing Her as the Mother of God, whenever he passed Her or spoke to Her alone, he did it with great external veneration and on bended knees. He would not allow Her to serve him, or wait upon him, or perform any other humble services, such as cleaning the house or washing the dishes and the like. All these things the most happy spouse wished to do himself, in order not to derogate from the dignity of the Queen.

But the heavenly Lady, who among the humble was the most humble and whom no one could surpass in humility, so managed all these things, that the palm of victory in all these virtues always remained with Her. She besought saint Joseph not to bend the knees to Her, for though this worship was due to the Lord whom She carried in her womb, yet as long as He was within unseen by any one no distinction was externally manifest between his and her own person. The saint therefore allowed himself to be persuaded and conformed to the wishes of the Queen of heaven; only at times, when She was not looking, he continued to give this worship to the Lord whom She bore in her womb, and also to Her as his Mother, intending thereby to honor Both according to the excellence of Each. In regard to the other works and services, an humble contention arose between them. For saint Joseph could not overcome his conviction as to the impropriety of allowing the great Queen and Lady to perform them, and therefore he sought to be beforehand with such household duties. His heavenly Spouse was filled with the same eagerness to seize upon occasions in advance of saint Joseph. As however he busied himself in these duties during the time which She spent in contemplation, he frustrated her continual desire of serving him and of performing all the duties of the household, which She considered as belonging to Her as a servant. In her affliction on this account, the heavenly Lady turned to the Lord with humble complaints, and besought Him to oblige saint Joseph not to hinder Her in the exercise of humility, as She desired. As this virtue is so powerful before the divine tribunal and has free access, no prayers accompanied by it is small. Humility makes all prayers effective and inclines the immutable Being of God to clemency. He heard Her petition and He ordered the angel guardian of the blessed husband to instruct him as follows: "Do not frustrate the humble desires of Her who is supreme over all the creatures of heaven and earth. Exteriorly allow Her to serve thee and interiorly treat Her with highest reverence, and at all times and in all places worship the incarnate Word. It is his will, equally with that of the heavenly Mother, to serve and not to be served, in order to teach the world the knowledge of life and the excellence of humility. In some of the work thou canst assist Her, but always reverence in Her the Lord of all creation."

Instructed by this command of the Most High, saint Joseph permitted the heavenly Princess to exercise her humility and so both of them were enabled to make an offering of their will to God: most holy Mary, by exercising the deepest humility and obedience toward her spouse in all her acts of virtue which She performed without failing in the least point of perfection; and saint Joseph by obeying the Almighty with a holy and prudent embarrassment, which was occasioned by seeing himself waited upon and served by Her, whom he had recognized as his Mistress and that of the world, and as the Mother of his God and Creator.

No human tongue can reproduce the celestial words and conversations of the most holy Mary and the blessed Joseph. I will adduce some of them in the following chapters, as far as I know how. Yet, who can declare the effects wrought in the sweet and devout heart of this saint in seeing himself not only constituted the husband of Her who was the true Mother of his Creator, but in finding himself also served by Her as if She was the humblest slave, while at the same time he beheld Her raised in sanctity and dignity above the highest seraphim and inferior only to God? If the divine right hand enriched with blessings the house of Obededom for having sheltered for a few months the figurative ark of the old Testament (I Par. 13, 4), what blessings did He not shower upon saint Joseph, to whom He entrusted the true ark and the Lawgiver himself enshrined in Her? Incomparable was the good fortune and happiness of this

saint! Not only because he had with him in his house
the living and true ark of the new Testament, the altar,
the sacrifice, and the temple, all left in his charge; but
also because he cared for them worthily and as a faithful
servant (Matth. 24, 45), constituted by the Lord himself
over his family to provide for all their necessities in the
right time as a most faithful dispenser (Os. 14, 20).
Let all generations and peoples acknowledge and bless
him, let them extol his merits; since the Most High has
favored none other in the same degree. I, an unworthy
and poor worm, in the light of such venerable sacraments,
exalt and magnify this Lord God, confessing Him as
holy, just, merciful, wise and admirable in the disposition of all his great works.

The humble but blessed house of Joseph contained three rooms, which occupied nearly all its space
and formed the exclusive dwelling place of the two
Spouses; for they kept neither a man- nor a maid-servant.
In one of the rooms saint Joseph slept, in another he
worked and kept the tools of his trade of carpentering;
the third was ordinarily occupied by the Queen of heaven
and was also her sleeping room. It contained a couch
made by the hands of saint Joseph. This arrangement
they had observed since their espousal and from the day
on which they had come to this, their dwelling. Before
knowing the dignity of his Spouse and Lady, saint Joseph
rarely went to see Her; for while She kept her retirement he was engaged in his work, unless some affair
made it absolutely necessary to consult Her. But after
he was informed of his good fortune, the holy man was
more solicitous for her welfare, and in order to renew
the joy of his heart he began to come often to the retreat
of the sovereign Lady, visiting Her and receiving her
commands. But he always approached Her with extreme

humility and reverential fear, and before he spoke to Her, he was careful to note in what She was engaged. Many times he saw Her in ecstasy raised from the earth and resplendent with most brilliant light; at other times in the company of her angels holding celestial intercourse with them; and at other times, he found Her prostrate upon the earth in the form of a cross, speaking to the Lord. Her most fortunate spouse was a participator in these favors. But whenever he found the great Lady in these occupations and postures, he would presume no farther than to look upon Her with profound reverence; and thereby he merited sometimes to hear the sweetest harmony of the celestial music, with which the angels regaled their Queen, and perceived a wonderful fragrancy which comforted him and filled him entirely with jubilation and joy of spirit.

The two holy spouses lived alone in their house, for as I have said, they had no servants of any kind, not only on account of their humility, but in order more fittingly to hide from any witnesses the wonders, which passed between them and which were not to be communicated to outsiders. Likewise the Princess of heaven did not leave her dwelling, except for very urgent causes in the service of God or her fellow-men. Whenever anything was necessary She asked that fortunate neighbor, who as I have said had served saint Joseph during the absence of Mary in the house of Zacharias. This woman received such a good return from Mary, that not only she herself became most holy and perfect, but her whole household and family was blessed by the help of the Queen and Mistress of the world. She was visited by most holy Mary in some of her sicknesses and with her family was copiously enriched by the blessings of heaven.

Never did saint Joseph see his heavenly Spouse

asleep, nor did he of his own experience know whether She ever slept, although he besought Her to take some rest, especially during the time of her sacred pregnancy. The resting-place of the Princess was the low couch, which I said had been constructed by saint Joseph; and on it were the coverings which served Her during her brief and holy sleep. Her undergarment was a sort of tunic made of cotton, but softer than the ordinary or common cloth. This tunic She never changed from the time since She left the temple, nor did it wear out or grow old or soiled, and no person ever saw it, nor did saint Joseph know that She wore that kind of a garment; for he never saw any other part of her clothing except the outside garments, which were open to the view of other persons. Those were of a gray color, as I have said (Part I. No. 400), and these only and her head-coverings were the garments, which the Queen changed now and then; not because they were soiled, but because, being visible to all, She wished to avoid notice by such strange sameness of outward appearance. Nothing that She wore upon her most pure and virginal body became soiled or worn; for She neither perspired, nor was She subject to the punishments, which are laid upon the sin-impregnated bodies of the children of Adam. She was in all respects most pure and the works of her hands were like crystal ornaments; and with the same purity She cared for the clothes and other necessities of saint Joseph. The food of which She partook, was most limited in kind and quantity; but She partook of some every day and in company of her spouse; she never ate meat, although he did, and She prepared it for him. Her sustenance was fruit, fishes, and ordinarily bread and cooked vegetables; but of all these She partook in exact measure and weight, only so much as was necessary for the nourishment of the body and the maintaining of the natural warmth without any superfluities that could pass over into excess of harmful corruption; the same rule She observed in regard to drink, although Her fervent acts of love often caused a superabundance of preternatural ardor. This rule, as to the quantity of her nourishment, She followed during her whole life, although as to the kind of food She adapted Herself to the various circumstances demanding a change, as I shall relate further on.

WORDS OF THE QUEEN.

My daughter, in the school of humility, which my whole life affords thee, I wish that thou be studious and diligent; and this should be thy first and principal care, if thou wishest to enjoy the sweet embraces of the Lord, assure thyself of his favor and possess the treasures of light, which are hidden to the proud (Matth. 11, 25). For without the trusty foundation of humility such treasures cannot be confided to any man. Let all thy ambition be to humble thyself in thy own estimation and thought, so that in thy exterior actions thou mayest truly exhibit this humility of thy interior. It must be a subject of confusion and a spur of humility for thee and for all the souls to have the Lord as their Father and Spouse, to see, that the presumption and pride of worldly wisdom is more powerful in its devotees, than humility and true self-knowledge is in the children of light. Consider the watchfulness, the untiring study and care of ambitious and aspiring men. Look upon their struggle to be esteemed in the world, their strivings never at rest, though so vain and worthless; how they conduct themselves outwardly according to the false notions which they have of themselves; how they pretend to be what they are not, and how they exert themselves to obtain through these false pretenses the treasures, which, though only earthly, they do not deserve. Hence it should be a cause of confusion and shame to the good, that deceit should urge on the sons of perdition with greater force than truth urges the elect; that the number of those, who in the world are anxious to strive in the service of their God and Creator, should be so small in comparison with the number of those who serve vanity; that there should be so few of the elect, though all are called (Matth. 20, 16).

CHAPTER III.

THE JOURNEY TO BETHLEHEM.

It had been decreed by the immutable will of Providence that the Onlybegotten of the Father should be born in the town of Bethlehem (Mich. 5, 2), and accordingly it had been foretold by the Saints and Prophets of foregone ages (Jerem. 10, 9); for the decrees of the absolute will of God are infallible, and since nothing can resist them (Esther 13, 9), sooner would heaven and earth pass away than that they fail of accomplishment (Matth. 24, 35). The fulfillment of this immutable decree the Lord secured by means of an edict of Cæsar Augustus for the whole Roman empire, ordering the registration or enumeration of all the world, as saint Luke says (Luke 2, 1). The Roman empire at that time embraced the greater part of what was then known of the earth and therefore they called themselves masters of the world, ignoring all the other nations. The object of this census was to make all the inhabitants acknowledge themselves as vassals of the emperor, and to pay a certain tax to their temporal lord; for this registration every one was to go to his native city in order to be inscribed. This edict was also proclaimed in Nazareth and came to the hearing of saint Joseph while he was on some errand. He returned to his house in sorrowful consternation and informed his heavenly Spouse of the news which had spread about concerning the edict. The most prudent Virgin answered: "Let not this edict of our temporal ruler cause thee any concern, my master and spouse, for all that happens to us is ordained by the Lord and King of heaven and earth; and in all events his Providence will assist and direct us (Eccli. 22, 28). Let us resign ourselves into his hands and we shall not be disappointed."

Most holy Mary was capable of being entrusted with all the mysteries of her most holy Son and She knew of the prophecies and their fulfillment; hence, also, that the Onlybegotten of the Father and her own was to be born in Bethlehem, a Stranger and an Unknown. But She said nothing of this to saint Joseph; for without being commissioned by the Lord She would reveal none of his secrets. All that She was not commanded to reveal She concealed with admirable prudence, notwithstanding her desire of consoling her most faithful and holy spouse. She wished to entrust Herself to his direction and arrangement without acting the part of those who are wise in their own conceit, as Wisdom warns us (Prov. 3, 7). They therefore conferred with each other about the course to be pursued; for already the pregnancy of the heavenly Lady was far advanced and her parturition was approaching. Saint Joseph said: "Queen of heaven and earth and my Mistress, if Thou hast no order to the contrary from the Almighty, it seems to me necessary that I go alone. Yet, although this order refers only to the heads of families, I dare not leave Thee without assistance, nor could I live without Thee, nor would I have a moment's peace away from Thee; for my heart could not come to any rest without seeing Thee.

They at the same time resolved upon the day of their departure, and Joseph diligently searched in the town of Nazareth for some beast of burden to bear the Mistress of the world. He could not easily find one because so many people were going to different towns in order to fulfill the requirements of the edict of the emperor. But after much anxious inquiry saint Joseph found an unpretentious little beast which, if we can call such creatures fortunate, was the most fortunate of all the irrational animals; since it was privileged not only to bear the Queen of all creation and the blessed fruit of her womb, the King of kings and the Lord of lords, but afterwards to be present at his Birth (Isaias 1, 3); and since it gave to its Creator the homage denied to Him by men, as I shall relate (No. 485). They provided the articles for the journey, which would last five days. The outfit of the heavenly travelers was the same as that which they had provided for their previous journey to the house of Zacharias on their visit to Elisabeth. They carried with them bread, fruit and some fishes, which ordinarily composed their nourishment. As the most prudent Virgin was enlightened regarding their protracted absence, She made use of prudent concealment in taking along the linens and clothes necessary for her heavenly delivery, for She wished to dispose all things according to the exalted intents of the Lord and in preparation for the events which She expected. Their house they left in charge of some neighbor until they should return.

The most pure Mary and the glorious saint Joseph departed from Nazareth for Bethlehem alone, poor and humble in the eyes of the world. None of the mortals thought more of them than what was warranted by their poverty and humility. But O the wonderful sacraments of the Most High, hidden to the proud, and unpenetrated by the wisdom of the flesh! They did not walk alone, poor or despised, but prosperous, rich and in magnificence. They were most worthy of the immense love of the eternal Father and most estimable in his eyes.

They carried with them the Treasure of heaven, the Deity itself. The whole court of the celestial ministers venerated them. All the inanimate beings recognized the living and true Ark of the Testament (Josue 3, 16) more readily than the waters of the Jordan recognized its type and shadow, when they courteously laid open and free the path for its passage and for those that followed it. They were accompanied by the ten thousand angels, which as mentioned (No. 450), were appointed by God himself as the servants of her Majesty during that whole journey. These heavenly squadrons marched along as their retinue in human forms visible to the heavenly Lady, more refulgent than so many suns. She herself walked in their midst better guarded and defended than the bed of Solomon, surrounded by the sixty valiant ones of Israel, girded with their swords (Cant. 3, 7). Besides these ten thousand angels there were many others, who descended from heaven as messengers of the eternal Father to his Onlybegotten made man in his most holy Mother, and who ascended from earth as their ambassadors with messages and treaties from them to the heavenly Father.

With these wonderful favors and delights, however, the Lord joined some hardships and inconveniences, which the divine Mother encountered on the way. For the concourse of people in the taverns, occasioned by the imperial edict, was very disagreeable and annoying to the modest and retiring Virgin-Mother and her spouse. On account of their poverty and timid retirement they were treated with less hospitality and consideration than others, especially the well-to-do; for the world judges and usually confers its favors according to outward appearance and according to personal influence. Our holy pilgrims were obliged repeatedly to listen to sharp reprimands in the taverns, at which they arrived tired out by their journey, and in some of them they were refused admittance as worthless and despicable people.   Several times they assigned to the Mistress of heaven and earth some corner of the hallway; while at others She did not fare even so well, being obliged to retire with her husband to places still more humble and unbecoming in the estimation of the world.   But in whatever places She tarried, how contemptible soever it might be considered, the courtiers of heaven established their court around their supreme King and sovereign Queen.   Immediately they surrounded and enclosed them like an impenetrable wall, securing the bridal chamber of Solomon against the terrors of the night.   Her most faithful spouse Joseph, seeing the Mistress of heaven so well guarded by the angelic hosts, betook himself to rest and sleep; for to this She urged him on account of the hardships of travel.   She, however, continued her celestial colloquies with the ten thousand angels of her retinue.

Thus variously and wonderfully assisted, our travelers arrived at the town of Bethlehem at four o'clock of the fifth day, a Saturday.   As it was at the time of the winter solstice, the sun was already sinking and the night was falling.   They entered the town, and wandered through many streets in search of a lodging-house or inn for staying over night.   They knocked at the doors of their acquaintances and nearer family relations; but they were admitted nowhere and in many places they met with harsh words and insults.   The most modest Queen followed her spouse through the crowds of people, while he went from house to house and from door to door.   Although She knew that the hearts and the houses of men were to be closed to them, and although to expose her state at her age to the public gaze was more painful to her modesty than to their failure to procure a night-lodging, She nevertheless wished to obey saint Joseph and suffer this indignity and unmerited shame. While wandering through the streets they passed the office of the public registry and they inscribed their names and paid the fiscal tribute in order to comply with the edict and not be obliged to return. They continued their search, betaking themselves to other houses. But having already applied at more than fifty different places, they found themselves rejected and sent away from them all. The heavenly spirits were filled with astonishment at these exalted mysteries of the Most High, which manifested the patience and meekness of his Virgin Mother and the unfeeling hardness of men. At the same time they blessed the Almighty in his works and hidden sacraments, since from that day on He began to exalt and honor poverty and humility among men.

It was nine o'clock at night when the most faithful Joseph, full of bitter and heartrending sorrow, returned to his most prudent Spouse and said: "My sweetest Lady, my heart is broken with sorrow at the thought of not only not being able to shelter Thee as Thou deservest and as I desire, but in not being able to offer Thee even any kind of protection from the weather, or a place of rest, a thing rarely or never denied to the most poor and despised in the world. No doubt heaven, in thus allowing the hearts of men to be so unmoved as to refuse us a night-lodging conceals some mystery. I now remember, Lady, that outside the city walls there is a cave, which serves as a shelter for shepherds and their flocks. Let us seek it out; perhaps it is unoccupied, and we may there expect some assistance from heaven, since we receive none from men on earth." The most prudent Virgin answered: "My spouse and my master, let not thy kindest heart be afflicted because the ardent wishes which the love of thy Lord excites in thee cannot be fulfilled. Since I bear Him in my womb, let us, I beseech thee, give thanks for having disposed events in this way. The place of which thou speakest shall be most satisfactory to me. Let thy tears of sorrow be turned into tears of joy, and let us lovingly embrace poverty, which is the inestimable and precious treasure of my most holy Son. He came from heaven in order to seek it, let us then afford Him an occasion to practice it in the joy of our souls; certainly I cannot be better delighted than to see thee procure it for me. Let us go gladly wherever the Lord shall guide us." The holy angels accompanied the heavenly pair, brilliantly lighting up the way, and when they arrived at the city gate they saw that the cave was forsaken and unoccupied. Full of heavenly consolation, they thanked the Lord for this favor, and then happened what I shall relate in the following chapter.

WORDS OF THE QUEEN.

My dearest daughter, if thou art of a meek and docile heart, these mysteries which thou hast written about and hast understood, will stir within thee sweet sentiments of love and affection toward the Author of such great wonders. I wish that, bearing them in mind, thou from this day on embrace with new and great esteem the contempt and neglect of the world. And tell me, dearest, if, in exchange for this forgetfulness and scorn of the world, God look upon thee with eyes of sweetest love, why shouldst thou not buy so cheaply what is worth an infinite price? What can the world give thee, even when it esteems thee and exalts thee most? And what dost thou lose, if thou despise it? Is its favor not all vanity and deceit (Ps. 4, 3)? Is it not all a fleeting and momentary shadow, which eludes the grasp of those that haste after it? Hence, if thou hadst all worldly advantage in thy possession, what great feat would it be to despise it as of no value? Consider how little thou dost in rejecting all of it for the love of God, for mine and that of the holy angels. And if the world does not neglect thee as much as thou shouldst desire, do thou on thy own behalf despise it, in order to remain free and unhampered to enjoy to the full extent the highest Good with the plenitude of his most delightful love and intercourse.

My most holy Son is such a faithful Lover of souls that He hast set me as the teacher and living example of the love of humility and true contempt of worldly vanity and pride. He ordained also for his own glory as well as for my sake that I, his Servant and Mother, should be left without shelter and be turned away by mortals, in order that afterwards his beloved souls might be so much the more readily induced to offer Him a welcome, thus obliging Him, by an artifice of love, to come and remain with them. He also sought destitution and poverty, not because He had any need of them for bringing the practice of virtues to the highest perfection, but in order to teach mortals the shortest and surest way for reaching the heights of divine love and union with God.

Thou knowest well, my dearest, that thou hast been incessantly instructed and exhorted by divine enlightenment to forget the terrestrial and visible and to gird thyself with fortitude (Prov. 31, 17), to raise thyself to the imitation of me, copying in thyself, according to thy capacity, the works and virtues manifested to thee in my life. This is the very first purpose of the knowledge which thou receivest in writing this history; for thou hast in me a perfect model, and by it thou canst arrange the converse and conduct of thy life in the same manner as I arranged mine in imitation of my sweetest Son. The dread with which this command to imitate me has inspired thee as a being above thy strength, thou must moderate and thou must encourage thyself by the words of my most holy Son in the Gospel of saint Matthew: "Be ye perfect as my heavenly Father is perfect" (Matth. 5, 8). This command of the Most High imposed upon his holy Church is not impossible of fulfillment, and, if his faithful children on their part dispose themselves properly, He will deny to none of them the grace of attaining this resemblance to the heavenly Father. All this my most holy Son has merited for them. But the degrading forgetfulness and neglect of men hinder them from maturing within themselves the fruits of his Redemption.

Of thee particularly I expect this perfection, and I invite thee to it by the sweet law of love which accompanies my instruction. Ponder and scrutinize, by the divine light, the obligation under which I place thee, and labor to correspond with it like a faithful and anxious child. Let no difficulty or hardship disturb thee, nor deter thee from any virtuous exercise, no matter how hard it may be. Nor be content with striving after the love of God and salvation of thyself alone; if thou wouldst be perfect in imitating me and fulfilling all that the Gospel teaches, thou must work for the salvation of other souls and the exaltation of the holy name of my Son, making thyself an instrument in his powerful hands for the accomplishment of mighty works to advance his pleasure and glory.

CHAPTER IV.

The palace which the supreme King of kings
and the Lord of lords had chosen for entertaining his
eternal and incarnate Son in this world was a most poor
and insignificant hut or cave, to which most holy Mary
and Joseph betook themselves after they had been denied
all hospitality and the most ordinary kindness by their
fellow-men, as I have described in the foregoing chapter.
This place was held in such contempt that though the
town of Bethlehem was full of strangers in want of night-
shelter, none would demean or degrade himself so far
as to make use of it for a lodging; for there was none
who deemed it suitable or desirable for such a purpose,
except the Teachers of humility and poverty, Christ our
Savior and his purest Mother. On this account the wisdom of the eternal Father had reserved it for Them, consecrating it in all its bareness, loneliness and poverty as
the first temple of light (Malachy 4, 2, Ps. 111, 4) and
as the house of the true Sun of justice, which was to
arise for the upright of heart from the resplendent Aurora
Mary, turning the night of sin into the daylight of grace.
Most holy Mary and saint Joseph entered the
lodging thus provided for them and by the effulgence of
the ten thousand angels of their guard they could easily
ascertain its poverty and loneliness, which they esteemed
as favors and welcomed with tears of consolation and
joy. Without delay the two holy travelers fell on their

knees and praised the Lord, giving Him thanks for his benefit, which they knew had been provided by his wisdom for his own hidden designs. Of this mystery the heavenly Princess Mary had a better insight; for as soon as She sanctified the interior of the cave by her sacred footsteps She felt a fullness of joy which entirely elevated and vivified Her. She besought the Lord to bless with a liberal hand all the inhabitants of the neighboring city, because by rejecting Her they had given occasion to the vast favors, which She awaited in this neglected cavern. It was formed entirely of the bare and coarse rocks, without any natural beauty or artificial adornment; a place intended merely for the shelter of animals; yet the eternal Father had selected it for the shelter and dwelling-place of his own Son.

The angelic spirits, who like a celestial militia guarded their Queen and Mistress, formed themselves into cohorts in the manner of court guards in a royal palace. They showed themselves in their visible forms also to saint Joseph; for on this occasion it was befitting that he should enjoy such a favor, on the one hand in order to assuage his sorrow by allowing him to behold this poor lodging thus beautified and adorned by their celestial presence, and on the other, in order to enliven and encourage him for the events which the Lord intended to bring about during that night, and in this forsaken place. The great Queen and Empress, who was already informed of the mystery to be transacted here, set about cleaning with her own hands the cave, which was so soon to serve as a royal throne and sacred mercy-seat; for neither did She want to miss this occasion for exercising her humility, nor would She deprive her only-begotten Son of the worship and reverence implied by this preparation and cleansing of his temple.

Saint Joseph, mindful of the majesty of his heavenly Spouse (which, it seemed to him, She was forgetting in her ardent longing for humiliation), besought Her not to deprive Him of this work, which he considered as his alone; and he hastened to set about cleaning the floor and the corners of the cave, although the humble Queen continued to assist him therein. As the holy angels were then present in visible forms, they were (according to our mode of speaking) abashed at such eagerness for humiliation, and they speedily emulated with each other to join in this work; or rather, in order to say it more succinctly, in the shortest time possible they had cleansed and set in order that cave, filling it with holy fragrance. Saint Joseph started a fire with the material which he had brought for that purpose. As it was very cold, they sat at the fire in order to get warm. They partook of the food which they had brought, and they ate this, their frugal supper, with incomparable joy of their souls. The Queen of heaven was so absorbed and taken up with the thought of the impending mystery of her divine delivery, that She would not have partaken of food if She had not been urged thereto by obedience to her spouse.

After their supper they gave thanks to the Lord as was their custom. Having spent a short time in this prayer and conferring about the mysteries of the incarnate Word, the most prudent Virgin felt the approach of the most blessed Birth. She requested her spouse saint Joseph to betake himself to rest and sleep as the night was already far advanced. The man of God yielded to the request of his Spouse and urged Her to do the same; and for this purpose he arranged and prepared a sort of couch with the articles of wear in their possession, making use of a crib or manger, that had been

left by the shepherds for their animals. Leaving most
holy Mary in the portion of the cave thus furnished, saint
Joseph retired to a corner of the entrance, where he
began to pray. He was immediately visited by the
divine Spirit and felt a most sweet and extraordinary
influence, by which he was wrapt and elevated into an
ecstasy. In it was shown him all that passed during that
night in this blessed cave; for he did not return to consciousness until his heavenly Spouse called him. Such
was the sleep which saint Joseph enjoyed in that night,
more exalted and blessed than that of Adam in paradise
(Gen. 21, 2).

The Queen of all creatures was called from her
resting-place by a loud voice of the Most High, which
strongly and sweetly raised Her above all created things
and caused Her to feel new effects of divine power; for
this was one of the most singular and admirable ecstasies
of her most holy life. Immediately also She was filled
with new enlightenment and divine influences, such as I
have described in other places, until She reached the clear
vision of the Divinity. The veil fell and She saw intuitively the Godhead itself in such glory and plenitude of
insight, as all the capacity of men and angels could not
describe or fully understand. All the knowledge of the
Divinity and humanity of her most holy Son, which She
had ever received in former visions was renewed and,
moreover, other secrets of the inexhaustible archives of
the bosom of God were revealed to Her. I have not
ideas or words sufficient and adequate for expressing
what I have been allowed to see of these sacraments by
the divine light; and their abundance and multiplicity convince me of the poverty and want of proper expression in
created language.

The Most High announced to his Virgin Mother,

that the time of his coming into the world had arrived and what would be the manner in which this was now to be fulfilled and executed. The most prudent Lady perceived in this vision the purpose and exalted scope of these wonderful mysteries and sacraments, as well in so far as related to the Lord himself as also in so far as they concerned creatures, for whose benefit they had been primarily decreed. She prostrated Herself before the throne of his Divinity and gave Him glory, magnificence, thanks and praise for Herself and for all creatures, such as was befitting the ineffable mercy and condescension of his divine love. At the same time She asked of the divine Majesty new light and grace in order to be able worthily to undertake the service and worship and the rearing up of the Word made flesh, whom She was to bear in Her arms and nourish with her virginal milk. This petition the heavenly Mother brought forward with the profoundest humility, as one who understood the greatness of this new sacrament. She held Herself unworthy of the office of rearing up and conversing as a Mother with a God incarnate of which even the highest seraphim are incapable. Prudently and humbly did the Mother of wisdom ponder and weigh this matter. And because She humbled Herself to the dust and acknowledged her nothingness in the presence of the Almighty, therefore his Majesty raised Her up and confirmed anew upon Her the title of *Mother of God*. He commanded Her to exercise this office and ministry of a legitimate and true Mother of Himself; that She should treat Him as the Son of the eternal Father and at the same time the Son of her womb. All this could be easily entrusted to such a Mother, in whom was contained an excellence that words cannot express.

The most holy Mary remained in this ecstasy and

beatific vision for over an hour immediately preceding her divine delivery. At the moment when She issued from it and regained the use of her senses She felt and saw that the body of the infant God began to move in her virginal womb; how, releasing and freeing Himself from the place which in the course of nature He had occupied for nine months, He now prepared to issue forth from that sacred bridal chamber. This movement not only did not cause any pain or hardship, as happens with the other daughters of Adam and Eve in their child-births; but filled Her with incomparable joy and delight, causing in her soul and in her virginal body such exalted and divine effects that they exceed all thoughts of men. Her body became so spiritualized with the beauty of heaven that She seemed no more a human and earthly creature. Her countenance emitted rays of light, like a sun incarnadined, and shone in indescribable earnestness and majesty, all inflamed with fervent love. She was kneeling in the manger, her eyes raised to heaven, her hands joined and folded at her breast, her soul wrapped in the Divinity and She herself was entirely deified. In this position, and at the end of the heavenly rapture, the most exalted Lady gave to the world the Onlybegotten of the Father and her own, our Savior Jesus, true God and man, at the hour of midnight, on a Sunday, in the year of the creation of the world five thousand one hundred and ninety-nine (5199), which is the date given in the Roman Church, and which date has been manifested to me as the true and certain one.

At the end of the beatific rapture and vision of the Mother ever Virgin, which I have described above, was born the Sun of Justice, the Onlybegotten of the eternal Father and of Mary most pure, beautiful, refulgent and immaculate, leaving Her untouched in her virginal integrity and purity and making Her more god-like and forever sacred; for He did not divide, but penetrated the virginal chamber as the rays of the sun penetrate the crystal shrine, lighting it up in prismatic beauty.

The infant God therefore was brought forth from the virginal chamber unencumbered by any corporeal or material substance foreign to Himself. But He came forth glorious and transfigured for the divine and infinite wisdom decreed and ordained that the glory of his most holy soul should in his Birth overflow and communicate itself to his body, participating in the gifts of glory in the same way as happened afterwards in his Transfiguration on mount Tabor in the presence of the Apostles (Matth. 17, 2). This miracle was not necessary in order to penetrate the virginal enclosure and to leave unimpaired the virginal integrity; for without this Transfiguration God could have brought this about by other miracles. Thus say the holy doctors, who see no other miracle in this Birth than that the Child was born without impairing the virginity of the Mother. It was the will of God that the most blessed Virgin should look upon the body of her Son, the God-man, for this first time in a glorified state for two reasons. The one was in order that by this divine vision the most prudent Mother should conceive the highest reverence for the Majesty of Him whom She was to treat as her Son, the true God-man. Although She was already informed of his two-fold nature, the Lord nevertheless ordained that by ocular demonstration She be filled with new graces, corresponding to the greatness of her most holy Son, which was thus manifested to Her in a visible manner. The second reason was to reward by this wonder the fidelity and holiness of the divine Mother; for her most pure and chaste eyes, that had turned away from all earthly things for love of her most holy Son, were to see Him at his very Birth in this glory and thus be rejoiced and rewarded for her loyalty and beautiful love.

The sacred evangelist Luke tells us that the Mother Virgin, having brought forth her firstbegotten Son, wrapped Him in swathing clothes and placed Him in a manger. He does not say that She received Him in her arms from her virginal womb; for this did not pertain to the purpose of his narrative. But the two sovereign princes, saint Michael and saint Gabriel, were the assistants of the Virgin on this occasion. They stood by at proper distance in human corporeal forms at the moment when the incarnate Word, penetrating the virginal chamber by divine power, issued forth to the light, and they received Him in their hands with ineffable reverence. In the same manner as a priest exhibits the sacred host to the people for adoration, so these two celestial ministers presented to the divine Mother her glorious and refulgent Son. All this happened in a short space of time. In the same moment in which the holy angels thus presented the divine Child to his Mother, both Son and Mother looked upon each other, and in this look, She wounded with love the sweet Infant and was at the same time exalted and transformed in Him. From the arms of the holy princes the Prince of all the heavens spoke to his holy Mother: "Mother, become like unto Me, since on this day, for the human existence, which thou hast today given Me, I will give thee another more exalted existence in grace, assimilating thy existence as a mere creature to the likeness of Me, who am God and Man." The most prudent Mother answered: "Trahe me post Te, curremus in odorem unguentorum tuorum" (Cant. 1, 3). Raise me, elevate me, Lord, and I will run after Thee in the odor of thy ointments. In the same way many of the hidden mysteries of the Canticles were fulfilled; and other sayings which passed between the infant God and the Virgin Mother had been recorded in that book of songs, as for instance: "My Beloved to me, and I to Him, and his desire is toward me" (Cant. 2, 16). "Behold thou art beautiful, my friend, and thy eyes are dove's eyes. Behold, my beloved, for thou art beautiful"; and many other sacramental words which to mention would unduly prolong this chapter.

The words, which most holy Mary heard from the mouth of her most holy Son, served to make Her understand at the same time the interior acts of his holiest soul united with the Divinity; in order that by imitating them She might become like unto Him. This was one of the greatest blessings, which the most faithful and fortunate Mother received at the hands of her Son, the true God and man, not only because it was continued from that day on through all her life, but because it furnished Her the means of copying his own divine life as faithfully as was possible to a mere creature. At the same time the heavenly Lady perceived and felt the presence of the most holy Trinity, and She heard the voice of the eternal Father saying: "This is my beloved Son, in whom I am greatly pleased and delighted" (Matth. 17, 5). The most prudent Mother made entirely god-like in the overflow of so many sacraments, answered: "Eternal Father and exalted God, Lord and Creator of the universe, give me anew thy permission and benediction to receive in my arms the Desired of nations (Agg. 2, 8); and teach me to fulfill as thy unworthy Mother and lowly slave, thy holy will." Immediately She heard a voice, which said: "Receive thy Onlybegotten Son, imitate Him and rear Him; and remember, that thou must sacrifice Him when I shall demand it of thee." The divine Mother answered: "Behold the creature of thy hands, adorn me with thy grace so that thy Son and my God receive me for his slave; and if Thou wilt come to my aid with thy Omnipotence, I shall be faithful in his service; and do Thou count it no presumption in thy insignificant creature, that she bear in her arms and nourish at her breast her own Lord and Creator."

After this interchange of Words, so full of mysteries, the divine Child suspended the miracle of his transfiguration, or rather He inaugurated the other miracle, that of suspending the effects of glory in his most holy body, confining them solely to his soul; and He now assumed the appearance of one capable of suffering. In this form the most pure Mother now saw Him and, still remaining in a kneeling position and adoring Him with profound humility and reverence, She received Him in her arms from the hands of the holy angels. And when She saw Him in her arms, She spoke to Him and said: "My sweetest Love and light of my eyes and being of my soul, Thou hast arrived in good hour into this world as the Sun of justice (Malach. 4, 2), in order to disperse the darkness of sin and death! True God of the true God, save thy servants and let all flesh see Him, who shall draw upon it salvation (Is. 9, 2). Receive me thy servant as thy slave and supply my deficiency, in order that I may properly serve Thee. Make me, my Son, such as Thou desirest me to be in thy service." Then the most prudent Mother turned toward the eternal Father to offer up to Him his Onlybegotten, saying: "Exalted Creator of all the Universe, here is the altar and the sacrifice acceptable in thy eyes (Malachy 3, 4). From this hour on, O Lord, look upon the human race with mercy; and inasmuch as we have deserved thy anger, it is now time that Thou be appeased in thy Son and mine. Let thy justice now come to rest, and let thy mercy be exalted; for on this account the Word has clothed itself in the semblance of sinful flesh (Rom. 8, 3), and became a Brother of mortals and sinners (Philip 2, 7). In this title I recognize them as brothers and I intercede for them from my inmost soul. Thou, Lord, hast made me the Mother of thy Onlybegotten without my merit, since this dignity is above all merit of a creature; but I partly owe to men the occasion of this incomparable good fortune; since it is on their account that I am the Mother of the Word made man and Redeemer of them all. I will not deny them my love, or remit my care and watchfulness for their salvation. Receive, eternal God, my wishes and petitions for that which is according to thy pleasure and good will."

The Mother of mercy turned also toward all mortals and addressed them, saying: "Be consoled ye afflicted and rejoice ye disconsolate, be raised up ye fallen, come to rest ye uneasy. Let the just be gladdened and the saints be rejoiced; let the heavenly spirits break out in new jubilee, let the Prophets and Patriarchs of limbo draw new hope, and let all the generations praise and magnify the Lord, who renews his wonders. Come, come ye poor; approach ye little ones, without fear, for in my arms I bear the Lion made a lamb, the Almighty, become weak, the Invincible subdued. Come to draw life, hasten to obtain salvation, approach to gain eternal rest, since I have all this for all, and it will be given to you freely and communicated to you without envy. Do not be slow and heavy of heart, ye sons of men; and Thou, O sweetest joy of my soul, give me permission to receive from Thee that kiss desired by all creatures." Therewith the most blessed Mother applied her most chaste and heavenly lips in order to receive the loving caresses of the divine Child, who on his part, as her true Son, had desired them from Her.

Holding Him in Her arms She thus served as the altar and the sanctuary, where the ten thousand angels adored in visible human forms their Creator incarnate. And as the most blessed Trinity assisted in an especial manner at the birth of the Word, heaven was as it were emptied of its inhabitants, for the whole heavenly court had betaken itself to that blessed cave of Bethlehem and was adoring the Creator in his garb and habit of a pilgrim (Phil. 2, 7). And in their concert of praise the holy angels intoned the new canticle: "Gloria in excelsis Deo, et in terra pax hominibus bonae voluntatis" (Luke 2, 14). In sweetest and sonorous harmony they repeated it, transfixed in wonder at the new miracles then being fulfilled and at the unspeakable prudence, grace, humility and beauty of that tender Maiden of fifteen years, who had become the worthy Trustee and Minister of such vast and magnificent sacraments.

It was now time to call saint Joseph, the faithful spouse of the most discreet and attentive Lady. As I have said above he was wrapped in ecstasy, in which he was informed by divine revelation of all the mysteries of this sacred Birth during this night. But it was becoming that he should see, and, before all other mortals, should in his corporeal faculties and senses be present and experience, adore and reverence the Word made flesh; for he of all others had been chosen to act as the faithful warden of this great sacrament. At the desire of his heavenly Spouse he issued from his ecstasy and, on being restored to consciousness, the first sight of his eyes was the divine Child in the arms of the Virgin Mother reclining against her sacred countenance and breast. There he adored Him in profoundest humility and in tears of joy. He kissed his feet in great joy and admiration, which no doubt would have taken away and destroyed life in him, if divine power had not preserved it; and he certainly would have lost all the use of his senses, if the occasion had permitted. When saint Joseph had begun to adore the Child, the most prudent Mother asked leave of her Son to arise (for until then She had remained on her knees) and, while saint Joseph handed Her the wrappings and swaddling-clothes, which She had brought, She clothed Him with incomparable reverence, devotion and tenderness. Having thus swathed and clothed Him, his Mother, with heavenly wisdom, laid Him in the crib, as related by saint Luke (Luke 2, 7). For this purpose She had arranged some straw and hay upon a stone in order to prepare for the God-Man his first resting-place upon earth next to that which He had found in her arms. According to divine ordainment an ox from the neighboring fields ran up in great haste and, entering the cave, joined the beast of burden brought by the Queen. The blessed Mother commanded them, with what show of reverence was possible to them to acknowledge and adore their Creator. The humble animals obeyed their Mistress and prostrated themselves before the Child, warming Him with their breath and rendering Him the service refused by men. And thus the God made man was placed between two animals, wrapped in swaddling-clothes and wonderfully fulfilling the prophecy, that "the ox knoweth his owner, and the ass his master's crib; but Israel hath not known me, and my people hath not understood." (Is. 13.)

WORDS OF THE QUEEN.

My daughter, if men would keep their heart disengaged and if they would rightly and worthily consider this great sacrament of the kindness of the Most High towards men, it would be a powerful means of conducting them in the pathway of life and subjecting them to the love of their Creator and Redeemer. For as men are capable of reasoning, if they would only make use of their freedom to treat this sacrament with the reverence due to its greatness, who would be so hardened as not to be moved to tenderness at the sight of their God become man, humiliated in poverty, despised, unknown, entering the world in a cave, lying in a manger surrounded by brute animals, protected only by a poverty-stricken Mother, and cast off by the foolish arrogance of the world? Who will dare to love the vanity and pride, which was openly abhorred and condemned by the Creator of heaven and earth in his conduct? No one can despise the humility, poverty and indigence, which the Lord loved and chose for Himself as the very means of teaching the way of eternal life. Few there are, who stop to consider this truth and example: and on account of this vile ingratitude only the few will reap the fruit of these great sacraments.

But if the condescension of my most holy Son was so great as to bestow so liberally upon thee his light and knowledge concerning these vast blessings, ponder well how much thou art bound to co-operate with this light. In order that thou mayest correspond to this obligation, I remind and exhort thee to forget all that is of earth and lose it out of thy sight; that thou seek nothing, or engage thyself with nothing except what can help thee to withdraw and detach thee from the world and its inhabitants; so that, with a heart freed from all terrestrial affection, thou dispose thyself to celebrate in it the mysteries of the poverty, humility and divine love of the incarnate God. Learn from my example the reverence, fear and respect, with which thou must treat Him, remembering how I acted, when I held Him in my arms; follow my example, whenever thou receivest Him in thy heart in the venerable sacrament of the holy Eucharist, wherein is contained the same God-Man, who was born of my womb. In this holy Sacrament thou receivest Him and possessest Him just as really, and He remains in thee just as actually, as I possessed Him and conversed with Him, although in another manner.

I desire that thou go even to extremes in this holy reverence and fear; and I wish that thou take notice and be convinced, that in entering into thy heart in the holy Sacrament, thy God exhorts thee in the same words, which thou hast recorded as spoken to me: become like unto Me. His coming down from heaven onto the earth, his being born in humility and poverty, his living and dying in it, giving such rare example of the contempt of the world and its deceits; the knowledge, which thou hast received concerning his conduct and which thou hast penetrated so deeply by divine intelligence: all these things should be for thee like living voices, which thou must heed and inscribe into the interior of thy heart. These privileges have all been granted to thee in order that thou discreetly use the common blessings to their fullest extent, and in order that thou mayest understand, how thankful thou must be to my most holy Son and Lord, and how thou shouldst strive to make as great a return for his goodness, as if He had come from heaven to redeem thee alone and as if He had instituted all his wonders and doctrines in the holy Church for none else than thee (Gal. 7, 12).

CHAPTER V.

THE ADORATION OF THE SHEPHERD; THE CIRCUMCISION.

After the courtiers of heaven had thus celebrated the birth of God made man near the portals of Bethlehem, some of them were immediately dispatched to different places, in order to announce the happy news to those, who according to the divine will were properly disposed to hear it. The holy prince Michael betook himself to the holy Patriarchs in limbo and announced to them, how the Onlybegotten of the eternal Father was already born into the world and was resting, humble and meek, as they had prophesied, in a manger between two beasts. He addressed also in a special manner holy Joachim and Anne in the name of the blessed Mother, who had enjoined this upon him; he congratulated them, that their Daughter now held in her arms the Desired of nations and Him, who had been foretold by all the Patriarchs and Prophets (Is. 7, 14; 9, 7, etc.). It was the most consoling and joyful day, which this great gathering of the just and the saints had yet had during their long banishment. All of them acknowledged this new Godman as the true Author of eternal salvation, and they composed and sang new songs of adoration and worship in his praise.

Another of the holy angels that attended and guarded the heavenly Mother was sent to saint Elisabeth and her son John. On hearing this news of the birth of the Redeemer, the prudent matron and her son, although he was yet of so tender an age, prostrated themselves upon the earth and adored their God made man in spirit and in truth (John 4, 23). The child which had been consecrated as his Precursor, was renewed interiorly with a spirit more inflamed than that of Elias, causing new admiration and jubilation in the angels themselves. Saint John and his mother requested our Queen through the angels, that She in the name of them both, adore her most holy Son and offer Him their services; all of which the heavenly Queen immediately fulfilled.

Amongst all these, the shepherds of that region, who were watching their flocks at the time of the birth of Christ, were especially blessed (Luke 2, 8); not only because they accepted the labor and inconvenience of their calling with resignation from the hand of God; but also because, being poor and humble, and despised by the world, they belonged in sincerity and uprightness of heart to those Israelites, who fervently hoped and longed for the coming of the Messias, speaking and discoursing of Him among themselves many times. They resembled the Author of life, as they were removed from the riches, vanity and ostentation of the world and far from its diabolical cunning (John 10, 14). They exhibited in the circumstances of their calling the office, which the good Shepherd had come to fulfill in knowing his Sheep and being known to them. Hence they merited to be called and invited, as the first fruits of the saints by the Savior himself, to be the very first ones, to whom the eternal and incarnate Word manifested Himself and by whom He wished to be praised, served and adored. Hence the archangel Gabriel was sent to them as they watched on the field, appearing to them in human form and with great splendor.

The shepherds found themselves suddenly enveloped and bathed in the celestial radiance of the angel, and at his sight, being little versed in such visions, they were filled with great fear. The holy prince reassured them and said: "Ye upright men, be not afraid: for I announce to you tidings of great joy, which is, that for you is born today the Redeemer Christ, our Lord, in the city of David. And as a sign of this truth, I announce to you, that you shall find the Infant wrapped in swaddling-clothes and placed in a manger" (Luke 2, 10, 12). At these words of the angel, suddenly appeared a great multitude of the celestial army, who in voices of sweet harmony sang to the Most High these words: "Glory to God in the highest and on earth peace to men of good will." Rehearsing this divine canticle, so new to the world, the holy angels disappeared. All this happened in the fourth watch of the night. By this angelic vision the humble and fortunate shepherds were filled with divine enlightenment and were unanimously impelled by a fervent longing to make certain of this blessing and to witness with their own eyes the most high mystery of which they had been informed.

The signs which the holy angels had indicated to them did not seem appropriate or proportioned for attesting the greatness of the Newborn to eyes of the flesh. For to lie in a manger and to be wrapped in swaddling-clothes, would not have been convincing proof of the majesty of a king, if these shepherds had not been illumined by divine light and been enabled to penetrate the mystery. As they were free from the arrogant wisdom of the world, they were easily made proficient in the divine wisdom. Conferring among themselves the thoughts excited by this message, they resolved to hasten in all speed to Bethlehem and see the wonder made known to them by the Lord. They departed without delay and entering the cave or portal, they found, as saint Luke tells us, Mary and Joseph, and the Infant lying in a manger. Seeing all this they recognized the truth of what they had heard of the Child. Upon this followed an interior enlightenment consequent upon seeing the Word made flesh; for when the shepherds looked upon Him, He also glanced at them, emitting from his countenance a great effulgence, which wounded with love the sincere heart of each of these poor yet fortunate men; with divine efficiency it changed them and renewed them, constituting them in a new state of grace and holiness and filling them with an exalted knowledge of the divine mysteries of the Incarnation and the Redemption of the human race.

Prostrating themselves on the earth they adored the Word made flesh. Not any more as ignorant rustics, but as wise and prudent men they adored Him, acknowledged and magnified Him as true God and man, as Restorer and Redeemer of the human race. The heavenly Lady and Mother of the Child took notice of all that they did interiorly and exteriorly; for She saw into their inmost hearts. In highest wisdom and prudence She preserved the memory of all these happenings and pondered them in her soul, (Luke 2, 19), comparing them with the other mysteries therein contained and with the holy prophecies and sayings of the Scriptures. As She was then the organ of the holy Spirit and the representative of the Infant, She spoke to the shepherds, instructing and exhorting them to persevere in divine love and in the service of the Most High. They also conversed with Her on their part and showed by their answers that they understood many of the mysteries. They remained in the cave from the beginning of dawn until mid-day, when, having given them something to eat, our great Queen sent them off full of heavenly grace and consolation.

When for the first time She placed the infant

God in his arms, the most holy Mary said to him: "My husband and my helper, receive in thy arms the Creator of heaven and earth and enjoy his amiable and sweet company, in order that my Lord and my God may be delighted and recompensed by thy faithful services (Prov. 8, 31). Take to thyself the Treasure of the eternal Father and participate in this blessing of the human race." And speaking interiorly to the divine Infant, She said: "Sweetest Love of my soul and Light of my eyes, rest in the arms of Joseph, my friend and spouse: do thou hold sweet intercourse with him and pardon me my shortcomings. Much do I feel the loss of Thee even for one instant, but I wish to communicate without envy the good I have received, to all that are worthy" (Wis. 7, 13). Her most faithful husband, acknowledging this new blessing, humbled himself to the earth and answered: "Lady and Sovereign of the world, my Spouse, how can I, being so unworthy, presume to hold in my arms God himself, in whose presence tremble the pillars of heaven? (Job 26, 11). How can this vile wormlet have courage to accept such an exalted favor? I am but dust and ashes, but do Thou, Lady, assist me in my lowliness and ask his Majesty to look upon me with clemency and make me worthy through his grace."

His desire of holding the infant God and his reverential fear of Him caused in saint Joseph heroic acts of love, of faith, of humility and profoundest reverence. Trembling with discreet fear He fell on his knees to receive Him from the hands of his most holy Mother, while sweetest tears of joy and delight copiously flowed from his eyes at a happiness so extraordinary. The divine Infant looked at him caressingly and at the same time renewed his inmost soul with such divine efficacy as no words will suffice to explain. He broke out in new canticles of praise at seeing himself thus enriched with such magnificent blessings and favors. After having for some time enjoyed in spirit the sweetest effects of holding in his arms the Lord, who contains heaven and earth (Is. 40, 12), He replaced Him into the arms of his fortunate Mother, both of them being on their knees in receiving and giving Him. Similar reverence the most prudent Mother observed every time She took Him up or relinquished Him, in which also saint Joseph imitated Her, as often as it was his happy lot to hold the incarnate Word. When they approached his Majesty, they also made three genuflections, kissing the earth and exciting heroic acts of humility, worship and reverence. Thus both the great Queen and the blessed Joseph observed all propriety in receiving or giving the Child from and to one another.

From the moment the most prudent Virgin found Herself chosen as the Mother of the divine Word, She began to ponder upon the labors and sufferings in store for her sweetest Son. As her knowledge of Scripture was so profound, She understood all the mysteries contained therein and She began to foresee and prepare with incomparable compassion for all that He was to suffer for the Redemption of Man. This sorrow, foreseen and expected with such a full knowledge of details, was a prolonged martyrdom for the most meek Mother of the sacrificial Lamb of God (Jer. 11, 19). But in regard to the Circumcision, which was to take place after the birth of the Child, the heavenly Lady had received no command or intimation of the will of the eternal Father. This uncertainty excited the loving solicitude and sweet plaints of the tender and affectionate Mother. Her prudent foresight enabled Her to conjecture, that, as her

most holy Son had come to honor and confirm his law
by fulfilling it and as He had moreover come in order
to suffer for men, He would be constrained by his burning
love and by other motives to undergo the pains of circumcision.

On the other hand her maternal love and compassion longed to exempt her sweet Child if possible,
from this suffering; moreover She knew, that circumcision was a rite instituted for cleansing the newborn
children from original sin, whereas the divine Infant
was entirely free from this guilt, not having contracted
it in Adam. In this hesitation between love of her divine
Son and obedience to the eternal Father, the most prudent Virgin practiced many heroic acts of virtue, unspeakably pleasing to his Majesty. Although She could
have easily escaped this uncertainty by directly asking the
Lord what was to be done; yet, being as humble as She
was prudent, She refrained. Neither would She ask her
angels; for with admirable wisdom, She awaited the
opportune time and occasion, assigned by divine Providence for all things, and She would not presume curiously
to search or pry into his decrees by consulting supernatural sources of information, especially in order to rid
Herself of any suffering. When any grave and doubtful affair arose, in which there was danger of offending
God, or some urgent undertaking for the good of creatures, in which it would be necessary to know the divine
will, She first asked permission to submit her petition for
enlightenment regarding the divine pleasure.

Most holy Mary issued from her prayer and requested saint Joseph to take the necessary steps for the
Circumcision of the divine Infant. With rarest prudence
She avoided telling Him anything of what She had been
told in answer to her prayer. She spoke as if She wished

to consult Him or ask his opinion in regard to the Circumcision, saying that the time appointed by law for the Circumcision of the Child had arrived and since they had not received any orders to the contrary, it seemed necessary to comply with it.   They themselves, She said, were more bound to please the Most High, to obey more punctually his precepts, and to be more zealous in the love and care of his most holy Son than all the rest of creatures, seeking to fufill in all things the divine pleasure in return for his incomparable favors.   To these words saint Joseph answered with the greatest modesty and discretion, saying, that, as no command to the contrary had been given concerning the Child he wished in all things to conform himself to the divine will manifested in the common law; that, although as God the incarnate Word was not subject to the law, yet He was now clothed with our humanity, and, as a most perfect Teacher and Savior, no doubt wished to conform with other men in its fulfillment.   Then he asked his heavenly Spouse how the Circumcision was to take place.

The most holy Mary answered, that the Circumcision should be performed substantially in the same way as it was performed on other children: but that She need not hand Him over or consign Him to any other person, but that She would herself hold Him in her arms.   And because the delicacy and tenderness of the Infant would make this ceremony more painful to Him than to other children, they should have at hand the soothing medicine, which was ordinarily applied at circumcision. Moreover, She requested saint Joseph to procure a crystal or glass vessel for preserving the sacred relic of the Circumcision of the divine Infant.   In the meanwhile the cautious Mother prepared some linen cloths to catch the sacred blood, which was now for the first time to be shed for our rescue, so that not one drop of it might be lost or fall upon the ground. After these preparations the heavenly Lady asked saint Joseph to inform the priest and request him to come to the cave where, without the necessity of bringing the Child to any other place, he might, as a fit and worthy minister of so hidden and great a sacrament, with his priestly hands perform the rite of the Circumcision.

Then most holy Mary and Joseph took counsel concerning the name to be given to the divine Infant in the Circumcision, and the holy spouse said: "My Lady, when the holy angel of the Most High informed me of this great sacrament, he also told me that thy most sacred Son should be called JESUS." The Virgin Mother answered: "This same name was revealed to me when He assumed flesh in my womb; and thus receiving this name from the Most High through the mouth of his holy angels, his ministers, it is befitting that we conform in humble reverence with the hidden and inscrutable judgments of his infinite wisdom in conferring it on my Son and Lord, and that we call Him JESUS. This name we will propose to the priest, for inscription in the register of the other circumcised children."

While the great Mistress of heaven and saint Joseph thus conversed with each other, innumerable angels descended in human forms from on high, clothed in shining white garments, on which were woven red embroideries of wonderful beauty. They had palms in their hands and crowns upon their heads and emitted a greater splendor than many suns. In comparison with the beauty of these holy princes all the loveliness seen in this world appeared repulsive. But pre-eminent in splendor were the devices or escutcheons on their breasts, on each of which the sweet name of Jesus was engraved or embossed. The effulgence which each of these escutcheons emitted exceeded that of all the angels together, and the variety of the beauty thus exhibited in this great multitude was so rare and exquisite as neither human tongue can express nor human imagination ever compass. The holy angels divided into two choirs in the cave, keeping their gaze fixed upon the King and Lord in the arms of his virginal Mother. The chiefs of these heavenly cohorts were the two princes, saint Michael and saint Gabriel, shining in greater splendor than the rest and bearing in their hands, as a special distinction, the most holy name of JESUS, written in larger letters on something like cards of incomparable beauty and splendor.

The two princes presented themselves apart from the rest before their Queen and said: "Lady, this is the name of thy Son (Matth. 1, 21), which was written in the mind of God from all eternity and which the blessed Trinity has given to thy Onlybegotten Son and our Lord as the signal of salvation for the whole human race; establishing Him at the same time on the throne of David. He shall reign upon it, chastise his enemies and triumph over them, making them his footstool and passing judgment upon them; He shall raise his friends to the glory of his right hand. But all this is to happen at the cost of suffering and blood; and even now He is to shed it in receiving this name, since it is that of the Savior and Redeemer; it shall be the beginning of his sufferings in obedience to the will of his eternal Father. We all are come as ministering spirits of the Most High, appointed and sent by the holy Trinity in order to serve the Onlybegotten of the Father and thy own in all the mysteries and sacraments of the law of grace. We are to accompany Him and minister to Him until He shall ascend triumphantly to the celestial Jerusalem and open the portals of heaven; afterwards we shall enjoy an especial accidental glory beyond that of the other blessed, to whom no such commission has been given." All this was witnessed by the most fortunate spouse Joseph conjointly with the Queen of heaven; but his understanding of these happenings was not so deep as hers, for the Mother of wisdom understood and comprehended the highest mysteries of the Redemption. Although saint Joseph understood many more mysteries than other mortals, yet he did not penetrate them in the same way as his heavenly Spouse. Both of them, however, were full of heavenly joy and admiration, and extolled the Lord in new canticles of glory. All that they experienced in these various and wonderful events surpasses human language, and certainly my own powers, and I cannot find adequate words for expressing my conceptions.

The priest came to the gates or cave of the Nativity, where the incarnate Word, resting in the arms of his Virgin Mother, awaited him. With the priest came also two other officials, who were to render such assistance as was customary at the performance of the rite. The rudeness of the dwelling at first astonished and somewhat disconcerted the priest. But the most prudent Queen spoke to him and welcomed him with such modesty and grace that his constraint soon changed into devotion and into admiration at the composure and noblest majesty of the Mother; and without knowing the cause he was moved to reverence and esteem for such an unusual personage. When the priest looked upon the face of Mary and of the Child in her arms he was filled with great devotion and tenderness, wondering at the contrast exhibited amid such poverty and in a place so lowly and despised. The priest thereupon proceeded to his duty and circumcised the Child, the true God and man. At the same time the Son of God, with immeasurable love, offered up to the eternal Father three sacrifices of so great value that each one would have been sufficient for the Redemption of a thousand worlds. The first was that He, being innocent and the Son of the true God, assumed the condition of a sinner (Phil. 2, 7) by subjecting Himself to a rite instituted as a remedy for original sin, and to a law not binding on Him (II Cor. 5, 21). The second was his willingness to suffer the pains of circumcision, which He felt as a true and perfect man. The third was the most ardent love with which He began to shed his blood for the human race, giving thanks to the eternal Father for having given Him a human nature capable of suffering for his exaltation and glory.

This prayerful sacrifice of JESUS our Savior the Father accepted, and, according to our way of speaking, He began to declare Himself satisfied and paid for the indebtedness of humanity. The incarnate Word offered these first fruits of his blood as pledges that He would give it all in order to consummate the Redemption and extinguish the debt of the sons of Adam. All these interior acts and movements of the Onlybegotten his most holy Mother perceived, and in her heavenly wisdom She penetrated the mystery of this sacrament, acting as his Mother and in concert with Her Son and Lord in all that He was doing and suffering. True to his human nature, the divine Infant shed tears as other children. Although the pains caused by the wounding were most severe, as well on account of the delicacy of his body as on account of the coarseness of the knife, which was made of flint, yet his tears were caused not so much by the sensible pain as by the supernatural sorrow caused by his knowledge of the hard-heartedness of mortals. For this was more rude and unyielding than the flint, resisting his sweetest love and the divine fire He had come to enkindle in the world and in the hearts of the faithful (Luke 12, 49).   Also the tender and affectionate Mother wept, like the guileless sheep, which raises its voice in unison with the innocent lamb.   In reciprocal love and compassion the Child clung to his Mother, while She sweetly caressed Him at her virginal breast and caught the sacred relics and the falling blood in the towel.

In the meanwhile the priest asked the parents what name they wished to give to the Child in Circumcision; the great Lady, always attentive to honor her spouse, asked saint Joseph to mention the name.   Saint Joseph turned toward Her in like reverence and gave Her to understand that He thought it proper this sweet name should first flow from her mouth.   Therefore, by divine interference, both Mary and Joseph said at the same time; "JESUS is his name."   The priest answered: "The parents are unanimously agreed, and great is the name which they give to the Child"; and thereupon he inscribed it in the tablet or register of names of the rest of the children.   While writing it the priest felt great interior movements, so that he shed copious tears; and wondering at what he felt yet not being able to account for, he said: "I am convinced that this Child is to be a great Prophet of the Lord.   Have great care in raising Him, and tell me in what I can relieve your needs."   Most holy Mary and Joseph answered the priest with humble gratitude and dismissed him after offering him the gift of some candles and other articles.

Being again left alone with the Child, most holy

Mary and Joseph celebrated anew the mystery of the Circumcision, commenting on the holy name of JESUS amid sweet canticles and tears of joy, the fuller knowledge of which (as also of other mysteries which I have mentioned) is reserved as an additional accidental glory to the saints in heaven. The most prudent Mother applied to the wound caused by the knife such medicines as were wont to be used on such occasions for other children, and during the time while the pain and the healing lasted She would not for a moment part with Him, holding Him in her arms day and night. The tender love of the heavenly Mother is beyond all comprehension or understanding of man; for her natural love was greater than any other mother was capable of, and her supernatural love exceeded that of all the angels and saints together. Her reverence and worship cannot be compared with that of any other created being. These were the delights of the incarnate Word (Prov. 8, 31), which He desired and longed for among the children of men; and this was the recompense, which his loving heart drew from the exceeding sanctity of the Virgin Mother for the sorrows occasioned Him by their behavior.

WORDS OF THE QUEEN.

My daughter, I wish thee to consider attentively the blessed favor conferred upon thee by being informed of the solicitous care and attention which I lavished upon my most holy and sweetest Son in the mysteries just now described. The Most High does not give thee this special light in order only to be regaled by the knowledge of these mysteries; but in order to imitate me in all these things as a faithful handmaid and in order to distinguish thyself in rendering thanks for his works in the same measure as thou art distinguished in knowing them more fully. Ponder, then, dearest, upon the small return given for the love of my Son and Lord by mortals, and how forgetful of thanks even his faithful continue to be. Assume it as thy task, as far as thy weak powers allow, to render satisfaction for this grievous offense: loving Him, thanking Him and serving Him with all thy powers, for all the other men who fail to do so. Therefore thou must be an angel in promptitude, most fervent and punctual on all occasions; thou must die to all earthly things, eliminating and crushing all human inclinations and rising upon the wings of love to the heights of love designed for thee by the Lord.

Thou art not ignorant of the sweet efficacy contained in the memory of the works performed by my most holy Son: and although thou canst so copiously avail thyself of the light given thee to be thankful: yet, in order that thou mayest fear so much the more the danger of forgetfulness, I particularly inform thee that the saints in heaven, comprehending by the divine light these mysteries, are astonished at themslves for not having paid more attention to them during their life. And if they were capable of pain, they would be deeply grieved for their tardiness and carlessness in not having set proper value upon the works for the Redemption, and for failing in the imitation of Christ. All the angels and saints, by an insight hidden to mortals, wonder at the cruelty of human hearts against themselves and against Christ their Redeemer. Men have compassion neither for the sufferings of the Lord, nor for the sufferings they themselves stand in danger of incurring. When the foreknown, in unending bitterness shall recognize their dreadful forgetfulness and their indifference to the works of Christ their Savior, their confusion and despair will be an intolerable punishment, and it alone will be a chastisement beyond all imagination; for they will then see the copiousness of the Redemption, which they have despised (Ps. 44, 11). Hear me, my daughter, and bend thy ears to these counsels and doctrines of eternal life. Cast out from thy faculties every image and affection toward human creatures and turn all the powers of thy heart and soul toward the mysteries and blessings of the Redemption. Occupy thyself wholly with them, ponder and weigh them, give thanks for them as if thou alone wert in existence, as if they had been wrought solely for thee, and singly for each human being in particular (Gal. 2, 20). Thus thou wilt find life and the way of life, proceeding thus thou canst not err; but thou shalt find therein the light of thy eyes and true peace.

CHAPTER VI.

THE ADORATION OF THE MAGI.

The three Magi Kings, who came to find the divine Infant after his birth, were natives of Persia, Arabia and Sabba (Ps. 71, 10), countries to the east of Palestine. Their coming was prophesied especially by David, and before him, by Balaam, who, having been hired by Balaac, king of the Moabites, to curse the Israelites, blessed them instead (Numb. 24, 17). In this blessing Balaam said, that he would see the King Christ, although not at once, and that he would behold Him, although not present; for he did not see Him with his own eyes, but through the Magi, his descendants many centuries after. He said, also, that a star would arise unto Jacob, which was Christ, who arose to reign forever in the house of Jacob (Luke 1, 32).

At the same time the holy angel, who had brought the news from Bethlehem to the kings, formed of the material air a most resplendent star, although not so large as those of the firmament; for it was not to ascend higher than was necessary for the purpose of its formation. It took its course through the atmospheric regions in order to guide and direct the holy Kings to the cave, where the Child awaited them. Its splendor was of a different kind from that of the sun and the other stars; with its most beautiful light it illumined the night like a brilliant torch, and it mingled its own most active brilliancy with that of the sun by day. On coming out of their palaces each one of the kings saw this new star (Matth. 2, 2) although each from a different standpoint, because it was only one star and it was placed in such distance and height that it could be seen by each one at the same time. As the three of them followed the guidance of this miraculous star, they soon met. Thereupon it immediately approached them much more closely, descending through many shifts of the aerial space and rejoicing them by shedding its refulgence over them at closer range. They began to confer among themselves about the revelation they had received and about their plans, finding that they were identical. They were more and more inflamed with devotion and with the pious desire of adoring the newborn God, and broke out in praise and admiration at the inscrutable works and mysteries of the Almighty.

The heavenly Mother awaited the pious and devout kings, standing with the Child in her arms. Amid the humble and poor surroundings of the cave, in incomparable modesty and beauty, She exhibited at same time a majesty more than human, the light of heaven shining in her countenance. Still more visible was this light in the Child, shedding through the cavern effulgent splendor, which made it like a heaven. The three kings of the East entered and at the first sight of the Son and Mother they were for a considerable space of time overwhelmed with wonder. They prostrated themselves upon the earth, and in this position they worshiped and adored the Infant, acknowledging Him as the true God and man, and as the Savior of the human race. By the divine power, which the sight of Him and his presence exerted in their souls, they were filled with new enlightenment. They perceived the multitude of angelic spirits, who as servants and ministers of the King of kings and Lord of lords attended upon him in reverential fear

(Heb. 1, 4).   Arising, they congratulated their and our Queen as Mother of the Son of the eternal Father; and they approached to reverence Her on their knees.   They sought her hand in order to kiss it, as they were accustomed to do to their queens in their countries.   But the most prudent Lady withdrew her hand, and offered instead that of the Redeemer of the world, saying: "My spirit rejoices in the Lord and my soul blesses and extols Him; because among all the nations He has called and selected you to look upon and behold that which many kings and prophets have in vain desired to see, namely, Him who is the eternal Word incarnate (Luke 10, 24). Let us extol and praise his name on account of the sacraments and mysteries wrought among his people; let us kiss the earth which He sanctifies by his real presence."

At these words of most holy Mary the three kings humiliated themselves anew, adoring the infant Jesus; they acknowledged the great blessings of living in the time when the Sun of justice was arising in order to illumine the darkness (Malachy 4, 2).   Thereupon they spoke to saint Joseph, congratulating him and extolling his good fortune in being chosen as the spouse of the Mother of God; and they expressed wonder and compassion at the great poverty, beneath which were hidden the greatest mysteries of heaven and earth.   In this intercourse they consumed three hours, and then the kings asked permission of most holy Mary to go to the city in order to seek a lodging, as they could find no room for themselves in the cave.   Some people had accompanied them; but the Magi alone participated in the light and the grace of this visit.   The others took notice merely of what passed exteriorly, and witnessed only the destitute and neglected condition of the Mother and her husband. Though wondering at the strange event, they perceived nothing of its mystery. The Magi took leave and departed, while most holy Mary and Joseph, being again alone with their Child, glorified his Majesty with new songs of praise, because his name was beginning to be known and adored among the Gentiles (Ps. 85, 9). What else the three wise men did will be related in the following chapter.

From the grotto of the Nativity, into which the three Kings had entered directly on their way to Jerusalem, they betook themselves to a lodging inside of the town of Bethlehem. They retired to a room where, in an abundance of affectionate tears and aspirations, they spent the greater part of the night, speaking of what they had seen, of the feelings and affections aroused in each, and of what each had noticed for himself in the divine Child and his Mother. During this conference they were more and more inflamed with divine love, amazed at the majesty and divine effulgence of the Infant Jesus; at the prudence, modesty and reserve of his Mother; at the holiness of her spouse Joseph, and the poverty of all three; at the humbleness of the place, where the Lord of heaven and earth had wished to be born. The devout kings felt a divine fire, which flamed up in their hearts, and, not being able to restrain themselves, they broke out into exclamations of sweet affection and acts of great reverence and love. "What is this that we feel?" they said. "What influence of this great King is it that moves us to such desires and affections? After this, how shall we converse with men? What can we do, who have been instructed in such new, hidden and supernatural mysteries? O greatness of his Omnipotence unknown to men and concealed beneath so much poverty! O humility unimaginable for mortals! Would that all be drawn to it, in order that they may not be deprived of such happiness!"

During these divine colloquies the Magi remembered the dire destitution of Jesus, Mary and Joseph in their cave, and they resolved immediately to send them some gifts in order to show their affection and to satisfy their desire of serving them, since they could not do anything else for them. They sent through their servants many of the presents, which they had already set aside for them, and others which they could procure. Most holy Mary and Joseph received these gifts with humble acknowledgment and they made a return not of empty-worded thanks, as other men are apt to make, but many efficacious blessings for the spiritual consolation of the three Kings. These gifts enabled our great Queen to prepare for her ordinary guests, the poor, an abundant repast; for the needy ones were accustomed to receive alms from Her, and, attracted still more by her sweet words, were wont to come and visit Her. The Kings went to rest full of incomparable joy in the Lord; and in their sleep the angels advised them as to their journey homeward.

On the following day at dawn they returned to the cave of the Nativity in order to offer to the heavenly King the special gifts which they had provided. Arriving they prostrated themselves anew in profound humility; and opening their treasures, as Scripture relates, they offered Him gold, incense and myrrh (Matth. 2, 11). They consulted the heavenly Mother in regard to many mysteries and practices of faith, and concerning matters pertaining to their consciences and to the government of their countries; for they wished to return well instructed and capable of directing themselves to holiness and perfection in their daily life. The great Lady heard them with exceeding pleasure and She conferred interiorly with the divine Infant concerning all that they had asked, in order to answer and properly to instruct these sons of the new Law. As a Teacher and an instrument of divine wisdom She answered all their questions, giving them such high precepts of sanctity that they could scarcely part from Her on account of the sweetness and attraction of her words. However, an angel of the Lord appeared to them, reminding them of the necessity and of the will of the Lord that they should return to their country. No wonder that her words should so deeply affect these Kings; for all her words were inspired by the holy Spirit and full of infused science regarding all that they had inquired and many other matters.

The heavenly Mother received the gifts of the Kings and in their name offered them to the Infant Jesus. His Majesty showed by signs of highest pleasure, that He accepted their gifts: they themselves became aware of the exalted and heavenly blessings with which He repaid them more than a hundredfold (Matth. 19, 29). According to the custom of their country they also offered to the heavenly Princess some gems of great value; but because these gifts had no mysterious signification and referred not to Jesus, She returned them to the Kings, reserving only the gifts of gold, incense and myrrh. In order to send them away more rejoiced, She gave them some of the clothes in which She had wrapped the infant God; for She neither had nor could have had any greater visible pledges of esteem with which to enrich them at their departure. The three Kings received these relics with such reverence and esteem that they encased them in gold and precious stones in order to keep them ever after. As a proof of their value these relics spread about such a copious fragrance that they revealed their presence a league in circumference. However, only those who believed in the coming of God into the world were able to perceive it; while the incredulous perceived none of the fragrance emitted by the relics. In their own countries the Magi performed great miracles with these relics.

The holy Kings also offered their property and possession to the Mother of the sweetest Jesus, or, if She did not wish to accept of them and preferred to live in this place, where her most holy Son had been born, they would build Her a house, wherein She could live more comfortably. The most prudent Mother thanked them for their offers without accepting them. On taking leave of Her, the three Kings besought Her from their inmost hearts not to forget them, which She promised and fulfilled; in the same way they asked of saint Joseph. With the blessing of Jesus, Mary and Joseph, they departed, so moved by tenderest affection that it seemed to them they had left their hearts all melted into sighs and tears in that place. They chose another way for their return journey, in order not to meet Herod in Jerusalem; for thus they had been instructed by the angel on the preceding night. On their departure from Bethlehem the same or a similar star appeared in order to guide them home, conducting them on their new route to the place where they had first met, whence each one separated to reach his own country.

WORDS OF THE QUEEN.

My daughter, great were the gifts which the Kings offered to my most holy Son; but greater still was the affection with which they offered them and the mystery concealed beneath them. On account of all this they were most acceptable to his Majesty. I wish that thou also offer up similar gifts, thanking Him for having made thee poor in condition and profession. For I

assure thee, my dearest, there is no more acceptable gift
to the Most High than voluntary poverty. There are
very few in the world in our days who use well the
temporal riches and offer them to their God and Lord
with the generosity and love of these holy Kings. The
poor of the Lord, so numerous in our day, experience
and give witness how cruel and avaricious human nature
has become; since in their great necessities they are so
little succored by the rich. This gross uncharitableness
of men offends the holy angels and grieves the Holy
Ghost, since they are bound to witness the nobility of
the souls so degraded and abased in the service of vile
greed of gold with all its evil powers (Eccles. 10, 20).
As if all things had been created for the individual use
of the rich, they appropriate them to themselves and deprive the poor, their brothers springing from the same
nature and flesh; and denying them even to God, who
created and preserves all things, and who can give or
take at will. It is most lamentable that while the rich
might purchase eternal life with their possessions, they
abuse them to draw upon themselves damnation as senseless and foolish creatures (Luke 14, 9).

This evil is common among the children of Adam;
and therefore voluntary poverty is so excellent and
safe a remedy. By it, making man willing to part
joyfully with his possessions for the sake of the poor, a
great sacrifice is offered to the Lord. Thou also canst
make such an offering of the things necessary for sustenance, giving a part of it to the poor and desiring, if it
were possible by thy labor and sweat, to help all of them.
Thy ceaseless offer, however, must be love, which is the
gold; continual prayer, which is the incense; and the
patient acceptance of labors and true mortifications,
which is the myrrh. All that thou dost for the Lord,

thou should offer up to Him with fervent affection and promptitude, without negligence or fear; for negligent works, and those not enlivened by love, are not an acceptable sacrifice in the eyes of his Majesty. In order to make those incessant offerings, it is necessary that divine faith and light continually inflame thy heart, having before thy eyes the great object of thy praise and exaltation, and the stimulus of love, by which thou art bound to the right hand of the Most High. Thus shouldst thou continue incessantly in this sweet exercise of love, so proper to the spouses of his Majesty; for their name implies such a continual payment of the debt of love and affection.

CHAPTER VII.

THE PRESENTATION OF THE INFANT JESUS IN THE TEMPLE.

The sacred humanity of Christ belonged to the eternal Father not only because it was created like other beings, but it was his special property by virtue of the hypostatic union with the person of the Word, for this person of the Word, being his Onlybegotten Son, was engendered of his substance, true God of true God. Nevertheless the eternal Father had decreed, that his Son should be presented to Him in the temple in mysterious compliance with the law, of which Christ our Lord was the end (Rom. 10, 4). It was established for no other purpose than that the just men of the old Testament should perpetually sanctify and offer to the Lord their first-born sons, in the hope that one thus presented might prove to be the Son of God and a Child of the Mother of the expected Messias (Exod. 13, 2). According to our way of thinking his Majesty acted like men, who are apt to repeat and enjoy over and over again a thing which has caused them enjoyment. For although the Father understood and knew all things in his infinite wisdom, He sought pleasure in the offering of the incarnate Word, which by so many titles already belonged to Him.

This will of the eternal Father, which was conformable to that of his Son in so far as He was God, was known to the Mother of life and of the human nature of the Word; for She saw that all his interior actions were in unison with the will of his eternal Father. Full of this holy science the great Princess passed the night before his presentation in the temple in divine colloquies. Speaking to the Father She said: "My Lord and God most high, Father of my Lord, a festive day for heaven and earth will be that, in which I shall bring and offer to Thee in thy holy temple the living Host, which is at the same time the Treasure of thy Divinity. Rich, O my Lord and God, is this oblation; and Thou canst well pour forth, in return for it, thy mercies upon the human race: pardoning the sinners, that have turned from the straight path, consoling the afflicted, helping the needy, enriching the poor, succoring the weak, enlightening the blind, and meeting those who have strayed away. This is, my Lord, what I ask of thee in offering to Thee thy Onlybegotten, who, by thy merciful condescension is also my Son. If Thou hast given Him to me as a God, I return Him to Thee as God and man; his value is infinite, and what I ask of Thee is much less. In opulence do I return to thy holy temple, from which I departed poor; and my soul shall magnify Thee forever, because thy divine right hand has shown itself toward me so liberal and powerful."

On the next morning, the Sun of heaven being now ready to issue from its purest dawning, the Virgin Mary, on whose arms He reclined, and being about to rise up in full view of the world, the heavenly Lady, having provided the turtle-dove and two candles, wrapped Him in swaddling-clothes and betook Herself with saint Joseph from their lodging to the temple. The holy angels, who had come with them from Bethlehem, again formed in procession in corporeal and most beautiful forms, just as has been said concerning the journey of the preceding day. On this occasion however the holy spirits added many other hymns of the sweetest and most entrancing harmony in honor of the infant God, which were heard only by the most pure Mary.   Besides the ten thousand, who had formed the procession on the previous day, innumerable others descended from heaven, who, accompanied by those that bore the shields of the holy name of Jesus, formed the guard of honor of the incarnate Word on the occasion of his presentation.   These however were not in corporeal shapes and only the heavenly Princess perceived their presence.   Having arrived at the temple-gate, the most blessed Mother was filled with new and exalted sentiments of devotion.   Joining the other women, She bowed and knelt to adore the Lord in spirit and in truth in his holy temple and She presented Herself before the exalted Majesty of God with his Son upon her arms (John 4, 23).   Immediately She was immersed in an intellectual vision of the most holy Trinity and She heard a voice issuing from the eternal Father, saying: "This is my beloved Son, in whom I am well pleased" (Matth. 27, 20).   Saint Joseph, the most fortunate of men, felt at the same time a new sweetness of the Holy Ghost, which filled him with joy and divine light.

The holy high-priest Simeon, moved by the Holy Ghost as explained in the preceding chapter, also entered the temple at that time (Luke 2, 7).   Approaching the place where the Queen stood with the infant Jesus in her arms, he saw both Mother and Child enveloped in splendor and glory.   The prophetess Anne, who, as the Evangelist says, had come at the same hour, also saw Mary and her Infant surrounded by this wonderful light. In the joy of their spirit both of them approached the Queen of heaven, and the priest received the Infant Jesus from her arms upon his hands.   Raising up his eyes to

heaven he offered Him up to the eternal Father, pronouncing at the same time these words so full of mysteries: "Now dost thou dismiss thy servant, O Lord, according to thy Word in peace. Because my eyes have
seen thy salvation, which thou hast prepared before the
face of all peoples: a light for the revelation of the gentiles, and the glory of thy people Israel" (Luke 2, 29).
It was as if He had said: "Now, Lord, thou wilt release
me from the bondage of this mortal body and let me go
free and in peace; for until now have I been detained in
it by the hope of seeing thy promises fulfilled and by the
desire of seeing thy Onlybegotten made man. Now that
my eyes have seen thy salvation, the Onlybegotten made
man, joined to our nature in order to give it eternal welfare according to the intention and eternal decree of thy
infinite wisdom and mercy, I shall enjoy true and secure
peace. Now, O Lord, Thou hast prepared and placed
before all mortals thy divine light that it may shine upon
the world and that all who wish may enjoy it throughout the universe and derive therefrom guidance and salvation. For this is the light which is revealed to the
gentiles for the glory of thy chosen people of Israel"
(John I, 9, 32).

Most holy Mary and saint Joseph heard this canticle of Simeon, wondering at the exalted revelation it
contained. The Evangelist calls them in this place the
parents of the divine Infant, for such they were in the
estimation of the people who were present at this event.
Simeon, addressing himself to the most holy Mother of
the Infant Jesus, then added: "Behold this Child is set
for the fall and for the resurrection of many in Israel,
and for a sign which shall be contradicted. And thy own
soul a sword shall pierce, that out of many hearts thoughts
may be revealed." Thus saint Simeon; and being a priest

he gave his blessing to the happy parents of the Child. Then also the prophetess Anne acknowledged the incarnate Word, and full of the Holy Ghost, she spoke of the mysteries of the Messias to many, who were expecting the redemption of Israel. By these two holy old people public testimony of the coming of the Redeemer was given to the world.

At the moment when the priest Simeon mentioned the sword and the sign of contradiction, which were prophetical of the passion and death of the Lord, the Child bowed its head. Thereby, and by many interior acts of obedience, Jesus ratified the prophecy of the priest and accepted it as the sentence of the eternal Father pronounced by his minister. All this the loving Mother noticed and understood; She presently began to feel the sorrow predicted by Simeon and thus in advance was She wounded by the sword, of which She had thus been warned. As in a mirror her spirit was made to see all the mysteries included in this prophecy; how her most holy Son was to be the stone of stumbling, the perdition of the unbelievers, and the salvation of the faithful; the fall of the synagogue and the establishment of the Church among the heathens; She foresaw the triumph to be gained over the devils and over death, but also that a great price was to be paid for it, namely the frightful agony and death of the Cross (Colos. 2, 15). She foresaw the boundless opposition and contradiction, which the Lord Jesus was to sustain both personally and in his Church (John 15, 20). At the same time She also saw the glory and excellence of the predestined souls. Most holy Mary knew it all and in the joy and sorrow of her most pure soul, excited by the prophecies of Simeon and these hidden mysteries, She performed heroic acts of virtue. All these sayings and happenings were indelibly impressed upon her memory, and, of all that She understood and experienced, She forgot not the least iota. At all times She looked upon her most holy Son with such a living sorrow, as we, mere human creatures with hearts so full of ingratitude, shall never be able to feel. The holy spouse saint Joseph was by these prophecies also made to see many of the mysteries of the Redemption and of the labors and sufferings of Jesus. But the Lord did not reveal them to him so copiously and openly as they were perceived and understood by his heavenly spouse; for in him these revelations were to serve a different purpose, and besides, saint Joseph was not to be an eye-witness of them during his mortal life.

The ceremony of the presentation thus being over, the great Lady kissed the hand of the priest and again asked his blessing. The same She did also to Anne, her former teacher; for her dignity as Mother of God, the highest possible to angels or men, did not prevent Her from these acts of deepest humility. Then, in the company of saint Joseph, her spouse, and of the fourteen thousand angels in procession, She returned with the divine Infant to her lodging. They remained, as I shall relate farther on, for some days in Jerusalem, in order to satisfy their devotion and during that time She spoke a few times with the priest about the mysteries of the Redemption and of the prophecies above mentioned.

When the most holy Mary and glorious saint Joseph returned from the presentation of the Infant Jesus in the temple, they concluded to stay in Jerusalem for nine days in order to be able each day to visit the temple and repeat the offering of the sacred Victim, their divine Son, thus rendering fitting thanks for the immense blessing for which they had been singled out from among all men. The heavenly Lady had a special veneration for this number in memory of the nine days, during which She had been prepared and adorned by God for the incarnation of the Word, as I have related in the first ten chapters of this second part; also in memory of the nine months, during which She had borne Jesus in her virginal womb. In honor of these events She wished to make this novena with her divine Child, presenting Him that many times to the eternal Father as an acceptable offering for her lofty purposes. They began the devotions of the novena every day before the third hour, praying in the temple until nightfall. They chose the most obscure and retired place, meriting thereby the invitation of the master of the banquet in the Gospel: "Friend, go up higher."

As an answer to her petitions He conceded to Her new and great privileges, among which was also this one, that, as long as the world should last, She should obtain all that She would ever ask for her clients; that the greatest sinners, if they availed themeselves of her intercession, should find salvation; that in the new Church and law of the Gospel She should be the Coöperatrix and Teacher of salvation with Christ her most holy Son. This was to be her privilege especially after his Ascension into heaven, when She should remain, as Queen of the universe, as the representative and instrument of the divine power on earth. This I will show more particularly in the third part of this history. Many other favors and mysteries the Most High confirmed upon the heavenly Mother in answer to her prayers. They, however, are beyond the reach of spoken language, and cannot be described by my short and limited terms.

In the course of these manifestations, on the fifth day of the novena after the presentation and purification, while the heavenly Lady was in the temple with the

Infant on her arms, the Deity revealed Itself to Her, although not intuitively, and She was wholly raised and filled by the Spirit. It is true, that this had been done to Her before; but as God's power and treasures are infinite, He never gives so much as not to be able to give still more to the creatures. In this abstractive vision the Most High visited anew his only Spouse, wishing to prepare Her for the labors, that were awaiting Her. Speaking to Her, He comforted Her saying: "My Spouse and my Dove, thy wishes and intentions are pleasing in my eyes and I delight in them always. But Thou canst not finish the nine days' devotion, which Thou hast begun, for I have in store for Thee other exercises of Thy love. In order to save the life of thy Son and raise Him up, Thou must leave thy home and thy country, fly with Him and thy spouse Joseph into Egypt, where Thou art to remain until I shall ordain otherwise: for Herod is seeking the life of the Child. The journey is long, most laborious and most fatiguing; do thou suffer it all for my sake; for I am, and always will be, with Thee."

Any other faith and virtue might have been disturbed (as the incredulous really have been) to see the powerful God flying from a miserable earthly being, and that He should do so in order to save his life, as if He, being both God and man, could be affected by the fear of death. But the most prudent and obedient Mother advanced no objection or doubt: She was not in the least disturbed or moved by this unlooked for order. Answering, She said: "My Lord and Master, behold thy servant with a heart prepared to die for thy love if necessary. Dispose of me according to thy will. This only do I ask of thy immense goodness, that, overlooking my want of merit and gratitude, Thou permit not my

Son and Lord to suffer, and that Thou turn all pains and labor upon me, who am obliged to suffer them." The Lord referred Her to saint Joseph, bidding Her to follow his directions in all things concerning the journey. Therewith She issued from her vision, which She had enjoyed without losing the use of her exterior senses and while holding in her arms the Infant Jesus. She had been raised up in this vision only as to the superior part of her soul; but from it flowed other gifts, which spiritualized her senses and testified to Her that her soul was living more in its love than in the earthly habitation of her body.

On account of the incomparable love, which the Queen bore toward her most holy Son, her maternal and compassionate heart was somewhat harrowed at the thought of the labors which She foresaw in the vision impending upon the infant God. Shedding many tears, She left the temple to go to her lodging-place, without manifesting to her spouse the cause of her sorrow. Saint Joseph therefore thought that She grieved on account of the prophecy of Simeon. As the most faithful Joseph loved Her so much, and as he was of a kind and solicitous disposition, he was troubled to see his Spouse so tearful and afflicted, and that She should not manifest to him the cause of this new affliction. This disturbance of his soul was one of the reasons why the holy angels spoke to him in sleep, as I have related above, when speaking of the pregnancy of the Queen. For in the same night, while saint Joseph was asleep, the angel of the Lord appeared to him, and spoke to him as recorded by saint Matthew: "Arise, take the Child and its Mother and fly into Egypt; there shalt thou remain until I shall return to give thee other advice; for Herod is seeking after the Child in order to take away its life." Immediately the holy spouse arose full of solicitude and sorrow, foreseeing also that of his most loving Spouse. Entering upon her retirement, he said: "My Lady, God wills that we should be afflicted; for his holy angel has announced to me the pleasure and the decree of the Almighty, that we arise and fly with the Child into Egypt, because Herod is seeking to take away its life. Encourage thyself, my Lady, to bear the labors of this journey and tell me what I can do for thy comfort, since I hold my life and being at the service of thy Child and of Thee."

"My husband and my master," answered the Queen, "if we have received from the hands of the Most High such great blessings of grace, it is meet that we joyfully accept temporal afflictions (Job 2, 13). We bear with us the Creator of heaven and earth; if He has placed us so near to Him, what arms shall be able to harm us, even if it be the arm of Herod? Wherever we carry with us all our Good, the highest treasure of heaven, our Lord, our guide and true light, there can be no desert; but He is our rest, our portion, and our country. All these goods we possess in having his company; let us proceed to fulfill his will." Then most holy Mary and Joseph approached the crib where the Infant Jesus lay; and where He, not by chance, slept at that time. The heavenly Mother uncovered Him without awakening Him; then the heavenly Mother, falling upon her knees, awakened the sweetest Infant, and took Him in her arms. Jesus, in order to move Her to greater tenderness and in order to show Himself as true man, wept a little (O wonders of the Most High in things according to our judgments so small)! Yet He was soon again quieted; and when the most holy Mother and saint Joseph asked his blessing He gave it them in visible manner. Gathering their poor clothing into the casket and loading it on the beast of burden which they had brought from Nazareth, they departed shortly after midnight, and hastened without delay on their journey to Egypt.

WORDS OF THE QUEEN.

My daughter, what thou must especially learn from this chapter is, that thou accustom thyself to humble thanksgiving for the benefits which thou receivest, since thou, among many generations, art so specially signalized by the riches of grace with which my Son and I visit thee without any merit of thine. I was wont to repeat many times this verse of David: "What shall I render to the Lord for all the things that he hath rendered to me?" (Ps. 15, 12). In such sentiments I humiliated myself to the dust, esteeming myself altogether useless among creatures. Therefore, if thou knowest what I did as Mother of God, consider what then is thy obligation, since thou must with so much truth confess thyself unworthy and undeserving of all thou receivest, and so poorly furnished for giving thanks and for making payment. Thou must supply thy insufficiency and thy misery by offering up to the eternal Father the living host of his onlybegotten Son, especially when thou receivest Him in the holy Sacrament and possessest Him within thee: for in this thou shouldst also imitate David, who, after asking the Lord what return he should make for all his benefits, answers: "I will take the chalice of salvation; and I will call upon the name of the Lord" (Ps. 115, 13). Thou must accept the salvation offered to thee and bring forth its fruits by the perfection of thy works, calling upon the name of the Lord, offering up his Onlybegotten. For He it is who gave the virtue of salvation, who merited it, who alone can be an adequate return for the blessings conferred upon the human race and upon thee especially. I have given Him human form in order that He might converse with men and become the property of each one. He conceals Himself under the appearances of bread and wine in order to accommodate Himself to the needs of each one, and that each one might consider Him as his personal property fit to offer to the eternal Father. In this way He furnishes to each one an oblation which no one could otherwise offer, and the Most High rests satisfied with it, since there is not anything more acceptable nor anything more precious in the possession of creatures.

In addition to this offering is the resignation with which souls embrace and bear with equanimity and patience the labors and difficulties of mortal life. My most holy Son and I were eminent Masters in the practice of this doctrine. My Son began to teach it from the moment in which He was conceived in my womb. For already then He began to suffer, and as soon as He was born into the world He and I were banished by Herod into a desert, and his sufferings continued until He died on the Cross. I also labored to the end of my life, as thou wilt be informed more and more in the writing of this history. Since, therefore, We suffered so much for creatures and for their salvation, I desire thee to imitate Us in this conformity to the divine will as being his spouse and my daughter. Suffer with a magnanimous heart, and labor to increase the possessions of thy Lord and Master, namely, souls, which are so precious in his sight and which He has purchased with his life-blood. Never shouldst thou fly from labors, difficulties, bitterness and sorrows, if by any of them thou canst gain a soul for the Lord, or if thou canst thereby induce it to leave the path of sin and enter the path of life. Let not the thought that thou art so useless and poor, or that thy desires and labor avail but little, discourage thee; since thou canst not know how the Lord will accept of them and in how far He shall consider Himself served thereby. At least thou shouldst wish to labor assiduously and eat no unearned bread in his house (Prov. 31, 27).

CHAPTER VIII.

THE FLIGHT TO EGYPT.

Our heavenly Pilgrims left Jerusalem and entered upon their banishment while yet the silence and obscurity of night held sway. They were full of solicitude for the Pledge of heaven, which they carried with them into a strange and unknown land. Although faith and hope strengthened them (for in no other beings could these virtues be more firmly and securely established than in our Queen and her most faithful spouse), nevertheless the Lord afforded them occasion for anxiety. Their love for the Infant Jesus would naturally excite in them anxiety and suffering on an occasion like this. They knew not what would happen during such a long journey, nor when it should end, nor how they would fare in Egypt, where they would be entire strangers, nor what comfort or convenience they would find there for raising the Child, nor even how they would be able to ward off great sufferings from Him on the way to Egypt. Therefore the hearts of these holy Parents were filled with many misgivings and anxious thoughts when they parted with so much haste from their lodging-place; but their sorrow was much relieved when the ten thousand heavenly courtiers above mentioned again appeared to them in human forms and in their former splendod and beauty, and when they again changed the night into the brightest day for the holy Pilgrims. As they set forth from the portals of the city the holy angels humiliated themselves and adored the incarnate Word in the arms of the Virgin

Mother. They also encouraged Her by again offering their homage and service, stating that it was the will of the Lord that they guide and accompany Her on the journey.

In this town of Gaza they remained two days, for saint Joseph and the beast of burden which carried the Queen were worn out by the fatigue of the journey. From that place they sent back the servant of saint Elisabeth, taking care to caution him not to tell any one of their whereabouts. But God provided still more effectually against this danger; for He took away from this man all remembrance of what saint Joseph had charged him to conceal, so that he retained only his message to saint Elisabeth. Most holy Mary expended the presents sent by Elisabeth in entertaining the poor; for She, who was Mother of the poor, could not bear to pass them by unassisted. Of the clothes sent to Her She made a cloak for the divine Infant, and one for saint Joseph, to shelter Them from the discomforts of the season and of the journey. She also used other things in their possession for the comfort of her Child and of saint Joseph. The most prudent Virgin would not rely on miraculous assistance whenever She could provide for the daily needs by her own diligence and labor; for in these matters She desired to subject Herself to the natural order and depend upon her own efforts. During the two days which they spent in that city the most pure Mary, in order to enrich it with great blessings, performed some wonderful deeds. She freed two sick persons from the danger of death and cured their ailments. She restored to another person, a crippled woman, the use of her limbs. In the souls of many, who met Her and conversed with Her, She caused divine effects of the knowledge of God and of a change of life. All of them felt themselves moved to praise their Creator. But neither Mary nor Joseph spoke a word about their native country, nor of the destination or object of their journey; for if this information had been added to the public notice caused by their wonderful actions, the attention of Herod's agents might have been drawn toward them, and they might have found sufficient inducement to follow them after their departure.

On the third day after our Pilgrims had touched Gaza, they departed from that city for Egypt. Soon leaving the inhabited parts of Palestine, they entered the sandy deserts of Bersabe, which they were obliged to traverse for sixty leagues in order to arrive and take their abode in Heliopolis, the present Cairo in Egypt. This journey through the desert consumed a number of days, for the distance they could travel each day was but short, not only on account of the laborious progress over the deep sand, but also on account of the hardships occasioned by the want of shelter. There were many incidents on their way through this solitude; I will mention some of them, from which others can be conjectured; for it is not necessary to relate all of them. In order to understand how much Mary and Joseph and also the Infant Jesus suffered on their pilgrimage, it must be remembered that the Almighty permitted his Onlybegotten, with his most holy Mother and saint Joseph, to suffer the inconveniences and hardships naturally connected with travel through this desert. And although the heavenly Lady made no complaints, yet She was much afflicted, which was also true of her most faithful husband. For both of them suffered many personal inconveniences and discomforts, while the Mother, in addition thereto, was afflicted still more on account of the sufferings of her Son and of saint Joseph; and the latter was deeply grieved not to be able by his diligence and care to ease the hardships of the Child and his Spouse.

During all this journey of sixty leagues through the desert they had no other night-shelter than the sky and open air; moreover, it was in the time of winter, for this journey took place in the month of February, only six days after the Purification, as was indicated in the last chapter. In the first night on these sandy plains they rested at the foot of a small hill, this being the only protection they could find. The Queen of heaven with the Child in her arms seated Herself on the earth, and with her husband She ate of the victuals brought with them from Gaza. The Empress of heaven also nursed the Infant Jesus at her breast and He on his part rejoiced his Mother and her husband by his contentment. In order to furnish them with some kind of shelter against the open air, however narrow and humble it might be, saint Joseph formed a sort of tent for the divine Word and most holy Mary by means of his cloak and some sticks. During that night the ten thousand angels who, full of marvel, assisted these earthly Pilgrims in visible human shapes, formed a guard around their King and Queen. The great Lady perceived that her divine Son offered up to the eternal Father the hardships and labors both of Himself and of Mary and Joseph. In these prayers and in the other acts of his deified Soul, the Queen joined him for the greater part of the night. The divine Infant slept for a short time in her arms, while She continued wakeful and engaged in heavenly colloquies with the Most High and his angels. Saint Joseph slept upon the ground, resting his head upon the chest, which contained the clothing and other articles of their baggage.

On the next day they pursued their journey and their little store of fruit and bread was soon exhausted, so that they began to suffer great want and to feel the hunger. Although Joseph was more deeply concerned, yet both of them felt this privation very much. On one of the first days of their journey they partook of no sustenance until nine o'clock at night, not having any more even of the coarse and poor food which until then had sustained them in their hardships and labor. As nature demanded some refreshment after the exertion and weariness of travel, and as there was no way of supplying their want by natural means, the heavenly Lady addressed Herself to the Most High in these words: "Eternal, great and powerful God, I give Thee thanks and bless Thee for thy magnificent bounty; and also that, without my merits, only on account of thy merciful condescension, Thou gavest me life and being and preservest me in it, though I am but dust and a useless creature. I have not made a proper return for all these benefits; therefore how can I ask for myself what I cannot repay? But, my Lord and Father, look upon thy Onlybegotten and grant me what is necessary to sustain my natural life and also that of my spouse, so that I may serve thy Majesty and thy Word made flesh for the salvation of men."

In order that the clamors of the sweetest Mother might proceed from yet greater tribulation, the Most High permitted the elements to afflict them more than at other times and in addition to the sufferings caused by their fatigue, destitution and hunger. For there arose a storm of wind and rain, which harassed and blinded them by its fury. This hardship grieved still more the tender-hearted and loving Mother on account of the delicate Child, which was not yet fifty days old. Although She tried to cover and protect Him as much as possible, yet She could not prevent Him from feeling the inclemency of the weather, so that He shed tears and shivered from the cold in the same manner as other children are wont to do. Then the anxious Mother, making use of her power as Queen and Mistress of creatures, commanded the elements not to afflict their Creator, but to afford Him shelter and refreshment, and wreak their vengeance upon Her alone. And, as related once before, at the occasion of the birth of Christ and of the journey to Jerusalem, again the wind immediately moderated and the storm abated, not daring to approach the Mother and Child. In return for this loving forethought, the Infant Jesus commanded his angels to assist his kindest Mother and to serve Her as a shield against the inclemency of the weather. They immediately complied and constructed a resplendent and beautiful globe round about and over their incarnate God, his Mother and her spouse. In this they were protected and defended more effectually than all the wealthy and powerful of the world in their palaces and rich garments. The same they did several times during the journey through the desert.

Nevertheless, they were in want of food, and they were destitute of other things unprovidable by their own mere human effort. But the Lord allowed them to fall into this need in order that, listening to the acceptable prayers of his Spouse, He might make provision also for this by the hands of the angels. They brought them delicious bread and well-seasoned fruits, and moreover a most delicious drink; all of which they administered and served with their own hands. Then all of them together sang hymns of praise and thanksgiving to the Lord, who gives food to all creatures at opportune times, in order that the poor may eat and be filled (Ps. 135, 25) whose eyes and hopes are fixed upon his kingly Providence and bounty. Of such a kind was

the delicate feast, with which the Lord regaled his three
exiled Wanderers in the desert of Bersabe (III Kings
19, 3), for it was the same desert in which Elias, fleeing
from Jezabel, was comforted by the hearth cake, brought
to him by the angel in order that he might travel to
Horeb mount.

So then the Infant Jesus, with his Mother and
saint Joseph, reached the inhabited country of Egypt.
On entering the towns the divine Infant, in the arms of
his Mother, raised his eyes and his hands to the Father
asking for the salvation of these inhabitants held captive
by satan.   And immediately He made use of his sovereign and divine power and drove the demons from the
idols and hurled them to the infernal abyss. Like lightning flashed from the clouds they darted forth and descended to the lowermost caverns of hell and darkness
(Luke 10, 4). At the same instant the idols crashed to
the ground, the altars fell to pieces, and the temples
crumbled to ruins. The cause of these marvelous
effects were known to the heavenly Lady, for She united
her prayers with those of her most holy Son as Co-opera-
trix of his salvation. Saint Joseph also knew this to be
the work of the incarnate Word; and He praised and
extolled Him in holy admiration. But the demons,
although they felt the divine power, knew not whence
this power proceeded.

The Egyptian people were astounded at these
inexplicable happenings; although among the more
learned, ever since the sojourn of Jeremias in Egypt, an
ancient tradition was current that a King of the Jews
would come and that the temples of the idols would be
destroyed. Yet of this prophecy the common people had
no knowledge, nor did the learned know how it was
to be fulfilled: and therefore the terror and confusion

was spread among all of them, as was prophesied by Isaias (Is. 9, 1). In this disturbance and fear, some, reflecting on these events, came to our great Lady and saint Joseph; and, in their curiosity at seeing these strangers in their midst, they also spoke to them about the ruin of their temples and their idols. Making use of this occasion the Mother of wisdom began to undeceive these people, speaking to them of the true God and teaching them that He is the one and only Creator of heaven and earth, who is alone to be adored, and acknowledged as God; that all others are but false and deceitful gods, nothing more than the wood, or clay, or metal of which they are made, having neither eyes, nor ears, nor any power; that the same artisans that made them, and any other man, could destroy them at pleasure; since any man is more noble and powerful than they; that the oracles which they gave forth were answers of the lying and deceitful demons within them; and that the latter had no power, since there is but one true God.

The heavenly Lady was so sweet and kind in her words, and at the same time so full of life and force; her appearance was so charming, and all her intercourse was accompanied by such salutary effects, that the rumor of the arrival of these strange Pilgrims quickly spread about in the different towns, and many people gathered to see and hear Them. Moreover, the powerful prayers of the incarnate Word wrought a change of hearts, and the crumbling of the idols caused an incredible commotion among these people, instilling into their minds knowledge of the true God and sorrow for their sins without their knowing whence or through whom these blessings came to them. Jesus, Mary and Joseph pursued their way through many towns of Egypt, performing these and many other miracles, driving out the demons not only from the idols, but out of many bodies possessed by them, curing many that were grievously and dangerously ill, enlightening the hearts by the doctrines of truth and eternal life. By these temporal benefits and others, so effectual in moving the ignorant, earthly-minded people, many were drawn to listen to the instructions of Mary and Joseph concerning a good and salutary life.

The traditions, which in many parts of Egypt kept alive the remembrance of wonders wrought by the incarnate Word, gave rise to differences of opinion among the sacred and other writers in regard to the city, in which our Exiles lived during their stay in Egypt. Some of them assert that they dwelt in this city, some in another. But all of them may be right and in accordance with facts, since each one may be speaking of a different period of the sojourn of our Pilgrims in Memphis, or Babylon of Egypt, or in Matarieh; for they visited not only these cities, but many others. I for my part have been informed that they passed through these and then reached Heliopolis, where they took up their abode. Their holy guardian angels instructed the heavenly Queen and saint Joseph, that They were to settle in this city. For, besides the ruin of the temples and idols, which, just as in other places, took place at their arrival here, the Lord had resolved to perform still other miracles for his glory and for the rescue of souls; and the inhabitants of this city, (according to the good fortune already prognosticated in its name as "City of the Sun"), were to see the Sun of justice and grace arise over them and shine upon them. Following these orders, saint Joseph sought to purchase for a suitable price some dwelling in the neighborhood; and the Lord ordained that he should find a poor and humble, yet serviceable house, at small distance from the city, just such as the Queen of heaven desired.

The most prudent Lady and her spouse, forsaken and destitute of all temporal help, accommodated themselves joyfully to the poverty of their little dwelling. Of the three rooms, which it contained, they assigned one to be the sanctuary or temple of the Infant Jesus under the tender care of the most pure Mother; there they placed the cradle and her bare couch, until, after some days, by the labor of the holy spouse, and through the kindness of some pious women, they could obtain wherewith to cover it. Another room was set aside for the sleeping place and oratory of saint Joseph. The third served as a workshop for plying his trade. In view of their great poverty, and of the great difficulty of sufficient employment as a carpenter, the great Lady resolved to assist him by the work of her hands to earn a livelihood. She immediately executed her resolve by seeking to obtain needlework through the intervention of the pious women, who, attracted by her modesty and sweetness, were beginning to have intercourse with Her. As all that She attended to or busied Herself with was so perfect, the reputation of her skill soon spread about, so that She never was in want of employment whereby to eke out the slender means of livelihood for her Son, the true God and man.

In order to obtain the indispensable victuals and clothing, furnish the house ever so moderately, and pay the necessary expenses, it seemed to our Queen that She must employ all day in work and consume the night in attending to her spiritual exercises. This She resolved upon, not for any motives of gain, or because She did not continue in her contemplations during the day; for this was her incessant occupation in the presence of the infant God, as I have so often said and shall repeat hereafter. But some of the hours, which She was wont to spend in special exercises, She wished to transfer to the night-time in order to be able to extend the hours of manual labor, not being minded to ask or expect God's miraculous assistance for anything which She could attain by greater diligence and additional labor on her own part. In all such cases we ask for miraculous help more for our own convenience than on account of necessity. The most prudent Queen asked the eternal Father to provide sustenance for her divine Son; but at the same time She continued to labor. Like one who does not trust in herself, or in her own efforts, She united prayer with her labors, in order to obtain the necessities of life like other men.

On account of the excessive heat prevailing in Egypt, and on account of many disorders rampant among the people, the distempers of the Egyptians were widespread and grievous. During the years of the stay of the Infant Jesus and his most holy Mother, pestilence devastated Heliopolis and other places. On this account, and on account of the report of their wonderful deeds, multitudes of people came to them from all parts of the country and returned home cured in body and soul. In order that the grace of the Lord might flow more abundantly, and in order that his kindest Mother might have assistance in her works of mercy, God, at the instance of the heavenly Mistress, ordained saint Joseph as her helper in the teaching and healing of the infirm. For this purpose He was endowed with new light and power of healing. The holy Mary began to make use of his assistance in the third year of their stay in Egypt; so that now he ordinarily taught and cured the men, while the blessed Lady attended to the women. Incredible was the fruit resulting from their labors in the souls of men; for her uninterrupted beneficence and the gracious efficacy of her words drew all toward our Queen, and her modesty and holiness filled them with devoted love. They offered her many presents and large possessions, anxious to see Her make use of them: but never did She receive anything for Herself, or reserve it for her own use; for they continued to provide for their wants by the labor of her hands and the earnings of saint Joseph. When at times the blessed Lady was offered some gift that seemed serviceable and proper for helping the needy and the poor, She would accept it for that purpose. Only with this understanding would She ever yield to the pious and affectionate importunities of devout persons; and even then She often made them a present in return of things made by her own hands. From what I have related we can form some idea how great and how numerous were the miracles wrought by the holy Family during their seven years' stay in Egypt and Heliopolis; for it would be impossible to enumerate and describe all of them.

Neither the tongue of creatures can describe, nor intellect comprehend, the vast merits and increase of sanctity accumulating in the most holy Mary through these continued and wonderful works; for in all things She acted with a prudence more than angelic. What moved Her to the greatest admiration, love and praise of the Almighty was to see how, at the intercession of Herself and her Son for the holy Innocents, his providence showed itself so liberal toward them. She knew as if She were present the great number of children that were killed and that all of them, though some were only eight days, two or six months old, and none of them over two years, had the use of their reason; that they all received a high knowledge of the being of God, perfect love, faith and hope, with which they performed heroic acts of faith, worship, and love of God, reverence and compassion for their parents. They prayed for their parents and, in reward for their sufferings, obtained for them light and grace for advance in spiritual things. They willingly submitted to martyrdom, in spite of the tenderness of their age, which made their sufferings so much the greater and consequently augmented their merits. A multitude of angels assisted them and bore them to limbo or to the bosom of Abraham. By their arrival they rejoiced the holy ancients and confirmed them in the hope of speedy liberation. All these were effects of the prayers of the divine Child and his Mother. Aware of all these wonders, She was inflamed with ardor and exclaimed: "Praise the Lord, ye children"; and joined with them in the praise of the Author of these magnificent works, so worthy of his Goodness and Omnipotence. Mary alone knew of them and appreciated them properly.

WORDS OF THE QUEEN.

My daughter, in what thou hast written I wish that thou learn a lesson from the very sorrow and apprehension with which thou hast performed this task. Well-founded is thy sorrow to see how such a noble creature as man, made according to the likeness and image of the Lord, endowed with such divine qualities, and gifted with the power of knowing, loving, seeing, and enjoying God eternally, should allow himself to be degraded and defiled by such brutal and abominable passions as to shed the innocent blood of those who can do no harm to any one. This should induce thee to weep over the ruin of so many souls; especially in the times in which thou livest, when that same ambition which incited Herod has kindled such great hatred and enmity among the children of the

Church, occasioning the ruin of countless souls and causing the waste and loss of the blood of my most holy Son, poured out for the salvation of men. Do thou bitterly deplore this loss.

But likewise be warned by what thou hast seen in others; ponder the effects of passions admitted into the heart; for if once they have mastered the heart, they will either smother it in lust when it finds success, or consume it with wrath at meeting any opposition. Fear thou, my daughter, this danger, not only on account of the results thou seest of ambition in Herod, but also on account of what thou seest going on every hour in other persons. Be very careful not to allow thyself to be mastered by anything, be it ever so small; for in order to start a great conflagration the smallest spark is sufficient. I have often repeated to thee this same warning, and I shall continue to do so more often in the future; for the greatest difficulty in practicing virtue consists in dying to all that is pleasurable to the senses. Thou canst not be a fit instrument in the hands of the Lord, such as He desires thee to be, if thou dost not cleanse thy faculties even of the images of all creatures, so that they do not find entrance into thy desires. I wish it to be to thee an inexorable law that all things, except God, his angels and saints, be to thee as if they did not exist. These should be thy sole possession; on this account the Lord has opened to thee his secrets, honors thee with his familiarity and intimacy, and for this purpose also do I honor thee with mine, that thou neither live nor wish to live without the Lord.

CHAPTER IX.

THE SWEET INTERCOURSE OF JESUS AND MARY; THEIR RETURN FROM EGYPT.

During one of the conversations of Mary with Joseph concerning the mysteries of the Lord, the Infant Jesus, having reached the age of one year, resolved to break the silence and speak in plain words to Joseph, who so faithfully fulfilled the duties of a foster-father. As I have already mentioned in chapter the tenth, He had thus conversed with his heavenly Mother from the time of his Birth. The two holy Spouses were speaking of the infinite being of God, of his goodness and excessive love, which induced Him to send his Onlybegotten Son as the Teacher and Savior of men, clothing Him in human form in order that He might converse with them and suffer the punishments of their depraved natures. Saint Joseph was lost in wonder at the works of the Lord and inflamed by affectionate gratitude and exaltation of the Lord. Seizing upon this occasion the infant God, resting upon the arms of his Mother as upon the seat of wisdom, began to speak to saint Joseph in an intelligible voice, saying: "My father, I came from heaven upon this earth in order to be the light of the world, and in order to rescue it from darkness of sin; in order to seek and know my sheep as a good Shepherd, to give them nourishment of eternal life, teach them the way of heaven, open its gates, which had been closed by their sins. I desire that you both be children of the Light, which you have so close at hand."

These words of the Infant Jesus, being full of divine life, filled the heart of the patriarch saint Joseph with new love, reverence and joy. He fell on his knees before the infant God with the profoundest humility and thanked Him for having called Him "father" by the very first word spoken to him. He besought the Lord with many tears to enlighten him and enable him to fulfill entirely his most holy will, to teach him to be thankful for the incomparable benefits flowing from his generous hands. Parents who love their children very much are touched with consolation and pride to see their children show great signs of wisdom and virtue; and even when this is not the case, they are naturally inclined to extol and make much of their childish pranks and sayings; for all this is the result of their tender affection for their young offspring. Although saint Joseph was not the natural, but the foster-father of Jesus, his love for Him exceeded by far all the love of parents for their children, since in him grace, or even natural love, was more powerful than in others, yea than in all the parents together. Hence the joy of his soul is to be measured by this love and appreciation of saint Joseph as being the foster-father of the Infant Jesus. For he at the same time heard himself called the father of the Son of the eternal Father, and saw Him so beautiful in grace, while listening to such exalted wisdom and knowledge in the Child.

During the whole of this first year his sweetest Mother had wrapped the infant God in clothes and coverings usual with other children; for He did not wish to be distinguished in this from others, and He wished to bear witness to his true humanity and to his love for mortals, enduring this inconvenience otherwise not required of Him. His boundless love for mortals inflamed Her with loving gratitude toward the Lord and produced in her heroic acts of many virtues. Seeing that the Child Jesus desired no footgear and only one garment, She said to Him: "My Son and my Lord, thy Mother has not the heart to allow Thee to go barefoot upon the ground at thy tender age; permit me, my Love, to provide some kind of covering to protect them. I also fear that the rough garment, which Thou askest of me, will wound thy tender body, if thou permit no linen to be worn beneath." "My Mother, I will permit a slight and ordinary covering for my feet until the time of my public preaching shall come, for this I must do barefooted. But I do not wish to wear linen, because it foments carnal pleasures, and is the causes of many vices in men. I wish to teach many by my example to renounce it for love and imitation of Me."

Immediately the great Queen set diligently about fulfilling the will of her most holy Son. Procuring some wool in its natural and uncolored state, She spun it very finely with her own hands and of it She wove a garment of one piece and without any seam, similar to knitted stuff, or rather like twilled cloth; for it was woven of twisted cords, not like smooth-woven goods. She wove it upon a small loom, by meshes, crocheting it of one seamless piece in a mysterious manner (John 19, 23). Two things were wonderful about it: that it was entirely even and uniform, without any folds, and that, at her request, the natural color was changed to a more suitable one, which was a mixture of brown and a most exquisite silver-gray, so that it could not be called either, appearing to be neither altogether brown, nor silvery, nor gray, but having a mixture of them all. She also wove a pair of sandals of strong thread, like hempen shoes, with which She covered the feet of the infant God. Besides these She made a half tunic of linen, which was to serve as an undergarment. In the next chapter I shall tell what happened when She clothed the Infant Jesus.

From the time the Child Jesus was on his feet

He commenced to retire and spent certain hours of the day in the oratory of his Mother. As the most prudent Mother was anxious to know his wishes in regard to her intercourse with Him, the Lord responded to her mute appeal, saying: "My Mother, enter and remain with Me always in order that thou mayest imitate Me in my works; for I wish that in thee be modeled and exhibited the high perfection which I desire to see accomplished in the souls. For if they had not resisted my first intentions (I Tim. 2, 4), they would have been endowed with my most abundant and copious gifts; but since the human race has hindered this, I have chosen thee as the vessel of all perfection and of the treasures of my right hand, which the rest of the creatures have abused and lost. Observe me therefore in all my actions for the purpose of imitating Me."

Thus the heavenly Lady was installed anew as the Disciple of her most holy Son. Thenceforward passed such great and hidden mysteries between these Two, that not until the day of eternity will they be known. Many times the divine Child prostrated Himself on the ground, at others He was raised from the ground in the form of a cross, earnestly praying to the eternal Father for the salvation of mortals. In all this his most loving Mother imitated Him. For to Her were manifest the interior operations of his most holy soul, just as well as the exterior movements of his body. Of this knowledge of most pure Mary I have spoken in other parts of this history and it is necessary to point it out often, because this was the source of the light which guided Her in her holy life. It was such a singular blessing, that all creatures together will not be able to understand or describe it by their united powers. The great Lady did not always enjoy visions of the Divinity; but always

the sight of the most holy humanity and soul of her Son
with all their activities. In a special manner She was
witness of the effects of the hypostatic and beatific union
of the humanity with the Divinity. Although She did
not always see this glory and this union substantially;
yet She perceived the interior acts by which his humanity
reverenced, loved and magnified the Divinity to which
it was united; and this privilege was reserved solely to
most holy Mary.

On these occasions it often happened that the
Child Jesus in the presence of his most holy Mother
wept and perspired blood, for this happened many times
before his agony in the garden. Then the blessed Lady
would wipe his face interiorly perceiving and knowing
the cause of this agony, namely the loss of the foreknown and of those who would be ungrateful for the
benefits of their Creator and Redeemer and in whom the
works of the infinite power and goodness of the Lord
would be wasted. At other times the blessed Mother
would find Him refulgent with heavenly light and surrounded by angels that sang sweet hymns of praise;
and She was made aware, that the heavenly Father was
pleased in his beloved and Onlybegotten Son (Matth.
17, 5). All these wonders commenced from the time
when at the age of one year He began to walk, witnessed only by his most holy Mother, whose heart was
to be the treasure-house of his wonders. The works of
love, praise and worshipful gratitude, his petitions for
the human race, all exceed my ability to describe. I must
refer the understanding of it to the faith and piety of the
Christians.

Many of the children of Heliopolis gathered
around the Child Jesus, as it is natural with children of
similar age and condition. Since they were free from

great malice and were not given to inquire, whether He was more than man, but freely admitted the heavenly light, the Master of truth welcomed them as far as was befitting. He instilled into them the knowledge of God and of the virtues; He taught and catechised them in the way of eternal life, even more abundantly than the adults. As his words were full of life and strength, He won their hearts and impressed his truths so deeply upon them, that all those, who had this good fortune, afterwards became great and saintly men; for in the course of time they ripened in themselves the fruit of this heavenly seed sown so early into their souls.

The Child Jesus reached the end of his seventh year while in Egypt, which was also the term set by the eternal Wisdom for his mysterious sojourn in that land. In order that the prophecies might be fulfilled, it was necessary that He return to Nazareth. This decree the eternal Father intimated to his most holy Son on a certain day in the presence of his holy Mother and while She was with Him in prayer. She saw it mirrored in his deified soul and She saw how He submitted to it in obedience to the Father. Therein the great Lady joined Him, although they had already become better acquainted and habituated to their present abode than to their own native city of Nazareth. Neither the Mother nor the Son made known to saint Joseph this new decree of heaven. But in that very night the angel of the Lord spoke to him in his sleep, as Matthew relates (Matth. 2, 19), and bade him take the Child and its Mother and return to the land of Israel; for Herod and those who with him had sought the life of the Child, were dead. So much value does the Almighty set on the proper order in created things, that, though Jesus was the true God and his Mother so highly exalted above saint

Joseph in sanctity, He did not permit the arrangements of this journey to proceed from his Son nor from his Mother, but from saint Joseph, who was the head of this Family. God intended to teach all mortals, that He wishes all things to be governed by the natural order set up by his Providence; and that the inferiors and subjects of the mystical body of the Church, even though they may excel in virtue and in certain other respects, must obey and submit to their superiors and prelates in the visible order.

They departed for Palestine in the company of angels as on their way thence. The great Queen sat on the ass with the divine Child on her lap and saint Joseph walked afoot, closely following the Son and Mother. On account of the loss of such great Benefactors their acquaintances and friends were very sorrowful at the news of their departure; with incredible weeping and sighing they saw Them leave, knowing and loudly complaining, that they were now losing all their consolation and refuge in their necessities. If the divine power had not interfered, the holy Family would have found great difficulty in leaving Heliopolis; for its inhabitants began to feel the night of their miseries secretly setting upon their hearts at the parting of the Sun, which had dispersed and brightened its darkness (John 1, 9). In traversing the inhabited country they passed through some towns of Egypt, where They scattered their graces and blessings. The news of their passage spreading about, all the sick, the afflicted and disconsolate gathered to seek Them out, and they found themselves relieved in body and soul. Many of the sick were cured, many demons were expelled without their knowing who it was that thus hurled them back to hell. Yet they felt the divine power, which compelled them and wrought such blessings among men.

They reached Nazareth, their home, for the Child was to be called a Nazarene. They found their former humble house in charge of the devout cousin of saint Joseph, who, as I have mentioned in the twelfth chapter of the third book, had offered to serve him while our Queen was absent in the house of Elisabeth. Before They had left Judea for Egypt, saint Joseph had written to this woman, asking her to take care of the house and what it contained. They found it all in good condition and his cousin received Them with great joy on account of her love for the great Queen, though at the same time she did not know of her dignity. The heavenly Lady entered with her Son and saint Joseph, and immediately She prostrated Herself in adoration of the Lord and in thanksgiving for having led Them, safe from the cruelty of Herod, to this retreat, and preserved Them in the dangers of their banishment and their long and arduous journeys. Above all did She render thanks for having returned in company with her Son, now grown both in years and in grace and virtue (Luke 2, 40).

Taking counsel with her divine Child She proceeded to set up a rule of life and regulate her pious practices; not that She had failed to observe a rule of life on her journey; for the most prudent Lady, in imitation of her Son, had always observed the most perfect order according to circumstances. But being now peacefully settled in her home She wished to include many exercises, which on the journey were impossible. Her greatest solicitude was always to co-operate with her most holy Son for the salvation of souls which was the work most urgently enjoined upon Her by the eternal Father. Toward this most high end our Queen directed all her practices in union with the Redeemer, and this was their constant occupation, as we shall see in the course of this second part. The holy Joseph also ordered his occupations and his work so as most worthily to earn sustenance for the divine Child and his Mother as well as for himself. That which in other sons of Adam is considered a punishment and a hardship was to this holy Patriarch a great happiness. For while others were condemned to sustain their natural life by the labor of their hands in the sweat of their brows, saint Joseph was blessed and consoled beyond measure to know, that he had been chosen by his labor and sweat to support God himself and his Mother, to whom belonged heaven and earth and all that they contain (Esther 13, 10).

The Queen of the angels herself undertook to pay the debt of gratitude due to saint Joseph for his labors and solicitude. Accordingly She provided his meals and attended to his comforts with incredible care and most loving gratitude. She was obedient to him in all things and humbled Herself before Him as if She were his handmaid and not his spouse, or, what is more, not the Mother of the Creator and Lord of all. She accounted Herself unworthy of existence and of being suffered to walk upon the earth; for She thought it just, that She should be in want of all things. In the consciousness of having been created out of nothing and therefore unable to make any return for either this benefit or, according to her estimation, for any of the others, She established in Herself such a rare humility, that She thought Herself less than the dust and unworthy to mingle with it. For the least favor She gave admirable thanks to the Lord, as to the first cause and origin of them all, and to creatures as to the instruments of his bounty. To some She gave thanks because they conferred favors upon Her, to others because they had denied them; and to others again because they bore with Her in patience.

She acknowledged Herself as indebted to all of them, though She filled them with the blessings of sweetness and placed Herself at the feet of all, seeking ingenious means and artifices to let no instant and no occasion pass for practicing the most perfect and exalted virtues to the admiration of the angels and the pleasure and the delight of the Most High.

WORDS OF THE QUEEN

My daughter, while journeying at the command of the Lord from one country to another and during the works enjoined upon me, my heart was never troubled nor my spirit cast down; for I always held myself prepared to fulfill entirely the will of God. Although the Lord made known to Me his high ends, yet this was not always done at the beginning, thus permitting me to endure so much the greater sufferings; for in obeying the Lord no further reason is necessary than that the Lord Creator so commands and disposes. The souls must accustom themselves to look for this motive alone and to learn solely to please the Lord, without distinguishing between fortunate or unfortunate events and without looking to their own inclinations. In this kind of wisdom I wish that thou advance. In imitation of me and to satisfy thy obligations toward my most holy Son, do thou receive prosperity or adversity in this mortal life with unmoved countenance and with equanimity and peace of mind. Let not the one grieve, nor the other vainly rejoice thee; but attend only to all that which the Almighty ordains according to his pleasure.

Human life is interwoven thus variously with both kinds of events; some of them according, others contrary to the likings of mortals; some which they abhor, others which they desire. As the human heart is limited

and narrow it immoderately inclines to extremes, bound-
lessly desiring what it loves and likes, and, on the other
hand, grieving and sorrowing at what it abhors and dis-
likes.   These changeful moods and fluctuations create
danger for all or many virtues.   The disorderly love for
one creature which it cannot attain, moves the soul presently to desire another, expecting a balm for its disappointment in the former.   And if it is successful, the
soul becomes involved and flurried in the desire of retaining what it possesses, thus casting itself by these
velleities into still greater disorders and passions.   Attend,
therefore, dearest, to this danger and attack it at the root
by preserving thy heart independent and riveted only on
the divine Providence, without ever allowing it to incline
toward what it desires or longs for, or to abhor what
is painful to it.   Let the will of the Lord be thy only
delight and joy.   Let neither thy desires draw thee on,
nor thy fears dishearten thee.   Let not thy exterior occupations, and much less thy regard or attention to creatures, ever impede thee or divert thee from thy holy
exercises, attending always to my example.   Seek thou
lovingly and diligently to follow in my footsteps.

BOOK FIVE

Concerning the Perfection with which the most Holy Mary copied and imitated the Activity of the Soul of Christ; how the Incarnate Word instructed Her in the Laws of grace, the Articles of Faith, the Sacraments, the Ten Commandments; and with what Alacrity and Noble Promptitude She Corresponded. Also concerning the Death of Saint Joseph, the Preaching of Saint John, the Fasting and the Baptism of our Redeemer, the call of the First Disciples and the Baptism of the Virgin Mary, our Blessed Lady

---

CHAPTER I.

INTERIOR TRIALS OF MARY; JESUS IN THE TEMPLE.

Already Jesus, Mary and Joseph had settled in Nazareth and thus changed their poor and humble dwelling into a heaven. In order to describe the mysteries and sacraments which passed between the divine Child and his purest Mother before his twelfth year and later on, until his public preaching, many chapters and many books would be required; and in them all, I would be able to relate but the smallest part in view of the vastness of the subject and the insignificance of such an ignorant woman as I am. Even with the light given me by this great Lady I can speak of only a few incidents and must leave the greater part unsaid. It is not possible or befitting to us mortals to comprehend all these mysteries in this life, since they are reserved for the future life.

Shortly after their return from Egypt to Nazareth the Lord resolved to try his most holy Mother in the same manner as He had tried Her in her childhood as the first-born Daughter of the new Law of grace, the most perfect copy of his ideals and the most pliant material, upon which, as on liquid wax, should be set the seal of his doctrine of holiness, so that the Son and the Mother might be the two true tablets of the new law of the world (Exod. 31, 18). For this purpose of the infinite wisdom He manifested to Her all the mysteries of the evangelical law and of his doctrine; and this was the subject of his instructions from the time of their return from Egypt until his public preaching, as we shall see in the course of this history. In these hidden sacraments the incarnate Word and his holy Mother occupied themselves during the twenty-three years of their stay in Nazareth. As all this concerned the heavenly Mother alone (whose life the holy Evangelists did not profess to narrate), the writers of the Gospel made no mention of it, excepting that which was related of the Child Jesus, when, in his twelfth year, he was lost in Jerusalem. During all those years Mary alone was the disciple of Christ.

In order to rear in the heart of the purest Virgin this edifice of holiness to a height beyond all that is not God, the Lord laid its foundations accordingly, trying the strength of her love and of all her other virtues. For this purpose the Lord withdrew Himself, causing Her to lose Him from her sight, which until then had caused Her to revel in continual joy and delight. I do not wish to say, that the Lord left Her bodily; but, still remaining with Her and in Her by an ineffable presence and grace, He hid Himself from her interior sight and suspended the tokens of his most sweet affection. The heavenly Lady in the meanwhile knew not the inward cause of this behavior, as the Lord gave Her no explanation. Moreover her divine Son, without any forewarning showed Himself very reserved and withdrew from her society. Many times He retired and spoke but few words to Her, and even these with great earnestness and majesty.

This unannounced and unexpected change was the crucible in which the purest gold of the love of our Queen was cleansed and assayed. Surprised at what was happening, She immediately took refuge in the humble opinion She had of Herself, deeming Herself unworthy of the vision of the Lord, who now had hidden Himself. She attributed it all to her want of correspondence and to her ingratitude for the blessings She had obtained from the most generous and exalted Father of mercies. The most prudent Queen did not feel so much the privation of his delightful caresses, as the dread of having displeased Him and of having fallen short in his service. This was the arrow that pierced Her heart with grief. One filled with such true and noble love could not feel less; for all delight of love is founded in the pleasure and satisfaction given by the lover to the one beloved, and therefore He cannot rest, when he suspects that the beloved is not contented or pleased. The loving sighs of his Mother were highly pleasing to her most holy Son. He was enamored with Her anew and the tender affection of his only and chosen One wounded his heart (Cant. 4, 9). But whenever the sweet Mother sought Him out in order to hold converse with Him He continued to show exterior reserve. Just as the flame of a forge or a conflagration is intensified by the application of insufficient water, so the flame of love in the heart of the sweetest Mother was fanned to an intenser blaze by this adversity.

The single-hearted Dove exercised Herself in heroic acts of all the virtues. She humbled Herself below the dust; She reverenced Her Son in deepest adoration; She blessed the Father, thanking Him for his admirable works and blessings and conforming Herself to his wishes and pleasure; She sought to know his will in order to fulfill it in all things; She unceasingly renewed her acts of faith, hope and burning love; and in all her actions and in all circumstances this most fragrant spike-nard gave forth the odor of sweetness for Him, the King of kings, who rested in her heart as in his flowery and perfumed couch (Cant. 1, 11). She persevered in her tearful prayers, with continual sighing and longing from her inmost heart; She poured forth her prayers in the presence of the Lord and recounted her tribulation before the throne of the God (Ps. 141, 3).

Upon the request of the loving Mother saint Joseph had made a couch, which She covered with a single blanket and upon which the Child Jesus rested and took his sleep; for from the time in which He had left the cradle, when they were yet in Egypt, He would not accept of any other bed or of more covering. Although He did not stretch Himself out on this couch, nor even always made use of it, He sometimes reclined in a sitting posture upon it, resting upon a poor pillow made of wool by the same Lady. When She spoke of preparing for Him a better resting-place, her most holy Son answered, that the only couch upon which He was to be stretched out, was that of his Cross, in order to teach men by his example (I Pet. 2, 21), that no one can enter eternal rest by things beloved of Babylon and that to suffer is our true relief in mortal life. Thence-forward the heavenly Lady imitated Him in this manner of taking rest with new earnestness and attention.

Thirty days passed in this conflict; and they equalled many ages in the estimation of Her, who deemed it impossible to live even one moment without the love and without the Beloved of her soul. After such delay (according to our way of speaking), the heart of the Child Jesus could no longer contain itself or resist further the immense force of his love for his sweetest Mother; for also the Lord suffered a delightful and wonderful violence in thus holding Her in such a suspense and affliction. It happened that the humble and sovereign Queen one day approached her Son Jesus, and, throwing Herself at his feet, with tears and sighs coming from her inmost heart, spoke to Him as follows: "My sweetest Love and highest Good, of what account am I, the insignificant dust and ashes, before thy vast power? What is the misery of a creature in comparison with thy endless affluence? In all things Thou excellest our lowliness and thy immense sea of mercy overwhelms our imperfections and defects. If I have not been zealous in serving Thee, as I am constrained to confess, do Thou chastise my negligence and pardon it. But let me, my Son and Lord, see the gladness of thy countenance, which is my salvation and the wished-for light of my life and being. Here at thy feet I lay my poverty, mingling it with the dust, and I shall not rise from it until I can again look into the mirror, which reflects my soul."

These and other pleadings, full of wisdom and most ardent love, the great Queen poured humbly forth before her most holy Son. And as his longings to restore Her to his delights were even greater than those of the blessed Lady, He pronounced with great sweetness these few words: "My Mother, arise." As these words were pronounced by Him, who is Himself the Word of the eternal Father, it had such an effect, that the heavenly Mother was instantly transformed and elevated into a most exalted ecstasy, in which She saw the

Divinity by an abstractive vision. In it the Lord received Her with sweetest welcome and embraces of a Father and Spouse, changing Her tears into rejoicing, her sufferings into delight and her bitterness into highest sweetness. The Lord manifested to Her great secrets of the scope of his new evangelical law. Wishing to write it entirely into her purest heart, the most holy Trinity appointed and destined Her as his first-born Daughter and the first disciple of the incarnate Word and set Her up as the model and pattern for all the holy Apostles, Martyrs, Doctors, Confessors, Virgins and other just of the new Church and of the law of grace, which the incarnate Word was to establish for the Redemption of man.

Some days after our Queen and Lady with her most holy Son and saint Joseph had settled in Nazareth, the time of the year in which the Jews were obliged to present themselves before the Lord in the temple of Jerusalem, was at hand. This commandment obliged the Jews to this duty three times each year, as can be seen in Exodus and Deuteronomy. But it obliged only the men, not the women (Exod. 23, 17); therefore the women could go or not, according to their devotion; for it was neither commanded nor prohibited to them. The heavenly Lady and her spouse conferred with each other as to what they should do in this regard. The holy husband much desired the company of the great Queen, his wife, and of her most holy Son; for he wished to offer Him anew to the eternal Father in the temple. The most pure Mother also was drawn by her piety to worship the Lord in the temple; but as in things of that kind She did not permit Herself to decide without the counsel and direction of the incarnate Word, her Teacher, She asked his advice upon this matter. They finally arranged, that two times a year saint Joseph was to go to Jerusalem by himself, while on the third occasion They would go together. The Israelites visited the temple on the feast of the Tabernacles (Deut. 16, 13), the feast of the Weeks, or Pentecost, and the feast of the unleavened Breads or the Pasch of the preparation. To this latter the sweetest Jesus, most pure Mary, and Joseph went up together. It lasted seven days and during that time happened what I shall relate in the next chapter. For the other solemnities saint Joseph went alone, leaving the Child and the Mother at home.

As I have said, Mary and Joseph repeated their visit to the temple at the feast of the unleavened Bread every year. Also when the divine Child was twelve years old and when it was time to allow the splendors of his inaccessible and divine light to shine forth, They went to the temple for this feast (Luke 2, 42). This festival of the unleavened Bread lasted seven days, according to the command of the divine law; and the more solemn days were the first and the last. On this account our heavenly Pilgrims remained in Jerusalem during the whole week, spending their time in acts of worship and devotion as the rest of the Jews, although on account of the sacraments connected with each of Them their worship and devotion was entirely different and greatly exalted above that of the others. The blessed Mother and holy Joseph received during these days favors and blessings beyond the conception of the human mind.

Having thus spent all the seven days of the feast They betook themselves on their way home to Nazareth. When his parents departed from Jerusalem and were pursuing their way homeward, the Child Jesus withdrew from them without their knowledge. For this purpose the Lord availed Himself of the separation of the men and women, which had become customary among the pilgrims for reasons of decency as well as for greater recollection during their return homeward. The children which accompanied their parents were taken in charge promiscuously either by the men or the women, since their company with either was a matter of indifference. Thus it happened that saint Joseph could easily suppose that the Child Jesus had remained with his most holy Mother, with whom He generally remained. The thought that She would go without Him was far from his mind, since the heavenly Queen loved and delighted in Him more than any other creature human or angelic. The great Lady did not have so many reasons for supposing that her most holy Son was in the company of saint Joseph: but the Lord himself so diverted her thoughts by holy and divine contemplations, that She did not notice his absence at first. When afterwards She became aware of her not being accompanied by her sweetest and beloved Son, She supposed that the blessed Joseph had taken Him along and that the Lord accompanied his foster-father for his consolation.

Thus assured, holy Mary and Joseph pursued their home journey for an entire day, as saint Luke tells us. As the pilgrims proceeded onwards they gradually thinned out, each taking his own direction and joining again with his wife or family. The most holy Mary and saint Joseph found themselves at length in the place where they had agreed to meet on the first evening after leaving Jerusalem. When the great Lady saw that the Child was not with saint Joseph and when the holy Patriarch found that He was not with his Mother, the two were struck dumb with amazement and surprise for quite a while. Both, governed in their judgment by their most profound humility, felt overwhelmed with self-reproach at their remissness in watching over their most holy Son and thus blamed themselves for his absence; for neither of them had any suspicion of the mysterious manner in which He had been able to elude their vigilance. After a time they recovered somewhat from their astonishment and with deepest sorrow took counsel with each other as to what was to be done (Luke 2, 45). The loving Mother said to saint Joseph: "My Spouse and my master, my heart cannot rest, unless we return with all haste to Jerusalem in order to seek my most holy Son." This they proceeded to do, beginning their search among their relations and friends, of whom, however, none could give them any information or any comfort in their sorrow; on the contrary their answers only increased their anxiety, since none of them had so much as seen their Son since their departure from Jerusalem.

Thus this sincerest Dove persevered in her tears and groans without cessation or rest, without sleeping or eating anything for three whole days. Although the ten thousand angels accompanied Her in corporeal forms and witnessed her affliction and sorrow, yet they gave Her no clue to find her lost Child. On the third day the great Queen resolved to seek Him in the desert where saint John was; for since She saw no indications that Archelaus had taken Him prisoner, She began to believe more firmly, that her most holy Son was with saint John. When She was about to execute her resolve and was on the point of departing for the desert, the holy angels detained Her, urging Her not to undertake the journey, since the divine Word was not there. She wanted also to go to Bethlehem, in the hope of finding Him in the cave of the Nativity; but this the holy angels likewise prevented, telling Her that He was not so far off. Although the blessed Mother heard these answers and well perceived that the holy angels knew the whereabouts of the Child Jesus, She was so considerate and reserved in her humility and prudence, that She gave no response, nor asked where She could find Him; for She understood that they withheld this information by command of the Lord. With such magnanimous reverence did the Queen of the angels treat the sacraments of the Most High and of his ministers and ambassadors (II Mach. 2, 9). This was one of the occasions in which the greatness of her queenly and magnanimous heart was made manifest.

Not all the sorrows suffered by all the martyrs ever reached the height of the sorrows of most holy Mary in this trial; nor will the patience, resignation and tolerance of this Lady ever be equalled, nor can they; for the loss of Jesus was greater to Her than the loss of anything created, while her love and appreciation of Him exceeded all that can be conceived by any other creature. Since She did not know the cause of the loss, her anxiety was beyond all measure, as I have already said. Moreover, during these three days the Lord left Her to her natural resources of nature and of grace, deprived of special privileges and favors; for, with the exception of the company and intercourse with the angels, He suspended all the other consolations and blessings so constantly vouchsafed to her most holy soul. From all this we can surmise what sorrow filled the loving heart of the heavenly Mother. But, O prodigy of holiness, prudence, fortitude and perfection! in such unheard of affliction and sorrow She was not disturbed, nor lost her interior or exterior peace, nor did She entertain a thought of anger or indignation, nor allowed Herself any improper movement or expression, nor fell into any excess of grief or annoyance, as is so common in great affliction with other children of Adam, who allow all their passions and faculties to be disarranged, yea even in small difficulties! The Mistress of all virtue held all her powers in heavenly order and harmony; though her sorrow was without comparison great and had pierced her inmost heart, She failed not in reverence and in the praise of the Lord, nor ceased in her prayers and petitions for the human race, and for the finding of her most holy Son.

With this heavenly wisdom and with greatest diligence She sought Him for three successive days, roaming through the streets of the city, asking different persons and describing to the daughters of Jerusalem the marks of her Beloved, searching the byways and the open squares of the city and thereby fulfilling what was recorded in the Canticles of Solomon (Cant. 5, 10). Some of the women asked Her what were the distinctive marks of her lost and only Son; and She answered in the words of the Spouse: "My Beloved is white and ruddy, chosen out of thousands." One of the women, hearing Her thus describing Him, said: "This Child, with those same marks, came yesterday to my door to ask for alms, and I gave some to Him; and his grace and beauty have ravished my heart. And when I gave Him alms, I felt myself overcome by compassion to see a Child so gracious in poverty and want." These were the first news the sorrowful Mother heard of her Onlybegotten in Jerusalem. A little respited in her sorrow, She pursued her quest and met other persons, who spoke of Him in like manner. Guided by this information She directed her steps to the hospital of the city, thinking that among the afflicted She would find the Spouse and the Originator of patient poverty among his own legitimate brethren and friends (Matth. 5, 40). Inquiring at that place, She was informed that a Child of that description had paid his visits to the inmates, leaving some alms and speaking words of much consolation to the afflicted.

The report of these doings of her Beloved caused sentiments of sweetest and most tender affection in the heart of the heavenly Lady, which She sent forth from her inmost heart as messengers to her lost and absent Son. Then the thought struck Her, that, since He was not with the poor, He no doubt tarried in the temple, as in the house of God and of prayer. The holy angels encouraged Her and said: "Our Queen and Lady, the hour of thy consolation is at hand: soon wilt Thou see the Light of thy eyes; hasten thy footsteps and go to the temple." The glorious patriarch saint Joseph at this moment again met his Spouse, for, in order to increase their chance of finding the divine Child, they had separated in different directions. By another angel he had now been likewise ordered to proceed to the temple. During all these three days he had suffered unspeakable sorrow and affliction, hastening from one place to another, sometimes without his heavenly Spouse, sometimes with Her. He was in serious danger of losing his life during this time, if the hand of the Lord had not strengthened Him and if the most prudent Lady had not consoled him and forced him to take some food and rest. His sincere and exquisite love for the divine Child made him so anxious and solicitous to find Him, that he would have allowed himself no time or care to take nourishment for the support of nature.

It was very near to the gate of the city, that the divine Child turned and hastened back through the streets. Foreseeing in his divine fore-knowledge all that was to happen, He offered it up to his eternal Father for the benefit of souls. He asked for alms during these three days in order to ennoble from that time on humble mendicity as the first-born of holy poverty. He visited the hospitals of the poor, consoling them and giving them the alms which He had received; secretly He restored bodily health to some and spiritual health to many, by enlightening them interiorly and leading them back to the way of salvation. On some of the benefactors, who gave Him alms, He performed these wonders with a greater abundance of grace and light; thus fulfilling from that time on the promise, which He was afterwards to make to his Church; that he who gives to the just and to the prophet in the name of a prophet, shall receive the reward of the just (Matth. 10, 41).

Having thus busied Himself with these and other works of his Father, He betook Himself to the temple. On the day which the Evangelist mentions it happened that also the rabbis, who were the learned and the teachers of the temple, met in a certain part of the buildings in order to confer among themselves concerning some doubtful points of holy Scriptures. On this occasion the coming of the Messias was discussed; for on account of the report of the wonderful events, which had spread about since the birth of the Baptist and the visit of the Kings of the east, the rumor of the coming of the Redeemer and of his being already in the world, though yet unknown, had gained ground among the Jews. They were all seated in their places filled with the sense of authority customary to those who are teachers and considered as learned. The Child Jesus came to the meeting of these distinguished men; and He that was the King of kings, and Lord of lords (Apoc. 19, 16), the infinite Wisdom itself (I Cor. 1, 24), and who corrects the wise (Wis. 7, 15), presented Himself before the teachers of this world as an humble disciple, giving them to understand that He had come to hear the discussion and inform Himself on the question treated of, namely: whether the Messias was already come, or, if not, concerning the time in which He should come into the world. Therefore the divine Child presented Himself to the disputants, manifesting the grace poured out over his lips (Ps. 44, 3). He stepped into their midst with exceeding majesty and grace, as one who would propose some doubt or solution. By his pleasing appearance He awakened in the hearts of these learned men a desire to hear Him attentively.

The scribes and learned men who heard Him were all dumbfounded. Convinced by his arguments they looked at each other and in great astonishment asked: "What miracle is this? and what prodigy of a boy! Whence has He come and who is the Child?" But though thus astonished, they did not recognize or suspect who it was, that thus taught and enlightened them concerning such an important truth. During this time and before Jesus had finished his argument, his most holy Mother and saint Joseph her most chaste spouse arrived, just in time to hear him advance his last arguments. When He had finished, all the teachers of the law arose with stupendous amazement. The heavenly Lady, absorbed in joy, approached her most loving Son and in the presence of the whole assembly, spoke to Him the words recorded by saint Luke: "Son, why hast Thou done so to us? Behold thy father and I have sought Thee sorrowing" (Luke 2, 48). This loving complaint the heavenly Mother uttered with equal reverence and affection, adoring Him as God and manifesting her maternal affliction. The Lord answered: "Why is it that you sought Me? Did you not know that I must be about my Father's business?"

The Evangelist says that they did not understand the mystery of these words (Luke 2, 50); for it was hidden at the time to most holy Mary and saint Joseph. And for two reasons; on the one hand, the interior joy of now reaping what they had sown in so much sorrow, and the visible presence of their precious Treasure, entirely filled the faculties of their souls; and on the other hand, the time for the full comprehension of what had just been treated of in this discussion had not yet arrived for them. Moreover, for the most solicitous Queen there was another hindrance just at that time, and it was, that the veil, concealing the interior of her most holy Son had again intervened and was not removed until some time later. The learned men departed, commenting in their amazement upon the wonderful event, by which they had been privileged to hear the teaching of eternal Wisdom, though they did not recognize it. Being thus left almost alone, the blessed Mother, embracing Him with maternal affection, said to Him: "Permit my longing heart, my son, to give expression to its sorrow and pain; so that it may not die of grief as long as it can be of use to Thee. Do not cast me off from thy sight; but accept me as thy slave. If it was my negligence, which deprived me of thy presence, pardon me and make me worthy of thy company, and do not punish me with thy absence." The divine Child received Her with signs of pleasure and offered Himself as her Teacher and Companion until the proper time should arrive. Thus was the dove-like and affectionate heart of the great Lady appeased, and They departed for Nazareth.

They arrived at Nazareth, where they occupied themselves in what I shall record later on. The evangelist Luke compendiously mentions all the mysteries in few words, saying the Child Jesus was subject to his

parents, namely most holy Mary and saint Joseph, and
that his heavenly Mother noted and preserved within
her heart all these events; and that Jesus advanced in
wisdom, and age, and grace with God and men (Luke
2, 52), of which, as far as my understanding goes, I
will speak later on. Just now I wish only to mention,
that the humility and obedience of our God and Master
toward his parents were the admiration of the angels.
But so was also the dignity and excellence of his most
blessed Mother, who thus merited that the incarnate God
should subject Himself and resign Himself to her care; so
much so, that She, with the assistance of saint Joseph,
governed Him and disposed of Him as her own.

To the obedience and subjection of her most holy
Son the great Lady on her part responded by heroic
works. Among her other excellences She conceived as
it were an incomprehensible humility and a most heartfelt gratitude for having regained the companionship of
her Son. This blessing, of which the heavenly Queen
deemed Herself unworthy, vastly increased in her most
pure heart her love and her anxiety to serve her divine
Son. And She was so constant in showing her gratitude,
so punctual and solicitous to serve Him, kneeling before
Him and lowering Herself to the dust, that it excited
the admiration of the highest seraphim. Moreover, She
sought with the closest attention to imitate Him in all
his actions as they became known to Her and exerted
Herself most anxiously to copy them and reproduce
them in her own life. The plenitude of her perfection
wounded the heart of our Christ and Lord, and, according to our way of speaking, held him bound to Her with
chains of invincible love. (Osee 11, 4). His being thus
bound as God and as Son to this heavenly Princess,
gave rise to such an interchange and divine reciprocity of

intense love, as surpasses all created understanding. For into the ocean of Mary's soul entered all the vast floods of the graces and blessings of the incarnate Word; and this ocean did not overflow (Eccles. 1, 7), because it contained the depth and expanse necessary to receive them.

WORDS OF THE QUEEN.

My daughter, all the works of my most holy Son and my own actions are full of mysterious instruction and doctrine for the mortals who contemplate them diligently and reverently. The Lord absented Himself from me in order that, seeking Him in sorrow and tears, I might find Him again in joy and with abundant fruits for my soul. I desire that thou imitate me in this mystery and seek Him with such earnestness, as to be consumed with a continual longing without ever in thy whole life coming to any rest until thou holdst Him and canst lose Him no more (Can. 5, 4). In order that thou mayest understand better this sacrament of the Lord, remember, that the infinite Wisdom made men capable of his eternal felicity and placed them on the way to this happiness, but left them in doubt of its attainment, as long as they have not yet acquired it and thus filled them with joyful hope and sorrowful fear of its final acquisition. This anxiety engenders in men a lifelong fear and abhorrence of sin, by which alone they can be deprived of beatitude and thus prevent them from being ensnared and misled by the corporeal and visible things of this earth. This anxiety the Creator assists by adding to the natural reasoning powers, faith and hope, which are the spurs of their love toward seeking and finding their last end. Besides these virtues and others infused at Baptism He sends his inspirations and helps to keep awake the soul in the absence of its Lord and to prevent forgetfulness of Him and of itself while deprived of his amiable presence. Thus it pursues the right course until it finds the great goal, where all its inclinations and longing shall be satiated.

Hence thou canst estimate the listless ignorance of mortals and how few stop to consider the mysterious order of the creation and justification and all the works of the Almighty tending toward this exalted end. From this forgetfulness flow so many evils endured by men while they appropriate so many earthly goods and deceitful delights, as if they could ever find in them their ultimate end. The height of perversity opposed to the order of the Creator, is that mortals in this transitory and short life rejoice in visible things as if they were their last end, while they ought, on the contrary, to make use of creatures to gain, not to lose, the highest Good. Do thou, therefore, my dearest, be mindful of this dangerous human folly. Consider all delights and joys of the world as insanity, its laughing as sorrow, sensible enjoyment as self deceit, as the source of foolishness, which intoxicates the heart and hinders and destroys all true wisdom. Live in constant and holy fear of losing eternal life and rejoice in nothing except in the Lord until thou obtainest full possession of Him.

CHAPTER II.

I have already said in former chapters, that our great Lady was the first and specially privileged Disciple of her most holy Son, chosen among all creatures as the model of the new evangelical law and its Author, according to which He was to mould all the saints of the new law and judge of all the results of the Redemption. In regard to Her the incarnate Word proceeded like a most skillful artist, who understands the art of painting and all that pertains to it most thoroughly; who, throwing all his powers into one chosen work, seeks to gain from it alone renown and fame as from the full exposition of his art. It is certain that all the holiness and glory of the saints was the result of the love and merits of Christ: (Eph. 2, 3) but in comparison with the excellence of Mary, they seem insignificant and as it were only rough sketches; for in all the saints are found defects (I John 1, 8). But this living image of the Onlybegotten was free from all imperfections; and the first strokes of his pencil in Her were of greater beauty than the last touches in the highest angels and saints. She is the model for all the perfection of holiness and virtues of all his elect, and the utmost limit to which the love of Christ can proceed in mere creatures. No one received any grace or glory that most holy Mary could not receive, and She received all that others were incapable of receiving; and her most blessed Son gave to Her all that She could receive and that He could communicate.

The multitude and variety of the saints silently enhance the Artificer of their great sanctity, and the greatness of the highest is made more conspicuous by the beauty of the lowest: but all of them together are a glorification of most holy Mary. For by her incomparable holiness they are all surpassed and they all partake of so much the greater felicity as they imitate Her, whose holiness redounds over all. If the most pure Mary has reached the highest pinnacle in the ranks of the just, She may also on this very account be considered as the instrument or the motive power through which the saints themselves have reached their station. As we must judge of her excellence (even if only from afar), by the labor which Christ the Lord applied for her formation, let us consider what labor He spent upon Her and how much upon the whole Church. To establish and to enrich his Church He deemed it sufficient to spend only three years in preaching, selecting the Apostles, teaching the people, and inculcating the evangelical law by his public life; and this was amply sufficient to accomplish the work enjoined upon Him by the eternal Father and to justify and sanctify all the true believers. But in order to stamp upon his most holy Mother the image of his holiness, He consumed not three years, but ten times three years, engaging in this work with all the power of his divine love, without ever ceasing hour after hour to add grace to grace, gifts to gifts, blessings to blessings, and holiness to holiness. And at the end of all this He still left Her in a state, in which He could continue to add excellence after his Ascension to his eternal Father as I will describe in the third part. Our reason is unbalanced, our words fail at the greatness of this incomparable Lady; for She is elect as the sun (Cant. 6, 9); and her effulgence cannot be borne by terrestrial eyes, nor comprehended by any earthly creatures.

Christ our Redeemer began to manifest his designs in regard to his heavenly Mother after they had come back from Egypt to Nazareth, as I have already mentioned; and from that time on He continued to follow up his purpose in his quality as Teacher and as the divine Enlightener in all the mysteries of the Incarnation and Redemption. After they returned from Jerusalem in his twelfth year, the great Queen had a vision of the Divinity, not an intuitive vision, but one consisting of intellectual images; one very exalted and full of the new influences of the Divinity and of the secrets of the Most High. She was especially enlightened in regard to the decrees of the divine Will concerning the law of grace, which was now to be established by the incarnate Word, and concerning the power, which was given to Him in the consistory of the most blessed Trinity. At the same time She saw how for this purpose the eternal Father consigned to His Son the seven-sealed book, of which saint John speaks (Apoc. 5, 1), and how none could be found either in heaven or on earth, who could unseal and open it, until the Lamb broke its seals by his Passion and Death and by his doctrines and merits. For in this figure God wished to intimate, that the secret of this book was nothing else than the new law of the Gospel and the Church founded upon it in this world.

Then the heavenly Queen saw in spirit, that, by the decree of the most blessed Trinity, She was to be the first one to read and understand this book; that her Onlybegotten was to open it for Her and manifest it all to Her, while She was to put it perfectly into practice; that She was the first one, who was to accompany the Word, and who was to occupy the first place next to Him on the way to heaven, which He had opened up for mortals and traced out in this book. In Her, as his true

Mother, was to be deposited this new Testament. She saw how the Son of the eternal Father and of Herself accepted this decree with great pleasure; and how his sacred humanity obeyed it with ineffable joy on her account.

She issued from this ecstatic vision and betook Herself to her most holy Son, prostrating Herself at his feet and saying: "My Lord, my Light and my Teacher, behold thy unworthy Mother prepared for the fulfillment of thy wishes admit me anew as thy disciple and servant and make use of me as the instrument of thy wisdom and power. Execute in me thy pleasure and that of thy eternal Father." Her most holy Son received Her with the majesty and authority of a divine Teacher and instructed Her in most exalted mysteries. In most persuasive and powerful words He explained to Her the profoundest meanings of the works enjoined upon Him by the eternal Father in regard to the Redemption of man, the founding of the Church and the establishment of the new evangelical law. He declared and reaffirmed, that in the execution of these high and hidden mysteries She was to be his Companion and Coadjutrix, receiving and enjoying the first-fruits of grace; and that therefore She, the most pure Lady, was to follow Him in his labors until his death on the Cross with a magnanimous and well prepared heart in invincible and unhesitating constancy. He added heavenly instruction such as enabled Her to prepare for the reception of the whole evangelical Law, the understanding and practice of all its precepts and counsels in their highest perfection. Other sacramental secrets concerning his works in this world the Child Jesus manifested to his most blessed Mother on this occasion. And the heavenly Lady met all his words and intentions with profound humility, obedience, reverence, thanksgiving and most ardent love.

WORDS OF THE QUEEN.

The Most High who in sheer goodness and bounty has given existence to all creatures and denies his providential care to none, faithfully supplies all souls with light, by which they can enter into the knowledge of Him and of eternal life provided they do not of their own free will prevent and obscure this light by sin or give up the quest of the kingdom of heaven. To the souls whom according to his secret judgments, He calls to his Church, He shows himself still more liberal. For with the grace of Baptism He infuses into them not only those virtues, which are called essentially infused and which the creature cannot merit by its own efforts; but also those, which are accidentally infused and which it can merit by its own labors and efforts. These the Lord gives freely beforehand, in order that the soul may be more prepared and zealous in the observance of his holy Law. In other souls, in addition to the common light of faith, the Lord in his clemency grants supernatural gifts of knowledge and virtue for the better understanding of the evangelical mysteries and for the more zealous practice of good works. In this kind of gifts He has been more liberal with thee than with many generations; obliging thee thereby to distinguish thyself in loving correspondence due to Him and to humble thyself before Him to the very dust.

In order that thou mayest be well instructed and informed, I wish to warn thee as a solicitous and loving Mother of the cunning of satan for the destruction of these works of the Lord. From the very moment in which mortals begin to have the use of their reason, each one of them is followed by many watchful and relentless demons. For as soon as the souls are in a position to raise their thoughts to the knowledge of their God and commence the practice of the virtues infused by Baptism, these demons, with incredible fury and astuteness, seek to root out the divine seed; and if they cannot succeed in this, they try to hinder its growth, and prevent it from bringing forth fruit by engaging men in vicious, useless, or trifling things. Thus they divert their thoughts from faith and hope and from the pursuit of other virtues, leading them to forget that they are Christians and diverting their attention from the knowledge of God and from the mysteries of the Redemption and of life eternal. Moreover the same enemy instills into the parents a base neglectfulness and carnal love for their offspring; and he incites the teachers to carelessness, so that the children find no support against evil in their education, but become depraved and spoiled by many bad habits, losing sight of virtue and of their good inclinations and going the way of perdition.

But the most kind Lord does not forget them in this danger and He renews in them his holy inspirations and special helps. He supplies them with the holy teachings of the Church by his preachers and ministers. He holds out to them the aid of the Sacraments and many other inducements to keep them on the path of life. That those who walk in the way of salvation are the smaller number, is due to the vice and depraved habits imbibed in youth and nourished in childhood. For that saying of Deuteronomy is very true: "As the days of thy youth, so also shall thy old age be" (Deut. 33, 25). Hence the demons gain courage and increase their tyrannical influence over souls in the early years of man's life, hoping that they will be able to induce men to commit so much the greater and the more frequent sins in later years, the more they have succeeded in drawing them into small and insignificant faults in their childhood. By these they draw them on to a state of blind presumption; for with each sin the soul loses more and more the power of resistance, subjects itself to the demon, and falls under the sway of its tyrannical enemies. The miserable yoke of wickedness is more and more firmly fastened upon it; it is trodden underfoot by its own iniquity and urged onward under the sway of the devil from one precipice to another, from abyss to abyss (Ps. 41, 8) : a chastisement merited by all those, that allow themselves to be overcome by evil-doing in the beginning. By these means Lucifer has hurled into hell so great a number of souls and continues so to hurl them every day, rising up in his pride against the Almighty. In this manner has he been able to introduce into the world his tyrannical power, spreading among men forgetfulness of death, judgment, heaven and hell, and casting so many nations from abyss to abyss of darkness and bestial errors, such as are contained in the heresies and false sects of the infidels. Do thou therefore beware of this terrible danger, my daughter, and let not the memory of the law of thy God, his precepts and commands, and the truths of the Catholic Church and the doctrines of the Gospels ever fail in thy mind. Let not a day pass in which thou dost not spend much time in meditating upon all these; and exhort thy religious and all those who listen to thee to do the same. For thy enemy and adversary is laboring with ceaseless vigilance to obscure thy understanding in forgetfulness of the divine law, seeking to withdraw thy will, which is a blind faculty, from the practice of justification. This, thou knowest, consists in acts of living faith, trustful hope, ardent love, all coming from a contrite and humble heart (Ps. 50, 19).

CHAPTER III.

The more our limited discourse seeks to make clear and extol the mysterious works of Christ, our Redeemer, and of his most holy Mother, the more evident it becomes, that mere human words are far from being able to compass the greatness of these sacraments; for, as Ecclesiasticus says, they surpass all our words of praise (Ecclus. 4, 33). Nor can we ever fathom or compass them, and there will always remain many greater secrets than those we have sought to explain. For those which we do explain are very insignificant, and we do not deserve to comprehend, nor to speak about the few, which we attempt to fathom. Inadequate is the intellect of the highest seraphim to weigh and pierce the secrets that passed between Jesus and Mary during the years in which They lived together. Especially is this true of the years, of which I am now speaking, during which the Teacher of life instructed Her in everything that was to happen in the law of grace; namely, how much this new law was to accomplish in this the sixth age of the world, which includes these sixteen hundred and fifty-seven years and all the unknown future until the end of the World. In all this the most blessed Lady was instructed in the school of her divine Son; for He foretold Her all by word of mouth, pointing out the time and place of each event, the kingdoms and provinces of their history during the existence of the Church.

All these hidden sacraments ordinarily transpired in that humble oratory of the Queen, where the greatest of all mysteries, the Incarnation of the divine Word in her virginal womb, had taken place. Though it was such a narrow and poorly furnished room, consisting merely of the bare and rude walls, yet it enclosed the grandeur of Him who is immense and shed forth all the majesty and sacredness, which since then is attached to the rich temples and innumerable sanctuaries of the world. In this holy of holies the Highpriest of the new Law ordinarily performed his prayers, which always concluded with fervent intercessions for men. At these times also He spoke to his Virgin Mother about all the works of the Redemption and communicated to Her the rich gifts and treasures of grace, which He had come to shower upon the children of light in the new Testament and in his holy Church. Many times did He beseech his eternal Father not to allow the sins and the ingratitude of men to hinder their Redemption. As Christ in his foreknowledge was always conscious of the sins of the human race and of the damnation of so many thankless souls, the thought of dying for them caused Him to sweat blood many times on these occasions. Although the Evangelists because they never intended to relate all the events of his life, mention this sweating of blood but once before his Passion, it is certain that this happened many times and in the presence of his most holy Mother; and this has been intimated to me several times.

During prayer our blessed Master sometimes assumed a kneeling posture, sometimes He was prostrate in the form of a cross or at other times raised in the air in this same position which He loved so much. In the presence of his Mother He was wont to pray: "O most blessed Cross! When shall thy arms receive mine, when shall I rest on thee and when shall my arms, nailed to thine, be spread to welcome all sinners? (Matth. 9, 13). But as I came from heaven for no other purpose than to invite them to imitate Me and associate with Me, they are even now and forever open to embrace and enrich all men. Come then, all ye that are blind, to the light. Come ye poor, to the treasures of my grace. Come, ye little ones, to the caresses and delights of your true Father. Come, ye afflicted and worn out ones, for I will relieve and refresh you (Matth. 11, 28). Come, ye just, since you are my possession and inheritance. Come all ye children of Adam, for I call upon you all. I am the way, the truth and the life (13, 6), and I will deny nothing that you desire to receive. My eternal Father, they are the works of thy hands, do not despise them; for I will offer Myself as a sacrifice on the Cross, in order to restore them to justice and freedom. If they be but willing I will lead them back to the bosom of thy elect and to their heavenly kingdom, where thy name shall be glorified."

At all these prayers the beloved Mother was present, and in her purest soul, as in the purest crystal, the light of the Onlybegotten was reflected. His interior and exterior prayers re-echoed in Her, causing Her to imitate his petitions and prayers in the same postures. When the great Lady for the first time saw Him sweat blood, her maternal heart was transfixed with sorrow and filled with astonishment at the effects caused in Christ, our Lord, by the sins and ingratitudes committed by men, foreseen by the Lord and known to Her. In the anguish of her heart She turned to her fellow mortals and exclaimed: "O children of men! Little do ye understand how highly the Lord esteems his image and likeness in you! For, as the price of your salvation, He offers his own blood and deems it little to shed all of it for you. O could I but unite your wills with mine, in order that I might bring you to love and obey Him! Blessed by his right hand be the grateful and the just among men, who will be faithful children of their Father! Let those be filled with light and with the treasures of grace, who will respond to the ardent desires of my Lord in regard to their salvation. Would that I could be the insignificant slave of the children of Adam and thereby induce and assist them to put an end to their sins and their own damnation! Lord and Master! Life and light of my soul! Who can be so hard of heart and so hostile to himself, that he should not feel himself urged on by thy blessings? Who can be so ungrateful and so unheedful, as to ignore thy most burning love? How can my heart bear with men, who, being so favored by thy bounty, are so coarse and rebellious? O children of Adam! Turn your inhuman cruelty upon me. Afflict and insult me as much as you will, only pay my beloved Lord the reverence and love which you owe to his endearments. Thou, my Son and Lord, art Light of light, Son of the eternal Father, figure of his substance (Heb. 1, 3), as everlasting, as immense, as infinite as He, equal to Him in essence and attributes, being with Him one God and one supreme Majesty (John 10, 30). Thou art chosen among thousands (Cant. 5, 10), beautiful above all the sons of men, holy, innocent and without defect of any kind. How then, eternal God, can mortals ignore the object of their most noble love? the Principle, which gives them existence? the End wherein consists their eternal true happiness? O that I could give my life in order that all might escape their error!"

Many other sentiments of burning love, far beyond the powers of my heart and tongue, this heavenly

Lady uttered in her dove-like sincerity; and in this love, and in profoundest reverence, She wiped the sweat from the face of her sweetest Son. At other times She found Him in quite a different condition, shining with glory and transfigured as afterwards on mount Tabor (Matth. 17, 2), in the midst of a great multitude of angels, who adored Him and in the sweet harmony of their voices gave praise and thanksgiving to the Onlybegotten of the Father made man. These celestial voices our blessed Lady heard and She joined hers with them. At other times this happened while He was not transfigured; for the divine will ordained that the sensitive part of the divine humanity of the Word should sometimes have this solace, while at other times it should enjoy also the transfiguring overflow of the glory of the soul into the body; yet this only at great intervals. But whenever the heavenly Mother found Him in this state and beheld his glorified body, or when She heard the hymns of the angels, She participated in these delights to such an extent, that, if her spirit had not been so strong, and if her Lord and Son had not fortified Her, She would have lost all her natural powers; and even as it was, the holy angels had to support the failing strength of her body on those occasions.

Many times, when her divine Son was in one of these states of suffering or joy, and was praying to the eternal Father or, as it were, conferring with Him concerning the highest mysteries of the Redemption, the Person of the Father approved or conceded his petitions for the relief of men, or showed to the most holy humanity of Christ the secret decrees of predestination, reprobation or condemnation of some souls. All this our blessed Lady heard, humbling Herself to the dust. With unequaled reverence and fear She adored the Omnipotent, and accompanied her Son in his prayers, petitions and thanksgivings, offered up to the eternal Father for mankind in praise of all his inscrutable judgments. Such secrets and mysteries the most prudent Virgin conferred in her heart, and stored them up in her memory, converting them into the material and nourishment of her fiery love. None of these blessings and secret favors were in her unprofitable or fruitless. To all of them She corresponded according to the inmost desires of her Lord. In all of them She fulfilled the highest intentions of the Almighty, and all his works found due response from Her as far as was possible from a mere creature.

WORDS OF THE QUEEN.

My daughter, one of the reasons why men should call me Mother of mercy, is the knowledge of my loving desire, that all be satiated with the flood of grace and taste the sweetness of the Lord as I myself. I call and invite all to come with me to the fountain of the Divinity. Let the most poor and afflicted approach, for if they respond and follow me, I will offer them my protection and help, and I will intercede for them with my Son and obtain for them the hidden manna, which will give to them nourishment and life (Apoc. 2, 27). Deny thyself and put off all the works of human weakness, and, by the true light, which thou hast received concerning the works of my Son and my own, contemplate and study thyself in this mirror, in order to arrive at that beauty, which the highest King seeks in thee.

Since this is the most powerful means for perfection in thy works, I wish that thou write this advice into thy heart. Whenever thou must perform any interior or exterior work, consider beforehand whether what thou art going to say or do corresponds with the doings of thy Lord, and whether thou hast the intention thereby to honor thy Lord and benefit thy neighbor.   As soon as thou art sure that this is thy motive, execute thy undertaking in union with Him and in imitation of Him; but if thou findest not this motive let the undertaking rest.   This was my invariable course in pursuing the imitation of my Lord and Teacher; though in me there was no reluctance toward the good, but only the desire of imitating Him perfectly.   In this imitation consists the fruit of his holy teaching, in which He urges us to do, what is most pleasing and acceptable to the eternal God.   Moreover from this day on be mindful not to undertake any work, not to speak or even think any of anything, without first asking my permission and consulting with me as thy Mother and Teacher. And as soon as I answer thee give thanks to the Lord; if I do not answer after continued inquiry, I promise and assure thee on the part of the Lord, that He will, nevertheless, give thee light as to what will be according to his most perfect will.   In all things, however, subject thyself to the guidance of thy spiritual director, and never forget this practice!

CHAPTER IV.

THE HAPPY DEATH OF SAINT JOSEPH.

Already eight years saint Joseph had been exercised by his infirmities and sufferings, and his noble soul had been purified more and more each day in the crucible of affliction and of divine love. As the time passed his bodily strength gradually diminished and he approached the unavoidable end, in which the stipend of death is paid by all of us children of Adam (Heb. 9, 27). In like manner also increased the care and solicitude of his heavenly Spouse, our Queen, assisting and serving him with unbroken punctuality. Perceiving, in her exalted wisdom, that the day and hour for his departure from this cumbrous earth was very near, the loving Lady betook Herself to her blessed Son and said to Him: "Lord God Most High, Son of the eternal Father and Savior of the world, by thy divine light I see the hour approaching which thou hast decreed for the death of thy servant Joseph. I beseech Thee, by thy ancient mercies and by thy infinite bounty, to assist him in that hour by thy almighty power. Let his death be as precious in thy eyes, as the uprightness of his life was pleasing to Thee, so that he may depart in peace and in the certain hope of the eternal reward to be given to him on the day in which Thou shalt open the gates of heaven for all the faithful. Be mindful, my Son, of the humility and love of thy servant; of his exceeding great merits and virtues; of the fidelity and solicitude by which this just man has supported Thee and me, thy humble handmaid, in the sweat of his brow."

Our Savior answered: "My Mother, thy request is pleasing to me, and the merits of Joseph are acceptable in my eyes. I will now assist him and will assign him a place among the princes of my people (Ps. 115, 15), so high that he will be the admiration of the angels and will cause them and all men to break forth in highest praise. With none of the human born shall I do as with thy spouse." The great Lady gave thanks to her sweetest Son for this promise; and, for nine days and nights before the death of saint Joseph he uninterruptedly enjoyed the company and attendance of Mary or her divine Son. By command of the Lord the holy angels, three times on each of the nine days, furnished celestial music, mixing their hymns of praise with the benedictions of the sick man. Moreover, their humble but most precious dwelling was filled with the sweetest fragrance and odors so wonderful that they comforted not only saint Joseph, but invigorated all the numerous persons who happened to come near the house.

One day before he died, being wholly inflamed with divine love on account of these blessings, he was wrapped in an ecstasy which lasted twenty-four hours. The Lord himself supplied strength for this miraculous intercourse. In this ecstasy he saw clearly the divine Essence, and, manifested therein, all that he had believed by faith: the incomprehensible Divinity, the mystery of the Incarnation and Redemption, the militant Church with all its Sacraments and mysteries. The blessed Trinity commissioned and assigned him as the messenger of our Savior to the holy Patriarchs and Prophets of limbo; and commanded him to prepare them for their issuing forth from this bosom of Abraham to eternal rest and happiness. All this most holy Mary saw reflected in the soul of her divine Son together with all the other mysteries, just as they had been made known to her beloved spouse, and She offered her sincerest thanks for all this to her Lord.

When saint Joseph issued from this ecstasy his face shone with wonderful splendor and his soul was entirely transformed by his vision of the essence of God. He asked his blessed Spouse to give him her benediction; but She requested her divine Son to bless him in her stead, which He did. Then the great Queen of humility, falling on her knees, besought saint Joseph to bless Her, as being her husband and head. Not without divine impulse the man of God fulfilled this request for the consolation of his most prudent Spouse. She kissed the hand with which he blessed Her and asked him to salute the just ones of limbo in her name. The most humble Joseph, sealing his life with an act of self-abasement, asked pardon of his heavenly Spouse for all his deficiencies in her service and love and begged Her to grant him her assistance and intercession in this hour of his passing away. The holy man also rendered humblest thanks to her Son for all the blessings of his life and especially for those received during this sickness. The last words which saint Joseph spoke to his Spouse were: "Blessed art Thou among all women and elect of all the creatures. Let angels and men praise Thee; let all the generations know, praise and exalt thy dignity; and may in Thee be known, adored and exalted the name of the Most High through all the coming ages; may He be eternally praised for having created Thee so pleasing in his eyes and in the sight of all the blessed spirits. I hope to enjoy thy sight in the heavenly fatherland."

Then this man of God, turning toward Christ, our Lord, in profoundest reverence, wished to kneel before Him. But the sweetest Jesus, coming near, received him in his arms, where, reclining his head upon them, Joseph said: "My highest Lord and God, Son of the eternal Father, Creator and Redeemer of the World, give thy blessing to thy servant and the works of thy hand; pardon, O most merciful King, the faults which I have committed in thy service and intercourse. I extol and magnify Thee and render eternal and heartfelt thanks to Thee for having, in thy ineffable condescension, chosen me to be the spouse of thy true Mother; let thy greatness and glory be my thanksgiving for all eternity." The Redeemer of the world gave him his benediction, saying: "My father, rest in peace and in the grace of my eternal Father and mine; and to the Prophets and Saints, who await thee in limbo, bring the joyful news of the approach of their redemption." At these words of Jesus, and reclining in his arms, the most fortunate saint Joseph expired and the Lord himself closed his eyes. At the same time the multitude of the angels, who attended upon their King and Queen, intoned hymns of praise in loud and harmonious voices. By command of the Lord they carried his most holy soul to the gathering-place of the Patriarchs and Prophets, where it was immediately recognized by all as clothed in the splendors of incomparable grace, as the putative father and the intimate friend of the Redeemer, worthy of highest veneration. Conformably to the will and mandate of the Lord, his arrival spread inutterable joy in this countless gathering of the saints by the announcement of their speedy rescue.

It is necessary to mention that the long sickness and sufferings which preceded the death of saint Joseph was not the sole cause and occasion of his passing away; for with all his infirmities he could have extended the term of his life, if to them he had not joined the fire of the intense love within his bosom. In order that his death might be more the triumph of his love than of the effects of original sin, the Lord suspended the special and miraculous assistance by which his natural forces were enabled to withstand the violence of his love during his lifetime. As soon as this divine assistance was withdrawn, nature was overcome by his love and the bonds and chains, by which this most holy soul was detained in its mortal body, were at once dissolved and the separation of the soul from the body in which death consists took place. Love was then the real cause of the death of saint Joseph, as I have said above. This was at the same time the greatest and most glorious of all his infirmities for in it death is but a sleep of the body and the beginning of real life.

The most fortunate of men, saint Joseph reached an age of sixty years and a few days. For at the age of thirty-three he espoused the blessed Virgin and he lived with Her a little longer than twenty-seven years as her husband. When saint Joseph died, She had completed the half of her forty-second year; for She was espoused to saint Joseph at the age of fourteen (as stated in the first part, book second, chapter twenty-second). The twenty-seven years of her married life completed her forty-first year, to which must be added the time from the eighth of September until the death of her blessed spouse. The Queen of heaven still remained in the same disposition of natural perfection as in her thirty-third year; for, as already stated in the thirteenth chapter of this book, She showed no signs of decline, or of more advanced age, or of weakness, but always remained in that same most perfect state of womanhood. She felt the natural sorrow due to the death of saint Joseph; for She loved him as her spouse, as a man pre-eminent in perfection and holiness, as her protector and benefactor.

I perceive a certain difference in the graces given to this great Patriarch and those vouchsafed to other saints; for many saints were endowed with graces and gifts that are intended not for the increase of their own sanctity, but for the advance of the service of the Most High in other souls; they were, so to say, gifts and graces freely given and not dependent upon the holiness of the receiver. But in our blessed Patriarch all the divine favors were productive of personal virtue and perfection; for the mysterious purpose, toward which they tended and helped along, was closely connected with the holiness of his own life. The more angelic and holy he grew to be, so much the more worthy was he to be the spouse of most holy Mary, the depository and treasure-house of heavenly sacraments. He was to be a miracle of holiness, as he really was. This marvelous holiness commenced with the formation of his body in the womb of his Mother. In this the providence of God himself interfered, regulating the composition of the four radical humors of his body with extreme nicety of proportion and securing for him that evenly tempered disposition which made his body a blessed earth fit for the abode of an exquisite soul and well-balanced mind (Wisdom 8, 19). He was sanctified in the womb of his mother seven months after his conception, and the leaven of sin was destroyed in him for the whole course of his life, never having felt any impure or disorderly movement. Although he did not receive the use of his reason together with this first sanctification, which consisted principally in justification from original sin, yet his mother at the time felt a wonderful joy of the Holy Ghost. Without understanding entirely the mystery she elicited great acts of virtue and believed that her Son, or whomever she bore in her womb, would be wonderful in the sight of God and men.

The holy child Joseph was born most beautiful and perfect of body and caused in his parents and in his relations an extraordinary delight, something like that caused by the birth of saint John the Baptist, though the cause of it was more hidden. The Lord hastened in him the use of his reason, perfecting it in his third year, endowing it with infused science and augmenting his soul with new graces and virtues. From that time the child began to know God by faith, and also by natural reasoning and science, as the cause and Author of all things. He eagerly listened and understood profoundly all that was taught him in regard to God and his works. At this premature age he already practiced the highest kinds of prayer and contemplation and eagerly engaged in the exercise of the virtues proper to his youth; so that, at the time when others come to the use of reason, at the age of seven years or more, saint Joseph was already a perfect man in the use of it and in holiness. He was of a kind disposition, loving, affable, sincere, showing inclinations not only holy but angelic, growing in virtue and perfection and advancing toward his espousal with most holy Mary by an altogether irreproachable life.

For the confirmation and increase of his good qualities was then added the intercession of the blessed Lady; for as soon as She was informed that the Lord wished Her to enter the married state with him, She earnestly besought the Lord to sanctify saint Joseph and inspire him with most chaste thoughts and desires in conformity with her own. The Lord listened to her prayer and permitted Her to see what great effects his right hand wrought in the mind and spirit of the patriarch saint Joseph. They were so copious, that they cannot be described in human words. He infused into his soul the most perfect habits of all the virtues and gifts. He balanced anew all his faculties and filled him with grace, confirming it in an admirable manner. In the virtue and perfection of chastity the holy spouse was elevated higher than the seraphim; for the purity, which they possessed without body, saint Joseph possessed in his earthly body and in mortal flesh; never did an image of the impurities of the animal and sensible nature engage, even for one moment, any of his faculties. This freedom from all such imaginations and his angelic simplicity fitted him for the companionship and presence of the most Pure among all creatures, and without this excellence he would not have been worthy of so great a dignity and rare excellence.

Also in the other virtues he was wonderfully distinguished, especially in charity; for he dwelt at the fountainhead of that living water, which flows on to eternal life (John 4, 14); he was in close proximity to that sphere of fire and was consumed without resistance. The best that can be said of the charity of our saint is what I have already said in the preceding chapter; namely, that his love of God was really the cause of his mortal sickness and of his death. The manner of his death was a privilege of his singular love, for his sweet sighs of love surpassed and finally put an end to those of his sickness, being far more powerful. As the objects of his love, Christ and his Mother, were present with him always and as both of Them were more closely bound to him than to any of the woman-born, his most pure and faithful heart was unavoidably consumed by the loving effects of such a close union. Blessed be the

Author of such great wonders and blessed be the most fortunate of mortals, saint Joseph, who so worthily corresponded to their love. He deserves to be known and extolled by all the generations of men and all nations, since the Lord has wrought such things with no other man and to none has He shown such love.

The divine visions and revelations vouchsafed to saint Joseph, I have particularly mentioned in the course of this history (Vol. II 422, 423, 471); but there were many more than can be described, and the greatest of them all was his having known the mysteries of the relation between Christ and his Mother and his having lived in their company for so many years as the putative father of the Lord and as the true spouse of the Queen of heaven. But I have been informed concerning certain other privileges conferred upon saint Joseph by the Most High on account of his great holiness, which are especially important to those who ask his intercession in a proper manner. In virtue of these special privileges the intercession of saint Joseph is most powerful: first, for attaining the virtue of purity and overcoming the sensual inclinations of the flesh; secondly, for procuring powerful help to escape sin and return to the friendship of God; thirdly, for increasing the love and devotion to most holy Mary; fourthly, for securing the grace of a happy death and protection against the demons in that hour; fifthly, for inspiring the demons with terror at the mere mention of his name by his clients; sixthly, for gaining health of body and assistance in all kinds of difficulties; seventhly, for securing issue of children in families. These and many other favors God confers upon those who properly and with good disposition seek the intercession of the spouse of our Queen, saint Joseph. I beseech all the faithful children of the Church to be very devout to him and they will experience these favors in reality, if they dispose themselves as they should in order to receive and merit them.

WORDS OF THE QUEEN.

My daughter, although thou hast described my spouse, saint Joseph, as the most noble among the princes and saints of the heavenly Jerusalem; yet neither canst thou properly manifest his eminent sanctity, nor can any of the mortals know it fully before they arrive at the vision of the Divinity. Then all of them will be filled with wonder and praise as the Lord will make them capable of understanding this sacrament. On the last day, when all men shall be judged, the damned will bitterly bewail their sins, which prevented them from appreciating this powerful means of their salvation, and availing themselves, as they easily could have, of this intercessor to gain the friendship of the just Judge. The whole human race has much undervalued the privileges and prerogatives conceded to my blessed spouse and they know not what his intercession with God is able to do. I assure thee, my dearest, that he is one of the greatly favored personages in the divine presence and has immense power to stay the arms of divine vengeance.

I desire that thou be very thankful to the divine condescension for vouchsafing thee so much light and knowledge regarding this mystery, and also for the favor which I am doing thee therein. From now on, during the rest of thy mortal life, see that thou advance in devotion and in hearty love toward my spouse, and that thou bless the Lord for thus having favored him with such high privileges and for having rejoiced me so much in the knowledge of all his excellences. In all thy necessities thou must avail thyself of his intercession.

Thou shouldst induce many to venerate him and see that thy own religious distinguish themselves in their devotion to him. That which my spouse asks of the Lord in heaven is granted upon the earth and on his intercession depend many and extraordinary favors for men, if they do not make themselves unworthy of receiving them. All these privileges were to be a reward for the amiable perfection of this wonderful saint and for his great virtues; for divine clemency is favorably drawn forth by them and looks upon saint Joseph with generous liberality, ready to shower down its marvelous mercies upon all those who avail themselves of his intercession.

CHAPTER V.

The love of our great Queen and Lady for her
divine Son must always remain the standard by which
we must measure as well her actions as all her emotions
either of joy or sorrow during her earthly life. But we
cannot measure the greatness of her love itself, nor can
the holy angels measure it, except by the love which they
see in God by the intuitive vision. All that can ever be
expressed by our inadequate words, similes and analogies,
is but the least portion of what this heavenly furnace of
love really contained. For She loved Jesus as the Son
of the eternal Father, equal to Him in essence and in
all the divine attributes and perfections; She loved Him
as her own natural Son, Son to Her in as far as He was
man, formed of her own flesh and blood; She loved Him
because as man He was the Saint of saints and the meritorious cause of all other holiness (Dan. 11, 24). He
was the most beautiful among the sons of men (Ps.
44, 3). He was the most dutiful Son of his Mother, her
most magnificent Benefactor; since it was He, that by his
sonship, had raised Her to the highest dignity possible
among creatures. He had exalted Her among all and
above all by the treasures of his Divinity and by conferring upon Her the dominion over all creation together
with favors, blessings and graces, such as were never to
be conferred upon any other being.

These motives and foundations of her love

were established and as it were, all comprehended in the wisdom of the heavenly Lady, together with many others, which only her exalted knowledge could appreciate. In her heart there was no hindrance of love, since it was the most innocent and pure; She was not ungrateful, because her profoundest humility urged Her to a most faithful correspondence; She was not remiss, because in Her the most abundant grace wrought with all its efficacy; She was not slow or careless, since She was filled with most zealous and diligent fervor; not forgetful, since her most faithful memory was constantly fixed upon the blessings received and upon the reasons and the precepts of deepest love. She moved in the sphere of the divine love itself, since She remained in his visible presence and attended the school of divine love of her Son, copying his works and his doings in his very company. Nothing was wanting to this peerless One among lovers for entertaining love without limitation of measure or manner. This most beautiful Moon then, being at its fullness, and looking into this Sun of justice just as it had risen like a divine aurora from height to height and reached the noontide splendor of the most clear light of grace; this Moon, Mary, detached from all material creatures and entirely transformed by the light of this Sun, having experienced on her part all the effects of his reciprocal love, favors and gifts, in the height of her blessedness, at a time when the loss of all these blessings in her Son made it most arduous, heard the voice of the eternal Father, calling Her as once He had called upon her prototype, Abraham, and demanding the deposit of all her love and hope, her beloved Isaac (Gen. 22, 1).

The most prudent Mother was not unaware, that the time of her sacrifice was approaching; for her sweetest Son had already entered the thirtieth year of his life and the time and place for satisfying the debt He had assumed was at hand. But in the full possession of the Treasure, which represented all her happiness, Mary was still considering its loss as far off, not having as yet had its experience. The hour therefore drawing near, She was wrapt in a most exalted vision and felt that She was being called and placed in the presence of throne of the most blessed Trinity. From it issued a voice of wonderful power saying to Her: "Mary, my Daughter and Spouse, offer to Me thy onlybegotten Son in sacrifice." By the living power of these words came to Her the light and intelligence of the Almighty's will, and in it the most blessed Mother understood the decree of the Redemption of man through the Passion and Death of her most holy Son, together with all that from now on would happen in the preaching and public life of the Savior. As this knowledge was renewed and perfected in Her, She felt her soul overpowered by sentiments of subjection, humility, love of God and man, compassion and tenderest sorrow for all that her Son was to suffer.

But with an undismayed and magnanimous heart She gave answer to the Most High: "Eternal King and omnipotent God of infinite wisdom and goodness, all that has being outside of Thee exists solely for thy mercy and greatness, and Thou art undiminished Lord of all. How then dost Thou command me, an insignificant wormlet of the earth, to sacrifice and deliver over to thy will the Son, whom thy condescension has given me? He is thine, eternal Father, since from all eternity before the morning star Thou hast engendered Him (Ps. 109, 3), and Thou begettest Him and shalt beget Him through all the eternities; and if I have clothed Him in the form of servant (Philip 2, 7) in my womb and from my own blood, and if I have nourished his humanity at my breast and ministered to it as a Mother: this most holy humanity is also thy property, and so am I, since I have received from Thee all that I am and that I could give Him. What then can I offer to Thee, that is not more thine than mine? I confess, most high King, that thy magnificence and beneficence are so liberal in heaping upon thy creatures thy infinite treasures, that in order to bind Thyself to them Thou wishest to receive from them as a free gift, even thy own onlybegotten Son, Him whom Thou begettest from thy own substance and from the light of thy Divinity. With Him came to me all blessings together and from his hands I received immense gifts and graces (Wis. 7, 11); He is the Virtue of my virtue, the Substance of my spirit, Life of my soul and Soul of my life, the Sustenance of all my joy of living. It would be a sweet sacrifice, indeed, to yield Him up to Thee who alone knowest his value; but to yield Him for the satisfaction of thy justice into the hands of his cruel enemies at the cost of his life, more precious than all the works of creation; this indeed, most high Lord, is a great sacrifice which Thou askest of his Mother. However let not my will but thine be done. Let the freedom of the human race be thus bought; let thy justice and equity be satisfied; let thy infinite love become manifest; let thy name be known and magnified before all creatures. I deliver Him over into thy hands before all creatures. I deliver over into thy hands my beloved Isaac, that He may be truly sacrificed; I offer my Son, the Fruit of my womb, in order that, according to the unchangeable decree of thy will, He may pay the debt contracted not by his fault, but by the children of Adam, and in order that in his Death He may fulfill all that thy holy Prophets, inspired by Thee, have written and foretold."

This sacrifice with all that pertained to it, was the greatest and the most acceptable that ever had been made to the eternal Father since the creation of the world, or ever will be made to the end, outside of that made by his own Son, the Redeemer; and hers was most intimately connected with and like to that, which He offered. If the greatest charity consists in offering one's life for the beloved, without a doubt most holy Mary far surpassed this highest degree of love toward men, as She loved Her Son much more than her own life. For in order to preserve the life of her Son, She would have given the lives of all men, if She had possessed them, yea and countless more. Among men there is no measure by which to estimate the love of that heavenly Lady, and it can be estimated only by the love of the eternal Father for his Son. As Christ says to Nikodemus (John 15, 7): so God loved the world, that He gave his only Son in order that none of those who believed in Him might perish; so this might also be said in its degree of the love of the Mother of mercy and in the same way do we owe to Her proportionately our salvation. For She also loved us so much, that She gave her only Son for our salvation; and if She had not given it in this manner, when it was asked of Her by the eternal Father on this occasion, the salvation of men could not have been executed by this same decree, since this decree was to be fulfilled on condition, that the Mother's will should coincide with that of the eternal Father. Such is the obligation which the children of Adam owe to most holy Mary.

Having accepted the offering of the great Lady, it was fitting that the most Blessed Trinity should reward and immediately pay Her by some favor, which would comfort Her in her sorrow and manifest more clearly the will of the eternal Father and the reasons for his command. Therefore the heavenly Lady, still wrapped in the same vision and raised to a more exalted ecstasy, in which She was prepared and enlightened in the manner elsewhere described (I, 623), the Divinity manifested Itself to Her by an intuitive and direct vision. In this vision, by the clear light of the essence of God, She comprehended the inclination of the infinite Good to communicate his fathomless treasures to the rational creatures by means of the works of the incarnate Word, and She saw the glory, that would result from these wonders to the name of the Most High. Filled with jubilation of her soul at the prospect of all these sacramental mysteries, the heavenly Mother renewed the offering of her divine Son to the Father; and God comforted Her with the life-giving bread of heavenly understanding, in order that She might with invincible fortitude assist the incarnate Word in the work of Redemption as his Coadjutrix and Helper, according to the disposition of infinite Wisdom and according as it really happened afterwards in the rest of her life.

Then most holy Mary issued forth from this exalted rapture in the description of which I will not further detain myself; for it was accompanied by the same circumstances as the other intuitive visions already mentioned. But by its effects and the strength imparted through it, She was now prepared to separate from her divine Son, who had already resolved to enter upon his fast in the desert in view of receiving his Baptism. He therefore called his Mother and, speaking to Her with the tokens of sweetest love and compassion, He said: "My Mother, my existence as man I derive entirely from thy substance and blood, of which I have taken the form of a servant in thy virginal womb (Phil. 2, 7). Thou also hast nursed Me at thy breast and taken care of Me by thy labors and sweat. For this reason I account Me more thine own and as thy Son, than any other ever acknowledged, or more than any ever will acknowledge himself as the son of his mother. Give Me thy permission and consent toward accomplishing the will of my eternal Father. Already the time has arrived, in which I must leave thy sweet intercourse and company and begin the work of the Redemption of man. The time of rest has come to an end and the hour of suffering for the rescue of the sons of Adam has arrived. But I wish to perform this work of my Father with thy assistance, and Thou art to be my companion and helper in preparing for my Passion and Death of the Cross. Although I must now leave Thee alone, my blessing shall remain with Thee, and my loving and powerful protection. I shall afterwards return to claim thy assistance and company in my labors; for I am to undergo them in the form of man, which Thou hast given Me."

With these words, while both Mother and Son were overflowing with abundant tears, the Lord placed his arms around the neck of the most tender Mother, yet Both maintaining a majestic composure such as befitted these Masters in the art of suffering. The heavenly Lady fell at the feet of her divine Son and, with ineffable sorrow and reverence, answered: "My Lord and eternal God: Thou art indeed my Son and in Thee is fulfilled all the force of love, which I have received of Thee: my inmost soul is laid open to the eyes of thy divine wisdom. My life I would account but little, if I could thereby save thy own, or if I could die for Thee many times. But the will of the eternal Father and thy own must be fulfilled and I offer my own will as a sacrifice for this fulfillment. Receive it, my Son and as Master of all my being; let it be an acceptable offering, and let thy divine protection never be wanting to me. It would be a much greater torment for me, not to be allowed to accompany Thee in thy labors and in thy Cross. May I merit this favor, my Son, and I ask it of Thee as thy true Mother in return for the human form, which Thou hast received of me." The most loving Mother also besought Him to take along some food from the house, or that He allow it to be sent to where He was to go. But the Savior would not consent to anything of the sort, at the same time enlightening his Mother of what was befitting for the occasion. They went together to the door of their poor house, where She again fell at his feet to ask his blessing and kiss his feet. The divine Master gave Her his benediction and then began his journey to the Jordan, issuing forth as the good Shepherd to seek his lost sheep and bring them back on his shoulders to the way of eternal life, from which they had been decoyed by deceit (Luke 15, 5).

When our Redeemer sought saint John in order to be baptized, He had already entered his thirtieth year, although not much of it had yet passed; for He betook Himself directly to the banks of the Jordan, where saint John was baptizing (Matth. 3, 13), and He received Baptism at his hands about thirty days after He had finished the twenty-ninth year of his life on the same day as is set aside for its celebration by the Church. I cannot worthily describe the sorrow of most holy Mary at his departure, nor the compassion of the Savior for Her. All words and description are far too inadequate to manifest what passed in the heart of the Son and Mother. As this was to be part of their meritorious sufferings, it was not befitting that the natural effects of their mutual loves should be diminished. God permitted these effects to work in Them to their full extent, and as far as was compatible with the holiness of both Mother and Son. Our divine Teacher found no relief in hastening his steps toward the goal of our Redemption, to which He was drawn by the force of his immense charity; nor was the thought of what He intended a lessening of the sense of loss, which She sustained at his departure; for all this only made more certain and more conspicuous the torments which He was to undergo. O my dearest Love! Why does not our ingratitude and hardness of heart allow us to meet Thee with a responsive love? Why does not the perfect uselessness of man, and still more, his ingratitude, influence Thee to desist? Without us, O my eternal Goodness and Life, Thou wilt be just as happy without us as with us, just as infinite in perfections, holiness and glory; we can add nothing to that which Thou hast in Thyself, since Thou art entirely independent of creatures. Why then, O my Love, dost Thou so anxiously seek us out and care for us? Why dost Thou, at the cost of thy Passion and the Cross, purchase our happiness? Without doubt, because thy incomprehensible love and goodness esteems it as thy own, and we alone insist in treating our own happiness as alien to Thee and to ourselves.

WORDS OF THE QUEEN.

My daughter, I wish that thou ponder and penetrate more and more this mystery of which thou hast written, so fixing it in thy soul, that thou wilt be drawn to imitate my example at least in some part of it. Consider then, that in the vision of the Divinity which I had on this occasion, I was made to comprehend the high value which the Lord sets upon the labors, the Passion and Death of my Son, and upon all those who were to imitate and follow Jesus in the way of the Cross. Knowing this, I not only offered to deliver my Son over to Passion and Death, but I asked Him to make me his companion and partaker of all his sorrows, sufferings and torments, which request the eternal Father granted. Then, in order to begin following in the footsteps of his bitterness, I besought my Son and Lord to deprive me of interior delights; and this petition was inspired in me by the Lord himself, because He wished it so, and because my own love taught me and urged me thereto. This desire for suffering and the wishes of my divine Son led me on in the way of suffering. He himself because He loved me so tenderly, granted me my desires; for those whom He loves, He chastises and afflicts (Prov. 3, 12). I as his Mother was not to be deprived of this blessed distinction of being entirely like unto Him, which alone makes this life most estimable. Immediately this will of the Most High, this my earnest petition, began to be fulfilled: I began to feel the want of his delightful caresses and He began to treat me with greater reserve. That was one of the reasons, why He did not call me Mother, but Woman, at the marriage-feast at Cana and at the foot of the Cross (John 2, 4, 19, 26); and also on other occasions, when He abstained from words of tenderness. So far was this from being a sign of a diminution of his love, that it was rather an exquisite refinement of his affection to assimilate me to Him in the sufferings which He chose for Himself as his precious treasure and inheritance.

Hence thou wilt understand the ignorance and error of mortals, and how far they drift from the way of light, when, as a rule, nearly all of them strive to avoid labor and suffering and are frightened by the royal and secure road of mortification and the Cross. Full of this deceitful ignorance, they do not only abhor resemblance to Christ's suffering and my own, and deprive themselves of the true and highest blessing of this life; but they make their recovery impossible, since all of them are weak and afflicted by many sins, for which the only remedy is suffering. Sin is committed by base indulgence and is repugnant to suffering sorrow, while tribulation earns the pardon of the just judge. By the bitterness of sorrow and affliction the vapors of sin are allayed; the excesses of the concupiscible and irascible passions are crushed; pride and haughtiness are humiliated; the flesh is subdued; the inclination to evil, to the sensible and earthly creatures, is repressed; the judgment is cleared; the will is brought within bounds and its desultory movements at the call of the passions, are corrected; and, above all, divine love and pity are drawn down upon the afflicted, who embrace suffering with patience, or who seek it to imitate my most holy Son. In this science of suffering are renewed all the blessed riches of the creatures; those that fly from them are insane, those that know nothing of this science are foolish.

CHAPTER VI.

BAPTISM OF CHRIST. HIS FAST. MARY'S DOINGS DURING
THESE EVENTS.

Leaving his beloved Mother in the poor dwelling at Nazareth, our Redeemer, without accompaniment of any human creature, but altogether taken up with the exercise of his most ardent charity, pursued his journey to the Jordan, where, in the neighborhood of a town called Bethany, otherwise called Betharaba, on the farther side of the river, his Precursor was preaching and baptizing. At the first steps from the house, our Redeemer, raising his eyes to the eternal Father, offered up to Him anew with an infinite love, whatever He was now about to begin for the salvation of mankind: his labors, sorrows, passion and death of the Cross, assumed for them in obedience to the eternal Will, the natural grief at parting as a true and loving Son from his Mother and at leaving her sweet company, which for twenty-nine years He had now enjoyed. The Lord of all creation walked alone, without show and ostentation of human retinue. The supreme King of kings and Lord of lords (Apoc. 19, 16), was unknown and despised by his own vassals, vassals so much his own, that they owed their life and preservation entirely to Him. His royal outfit was nothing but the utmost poverty and destitution.

While proceeding on his way to the Jordan our Savior dispensed his ancient mercies by relieving the necessities of body and soul in many of those whom He encountered at different places. Yet this was always

435

done in secret; for before his Baptism He gave no public token of his divine power and his exalted office. Before appearing at the Jordan, He filled the heart of saint John with new light and joy, which changed and elevated his soul. Perceiving these new workings of grace within himself, he reflected upon them full of wonder, saying: "What mystery is this? What presentiments of happiness? From the moment when I recognized the presence of my Lord in the womb of my mother, I have not felt such stirring of my soul as now! Is it possible that He is now happily come, or that the Savior of the world is now near me?" Upon this enlightenment of the Baptist followed an intellectual vision, wherein he perceived with greater clearness the mystery of the hypostatic union of the person of the Word with the humanity and other mysteries of the Redemption. In the fulness of this intellectual light he gave the testimonies, which are recorded by saint John in his Gospel and which occurred while the Lord was in the desert and afterwards, when He returned to the banks of the Jordan. The Evangelist mentions one of these public testimonies as happening at the interpellation of the Jews, and the other when the Precursor exclaimed: "Behold the lamb of God," as I shall narrate later on (John 1, 36). Although the Baptist had been instructed in great mysteries, when he was commanded to go forth to preach and baptize; yet all of them were manifested to him anew and with greater clearness and abundance on this occasion, and he was then notified that the Savior of the world was coming to be baptized.

The Lord then joined the multitude and asked Baptism of saint John as one of the rest. The Baptist knew Him and, falling at his feet, hesitated, saying: "I have need of being baptized, and Thou, Lord, askest

Baptism of me?" as is recorded by saint Matthew. But the Savior answered: "Suffer it to be so now. For so it becometh us to fulfill all justice."

When saint John had finished baptizing our Lord, the heavens opened and the Holy Ghost descended visibly in the form of a dove upon his head and the voice of his Father was heard: "This is my beloved Son, in whom I am well pleased" (Matth. 3, 17). Many of the bystanders heard this voice, namely, those who were not unworthy of such a wonderful favor; they also saw the Holy Ghost descending upon the Savior. This was the most convincing proof which could ever be given of the Divinity of the Savior, as well on the part of the Father, who acknowledged Him his Son, as also in regard to the nature of the testimony given; for without any reserve was Christ manifested as the true God, equal to his eternal Father in substance and in perfection. The Father himself wished to be the first to testify to the Divinity of Christ in order that by virtue of his testimony all the other witnesses might be ratified. There was also another mystery in this voice of the eternal Father: it was as it were a restoration of the honor of his Son before the world and a recompense for his having thus humiliated Himself by receiving the Baptism of the remission of sins, though He was entirely free from fault and never could have upon Him the guilt of sin (Heb. 7, 26).

Let us return now to the main subject of this history, namely, to the occupations of our great Queen and Lady. As soon as her most holy Son was baptized, although She knew by the divine light of his movements, the holy angels who had attended upon their Lord brought Her intelligence of all that had happened at the Jordan; they were those that carried the ensigns or shields of the passion of the Savior, as described in the first part. To celebrate all these mysteries of Christ's Baptism and the public proclamation of his Divinity, the most prudent Mother composed new hymns and canticles of praise and of incomparable thanksgiving to the Most High and to the incarnate Word. All his actions of humility and prayers She imitated, exerting Herself by many acts of her own to accompany and follow Him in all of them. With ardent charity She interceded for men, that they might profit by the sacrament of Baptism and that it might be administered all over the world. In addition to these prayers and hymns of thanksgiving, She asked the heavenly courtiers to help Her in magnifying her most holy Son for having thus humiliated Himself in receiving Baptism at the hands of one of his creatures.

Without delay Christ our Lord pursued his journey from the Jordan to the desert after his Baptism. Only his holy angels attended and accompanied Him, serving and worshipping Him, singing the divine praises on account of what He was now about to undertake for the salvation of mankind. He came to the place chosen by Him for his fast: a desert spot among bare and beetling rocks, where there was also a cavern much concealed. Here He halted, choosing it for his habitation during the days of his fast (Matth. 4, 1). In deepest humility He prostrated Himself upon the ground which was always the prelude of his prayer and that of his most blessed Mother. He praised the eternal Father and gave Him thanks for the works of his divine right hand and for having according to his pleasure afforded Him this retirement. In a suitable manner He thanked even this desert for accepting his presence and keeping Him hidden from the world during the time He was to spend there.

He continued his prayers prostrate in the form of a cross, and this was his most frequent occupation in the desert; for in this manner He often prayed to the eternal Father for the salvation of men.

After the Savior had begun his fast He persevered therein without eating anything for forty days, offering up his fast to the eternal Father as a satisfaction for the disorder and sins to which men are drawn by the so vile and debasing, yet so common and even so much esteemed vice of gluttony. Just as our Lord overcame this vice so He also vanquished all the rest, and He made recompense to the eternal Judge and supreme Legislator for the injuries perpetrated through these vices by men. According to the enlightenment vouchsafed to me, our Savior, in order to assume the office of Preacher and Teacher and to become our Mediator and Redeemer before the Father, thus vanquished all the vices of mortals and He satisfied the offenses committed through them by the exercises of the virtues contrary to them, just as He did in regard to gluttony. Although He continued this exercise during all his life with the most ardent charity, yet during his fast He directed in a special manner all his efforts toward this purpose.

A loving Father, whose sons have committed great crimes for which they are to endure the most horrible punishment, sacrifices all his possessions in order to ward off their impending fate: so our most loving Father and Brother, Jesus Christ, wished to pay our debts. In satisfaction for our pride He offered his profound humility; for our avarice, his voluntary poverty and total privation of all that was his; for our base and lustful inclinations, his penance and austerity; for our hastiness and vengeful anger, his meekness and charity toward his enemies; for our negligence and laziness, his ceaseless labors; for our deceitfulness and our envy, his candid and upright sincerity and truthfulness and the sweetness of his loving intercourse.   In this manner He continued to appease the just Judge and solicited pardon for us disobedient and bastard children; and He not only obtained this pardon for them, but He merited for them new graces and favors, so that they might make themselves worthy of his company and of the vision of his Father and his own inheritance for all eternity. Though He could have obtained all this for us by the most insignificant of his works; yet He acted not like we. He demonstrated his love so abundantly, that our ingratitude and hardness of heart will have no excuse.

In order to keep informed of the doings of our Savior the most blessed Mary needed no other assistance than her continual visions and revelations; but in addition to all these, She made use of the service of her holy angels, whom She sent to her divine Son.   The Lord himself thus ordered it, in order that, by means of these faithful messengers, both He and She might rejoice in the sentiments and thoughts of their inmost hearts faithfully rehearsed by these celestial messengers; and thus They each heard the very same words as uttered by Each, although both Son and Mother already knew them in another way.   As soon as the great Lady understood that our Redeemer was on the way to the desert to fulfill his intention, She locked the doors of her dwelling, without letting any one know of her presence; and her retirement during the time of our Lord's fast was so complete, that her neighbors thought that She had left with her divine Son.   She entered into her oratory and remained there for forty days and nights without ever leaving it and without eating anything, just as She knew was done by her most holy Son. Both of them observed the same course of rigorous fasting. In all his prayers and exercises, his prostrations and genuflections She followed our Savior, not omitting any of them; moreover She performed them just at the same time; for, leaving aside all other occupations, She thus profited by the information obtained from the angels and by that other knowledge, which I have already described. Whether He was present or not, She knew the interior operations of the soul of Christ. All his bodily movements, which She had been wont to perceive with her own senses, She now knew by intellectual vision or through her holy angels.

While the Savior was in the desert He made every day three hundred genuflections, which also was done by our Queen Mary in her oratory; the other portions of her time She spent in composing hymns with the angels, as I have said in the last chapter. Thus imitating Christ the Lord, the Holy Queen co-operated with Him in all his prayers and petitions, gaining the same victories over the vices, and on her part proportionately satisfying for them by her virtues and her exertions. Thus it happened, that, while Christ as our Redeemer gained for us so many blessings and abundantly paid all our debts, most holy Mary, as his Helper and our Mother, lent us her merciful intercession and became our Mediatrix to the fullest extent possible to a mere creature.

Christ the Savior permitted Lucifer to remain under the false impression, that He was a mere human creature though very holy and just; He wished to raise his courage and malice for the contest, for such is the effect of any advantages espied by the devil in his attacks upon the victims of his temptations. Rousing his courage by his own arrogance, he began this battle in the wilderness with greater prowess and fierceness than the demons ever exhibited in their battles with men. Lucifer and his satellites strained all their power and malice, lashing themselves into fury against the superior strength which they soon found in Christ our Lord. Yet our Savior tempered all his actions with divine wisdom and goodness, and in justice and equity concealed the secret source of his infinite power, exhibiting just so much as would suffice to prove Him to be a man so far advanced in holiness as to be able to gain these victories against the infernal foes. In order to begin the battle as man, He directed a prayer to the eternal Father from his inmost soul, to which the intelligence of the demon could not penetrate, saying: "My Father and eternal God, I now enter into battle with the enemy in order to crush his power and humble his pride and his malice against my beloved souls. For thy glory and for the benefit of souls I submit to the daring presumption of Lucifer. I wish thereby to crush his head in order that when mortals are attacked by his temptations without their fault, they may find his arrogance already broken. I beseech Thee, my Father, to remember my battle and victory in favor of mortals assailed by the common enemy. Strengthen their weakness through my triumph, let them obtain victory; let them be encouraged by my example, and let them learn from Me how to resist and overcome their enemies."

During this battle the holy angels that attended upon Christ were hidden from the sight of Lucifer, in order that he might not begin to understand and suspect the divine power of our Savior. The holy spirits gave glory and praise to the Father and the Holy Ghost, who rejoiced in the works of the incarnate Word. The most

blessed Virgin also from her oratory witnessed the
battle in the manner to be described below. The temptation of Christ began on the thirty-fifth day of his fast
in the desert, and lasted to the end of the fast, as related
by the Evangelists. Lucifer assumed the shape of a
man and presented himself before the Lord as a stranger,
who had never seen or known Him before. He clothed
himself in refulgent light, like that of an angel, and,
conjecturing that the Lord after his long fast must be
suffering great hunger, he said to Him: "If Thou be
the Son of God, command that these stones be made
bread" (Matth. 4, 3). By thus cunningly resting his
advice on the supposition of his being the Son of God,
the demon sought some information on what was giving
him the greatest concern. But the Savior of the world
answered only in these few words: "Not in bread alone
doth man live, but in every word that proceedeth from
the mouth of God."

Lucifer found himself repulsed by the force of
this answer and by the hidden power which accompanied
it; but he wished to show no weakness, nor desist from
the contest. The Lord allowed the demon to continue
in his temptation and for this purpose permitted Himself
to be carried by the devil bodily to Jerusalem and to be
placed on the pinnacle of the temple. Here the Lord
could see multitudes of people, though He himself was
not seen by anybody. Lucifer tried to arouse in the
Lord the vain desire of casting Himself down from this
high place, so that the crowds of men, seeing Him un-
hurt, might proclaim Him as a great and wonderful man
of God. Again using the words of the holy Scriptures,
he said to Him: "If Thou be the Son of God, cast
Thyself down, for it is written (Ps. 90, 11): that He
hath given his angels charge over Thee, and in their

hands they shall bear Thee up, lest perhaps Thou dash thy foot against a stone" (Matth. 4, 6). The heavenly spirits who accompanied their King, were full of wonder, that He should permit Lucifer to carry Him bodily in his hands, solely for the benefit of mortal man. With the prince of darkness were gathered innumerable demons; for on that occasion hell was almost emptied of its inhabitants in order to furnish assistance for this enterprise. The Author of wisdom answered: "It is also written: Thou shalt not tempt the Lord thy God" (Deut. 6, 16). While giving these answers the Redeemer of the world exhibited a matchless meekness, profoundest humility, and a majesty so superior to all the attempts of satan, as was of itself alone sufficient to crush Lucifer's arrogance and to cause him torments and confusion never felt before.

Being thus foiled, he attacked our Lord in still another way, seeking to rouse his ambition by offering Him some share in his dominion. For this purpose he took the Lord upon a high mount, from whence could be seen many lands, and said to Him with perfidious daring: "All these will I give to Thee, if falling down, Thou wilt adore me" (Matth. 4, 9). Exorbitant boldness, and more than insane madness and perfidy! Offering to the Lord what he did not possess, nor ever could give, since the earth, the stars, the kingdoms, principalities, riches and treasures, all belong to the Lord, and He alone can give or withhold them when it serves and pleases Him! Never can Lucifer give anything, even not of the things of the earth, and therefore all his promises are false. The King and Lord answered with imperial majesty: "Begone, satan, for it is written: The Lord thy God thou shalt adore, and Him only shalt thou serve." By this command, "Begone satan," Christ the Redeemer took away from Lucifer permission further to tempt Him, and hurled him and all his legions into the deepest abysses of hell. There they found themselves entirely crushed and buried in its deepest caverns, unable to move for three days. When they were permitted again to rise, seeing themselves thus vanquished and annihilated, they began to doubt whether He, who had so overwhelmed them, might not be the incarnate Son of God. In this doubt and uncertainty they remained, without ever being able to come to certain conviction until the death of the Savior. Lucifer was overcome by hellish wrath at his defeat and was almost consumed in his fury.

Our divine Conqueror Christ then sang hymns of praise and thanks to the eternal Father for having given Him this triumph over the common enemy of God and man; and amid the triumphal songs of a multitude of angels, He was borne back to the desert. They carried Him in their hands, although He had not need of their help, since He could make use of his own divine power; but this service of the angels was due to Him in recompense for enduring the audacity of Lucifer in carrying to the pinnacle of the temple and to the mountain top the sacred humanity of Christ, in which dwelt substantially and truly the Divinity itself. It would never have entered into the thoughts of man, that the Lord should give such a permission to satan, if it had not been made known to us in the Gospels.

Let us return to Nazareth, where, in her oratory, the Princess of the angels had witnessed the battles of her most holy Son. She had seen them all by the divine light already described and by the uninterrupted messages of her angels, who brought them back and forth between the Savior and the blessed Queen. She repeated the same prayers as the Lord and at the same time! She entered likewise into the conflict with the dragon, although invisibly and spiritually. From her retreat She anathemized and crushed Lucifer and his followers, co-operating in all the doings of Christ in our favor. When She perceived that the demon carried the Lord from place to place, She wept bitterly, because the malice of sin reduced the King of kings to such misusage. In honor of all the victories, which He gained over the devil, She composed hymns of praise to the Divinity and the most holy humanity of Christ, while the angels set them to music and were sent with them to congratulate Him for the blessings won for the human race. Christ on his part sent back the angels with words of sweet consolation and rejoicing on account of his triumphs over Lucifer.

The Master directed his most faithful steps toward the Jordan, where his great Precursor saint John was still preaching and baptizing. By his presence and appearance there He wished to secure new testimony of his mission and Divinity through the mouth of saint John. Moreover He was drawn by his own love to see and speak with him, for during his Baptism the heart of the Precursor had become inflamed and wounded by the divine love of the Savior, which so resistlessly attracted all creatures. In the hearts which were well disposed, as was that of saint John, the fire of love burned with so much the greater ardor and violence. When the Baptist saw the Savior coming to him the second time, his first words were those recorded by the Evangelist: "Behold the Lamb of God, behold Him who taketh away the sin of the world." Saint John gave this testimony while pointing out the Lord with his finger to those who were listening to his instructions and were receiving Baptism at his hands. He added: "This is He of whom I said: after me there cometh a Man, who is preferred before me; because He was before me. And I knew Him not; but that He may be made manifest in Israel, therefore I am come baptizing with water."

The two first disciples of Christ who were with saint John at the time, heard this testimony and, moved by it and by the light and grace interiorly imparted to them, they began to follow the Lord. Benignantly turning to them the Lord asked them, that they sought (John 1, 38). They answered that they wished to know where He lived; and the Lord bade them follow. They were with Him that day as saint John tells us. One of them, he says, was saint Andrew, the brother of saint Peter; the other he does not mention. But I was made to understand that it was saint John himself, who, in his great modesty, did not wish to give his name. These two, then, saint John and saint Andrew, were the first fruits of the Baptist's apostolate, being the first of the disciples of the Baptist who followed the Savior in consequence of his express testimony and without being outwardly called by the Lord. Saint Andrew immediately sought his brother Simon and took him along, saying that he had found the Messias, who called Himself Christ. Looking upon Peter He said: "Thou art Simon the son of Jona: thou shalt be called Cephas, which is interpreted Peter." All this happened within the confines of Judea and on the next day the Lord entered Galilee. There He found saint Philip and called him to his following. Philip immediately sought Nathanael and brought him to Jesus, telling him what had happened and that they had found the Messias in the Person of Jesus of Nazareth. Nathanael, having spoken with the Lord as recorded in the first chapter of saint John's Gospel, joined as the fifth of the disciples of Christ.

With these five disciples, the first stones in the foundation of the new Church, Christ, the Savior, entered Galilee for the purpose of beginning his public preaching and baptizing. In the Apostles thus called He enkindled, from the moment of their joining the Master, a new light and fire of divine love and showered upon them the sweetness of his blessings (Ps. 20, 4). It is not possible worthily to describe the labors undergone by the divine Teacher in the vocation and education of these and of the other disciples, in order to found upon them the Church. He sought them out with great diligence and solicitude; He urged them on frequently by the powerful and efficacious help of his grace; He enlightened their hearts and enriched them with incomparable gifts and blessings; He received them with admirable kindness; He nourished them with the sweetest milk of his doctrines; He bore with them with invincible patience; He caressed them as a most loving Father caresses his tender and darling sons. As our nature is base and uncouth material for the exalted and exquisite aspirations of the Spirit, and as they were to be not only perfect disciples, but consummate masters of perfection in the world and in the Church, the work of transforming and raising them from their rough natural state into such a heavenly and divine position by his instructions and example, necessarily was a vast enterprise. In the performance of this work the Lord has left a most exalted example of patience, meekness and charity for all the prelates, princes and whoever is charged with the guidance of subjects. Not less significant for us sinners are the proofs of his fatherly kindness: for He was not satisfied with simply bearing with their faults and defects, their natural inclinations and passions: but He allowed his tender kindness to overflow thus wonderfully toward them, in order that we might be cheered on to trust Him and not permit ourselves to be dismayed amidst the countless imperfections and weaknesses natural to our earthly existence.

By the means already mentioned the Queen of heaven was informed of all the wonderful doings of our Savior in the vocation of the Apostles and disciples and in his public preaching. She gave thanks to the eternal Father for these the first disciples, acknowledging and admitting them in imitation of her Son as her spiritual children, and offering them to the divine Majesty with new songs of praise and joy. On this occasion of the choice of the first disciples She was favored by a new revelation of the Most High in which She was informed again of his holy and eternal decree concerning the Redemption of man and of the manner in which it was to be executed in the preaching of his most holy Son.

The five disciples of the Lord begged Him to grant them the consolation of seeing and reverencing his Mother. In accordance with their petition, He journeyed directly to Nazareth through Galilee, continuing to preach and teach publicly on the way and proclaiming Himself as the Master of truth and eternal life. Many, carried away by the force of his doctrines and by the light and grace overflowing into their hearts, began to listen to Him and to follow Him; though He did not, for the present, call any more to be his disciples. It is worthy of notice that though the five disciples had conceived such an ardent devotion to the heavenly Lady and though they saw with their own eyes how worthy She was of her eminent position among creatures, yet they all maintained strict silence about their thoughts.

The Savior then pursued his way to Nazareth, instructing his new children and disciples not only in the mysteries of faith, but in all virtues by word and example, as He continued to do during the whole period of his evangelical preaching. With this in view He searched out the poor and afflicted, consoled the sick and sorrowful, visited the infirmaries and prisons, performing miracles of mercy as well for body as for soul. Yet He did not profess Himself as the Author of any miracles until he attended the marriage feast at Cana, as I shall relate in the next chapter. While the Savior proceeded on his journey his most holy Mother prepared to receive Him and his disciples at Nazareth; for She was aware of all that happened, and therefore hospitably set her poor dwelling in order and solicitously procured the necessary victuals beforehand for their entertainment. Thus, just as the Son had in her absence instilled into their minds the reverence for the dignity of his Mother, so the most prudent and faithful Mother, in the presence of her Son, wished to instruct them in regard to the worship due to their divine Master, as to their God and Redeemer. The profound humility and worship with which the great Lady received Christ the Savior filled the disciples with new devotion and reverential fear for their divine Master; henceforth She served them as an example and model of true devotion, entering at once into her office as Instructress and spiritual Mother of the disciples of Christ by showing them how to converse with their God and Redeemer. They were immediately drawn toward their Queen and cast themselves on their knees before Her, asking to be received as her sons and servants. The first to do this was saint John, who from that time on distinguished himself in exalting and reverencing Mary before all the Apostles, while She on her part received him with an especial love; for, besides his excelling in virginal chastity, he was of a meek and humble disposition.

The great Lady received them all as her guests, serving them their meals and combining the solicitude of a Mother with the modesty and majesty of a Queen, so that She caused admiration even in the holy angels. She served her divine Son on her knees in deepest reverence. At the same time She spoke of the Majesty of their Teacher and Redeemer to the Apostles instructing them in the great doctrines of the Christian faith. During that night, when the Apostles had retired, the Savior betook himself to the oratory of his purest Mother as He had been wont to do, and She, the most Humble among the humble, placed Herself at his feet as in the years gone by. In regard to the practice of humility, all that She could do seemed little to the great Queen, and much less than She ought to in view of his infinite love and the immense gifts received at his hands. She confessed Herself as useless as the dust of the earth. The Lord lifted Her from the ground and spoke to Her words of life and eternal salvation, yet quietly and serenely. For at this period He began to treat Her with greater reserve in order to afford Her a chance of merit, as I have mentioned when I spoke of this departure for the desert and for his Baptism.

WORDS OF THE QUEEN.

My daughter, I see thee much moved to emulation and desire by the great happiness of the disciples of my most holy Son, and especially that of saint John, my favored servant. It is certain that I loved him in a special manner; because he was most pure and candid as a dove; and in the eyes of the Lord he was very pleasing, both on account of his purity and on account of his love toward me. His example should serve thee as a spur to do that which my Son and I expect of thee. Thou art aware, my dearest, that I am the most pure Mother and that I receive with maternal affection all those who fervently and devoutly desire to be my children and servants in the Lord. By the love which He has given me, I shall embrace them with open arms and shall be their Intercessor and Advocate. Thy poverty, uselessness and weakness shall be for me only a more urgent motive for manifesting toward thee my most liberal kindness. Therefore, I call upon thee to become my chosen and beloved daughter in the holy Church.

I shall, however, make the fulfillment of my promise depend upon a service on thy part: namely, that thou have a true and holy emulation of the love with which I loved saint John, and of all the blessings flowing from it, by imitating him as perfectly as thy powers will allow. Hence, thou must promise to fulfill all that I now command thee, without failing in the least point. I desire, then, that thou labor until all love of self die within thee, that thou suppress all the effects of the first sin until all the earthly inclinations consequent upon it are totally extinguished; that thou seek to restore within thee that dove-like sincerity and simplicity which destroys all malice and duplicity. In all thy doings thou must be an angel, since the condescension of the Most High with thee was so great as to furnish thee with the light and intelligence more of an angel than that of a human creature. I have procured for thee these great blessings and, therefore, it is but reasonable on my part to expect thee to correspond with them in thy works and in thy thoughts. In regard to me thou must cherish a continual affection and loving desire of pleasing and serving me, being always attentive to my counsels and having thy eyes fixed upon me in order to know and execute what I command. Then shalt thou be my true daughter, and I shall be thy Protectress and loving Mother.

BOOK SIX

The Marriage at Cana; How Most Holy Mary Accompanied the Redeemer of the World In His Preaching; the Humility shown by the Heavenly Queen in regard to the Miracles Wrought by Her Divine Son; the Transfiguration of the Lord; His Entrance into Jerusalem; His Passion and Death; His Triumph over Lucifer and his Demons by His Death on the Cross; the Most Sacred Resurrection of the Savior and His Wonderful Ascension into Heaven

CHAPTER I.

MARY ACCOMPANIES JESUS ON HIS JOURNEYS.

It would not be foreign to the purpose of this history to describe the miracles and the heroic works of Christ, our Redeemer and Master; for in almost all of them his most blessed and holy Mother concurred and took a part. But I cannot presume to undertake a work so arduous and so far above human strength and capacity. For the Evangelist saint John, after having described many miracles of Christ, says at the end of his Gospel, that Jesus did many other things, which, if they were all described, could not be contained in all the books of the world (John 21, 25). If such a task seemed so impossible to the Evangelist, how much more to an ignorant woman, more useless than the dust of the earth? All that is necessary and proper, and abundantly sufficient for founding and preserving the Church has been written by the four Evangelists; and it is not necessary to repeat it in this history. Yet in order to compose this history and in order not to pass over in silence so many great works of the exalted Queen, which have not been mentioned, it is necessary to touch on a few particulars. Moreover, I think, that to write of them and thus fasten them in my memory will be both consoling and useful for my advancement. The others, which the Evangelists recorded in their Gospels and of which I have not been commanded to write, are better preserved for the beatific vision, where the saints shall see them manifested to them by the Lord and where they will eternally praise Him for such magnificent works.

From Cana in Galilee Christ, the Redeemer, walked to Capernaum, a large and populous city near the sea of Tiberias. Here, according to saint John (John 2, 12), He remained some days, though not many; for as the time of the Pasch was approaching, He gradually drew nigh to Jerusalem in order to celebrate this feast on the fourteenth of the moon of March. His most blessed Mother, having rid Herself of her house in Nazareth, accompanied Him thenceforth in his tours of preaching and of teaching to the very foot of the Cross. She was absent from Him only a few times, as when the Lord absented Himself on Mount Tabor (Matth. 17, 1), or on some particular conversions, as for instance that of the Samaritan woman, or when the heavenly Lady herself remained behind with certain persons in order to instruct and catechize them. But always after a short time, She returned to her Lord and Master, following the Sun of justice until it sank into the abyss of Death. During these journeys the Queen of heaven proceeded on foot, just as her divine Son. If even the Lord was fatigued on the way, as saint John says (John 4, 61), how much more fatigued was this purest Lady? What hardships did She not endure on such arduous journeys in all sorts of weather? Such is the rigorous treatment accorded by the Mother of mercy to her most delicate body! What She endured in these labors alone is so great that not all the mortals together can ever satisfy their obligations to Her in this regard. Sometimes by permission of the Lord, She suffered such great weakness and pains that He was constrained to relieve Her miraculously. At other times he commanded Her to rest Herself at some stopping-place for a few days; while again on certain occasions, He gave such lightness to her body, that She could move about without difficulty as if on wings.

As I have already mentioned, the heavenly Lady had the whole doctrine of the evangelical law written in her heart. Nevertheless She was as solicitous and attentive as a new disciple to the preaching and doctrine of her divine Son, and She had instructed her angels to report to Her, if necessary, the sermons of the Master whenever She was absent. To the sermons of her Son She always listened on her knees, thus according to the utmost of her powers showing the reverence and worship due to his Person and doctrine. As She was aware at each moment, of the interior operations of the Soul of Christ, and of his continual prayers to the eternal Father for the proper disposition of the hearts of his hearers and for the growth of the seed of his doctrine into eternal life, the most loving Mother joined the divine Master in his petitions and prayers and in securing for them the blessings of her most ardent and tearful charity. By her attention and reverence She taught and moved others to appreciate duly the teaching and instructions of the Savior of the world. She also knew the interior of those that listened to the preaching of the Lord, their state of grace or sin, their vices and virtues. This various and hidden knowledge, so far above the capacity of men, caused in the heavenly Mother many wonderful effects of highest charity and other virtues; it inflamed Her with zeal for the Honor of the Lord and with ardent desires, that the fruits of the Redemption be not lost to the souls, while at the same time, the danger of their loss to the souls through sin moved Her to exert Herself in the most fervent prayer for their welfare. She felt in her heart a piercing and cruel sorrow, that God should not be known, adored and served by all his creatures: and this sorrow was in proportion to the unequaled knowledge and understanding She had of all these mysteries. For the souls, that would not give entrance to divine grace and virtue, She sorrowed with ineffable grief, and was wont to shed tears of blood at the thought of their misfortune. What the great Queen suffered in this her solicitude and in her labors exceeds beyond all measure the pains endured by all the martyrs of the world.

All the followers of the Savior, and whomever He received into his ministry, She treated with incomparable prudence and wisdom, especially those whom She held in such high veneration and esteem as the Apostles of Christ. As a Mother She took care of all, and as a powerful Queen She procured necessaries for their bodily nourishment and comforts. Sometimes, when She had no other resources, She commanded the holy angels to bring provisions for them and for the women in their company. In order to assist them toward advancing in the spiritual life, the great Queen labored beyond possibility of human understanding; not only by her continual and fervent prayers for them but by her precious example and by her counsels, with which She nourished and strengthened them as a most prudent Mother and Teacher. When the Apostles or disciples were assailed by any doubts, which frequently happened in the beginning, or when they were attacked by some secret temptation, the great Lady immediately hastened to their assistance in order to enlighten and encourage them by the peerless light and charity shining forth in Her; and by the sweetness of her words they were exquisitely consoled and rejoiced. They were enlightened by her wisdom, chastened by her humility, quieted by her modesty, enriched by all the blessings that flowed from this storehouse of all the gifts of the Holy Ghost. For all these benefits, for the calling of the disciples, for the conversion and perseverance of the just, and for all the works of grace and virtue, She made a proper return to God, celebrating these events in festive hymns.

As the Evangelists tell us, some of the women of Galilee followed Christ the Redeemer on his journeys. Saint Matthew, saint Mark and saint Luke tell us that some of those whom He had cured of demoniacal possession and of other infirmities, accompanied and served Him (Matth. 27; Mark 15; Luke 8); for the Master of eternal life excluded no sex from his following, imitation and doctrine. Hence some of the women attended upon Him and served Him from the very beginning of his preaching. The divine wisdom so ordered it for certain purposes, among which was also the desire to provide proper companions for his blessed Mother during these travels. Our Queen interested Herself in a special manner in these pious and holy women, gathering them around Her, teaching and catechising them and bringing them as listeners to the sermons of her divine Son. Although She herself was fully enlightened and instructed in the evangelical doctrine and abundantly able to teach them the way of eternal life, nevertheless, partly in order to conceal this secret of her heart, She always availed Herself of the sayings of Christ in his public preaching as a text for her instructions and exhortations, whenever She taught these and many other women who came to Her either before or after hearing the Savior of the world.

One of the great miracles of divine omnipotence and a wonder of wonders was the conduct of the most holy Mary toward the Apostles and disciples of her Son and Savior Christ. A full account of her wisdom is impossible to human tongue, and if I would wish to describe no more than what I have been made to understand concerning this matter, I would be obliged to write a large volume. I will touch upon it in this chapter and as occasion requires in the rest of this history. All that I can say is very little, yet from it the faithful can infer enough for their instruction. All those whom the Savior received into his divine school, were to see and treat familiarly his most blessed Mother. Hence He infused into their hearts an especial reverence and devotion toward that blessed Lady. But though this infused reverence was common to all, it was not equal in all the disciples; for the Lord distributed his gifts according to his free will in reference to their dispositions and in accordance with the duties and offices for which each one was destined. By conversation and familiar intercourse with their great Queen and Lady their reverential love and devotion was to grow and increase; for the blessed Lady spoke to all, loved them, consoled them, instructed and assisted them in their necessities, without ever permitting them to leave Her conversation and presence unreplenished by interior joy and consolation greater than they had asked for. Yet the measure of good fruit derived from them was dependent upon the disposition of the heart of those that received these favors.

They were all enabled to begin their intercourse with the Mother of God in high admiration of her prudence, wisdom, purity, holiness and great majesty, and were made sensible of a sweetness in Her inexpressibly humble and pleasing. This was so ordained by the Most High, because as I have said in the fifth book, chapter twenty-second, it was not yet time to reveal this mystic Ark of the new Testament to the world. Thus, just as the Lord, however much He wished to break forth in her praise, could not manifest it in words and concentrated it within his heart; so the holy Apostles, sweetly constrained into silence, found a vent for their fervent feelings in a so much the more intense love of most holy Mary and praise of her Maker. As the great Lady, on account of her peerless insight knew the natural disposition of each of the disciples, his measure of grace, his present condition and future office, She proceeded according to this knowledge in her petitions and prayers, in her instructions and conversings with them, and in the favors She obtained for each in support of his vocation. Such a loving zeal in the conduct of a mere Creature so entirely pleasing to the wishes of his Lord, excited a new and boundless admiration in the holy angels. Of no less admiration was the hidden providence of the Almighty by which the Apostles were made to correspond to the blessings and favors received by them at the intercession of the most holy Mother. All this caused a divine harmony of action, hidden to men and manifest only to the heavenly spirits.

Especially signalized for the reception of these

sacramental favors were saint Peter and saint John; the former because he was destined to be the vicar of Christ and head of the militant Church and because he therefore deserved the special reverence and love of the holy Mother; the latter because he was to take the place of the Lord after his Passion in attending upon and conversing with the heavenly Lady upon earth. As therefore the government and custody of the mystic Church, namely of Mary immaculate and of the visible militant Church, namely the faithful on earth, was to be divided between these two Apostles, it was no wonder, that they should be singularly favored by the great Queen of the world. But as saint John was chosen to serve Mary and attain the dignity of an adopted son of the Mistress of heaven, he at once began to experience special urgings of grace and signalize himself in the service of the most holy Mary. Although all the Apostles excelled in devotion to the Queen beyond our power of understanding or conception the evangelist saint John penetrated deeper into the mysteries of this City of God and received through Her such divine enlightenment as to excel all the other Apostles. This is also evident from his Gospel (John 21, 20); all the divine insight therein manifested he received through the Queen of heaven, and the distinction of being called the beloved disciple of Jesus, he gained by his love toward the most blessed Mother. As this love was reciprocated by the heavenly Lady, he became the most beloved disciple both of Jesus and Mary.

The Evangelist besides chastity and virginal purity, possessed some other virtues which were especially pleasing to the Queen; among them were a dovelike simplicity, as is manifest from his writings, and a great gentleness and humility, which made him most meek and tractable. The heavenly Mother always looked upon the peaceful and the humble as the most faithful imitators of her divine Son. On this account the blessed Queen favored saint John above all the other Apostles and he himself became more and more anxious to serve Her with ever increasing reverential love and affection. From the very first moment of his vocation saint John commenced to excel all the rest in piety toward the Mother Mary and to fulfill the least of her wishes as her most humble slave. He attended upon Her more assiduously than the rest; and whenever it was possible he sought to be in her company and take upon himself some of the bodily labors connected with her present life. Sometimes it happened that the fortunate Apostle competed with the holy angels in his zeal for thus assisting the great Queen; while She still more eagerly sought to perform these works of humility Herself; for in this virtue She triumphed over all other creatures and none of them could ever hope in the least to surpass or equal Her in acts of humility. The beloved disciple was very diligent in reporting to the heavenly Lady the works and miracles wrought by the Savior, whenever She herself could not be present, and in informing Her of the new disciples converted by his teaching. He was constantly alert and studious to serve Her in the least of her wishes, fulfilling each one of them with a loving eagerness.

I will, however, say something of that which has been made known to me concerning the wicked Apostle Judas; for it belongs to this history and less is known of him. It will at the same time be a warning to the obstinate and an admonition for those little devoted to the most blessed Mary; for it is a sad truth that there should be any mortals who entertain little love toward a Creature so lovable, and One whom the infinite God

himself loves without bound or measure; whom the
angels love with all their heavenly powers, the Apostles
and saints from their inmost souls, whom all creatures
should eagerly strive to love, and who never can be
loved according to her merits. Yet this unhappy Apostle
strayed from the royal road of divine love and its blessings. The understanding, which has been given me concerning this defection for the purpose of making it known
in this history, is contained in the following paragraphs.

Judas was attracted to the school of Christ our
Teacher by his forceful doctrines, and was filled with
the same good intentions which moved the others.
Powerfully drawn by these motives, he asked the Savior
to admit him among his disciples, and the Savior received
him with the bowels of a loving Father, who rejects
none that come to Him in search of truth. In the beginning Judas merited special favors and forged ahead
of some of the other disciples, deserving to be numbered
among the twelve Apostles; for the Savior loved his
soul according to its present state of grace and his good
works, just as He did the others. The Mother of grace
and mercy observed the same course with him, although
by her infused knowledge She immediately became aware
of the perfidious treachery with which he was to end his
apostolate. She did not, on this account, deny him her
intercession and maternal love; but she applied Herself
even more zealously to justify as far as possible the cause
of her divine Son against this perfidious and unfortunate
man, in order that his wickedness, as soon as it should
be put into action, might not have the shadow of an excuse before men. Well knowing that such a character
as his could not be overcome by rigor, but would only
be driven by it to so much the greater obstinacy, the
most prudent Lady took care, that none of the wants or

the comforts of Judas should be ignored and She began to treat him, speak and listen to him more gently and lovingly than to all the rest. This She carried so far, that Judas, when the disciples once disputed among themselves concerning their standing with the Queen (as, according to the Evangelist [Luke 22, 24], it happened also concerning the Redeemer), never experienced the least jealousy or doubt in this matter; for the blessed Lady in the beginning always distinguished him by tokens of special love and he, at that time, also showed himself thankful for these favors.

But as Judas found little support in his natural disposition, and as the disciples, not being as yet confirmed in virtue and not as yet even in grace, were guilty of some human failings, the imprudent man began to compliment himself on his perfection and to take more notice of the faults of his brethren than of his own (Luke 4, 41). He permitted himself thus to be deceived, making no effort to amend or repent, he allowed the beam in his own eyes to grow while watching the splinters in the eyes of others. Complaining of their little faults and seeking, with more presumption than zeal, to correct the weaknesses of his brethren, he committed greater sins himself. Among the other Apostles he singled out saint John, looking upon him as an intermeddler and accusing him in his heart of ingratiating himself with the Master and his blessed Mother. The fact that he received so many special favors from Them was of no avail to deter him from this false assumption. Yet so far Judas had committed only venial sins and had not lost sanctifying grace. But they argued a very bad disposition, in which he wilfully persevered. He had freely entertained a certain vain complacency in himself; this at once called into existence a certain amount of envy, which brought on a calumnious spirit and harshness in judging of the faults of his brethren. These sins opened the way for greater sins; for immediately the fervor of his devotion decreased, his charity toward God and men grew cold, and his interior light was lost and extinguished; he began to look upon the Apostles and upon the most holy Mother with a certain disgust and find little pleasure in their intercourse and their heavenly activity.

The most prudent Lady perceived the growth of this defection in Judas. Eagerly seeking his recovery and salvation before he should cast himself entirely into the death of sin, She spoke to him and exhorted him as her beloved child and with extreme sweetness and force of reasoning. Although at times this storm of tormenting thoughts, which had begun to rise in the breast of Judas, was allayed; yet it was only for a short time, and soon it arose and disturbed him anew. Giving entrance to the devil into his heart, he permitted a furious rage against the most meek Dove to take possession of him. With insidious hypocrisy he sought to deny his sins or palliate them by alleging other reasons for his conduct: as if he could ever deceive Jesus and Mary and hide from Them the secrets of his heart. Thereby he lost his interior reverence for the Mother of mercy, despising her exhortations and openly reproaching Her for her gentle words and reasonings. This ungrateful presumption threw him from the state of grace, the Lord was highly incensed and deservedly left him to his own evil counsels. By thus designedly rejecting the kindness and the intercession of most holy Mary, he closed against himself the gates of mercy and of his only salvation. His disgust with the sweetest Mother soon engendered in him an abhorrence of his Master; he grew dissatisfied with his doctrines and began to look upon the life of an Apostle and intercourse with the disciples as too burdensome.

Nevertheless divine Providence did not abandon him immediately, but continued to send him interior assistance, although in comparison with former helps they were of a kind more common and ordinary. They were, however, in themselves sufficient for his salvation, if he would have made use of them. To these graces were added the gentle exhortations of the kindest Mistress, urging him to restrain himself and to humble himself and ask pardon of his divine Master. She offered him mercy in his name and her own kind assistance in obtaining it, promising to do penance for him, if he would consent to be sorry for his sins and amend his life. All these advances did the Mother of grace make in order to prevent the fall of Judas. She was well aware, that not seeking to arise from a fall and to persevere in sin was a much greater evil than to have fallen. The conscience of this proud disciple could not but reproach him with his wickedness; but becoming hardened in his heart, he began to dread the humiliation, which would have been to his credit, and he fell into still greater sins. In his pride he rejected the salutary counsels of the Mother of Christ and chose rather to deny his guilt, protesting with a lying tongue, that he loved his Master and all the rest, and that there was no occasion for amending his conduct in this regard.

In order that I may not incur the blame of concealing what belongs to this chapter, I will mention another cause of the ruin of Judas. When the number of the Apostles and disciples increased, the Lord resolved to appoint one of them to take charge of the alms received; thus to supply the common needs and pay the imperial tribute. Jesus made known his wishes to all

indiscriminately without addressing Himself to any one
in particular. While all of them feared such an office
and sought to evade it, Judas immediately strove to
obtain it. In order to secure his appointment he humbled
himself so far as to ask saint John to speak to the most
holy Queen and induce Her to arrange this matter for
him with her Son. Saint John yielded to the request
of Judas and spoke to the most prudent Mother; but
She, knowing that this request of Judas was not proper
or just, but proceeded from ambition and avarice, did
not wish to propose it to the divine Master. The same
kind of influence Judas sought to bring into play through
saint Peter and other Apostles, without success; for the
Lord in his goodness wished to stay his ruin, and justify
his cause before men, if He should grant the request.
At this resistance the heart of Judas, already corrupted
by avarice, instead of quietly yielding, was consumed
with unhappy desires for the office, and the devil stirred
up thoughts of vilest ambition, such as would have been
most improper and wicked in any one, and hence were
much more culpable in Judas, who had been a disciple
in the school of highest perfection and who had lived in
the light of the Sun of justice and its beautiful Moon,
Mary! Neither in the day of abundant graces, when the
Sun Jesus lighted his paths, nor in the night of temptations, when the Moon Mary disclosed to him the wiles
of the poisonous serpent, could he have failed to become
aware of the wickedness of such suggestions. But, as he
flew from the light and cast himself willfully into darkness, he presumed to ask most holy Mary in a direct
manner for her influence in obtaining his object. He
had lost all fear and hid his avarice in the cloak of
virtue. Approaching Her, he said that he had made his
request through saint Peter and saint John, with the sole

desire of diligently serving Her and his divine Master, since not all would attend to the duties of this office with proper solicitude; and that, therefore, he now asked Her to obtain the position of purser for him from the Master.

The great Lady answered him with extreme gentleness: "Consider well, my dearest, what thou askest, and examine whether thy intentions are upright. Ponder well, whether it is good for thee to seek that which all thy brethren fear and refuse to accept, unless they shall be compelled thereto by the command of their Lord and Master. He loves thee more than thou lovest thyself and without doubt knows what will benefit thee; resign thyself to his most holy will, change thy purpose, and seek to grow rich in humility and poverty. Rise from thy fall, for I will extend thee a helpful hand and my Son will show thee his loving mercy." Who would not have yielded to these sweetest words and such urgent advice, spoken by such an amiable and heavenly Creature as was most holy Mary? But this fierce and adamantine heart was not softened or moved. On the contrary, the soul of Judas was offended and enraged against the heavenly Lady for thus offering him a means of escaping from his dreadful danger. Boundless ambition and avarice roused his fury against Her who seemed to hinder him in his projects and he considered her well-meant advice as an insult. But the most meek and loving Dove pretended not to notice his obstinacy and said nothing more to him at that time.

After his interview with most holy Mary, the avarice of Judas would not allow him to rest; casting off all modesty and natural shame (and the least spark of faith), Judas now resolved to apply to his divine Master and Savior. Clothing himself like a consummate hypocrite in the garb of a sheep, he went to his Master and said: "Master, I wish to fulfill thy wishes and serve Thee as thy purser and as the dispenser of the alms which we receive; I will look to the interests of the poor, fulfilling thy doctrine that we should do unto others as we wish them to do unto us, and I will see to it that alms are distributed according to thy wishes, more profitably and orderly than hitherto." Such reasoning the specious hypocrite boldly used, committing many enormous sins in one and the same act. For, first of all he lied, concealing his real intention. Then, being ambitious of an honor which he did not merit, he neither wished to appear in his true light nor did he wish to be in truth what he merely pretended to be. He also blamed his brethren, discrediting them and praising himself: the ordinary course of those who are ambitious. What is especially to be noticed in this conduct of Judas is that he showed his loss of infused faith; for he attempted to deceive Christ, his divine Master, by wearing the cloak of hypocrisy. For, if he had firmly believed that Christ was true God and man who penetrated into the secrets of the heart, he could not have hoped to be able to deceive Him; nor would he have attempted such double dealing, not only because he would have known Christ as the omniscient God, but because he would not have hoped to impose upon the infused and beatific science of Christ as man. Hence Judas had lost belief in all these prerogatives, and to his other sins, added the sin of heresy.

But let us return to the answer given to Judas by the Master, whom he asked to make him purser. We shall see how hidden and terrible are the judgments of the Most High. The Redeemer wished to ward off from him the danger which lay behind this request and which threatened the avaricious Apostle with final perdition. In order that Judas might not excuse himself under plea of ignorance, the Lord answered him: "Dost thou know, Judas, what thou seekest and what thou askest? Be not so cruel toward thy own self as to solicit and seek to obtain the poison and the arms which may cause thy death." Judas replied: "Master I desire to serve Thee by employing my strength in the service of thy faithful followers and in this way I can do it better than in any other; for I offer to fulfill all the duties of this office without fail." This daring presumption of Judas in seeking and coveting danger, justified the cause of God in allowing him to enter and perish in the danger thus sought and coveted. He resisted the light (Eccli. 15, 17), and hardened himself against it, water and fire was shown him, life and death: he stretched forth his hand and chose perdition.

WORDS OF THE QUEEN.

My daughter, all that thou hast written in this chapter is a most important warning for all those that live in the flesh and in the imminent danger of losing their eternal happiness. It should teach them to seek my most kind and powerful intercession and to fear the judgments of the Most High; for in this lies an efficacious means of salvation and of meriting higher reward for the Lord. I wish to remind thee once more, that among the secrets revealed to the beloved John at the last Supper, was also this, that he had become the beloved disciple of Christ on account of his love toward me, and that Judas fell because he despised the mercy and kindness which I had shown him. At that time, also, the Evangelist understood other great mysteries communicated and wrought in me; that I should take part in the labor and suffering of the Passion and that he should have special charge of me. My dearest, the purity which I require of thee must be greater than that of an angel; and if thou strive after it thou wilt become my dearest child, as saint John, and a most beloved and favored spouse of my Son and Lord. His example and the ruin of Judas should continually serve thee as a stimulus and as a warning, to seek only after my love and to be sincerely thankful for the love shown thee without thy merit.

CHAPTER II.

Our Redeemer and Master Jesus had already consumed more than two years and a half in preaching and performing wonders, and He was approaching the time predestined by the eternal wisdom for satisfying divine justice for redeeming the human race through his Passion and Death and thus to return to his eternal Father. Since all his works were ordered with the highest wisdom for our instruction and salvation, the Lord resolved to prepare and strengthen some of his Apostles for the scandal of his Passion by manifesting to them beforehand in its glory that same body, which He was so soon to exhibit in the disfigurement of the Cross. Thus would they be reassured by the thought, that they had seen it transfigured in glory before they looked upon it disfigured by his sufferings. This he had promised a short time before in the presence of all, although not to all, but only to some of his disciples, as is recorded by saint Matthew (Matth. 16, 28). For his Transfiguration He selected a high mountain in the center of Galilee, two leagues east of Nazareth and called Mount Tabor. Ascending to its highest summit with the three Apostles, Peter, and the two brothers James and John, He was transfigured before them (Matth. 17, 1; Mark 9, 1; Luke 9, 28). The three Evangelists tell us that besides these Apostles, were present also the two prophets, Moses and Elias, discoursing with Jesus about his Passion, and that, while He was thus transfigured, a voice resounded from heaven in the name of the eternal Father, saying: "This is my beloved Son, in whom I am well pleased: hear ye Him."

The Evangelists do not say that most holy Mary was present at this Transfiguration, nor do they say that She was not there; this did not fall within their purpose, and they did not think it proper to speak of the hidden miracle by which She was enabled to be there. For the purpose of recording this event here, I was given to understand that at the same time in which some of the holy angels were commissioned to bring the soul of Moses and Elias from their abode, others of her own guard carried the heavenly Lady to Mount Tabor, in order to witness the Transfiguration of her divine Son, for without a doubt She really witnessed it. There was no necessity of confirming the most holy Mother in her faith, as was necessary with the Apostles; for She was invincibly confirmed in faith.

But no human ingenuity can suffice fully to describe the effects of this glorious vision of her Son on her most holy soul. With inmost gratitude and deepest penetration She began to ponder upon what She had seen and heard; exalted praise of the omnipotent God welled forth from her lips, when She considered how her eyes had seen refulgent in glory that same bodily substance, which had been formed of her blood, carried in her womb and nursed at her breast; how She had with her own ears heard the voice of the eternal Father acknowledge her Son as his own and appoint Him as the Teacher of all the human race. With her holy angels She composed new canticles to celebrate an event so full of festive joy for her soul and for the most sacred humanity of her Son. I will not expatiate upon this mystery, nor discuss in what the Transfiguration of the body of Jesus really consisted. It is enough to know that his countenance began to shine like the sun and his garments became whiter than the snow (Matth. 17, 2).

After the Transfiguration the most blessed Mother was brought back to her house in Nazareth; her divine Son descended the mountain and immediately came to visit her in order to take final leave of his parental province and set out for Jerusalem. There, on the following Pasch, which was to be for Him the last upon earth, He was to enter upon his Passion. Having spent only a few days at Nazareth, He departed with his Mother, his disciples and Apostles and some of the holy women, traveling about through Galilee and Samaria before entering Judea and Jerusalem. The Evangelist saint Luke writes of this journey where he says, that He set his face toward Jerusalem (Luke 9, 51); for He journeyed to Jerusalem with a joyous countenance and full of desire to enter upon his sufferings, in order thereby, according to his own most ardent and generous desire, to sacrifice Himself for the human race. He was not to return to Galilee, where He had wrought so many miracles. Knowing this at his departure from Nazareth, He glorified his eternal Father and, in the name of his sacred humanity, gave thanks for having, in that house and neighborhood, received the human form and existence which He was now to deliver over to suffering and death. Of the prayers of Christ our Lord on this occasion I will record as far as I can the following one:

"My eternal Father, in compliance with thy will I gladly haste to satisfy thy justice by suffering even unto death. Thus shall I reconcile to Thee all the children of Adam, paying their debts and opening to them the gates of heaven which have been closed against them. I shall seek those who have turned away and lost themselves, so that they may be restored by the force of my love. I shall find and gather together the lost of the house of Jacob (Is. 56, 8), raise up the fallen, enrich the poor, refresh the thirsty, cast down the haughty and exalt the humble. I wish to vanquish hell and enhance the glories of the triumph over Lucifer (I John 3, 8), and over the vices which he has sown into the world. I wish to raise up the standard of the Cross, beneath which virtue, and all those that put themselves under its protection, are to fight their battles. I wish to satiate my heart with insults and affronts, which are so estimable in thy eyes. I wish to humiliate Myself even to death at the hands of my enemies, in order that our chosen friends may be consoled in their tribulations and that they may be honored by high rewards, whenever they choose to humiliate themselves in suffering the same persecutions. O beloved Cross! When shalt thou receive Me in thy arms? O sweet ignominies and affronts! When shalt thou bear Me on to overcome death through the sufferings of my entirely guiltless flesh? Ye pains, affronts, ignominies, scourges, thorns, torments, death, come to Me, who wish to embrace you, yield yourselves to my welcome, since I well understand your value. If the world abhors you, I long for you. If the world, in its ignorance, despises you, I, who am truth and wisdom, love and embrace you. Come then to Me, for in welcoming you as man, I exalt you as the true God and am ready to efface the touch of sin from you and from all that will embrace you. Come to Me, ye pains, and disappoint Me not; heed not my Omnipotence, for I shall permit you to exert your full force upon my humanity. You shall not be rejected and abhorred by Me as you are by mortals. The deceitful fascination of the children of Adam in vainly judging the poor and the afflicted of this world as unhappy, shall now disappear; for if they see their true God, their Creator, Master and Father, suffering horrible insults, scourgings, the ignominious torment and destitution of the Cross, they will understand their error and esteem it as an honor to follow their crucified God."

I cannot worthily express all the thoughts and affections of the Mistress of the world in this her departure from Nazareth, her prayers and petitions to the eternal Father, her most sweet and sorrowful conversations with her divine Son, the greatness of her grief and the vastness of her merits. For, on account of the conflict between the love of a true Mother, by which She naturally desired to preserve Him from the terrible torments, and the conformity of her will with that of Jesus and of his eternal Father, her heart was pierced by the sword of sorrow, prophesied by Simeon (Luke 2, 35). In her affliction She complained to her divine Son in words of deepest prudence and wisdom, yet also of sweetest sorrow, that She should be unable to prevent his sufferings, or at least die with Him. These sorrows of the Mother of God exceeded the sufferings of all the martyrs who have died or will die for love of God to the end of the world. In such a state of mind and affection the Sovereigns of the world pursued their way from Nazareth toward Jerusalem through Galilee, which the Savior was not to revisit in this life. As the end of his labors for the salvation of men drew to a close, his miraculous works increased in number, and, as the sacred writers of the Gospels relate, they became especially numerous in the last months intervening between his departure from Galilee and the day of his entrance into Jerusalem. Until that day, after having celebrated the feast or the Pasch of the Tabernacles, the Savior traveled about and labored in Judea, awaiting the appointed time, when, according to his will, He was to offer Himself in sacrifice.

Our Savior continued to perform his miracles in Judea. Among them was also the resurrection of Lazarus in Bethany, whither He had been called by the two sisters, Martha and Mary. As this miracle took place so near to Jerusalem, the report of it was soon spread throughout the city. The priests and Pharisees, being irritated by this miracle, held a council (John 9, 17), in which they resolved upon the death of the Redeemer and commanded all those that had any knowledge of his whereabouts, to make it known; for after the resurrection of Lazarus, Jesus retired to the town of Ephrem, until the proximate feast of the Pasch should arrive. As the time of celebrating it by his own Death drew nigh, He showed Himself more openly with his twelve disciples, the Apostles; and He told them privately that they should now get themselves ready to go to Jerusalem, where the Son of man, He himself, should be delivered over to the chiefs of the Pharisees, bound as a prisoner, scourged, and ill-treated unto the death of the Cross (Matth. 20, 18). In the meanwhile the priests kept a sharp watch to find Him among those who came to celebrate the Pasch. Six days previous He again visited Bethania, where He had called Lazarus to life, and where He was entertained by the two sisters. They arranged a banquet for the Lord and his Mother, and for all of his company. Among those that were at table with Them, was also Lazarus, whom He had brought back to life a few days before.

Thursday, the eve of the Passion and Death of the Savior, had arrived; at earliest dawn the Lord called upon his most beloved Mother and She, hastening to prostrate Herself at his feet, responded; "Speak, my Lord and Master, for thy servant heareth." Raising Her up from the ground, He spoke to Her in words of soothing and tenderest love: "My Mother, the hour decreed by the eternal wisdom of my Father for accomplishing the salvation and restoration of the human race and imposed upon Me by his most holy and acceptable will, has now arrived; it is proper that now We subject to Him our own will, as We have so often offered to do. Give Me thy permission to enter upon my suffering and death, and, as my true Mother, consent that I deliver Myself over to my enemies in obedience to my eternal Father. In this manner do Thou also willingly co-operate with Me in this work of eternal salvation, since I have received from Thee in thy virginal womb the form of a suffering and mortal man in which I am to redeem the world and satisfy the divine justice. Just as thou, of thy own free will, didst consent to my Incarnation, so I now desire thee to give consent also to my passion and death of the Cross. To sacrifice Me now of thy own free will to the decree of my eternal Father, this shall be the return which I ask of thee for having made thee my Mother; for He has sent Me in order that by the sufferings of my flesh I might recover the lost sheep of his house, the children of Adam" (Matth. 18, 11).

These and other words of the Savior, spoken on that occasion, pierced the most loving heart of Mary and cast Her into the throes of a sorrow greater than She had ever endured before. For now had arrived that dreadful hour, whence there was no issue for her pains, neither in an appeal to the swift-fleeting time nor to any other tribunal against the inevitable decree of the eternal Father, that had fixed the term of her beloved Son's life. When now the most prudent Mother looked upon Him as her God, infinite in his attributes and perfections, and as the true Godman in hypostatical union with the person of the Word, and beheld Him sanctified and ineffably exalted by this union with the Godhead: She remembered the obedience He had shown Her as his Mother during so many years and the blessings He had conferred upon Her during his long intercourse with Her; She realized that soon She was to be deprived of this blessed intercourse and of the beauty of his countenance, of the vivifying sweetness of his words; that She was not only to lose all this at once, but moreover that She was to deliver Him over into the hands of such wicked enemies, to ignominies and torments and to the bloody sacrifice of a death on the Cross. How deeply must all these considerations and circumstances, now so clearly before Her mind, have penetrated into her tender and loving heart and filled it with a sorrow unmeasurable! But with the magnanimity of a Queen, vanquishing this invincible pain, She prostrated Herself at the feet of Her divine Son and Master, and, in deepest reverence, kissing his feet, answered:

"Lord and highest God, Author of all that has being, though Thou art the Son of my womb, I am thy handmaid; the condescension of thy ineffable love alone has raised me from the dust to the dignity of being thy Mother. It is altogether becoming that I, vile wormlet, acknowledge and thank thy most liberal clemency by obeying the will of the eternal Father and thy own. I offer myself and resign myself to his divine pleasure, in order that in Me, just as in Thee, my Son and Lord, his eternal and adorable will be fulfilled. The greatest sacrifice which I can make, is that I shall not be able to die with Thee, and that our lot should not be inverted; for to suffer in imitation of Thee and in thy company would be a great relief for my pains, and all torments would be sweet, if undergone in union with thine. That Thou shouldst endure all these torments for the salvation of mankind shall be my only relief in my pains. Receive, O my God, this sacrifice of my desire to die with Thee, and of my still continuing to live, while thou, the most innocent Lamb and figure of the substance of thy eternal Father undergoest Death (Heb. 1, 3). Receive also the agonies of my sorrow to see the inhuman cruelty of thy enemies executed on thy exalted Person because of the wickedness of the human kind. O ye heavens and elements and all creatures within them, ye sovereign spirits, ye Patriarchs and Prophets, assist me to deplore the death of my Beloved, who gave you being, and bewail with me the misery of men, who are the cause of this Death, and who, failing to profit of such great blessings, shall lose that eternal life so dearly bought! O unhappy you, that are foreknown as doomed! and O ye happy predestined, who shall wash your stoles in the blood of the Lamb (Apoc. 7, 14), you, who knew how to profit by this blessed sacrifice, praise ye the Lord Almighty! O my Son and infinite delight of my soul, give fortitude and strength to thy afflicted Mother; admit Her as thy disciple and companion, in order that she may participate in thy Passion and Cross, and in order that the eternal Father may receive the sacrifice of thy Mother in union with thine."

With these and other expressions of her sentiments, which I cannot all record in words, the Queen of heaven answered her most holy Son, and offered Herself as a companion and a coadjutrix in his Passion.

Thereupon, thoroughly instructed and prepared by divine light for all the mysteries to be wrought by the Master of life towards accomplishing all his great ends, the most pure Mother, having the Lord's permission, added another request in the following words: "Beloved of my soul and light of my eyes, my Son, I am not worthy to ask Thee what I desire from my inmost soul; but Thou, O Lord, art the life of my hope, and in this my trust I beseech Thee, if such be thy pleasure, to make me a participant in the ineffable Sacrament of thy body and blood. Thou hast resolved to institute it as a pledge of thy glory and I desire in receiving Thee sacramentally in my heart to share the effects of this new and admirable Sacrament. Well do I know, O Lord, that no creature can ever merit such an exquisite blessing, which Thou hast resolved to set above all the works of thy magnificence; and in order to induce Thee to confer it upon me, I have nothing else to offer except thy own self and all thy infinite merits. If by perpetuating these merits through the same humanity which thou hast received from my womb, creates for me a certain right, let this right consist not so much in giving Thyself to me in this Sacrament, as in making me thine by this new possession, which restores to me thy sweetest companionship. All my desires and exertions I have devoted to the worthy reception of this holy Communion from the moment in which Thou gavest me knowledge of it and ever since it was thy fixed decree to remain in the holy Church under the species of consecrated bread and wine. Do Thou then, my Lord and God, return to thy first habitation which Thou didst find in thy beloved Mother and thy slave, whom Thou hast prepared for thy reception by exempting Her from the common touch of sin. Then shall I receive within me the humanity, which I have communicated to Thee from my own blood, and thus shall we be united in a renewed and close embrace. This prospect enkindles my heart with most ardent love, and may I never be separated from Thee, who art the infinite Good and the Love of my soul."

Our Savior, having thus parted with his most beloved Mother and sorrowful Spouse, and taking along with Him all his Apostles, a little before midday of the Thursday of the last Supper, departed on his last journey from Bethany to Jerusalem. At the very outset He raised his eyes to the eternal Father, and, confessing Him in words of thankfulness and praise, again professed his most ardent love and most lovingly and obediently offered to suffer and die for the Redemption of the human race. This prayer and sacrifice of our Savior and Master sprang from such ineffable love and ardor of his spirit, that it cannot be described; all that I say of it seems to me rather a gainsaying of the truth and of what I desire to say. "Eternal Father and my God," said Christ our Lord, "in compliance with thy holy will I now go to suffer and die for the liberation of men, my brethren and the creatures of thy hands. I deliver Myself up for their salvation and to gather those who have been scattered and divided by the sin of Adam.

WORDS OF THE QUEEN.

My daughter, as thy soul has been furnished with special gifts of enlightenment, I call and invite thee anew to cast thyself into the sea of mysteries contained in the passion and death of my divine Son. Direct all thy faculties and strain all the powers of thy heart and soul, to make thyself at least somewhat worthy of understanding and meditating upon the ignominies and sorrows of the Son of the eternal Father in his death on the Cross for the salvation of men; and also of considering my doings and sufferings in connection with his bitterest Passion.

This science, so much neglected by men, I desire that thou, my daughter, study and learn, so as to be able to follow thy Spouse and imitate me, who am thy Mother and Teacher. Writing down and feeling deeply all that I shall teach thee of these mysteries, thou shouldst detach thyself entirely of human and earthly affections and of thy own self, so as freely to follow our footsteps in destitution and poverty.

I wish thee also to ponder, what a horrible crime it is in the eyes of the Lord, in mine, and in those of all the saints, that men should despise and neglect the frequent reception of the holy Communion, and that they should approach it without preparation and fervent devotion. Principally in order that thou mayest understand and record this warning, I have manifested to thee, what I did on that occasion and how I prepared myself so many years for receiving my most blessed Son in the holy Sacrament and also the rest, which thou art yet to write for the instruction and confusion of men. For if I, who was innocent of any hindering sin and filled with all graces, sought to increase my fitness for this favor by such fervent acts of love, humility and gratitude, consider what efforts thou and the other children of the Church, who every day and hour incur new guilt and blame, must make in order to fit yourselves for the beauty of the Divinity and humanity of my most holy Son? What excuse can those men give in the last judgment, who have despised this ineffable love and blessing, which they had always present in the holy Church, ready to fill them with the plenitude of his gifts, and who rather sought diversion in worldly pleasures and attended upon the outward and deceitful vanities of this earthly life? Be thou amazed at this insanity as were the holy angels, and guard thyself against falling into the same error.

CHAPTER III.

Christ had partaken of the prescribed supper with his disciples reclining on the floor around a table, which was elevated from it little more than the distance of six or seven fingers; for such was the custom of the Jews. But after the washing of the feet He ordered another, higher table to be prepared, such as we now use for our meals. By this arrangement He wished to put an end to the legal suppers and to the lower and figurative law and establish the new Supper of the law of grace. From that time on He wished the sacred mysteries to be performed on the tables or altars, which are in use in the Catholic Church. The table was covered with a very rich cloth and upon it was placed a plate or salver and a large cup in the form of a chalice, capacious enough to hold the wine. All this was done in pursuance of the will of Christ our Savior, who by his divine power and wisdom directed all these particulars. The master of the house was inspired to offer these rich vessels, which were made of what seemed a precious stone like emerald. The Apostles often used it afterwards in consecrating, whenever the occasion permitted it. The Lord seated himself at this table with the Apostles and some of the other disciples, and then ordered some unleavened bread to be placed on the table and some wine to be brought, of which He took sufficient to prepare the chalice.

Then the Master of life spoke words of most endearing love to his Apostles, and, though his sayings were wont to penetrate to the inmost heart at all times, yet on this occasion they were like the flames of a great fire of charity, which consumed the souls of his hearers. He manifested to them anew the most exalted mysteries of his Divinity, humanity and of the works of the Redemption. He enjoined upon them peace and charity, of which He was now to leave a pledge in the mysteries about to be celebrated. He reminded them, that in loving one another, they would be loved by the eternal Father with the same love in which He was beloved. He gave them an understanding of the fulfillment of this promise in having chosen them to found the new Church and the law of grace. He renewed in them the light concerning the supreme dignity, excellence and prerogatives of his most pure Virgin Mother.

Thereupon Christ our Lord took into his venerable hands the bread, which lay upon the plate, and interiorly asked the permission and co-operation of the eternal Father, that now and ever afterwards in virtue of the words about to be uttered by Him, and later to be repeated in his holy Church, He should really and truly become present in the host, Himself to yield obedience to these sacred words. While making this petition He raised his eyes toward heaven with an expression of such sublime majesty, that He inspired the Apostles, the angels and his Virgin Mother with new and deepest reverence. Then He pronounced the words of consecration over the bread, changing its substance into the substance of his true body and immediately thereupon He uttered the words of consecration also over the wine, changing it into his true blood. As an answer to these words of consecration was heard the voice of the eternal Father, saying: "This is my beloved Son, in whom I delight, and shall take my delight to the end of the world;

and He shall be with men during all the time of their banishment." In like manner was this confirmed by the Holy Ghost. The most sacred humanity of Christ, in the Person of the Word, gave tokens of profoundest veneration to the Divinity contained in the Sacrament of his body and blood. The Virgin Mother, in her retreat, prostrated Herself on the ground and adored her Son in the blessed Sacrament with incomparable reverence. Then also the angels of her guard, all the angels of heaven, and among them likewise the souls of Enoch and Elias, in their own name and in the name of the holy Patriarchs and Prophets of the old law, fell down in adoration of their Lord in the holy Sacrament.

All the Apostles and disciples, who, with the exception of the traitor, believed in this holy Sacrament, adored it with great humility and reverence according to each one's disposition. The great high priest Christ raised up his own consecrated body and blood in order that all who were present at this first Mass might adore it in a special manner, as they also did. During this elevation his most pure Mother, saint John, Enoch and Elias, were favored with an especial insight into the mystery of his presence in the sacred species. They understood more profoundly, how, in the species of the bread, was contained his body and in those of the wine, his blood; how in both, on account of the inseparable union of his soul with his body and blood, was present the living and true Christ; how with the Person of the Word, was also therein united the Person of the Father and of the Holy Ghost; and how therefore, on account of the inseparable existence and union of the Father, Son and Holy Ghost, the holy Eucharist contained the perfect humanity of the Lord with the three divine Persons of the Godhead. All this was understood most profoundly by the heavenly Lady and by the others according to their degree. They understood also the efficacy of the words of the consecration, now endowed with such divine virtue, that as soon as they are pronounced with the intention of doing what Christ did at that time, by any priest since that time over the proper material, they would change the bread into his body and the wine into his blood, leaving the accidents to subsist in a new way and without their proper subject. They saw, that this change would take place so certainly and infallibly, that heaven and earth would sooner fall to pieces, than that the effect of these words of consecration, when pronounced in the proper manner by the sacerdotal minister of Christ, should ever fail.

The heavenly Queen understood also by a special vision how the most sacred body of Christ is hidden beneath the accidents of bread and wine without change in them or alteration of the sacred humanity; for neither can the Body be the subject of the accidents, nor can the accidents be the form of the body. The accidents retain the same extension and qualities as before, and each of their parts retain the same position after the host has been consecrated; and the sacred body is present in an invisible form, also retaining the same size without intermingling of parts. It remains in the whole host, and all of it in every particle of the host, without being strained by the host, or the host by the body. For neither is the extension of his body correlative with the accidental species, nor do they depend upon the sacred body for their existence. They therefore have a totally different mode of existence and the body interpenetrates the accidents without hindrance.

Still greater was my admiration when Jesus our God, having raised the most holy Sacrament, as I said before, for their adoration, divided it by his own sacred hands, first partook of it Himself as being the First and Chief of all the priests. Recognizing Himself, as man, inferior to the Divinity, which He was now to receive in this his own consecrated body and blood. He humiliated and, as it were, with a trembling of the inferior part of his being, shrank within Himself before that Divinity, thereby not only teaching us the reverence with which holy Communion is to be received; but also showing us what was his sorrow at the temerity and presumption of many men during the reception and handling of this exalted and sublime Sacrament. The effects of holy Communion in the body of Christ were altogether miraculous and divine; for during a short space of time the gifts of glory flowed over in his body just as on mount Tabor, though the effects of this transfiguration were manifest only to his blessed Mother, and partly also to saint John, Enoch and Elias. This was the last consolation He permitted his humanity to enjoy as to its inferior part during his earthly life, and from that moment until his Death He rejected all such alleviation. The Virgin Mother, by a special vision, also understood how Christ her divine Son received Himself in the blessed Sacrament and what was the manner of its presence in his divine Heart. All this caused inestimable affection in our Queen and Lady.

While receiving his own body and blood Christ our Lord composed a canticle of praise to the eternal Father and offered Himself in the blessed Sacrament as a sacrifice for the salvation of man. He took another particle of the consecrated bread and handed it to the archangel Gabriel who brought and communicated it to the most holy Mary. By having such a privilege conferred on one of their number, the holy angels considered themselves sufficiently recompensed for being excluded from the sacerdotal dignity and for yielding it to man. The privilege of merely having even one of their number hold the sacramental body of their Lord and true God filled them with a new and immense joy. In abundant tears of consolation the great Queen awaited holy Communion. When saint Gabriel with innumerable other angels approached, She received it, the first after her Son, imitating his self-abasement, reverence and holy fear. The most blessed Sacrament was deposited in the breast and above the heart of the most holy Virgin Mother, as in the most legitimate shrine and tabernacle of the Most High. There the ineffable sacrament of the holy Eucharist remained deposited from that hour until after the Resurrection, when saint Peter said the first Mass and consecrated anew, as I shall relate in its place.

After having thus favored the heavenly Princess, our Savior distributed the sacramental bread to the Apostles (Luke 22, 17), commanding them to divide it among themselves and partake of it. By this commandment He conferred upon them the sacerdotal dignity and they began to exercise it by giving Communion each to Himself. This they did with the greatest reverence, shedding copious tears and adoring the body and blood of our Lord, whom they were receiving. They were established in the power of the priesthood, as being founders of the holy Church and enjoying the distinction of priority over all others (Ephes. 2, 20). Then saint Peter, at the command of Christ the Lord, administered two of the particles of holy Communion to the two patriarchs, Enoch and Elias. This holy Communion so rejoiced these two holy men, that they were encouraged anew in their hope of the beatific vision, which for them was to be deferred for so many ages, and they were strengthened to live on in this hope until the end of the world. Having given most fervent and humble thanks to the Almighty for this blessing, they were brought back to their abiding-place by the hands of the holy angels. The Lord desired to work this miracle in order to pledge Himself to include the ancient natural and written laws in the benefits of the Incarnation, Redemption and general resurrection; since all these mysteries were contained in the most holy Eucharist. By thus communicating Himself to the two holy men, Enoch and Elias, who were still in their mortal flesh, these blessings were extended over the human race such as it existed under the natural and the written laws, while all the succeeding generations were to be included in the new law of grace, the Apostles at the head. This was all well understood by Enoch and Elias, and, returning to the midst of their contemporaries, they gave thanks to their and our Redeemer for this mysterious blessing.

WORDS OF THE QUEEN.

O my daughter! Would that the believers in the holy Catholic faith opened their hardened and stony hearts in order to attain to a true understanding of the sacred and mysterious blessing of the holy Eucharist! If they would only detach themselves, root out and reject their earthly inclinations, and, restraining their passions, apply themselves with living faith to study by the divine light their great happiness in thus possessing their eternal God in the holy Sacrament and in being able, by its reception and constant intercourse, to participate in the full effects of this heavenly manna! If they would only worthily esteem this precious gift, begin to taste its sweetness, and share in the hidden power of their omnipotent God! Then nothing would ever be wanting to them in their exile. In this, the happy age of the law of grace, mortals have no reason to complain of their weakness and their passions; since in this bread of heaven they have at hand strength and health. It matters not that they are tempted and persecuted by the demon; for by receiving this Sacrament frequently they are enabled to overcome him gloriously. The faithful are themselves to blame for all their poverty and labors, since they pay no attention to this divine mystery, nor avail themselves of the divine powers, thus placed at their disposal by my most holy Son. I tell thee truly, my dearest, that Lucifer and his demons have such a fear of the most holy Eucharist, that to approach it, causes them more torments than to remain in hell itself. Although they do enter churches in order to tempt souls, they enter them with aversion, forcing themselves to endure cruel pains in the hope of destroying a soul and drawing it into sin, especially in the holy places and in the presence of the holy Eucharist. Their wrath against the Lord and against the souls alone could induce them to expose themselves to the torment of his real sacramental presence.

Whenever He is carried through the streets they usually fly and disperse in all haste; and they would not dare to approach those that accompany Him, if by their long experience they did not know, that they will induce some to forget the reverence due to their Lord. Therefore they make special efforts to tempt the faithful in the churches; for they know what great injury they can thereby do to the Lord himself, who in his sacramental love is there waiting to sanctify men and to receive the return of his sweetest and untiring love. Hence thou canst also understand the strength of those who prepare themselves to partake of this bread of the angels and how the demons fear the souls, who receive the Lord worthily and devoutly and who strive to preserve themselves in this purity until the next Communion. But there are very few who live with this intention, and the enemy is ceaselessly alert in striving to throw them back into their forgetfulness, distraction and indifference, so that he may not be obliged to encounter such powerful weapons in the hands of men. Write this admonition in thy heart; and since without thy merit the Almighty has ordained, that thou receive holy Communion daily, seek by all possible means to preserve thyself in the good dispositions from one Communion to the other. It is the will of the Lord and my own, that with this sword thou fight the battles of the Almighty in the name of the holy Church against the invisible enemies. For in our days they are heaping affliction and sorrow upon the mistress of nations, while there is none to console her or to take it to heart (Thren. 1, 10). Do thou thyself weep for the same reason and let thy heart be torn in sorrow. But while the omnipotent and just Judge who is so greatly incensed against the Catholics for having outraged his justice by their unmeasurable and continual transgressions even under the aegis of their grand faith, none are found to consider and weigh the fearful damage, nor to approach the easy remedy of receiving the holy Eucharist with a contrite and humble heart; nor does any one ask for my intercession.

Though all the children of the Church largely incur this fault, yet more to be blamed are the unworthy and wicked priests; for by the irreverence with which they treat the blessed Sacrament the other Catholics have been drawn to undervalue it. If the people see that their priests approach the divine mysteries with holy fear and trembling, they learn to treat and receive their God in like manner. Those that so honor Him shall shine in heaven like the sun among the stars; for the glory of my divine Son's humanity will redound in a special measure in those who have behaved well toward Him in the blessed Sacrament and have received Him with all reverence; whereas this will not happen to those who have not frequented this holy table with devotion. Moreover the devout will bear on their breast, where they have so often harbored the holy Eucharist, most beautiful and resplendent inscriptions, showing that they were most worthy tabernacles of the holy Sacrament. This will be a great accidental reward for them and a source of jubilation and admiration for the holy angels and all the rest of the blessed. They will also enjoy the special favor of being able to penetrate deeper into the mystery of the presence of the Lord in the sacrament and to understand all the rest of the wonders hidden therein. This will be such a privilege, that it alone would suffice for their eternal happiness, even if there were no other enjoyment in heaven. Moreover the essential glory of those, who have worthily and devoutly received the holy Eucharist, will in several respects exceed the glory of many martyrs who have not received the body and blood of the Lord.

I wish thee also to hear, my dearest daughter, from my own mouth, what were my sentiments when in mortal life I was about to receive holy Communion. In order that thou mayest better understand what I say, reflect on all I have commanded thee to write about my gifts, merits and labors in life. I was preserved from original sin and, at the instant of my Conception, I received the knowledge and vision of the Divinity, as thou hast often recorded. I knew more than all the saints; I surpassed the highest seraphim in love; I never committed any fault; I constantly practiced all the virtues in a heroic degree and in the least of them I was greater than all the saints in their highest perfection; the intention and object of my actions were most exalted and my habits and gifts were noble without measure; I imitated my most holy Son most closely; I labored most faithfully; I suffered with eagerness and co-operated with the doings of the Lord exactly as was becoming to me; I ceased not to exercise my love and gain new and supereminent merits of grace. Yet I thought myself to have been fully repaid by being allowed to receive Him even once in the holy Eucharist; yea, I did not consider myself worthy of this one favor. Reflect then what should be thy sentiments, and those of the rest of the children of Adam, on being admitted to the reception of this admirable Sacrament. And if for the greatest of saints one holy Communion is a superabundant reward, what must the priests and the faithful think, when they are allowed to receive it so frequently? Open thy eyes in the deep darkness and blindness which overwhelm men around thee, and raise them up to the divine brightness in order to understand these mysteries. Look upon all thy works as insufficient, all thy sufferings as most insignificant, all thy thanksgiving as falling far short of what thou owest for such an exquisite blessing as that of possessing in the holy Church, Christ my divine Son, present in the holy Sacrament in order to enrich all the faithful. If thou hast not wherewith to show thy thanks for this and the other blessings which thou receivest, at least humiliate thyself to the dust and remain prostrate upon it; confess thyself unworthy in all the sincerity of thy heart. Magnify the Most High, bless and praise Him, preserving thyself at all times worthy to receive Him and to suffer many martyrdoms in return for such a favor.

CHAPTER IV.

By the wonderful mysteries, which our Savior
Jesus had celebrated in the Cenacle, the reign which,
according to his inscrutable decree, his eternal Father had
consigned to Him, was well established; and the Thursday night of his last Supper having already advanced
some hours, He chose to go forth to that dreadful battle
of his suffering and death by which the Redemption was
to be accomplished. The Lord then rose to depart from
the hall of the miraculous feast and also most holy
Mary left her retreat in order to meet Him on the way.
At this face to face meeting of the Prince of eternity
and of the Queen, a sword of sorrow pierced the heart
of Son and Mother, inflicting a pang of grief beyond
all human and angelic thought. The sorrowful Mother
threw Herself at the feet of Jesus, adoring Him as her
true God and Redeemer. The Lord, looking upon Her
with a majesty divine and at the same time with the
overflowing love of a Son, spoke to Her only these
words: "My Mother, I shall be with thee in tribulation;
let Us accomplish the will of the eternal Father and the
salvation of men." The great Queen offered Herself
as a sacrifice with her whole heart and asked his blessing. Having received this She returned to her retirement, where, by a special favor of the Lord, she was
enabled to see all that passed in connection with her
divine Son. Thus She was enabled to accompany Him

and co-operate with Him in his activity as far as devolved upon Her. The owner of the house, who was present at this meeting, moved by a divine impulse, offered his house and all that it contained to the Mistress of heaven, asking Her to make use of all that was his during her stay in Jerusalem; and the Queen accepted his offer with humble thanks. The thousand angels of her guard, in forms visible to Her, together with some of the pious women of her company, remained with the Lady.

Our Redeemer and Master left the house of the Cenacle with all the men, who had been present at the celebration of the mysterious Supper; and soon many of them dispersed in the different streets in order to attend to their own affairs. Followed by his twelve Apostles, the Lord directed his steps toward mount Olivet outside and close to the eastern walls of Jerusalem. Judas, alert in his treacherous solicitude for the betrayal of his divine Master, conjectured that Jesus intended to pass the night in prayer as was his custom. This appeared to him a most opportune occasion for delivering his Master into the hands of his confederates, the scribes and the pharisees. Having taken this dire resolve, he lagged behind and permitted the Master and his Apostles to proceed. Unnoticed by the latter he lost them from view and departed in all haste to his own ruin and destruction. Within him was the turmoil of sudden fear and anxiety, interior witnesses of the wicked deed he was about to commit. Driven on in the stormy hurricane of thoughts raised by his bad conscience, he arrived breathless at the house of the high priests. On the way it happened, that Lucifer, perceiving the haste of Judas in procuring the death of Jesus Christ, and (as I have related in chapter the tenth), fearing that after all Jesus might be the true Messias, came toward him in the shape of a very wicked man, a friend of Judas acquainted with the intended betrayal. In this shape Lucifer could speak to Judas without being recognized. He tried to persuade him that this project of selling his Master did at first seem advisable on account of the wicked deeds attributed to Jesus; but that, having more naturally considered the matter, he did not now deem it advisable to deliver Him over to the priests and pharisees; for Jesus was not so bad as Judas might imagine; nor did He deserve death; and besides He might free Himself by some miracles and involve his betrayer into great difficulties.

In the meanwhile our divine Lord with the eleven Apostles was engaged in the work of our salvation and the salvation of those who were scheming his death. Unheard of and wonderful contest between the deepest malice of man and the unmeasurable goodness and charity of God! If this stupendous struggle between good and evil began with the first man, it certainly reached its highest point in the death of the Repairer; for then good and evil stood face to face and exerted their highest powers: human malice in taking away the life and honor of the Creator and Redeemer, and his immense charity freely sacrificing both for men. According to our way of reasoning, it was as it were necessary that the most holy soul of Christ, yea that even his Divinity, should revert to his blessed Mother, in order that He might find some object in creation, in which his love should be recompensed and some excuse for disregarding the dictates of his justice. For in this Creature alone could He expect to see his Passion and Death bring forth full fruit; in her immeasurable holiness did his justice find some compensation for human malice; and in the humility and constant charity of this great Lady could be deposited the treasures of his merits, so that afterwards, as the new Phœnix from the rekindled ashes, his Church might arise from his sacrifice. The consolation which the humanity of Christ drew from the certainty of his blessed Mother's holiness gave Him strength and, as it were, new courage to conquer the malice of mortals; and He counted Himself well recompensed for suffering such atrocious pains by the fact that to mankind belonged also his most beloved Mother.

Our Savior pursued his way across the torrent of Cedron (John 18, 1) to mount Olivet and entered the garden of Gethsemani. Then He said to all the Apostles: "Wait for Me, and seat yourselves here while I go a short distance from here to pray (Matth. 26, 36); do you also pray, in order that you may not enter into temptation" (Luke 22, 40). The divine Master gave them this advice, in order that they might be firm in the temptations, of which He had spoken to them at the Supper: that all of them should be scandalized on account of what they should see Him suffer that night, that Satan would assail them to sift and stir them up by his false suggestions; for the Pastor (as prophesied) was to be illtreated and wounded and the sheep were to be dispersed (Zach. 13, 7). Then the Master of life, leaving the band of eight Apostles at that place and taking with Him saint Peter, saint John, and saint James, retired to another place, where they could neither be seen nor heard by the rest (Mark 14, 33). Being with the three Apostles He raised his eyes up to the eternal Father confessing and praising Him as was his custom; while interiorly He prayed in fulfillment of the prophecy of Zacharias, permitting death to approach the most innocent of men and commanding the sword of divine justice to be unsheathed over the Shepherd and descend upon the Godman with all its deathly force. In this prayer Christ our Lord offered Himself anew to the eternal Father in satisfaction of his justice for the rescue of the human race; and He gave consent, that all the torments of his Passion and Death be let loose over that part of his human being, which was capable of suffering. From that moment He suspended and restrained whatever consolation or relief would otherwise overflow from the impassable to the passable part of his being, so that in this dereliction his passion and sufferings might reach the highest degree possible. The eternal Father granted these petitions and approved this total sacrifice of the sacred humanity.

This prayer was as it were the floodgate through which the rivers of his suffering were to find entrance like the resistless onslaught of the ocean, as was foretold by David (Ps. 68, 2). And immediately He began to be sorrowful and feel the anguish of his soul and therefore said to the Apostles: "My soul is sorrowful unto death" (Mark 14, 34).

He threw himself with his divine face upon the ground and prayed to the eternal Father: "Father, if it is possible, let this chalice pass from Me" (Matth. 24, 38). This prayer Christ our Lord uttered, though He had come down from heaven with the express purpose of really suffering and dying for men; though He had counted as naught the shame of his Passion, had willingly embraced it and rejected all human consolation; though He was hastening with most ardent love into the jaws of death, to affronts, sorrows and afflictions; though He had set such a high price upon men, that He determined to redeem them at the shedding of his life-blood. Since by virtue of his divine and human wisdom and his inextinguishable love He had shown Himself so superior to the natural fear of death, that it seems this petition did not arise from any motive solely coming from Himself. That this was so in fact, was made known to me in the light which was vouchsafed me concerning the mysteries contained in this prayer of the Savior.

This agony of Christ our Savior grew in proportion to the greatness of his charity and the certainty of his knowledge, that men would persist in neglecting to profit by his Passion and Death (Luke 22, 44). His agony increased to such an extent, that great drops of bloody sweat were pressed from Him, which flowed to the very earth. Although this prayer was uttered subject to a condition and failed in regard to the reprobate who fell under this condition; yet He gained thereby a greater abundance and secured a greater frequency of favors for mortals. Through it the blessings were multiplied for those who placed no obstacles, the fruits of the Redemption were applied to the saints and to the just more abundantly, and many gifts and graces, of which the reprobates made themselves unworthy, were diverted to the elect. The human will of Christ, conforming itself to that of the Divinity, then accepted suffering for each respectively: for the reprobate, as sufficient to procure them the necessary help, if they would make use of its merits, and for the predestined, as an efficacious means, of which they would avail themselves to secure their salvation by co-operating with grace. Thus was set in order, and as it were realized, the salvation of the mystical body of his holy Church, of which Christ the Lord was the Creator and Head.

As a ratification of this divine decree, while yet our Master was in his agony, the eternal Father for the third time sent the archangel Michael to the earth in order to comfort Him by a sensible message and confirmation of what He already knew by the infused science of his most holy soul; for the angel could not tell our Lord anything He did not know, nor could he produce any additional effect on his interior consciousness for this purpose.

Let us now return to the Cenacle, where the Queen of heaven had retired with the holy women of her company. From her retreat, by divine enlightenment, She saw most clearly all the mysteries and doings of her most holy Son in the garden. At the moment when the Savior separated Himself with the three Apostles Peter, John and James, the heavenly Queen separated Herself from the other women and went into another room. Upon leaving them She exhorted them to pray and watch lest they enter into temptation, but She took with Her the three Marys, treating Mary Magdalen as the superior of the rest. Secluding Herself with these three as her more intimate companions, She begged the eternal Father to suspend in Her all human alleviation and comfort, both in the sensitive and in the spiritual part of her being, so that nothing might hinder Her from suffering to the highest degree in union with her divine Son. She prayed that She might be permitted to feel and participate in her virginal body all the pains of the wounds and tortures about to be undergone by Jesus. This petition was granted by the blessed Trinity and the Mother in consequence suffered all the torments of her most holy Son in exact duplication, as I shall relate later. Although they were such, that, if the right hand of the Almighty had not preserved Her, they would have caused her death many times over; yet, on the other hand, these sufferings, inflicted by God himself, were like a pledge and a new lease of life. For in her most ardent love She would have considered it incomparably more painful to see her divine Son suffer and die without being allowed to share in his torments.

The three Marys were instructed by the Queen to accompany and assist Her in her affliction, and for this purpose they were endowed with greater light and grace than the other women. In retiring with them the most pure Mother began to feel unwonted sorrow and anguish and She said to them: "My soul is sorrowful, because my beloved Son is about to suffer and die, and it is not permitted me to suffer and die of his torments. Pray, my friends, in order that you may not be overcome by temptation." Having said this She went apart a short distance from them, and following the Lord in his supplications. She, as far as was possible to Her and as far as She knew it to be conformable to the human will of her Son, continued her prayers and petitions, feeling the same agony as that of the Savior in the garden. She also returned at the same intervals to her companions to exhort them, because She knew of the wrath of the demon against them. She wept at the perdition of the foreknown; for She was highly enlightened in the mysteries of eternal predestination and reprobation. In order to imitate and co-operate in all things with the Redeemer of the world, the great Lady also suffered a bloody sweat, similar to that of Jesus in the garden, and by divine intervention She was visited by the archangel saint Gabriel, as Christ her Son was visited by the archangel Michael. The holy prince expounded to Her the will of the Most High in the same manner as saint Michael had expounded it to Christ the Lord. In both of them the prayer offered and the cause of sorrow was the same; and therefore They were also proportionally alike to one another in their actions and in their knowledge.

While they were approaching, the Lord returned the third time to his Apostles and finding them asleep spoke to them: "Sleep ye now, and take your rest. It is enough: the hour is come; behold the Son of man shall be betrayed into the hands of sinners. Rise up, let us go. Behold he that will betray Me is at hand" (Mark 14, 41). Such were the words of the Master of holiness to the three most privileged Apostles; He was unwilling to reprehend them more severely than in this most meek and loving manner. Being oppressed, they did not know what to answer their Lord, as Scripture says (Mark 14, 40). They arose and Jesus went with them to join the other eight disciples. He found them likewise overcome and oppressed by their great sorrow and fallen asleep. The Master then gave orders, that all of them together, mystically forming one body with Him their Head, should advance toward the enemies, thereby teaching them the power of mutual and perfect unity for overcoming the demons and their followers and for avoiding defeat by them. For a triple cord is hard to tear, as says Ecclesiastes (4, 12), and he that is mighty against one, may be overcome by two, that being the effect of union. The Lord again exhorted all the Apostles and forewarned them of what was to happen. Already the confused noise of the advancing band of soldiers and their helpmates began to be heard. Our Savior then proceeded to meet them on the way, and, with incomparable love, magnanimous courage and tender piety prayed interiorly: "O sufferings longingly desired from my inmost soul, ye pains, wounds, affronts, labors, afflictions and ignominious death, come, come, come quickly, for the fire of love, which burns for the salvation of men, is anxious to see you meet the Innocent one of all creatures. Well do I know your value, I have sought, desired, and solicited you and I meet you joyously of my own free will; I have purchased you by my anxiety in searching for you and I esteem you for your merits. I desire to remedy and enhance your value and raise you to highest dignity. Let death come, in order that by my accepting it without having deserved it I may triumph over it and gain life for those who have been punished by death for their sins (Osee 13, 14). I give permission to my friends to forsake Me; for I alone desire and am able to enter into this battle and gain for them triumph and victory" (Is. 53, 3).

During these words and prayers of the Author of life Judas advanced in order to give the signal upon which he had agreed with his companions (Matth. 26, 48), namely the customary, but now feigned kiss of peace, by which they were to distinguish Jesus as the One whom they should single out from the rest and immediately seize. These precautions the unhappy disciple had taken, not only out of avarice for the money and hatred against his Master, but also, on account of the fear with which he was filled. For he dreaded the inevitable necessity of meeting Him and encountering Him in the future, if Christ was not put to death on this occasion. Such a confusion he feared more than the death of his soul, or the death of his divine Master, and, in order to forestall it, he hastened to complete his treachery and desired to see the Author of life die at the hands of his enemies. The traitor then ran up to the meekest Lord, and, as a consummate hypocrite, hiding his hatred, he imprinted on his countenance the kiss of peace, saying: "God save Thee, Master." By this so treacherous act the perdition of Judas was matured and God was justified in withholding his grace and help. On the part of the unfaithful disciple, malice and temerity reached their highest degree; for, interiorly denying or disbelieving the uncreated and created wisdom by which

Christ must know of his treason, and ignoring his power to destroy him, he sought to hide his malice under the cloak of the friendship of a true disciple; and all this for the purpose of delivering over to such a frightful and cruel death his Creator and Master, to whom he was bound by so many obligations. In this one act of treason he committed so many and such formidable sins, that it is impossible to fathom their immensity; for he was treacherous, murderous, sacrilegious, ungrateful, inhuman, disobedient, false, lying, impious and unequalled in hypocrisy; and all this was included in one and the same crime perpetrated against the person of God made man.

The most pure Mother of Christ our Lord was most attentive to all that passed in his capture, and by means of her clear visions saw it more clearly than if She had been present in person; for by means of her supernatural visions She penetrated into all the mysteries of his words and actions. When She beheld the band of soldiers and servants issuing from the house of the high priest, the prudent Lady foresaw the irreverence and insults with which they would treat their Creator and Redeemer; and in order to do what was within her power, She invited the holy angels and many others in union with Her to render adoration and praise to the Lord of creation as an offset to the injuries and affronts He would sustain at the hands of those ministers of darkness. The same request She made to the holy women who were praying with Her. She told them, that her most holy Son had now given permission to his enemies to take him prisoner and illtreat him, and that they were about to make use of this permission in a most impious and cruel manner. Assisted by the holy angels and the pious women the faithful Queen engaged in interior and exterior acts of devoted faith and love, confessing, adoring, praising and magnifying the infinite Deity and the most holy humanity of her Creator and Lord. The holy women imitated Her in the genuflections and prostrations, and the angelic princes responded to the canticles with which She magnified, celebrated and glorified the Divinity and humanity of Christ. In the measure in which the children of malice increased their irreverence and injuries, She sought to compensate them by her praise and veneration. Thus She continued to placate the divine justice, lest it should be roused against his persecutors and destroy them; for only most holy Mary was capable of staying the punishment of such great offenses.

And the great Lady not only placated the just Judge, but even obtained favors and blessings from the divine clemency for the very persons who irritated Him and thus secured a return of good for those who were heaping wrongs upon Christ the Lord for his doctrine and benefits. This mercy attained its highest point in the disloyal and obstinate Judas; for the tender Mother, seeing him deliver Jesus by the kiss of feigned friendship, and considering how shortly before his mouth had contained the sacramental body of the Lord, with whose sacred countenance so soon after those same foul lips were permitted to come in contact, was transfixed with sorrow and entranced by charity. She asked the Lord to grant new graces, whereby this man, who had enjoyed the privilege of touching the face whereon angels desire to look, might, if he chose to use them, save himself from perdition. In response to this prayer of most holy Mary, her Son and Lord granted Judas powerful graces in the very consummation of his treacherous delivery. If the unfortunate man had given heed and had commenced to respond to them, the Mother of mercy would have obtained for him many others and at last also pardon for his sin. She has done so with many other great sinners, who were willing to give that glory to Her, and thus obtain eternal glory for themselves. But Judas failed to realize this and thus lost all chance of salvation, as I shall relate in the next chapter.

When the servants of the high priest laid hands on and bound the Savior, the most blessed Mother felt on her own hands the pains caused by the ropes and chains, as if She Herself was being bound and fettered; in the same manner She felt in her body the blows and torments further inflicted upon the Lord, for, I have already said, this favor was granted to his Mother, as we shall see in the course of the Passion. This her sensible participation in his sufferings was some kind of relief of the pain, which She would have suffered in her loving soul at the thought of not being with Him in his torments.

WORDS OF THE QUEEN.

My daughter, in all that thou art made to understand and write concerning these mysteries, thou drawest upon thyself (and upon mortals) a severe judgment, if thou dost not overcome thy pusillanimity, ingratitude and baseness by meditating day and night on the Passion and Death of Jesus crucified. This is the great science of the saints, so little heeded by the worldly; it is the bread of life and the spiritual food of the little ones, which gives wisdom to them and the want of which starves the lovers of this proud world (Wis. 15, 3). In this science I wish thee to be studious and wise, for with it thou canst buy thyself all good things (Wis. 7, 11). My Son and Lord taught us this science when He said: "I am the way, the truth and the life: no one

cometh to my Father except through Me" (John 14, 6).
Tell me then, my daughter: if my Lord and Master has
made Himself the life and the way for men through his
Passion and Death, is it not evident that in order to
go that way and live up to this truth, they must follow
Christ crucified, afflicted, scourged and affronted? Consider the ignorance of men who wish to come to the
Father without following Christ, since they expect to
reign with God without suffering or imitating his Passion, yea without even a thought of accepting any part
of his suffering and Death, or of thanking Him for it.
They want it to procure for them the pleasures of this
life as well as of eternal life, while Christ their Creator
has suffered the most bitter pains and torments in order
to enter heaven and to show them by his example how
they are to find the way of light.

Eternal rest is incompatible with the shame of
not having duly labored for its attainment. He is not
a true son of his father, who does not imitate him, nor
he a good disciple, who does not follow his Master,
nor he a good servant, who does not accompany his
lord; nor do I count him a devoted child, who does not
suffer with me and my divine Son. But our love for
the eternal salvation of men obliges us, who see them
forgetful of this truth and so adverse to suffering, to
send them labors and punishments, so that if they do
not freely welcome them, they may at least be forced to
undergo them and so be enabled to enter upon the way
of salvation. And yet even all this is insufficient, since
their inclinations and their blind love of visible things
detains them and makes them hard and heavy of heart;
they rob them of remembrance and affection toward
these higher things, which might raise them above themselves and above created things. Hence it comes, that

men do not find joy in their tribulations, nor rest in their labors, nor consolation in their sorrows, nor any peace in adversities. For, altogether different from the saints who glory in tribulation as the fulfillment of their most earnest desires, they desire none of it and abhor all that is painful. In many of the faithful this ignorance goes still farther; for some of them expect to be distinguished by God's most intimate love, others, to be pardoned without penance, others, to be highly favored. Nothing of all this will they attain, because they do not ask in the name of Christ the Lord and because they do not wish to imitate Him and follow Him in his Passion.

Therefore, my daughter, embrace the Cross and do not admit any consolation outside of it in this mortal life. By contemplating and feeling within thyself the sacred Passion thou wilt attain the summit of perfection and attain the love of a spouse. Bless and magnify my most holy Son for the love with which He delivered Himself up for the salvation of mankind. Little do mortals heed this mystery; but I, as an Eyewitness, assure thee, next to ascending to the right hand of his eternal Father, nothing was so highly estimated and so earnestly desired by Him, as to offer Himself for suffering and death and to deliver Himself up entirely to his enemies. I wish also that thou lament with great sorrow the fact that Judas, in his malice and treachery, has many more followers than Christ. Many are the infidels, many the bad Catholics, many the hypocrites, who under the name of a Christian, sell and deliver Him and wish to crucify Him anew. Bewail all these evils, which thou understandest and knowest, in order that thou mayest imitate and follow me in this matter.

CHAPTER V.

Having been taken prisoner and firmly bound, the most meek Lamb Jesus was dragged from the garden to the house of the highpriests, first to the house of Annas (John 18, 13). The turbulent band of soldiers and servants, having been advised by the traitorous disciple that his Master was a sorcerer and could easily escape their hands, if they did not carefully bind and chain Him securely before starting on their way, took all precautions inspired by such a mistrust (Mark 14, 44). Lucifer and his compeers of darkness secretly irritated and provoked them to increase their impious and sacrilegious illtreatment of the Lord beyond all bounds of humanity and decency. As they were willing accomplices of Lucifer's malice, they omitted no outrage against the person of their Creator within the limits set them by the Almighty. They bound Him with a heavy iron chain with such ingenuity, that it encircled as well the waist as the neck. The two ends of the chain, which remained free, were attached to large rings or handcuffs, with which they manacled the hands of the Lord, who created the heavens, the angels and the whole universe. The hands thus secured and bound, they fastened not in front, but behind. This chain they had brought from the house of Annas the highpriest, where it had served to raise the portcullis of a dungeon. They had wrenched it from its place and provided it with padlock handcuffs. But they were not satisfied with this unheard-of way of securing a prisoner; for in their distrust they added two pieces of strong rope: the one they wound around the throat of Jesus and, crossing it at the breast, bound it in heavy knots all about the body, leaving two long ends free in front, in order that the servants and soldiers might jerk Him in different directions along the way. The second rope served to tie his arms, being bound likewise around his waist. The two ends of this rope were left hanging free to be used by two other executioners for jerking Him from behind.

The Author of our salvation, hiding his power of annihilating his enemies in order that our Redemption might be the more abundant, submitted to all the consequences of the impious fury which Lucifer and his hellish squadron fomented in the Jews. They dragged Him bound and chained under continued ill-treatment to the house of Annas, before whom they presented Him as a malefactor worthy of death. It was the custom of the Jews to present thus bound those criminals who merited capital punishment; and they now made use of this custom in regard to Jesus, in order to intimate his sentence even before the trial. The sacrilegious priest Annas seated himself in proud and arrogant state on the platform or tribunal of a great hall. Immediately Lucifer placed himself at his side with a multitude of evil spirits.

Imperiously and haughtily the highpriest asked Him about his disciples (John 18, 19!), and what doctrine He was preaching and teaching. This question was put merely for the purpose of misinterpreting his answer, if Jesus should utter any word that afforded such a chance. But the Master of holiness, who is the Guide and the Corrector of the most wise (Wis. 7, 15), offered to the eternal Father the humiliation of being presented as a criminal before the highpriest and of being questioned by him as a prevaricator and author of a false doctrine. Our Redeemer with an humble and cheerful countenance answered the question as to his doctrines: "I have spoken openly to the world: I have always taught in the synagogue and in the temple, whither all the Jews resort: and in secret I have spoken nothing. Why askest thou Me? ask these, who have heard what I have spoken unto them: behold they know what I have said." As the doctrine of Christ our Lord came from his eternal Father, He spoke for it and defended its honor. He referred them to his hearers, both because those by whom He was now surrounded, would not believe Him and wished to distort all He should say, and because the truth and force of his teachings recommended and forced themselves upon the minds of his greatest enemies by their own excellence.

Concerning the Apostles He said nothing, because it was not necessary on this occasion and because they were not reflecting much credit upon their Master by their present conduct. Though his answer was so full of wisdom and so well suited to the question, yet one of the servants of the highpriest rushed up with raised hand and audaciously struck the venerable and sacred face of Jesus, saying: "Answerest Thou the high priest so?" The Lord accepted this boundless injury, praying for the one who had inflicted it; and holding Himself ready, if necessary, to turn and offer the other cheek for a second stroke, according to the doctrine He had himself inculcated (Matth. 5, 39). But in order that the atrocious and daring offender might not shamelessly boast of his wickedness, the Lord replied with great tranquillity and meekness: "If I have spoken evil, give testimony of the evil; if well, why strikest thou

Me?" O sight most astounding to the supernal spirits! Since this is He, at the mere sound of whose voice the foundations of the heavens tremble and ought to tremble and the whole firmament is shaken! While this ill-treatment of the Lord was going on, saint Peter and the other disciple, who was none other than saint John, arrived at the house of Annas. Saint John, as being well known there, readily obtained entrance, while saint Peter remained outside. Afterwards the servant maid, who was an acquaintance of saint John, allowed also him to enter and see what would happen to the Lord (John 18, 16). The two disciples remained in the portico adjoining the court-hall of the priest, and saint Peter approached the fire, which the soldiers, on account of the coldness of the night, had built in the enclosure near the portico. The servant maid, on closer inspection, noticed the depressed bearing of saint Peter. Coming up to him she recognized him as a disciple of Jesus, and said: "Art thou not perhaps one of the disciples of this Man?" This question was asked by the maid with an air of contempt and reproach. Peter in his great weakness and hesitancy yielded to a sense of shame. Overcome also by his fear he answered: "I am not his disciple." Having given this answer, he slipped away to avoid further conversation, and left the premises. But he soon afterwards followed his Master to the house of Caiphas, where he denied Him again at two different times, as I shall relate farther on.

The denial of Peter caused greater pain to the Lord than the buffet which He had received; for this sin was directly opposed and abhorrent to his immense charity, while pains and sufferings were sweet and welcome to Him, since He could thereby atone for our sins. After this first denial of Peter, Christ prayed for him to his eternal Father and ordained that through the intercession of the blessed Mary he should obtain pardon even after the third denial. The great Lady witnessed all that passed from her oratory, as I have said. As She contained in her own breast the propitiatory and sacrifice of her Son and Lord in sacramental form, She directed her petitions and loving aspirations to Him, eliciting most heroic acts of compassion, thanksgiving, adoration and worship. She bitterly wept over the denial of saint Peter, and ceased not, until She perceived that the Lord would not refuse him the necessary helps for effectually rising from his fall.

The whole rabble of infernal spirits and merciless foes of Christ left the house of Annas and dragged our Lord Savior through the streets to the house of Caiphas, exercising upon Him all the cruelty of their ignominious fury. The highpriests and his attendants broke out in loud derision and laughter, when they saw Jesus brought amid tumultuous noise into their presence and beheld Him now subject to their power and jurisdiction without hope of escape. O mystery of the most exalted wisdom of heaven! O foolishness and ignorance of hell, and blind stupidity of mortals! What a distance immeasurable do I see between the doings of the Most High and yours!

The highpriest Caiphas, filled with a deadly envy and hatred against the Master of life, was seated in his chair of state or throne. With him were Lucifer and all his demons, who had come from the house of Annas. The scribes and pharisees, like bloodthirsty wolves, surrounded the gentle Lamb; all of them were full of the exultation of the envious, who see the object of their envy confounded and brought down. By common consent they sought for witnesses, whom they could bribe to bring false testimonies against Jesus our Savior (Matth. 26, 59). Those that had been procured, advanced to proffer their accusations and testimony; but their accusations neither agreed with each other, nor could any of their slander be made to apply to Him, who of his very nature was innocence and holiness (Mark 25, 56; Heb. 7, 26).

Our Savior Jesus answered not a word to all the calumnies and lies brought forward against his innocence. Caiphas, provoked by the patient silence of the Lord, rose up in his seat and said to Him: "Why dost Thou not answer to what so many witnesses testify against Thee?" But even to this the Lord made no response. For Caiphas and the rest were not only indisposed to believe Him; but they treacherously wished to make use of his answer in order to calumniate Him and satisfy the people in their proceedings against the Galileean, so that they might not be thought to have condemned Him to death without cause. This humble silence, which should have appeased the wicked priest, only infuriated him so much the more because it frustrated his evil purpose. Lucifer, who incited the high priest and all the rest, intently watched the conduct of the Savior. But the intention of the dragon was different from that of the high priest. He merely wanted to irritate the Lord, or to hear some word, by which he could ascertain whether he was true God.

With this purpose satan stirred up Caiphas to the highest pitch of rage and to ask in great wrath and haughtiness: "I adjure Thee by the living God, that Thou tell us, if Thou be the Christ, the Son of God." This question of the highpriest certainly convicted him at once of the deepest folly and of dreadful blasphemy; for if it was sincere, he had permitted Christ to be brought before his tribunal in doubt whether He was the true God or not, which would make him guilty of the most formidable and audacious crime. The doubt in such a matter should have been solved in quite another way, conformable to the demands of right reason and justice. Christ our Savior, hearing Himself conjured by the living God, inwardly adored and reverenced the Divinity, though appealed to by such sacrilegious lips. Out of reverence for the name of God He therefore answered: "Thou hast said: I am He. Nevertheless I say to you, hereafter you shall see the Son of man (who I am) sitting on the right hand of the power of God, and coming in the clouds of heaven" (Matth. 26, 64).

But the highpriest, furious at the answer of the Lord, instead of looking upon it as a solution of his doubt, rose once more in his seat, and rending his garments as an outward manifestation of his zeal for the honor of God, loudly cried out: "He hath blasphemed; what further need have we of witnesses? Behold, now you have heard the blasphemy: what think you?" (Matth. 26, 65.) The real blasphemy however consisted rather in these words of Caiphas, since he denied the certain fact that Christ was the Son of God by his very nature, and since he attributed to the divine Personality sinfulness, which was directly repugnant to his very nature. Such was the folly of the wicked priest, who by his office should have recognized and proclaimed the universal truth. He made of himself an execrable blasphemer in maintaining that He, who is holiness itself, had blasphemed. Having previously, with satanical instinct, abused his high office in prophesying that the death of one man is better than the ruin of all the people, he now was hindered by his sins from understanding his own prophecy.   As the example and the opinions of princes and prelates powerfully stirs up the flattery and subserviency of inferiors, that whole gathering of wickedness was incensed at the Savior Jesus: all exclaimed in a loud voice: "He is guilty of death (Matth. 26, 66), let Him die, let Him die!" Roused by satanic fury they all fell upon their most meek Master and discharged upon Him their wrath.   Some of them struck Him in the face, others kicked Him, others tore out his hair, others spat upon his venerable countenance, others slapped or struck Him in the neck, which was a treatment reserved among the Jews only for the most abject and vile of criminals. All these affronts, reproaches and insults were seen and felt by the most holy Mary, causing in Her the same pains and wounds in the same parts of her body and at the same time as inflicted upon the Lord.   The only difference was, that in our Lord the blows and torments were inflicted by the Jews themselves, while in his most pure Mother they were caused by the Almighty in a miraculous manner and upon request of the Lady.   According to natural laws, the vehemence of her interior sorrow and anxiety would have put an end to her life; but She was strengthened by divine power, so as to be able to continue to suffer with her beloved Son and Lord.

The interior acts performed by the Savior under these barbarous and unheard of persecutions, cannot be fathomed by human reason or faculties.   Mary alone understood them fully, so as to be able to imitate them with the highest perfection.   But as the divine Master now experienced in his own Person, how necessary his sympathy would be for those who were to follow him and practice his doctrine, He exerted Himself so much the more in procuring for them grace and blessings on this occasion, in which He was teaching them by his own example the narrow way of perfection. In the midst of these injuries and torments, and those which followed thereafter, the Lord established for his perfect and chosen souls the beatitudes, which He had promised and proposed to them some time before. He looked upon the poor in spirit, who were to imitate Him in this virtue and said: "Blessed are you in being stripped of the earthly goods; for by my Passion and Death I am to entail upon you the heavenly kingdom as a secure and certain possession of voluntary poverty. Blessed are those who meekly suffer and bear adversities and tribulations; for, besides the joy of having imitated Me, they shall possess the land of the hearts and the good will of men through the peacefulness of their intercourse and the sweetness of their virtues. Blessed are they that weep while they sow in tears; for in them, they shall receive the bread of understanding and life, and they shall afterwards harvest the fruits of everlasting joy and bliss."

"Blessed are also those who hunger and thirst for justice and truth; for I shall earn for them satiation far beyond all their desires, as well in the reign of grace as in the reign of glory. Blessed are they, who, imitating Me in my offers of pardon and friendship, mercifully pity those that offend and persecute them; for I promise them the fulness of mercy from my Father. Blessed be the pure of heart, who imitate Me in crucifying their flesh in order to preserve the purity of their souls. I promise them the vision of peace and of my Divinity, by becoming like unto Me and by partaking of Me. Blessed are the peaceful, who, yielding their rights, do not resist the evil-minded and deal with them with a sincere and tranquil heart without vengeance;

they shall be called my children, because they imitate my eternal Father and I shall write them in my memory and in my mind as my adopted sons. Those that suffer persecution for justice's sake, shall be the blessed heirs of my celestial kingdom, since they suffer with Me; and where I am, there also they shall be in eternity. Rejoice, ye poor; be consoled all ye that are and shall be afflicted; glory in your lot, ye little ones and despised ones of this world, you who suffer in humility and longanimity, suffer with an interior rejoicing; since all of you are following Me in the path of truth. Renounce vanity, despise the pomp and haughtiness of the false and deceitful Babylon; pass ye through the fires and the waters of tribulation until you reach Me, who am the light, the truth and your guide to the eternal rest and refreshment."

By the ill-treatment, which the Lord received in the presence of Caiphas, the wrath of this highpriest and of all his supporters and ministers was much gratified, though not at all satiated. But as it was already past midnight, the whole council of these wicked men resolved to take good care, that the Savior be securely watched and confined until the morning, lest He should escape while they were asleep. For this purpose they ordered Him to be locked, bound as He was, in one of the subterranean dungeons, a prison cell set apart for the most audacious robbers and criminals of the state. Scarcely any light penetrated into this prison to dispel its darkness. It was filled with such uncleanness and stench, that it would have infected the whole house, if it had not been so remote and so well enclosed; for it had not been cleaned for many years, both because it was so deep down and because of the degradation of the criminals that were confined in it; for none thought it worth while making it more habitable than for mere wild beasts, unworthy of all human kindness.

WORDS OF THE QUEEN.

My daughter, to great deeds art thou called and invited on account of the divine enlightenment thou receivest concerning the mysteries of the sufferings of my most holy Son and of myself for the human race, and on account of the knowledge which thou hast obtained concerning the small return made by heartless and ungrateful men for all our pains. Thou livest yet in mortal flesh and art thyself subject to this ignorance and weakness; but by the force of truth thou art now roused to great wonder, sorrow and compassion at the want of attention displayed by mortals toward these great sacraments and at the losses sustained by them through their lukewarmness and negligence. What then are the thoughts of the angels and saints, and what are my thoughts in beholding this world and all the faithful in such a dangerous and dreadful state of carelessness, when they have the Passion and Death of my divine Son before their eyes, and when they have me, for their Mother and Intercessor and his most pure life and mine for an example? I tell thee truly, my dearest, only my intercession and the merits of his Son, which I offer to the eternal Father, can delay the punishment and placate his wrath, can retard the destruction of the world and the severe chastisement of the children of the Church, who know his will and fail to fulfill it (John 15, 15). But I am much incensed to find so few who condole with me and try to console my Son in his sorrows, as David says (Ps. 68, 21). This hardness of heart will cause great confusion to them on the day of judgment; since they will then see with irreparable sorrow, not only that they were ungrateful, but inhuman and cruel toward my divine Son, toward me and toward themselves.

Consider then thy duty, my dearest, and raise thyself above all earthly things and above thyself; for I am calling thee and choose thee to imitate and follow me into the solitude, in which I am left by creatures, whom my Son and I have pursued with so many blessings and favors. Weigh in thy heart, how much it cost my Lord to reconcile mankind to the eternal Father (Colos. 1, 22) and regain for them his friendship. Weep and afflict thyself that so many should live in such forgetfulness and that so many should labor with all their might at destroying and losing what was bought by the blood of God itself and all that I from the first moment of my Conception have sought to procure and am procuring for their salvation. Awaken in thy heart the deepest grief, that in his holy Church there should be many followers of the hypocritical and sacrilegious priests who, under cover of a false piety, still condemn Christ; that pride and sumptuousness with other grave vices should be raised to authority and exalted, while humility, truth, justice and all virtues be so oppressed and debased and avarice and vanity should prevail. Few know the poverty of Christ, and fewer embrace it. Holy faith is hindered and is not spread among the nations on account of the boundless ambition of the mighty of this earth; in many Catholics it is inactive and dead; and whatever should be living, is near to death and to eternal perdition. The counsels of the Gospel are forgotten, its precepts trodden under foot, charity almost extinct. My son and true God offers his cheeks in patience and meekness to be buffeted and wounded (Thren. 3, 30). Who pardons an insult for the sake of imitating Him? Just the contrary is set up as law in this world, not only by the infidels, but by the very children of the faith and of light.

In recognizing these sins I desire that thou imitate me in what I did during the Passion and during my whole life, namely practice the virtues opposed to these vices. As a recompense for their blasphemies, I blessed God; for their oaths, I praised Him; for their unbelief, I excited acts of faith, and so for all the rest of the sins committed. This is what I desire thee to do while living in this world. Fly also the dangerous intercourse with creatures, taught by the example of Peter, for thou art not stronger than he, the Apostle of Christ; and if thou fall in thy weakness, weep over thy fault and immediately seek my intercession. Make up for thy ordinary faults and weaknesses by thy patience in adversities, accept them with a joyous mien and without disturbance, no matter what they may be, whether they be sickness or the molestations coming from creatures, or whether they arise from the opposition of the flesh to the spirit, or from the conflicts with visible or invisible enemies. In all these things canst thou suffer and must thou bear up in faith, hope and magnanimous sentiment. I remind thee, that there is no exercise more profitable and useful for the soul than to suffer: for suffering gives light, undeceives, detaches the heart from visible things and raises it up to the Lord. He will come to meet those in suffering, because He is with the afflicted and sends to them his protection and help (Ps. 40, 15).

CHAPTER VI.

JESUS BROUGHT BEFORE PILATE. THE SCOURGING AND
CROWNING WITH THORNS.

At the dawn of Friday morning, say the Evangelists (Matth. 27, 1; Mark 15, 1; Luke 22, 66; John 11, 47), the ancients, the chief priests and scribes, who according to the law were looked upon with greatest respect by the people, gathered together in order to come to a common decision concerning the death of Christ. This they all desired; however they were anxious to preserve the semblance of justice before the people. This council was held in the house of Caiphas, where the Lord was imprisoned. Once more they commanded Him to be brought from the dungeon to the hall of the council in order to be examined. The satellites of justice rushed below to drag Him forth bound and fettered as He was.

They again asked Him to tell them, whether He was the Christ (Luke 22, 1), that is, the Anointed. Just as all their previous questions, so this was put with the malicious determination not to listen or to admit the truth, but to calumniate and fabricate a charge against Him. But the Lord, being perfectly willing to die for the truth, denied it not; at the same time He did not wish to confess it in such a manner that they could despise it, or borrow out of it some color for their calumny; for this was not becoming his innocence and wisdom. Therefore He veiled his answer in such a way, that if the pharisees chose to yield to even the least kindly feeling, they would be able to trace up the mystery hidden in his words; but if they had no such feeling, then should it become clear through their answer, that the evil which they imputed to Him was the result of their wicked intentions and lay not in his answer. He therefore said to them: "If I tell you that I am He of whom you ask, you will not believe what I say; and if I shall ask you, you will not answer, nor release Me. But I tell you, that the Son of man, after this, shall seat Himself at the right hand of the power of God" (Luke 22, 67). The priests answered: "Then thou art the Son of God?" and the Lord replied: "You say that I am." This was as if He had said: You have made a very correct inference, that I am the Son of God; for my works, my doctrines, and your own Scripture, as well as what you are now doing with Me, testify to the fact, that I am the Christ, the One promised in the law.

But this council of the wicked was not disposed to assent to divine truth, although they themselves inferred it very correctly from the antecedents and could easily have believed it. They would neither give assent nor belief, but preferred to call it a blasphemy deserving death. Since the Lord had now reaffirmed what He had said before, they all cried out: "What need have we of further witnesses, since He himself asserts it by his own lips?" And they immediately came to the unanimous conclusion that He should, as one worthy of death, be brought before Pontius Pilate, who governed Judea in the name of the Roman emperor and was the temporal Lord of Palestine.

The sun had already arisen while these things happened and the most holy Mother, who saw it all from afar, now resolved to leave her retreat and follow her divine Son to the house of Pilate and to his death on the Cross. When the great Queen and Lady was about to set forth from the Cenacle, saint John arrived, in order to give an account of all that was happening; for the beloved disciple at that time did not know of the visions, by which all the doings and sufferings of her most holy Son were manifest to the blessed Mother. After the denial of saint Peter, saint John had retired and had observed, more from afar what was going on. Recognizing also the wickedness of his flight in the garden, he confessed it to the Mother of God and asked her pardon as soon as he came into her presence; and then he gave an account of all that passed in his heart and of what he had done and what he had seen in following his Master.   Saint John thought it well to prepare the afflicted Mother for her meeting with her most holy Son, in order that She might not be overcome by the fearful spectacle of his present condition.   Therefore He sought to impress Her beforehand with some image of his sufferings by saying: "O my Lady, in what a state of suffering is our divine Master! The sight of Him cannot but break one's heart; for by the buffets and the blows and by the spittle, his most beautiful countenance is so disfigured and defiled, that Thou wilt scarcely recognize Him with thy own eyes."   The most prudent Lady listened to his description, as if She knew nothing of the events; but She broke out in bitterest tears of heart-rending sorrow.   The holy women, who had came forth with the Lady, also listened to saint John, and all of them were filled with grief and terror at his words. The Queen of heaven asked the Apostle to accompany Her and the devout women, and, exhorting them all, She said: "Let us hasten our steps, in order that my eyes may see the Son of the eternal Father, who took human form in my womb; and you shall see, my dearest friends, to what the love of mankind has driven Him, my Lord and God, and what it costs Him to redeem men from sin and death, and to open for them the gates of heaven."

The Queen of heaven set forth through the streets of Jerusalem accompanied by saint John and by some holy women. Of these not all, but only the three Marys and other very pious women, followed Her to the end. With Her were also the angels of her guard, whom She asked to open a way for Her to her divine Son. The holy angels obeyed and acted as her guard. On the streets She heard the people expressing their various opinions and sentiments concerning the sorrowful events now transpiring in reference to Jesus of Nazareth. The more kindly hearted lamented over his fate, and they were fewest in number. Others spake about the intention of his enemies to crucify Him; others related where He now was and how He was conducted through the streets, bound as a criminal; others spoke of the illtreatment He was undergoing; others asked, what evil He had done, that He should be so misused; others again in their astonishment and in their doubts, exclaimed: To this then have his miracles brought Him! Without a doubt they were all impostures, since He cannot defend or free Himself!

Through the swarming and confused crowds the angels conducted the Empress of heaven to a sharp turn of the street, where She met her most holy Son. With the profoundest reverence She prostrated Herself before his sovereign Person and adored it more fervently and with a reverence more deep and more ardent than ever was given or ever shall be given to it by all the creatures. She arose and then the Mother and Son looked upon each other with ineffable tenderness, interiorly conversing with each other in transports of an unspeakable sorrow. The most prudent Lady stepped aside and then followed Christ our Lord, continuing at a distance her interior communication with Him and with the eternal Father. The words of her soul are not for the mortal and corruptible tongue.

The image of her divine Son, thus wounded, defiled and bound, remained so firmly fixed and imprinted in the soul of our Queen, that during her life it was never effaced, and remained in her mind as distinctly, as if She were continually beholding Him with her own eyes. Christ our God arrived at the house of Pilate, followed by many of the council and a countless multitude of the people. The Jews, wishing to preserve themselves as clean before the law as possible for the celebration of the Pasch and the unleavened bread, excused themselves before Pilate for their refusing to enter the pretorium or court of Pilate in presenting Jesus. As most absurd hypocrites they paid no attention to the sacrilegious uncleanness, with which their souls were affected in becoming the murderers of the innocent Godman. Pilate, although a heathen, yielded to their ceremonious scruples, and seeing that they hesitated to enter his pretorium, he went out to meet them. According to the formality customary among the Romans, he asked them (John 18, 28): "What accusation have you against this Man?" They answered: "If He were not a criminal, we would not have brought Him to thee thus bound and fettered." This was as much as to say: We have convinced ourselves of the misdeeds and we are so attached to justice and to our obligations, that we would not have begun any proceedings against Him, if He were not a great malefactor. But Pilate pressed his inquiry and said: "What then are the misdeeds, of which He has made Himself guilty?" They answered: "He is convicted of disturbing the commonwealth, He wishes to make Himself our king and forbids paying tribute to Cæsar (Luke 23, 2); He claims to be the son of God, and has preached a new doctrine, commencing in Galilee, through all Judea and Jerusalem." "Take Him then yourselves," said Pilate, "and judge Him according to your laws; I do not find a just cause for proceeding against Him." But the Jews replied: "It is not permitted us to sentence any one to death, nor to execute such a sentence."

The most holy Mary, with saint John and the women who followed Her, was present at this interview; for the holy angels made room for them where they could hear and see all that was passing. Shielded by her mantle She wept tears of blood, pressed forth by the sorrow which pierced her virginal heart. In her interior acts of virtue She faithfully reproduced those practiced by her most holy Son, while in her pains and endurance She copied those of his body. She asked the eternal Father to grant Her the favor of not losing sight of her divine Son, as far as was naturally possible, until his Death; and this was conceded to Her, excepting during the time in which He was in prison.

One of the accusations of the Jews and the priests before Pilate was, that Jesus our Savior had begun to stir up the people by his preaching in the province of Galilee (Luke 23, 6). This caused Pilate to inquire, whether He was a Galileean; and as they told him, that Jesus was born and raised in that country, he thought this circumstance useful for the solution of his difficulties in regard to Jesus and for escaping the molestations of the Jews, who so urgently demanded his death. Herod was at that time in Jerusalem, celebrating the Pasch of the Jews. He was the son of the first Herod, who had murdered the Innocents to procure the death of Jesus soon after his birth (Matth 2, 16). This murderer had become a proselyte of the Jews at the time of his marriage with a Jewish woman. On this account his son Herod likewise observed the law of Moses, and he had come to Jerusalem from Galilee, of which he was governor. Pilate was at enmity with Herod, for the two governed the two principal provinces of Palestine, namely, Judea and Galilee, and a short time before it had happened that Pilate, in his zeal for the supremacy of the Roman empire, had murdered some Galileeans during a public function in the temple, mixing the blood of the insurgents with that of the holy sacrifices. Herod was highly incensed at this sacrilege, and Pilate, in order to afford him some satisfaction without much trouble to himself, resolved to send to him Christ the Lord to be examined and judged as one of the subjects of Herod's sway. Pilate also expected that Herod would set Jesus free as being innocent and a Victim of the malice and envy of the priests and scribes.

When Herod was informed that Pilate would send Jesus of Nazareth to him, he was highly pleased. He knew that Jesus was a great friend of John the Baptist, whom he had ordered to be put to death (Mark 6, 27), and had heard many reports of his preaching. In vain and foolish curiosity he harbored the desire of seeing Jesus do something new and extraordinary for his entertainment and wonder (Luke 23, 8). The Author of life therefore came into the presence of the murderer Herod, against whom the blood of the Baptist was calling more loudly to this same Lord for vengeance, than in its time the blood of Abel (Gen. 4, 10). But the unhappy adulterer, ignorant of the terrible judgment of the Almighty, received Him with loud laughter as an enchanter and conjurer. In this dreadful misconception he commenced to examine and question Him, persuaded that he could thereby induce Him to work some miracle to satisfy his curiosity. But the Master of wisdom and prudence, standing with an humble reserve before his most unworthy judge, answered him not a word. For on account of his evil-doing he well merited the punishment of not hearing the words of life, which he would certainly have heard if he had been disposed to listen to them with reverence.

The princes and priests of the Jews stood around, continually rehearsing the same accusations and charges which they had advanced in the presence of Pilate. But the Lord maintained silence also in regard to these calumnies, much to the disappointment of Herod. In his presence the Lord would not open his lips, neither in order to answer his questions, nor in order to refute the accusations. Herod was altogether unworthy of hearing the truth, this being his greatest punishment and the punishment most to be dreaded by all the princes and the powerful of this earth. Herod was much put out by the silence and meekness of our Savior and was much disappointed in his vain curiosity. But the unjust judge tried to hide his confusion by mocking and ridiculing the innocent Master with his whole cohort of soldiers and ordering him to be sent back to Pilate.

Pilate was again confronted with Jesus in his palace and was bestormed anew by the Jews to condemn Him to death of the cross. Convinced of the innocence of Christ and of the mortal envy of the Jews, he was much put out at Herod's again referring the disagreeable decision to his own tribunal. Feeling himself obliged in his quality of judge to give this decision, he sought to placate the Jews in different ways. One of these was a private interview with some of the servants and friends of the highpriests and priests. He urged them to prevail upon their masters and friends, not any more to ask for the release of the malefactor Barabbas, but instead demand the release of our Redeemer; and to be satisfied with some punishment he was willing to administer before setting Him free. This measure Pilate had taken before they arrived a second time to press their demand for a sentence upon Jesus. The proposal to choose between freeing either Barabbas or Jesus was made to the Jews, not only once, but two or three times. The first time before sending Him to Herod and the second time after his return; this is related by the Evangelists with some variation, though not essentially contradicting truth (Matth. 27, 17). Pilate spoke to the Jews and said: "You have brought this Man before me, accusing Him of perverting the people by his doctrines; and having examined Him in your presence, I was not convinced of the truth of your accusations. And Herod, to whom I have sent Him and before whom you repeated your accusations, refused to condemn Him to death. It will be sufficient to correct and chastise Him for the present, in order that He may amend. As I am to release some malefactor for the feast of the Pasch, I will release Christ, if you will have Him freed, and punish Barabbas." But the multitude of the Jews, thus informed how much Pilate desired to set Jesus free, shouted with one voice: "Enough, enough, not Christ, but Barabbas deliver unto us."

While Pilate was thus disputing with the Jews in the pretorium, his wife, Procula, happened to hear of his doings and she sent him a message telling him: "What hast thou to do with this Man? Let him go free; for I warn thee that I have had this very day some visions in regard to Him!" This warning of Procula originated through the activity of Lucifer and his demons. For they, observing all that was happening in regard to the person of Christ and the unchangeable patience with which He bore all injuries, were more and more confused and staggered in their rabid fury. Despairing of success the demons betook themselves to the wife of Pilate and spoke to her in dreams, representing to her that this Man was just and without guilt, that if her husband should sentence Him he would be deprived of his rank and she herself would meet with great adversity. They urged her to advise Pilate to release Jesus and punish Barabbas, if she did not wish to draw misfortune upon their house and their persons.

Procula was filled with great fear and terror at these visions, and as soon as she heard what was passing between the Jews and her husband, she sent him the message mentioned by saint Matthew, not to meddle with this Man nor condemn One to death, whom she held to be just. The demon also injected similar misgivings into the mind of Pilate and these warnings of his wife only increased them. Yet, as all his considerations rested upon worldly policy, and as he had not co-operated with the true helps given him by the Savior, all these fears retarded his unjust proceedings only so long as no other more powerful consideration arose, as will be seen in effect. But just now he began for the third time to argue (as saint Luke tells us), insisting upon the innocence of Christ our Lord and that he found no crime in Him nor any guilt worthy of death, and therefore he would punish and then dismiss Him (Luke 23, 22). As we shall see in the next chapter, he did really punish Christ in order to see whether the Jews would be satisfied. But the Jews, on the contrary, demanded that Christ be crucified. Thereupon Pilate asked for water and released

Barabbas. Then he washed his hands in the presence of all the people, saying: "I have no share in the death of this just Man, whom you condemn. Look to yourselves in what you are doing, for I wash my hands in order that you may understand they are not sullied in the blood of the Innocent." Pilate thought that by this ceremony he could excuse himself entirely and that he thereby could put its blame upon the princes of the Jews and upon the people who demanded it. The wrath of the Jews was so blind and foolish that for the satisfaction of seeing Jesus crucified, they entered upon this agreement with Pilate and took upon themselves and upon their children the responsibility for this crime. Loudly proclaiming this terrible sentence and curse, they exclaimed: "His blood come upon us and upon our children" (Matth. 27, 25).

In the house of Pilate, through the ministry of the holy angels, our Queen was placed in such a position that She could hear the disputes of the iniquitous judge with the scribes and priests concerning the innocence of Christ our Savior, and concerning the release of Barabbas in preference to Him. All the clamors of these human tigers She heard in silence and admirable meekness, as the living counterpart of her most holy Son. Although She preserved the unchanging propriety and modesty of her exterior, all the malicious words of the Jews pierced her sorrowful heart like a two-edged sword. But the voices of her unspoken sorrows resounded in the ears of the eternal Father more pleasantly and sweetly than the lamentation of the beautiful Rachel who, as Jeremias says, was beweeping her children because they cannot be restored (Jer. 31, 15). Our most beautiful Rachel the purest Mary, sought not revenge, but pardon for her enemies, who were depriving Her of the Only-begotten of the Father and her only Son. She imitated all the actions of the most holy Soul of Christ and accompanied Him in the works of most exalted holiness and perfection; for neither could her torments hinder her charity, nor her affliction diminish her fervor, nor could the tumult distract her attention, nor the outrageous injuries of the multitudes prevent her interior recollection: under all circumstances She practiced the most exalted virtues in the most eminent degree.

Such was the implacable fury of the priests and of their confederates, the pharisees, against the Author of life. For Lucifer, despairing of being able to hinder his murder by the Jews, inspired them with his own dreadful malice and outrageous cruelty. Pilate, placed between the known truth and his human and terrestrial considerations, chose to follow the erroneous leading of the latter, and order Jesus to be severely scourged, though he had himself declared Him free from guilt (John 19, 1). Thereupon those ministers of satan, with many others, brought Jesus our Savior to the place of punishment, which was a courtyard or enclosure attached to the house and set apart for the torture of criminals in order to force them to confess their crimes. It was surrounded by a low, open building, surrounded by columns, some of which supported the roof, while others were lower and stood free. To one of these columns, which was of marble, they bound Jesus very securely; for they still thought Him a magician and feared his escape.

They first took off the white garment with not less ignominy than when they clothed Him therein in the house of the adulterous homicide Herod. In loosening the ropes and chains, which He had borne since his capture in the garden, they cruelly widened the wounds which his bonds had made in his arms and wrists. Having freed his hands, they commanded Him with infamous blasphemies to despoil Himself of the seamless tunic which He wore. This was the identical garment with which his most blessed Mother had clothed Him in Egypt when He first began to walk.

Thus the Lord stood uncovered in the presence of a great multitude and the six torturers bound Him brutally to one of the columns in order to chastise Him so much the more at their ease. Then, two and two at a time, they began to scourge Him with such inhuman cruelty, as was possible only in men possessed by Lucifer, as were these executioners. The first two scourged the innocent Savior with hard and thick cords, full of rough knots, and in their sacrilegious fury strained all the powers of their body to inflict the blows. This first scourging raised in the deified body of the Lord great welts and livid tumors, so that the sacred blood gathered beneath the skin and disfigured his entire body. Already it began to ooze through the wounds. The first two having at length desisted, the second pair continued the scourging in still greater emulation; with hardened leather thongs they leveled their strokes upon the places already sore and caused the discolored tumors to break open and shed forth the sacred blood until it bespattered and drenched the garments of the sacrilegious torturers, running down also in streams to the pavement. Those two gave way to the third pair of scourgers, who commenced to beat the Lord with extremely tough rawhides, dried hard like osier twigs. They scourged Him still more cruelly, because they were wounding, not so much his virginal body, as cutting into the wounds already produced by the previous scourging. Besides they had been secretly incited to greater fury by the demons, who were filled with new rage at the patience of Christ.

As the veins of the sacred body had now been opened and his whole Person seemed but one continued wound, the third pair found no more room for new wounds. Their ceaseless blows inhumanly tore the immaculate and virginal flesh of Christ our Redeemer and scattered many pieces of it about the pavement; so much so that a large portion of the shoulder-bones were exposed and showed red through the flowing blood; in other places also the bones were laid bare larger than the palm of the hand. In order to wipe out entirely that beauty, which exceeded that of all other men (Ps. 44, 3), they beat Him in the face and in the feet and hands, thus leaving unwounded not a single spot in which they could exert their fury and wrath against the most innocent Lamb. The divine blood flowed to the ground, gathering here and there in great abundance. The scourging in the face, and in the hands and feet, was unspeakably painful, because these parts are so full of sensitive and delicate nerves. His venerable countenance became so swollen and wounded that the blood and the swellings blinded Him. In addition to their blows the executioners spirted upon his Person their disgusting spittle and loaded Him with insulting epithets (Thren. 3, 30). The exact number of blows dealt out to the Savior from head to foot was 5,115. The great Lord and Author of all creation who, by his divine nature was incapable of suffering, was, in his human flesh and for our sake, reduced to a man of sorrows as prophesied, and was made to experience our infirmities, becoming the last of men (Is. 53, 3), a man of sorrows and the outcast of the people.

The multitudes who had followed the Lord, filled up the courtyard of Pilate's house and the surrounding streets; for all of them waited for the issue of this event, discussing and arguing about it according to each one's views.   Amid all this confusion the Virgin Mother endured unheard of insults, and She was deeply afflicted by the injuries and blasphemies heaped upon her divine Son by the Jews and gentiles.   When they brought Jesus to the scourging place She retired in the company of the Marys and saint John to a corner of the courtyard. Assisted by her divine visions, She there witnessed all the scourging and the torments of our Savior.   Although She did not see it with the eyes of her body nothing was hidden to Her, no more than if She had been standing quite near.   Human thoughts cannot comprehend how great and how diverse were the afflictions and sorrows of the great Queen and Mistress of the angels: together with many other mysteries of the Divinity they shall become manifest in the next life, for the glory of the Son and Mother.   I have already mentioned in other places of this history, and especially in that of the Passion, that the blessed Mother felt in her own body all the torments of her Son.   This was true also of the scourging, which She felt in all the parts of her virginal body, in the same intensity as they were felt by Christ in his body.   Although She shed no blood except what flowed from her eyes with her tears, nor was lacerated in her flesh; yet the bodily pains so changed and disfigured Her, that saint John and the holy women failed to find in Her any resemblance of Herself.   Besides the tortures of the body She suffered ineffable sorrows of the soul; there sorrow was augmented in proportion to the immensity of her insight (Eccles. 1, 18).   For her sorrows flowed not only from the natural love of a mother and a supreme love of Christ as her God, but it was proportioned to her power of judging more accurately than all creatures of the innocence of Christ, the dignity of his divine Person, the atrocity of the insults coming from the perfidious Jews and the children of Adam, whom He was freeing from eternal death.

Thereupon they took Jesus to the pretorium, where, with the same cruelty and contempt, they again despoiled him of his garments and in order to deride Him before all the people as a counterfeit king, clothed Him in a much torn and soiled mantle of purple color. They placed also upon his sacred head a cap made of woven thorns, to serve Him as a crown (John 19, 2). This cap was woven of thorn branches and in such a manner that many of the hard and sharp thorns would penetrate into the skull, some of them to the ears and others to the eyes. Hence one of the greatest tortures suffered by the Lord was that of the crown of thorns. Instead of a sceptre they placed into his hands a contemptible reed. They also threw over His shoulders a violet colored mantle, something of the style of capes worn in churches; for such a garment belonged to the vestiture of a king. In this array of a mock-king the perfidious Jews decked out Him, who by his nature and by every right was the King of kings and the Lord of lords (Apoc. 19, 16). Then all the soldiers, in the presence of the priests and pharisees, gathered around Him and heaped upon Him their blasphemous mockery and derision. Some of them bent their knees and mockingly said to Him: God save Thee, King of the Jews. Others buffeted Him; others snatched the cane from his hands and struck Him on his crowned head; others ejected their disgusting spittle upon Him; all of them, instigated by furious demons, insulted and affronted Him in different manners.

It seemed to Pilate that the spectacle of a man so illtreated as Jesus of Nazareth would move and fill with shame the hearts of that ungrateful people. He therefore commanded Jesus to be brought from the pretorium to an open window, where all could see Him crowned with thorns, disfigured by the scourging and the ignominious vestiture of a mock-king. Pilate himself spoke to the people, calling out to them: "Ecce Homo," "Behold, what a man!" (John 19, 5). See this Man, whom you hold as your enemy! What more can I do with Him than to have punished Him in this severe manner? You certainly have nothing more to fear from Him.

When the Blessed among women, most holy Mary, saw her divine Son as Pilate showed Him to the people and heard him say: "Ecce homo!" She fell upon her knees and openly adored Him as the true Godman. The same was also done by saint John and the holy women, together with all the holy angels of the Queen and Lady; for they saw that not only Mary, as the Mother of the Savior, but that God himself desired them thus to act.

WORDS OF THE QUEEN.

Think well, then, my dearest, which of these lots thou wishest to choose in the sight of my Son and me. If thou seest thy Redeemer, thy Spouse and thy Chief tormented, afflicted, crowned with thorns and saturated with reproaches and at the same time desirest to have a part in Him and be a member of his mystical body, it is not becoming, or even possible, that thou live steeped in the pleasures of the flesh. Thou must be the persecuted and not a persecutor, the oppressed and not the oppressor; the one that bears the cross, that encounters the scandal, and not that gives it; the one that suffers, and at the same time makes none of the neighbors suffer. On the contrary, thou must exert thyself for their conversion and salvation in as far as is compatible with the perfection of thy state and vocation. This is the portion of the friends of God and the inheritance of his children in mortal life; in this consists the participation in grace and glory, which by his torments and reproaches and by his death of the Cross my Son and Lord has purchased for them. I too have co-operated in this work and have paid the sorrows and afflictions, which thou hast understood and which I wish thou shalt never allow to be blotted out from my inmost memory. The Almighty would indeed have been powerful enough to exalt his predestined in this world, to give them riches and favors beyond those of others, to make them strong as lions for reducing the rest of mankind to their invincible power. But it was inopportune to exalt them in this manner, in order that men might not be led into the error of thinking that greatness consists in what is visible and happiness in earthly goods; lest, being induced to forsake virtues and obscure the glory of the Lord, they fail to experience the efficacy of divine grace and cease to aspire toward spiritual and eternal things. This is the science which I wish thee to study continually and in which thou must advance day by day, putting into practice all that thou learnest to understand and know.

CHAPTER VII.

THE WAY OF THE CROSS.

The sentence of Pilate against our Savior having been published in a loud voice before all the people, the executioners loaded the heavy Cross, on which He was to be crucified, upon his tender and wounded shoulders. In order that He might carry it they loosened the bonds holding his hands, but not the others, since they wished to drag Him along by the loose ends of the ropes that bound his body. In order to torment Him the more they drew two loops around his throat. The Cross was fifteen feet long, of thick and heavy timbers. The herald began to proclaim the sentence and the whole confused and turbulent multitude of the people, the executioners and soldiers, with great noise, uproar and disorder began to move from the house of Pilate to mount Calvary through the streets of Jerusalem. The Master and Redeemer of the world, Jesus, before receiving the Cross, looked upon it with a countenance full of extreme joy and exultation such as would be shown by a bridegroom looking at the rich adornments of his bride, and on receiving it, He addressed it as follows:

"O Cross, beloved of my soul, now prepared and ready to still my longings, come to Me, that I may be received in thy arms, and that, attached to them as on an altar, I may be accepted by the eternal Father as the sacrifice of his everlasting reconciliation with the human race. In order to die upon thee, I have descended from heaven and assumed mortal and passible flesh; for thou

542

art to be the sceptre with which I shall triumph over all my enemies, the key with which I shall open the gates of heaven for all the predestined (Is. 22, 22), the sanctuary in which the guilty sons of Adam shall find mercy, and the treasurehouse for the enrichment of their poverty. Upon thee I desire to exalt and recommend dishonor and reproach among men, in order that my friends may embrace them with joy, seek them with anxious longings, and follow Me on the path which I through thee shall open up before them. My Father and eternal God, I confess Thee as the Lord of heaven and earth (Matth. 11, 25), subjecting Myself to thy power and to thy divine wishes, I take upon my shoulders the wood for the sacrifice of my innocent and passible humanity and I accept it willingly for the salvation of men. Receive Thou, eternal Father, this sacrifice as acceptable to thy justice, in order that from today on they may not any more be servants, but sons and heirs of thy kingdom together with Me" (Rom. 8, 17).

None of these sacred mysteries and happenings were hidden from the great Lady of the world, Mary; for She had a most intimate knowledge and understanding of them, far beyond that of all the angels. The events, which She could not see with the eyes of her body, She perceived by her intelligence and revealed science, which manifested to Her the interior operation of her most holy Son. By this divine light She recognized the infinite value of the wood of the Cross after once it had come in contact with the deified humanity of Jesus our Redeemer. Immediately She venerated and adored it in a manner befitting it. The same was also done by the heavenly spirits attending upon the Queen. She imitated her divine Son in the tokens of affections, with which He received the Cross, addressing it in the words suited to her office as Coadjutrix of the Redeemer. By her prayers to the eternal Father She followed Him in his exalted sentiments as the living original and exemplar, without failing in the least point. When She heard the voice of the herald publishing and rehearsing the sentence through the streets, the heavenly Mother, in protest against the accusations contained in the sentence and in the form of comments on the glory and honor of the Lord, composed a canticle of praise and worship of the innocence and sinlessness of her all-holy Son and God. The most loving Mother was so admirably faithful in her sufferings and in imitating the example of Christ our God, that She never permitted Herself any easement either of her bodily pains, such as rest, or nourishment, or sleep; nor any relaxation of the spirit, such as any consoling thoughts or considerations, except when She was visited from on high by divine influence. Then only would She humbly and thankfully accept relief, in order that She might recover strength to attend still more fervently to the object of her sorrows and to the cause of his sufferings. The same wise consideration She applied to the malicious behavior of the Jews and their servants, to the needs of the human race, to their threatening ruin, and to the ingratitude of men, for whom He suffered. Thus She perfectly and intimately knew of all these things and felt it more deeply than all the creatures.

Another hidden and astonishing miracle was wrought by the right hand of God through the instrumentality of the blessed Mary against Lucifer and his infernal spirits. It took place in the following manner: The dragon and his associates, though they could not understand the humiliation of the Lord, were most attentive to all that happened in the Passion of the Lord.

Now, when He took upon Himself the Cross, all these enemies felt a new and mysterious tremor and weakness, which caused in them great consternation and confused distress. Conscious of these unwonted and invincible feelings the prince of darkness feared, that in the Passion and Death of Christ our Lord some dire and irreparable destruction of his reign was imminent. In order not to be overtaken by it in the presence of Christ our God, the dragon resolved to retire and fly with all his followers to the caverns of hell. But when he sought to execute this resolve, he was prevented by the great Queen and Mistress of all creation; for the Most High, enlightening Her and intimating to Her what She was to do, at the same time invested Her with his power. The heavenly Mother, turning toward Lucifer and his squadrons, by her imperial command hindered them from flying; ordering them to await and witness the Passion to the end on mount Calvary. The demons could not resist the command of the mighty Queen; for they recognized and felt the divine power operating in Her. Subject to her sway they followed Christ as so many prisoners dragged along in chains to Calvary, where the eternal wisdom had decreed to triumph over them from the throne of the Cross, as we shall see later on. There is nothing which can exemplify the discouragement and dismay, which from that moment began to oppress Lucifer and his demons. According to our way of speaking, they walked along to Calvary like criminals condemned to a terrible death, and seized by the dismay and consternation of an inevitable punishment.

The executioners, bare of all human compassion and kindness, dragged our Savior Jesus along with incredible cruelty and insults. Some of them jerked Him

forward by the ropes in order to accelerate his passage,
while others pulled from behind in order to retard it.
On account of this jerking and the weight of the Cross
they caused Him to sway to and fro and often to fall
to the ground. By the hard knocks He thus received on
the rough stones great wounds were opened, especially
on the two knees and they were widened at each repeated fall. The heavy Cross also inflicted a wound
on the shoulder on which it was carried. The unsteadi-
ness caused the Cross sometimes to knock against his
sacred head, and sometimes the head against the Cross;
thus the thorns of his crown penetrated deeper and
wounded the parts, which they had not yet reached. To
these torments of the body the ministers of evil added
many insulting words and execrable affronts, ejecting
their impure spittle and throwing the dirt of the pavement into his face so mercilessly, that they blinded the
eyes that looked upon them with such divine mercy.
Thus they of their own account condemned themselves
to the loss of the graces, with which his very looks were
fraught. By the haste with which they dragged Him
along in their eagerness to see Him die, they did not
allow Him to catch his breath; for his most innocent
body, having been in so few hours overwhelmed with
such a storm of torments, was so weakened and bruised,
that to all appearances He was ready to yield up life
under his pains and sorrows.

From the house of Pilate the sorrowful and
stricken Mother followed with the multitudes on the
way of her divine Son, accompanied by saint John and
the pious women. As the surging crowds hindered Her
from getting very near to the Lord, She asked the
eternal Father to be permitted to stand at the foot of
the Cross of her blessed Son and see Him die with

her own eyes. With the divine consent She ordered her holy angels to manage things in such a way as to make it possible for Her to execute her wishes. The holy angels obeyed Her with great reverence; and they speedily led the Queen through some bystreet, in order that She might meet her Son. Thus it came that both of Them met face to face in sweetest recognition of each Other and in mutual renewal of each other's interior sorrows. Yet They did not speak to one another, nor would the fierce cruelty of the executioners have permitted such an intercourse. But the most prudent Mother adored her divine Son and true God, laden with the Cross; and interiorly besought Him, that, since She could not relieve Him of the weight of the Cross and since She was not permitted to command her holy angels to lighten it, He would inspire these ministers of cruelty to procure some one for his assistance. This prayer was heard by the Lord Christ; and so it happened, that Simon of Cyrene was afterwards impressed to carry the Cross with the Lord (Matth. 27, 32). The pharisees and the executioners were moved to this measure, some of them out of natural compassion, others for fear lest Christ, the Author of life, should lose his life by exhaustion before it could be taken from Him on the Cross.

Beyond all human thought and estimation was the sorrow of the most sincere Dove and Virgin Mother while She thus witnessed with her own eyes her Son carrying the Cross to Mount Calvary; for She alone could fittingly know and love Him according to his true worth. It would have been impossible for Her to live through this ordeal, if the divine power had not strengthened Her and preserved Her life. With bitterest sorrow She addressed the Lord and spoke to Him in her heart:

"My Son and eternal God, light of my eyes and life of my soul, receive, O Lord, the sacrifice of my not being able to relieve Thee of the burden of the Cross and carry it myself, who am a daughter of Adam; for it is I who should die upon it in love of Thee, as Thou now wishest to die in most ardent love of the human race. O most loving Mediator between guilt and justice! How dost Thou cherish mercy in the midst of so great injuries and such heinous offenses! O charity without measure or bounds, which permits such torments and affronts in order to afford it a wider scope for its ardor and efficacy! O infinite and sweetest love, would that the hearts and the wills of men were all mine, so that they could give no such thankless return for all that Thou endurest! O who will speak to the hearts of the mortals to teach them what they owe to Thee, since Thou hast paid so dearly for their salvation from ruin!"

WORDS OF THE QUEEN.

I desire that the fruit of the obedience with which thou writest the history of my life shall be, that thou become a true disciple of my most holy Son and of myself. The main purpose of the exalted and venerable mysteries, which are made known to thee, and of the teachings, which I so often repeat to thee, is that thou deny and strip thyself, estranging thy heart from all affection to creatures, neither wishing to possess them nor accept them for other uses. By this precaution thou wilt overcome the impediments, which the devils seek to place in the way of the dangerous softness of thy nature. I who know thee, thus advise and lead thee by the way of instruction and correction as thy Mother and Instructress. By the divine teaching thou knowest the mysteries of the Passion and Death of

Christ and the one true way of life, which is the Cross; and thou knowest that not all who are called, are chosen. Many there are who wish to follow Christ and very few who truly dispose themselves to imitate Him; for as soon as they feel the sufferings of the Cross they cast it aside. Laborious exertions are very painful and averse to human nature according to the flesh; and the fruits of the spirit are more hidden and few guide themselves by the light. On this account there are so many among mortals, who, forgetful of the eternal truths, seek the flesh and the continual indulgence of its pleasures. They ardently seek honors and fly from injuries: they strive after riches, and contemn poverty; they long after pleasure and dread mortification. All these are enemies of the Cross of Christ (Phil. 3, 18), and with dreadful aversion they fly from it, deeming it sheer ignominy, just like those who crucified Christ, the Lord.

Another deceit has spread through the world: many imagine that they are following Christ their Master, though they neither suffer affliction nor engage in any exertion or labor. They are content with avoiding boldness in committing sins, and place all their perfection in a certain prudence or hollow self-love, which prevents them from denying anything to their will and from practicing any virtues at the cost of their flesh. They would easily escape this deception, if they would consider that my Son was not only the Redeemer, but their Teacher; and that He left in this world the treasures of his Redemption not only as a remedy against its eternal ruin, but as a necessary medicine for the sickness of sin in human nature. No one knew so much as my Son and Lord; no one could better understand the quality of love than the divine Lord, who was and is wisdom and charity itself; and no one was more able to fulfill all his wishes (I John 4, 16). Nevertheless, although He well could do it, He chose not a life of softness and ease for the flesh, but one full of labors and pains; for He judged his instructions to be incomplete and insufficient to redeem man, if He failed to teach them how to overcome the demon, the flesh and their own self. He wished to inculcate, that this magnificent victory is gained by the Cross, by labors, penances, mortifications and the acceptance of contempt: all of which are the trade-marks and evidences of true love and the special watchwords of the predestined.

CHAPTER VIII.

Our Savior then, the new and true Isaac, the Son of the eternal Father, reached the mountain of sacrifice, which is the same one to which his prototype and figure, Isaac, was brought by the patriarch Abraham (Gen. 22, 9). Upon the most innocent Lamb of God was to be executed the rigor of the sentence, which had been suspended in favor of the son of the Patriarch. Mount Calvary was held to be a place of defilement and ignominy, as being reserved for the chastisement of condemned criminals, whose cadavers spread around it their stench and attached to it a still more evil fame. Our most loving Jesus arrived at its summit so worn out, wounded, torn and disfigured, that He seemed altogether transformed into an object of pain and sorrows.

When the most prudent Mother perceived that now the mysteries of the Redemption were to be fulfilled and that the executioners were about to strip Jesus of his clothes for crucifixion, She turned in spirit to the eternal Father and prayed as follows: "My Lord and eternal God, Thou art the Father of thy only-begotten Son. By eternal generation He is engendered, God of the true God, namely Thyself, and as man He was born of my womb and received from me this human nature, in which He now suffers. I have nursed and sustained Him at my own breast; and as the best of sons that ever can be born of any creature, I love Him with maternal love. As his Mother I have a natural right in the Person of his most holy humanity and thy Providence will never infringe upon any rights held by thy creatures. This right of a Mother then, I now yield to Thee and once more place in thy hands thy and my Son as a sacrifice for the Redemption of man. Accept, my Lord, this pleasing offering, since this is more than I can ever offer by submitting my own self as a victim or to suffering. This sacrifice is greater, not only because my Son is the true God and of thy own substance, but because this sacrifice costs me a much greater sorrow and pain. For if the lots were changed and I should be permitted to die in order to preserve his most holy life, I would consider it a great relief and the fulfillment of my dearest wishes." The eternal Father received this prayer of the exalted Queen with ineffable pleasure and complacency. The patriarch Abraham was permitted to go no further than to prefigure and attempt the sacrifice of a son, because the real execution of such a sacrifice God reserved to Himself and to his Onlybegotten. Nor was Sara, the mother of Isaac, informed of the mystical ceremony, this being prevented not only by the promptness of Abraham's obedience, but also because he mistrusted, lest the maternal love of Sara, though she was a just and holy woman, should impel her to prevent the execution of the divine command. But not so was it with most holy Mary, to whom the eternal Father could fearlessly manifest his unchangeable will in order that She might, as far as her powers were concerned, unite with Him in the sacrifice of his Onlybegotten.

It was already the sixth hour, which corresponds to our noontime, and the executioners, intending to crucify the Savior naked, despoiled Him of the seamless tunic and of his garments. As the tunic was large and without opening in front, they pulled it over the head of

Jesus without taking off the crown of thorns; but on account of the rudeness with which they proceeded, they inhumanly tore off the crown with the tunic. Thus they opened anew all the wounds of his head, and in some of them remained the thorns, which, in spite of their being so hard and sharp, were wrenched off by the violence with which the executioners despoiled Him of his tunic and, with it, of the crown. With heartless cruelty they again forced it down upon his sacred head, opening up wounds upon wounds. By the rude tearing off of the tunic were renewed also the wounds of his whole body, since the tunic had dried into the open places and its removal was, as David says, adding new pains to his wounds (Ps. 68, 27). Four times during the Passion did they despoil Jesus of his garments and again vest Him. The first time in order to scourge Him at the pillar; the second time in order to clothe Him in the mock purple; the third, when they took this off in order to clothe Him in his tunic; the fourth, when they finally took away his clothes. This last was the most painful, because his wounds were more numerous, his holy humanity was much weakened, and there was less shelter against the sharp wind on mount Calvary; for also this element was permitted to increase the sufferings of his death-struggle by sending its cold blasts across the mount.

The holy Cross was lying on the ground and the executioners were busy making the necessary preparations for crucifying Him and the two thieves. In the meanwhile our Redeemer and Master prayed to the Father in the following terms:

"Eternal Father and my Lord God, to the incomprehensible Majesty of thy infinite goodness and justice I offer my entire humanity and all that according to thy will it has accomplished in descending from thy bosom to assume passible and mortal flesh for the Redemption of men, my brethren. I offer Thee, Lord, with Myself, also my most loving Mother, her love, her most perfect works, her sorrows, her sufferings, her anxious and prudent solicitude in serving Me, imitating Me and accompanying Me unto death. I offer Thee the little flock of my Apostles, the holy Church and congregation of the faithful, such as it is now and as it shall be to the end of the world; and with it I offer to Thee all the mortal children of Adam. All this I place in thy hands as the true and almighty Lord and God. As far as my wishes are concerned, I suffer and die for all, and I desire that all shall be saved, under the condition that all follow Me and profit of my Redemption. Thus may they pass from the slavery of the devil to be thy children, my brethren and co-heirs of the grace merited by Me. Especially, O my Lord, do I offer to Thee the poor, the despised and afflicted, who are my friends and who follow Me on the way to the Cross. I desire that the just and the predestined be written in thy eternal memory. I beseech Thee, my Father, to withhold thy chastisement and not to raise the scourge of thy justice over men; let them not be punished as they merit for their sins. Be Thou from now on their Father as Thou art mine. I beseech Thee also, that they may be helped to ponder upon my Death in pious affection and be enlightened from above; and I pray for those who are persecuting Me, in order that they may be converted to the truth. Above all do I ask Thee for the exaltation of thy ineffable and most holy name."

This prayer and supplication of our Savior Jesus were known to the most blessed Mother, and She imitated Him and made the same petitions to the eternal Father in as far as She was concerned. The most prudent Virgin never forgot or disregarded the first word which She had heard from the mouth of her divine Son as an infant: "Become like unto Me, my Beloved." His promise, that in return for the new human existence which She had given Him in her virginal womb, He would, by his almighty power, give Her a new existence of divine and eminent grace above all other creatures, was continually fulfilled.

In order to find the places for the auger-holes on the Cross, the executioners haughtily commanded the Creator of the universe (O dreadful temerity!), to stretch Himself out upon it. The Teacher of humility obeyed without hesitation. But they, following their inhuman instinct of cruelty, marked the places for the holes, not according to the size of his body, but larger, having in mind a new torture for their Victim. This inhuman intent was known to the Mother of light, and the knowledge of it was one of the greatest afflictions of her chastest heart during the whole Passion. She saw through the intentions of these ministers of sin and She anticipated the torments to be endured by her beloved Son when his limbs should be wrenched from their sockets in being nailed to the Cross. But She could not do anything to prevent it, as it was the will of the Lord to suffer these pains for men. When He rose from the Cross, and they set about boring the holes, the great Lady approached and took hold of one of his hands, adoring Him and kissing it with greatest reverence. The executioners allowed this because they thought that the sight of his Mother would cause so much the greater affliction to the Lord; for they wished to spare Him no sorrow they could cause Him. But they were ignorant of the hidden mysteries; for the Lord during his Passion had no greater source of consolation and interior joy than to see in the soul of his most blessed Mother, the beautiful likeness of Himself and the full fruits of his Passion and Death. This joy, to a certain extent, comforted Christ our Lord also in that hour.

Presently one of the executioners seized the hand of Jesus our Savior and placed it upon the auger-hole, while another hammered a large and rough nail through the palm. The veins and sinews were torn, and the bones of the sacred hand, which made the heavens and all that exists, were forced apart. When they stretched out the other hand, they found that it did not reach up to the auger-hole; for the sinews of the other arm had been shortened and the executioners had maliciously set the holes too far apart, as I have mentioned above. In order to overcome the difficulty, they took the chain, with which the Savior had been bound in the garden, and looping one end through a ring around his wrist, they, with unheard of cruelty, pulled the hand over the hole and fastened it with another nail. Thereupon they seized his feet, and placing them one above the other, they tied the same chain around both and stretched them with barbarous ferocity down to the third hole. Then they drove through both feet a large nail into the Cross. Thus the sacred body, in which dwelled the Divinity, was nailed motionless to the holy Cross, and the handiwork of his deified members, formed by the Holy Ghost, was so stretched and torn asunder, that the bones of his body, dislocated and forced from their natural position, could all be counted. The bones of his breast, of his shoulders and arms, and of his whole body yielded to the cruel violence and were torn from their sinews.

Then they dragged the lower end of the Cross with the crucified God near to the hole, wherein it was to be planted. Some of them getting under the upper part of the Cross with their shoulders, others pushing upward with their halberds and lances, they raised the Savior on his Cross and fastened its foot in the hole they had drilled into the ground. Thus our true life and salvation now hung in the air upon the sacred wood in full view of the innumerable multitudes of different nations and countries. I must not omit mentioning another barbarity inflicted upon the Lord as they raised Him: for some of them placed the sharp points of their lances and halberds to his body and fearfully lacerating Him under the armpits in helping to push the Cross into position. At this spectacle new cries of protest arose with still more vehemence and confusion from the multitude of people. The Jews blasphemed, the kind-hearted lamented, the strangers were astounded, some of them called the attention of the bystanders to the proceedings, others turned away their heads in horror and pity; others took to themselves a warning from this spectacle of suffering, and still others proclaimed Him a just Man. All these different sentiments were like arrows piercing the heart of the afflicted Mother. The sacred body now shed much blood from the nail wounds, which, by its weight and the shock of the Cross falling into the hole, had widened. They were the fountains, now opened up, to which Isaias invites us to hasten with joy to quench our thirst and wash off the stains of our sins (Is. 12, 3). No one shall be excused who does not quickly approach to drink of them.

Then they crucified also the two thieves and planted their crosses to the right and the left of the Savior; for thereby they wished to indicate that He deserved the most conspicuous place as being the greatest malefactor. The pharisees and priests, forgetting the two thieves, turned all the venom of their fury against the sinless and holy One by nature. Wagging their heads in scorn and mockery (Matth. 27, 39) they threw stones and dirt at the Cross of the Lord and his royal Person, saying: "Ah Thou, who destroyest the temple and in three days rebuildest it, save now Thyself; others He has made whole, Himself He cannot save; if this be the Son of God let Him descend from the Cross, and we will believe in Him" (Matth. 27, 42). The two thieves in the beginning also mocked the Lord and said: "If Thou art the Son of God, save Thyself and us." These blasphemies of the two thieves caused special sorrow to our Lord, since they were so near to death and were losing the fruit of their death-pains, by which they could have satisfied in part for their justly punished crimes. Soon after, however, one of them availed himself of the greatest opportunity that a sinner ever had in this world, and was converted from his sins.

As the wood of the Cross was the throne of his majesty and the chair of the doctrine of life, and as He was now raised upon it, confirming his doctrine by his example, Christ now uttered those words of highest charity and perfection: "Father, forgive them, for they know not what they do!" (Luke 23, 34.) This principle of charity and fraternal love the divine Teacher had appropriated to Himself and proclaimed by his own lips (John 15, 12; Matth. 15, 44). He now confirmed and executed it upon the Cross, not only pardoning and loving his enemies, but excusing those under the plea of ignorance whose malice had reached the highest point possible to men in persecuting, blaspheming and crucifying their God and Redeemer. Such was the difference between the behavior of ungrateful men favored with so great enlightenment, instruction and blessing; and the behavior of Jesus in his most burning charity while suf-

fering the crown of thorns, the nails, and the Cross and
unheard of blasphemy at the hands of men. O incomprehensible love! O ineffable sweetness! O patience inconceivable to man, admirable to the angels and fearful
to the devils! One of the two thieves, called Dismas,
became aware of some of the mysteries. Being assisted
at the same time by the prayers and intercession of most
holy Mary, he was interiorly enlightened concerning
his Rescuer and Master by the first word on the Cross.
Moved by true sorrow and contrition for his sins, he
turned to his companion and said: "Neither dost thou
fear God, seeing that thou art under the same condemnation? And we indeed justly, for we receive the due reward of our deeds; but this Man hath done no evil."
And thereupon speaking to Jesus, he said: "Lord, remember me when Thou shalt come into thy kingdom!"
(Luke 23, 40.)

In this happiest of thieves, in the centurion, and
in the others who confessed Jesus Christ on the Cross,
began to appear the results of the Redemption. But the
one most favored was this Dismas, who merited to hear
the second word of the Savior on the Cross: "Amen, I
say to thee, this day shalt thou be with Me in Paradise."

Having thus justified the good thief, Jesus turned
his loving gaze upon his afflicted Mother, who with
saint John was standing at the foot of the Cross. Speaking to both, he first addressed his Mother, saying:
"Woman, behold thy son!" and then to the Apostle:
"Behold thy Mother!" (John 19, 26.) The Lord called
Her Woman and not Mother, because this name of
Mother had in it something of sweetness and consolation, the very pronouncing of which would have been a
sensible relief. During his Passion He would admit
of no exterior consolation, having renounced for that

time all exterior alleviation and easement, as I have mentioned above. By this word "woman" he tacitly and by implication wished to say: Woman blessed among all women, the most prudent among all the daughters of Adam, Woman, strong and constant, unconquered by any fault of thy own, unfailing in my service and most faithful in thy love toward Me, which even the mighty waters of my Passion could not extinguish or resist (Cant. 8, 7), I am going to my Father and cannot accompany Thee further; my beloved disciple will attend upon Thee and serve Thee as his Mother, and he will be thy son. All this the heavenly Queen understood. The holy Apostle on his part received Her as his own from that hour on; for he was enlightened anew in order to understand and appreciate the greatest treasure of the Divinity in the whole creation next to the humanity of Christ our Savior. In this light He reverenced and served Her for the rest of her life, as I will relate farther on. Our Lady also accepted him as her son in humble subjection and obedience.

Already the ninth hour of the day was approaching, although the darkness and confusion of nature made it appear to be rather a chaotic night. Our Savior spoke the fourth word from the Cross in a loud and strong voice, so that all the bystanders could hear it: "My God, my God, why hast thou forsaken Me?" (Matth. 27, 46.) Although the Lord had uttered these words in his own Hebrew language, they were not understood by all. Since they began with: "Eli, eli," some of them thought He was calling upon Elias, and a number of them mocked Him saying: "Let us see whether Elias shall come to free Him from our hands?" He grieved that his copious and superabundant Redemption, offered for the whole human race, should not be efficacious in the reprobate and that He should find Himself deprived of them in the eternal happiness, for which He had created and redeemed them. As this was to happen in consequence of the decree of his Father's eternal will, He lovingly and sorrowfully complained of it in the words: "My God, my God, why hast Thou forsaken Me?" that is, in so far as God deprived Him of the salvation of the reprobate.

In confirmation of this sorrow the Lord added: "I thirst!" The sufferings of the Lord and his anguish could easily cause a natural thirst. But for Him this was not a time to complain of this thirst or to quench it; and therefore Jesus would not have spoken of it so near to its expiration, unless in order to give expression to a most exalted mystery. He was thirsting to see the captive children of Adam make use of the liberty, which He merited for them and offered to them, and which so many were abusing. He was athirst with the anxious desire that all should correspond with Him in the faith and love due to Him, that they profit by his merits and sufferings, accept his friendship and grace now acquired for them, and that they should not lose the eternal happiness which He was to leave as an inheritance to those that wished to merit and accept it. This was the thirst of our Savior and Master; and the most blessed Mary alone understood it perfectly and began, with ardent affection and charity, to invite and interiorly to call upon all the poor, the afflicted, the humble, the despised and downtrodden to approach their Savior and thus quench, at least in part, his thirst which they could not quench entirely. But the perfidious Jews and the executioners, evidencing their unhappy hard-heartedness, fastened a sponge soaked in gall and vinegar to a reed and mockingly raised it to his mouth, in order that He might drink of it. Thus was fulfilled the prophecy of David: "In my thirst they gave me vinegar to drink" (John 16, 28; Ps. 68, 22).

In connection with this same mystery the Savior then pronounced the sixth word: "Consummatum est," "It is consummated" (John 19, 29). Now is consummated this work of my coming from heaven and I have obeyed the command of my eternal Father, who sent Me to suffer and die for the salvation of mankind. Now are fulfilled the holy Scriptures, the prophecies and figures of the old Testament, and the course of my earthly and mortal life assumed in the womb of my Mother. Now are established on earth my example, my doctrines, my Sacraments and my remedies for the sickness of sin. Now is appeased the justice of my eternal Father in regard to the debt of the children of Adam. Now is my holy Church enriched with the remedies for the sins committed by men; the whole work of my coming into the world is perfected in so far as concerns Me, its Restorer; the secure foundation of the triumphant Church is now laid in the Church militant, so that nothing can overthrow or change it. These are the mysteries contained in the few words: "Consummatum est."

Having finished and established the work of Redemption in all its perfection, it was becoming that the incarnate Word, just as He came forth from the Father to enter mortal life (John 16, 8), should enter into immortal life of the Father through death. Therefore Christ our Savior added the last words uttered by Him: "Father, into thy hands I commend my spirit." The Lord spoke these words in a loud and strong voice, so that the bystanders heard them. In pronouncing them He raised his eyes to heaven, as one speaking with the eternal Father, and with the last accent He gave up his spirit and inclined his head. By the divine force of these words Lucifer with all his demons were hurled into the deepest caverns of hell, there they lay motionless, as I shall relate in the next chapter. The invincible Queen and Mistress of all virtues understood these mysteries beyond the understanding of all creatures, as She was the Mother of the Savior and the Coadjutrix of his Passion. In order that She might participate in it to the end, just as She had felt in her own body the other torments of her Son, She now, though remaining alive, felt and suffered the pangs and agony of his death. She did not die in reality; but this was because God miraculously preserved her life, when according to the natural course death should have followed. This miraculous aid was more wonderful than all the other favors She received during the Passion. For this last pain was more intense and penetrating; and all that the martyrs and the men sentenced to death have suffered from the beginning of the world cannot equal what the blessed Mary suffered during the Passion. The great Lady remained at the foot of the Cross until evening, when the sacred body (as I shall relate) was interred. But in return for this last anguish of death, all that was still of this mortal life in the virginal body of the purest Mother, was more than ever exalted and spiritualized.

WORDS OF THE QUEEN.

My daughter, seek with all the powers of thy mind during thy whole life to remember the mysteries manifested to thee in this chapter. I, as thy Mother and thy Instructress, shall ask the Lord by his divine power to impress in thy heart the knowledge, which I have vouchsafed thee, in order that it may remain fixed and ever present to thee as long as thou livest. In virtue of this blessing keep in thy memory Christ crucified, who is my divine Son and thy Spouse, and never forget the sufferings of the Cross and the doctrine taught by Him upon it. This is the mirror by which thou must arrange all thy adornments and the source from which thou art to draw thy interior beauty, like a true daughter of the Prince (Ps. 44, 14), in order that thou mayest be prepared, proceed and reign as the spouse of the supreme King. As this honorable title obliges thee to seek with all thy power to imitate Him as far as is becoming thy station and possible to thee by his grace, and as this is to be the true fruit of my doctrine, I wish that from today on thou live crucified with Christ, entirely assimilated to thy exemplar and model and dead to this earthly life (II Cor. 5, 15).

CHAPTER IX.

MARY THE HEIRESS OF THE MERITS OF CHRIST.

Of many of the sacraments and mysteries connected with the doings of Christ our Savior on the Cross the Evangelists make no mention; and we as Catholics can only form prudent conjectures founded upon the infallible certainty of our faith. But among those which have been manifested to me in this history, and concerning this part of the Passion, is a prayer, which Christ addressed to his eternal Father before speaking the seven words on the Cross recorded by the Evangelists. I call it a prayer because it was addressed to the Father; but in reality it was a last bequest or testament, which He made as a true and most wise Father in order to consign his possessions to his family, that is, to the whole human race. Even natural reason teaches us, that he who is the head of a family or the lord over many or few possessions, would not be a prudent dispenser of his goods, and inattentive to his office or dignity, if at the hour of his death he would not make known his will in regard to the disposition of his goods and his estate, in order that each one of his family may know what belongs to him and may possess it justly and peacefully without recourse to lawsuits. Although earthly things could not disturb our Savior, since He neither possessed them, nor, if He had possessed any, could He be embarrassed by them in his infinite power; yet it was fitting, that He should in that hour dispose of the spiritual riches and treasures which He had amassed for mankind in the course of his pilgrimage.

Of these eternal goods the Saviour made his last disposition on the Cross, distributing them and pointing out those who should be legitimate heirs and those who should be disinherited, and mentioning the reasons for the one as well as the other. All this He did in conference with his eternal Father, as the supreme Lord and most just Judge of all creatures; for in this testament are rehearsed the mysteries of the predestination of the saints and of the reprobation of the wicked. It was a testament hidden and sealed for mankind; only the blessed Mary understood it, because, in addition to her being informed of the operations of the divine Soul of Christ, She was also to be the universal Heiress of all creation. As She was the Coadjutrix of salvation, She was also to be the testamentary Executrix. For the Son placed all things in her hands, just as the Father had assigned the whole creation to Him. She was to execute his will and she was to distribute all the treasures acquired and due to her Son as God on account of his infinite merits. This understanding has been given me as part of this history for the exaltation of our Queen and in order that sinners might approach Her as the Custodian of all the treasures gained by her Son and our Redeemer in the sight of his eternal Father. All help and assistance is in the hands of most holy Mary and She is to distribute it according to her most sweet kindness and liberality.

When the holy wood of the Cross had been raised on mount Calvary, bearing aloft with it the incarnate Word crucified before speaking any of the seven words, Christ prayed interiorly to his heavenly Father and said: "My Father and eternal God, I confess and magnify Thee from this tree of the Cross, and I offer

Thee a sacrifice of praise in my Passion and Death; for, by the hypostatic union with the divine nature, Thou hast raised my humanity to the highest dignity, that of Christ, the Godman, anointed with thy own Divinity. I confess Thee on account of the plenitude of the highest possible graces and glory, which from the first instant of my Incarnation Thou hast communicated to my humanity, and because from all eternity up to this present hour Thou hast consigned to me full dominion of the universe both in the order of grace and of nature. Thou hast made Me the Lord of the heavens and of the elements (Matth. 28, 18), of the sun, the moon and the stars; of fire and air, of the earth and the sea, of all the animate and inanimate creatures therein; Thou hast made Me the Disposer of the seasons, of the days and nights, with full lordship and possession according to my free will, and Thou hast set Me as the Head, the King and Lord of all angels and men (Ephes. 1, 21), to govern and command them, to punish the wicked and to reward the good (John 5, 22); Thou hast given Me the dominion and power of disposing all things from highest heavens to deepest abysses of hell (Apoc. 20, 1). Thou hast placed in my hands the eternal justification of men, the empires, kingdoms and principalities, the great and the little, the rich and the poor; and of all that are capable of thy grace and glory, Thou hast made Me the Justifier, the Redeemer and Glorifier, the universal Lord of all the human race, of life and death, of the holy Church, its treasures, laws and blessings of grace: all hast Thou, my Father, consigned to my hands, subjected to my will and my decrees, and for this I confess, exalt and magnify thy holy name."

"Now, at this moment, my Lord and eternal

Father, when I am returning from this world to thy right hand through this death on the Cross, by which I completed the task of the Redemption of men assigned to Me, I desire that this same Cross shall be the tribunal of our justice and mercy. Nailed to it, I desire to judge those for whom I give my life. Having justified my cause, I wish to dispense the treasures of my coming into the world and of my Passion and Death to the just and the reprobate according as each one merits by his works of love or hatred. I have sought to gain all mortals and invited them to partake of my friendship and grace; from the first moment of my Incarnation I have ceaselessly labored for them; I have borne inconveniences, fatigues, insults, ignominies, reproaches, scourges, a crown of thorns, and now suffer the bitter death of the Cross; I have implored thy vast kindness upon all of them; I have watched in prayer, fasted and wandered about teaching them the way of eternal life. As far as in Me lay I have sought to secure eternal happiness for all men, just as I merited it for all, without excluding any one. I have established and built up the law of grace and have firmly and forever established the Church in which all human beings can be saved."

"But in our knowledge and foresight We are aware, my God and Father, that on account of their malice and rebellious obstinacy not all men desire to accept our eternal salvation, nor avail themselves of our mercy and of the way I have opened to them by my labors, life and death; but that many will prefer to follow their sinful ways unto perdition. Thou art just, my Lord and Father, and most equitable are thy judgments (Ps. 68, 137); and therefore it is right, since Thou hast made Me the Judge of the living and the dead, of the good and the bad (Act 10, 3), that I give to the good the reward of having served and followed Me, and to sinners the chastisement of their perverse obstinacy; that the just should share in my goods, and the wicked be deprived of the inheritance, which they refuse to accept. Now then, my eternal Father, in my and thy name and for thy glorification, I make my last bequest according to my human will, which is conformable to thy eternal and divine will. First shall be mentioned my most pure Mother, who gave Me human existence; Her I constitute my sole and universal Heiress of all the gifts of nature, of grace and of glory that are mine. She shall be Mistress and Possessor of them all. The gifts of grace, of which as a mere creature She is capable, She shall actually receive now, while those of glory I promise to confer upon Her in their time. I desire that She shall be Mistress of angels and men, claim over them full possession and dominion and command the service and obedience of all. The demons shall fear Her and be subject to Her. All the irrational creatures, the heavens, the stars, the planets, the elements with all the living beings, the birds, the fishes and the animals contained in them, shall likewise be subject to Her and acknowledge Her as Mistress, exalting and glorifying Her with Me. I wish also that She be the Treasurer and Dispenser of all the goods in heaven and on earth. Whatever She ordains and disposes in my Church for my children, the sons of men, shall be confirmed by the three divine Persons; and whatever She shall ask for mortals now, afterwards and forever, We shall concede according to her will and wishes."

"To the holy angels, who have obeyed thy holy and just will, I assign as habitation the highest heavens as their proper and eternal abode, and with it the joys of eternal vision and fruition of our Divinity. I desire that they enjoy its everlasting possession together with our company and friendship. I decree, that they recognize my Mother as their legitimate Queen and Lady, that they serve Her, accompany and attend upon Her, bear Her up in their hands in all places and times, obeying Her in all that She wishes to ordain and command. The demons, rebellious to our perfect and holy will, I cast out and deprive of our vision and company; again do I condemn them to our abhorrence, to eternal loss of our friendship and glory, to privation of the vision of my Mother, of the saints and of my friends, the just. I appoint and assign to them as their eternal dwelling the place most remote from our royal throne, namely the infernal caverns, the centre of the earth, deprived of light and full of the horrors of sensible darkness (Jude 6). I decree this to be their portion and inheritance, as chosen by them in their pride and obstinacy against the divine Being and decrees. In those eternal dungeons of darkness they shall be tormented by everlasting and inextinguishable fire."

"From the multitudes of men, in the fulness of my good will, I call, select and separate all the just and the predestined, who through my grace save themselves by imitating Me, doing my will and obeying my holy law. These, next to my most pure Mother, I appoint as the inheritors of all my mysteries, my blessings, my sacramental treasures, of the mysteries concealed in the holy Scriptures; of my humility, meekness of heart; of the virtues of faith, hope, and charity; of prudence, justice, fortitude and temperance; of my divine gifts and favors; of my Cross, labors, contempt, poverty and nakedness. This shall be their portion and inheritance in this present and mortal life. Since they must choose these in order to labor profitably,

I assign to them the trials I have chosen for Myself in this life, as a pledge of my friendship, in order that they may undergo them with joy. I offer them my protection and defense, my holy inspirations, my favors and powerful assistance, my blessings and my justification, according to each one's disposition and degree of love. I promise to be to them a Father, a Brother and a Friend, and they shall be my chosen and beloved children, and as such I appoint them as the inheritors of all my merits and treasures without limitation. I desire that all who dispose themselves, shall partake of the goods of my holy Church and of the Sacraments; that, if they should lose my friendship, they shall be able to restore themselves and recover my graces and blessings through my cleansing blood. For all of them shall be open the intercession of my Mother and of the saints, and She shall recognize them as her children, shielding them and holding them as her own. My angels shall defend them, guide them, protect them and bear them up in their hands lest they stumble, and if they fall, they shall help them to rise" (Ps. 90, 11, 12).

"Likewise it is my will that my just and chosen ones shall stand high above the reprobate and the demons, that they shall be feared and obeyed by my enemies; that all the rational and irrational creatures shall serve them; that all the influences of the heavens, the planets and the stars shall favor them and give them life; that the earth, its elements and animals, shall sustain them; all the creatures, that are mine and serve Me, shall be theirs, and shall serve also them as my children and friends (I Cor. 3, 22; Wis. 16, 24), and their blessing shall be in the dew of heaven and in the fruits of the earth (Genes. 27, 28). I wish to hold with them my delights (Pros. 8, 31), communicate to them my secrets, converse with them intimately and live with them in the militant Church in the species of bread and wine, as an earnest and an infallible pledge of the eternal happiness and glory promised to them; of it, I make them partakers and heirs, in order that they may enjoy it with Me in heaven by perpetual right and in unfailing beatitude."

"I consent that the foreknown and reprobate (though they were created for another and much higher end), shall be permitted to possess as their portion and inheritance the concupiscence of the flesh and the eyes (John 1, 2-16), pride in all its effects; that they eat and be satisfied with the dust of the earth, namely, with riches; with the fumes and the corruption of the flesh and its delights, and with the vanity and presumption of the world. For such possessions have they labored, and applied all the diligence of their mind and body; in such occupations have they consumed their powers, their gifts and blessings bestowed upon them by Us, and they have of their own free will chosen deceit, despising the truth I have taught them in the holy law (Rom. 2, 8). They have rejected the law which I have written in their hearts and the one inspired by my grace; they have despised my teachings and my blessings, and listened to my and their own enemies; they have accepted their deceits, have loved vanity (Ps. 4, 3), wrought injustice, followed their ambitions, sought their delight in vengeance, persecuted the poor, humiliated the just, mocked the simple and the innocent, strove to exalt themselves and desired to be raised above all the cedars of Lebanon in following the laws of injustice" (Ps. 36, 35).

"Since they have done all this in opposition to our divine goodness and remained obstinate in their

malice, and since they have renounced the rights of sonship merited for them by Me, I disinherit them of my
friendship and glory. Just as Abraham separated the
children of the slave, setting aside some possessions
for them and reserving the principal heritage for Isaac,
the son of the freedwoman Sarah (Gen. 25, 5), thus I
set aside their claims on my inheritance by giving them
the transitory goods, which they themselves have chosen.
Separating them from our company and from that of
my Mother, of the angels and saints, I condemn them
to the eternal dungeons and the fire of hell in the company of Lucifer and his demons, whom they have freely
served, I deprive them forever of all hope of relief.
This is, O my Father, the sentence which I pronounce
as the Head and the Judge of men and angels (Eph. 4,
15; Col. 2, 10), and this is the testament made at my
Death, this is the effect of my Redemption, whereby
each one is rewarded with that which he has justly
merited according to his works and according to thy
incomprehensible wisdom in the equity of thy strictest
justice" (II Tim. 4, 8). Such was the prayer of
Christ our Savior on the Cross to his eternal Father.
It was sealed and deposited in the heart of the most holy
Mary as the mysterious and sacramental testament, in
order that through her intercession and solicitous care it
might at its time, and even from that moment, be executed in the Church, just as it had before this time
been prepared and perfected by the wise providence of
God, in whom all the past and the future is always one
with the present.

CHAPTER X.

The hidden and venerable mysteries of this chapter correspond to many others scattered through the whole extent of this history. One of them is, that Lucifer and his demons in the course of the life and miracles of our Savior, never could ascertain fully whether the Lord was true God and Redeemer of the world, and consequently what was the dignity of the most holy Mary. This was so disposed by divine Providence, in order that the whole mystery of the Incarnation and the Redemption of the human race might be more fittingly accomplished. Lucifer, although knowing that God was to assume human flesh, nevertheless knew nothing of the manner and the circumstances of the Incarnation. As he was permitted to form an opinion of this mystery in accordance with his pride, he was full of hallucinations, sometimes believing Christ to be God on account of his miracles, sometimes rejecting such an opinion on account of seeing Him poor, humiliated, afflicted and fatigued. Harassed by these contradicting evidences, he remained in doubt and continued his inquiries until the predestined hour of Christ's Death on the Cross, where, in virtue of the Passion and Death of the sacred humanity, which he had himself brought about, he was to be both undeceived and vanquished by the full solution of these mysteries.

Lucifer and his demons, as soon as they saw the Lord taking the Cross upon his sacred shoulders, wished to fly and cast themselves into hell; for at that moment they began to feel with greater force the operations of his divine power. By divine intervention this new torment made them aware that the Death of this innocent Man, whose destruction they had plotted and who could not be a mere man, threatened great ruin to themselves. They therefore desired to withdraw and they ceased to incite the Jews and the executioners, as they had done hitherto. But the command of the most blessed Mary, enforced by the divine power, detained them and, enchained like fiercest dragons, compelled them to accompany Christ to Calvary. The ends of the mysterious chain that bound them were placed into the hands of Mary, the great Queen, who, by the power of her divine Son, held them all in subjection and bondage. Although they many times sought to break away and raged in helpless fury, they could not overcome the power of the heavenly Lady. She forced them to come to Calvary and stand around the Cross, where She commanded them to remain motionless and witness the end of the great mysteries there enacted for the salvation of men and the ruin of themselves.

Lucifer and his infernal hosts were so overwhelmed with pains and torments by the presence of the Lord and his blessed Mother, and with the fear of their impending ruin, that they would have felt greatly relieved to be allowed to cast themselves into the darkness of hell. As this was not permitted them, they fell upon one another and furiously fought with each other like hornets disturbed in their nest, or like a brood of vermin confusedly seeking some dark shelter. But their rabid fury was not that of animals, but that of demons more cruel than dragons.

The time had now come for this ancient dragon

to be vanquished by the Master of life. As this was to be the hour of his disillusionment, and as this poisonous asp was not to escape it by stopping his ears to the voice of the Enchanter (Ps. 57, 5), the Lord began to speak the seven words from his Cross, at the same time providing that Lucifer and his demons should understand the mysteries therein contained. For it was by this disclosure that the Lord wished to triumph over them, over sin and death, and despoil them of their tyrannous power over the human race. The Savior then pronounced the first word: "Father, forgive them, for they know not what they do!" (Luke 23, 34). By these words the princes of darkness came to the full conviction, that Christ our Lord was speaking to the eternal Father, that He was his natural Son and the true God with Him and the Holy Ghost, that He had permitted death in his most sacred and perfect humanity, united to the Divinity for the salvation of the whole human race; that now He offered his infinitely precious merits for the pardon of the sins of all those children of Adam, who should avail themselves thereof for their rescue, not excepting even the wretches that crucified Him. At this discovery Lucifer and his demons were thrown into such fury and despair that they instantly wished to hurl themselves impetuously to the depths of hell and strained all their powers to accomplish it in spite of the powerful Queen.

In the second word spoken by the Lord to the fortunate thief: "Amen I say to thee, today thou shalt be with Me in paradise," the demons understood that the fruits of the Redemption in the justification of sinners ended in the glorification of the just. They were made aware that from this hour the merits of Christ would commence to act with a new force and strength, that through them should be opened the gates of Paradise, which had been closed by the first sin, and that from now on men would enter upon eternal happiness and occupy their destined heavenly seats, which until now had been impossible for them. They perceived the power of Christ to call sinners, justify and beautify them, and they felt the triumphs gained over themselves by the exalted virtues, the humility, patience, meekness and all the virtues of his life. The confusion and torment of Lucifer at seeing this cannot be explained by human tongue; but it was so great, that he humiliated himself so far as to beg the most blessed Virgin to permit them to descend into hell and be cast out from her presence; but the great Queen would not consent, as the time had not yet arrived.

At the third word spoken by the Lord to his Mother: "Woman, behold thy son!" the demons discovered that this heavenly Lady was the true Mother of the Godman, the same Woman whose likeness and prophetic sign had been shown to them in the heavens at their creation, and who was to crush their head as announced by the Lord in the terrestrial paradise. They were informed of the dignity and excellence of this great Lady over all creatures, and of her power which they were even now experiencing. As they had from the beginning of the world and from the creation of the first woman, used all their astuteness to find out who this great woman that was announced in the heavens could be, and as they now discovered Her in Mary, whom they had until now overlooked, these dragons were seized with inexpressible fury; their having been thus mistaken crushed their arrogance beyond all their other torments, and in their fury they raged against their own selves like bloodthirsty lions, while their helpless wrath against the heavenly Lady was increased a thousandfold. Moreover, they discerned that saint John was appointed by Christ our Lord as the angel guardian of his Mother, endowed with the powers of the priesthood. This they understood to be in the nature of a threat against their own wrath, which was well known to saint John. Lucifer saw not only the power of the Evangelist, but that given to all the priests in virtue of their participation in the dignity and power of our Redeemer; and that the rest of the just, even though no priests, were placed under the special protection of the Lord and made powerful against hell. All this paralyzed the strength of Lucifer and his demons.

The fourth word of Christ was addressed to the eternal Father: "God, my God, why hast Thou forsaken Me?" The evil spirits discovered in these words that the charity of God toward men was boundless and everlasting; that, in order to satisfy it, He had mysteriously suspended the influence of the Divinity over his most sacred humanity, thus permitting his sufferings to reach the highest degree and to draw from them the most abundant fruits; that He was aware and lovingly complained of his being deprived of the salvation of a part of the human race; how ready He was to suffer more, if such would be ordained by the eternal Father. Man's good fortune in being so beloved by God increased the envy of Lucifer and his demons, and they foresaw the divine Omnipotence following out this immense love without limitation. This knowledge crushed the haughty malice of the enemies and they were made well aware of their own weakness and helplessness in opposing this love, if men themselves should not choose to neglect its influence.

The fifth word of Christ, "I thirst," confirmed Christ's triumph over the devil and his followers; they were filled with wrath and fury because the Lord clearly let them see their total overthrow. By these words they understood Him to say to them: If what I suffer for men and my love for them seem great to you, be assured that my love for them is still unsatiated, that it continues to long for their eternal salvation, and that the mighty waters of torments and sufferings have not extinguished it (Cant. 8, 7). Much more would I suffer for them, if it were necessary, in order to deliver them from your tyranny and make them powerful and strong against your malice and pride.

In the sixth word of the Lord: "It is consummated!" Lucifer and his hordes were informed that the mystery of the Incarnation and Redemption was now accomplished and entirely perfected according to the decree of divine wisdom. For they were made to feel that Christ our Redeemer had obediently fulfilled the will of the eternal Father; that He had accomplished all the promises and prophecies made to the world by the ancient Fathers; that his humility and obedience had compensated for their own pride and disobedience in heaven in not having subjected themselves and acknowledged Him as their Superior in human flesh; and that they were now through the wisdom of God justly humbled and vanquished by the very Lord whom they despised. The great dignity and the infinite merits of Christ demanded that in this very hour He should exercise his office and power of Judge over angels and men, such as had been conceded to Him by the eternal Father. He now applied this power by hurling this sentence at Lucifer and all his followers, that, being condemned to eternal fire, they instantly depart into the deepest dungeons of hell. This very sentence was included in the pronouncing of the seventh word: "Father, into thy hands I commend my spirit!" (Luke 23, 46.)   The mighty Queen and Mother concurred with the will of her Son Jesus and united with his her command that Lucifer and all demons depart to the infernal depths.   In virtue of these decrees of the supreme King and of the Queen, the evil spirits were routed from Calvary and precipitated to deepest hell more violently and suddenly than a flash of light through the riven clouds.

The rout of Lucifer and his angels from Calvary to the abyss of hell was more violent and disastrous than their first expulsion from heaven.   Though, as holy Job says (Job 10, 21), that place is a land of darkness, covered with the shades of death, full of gloomy disorder, misery, torments and confusion; yet on this occasion the chaos and disorder was a thousandfold increased; because the damned were made to feel new horror and additional punishments at the sudden meeting of the ferocious demons in their rabid fury.   It is certain that the devils have not the power of assigning the damned to a place of greater or lesser torment; for all their torments are decreed by divine justice according to the measure of the demerits of each of the condemned.

As soon as Lucifer was permitted to proceed in these matters and arise from the consternation in which he remained for some time, he set about proposing to his fellow-demons new plans of his pride.   For this purpose he called them all together and placing himself in an elevated position, he spoke to them: "To you, who have for so many ages followed and still follow my standards for the vengeance of my wrongs, is known the injury which I have now sustained at the hands of this Mangod, and how for thirty-three years He has led me about in deceit, hiding his Divinity and concealing the operations of his soul, and how He has now triumphed over us by the very Death which we have brought upon Him. Before He assumed flesh I hated Him and refused to acknowledge Him as being more worthy than I to be adored by the rest of creation. Although on account of this resistance I was cast out from heaven with you and was degraded to this abominable condition so unworthy of my greatness and former beauty, I am even more tormented to see myself thus vanquished and oppressed by this Man and by his Mother. From the day on which the first man was created I have sleeplessly sought to find Them and destroy Them; or if I should not be able to destroy Them, I at least wished to bring destruction upon all his creatures and induce them not to acknowledge Him as their God, and that none of them should ever draw any benefit from his works. This has been my intent, to this all my solicitude and efforts were directed. But in vain, since He has overcome me by his humility and poverty, crushed me by his patience, and at last has despoiled me of the sovereignty of the world by his Passion and frightful Death. This causes me such an excruciating pain, that, even if I succeeded in hurling Him from the right hand of his Father, where He sits triumphant, and if I should draw all the souls redeemed down into this hell, my wrath would not be satiated or my fury placated."

"Is it possible that the human nature, so inferior to my own, shall be exalted above all the creatures! That it should be so loved and favored, as to be united to the Creator in the person of the eternal Word! That He should first make war upon me before executing this work, and afterwards overwhelm me with such confusion! From the beginning I have held this humanity as my greatest enemy; it has always filled me with intolerable abhorrence. O men, so favored and gifted by your God, whom I abhor, and so ardently loved by Him! How shall I hinder your good fortune? How shall I bring upon you my unhappiness, since I cannot destroy the existence you have received? What shall we now begin, O my followers? How shall we restore our reign? How shall we recover our power over men? How shall we overcome them? For if men from now on shall not be most senseless and ungrateful, if they are not worse disposed than we ourselves toward this Godman, who has redeemed them with so much love, it is clear that all of them will eagerly follow Him; none will take notice of our deceits; they will abhor the honors which we insidiously offer them, and will love contempt; they will seek the mortification of the flesh and will discover the danger of carnal pleasure and ease; they will despise riches and treasures, and love the poverty so much honored by their Master; and all that we can offer to their appetites they will abhor in imitation of their true Redeemer. Thus will our reign be destroyed, since no one will be added to our number in this place of confusion and torments; all will reach the happiness which we have lost, all will humiliate themselves to the dust and suffer with patience; and my wrath and haughtiness will avail me nothing."

"Ah, woe is me, what torment does this mistake cause me! When I tempted Him in the desert, the only result was to afford Him a chance to leave the example of this victory, by following which men can overcome me so much the more easily. My persecutions only brought out more clearly his doctrine of humility and patience. In persuading Judas to betray Him, and the Jews to subject Him to the deadly torture of the Cross, I merely hastened my ruin and the salvation of men, while the doctrine I sought to blot out was only the more firmly implanted. How could One who is God humiliate Himself to such an extent? How could He bear so much from men who are evil? How could I myself have been led to assist so much in making this salvation so copious and wonderful? O how godlike is the power of that Man which could torment and weaken me so? And how can this Woman, his Mother and my Enemy, be so mighty and invincible in her opposition to me? New is such power in a mere creature, and no doubt She derived it from the divine Word, whom She clothed in human flesh. Through this Woman the Almighty has ceaselessly waged war against me, though I have hated Her in my pride from the moment I recognized Her in her image or heavenly sign. But if my proud indignation is not to be assuaged, I benefit nothing by my perpetual war against this Redeemer, against his Mother and against men. Now then, ye demons who follow me, now is the time to give way to our wrath against God. Come all of ye to take counsel what we are to do; for I desire to hear your opinions."

Some of the principal demons gave their answers to this dreadful proposal, encouraging Lucifer by suggesting diverse schemes for hindering the fruit of the Redemption among men. They all agreed that it was not possible to injure the person of Christ, to diminish the immense value of his merits, to destroy the efficacy of the Sacraments, to falsify or abolish the doctrine which Christ had preached; yet they resolved that, in accordance with the new order of assistance and favor established by God for the salvation of men, they should now seek new ways of hindering and preventing the work of God by so much the greater deceits and temptations. In reference to these plans some of the astute and malicious demons said: "It is true, that men now have at their disposal a new and very powerful doctrine and law, new and efficacious Sacraments, a new Model and Instructor of virtues, a powerful Intercessor and Advocate in this Woman; yet the natural inclinations and passions of the flesh remain just the same, and the sensible and delectable creatures have not changed their nature. Let us then, making use of this situation with increased astuteness, foil as far as in us lies the effects of what this Godman has wrought for men. Let us begin strenuous warfare against mankind by suggesting new attractions, exciting them to follow their passions in forgetfulness of all else. Thus men, being taken up with these dangerous things, cannot attend to the contrary."

Acting upon this counsel they redistributed the spheres of work among themselves, in order that each squadron of demons might, with a specialized astuteness, tempt men to different vices. They resolved to continue to propagate idolatry in the world, so that men might not come to the knowledge of the true God and the Redemption. Wherever idolatry would fail, they concluded to establish sects and heresies, for which they would select the most perverse and depraved of the human race as leaders and teachers of error. Then and there was concocted among these malignant spirits the sect of Mahomet, the heresies of Arius, Pelagius, Nestorius, and whatever other heresies have been started in the world from the first ages of the Church until now, together with those which they have in readiness, but which it is neither necessary nor proper to mention here. Lucifer showed himself content with these infernal counsels as being opposed to divine truth and destructive of the very foundation of man's rescue, namely divine faith. He lavished flattering praise and high offices upon those demons, who showed themselves willing and who undertook to find the impious originators of these errors.

Some of the devils charged themselves with perverting the inclinations of children at their conception and birth; others to induce parents to be negligent in the education and instruction of their children, either through an inordinate love or aversion, and to cause a hatred of parents among the children. Some offered to create hatred between husbands and wives, to place them in the way of adultery, or to think little of the fidelity promised to their conjugal partners. All agreed to sow among men the seeds of discord, hatred and vengeance, proud and sensual thoughts, desire of riches or honors, and by suggesting sophistical reasons against all the virtues Christ has taught; above all they intended to weaken the remembrance of his Passion and Death, of the means of salvation, and of the eternal pains of hell. By these means the demons hoped to burden all the powers and the faculties of men with solicitude for earthly affairs and sensual pleasures, leaving them little time for spiritual thoughts and their own salvation.

Lucifer heard these different suggestions of the demons, and answering them, he said: "I am much beholden to you for your opinions: I approve of them and adopt them all; it will be easy to put them into practice with those, who do not profess the law given by this Redeemer to men, though with those who accept and embrace these laws, it will be a difficult enterprise. But against this law and against those that follow it, I intend to direct all my wrath and fury and I shall most bitterly persecute those who hear the doctrine of this Redeemer and become his disciples; against these must our most relentless battle be waged to the end of the world. In this new Church I must strive to sow my cockle (Matth. 14, 25), the ambitions, the avarice, the sensuality, and the deadly hatreds, with all the other vices, of which I am the head. For if once these sins multiply and increase among the faithful, they will, with their concomitant malice and ingratitude, irritate God and justly deprive men of the helps of grace left to them by the merits of the Redeemer. If once they have thus despoiled themselves of these means of salvation, we shall have assured victory over them. We must also exert ourselves to weaken piety and all that is spiritual and divine; so that they do not realize the power of the Sacraments and receive them in mortal sin, or at least without fervor and devotion. For since these Sacraments are spiritual, it is necessary to receive them with well-disposed will, in order to reap their fruits. If once they despise the medicine, they shall languish in their sickness and be less able to withstand our temptations; they will not see through our deceits, they will let the memory of their Redeemer and of the intercession of his Mother slip from their minds. Thus will their foul ingratitude make them unworthy of grace and so irritate their God and Savior, as to deprive them of his helps. In all this I wish, that all of you assist me strenuously, losing neither time nor occasion for executing my commands."

It is not possible to rehearse all the schemes of this dragon and his allies concocted at that time against the holy Church and her children, in order that these waters of Jordan might be swallowed up in his throat (Job 40, 18). It is enough to state that they spent nearly a full year after the Death of Christ in conferring and considering among themselves the state of the world up to that time and the changes wrought by Christ our God and Master through his Death and after having manifested the light of his faith by so many miracles, blessings and examples of holy men. If all these labors have not sufficed to draw all men to the way of salvation, it can be easily understood, that Lucifer should have prevailed and that his wrath should be so great, as to cause us justly to say with saint John: "Woe to the earth, for satan is come down to you full of wrath and fury!" But alas! that truths so infallible and so much to be dreaded and avoided by men, should in our days be blotted from the minds of mortals to the irreparable danger of the whole world! Our enemy is astute, cruel and watchful: we sleepy, lukewarm and careless! What wonder that Lucifer has intrenched himself so firmly in the world, when so many listen to him, accept and follow his deceits, so few resist him, and entirely forget the eternal death, which he so furiously and maliciously seeks to draw upon them? I beseech those, who read this, not to forget this dreadful danger. If they are not convinced of this danger through the evil condition of the world and through the evils each one experiences himself, let them at least learn of this danger by the vast and powerful remedies and helps, which the Savior thought it necessary to leave behind in his Church. For He would not have provided such antidotes if our ailment and danger of eternal death were not so great and formidable.

WORDS OF THE QUEEN.

This close imitation and living reproduction of Christ, confronting the demons in the first children of the Church, they feared so much, that they dared not approach and they precipitously fled from the Apostles and the just ones imbued with the doctrines of my divine Son. In them were offered up to the Almighty the first fruits of grace, and of Redemption. What is seen in the saints and in perfect Christians in those times, would happen in the present times with all the Catholics if they would accept grace and work with it instead of permitting it to go to waste, and if they would seek the way of the Cross; for Lucifer fears it just as much now as in the times thou hast been writing of. But soon the charity, zeal and devotion in many of the faithful began to grow cold and they forgot the blessings of the Redemption; they yielded to their carnal inclinations and desires, they loved vanity and avarice, and permitted themselves to be fascinated and deceived by the false pretenses of Lucifer, obscuring the glory of their Savior and inveigling them into the meshes of their mortal enemies. This foul ingratitude has thrown the world into the present state and has encouraged the demons to rise up in their pride against God, audaciously presuming to possess themselves of all the children of Adam on account of this forgetfulness and carelessness of Catholics. They presume to plot the destruction of the whole Church by the perversion of so many who have fallen away from it; and by inducing those who are in it, to think little of it, or by hindering them from producing the fruits of the blood and death of their Redeemer. The greatest misfortune is, that many Catholics fail to recognize this great damage and do not seriously think of a remedy, although they can presume that the times, of which Jesus forewarned the women of Jerusalem, have arrived; namely, those in which the sterile should be happy, and in which many would call upon the mountains and the hills to cover and fall upon them, in order not to see the devastation of wickedness cutting down the sons of perdition, the dried trees, barren of all the fruits of virtue.

CHAPTER XI.

The fullness of wisdom in the soul of our great Queen and Lady amid all her sorrows permitted no defect or remissness in noticing and attending to all the duties of each occasion and at all times. By this heavenly foresight She met her obligations and practiced the highest and most eminent of all the virtues. As I have said, the Queen retired, after the burial of Christ, to the house of the Cenacle. Remaining in the hall of the last Supper in the company of saint John, the Marys, and the other women who had followed Christ from Galilee, She spoke to them and the Apostle, thanking them in profound humility and abundant tears for persevering with Her up to this time throughout the Passion of her beloved Son and promising them in his name the reward of having followed Him with so much constancy and devotion. At the same time She offered Herself as a servant and as a friend to those holy women. All of them with Saint John acknowledged this great favor, kissed her hands and asked for her blessing. They also begged her to take some rest and some bodily refreshment. But the Queen answered: "My rest and my consolation shall be to see my Son and Lord arisen from the dead. Do you, my dearest friends, satisfy your wants according to your necessities, while I retire alone with my Son." In her retirement during this evening the great Lady contemplated the doings of the most holy soul of her Son after it left the sacred body. For from the first the blessed Mother knew that the soul of Christ, united to the Divinity, descended to limbo in order to release the holy Fathers from the subterranean prison, where they had been detained since the death of the first just man that had died in expectance of the advent of the Redeemer of the whole human race. By the presence of the most holy Soul this obscure cavern was converted into a heaven and was filled with a wonderful splendor; and to the souls therein contained was imparted the clear vision of the Divinity. In one instant they passed from the state of long-deferred hope to the possession of glory, and from darkness to the inaccessible light, which they now began to enjoy. All of them recognized their true God and Redeemer, and gave him thanks and glory, breaking forth in canticles of praise saying: "The Lamb that was slain is worthy to receive power and Divinity, and wisdom, and strength, and honor, and glory and benediction. Thou hast redeemed us, Lord, in thy blood, out of every tribe, and tongue, and people, and nation; and hast made us to our God a kingdom and priests, and we shall reign on the earth (Apoc. 59, 12). Thine is, O Lord, the power, thine the reign, and thine is the glory of thy works." Then the Lord commanded the angels to bring all the souls in purgatory, and this was immediately done. As if in earnest of the human Redemption they were absolved then and there by the Redeemer from the punishments still due to them, and they were glorified with the other souls of the just by the beatific vision. Thus on that day of the presence of the King were depopulated the prisonhouses of both limbo and purgatory.

The divine soul of Christ our Redeemer remained in limbo from half past three of Friday afternoon, until after three of the Sunday morning following.

During this hour He returned to the Sepulchre as the victorious Prince of the angels and of the saints, whom He had delivered from those nether prisons as spoils of his victory and as an earnest of his glorious triumph over the chastised and prostrate rebels of hell. In the sepulchre were many angels as its guard, venerating the sacred body united to the Divinity. Some of them, obeying the command of their Queen and Mistress, had gathered the relics of the sacred blood shed by her divine Son, the particles of flesh scattered about, the hair torn from his divine face and head, and all else that belonged to the perfection and integrity of his most sacred humanity. On these the Mother of prudence lavished her solicitous care. The angels took charge of these relics, each one filled with joy at being privileged to hold the particles, which he was able to secure. Before any change was made, the body of the Redeemer was shown to the holy Fathers, in the same wounded, lacerated and disfigured state in which it was left by the cruelty of the Jews. Beholding Him thus disfigured in death, the Patriarchs and Prophets and other saints adored Him and again confessed Him as the incarnate Word, who had truly taken upon Himself our infirmities and sorrows (Is. 53, 4) and paid abundantly our debts, satisfying in his innocence and guiltlessness for what we ourselves owed to the justice of the eternal Father. There did our first parents Adam and Eve see the havoc wrought by their disobedience, the priceless remedy it necessitated, the immense goodness and mercy of the Redeemer. As they felt the effects of his copious Redemption in the glory of their souls, they praised anew the Omnipotent and Saints of saints, who had with such marvelous wisdom wrought such a salvation.

Then, in the presence of all those saints, through the ministry of those angels, were united to the sacred body all the relics, which they had gathered, restoring it to its natural perfection and integrity. In the same moment the most holy soul reunited with the body, giving it immortal life and glory. Instead of the winding-sheets and the ointments, in which it had been buried, it was clothed with the four gifts of glory, namely: with clearness, impassibility, agility and subtility (John 19, 40). These gifts overflowed from the immense glory of the soul of Christ into the sacred body. Although these gifts were due to it as a natural inheritance and participation from the instant of its conception, because from that very moment his soul was glorified and his whole humanity was united to the Divinity; yet they had been suspended in their effects upon the purest body, in order to permit it to remain passable and capable of meriting for us our own glory. In the Resurrection these gifts were justly called into activity in the proper degree corresponding to the glory of his soul and to his union with the Divinity. As the glory of the most holy soul of Christ our Savior is incomprehensible and ineffable to man, it is also impossible entirely to describe in our words or by our examples the glorious gifts of his deified body; for in comparison to its purity, crystal would be obscure. The light inherent and shining forth from his body so far exceeds that of the others, as the day does the night, or as many suns the light of one star; and all the beauty of creatures, if it were joined, would appear ugliness in comparison with his, nothing else being comparable to it in all creation.

The excellence of these gifts in the Resurrection were far beyond the glory of his Transfiguration or that manifested on other occasions of the kind mentioned in this history. For on these occasions He received it transitorily and for special purposes, while now He received it in plenitude and forever. Through impassibility his body became invincible to all created power, since no power can ever move or change Him. By subtility the gross and earthly matter was so purified, that it could now penetrate other matter like a pure spirit. Accordingly He penetrated through the rocks of the sepulchre without removing or displacing them, just as He had issued forth from the womb of his most blessed Mother. Agility so freed Him from the weight and slowness of matter, that it exceeded the agility of the immaterial angels, while He himself could move about more quickly than they, as shown in his apparitions to the Apostles and on other occasions. The sacred wounds, which had disfigured his body, now shone forth from his hands and feet and side so refulgent and brilliant, that they added a most entrancing beauty and charm. In all this glory and heavenly adornment the Savior now arose from the grave; and in the presence of the saints and Patriarchs He promised universal resurrection in their own flesh and body to all men, and that they moreover, as an effect of his own Resurrection, should be similarly glorified. As an earnest and as a pledge of the universal resurrection, the Lord commanded the souls of many saints there present to reunite with their bodies and rise up to immortal life. Immediately this divine command was executed, and their bodies arose, as is mentioned by saint Matthew, in anticipation of this mystery (Matthew 27, 52). Among them was saint Anne, saint Joseph and saint Joachim, and others of the ancient Fathers and Patriarchs, who had distinguished themselves in the faith and hope of the Incarnation, and had desired and prayed for it with greater earnestness to the Lord. As a reward for their zeal, the resurrection and glory of their bodies was now anticipated.

Of all these mysteries the great Queen of heaven was aware and She participated in them from her retreat in the Cenacle. In the same instant in which the most holy soul of Christ entered and gave life to his body the joy of her immaculate soul, which I mentioned in the foregoing chapter as being restrained and, as it were, withheld, overflowed into her immaculate body. And this overflow was so exquisite in its effects, that She was transformed from sorrow to joy, from pain to delight, from grief to ineffable jubilation and rest. It happened that just at this time the Evangelist John, as he had done on the previous morning, stepped in to visit her and console Her in her bitter solitude, and thus unexpectedly, in the midst of splendor and glory, met Her, whom he had before scarcely recognized on account of her overwhelming sorrow. The Apostle now beheld Her with wonder and deepest reverence and concluded that the Lord had risen, since his blessed Mother was thus transfigured with joy.

In this new joy and under the divine influences of her supernatural vision the great Lady began to prepare Herself for the visit of the Lord, which was near at hand. While eliciting acts of praise, and in her canticles and prayers, She immediately felt within Her a new kind of jubilation and celestial delight, reaching far beyond the first joy, and correspondng in a wonderful manner to the sorrows and tribulations She had undergone in the Passion; and this new favor was different and much more exalted than the joys overflowing naturally from her soul into her body. Moreover She perceived within Herself another third and still more different effect, implying new divine favors.

The blessed Mary being thus prepared, Christ our Savior, arisen and glorious, in the company of all the Saints and Patriarchs, made his appearance. The ever humble Queen prostrated Herself upon the ground and adored her divine Son; and the Lord raised Her up and drew Her to Himself. In this contact, which was more intimate than the contact with the humanity and the wounds of the Savior sought by Magdalen, the Virgin Mother participated in an extraordinary favor, which She alone, as exempt from sin, could merit. Although it was not the greatest of the favors She attained on this occasion, yet She could not have received it without failing of her faculties, if She had not been previously strengthened by the angels and by the Lord himself. This favor was, that the glorious body of the Son so closely united itself to that of his purest Mother, that He penetrated into it or She into his, as when, for instance, a crystal globe takes up within itself the light of the sun and is saturated with the splendor and beauty of its light. In the same way the body of the most holy Mary entered into that of her divine Son by this heavenly embrace; it was, as it were, the portal of her intimate knowledge concerning the glory of the most holy soul and body of her Lord. As a consequence of these favors, constituting higher and higher degrees of ineffable gifts, the spirit of the Virgin Mother rose to the knowledge of the most hidden sacraments. In the midst of them She heard a voice saying to Her: "My beloved, ascend higher!" (Luke 18, 10). By the power of these words She was entirely transformed and saw the Divinity clearly and intuitively, wherein She found complete, though only temporary, rest and reward for all her sorrows and labors.　Silence alone here is proper, since reason and language are entirely inadequate to comprehend or express what passed in the blessed Mary during this beatific vision, the highest She had until then enjoyed.　Let us celebrate this day in wonder and praise, with congratulations and loving and humble thanks for what She then merited for us, and for her exaltation and joy.

For some hours the heavenly Princess continued to enjoy the essence of God with her divine Son, participating now in his triumph as She had in his torments. Then by similar degrees She again descended from this vision and found Herself in the end reclining on the right arm of the most sacred humanity and regaled in other ways by the right hand of his Divinity (Cant. 2, 6). She held sweetest converse with her Son concerning the mysteries of his Passion and of his glory.　In these conferences She was again inebriated with the wine of love and charity, which now She drank unmeasured from the original fount.　All that a mere creature can receive was conferred upon the blessed Mary on this occasion; for, according to our way of conceiving such things, the divine equity wished to compensate the injury (thus I must call it, because I cannot find a more proper word), which a Creature so pure and immaculate had undergone in suffering the sorrows and torments of the Passion.　For, as I have mentioned many times before, She suffered the same pains as her Son, and now in this mystery She was inundated with a proportionate joy and delight.

WORDS OF THE QUEEN.

Each of these gifts are correspondingly augmented in him who in the state of grace performs the least meritorious work, even if it be no more than removing a straw or giving a cup of water for the love of God (Matth. 10, 42). For each of the most insignificant works the creature gains an increase of these gifts; an increase of clearness exceeding many times the sunlight and added to its state of blessedness; an increase of impassibility, by which man recedes from human and earthly corruption farther than what all created efforts and strength could ever effect in resisting or separating itself from such infirmity or changefulness; an increase of subtility, by which he advances beyond all that could offer it resistance and gains new power of penetration; an increase of agility, surpassing all the activity of birds, of winds, and all other active creatures, such as fire and the elements tending to their centre. From this increase of the gifts of the body merited by good works, thou wilt understand the augmentation of the gifts of the soul; for those of the body are derived from those of the soul and correspond with them. In the beatific vision each merit secures greater clearness and insight into the divine attributes and perfections than that acquired by all the doctors and enlightened members of the Church. Likewise the gift of apprehension, or possession of the divine Object, is augmented; for the security of the possession of the highest and infinite Good makes the tranquillity and rest of its enjoyment more estimable than if the soul possessed all that is precious and rich, desirable and worthy of attainment in all creation, even if possessed all at one time. Fruition, the third gift of the soul, on account of the love with which man performs the smallest acts, so exalts the degrees of functional love, that the greatest love of men here on earth can never be compared thereto; nor can the delight resulting therefrom ever be compared with all the delights of this mortal life.

CHAPTER XII.

THE ASCENSION OF CHRIST.

A few days before the Ascension of the Lord, while the blessed Mary was engaged in the one of the above-mentioned exercises, the eternal Father and the Holy Ghost appeared in the Cenacle upon a throne of ineffable splendor surrounded by the choirs of angels and saints there present and other heavenly spirits, which had now come with the divine Persons. Then the incarnate Word ascended the throne and seated Himself with the other Two. The ever humble Mother of the Most High, prostrate in a corner of a room, in deepest reverence adored the most blessed Trinity, and in it her own incarnate Son. The eternal Father commanded two of the highest angels to call Mary, which they did by approaching Her, and in sweetest voices intimating to Her the divine will. She arose from the dust with the most profound humility, modesty and reverence. Accompanied by the angels She approached the foot of the Throne, humbling herself anew. The eternal Father said to Her: "Beloved, ascend higher!" (Luke 14, 10). As these words at the same time effected what they signified, She was raised up and placed on the throne of royal Majesty with the three divine Persons. New admiration was caused in the saints to see a mere Creature exalted to such dignity. Being made to understand the sanctity and equity of the works of the Most High, they gave new glory and praise proclaiming Him immense, Just, Holy and Admirable in all his counsels.

The Father then spoke to the blessed Mary saying: "My Daughter, to Thee do I entrust the Church founded by my Onlybegotten, the new law of grace He established in the world, and the people, which He redeemed: to Thee do I consign them all." Thereupon also the Holy Ghost spoke to Her: "My Spouse, chosen from all creatures, I communicate to Thee my wisdom and grace together with which shall be deposited in thy heart the mysteries, the works and teachings and all that the incarnate Word has accomplished in the world." And the Son also said: "My most beloved Mother, I go to my Father and in my stead I shall leave Thee and I charge Thee with the care of my Church; to Thee do I commend its children and my brethren, as the Father has consigned them to Me." Then the three Divine Persons, addressing the choir of holy angels and the other saints, said: "This is the Queen of all created things in heaven and earth; She is the Protectress of the Church, the Mistress of creatures, the Mother of piety, the Intercessor of the faithful, the Advocate of sinners, the Mother of beautiful love and holy hope (Eccli. 24, 24); She is mighty in drawing our will to mercy and clemency. In Her shall be deposited the treasures of our grace and her most faithful heart shall be the tablet whereon shall be written and engraved our holy law. In Her are contained the mysteries of our Omnipotence for the salvation of mankind. She is the perfect work of our hands, through whom the plenitude of our desires shall be communicated and satisfied without hindrance in the currents of our divine perfections. Whoever shall call upon Her from his heart shall not perish; whoever shall obtain her intercession shall secure for himself eternal life. What She asks of Us, shall be granted, and We shall always hear her requests and prayers and fulfill her will; for She has consecrated Herself perfectly to what pleases Us." The most blessed Mary, hearing Herself thus exalted, humiliated Herself so much the deeper the more highly She was raised by the right hand of the Most High above all the human and angelic creatures. As if She were the least of all, She adored the Lord and offered Herself, in the most prudent terms and in the most ardent love, to work as a faithful servant in the Church and to obey promptly all the biddings of the divine will. From that day on She took upon Herself anew the care of the evangelical Church, as a loving Mother of all its children; She renewed all the petitions She had until then made, so that during the whole further course of her life they were most fervent and incessant, as we shall see in the third part, where will appear more clearly what the Church owes to this great Queen and Lady, and what blessings She gained and merited for it.

On that same day, by divine dispensation, while the Lord was at table with the eleven Apostles, other disciples and pious women gathered at the Cenacle to the number of one hundred and twenty; for the divine Master wished them to be present at his Ascension. Moreover, just as He had instructed the Apostles, so He now wanted to instruct these faithful respectively in what each was to know before his leaving them and ascending into heaven. All of them being thus gathered and united in peace and charity within those walls in the hall of the last Supper, the Author of life manifested Himself to them as a kind and loving Father and said to them:

"My sweetest children, I am about to ascend to my Father, from whose bosom I descended in order to rescue and save men. I leave with you in my stead my own Mother as your Protectress, Consoler and Advocate, and as your Mother, whom you are to hear and obey in all things. Just as I have told you, that he who sees Me sees my Father, and he who knows Me, knows also Him; so I now tell you, that He who knows my Mother, knows Me; he who hears Her, hears Me; and who honors Her, honors Me. All of you shall have Her as your Mother, as your Superior and Head, and so shall also your successors. She shall answer your doubts, solve your difficulties; in Her, those who seek Me shall always find Me; for I shall remain in Her until the end of the world, and I am in Her now, although you do not understand how." This the Lord said, because He was sacramentally present in the bosom of his Mother; for the sacred species, which She had received at the last Supper, were preserved in Her until consecration of the first Mass, as I shall relate further on. The Lord thus fulfilled that which He promised in saint Matthew: "I am with you to the consummation of the world" (Matth. 28, 20). The Lord added and said: "You will have Peter as the supreme head of the Church, for I leave him as my Vicar; and you shall obey him as the chief highpriest. Saint John you shall hold as the son of my Mother; for I have chosen and appointed him for this office on the Cross." The Lord then looked upon his most beloved Mother, who was there present, and intimated his desire of expressly commanding that whole congregation to worship and reverence Her in a manner suited to the dignity of Mother of God, and of leaving this command under form of a precept for the whole Church. But the most humble Lady besought her Onlybegotten to be pleased not to secure Her more honor than was absolutely necessary for executing all that He had charged Her with; and that the new children of the Church should not be induced to show Her greater honor than they had shown until then. On the contrary, She desired to divert all the sacred worship of the Church immediately upon the Lord himself and to make the propagation of the Gospel redound entirely to the exaltation of his holy name. Christ our Savior yielded to this most prudent petition of his Mother, reserving to Himself the duty of spreading the knowledge of Her at a more convenient and opportune time; yet in secret He conferred upon Her new extraordinary favors, as shall appear in the rest of this history.

In considering the loving exhortations of their divine Master, the mysteries which He had revealed to them, and the prospect of his leaving them, that whole congregation was moved to their inmost hearts; for He had enkindled in them the divine love by the vivid faith of his Divinity and humanity. Reviving within them the memory of his words and his teachings of eternal life, the delights of his most loving intercourse and company, and sorrowfully realizing, that they were now all at once to be deprived of these blessings, they wept most tenderly and sighed from their inmost souls. They longed to detain Him, although they could not, because they saw it was not befitting; words of parting rose to their lips, but they could not bring themselves to utter them; each one felt sentiments of sorrow arising amid feelings both of joy and yet also of pious regret. How shall we live without such a Master? they thought. Who can ever speak to us such words of life and consolation as He? Who will receive us so lovingly and kindly? Who shall be our Father and protector? We shall be helpless children and orphans in this world. Some of them broke their silence and exclaimed: "O most loving Lord and Father! O joy and life of our souls! Now that we know Thee as our Redeemer, Thou departest and leavest us! Take us along with Thee, O Lord; banish us not from thy sight. Our blessed Hope, what shall we do without thy presence? Whither shall we turn, if Thou goest away? Whither shall we direct our steps, if we cannot follow Thee, our Father, our Chief, and our Teacher?" To these and other pleadings the Lord answered by bidding them not to leave Jerusalem and to persevere in prayer until He should send the Holy Spirit, the Consoler, as promised by the Father and as already foretold to the Apostles at the last Supper. Thereupon happened, what I shall relate in the next chapter.

The most auspicious hour, in which the Only-begotten of the eternal Father, after descending from heaven in order to assume human flesh, was to ascend by his own power and in a most wonderful manner to the right hand of God, the Inheritor of his eternities, one and equal with Him in nature and infinite glory. He was to ascend, also, because He had previously descended to the lowest regions of the earth, as the Apostle says (Ephes. 4, 9), having fulfilled all that had been written and prophesied concerning his coming into the world, his Life, Death and the Redemption of man, and having penetrated, as the Lord of all, to the very centre of the earth. By this Ascension he sealed all the mysteries and hastened the fulfillment of his promise, according to which He was, with the Father, to send the Paraclete upon his Church after He himself should have ascended into heaven (John 16, 7). In order to celebrate this festive and mysterious day, Christ our Lord selected as witnesses the hundred and twenty persons, to whom, as related in the foregoing chapter, He had spoken in the Cenacle. They were the most holy Mary, the eleven Apostles, the seventy-two disciples, Mary Magdalen, Lazarus their brother, the other Marys and the faithful men and women making up the above-mentioned number of one hundred and twenty.

With this little flock our divine Shepherd Jesus left the Cenacle, and, with his most blessed Mother at his side, He conducted them all through the streets of Jerusalem. The Apostles and all the rest in their order, proceeded in the direction of Bethany, which was less than half a league over the brow of mount Olivet. The company of angels and saints from limbo and purgatory followed the Victor with new songs of praise, although Mary alone was privileged to see them. The Resurrection of Jesus of Nazareth was already divulged throughout Jerusalem and Palestine. Although the perfidious and malicious princes and priests had spread about the false testimony of his being stolen by the disciples, yet many would not accept their testimony, nor give it any credit. It was divinely provided, that none of the inhabitants of the city, and none of the unbelievers or doubters, should pay any attention to this holy procession, or hinder it on its way from the Cenacle. All, except the one hundred and twenty just, who were chosen by the Lord to witness his Ascension into heaven, were justly punished by being prevented from noticing this wonderful mystery, and the Chieftain and Head of this procession remained invisible to them.

The Lord having thus secured them this privacy, they all ascended mount Olivet to its highest point. There they formed three choirs, one of the angels, another of the saints, and a third of the Apostles and faithful, which again divided into two bands, while Christ the Savior presided. Then the most prudent

Mother prostrated Herself at the feet of her Son and, worshipping Him with admirable humility, She adored Him as the true God and as the Redeemer of the world, asking his last blessing. All the faithful there present imitated Her and did the same. Weeping and sighing, they asked the Lord, whether He was now to restore the kingdom of Israel (Acts 1, 6). The Lord answered, that this was a secret of the eternal Father and not to be made known to them; but, for the present, it was necessary and befitting, that they receive the Holy Ghost and preach, in Jerusalem, in Samaria and in all the world, the mysteries of the Redemption of the world.

Jesus, having taken leave of this holy and fortunate gathering of the faithful, his countenance beaming forth peace and majesty, joined his hands and, by his own power, began to raise Himself from the earth, leaving thereon the impression of his sacred feet. In gentlest motion He was wafted toward the aerial regions, drawing after Him the eyes and the hearts of those first-born children, who amid sighs and tears vented their affection. And as, at the moving of the first Cause of all motion, it is proper that also the nether spheres should be set in motion, so the Savior Jesus drew after Him also the celestial choirs of the angels, the holy Patriarchs and the rest of the glorified saints, some of them with body and soul, others only as to their soul. All of them in heavenly order were raised up together from the earth, accompanying and following their King, their Chief and Head. The new and mysterious sacrament, which the right hand of the Most High wrought on this occasion for his most holy Mother, was that He raised Her up with Him in order to put Her in possession of the glory, which He had assigned to Her as his true Mother and which She had by her merits prepared and earned for Herself. Of this favor the great Queen was capable even before it happened; for her divine Son had offered it to Her during the forty days which He spent in her company after his Resurrection. In order that this sacrament might be kept secret from all other living creatures at that time, and in order that the heavenly Mistress might be present in the gathering of the Apostles and the faithful in their prayerful waiting upon the coming of the Holy Ghost (Acts 1, 14), the divine power enabled the blessed Mother miraculously to be in two places at once; remaining with the children of the Church for their comfort during their stay in the Cenacle and at the same time ascending with the Redeemer of the world to his heavenly throne, where She remained for three days. There She enjoyed the perfect use of all her powers and faculties, whereas She was more restricted in the use of them during that time in the Cenacle.

Amidst this jubilee and other rejoicings exceeding all our conceptions that new divinely arranged procession approached the empyrean heavens. Between the two choirs of angels and saints, Christ and his most blessed Mother made their entry. All in their order gave supreme honor to Each respectively and to Both together, breaking forth in hymns of praise in honor of the Authors of grace and of life. Then the eternal Father placed upon the throne of his Divinity at his right hand, the incarnate Word, and in such glory and majesty, that He filled with new admiration and reverential fear all the inhabitants of heaven. In clear and intuitive vision they recognized the infinite glory and perfection of the Divinity inseparably and substantially united in one personality to the most holy humanity, beautified and exalted by the pre-eminence and glory due to this union, such as eyes have not seen, nor ears heard, nor ever has entered into the thoughts of creatures (Is. 54, 4).

On this occasion the humility and wisdom of our most prudent Queen reached their highest point; for, overwhelmed by such divine and admirable favors, She hovered at the footstool of the royal throne, annihilated in the consciousness of being a mere earthly creature. Prostrate She adored the Father and broke out in new canticles of praise for the glory communicated to his Son and for elevating in Him the deified humanity to such greatness and splendor. Again the angels and saints were filled with admiration and joy to see the most prudent humility of their Queen, whose living example of virtue, as exhibited on that occasion, they emulated among themselves in copying. Then the voice of the eternal Father was heard saying: "My Daughter, ascend higher!" Her divine Son also called Her, saying: "My Mother, rise up and take possession of the place, which I owe Thee for having followed and imitated Me." The Holy Ghost said: "My Spouse and Beloved, come to my eternal embraces!" Immediately was proclaimed to all the blessed the decree of the most holy Trinity, by which the most blessed Mother, for having furnished her own life-blood toward the Incarnation and for having nourished, served, imitated and followed Him with all the perfection possible to a creature, was exalted and placed at the right hand of her Son for all eternity. None other of the human creatures should ever hold that place or position, nor rival Her in the unfailing glory connected with it; but it was to be reserved to the Queen and to be her possession by right after her earthly life, as of one who pre-eminently excelled all the rest of the saints.

In fulfillment of this decree, the most blessed
Mary was raised to the throne of the holy Trinity at
the right hand of her Son.   At the same time She,
with all the saints, was informed, that She was given
possession of this throne not only for all the ages of
eternity, but that it was left to her choice to remain
there even now and without returning to the earth.
For it was the conditional will of the divine Persons,
that as far as they were concerned, She should now
remain in that state.   In order that She might make
her own choice, She was shown anew the state of the
Church upon earth, the orphaned and necessitous condition of the faithful, whom She was left free to assist.
This admirable proceeding of the divine Providence
was to afford the Mother of mercy an occasion of going
beyond, so to say, even her own Self in doing good
and in obliging the human race with an act of tenderest
love similar to that of her Son in assuming a passible
state and in suspending the glory due to his body during
and for our Redemption.   The most blessed Mother
imitated Him also in this respect, so that She might be in
all things like the incarnate Word.   The great Lady
therefore, having clearly before her eyes all the sacrifices included in this proposition, left the throne and,
prostrating Herself at the feet of the Three Persons,
said: "Eternal and almighty God, my Lord, to accept
at once this reward, which thy condescending kindness
offers me, would be to secure my rest; but to return
to the world and continue to labor in mortal life for
the good of the children of Adam and the faithful of
thy holy Church, would be to the glory and according
to the pleasure of thy Majesty and would benefit my
sojourning and banished children on earth.   I accept
this labor and renounce for the present the peace and

joy of thy presence. Well do I know, what I possess and receive, but I will sacrifice it to further the love Thou hast for men. Accept, Lord and Master of all my being, this sacrifice and let thy divine strength govern me in the undertaking confided to me. Let faith in Thee be spread, let thy holy name be exalted, let thy holy Church be enlarged, for Thou hast acquired it by the blood of thy Onlybegotten and mine; I offer myself anew to labor for thy glory and for the conquest of the souls, as far as I am able."

Such was the sacrifice made by the most loving Mother and Queen, one greater than ever was conceived by creature, and it was so pleasing to the Lord, that He immediately rewarded it by operating in Her those purifications and enlightenments, which I have at other times mentioned as necessary to the intuitive vision of the Divinity; for so far She had on this occasion seen It only by abstractive vision. Thus elevated She partook of the beatific vision and was filled with splendor and celestial gifts, altogether beyond the power of man to describe or conceive in mortal life.

In order to finish this chapter, and with it this second part, I return to the congregation of the faithful, whom we left so sorrowful on mount Olivet. The most holy Mary did not forget them in the midst of her glory; as they stood weeping and lost in grief and, as it were, absorbed in looking into the aerial regions, into which their Redeemer and Master had disappeared, She turned her eyes upon them from the cloud on which She had ascended, in order to send them her assistance. Moved by their sorrow, She besought Jesus lovingly to console these little children, whom He had left as orphans upon the earth. Moved by the prayers of his Mother, the Redeemer of the human race sent down two angels in white and resplendent garments, who appeared to all the disciples and the faithful and spoke to them: "Ye men of Galilee, do not look up to heaven in so great astonishment, for this Lord Jesus, who departed from you and has ascended into heaven, shall again return with the same glory and majesty in which you have just seen Him" (Acts 1, 11). By such words and others which they added they consoled the Apostles and disciples and all the rest, so that they might not grow faint, but in their retirement hope for the coming and the consolation of the Holy Ghost promised by their divine Master.

WORDS OF THE QUEEN.

My daughter, thou wilt appropriately close this second part of my life by remembering the lesson concerning the most efficacious sweetness of the divine love and the immense liberality of God with those souls, that do not hinder its flowing. It is in conformity with the inclinations of his holy and perfect will to regale rather than afflict creatures, to console them rather than cause them sorrow, to reward them rather than to chastise them, to rejoice rather than grieve them. But mortals ignore this divine science, because they desire from the hands of the Most High such consolations, delights and rewards, as are earthly and dangerous, and they prefer them to the true and more secure blessings. The divine Love then corrects this fault by the lessons conveyed in tribulations and punishments. Human nature is slow, coarse and uneducated; and if it is not cultivated and softened, it gives no fruit in season, and on account of its evil inclinations, will never of itself become fit for the most loving and sweet intercourse with the highest Good. Therefore it must be shaped and reduced by the hammer of adversities, refined in the crucible of tribulation, in order that it may become fit and capable of the divine gifts and favors and may learn to despise terrestrial and fallacious goods, wherein death is concealed.

I counted for little all that I endured, when I saw the reward which the divine Goodness had prepared for me; and therefore He ordained, in his admirable Providence, that I should return to the militant Church of my own free will and choice. This I knew would redound to my greater glory and to the exaltation of his holy name, while it would provide assistance to his Church and to his children in an admirable and holy manner (I Tim. 1, 17). It seemed to me a sacred duty, that I deprive myself of the eternal felicity of which I was in possession and, returning from heaven to earth, gain new fruits of labor and love for the Almighty; all this I owed to the divine Goodness, which had raised me up from the dust. Learn therefore, my beloved, from my example, and excite thyself to imitate me most eagerly during these times, in which the holy Church is so disconsolate and overwhelmed by tribulations and in which there are none of her children to console her. In this cause I desire that thou labor strenuously, ready to suffer in prayer and supplication, and crying from the bottom of thy heart to the Omnipotent. And if it were necessary thou shouldst be willing to give thy life. I assure thee, my daughter, thy solicitude shall be very pleasing in the eyes of my divine Son and in mine.

Let it all be for the glory and honor of the Most High, the King of the ages, the Immortal and Invisible (I Tim. 1, 17), and for that of his Mother, the most blessed Mary, through all the eternities!

PART THIRD

BOOKS VII, VIII

THE CORONATION

BOOK SEVEN

How the divine Right Hand showered upon the Queen of Heaven highest
Gifts, in order that She might labor in the holy Church; the Coming
of the Holy Ghost; the copious Fruit of the Redemption and the
Preaching of the Apostles; the first Persecution of the Church,
the Conversion of saint Paul and the arrival of saint James
in Spain; the Apparition of the Mother of God in Saragossa, and the Founding of the Pilgrimage of our
Lady of the Pillar.

CHAPTER I.

DESCENT OF THE HOLY GHOST; MARY'S INTUITIVE VISION
OF HIM.

In the company of the great Queen of heaven,
and encouraged by Her, the twelve Apostles and the rest
of the disciples and faithful joyfully waited for the fulfillment of the promise of the Savior, that He would
send them the Holy Ghost, the Consoler, who should
instruct them and administer unto them all that they
had heard in the teaching of their Lord (John 14, 26).
They were so unanimous and united in charity, that
during all these days none of them had any thought,
affection or inclination contrary to those of the rest.
They were of one heart and soul in thought and action.
Although the election of saint Mathias had occurred,
not the least movement or sign of discord arose among
all those first-born children of the Church; yet this was
a transaction, which is otherwise apt to arouse differences
of opinion in the most excellently disposed; since each
one is apt to follow his own insight and does not easily

yield to the opinion of others. But into this holy congregation no discord found entrance, because they were united in prayer, in fasting and in the expectation of the Holy Ghost, who does not seek repose in discordant and unyielding hearts. In order that it may be inferred, how powerful was this union in charity, not only for disposing them toward the reception of the Holy Ghost, but for overcoming and dispersing the evil spirits, I will say; that the demons, who since the death of the Savior had lain prostrate in hell, felt in themselves a new kind of oppression and terror, resulting from the virtues of those assembled in the Cenacle. Although they could not explain it to themselves, they perceived a new terrifying force, emanating from that place, and when they perceived the effects of the doctrine and example of Christ in the behavior of the disciples, they feared the ruin of their dominion.

The Queen of the angels, most holy Mary, in the plenitude of her wisdom and grace, knew the time and predestined hour for the sending of the Holy Ghost upon the apostolic college. When the days of Pentecost were about to be fulfilled (Act 2, 1), (which happened fifty days after the Resurrection of the Lord our Redeemer), the most blessed Mother saw, how in heaven the humanity (John 14, 26) of the Word conferred with the eternal Father concerning the promised sending of the divine Paraclete to the Apostles, and that the time predetermined by his infinite wisdom for planting the faith and all his gifts in his holy Church, was at hand. The Lord also referred to the merits acquired by Him in the flesh through his most holy Life, Passion and Death, to the mysteries wrought by Him for the salvation of the human race and to the fact, that He was the Mediator, Advocate and Intercessor between the eternal Father and men, and that among them lived his sweetest Mother, in whom the divine Persons were so well pleased. He besought his Father also, that, besides bringing grace and the invisible gifts the Holy Ghost appear in the world in visible form, that so the evangelical law might be honored before all the world; that the Apostles and faithful, who were to spread the divine truth, might be encouraged, and that the enemies of the Lord, who had in this life persecuted and despised Him unto the death of the Cross, might be filled with terror.

This petition of our Redeemer in heaven was supported on earth by most holy Mary in a manner befitting the merciful Mother of the faithful. Prostrated upon the earth in the form of a cross and in profoundest humility, She saw, how in that consistory of the blessed Trinity, the request of the Savior was favorably accepted, and how, to fulfill and execute it, the persons of the Father and the Son, as the Principle from which the Holy Ghost proceeded, decreed the active mission of the Holy Spirit; for to these Two is attributed the sending of the third Person, because He proceeds from Both; and the third Person passively took upon Himself this mission and consented to come into the world.

On Pentecost morning the blessed Virgin Mary exhorted the Apostles, the disciples and the pious women, numbering about one hundred and twenty, to pray more fervently and renew their hopes, since the hour was at hand in which they were to be visited by the divine Spirit from on high. At the third hour (nine o'clock), when all of them were gathered around their heavenly Mistress and engaged in fervent prayer, the air resounded with a tremendous thunder and the blowing of a violent wind mixed with the brightness of fire or lightning, all centering upon the house of the Cenacle. The house was enveloped in light and the divine fire was poured out over all of that holy gathering (Acts 2, 2). Over the head of each of the hundred and twenty persons appeared a tongue of that same fire, in which the Holy Ghost had come, filling each one with divine influences and heavenly gifts and causing at one and the same time the most diverse and contrary effects in the Cenacle and in the whole of Jerusalem, according to the diversity of the persons affected.

In the most holy Mary these effects were altogether divine, and most wonderful in the sight of all the heavenly courtiers; for as regard us men, we are incapable of understanding and explaining them. The purest Lady was transformed and exalted in God; for She saw intuitively and clearly the Holy Ghost, and for a short time enjoyed the beatific vision of the Divinity. Of his gifts and divine influences She by Herself received more than all the rest of the saints. Her glory for that space of time, exceeded that of the angels and of the blessed. She alone gave to the Lord more glory, praise and thanksgiving than all the universe for the benefit of the descent of his Holy Spirit upon his Church and for his having pledged Himself so many times to send Him and through Him to govern it to the end of the world. The blessed Trinity was so pleased with the conduct of Mary on this occasion, that It considered Itself fully repaid and compensated for having created the world; and not only compensated, but God acted as if He were under a certain obligation for possessing such a peerless Creature, whom the Father could look upon as his Daughter, the Son as his Mother, and the Holy Ghost as his Spouse; and whom (according to our way of thinking) He was now obliged to visit and enrich after having conferred upon Her such high dignity. In this exalted and blessed Spouse were renewed all the gifts and graces of the Holy Spirit, creating new effects and operations altogether beyond our capacity to understand.

The Apostles, as saint Luke says (Acts 2, 11), were also replenished and filled with the Holy Ghost; for they received a wonderful increase of justifying grace of a most exalted degree. The twelve Apostles were confirmed in this sanctifying grace and were never to lose it. In all of them, according to each one's condition, were infused the habits of the seven gifts: Wisdom, Understanding, Science, Piety, Counsel, Fortitude and Fear. In this magnificent blessing, as new as it was admirable in the world, the twelve Apostles were created fit ministers of the new Testament and founders of the evangelical Church for the whole world: for this new grace and blessing communicated to them a divine strength most efficacious and sweet, which inclined them to practice the most heroic virtue and the highest sanctity. Thus strengthened they prayed, they labored willingly and accomplished the most difficult and arduous tasks, engaging in their labors not with sorrow or from necessity, but with the greatest joy and alacrity.

In all the rest of the disciples and the faithful, who received the Holy Ghost in the Cenacle, the Most High wrought proportionally and respectively the same effects, except that they were not confirmed in grace like the Apostles. According to the disposition of each the gifts of grace were communicated in greater or less abundance in view of the ministry they were to hold in the holy Church. The same proportion was maintained in regard to the Apostles; yet saint Peter and saint John were more singularly favored on account of the high offices assigned to them: the one to govern the Church as its head, and the other to attend upon and serve the Queen and Mistress of heaven and of earth, most holy Mary. The sacred text of saint Luke says, that the Holy Ghost filled the whole house in which this happy congregation was gathered (Acts 2, 7), not only because all of them were filled with the Holy Ghost and his admirable gifts, but because the house itself was filled with wonderful light and splendor. This plenitude of wonders and prodigies overflowed and communicated itself also to others outside of the Cenacle; for it caused diverse and various effects of the Holy Spirit among the inhabitants of Jerusalem and its vicinity. All those, who with some piety had compassioned our Savior Jesus in his Passion and Death, deprecating his most bitter torments and reverencing his sacred Person, were interiorly visited with new light and grace, which disposed them afterwards to accept the doctrine of the Apostles. Those that were converted by the first sermon of saint Peter, were to a great extent of the number of those who, by their compassion and sorrow at the death of the Lord, had merited for themselves such a great blessing. Others of the just who were in Jerusalem outside of the Cenacle, also felt great interior consolations, by which they were moved and predisposed by new effects of grace wrought in each one proportionately by the Holy Ghost.

Not less wonderful, although more hidden, were some contrary effects produced on that day by the Holy Ghost in Jerusalem. By the dreadful thunders and violent commotion of the atmosphere and the lightnings accompanying his advent, He disturbed and terrified the enemies of the Lord in that city, each one according to his own malice and perfidy. This chastisement was particularly evident in those who had actively concurred in procuring the death of Christ, and who had signalized themselves in their rabid fury against Him. All these fell to the ground on their faces and remained thus for three hours. Those that had scourged the Lord were suddenly choked in their own blood, which shot forth from their veins in punishment for shedding that of the Master. The audacious servant, who had buffeted the Lord, not only suddenly died, but was hurled into hell body and soul. Others of the Jews, although they did not die, were chastised with intense pains and abominable sicknesses. These disorders, consequent upon shedding the blood of Christ, descended to their posterity and even to this day continue to afflict their children with most horrible impurities. This chastisement became notorious in Jerusalem, although the priests and pharisees diligently sought to cover it up, just as they had tried to conceal the Resurrection of the Savior. As these events, however, were not so important, neither the Apostles nor the Evangelists wrote about them, and in the confusion of the city the multitude soon forgot them.

WORDS OF THE QUEEN.

My daughter, in small esteem and thankfulness do the children of the Church hold this blessing of the Most High, by which, in addition to sending of his Son as their Master and Redeemer, He sent also the Holy Ghost into his Church. So great was the love, by which He sought to draw them to Himself, that, in order to make them sharers of his divine perfections, He sent them first the Son, who is wisdom (John 3, 16) and afterwards the Holy Ghost, who is love, so that all might be enriched in the manner in which they were capable. The divine Spirit, in coming for the first time upon the Apostles and the others gathered with them, intended it as a pledge and testimony, that He would confer the same favor on the rest of the children of the Church, of light and of the Gospel, and that He was ready to communicate his gifts to all, if all will dispose themselves toward receiving them. In witness to this truth the Holy Ghost came upon many of the faithful in visible form and with visible effects (Acts 8, 17; 10, 44; 11, 15), because they were truly faithful servants, humble and sincere, pure and ready of heart to receive Him. Also in our times He comes to many just souls, although not with such open manifestations, because it is neither necessary nor proper. The interior effects and gifts are all of the same nature, acting according to the disposition and state of the one who receives them.

Blessed is the soul which sighs and aspires after this blessing and seeks to participate in this divine fire, which enkindles, enlightens and consumes all that is terrestrial and carnal, which purifies and raises it up to a new existence, union and participation with God himself.

CHAPTER II.

On account of the visible and open signs, by
which the Holy Ghost descended upon the Apostles, the
whole city of Jerusalem with its inhabitants was stirred
to wonder.   When the news of the astounding events at
the house of the Cenacle spread about, the multitude of
the people gathered in crowds to know more of the happenings (Acts 2, 6).   On that day was being celebrated
one of the paschs or feasts of the Jews; and as well
on this account, as on account of the special dispensation
of heaven, the city was crowded with foreigners and
strangers from all parts of the world.   For to them the
Most High wished to manifest the wonders of the first
preaching and spreading of the new law of grace, which
the incarnate Word, our Redeemer and Master, had ordained for the salvation of men.

The sacred Apostles, who were filled with charity
by the plenitude of the gifts of the Holy Ghost and who
knew that all Jerusalem was gathering at the doors of
the Cenacle, asked permission of their Mistress and
Queen to go forth and preach to them; in order that
such great graces might not even for a moment fail
to redound to the benefit of souls and to new glory
of their Author.   They all left the house of the Cenacle
and, placing themselves before the multitudes, began
to preach the mysteries of the faith and of eternal life.
Though until then they had been so shy and seclusive,

they now stepped forth with unhesitating boldness and poured forth burning words, that like a flashing fire penetrated to the souls of their hearers.

This miracle, that all the men of so many different tongues then assembled in Jerusalem should hear the Apostles in their own language, joined to the doctrine which they preached, caused great astonishment. Yet I wish to remark, that though all the Apostles, on account of the plenitude of science and of gifts gratuitously received, were able to speak in the languages of all nations, because that was necessary for the preaching of the Gospel, yet on that occasion they all spoke the language of Palestine. Using only this idiom they were understood by all the different nationalities there present, as if they had spoken in the several idioms. This miracle the Lord wrought at the time in order that they might be understood and believed by those different nations, and in order that saint Peter might not be obliged to repeat in the different languages of those present, what he preached to them concerning the mysteries of faith. He preached only once and all heard and understood him, each in his own language, and so it happened also with the other Apostles. For if each one had spoken in the language of those who heard them, and which they knew as their mother tongue, it would have been necessary for them to repeat what they said at least seven or eight times according to the different nationalities mentioned by saint Luke (Acts 2, 9). This would have consumed a longer time than is intimated by the sacred text, and it would have caused great confusion and trouble to repeat the same doctrines over and over again or to speak so many languages on one occasion; nor would the miracle be so intelligible to us as the one mentioned.

The people who heard the Apostles did not understand the miracle, although they wondered at hearing each their own idiom. What saint Luke says about their speaking different languages, must be understood as meaning, that the Apostles were then and there able to understand them, as I shall mention later on (Acts 2, 4), and because on that day, those that came to the Cenacle understood them all speaking in their own language. But this miracle and wonderment caused in their hearers different effects and opinions, according to the dispositions of each one. Those that listened piously received a deep understanding of the Divinity and of the Redemption of man, now so eloquently and fervently propounded to them. They were moved eagerly to desire the knowledge of the truth; by the divine light they were filled with compunction and sorrow for their sins and with desire of divine mercy and forgiveness. With tears in their eyes they cried out to the Apostles and asked what they must do to gain eternal life. Others, who hardened their hearts, altogether untouched by the divine truths preached by them, became indignant at the Apostles, and instead of yielding to them, called them innovators and adventurers. Many of the Jews, more impious in their perfidy and envy, inveighed against the Apostles, saying they were drunk and insane (Acts 2, 13). Among these were some of those who had again come to their senses after having fallen to the ground at the thunder caused by the coming of the Holy Ghost;

The three thousand, who were converted by the first sermon of saint Peter, were from all the nations then gathered in Jerusalem, so that forthwith all nations, without excluding any, might partake of the fruits of the Redemption, all might be gathered to the Church, and all might experience the grace of the Holy Spirit;

for the holy Church was to be composed of all nations and tribes. Many were Jews, who had followed Christ our Savior with kindly feelings and witnessed his sufferings and Death with compassion, as I said above. Some also of those, who had concurred in his Passion, were converted, though these were few, because many would not alter their disposition; for, if they had done so, all of them would have been admitted to mercy and received pardon for their error. After their preaching the Apostles retired that evening within the Cenacle, in order to give an account to the Mother of mercy, the purest Mary. With them also entered a great number of the new children of the Church, in order that they might come to know and venerate the Mother of mercy.

But the great Queen of the angels was ignorant of nothing that had happened; for from her retreat She had heard the preaching of the Apostles and She knew the secret hearts and thoughts of all the hearers. The tenderest Mother remained prostrate with her face upon the ground during the whole time, tearfully praying for the conversion of all that subjected themselves to the faith of the Savior, and for all the rest, if they should consent to co-operate with the helps and the graces of the Lord. In order to help the Apostles in their great work of beginning to preach, and the bystanders in properly listening to them, the most holy Mary sent many of her accompanying angels with holy inspirations, encouraging the sacred Apostles and giving them strength to inquire and to manifest more explicitly the hidden mysteries of the humanity and Divinity of Christ our Redeemer. The angels fulfilled all the commands of their Queen, while She Herself exercised her own power and gifts according to the circumstances of the occasion. When the Apostles came to Her with those copious first-fruits of their preaching and of the Holy Ghost, She received them with incredible joy and sweetness and with the most loving kindness of a true Mother.

The Apostle saint Peter spoke to the recently converted and said to them: "My brethren, and servants of the Most High, this is the Mother of our Redeemer and Master, Jesus Christ, whose faith you have received in acknowledging Him as true God and man. She has given Him the human form, conceiving Him in her womb, and She bore Him, remaining a Virgin before, during and after his birth. Receive Her as your Mother, as your Refuge and Intercessor, for through Her you and we shall receive light, direction, and release from our sins and miseries." At these words of the Apostle and at the sight of most holy Mary these new adherents of the faith were filled with admirable light and consolation; for this privilege of conferring great interior blessings and of giving light to those who looked upon Her with pious veneration, was renewed and extended in Her at the time when She was at the right hand of her divine Son in Heaven. As all of those faithful partook of these blessings in the presence of their Queen, they prostrated themselves at her feet and with tears besought her assistance and blessing. But the humble and prudent Queen evaded this latter, because of the presence of the Apostles, who were priests, and of saint Peter, the Vicar of Christ. Then this Apostle said to Her: "Lady, do not refuse to these faithful what they piously ask for the consolation of their souls." The blessed Mary obeyed the head of the Church and in humble serenity of a Queen She gave her blessing to the newly converted.

The love which filled their hearts made them desire to hear from their heavenly Mother some words of consolation; yet their humility and reverence prevented them from asking for this favor. As they perceived how obediently She had yielded to saint Peter, they turned to him and begged him to ask Her not to send them away without some word of encouragement. Saint Peter, though he considered this favor very proper for these souls who had been born again to Christ by his preaching and that of the other Apostles, nevertheless, aware that the Mother of Wisdom knew well what was to be done, presumed to say no more than these words; "Lady, listen to the petitions of thy servants and children." Then the great Lady obeyed and said to the converts: "My dearest brethren in the Lord, give thanks and praise with your whole hearts to the Almighty God, because from among all men He has called and drawn you to the sure path of eternal life in the knowledge of the holy faith you have received. Be firm in your confession of it from all your hearts and in hearing and believing all that the law of grace contains as preached and ordained by its true Teacher Jesus, my Son and your Redeemer. Be eager to hear and obey his Apostles, who teach and instruct you, so that you may be signed and marked by Baptism in the character of children of the Most High. I offer myself as your handmaid to assist you in all that serves toward your consolation, and I shall ask Him to look upon you as a kind Father and to manifest to you the true joy of his countenance, communicating to you also his grace."

By this sweetest of exhortations those new children of the Church were filled with consolation, light, veneration and admiration of what they saw of the Mistress of the world; asking again for her blessing, they for that day left her presence, renewed and replete with the wonderful gifts of the Most High. The Apostles and disciples from that day on continued without intermission their preaching and their miracles, and through the entire octave they instructed not only the three thousand, who had been converted on Pentecost day, but multitudes of others, who day by day accepted the faith.   Since they came from all parts of the world, they conversed and spoke with each one in his own language; for as I have said above, they spoke in various languages from that time on.   This grace was given not only to the Apostles, although it was more complete and noticeable in them; also the disciples and all the one hundred and twenty, who were in the Cenacle at the time, and also the holy women, who received the Holy Ghost, were thus favored. This was really necessary at the time on account of the great multitudes, who came to the faith.   Although all the men and many of the women came to the Apostles, yet many, after having heard them, went to Magdalen and her companions, who catechized, instructed and converted them and others that came at the report of the miracles they performed.   For this gift was also conferred on the women, who, by the imposition of hands, cured all the sicknesses, gave sight to the blind, tongue to the mute, motion to the lame, and life to many of the dead.   These and other wonders were principally wrought by the Apostles, nevertheless both their miracles and those of the women excited the wonder and astonishment of all Jerusalem; so that nothing else was talked about except the prodigies and the preaching of the Apostles of Jesus, of his disciples, and followers of his doctrine.

This was the happy beginning and the golden age of the evangelical Church, where the rushing of the stream rejoiced the city of God (Ps. 45, 5) and the current of grace and the gifts of the Holy Ghost fertilized this new paradise recently planted by the hands of the Savior Jesus, while in its midst stood the tree of life, most holy Mary. Then was faith alive, hope firm, charity ardent, sincerity pure, humility true, justice most equitable, when the faithful neither knew avarice nor followed vanity, when they trod under foot vain pomp, were free from covetousness, pride, ambition, which later prevailed among the professors of the faith, who while confessing themselves followers of Christ, denied Him in their works.

It will be possible in this third part to describe only a minute portion of the wonderful and great works accomplished by the mighty Queen in the primitive Church; but from those which I will describe, and from her life in this world after the Ascension, much can be inferred. For She did not rest or lose one moment or occasion of conferring some singular favor either upon the whole Church or some of its members. For She consumed Herself either in praying and beseeching her divine Son, without ever experiencing a refusal; or in exhorting, instructing, counseling, and, as Treasurer and Dispenser of the divine favors, distributing graces in diverse manners among the children of the Gospel. Among the hidden mysteries, which were made known to me concerning this power of the blessed Mary, was also this, that in those first ages, during which She lived in the holy Church, the number of the damned was proportionately very small; and that, comparatively, in those few years a greater number were saved than in many succeeding ages.

I acknowledge, that, if the lapse of time had decreased the power, the charity and clemency of that highest Sovereign, the good fortune of those living in that happy time might cause a holy envy in those living by the light of faith in our more protracted and less favored times. It is true we have not the happiness of seeing

Her, conversing with Her and listening to Her with our bodily senses; and in this respect those first children of the Church were more fortunate. But let us all remember, that in the heavenly knowledge and charity of this most loving Mother we were all present to Her, also during those times (Vol. III., 78); for She saw and knew us all in the order and succession in which we were to be born in the Church; and She prayed and interceded for us no less than for those who lived in her times. Nor is She at present less powerful in heaven, than She was then upon earth; nor less our Mother, than of those first children; and She held us as her own, just as well as them. But alas! that our faith and our fervor and devotion should be so very different! Not She has changed, nor is her love less ardent, nor would we experience less of her intercession and protection, if in these troubled times we would hasten to Her with the same sentiments of humility and fervor, asking for her prayers and trustfully relying upon Her for help, as was the case with those devoted Christians in the first beginning. Without a doubt the whole Catholic Church would then immediately experience the same assistance of the Queen throughout the whole world.

Many of those new faithful, highly impressed with her greatness by their conversation with the heavenly Mistress, returned to present to Her jewels and the richest gifts; especially the women despoiled themselves of fineries to lay them at her feet. But She would receive or permit none of these gifts. When it seemed to Her appropriate not to refuse entirely, She secretly inspired the minds of the givers to bring them to the Apostles, in order that they might be equitably and justly distributed in charity among the most poor and needy of the faithful. But the humble Mother gratefully acknowledged

them as if they had been given to Her. The poor and
the sick She received with ineffable kindness, and many
of them she cured of inveterate and long-standing infirmities. Through the hands of saint John She supplied
many secret wants, never omitting the least point of virtue. As the Apostles and disciples were engaged all day
in preaching the faith and in converting those that came,
the great Queen busied Herself in preparing their food
and attending to their comfort; and at stated times She
served the priests on her knees and with incredible humility and reverence asked to kiss their hands. This She
observed especially with the Apostles, knowing and beholding their souls confirmed in grace, endowed with
all that the Holy Ghost had wrought in them and exalted
by their dignity of being the highpriests and the founders of the Church (Eph. 2, 20). Sometimes She saw
them clothed in great splendor, which elicited from
Her increased reverence and veneration.

WORDS OF THE QUEEN.

My daughter, in what thou hast come to know
of the events related in this chapter, thou wilt find a
great deal that points to the mystery of the predestination of souls. Be convinced that, since the Redemption
was so overflowing and copious, it was sufficient for the
salvation of all men (Rom. 5, 20). The divine truth
was made known to all, whoever heard its preaching or
who saw the effects of the coming of the Godman into
the world. Besides the outward preaching and knowledge of the remedy, all received interior inspirations and
helps in order to seek and accept the means. You are
surprised that, in spite of all this, only three thousand
were converted by the first sermon of the Apostle among
all that great multitude then in Jerusalem. It should

cause a greater surprise that in our times so few are converted to the way of eternal life, as the Gospel is more widespread, its preaching is frequent, its ministers numerous, the light of the Church clearer and the knowledge of the divine mysteries more definite. With all this men are blinder, the hearts more hardened, pride more inflated, avarice more bold, and all the vices are practiced without fear of God and without consideration.

In this most perverse and unhappy state mortals cannot complain of the most high and equitable providence of the Lord, who offers to all and every one his fatherly mercy, and points out to them both the way of life and the way of death; so that if any man hardens his heart, God can permit it in strictest justice. The reprobate will have none but themselves to blame, if afterwards, when there is no more time, they shall be uselessly dismayed with what in opportune time they could and should have known. If in the short and transient life, which is given to them in order to merit the eternal, they close their eyes and ears to the truth and to the light, and if they listen to the demon, giving themselves up to all the promptings of his malice; if they thus abuse the goodness and clemency of the Lord, what can they then allege as their excuse? If they do not know how to pardon an injury and for the slightest offense meditate the direst vengeance; if, for the sake of increasing their property, they pervert the entire order of reason and of natural brotherhood; if for a passing delight they forget the eternal pains, and if, in addition to all this, they despise the warnings, helps and admonitions sent to them by God to inspire them with the fear of perdition and induce them to avoid it, how shall they afterwards find fault with the divine clemency? Let then mortals, who have sinned against God, undeceive themselves: without penance there shall be no grace, without reform no pardon, without pardon no glory. But just as these are not conceded to those that are unworthy, so they are also never denied to those that are worthy; nor is ever the mercy of God withheld from any one who seeks to obtain it.

CHAPTER III.

As the Apostles continued their preaching and wonders in Jerusalem the number of the faithful increased and, as saint Luke says in the fourth chapter of the Acts, after seven days reached five thousand. All of them were busy catechising the newcomers in preparation for Baptism, though that work was done principally by the disciples; for the Apostles were preaching and were conducting some controversies with the pharisees and sadducees. The Queen, with the assistance of her angels and of the other Marys, proceeded to prepare and adorn the hall, in which her divine Son had celebrated the last Supper; and with her own hands She cleansed it and scrubbed it for his return in the consecration to be performed on the next day. She asked the owner to furnish it in the same way as I have described for the Thursday of the Last Supper and the devout host deferred to her wishes with deepest reverence. She also prepared the unleavened bread and the wine necessary for the consecration, together with the same paten and chalice in which the Savior had consecrated. For the Baptism She provided pure water and the basins for administering it with ease and reverence. Then the loving Mother retired and passed the night in most fervent aspirations, prostrations, thanksgiving and other exercises of exalted prayer; offering to the eternal Father all that She, in her heavenly wisdom, knew would help worthily to prepare Herself and all the rest for the worthy administration of Baptism.

Early the next day, which was the octave of the coming of the Holy Ghost, all the faithful and catechumens gathered with the Apostles and disciples in the house of the Cenacle. Saint Peter preached to this gathering instructing them in the nature and excellence of Baptism, the need in which they stood of it and its divine effects, how they would, through it, be made members of the mystical body of the Church, receive an interior character; be regenerated to a new existence as children of God and inheritors of his glory through the remission of sins and sanctifying grace. He exhorted them to the observance of the divine law, to which they subjected themselves by their own free will, and to humble thanksgiving for this benefit and for all the others, which they received from the hands of the Most High. He explained to them also the mysterious and sacred truth of the holy Eucharist, which was to be celebrated in the consecration of the true body and blood of Jesus Christ, and he admonished all those especially, who were to receive holy Communion after their Baptism.

Through this sermon all the converts were inspired with additional fervor; for their dispositions were altogether sincere, the words of the Apostles full of life and penetration, and the interior grace very abundant. Then the Apostles themselves began to baptize amid the most devout and orderly attention of the others. The catechumens entered one door of the Cenacle and after being baptized, they passed out through another, while the disciples and other of the faithful acted as ushers. The most holy Mary was present at the entire ceremony, although keeping to one side of the hall. She prayed for all of them and broke forth in canticles of praise. She recognized the effects of Baptism in each one, according to the greater or less degree of virtues infused in their souls. She beheld them renewed and washed in the blood of the Lamb, and their souls restored to a divine purity and spotlessness. In witness of these effects, a most clear light, visible to all that were present, descended upon each one that was baptized. By this miracle God wished to authenticate the first beginnings of this Sacrament in his holy Church, and to console both those first children and us, who are made partakers of this blessing without much adverting to it or giving thanks for it.

This administration of Baptism was continued on that day until all were baptized, although there were about five thousand to receive it. While the baptized were making their thanksgiving for this admirable blessing, the Apostles with all the disciples and the faithful spent some time in prayer. All of them prostrated themselves on the ground adoring the infinite and immutable God, and confessing their own unworthiness of receiving Him in the most august sacrament of the Altar. In this profound humility and adoration they prepared themselves more immediately for Communion. And then they recited the same psalms and prayers which Christ had recited before consecrating, imitating faithfully that sacred function just as they had seen it performed by their divine Master. Saint Peter took in his hands the unleavened bread, and, after raising up his eyes to heaven with admirable devotion, he pronounced over the bread the words of consecration of the most holy body of Christ, as had been done before the Lord Jesus (II Cor. 9, 24). Immediately the Cenacle was filled with the visible splendor of innumerable angels; and this light converged in a most singular manner on the Queen of heaven and earth and was seen by all those present. Then saint Peter consecrated the chalice and performed all the ceremonies, which Christ had observed with the consecrated body and blood, raising them up for the adoration of all the faithful. The Apostle partook himself of the Sacrament and communicated it to the eleven Apostles as most holy Mary had instructed him. Thereupon, at the hands of saint Peter, the heavenly Mother partook of it, while the celestial spirits there present attended with ineffable reverence. In approaching the altar the great Lady made three profound prostrations, touching the ground with her face.

She returned to her place, and it is impossible to describe in words the effects of this participation of the holy Eucharist in this most exalted of creatures. She was entirely transformed and elevated, completely absorbed in this divine conflagration of the love of her most holy Son, whom She had now received bodily. She remained in a trance, elevated from the floor; but the holy angels shielded Her somewhat from view according to her own wish, in order that the attention of those present might not be unduly attracted by the divine effects apparent in Her. The disciples continued to distribute holy Communion, first to the disciples and then to the others who had been believers before the Ascension. But of the five thousand newly baptized only one thousand received Communion on that day; because not all were entirely prepared or furnished with the insight and attention required for receiving the Lord in this great sacrament and mystery of the Altar.

To explain the rare and prodigious favor, that the sacramental body of Christ in the sacred species should be preserved continually in the bosom of Mary, it is not necessary to seek for another cause than that underlying all the other favors with which God distinguished this great Lady, namely: that it was his holy will and according to his infinite wisdom, by which He performs according to measure and weight all that is befitting (Wis. 11, 21). Christian prudence and piety will be content to know as a reason, that God had singled this mere Creature out to be his natural Mother, and that therefore She alone, of all creatures, deserved this distinction. As this miracle of her Mothership was unique and without parallel, it would be shameful ignorance to seek proofs of what the Lord did in Her by comparing it with what He did or ever will do in other souls; since Mary alone rises supereminently above the common order of all. Yet, though all this is true, the Lord nevertheless wishes that by the light of faith and by other enlightenment, we seek the reasons of the propriety and equity, according to which the powerful arm of the Almighty wrought these wonders in his most worthy Mother, so that in them we may know and bless Him in Her and through Her; and so that we may understand, how secure our salvation, all our hope, and our lot are in the hands of that powerful Queen, toward whom her Son has directed all the excess of his love. In accordance with these truths I will explain what has been made known to me of this mystery.

The heavenly Mother lived thirty-three years in the company of her Son and true God; and from the time when He was born of her virginal womb She never left Him to the time of his death on the Cross. She nursed Him, served Him, followed Him and imitated Him, conducting Herself always as a Mother, Daughter and Spouse, as a most faithful Servant and Friend; She enjoyed the sight of Him, his conversation, his doctrine and the favors, which, by all these meritorious services, She attained in this mortal life. Christ ascended into heaven, and the force of love and right reason demanded,

that He should take to heaven with Him his most loving
Mother, in order that He should not be deprived of Her
there, nor She in this world of his presence and company.
But the most ardent love which both of Them had for
men, dissolved in a manner these bonds of union, inducing our kindest Mother to return to the world in order to establish the Church; and moving the Son to give
his consent to her absence from Him during that time.
But as the Son of God was powerful enough to recompense Her for this privation to a certain extent, it became for Him an obligation of his love to make such a
recompense. And the fulfillment of this obligation would
not have been so publicly acknowledged or made so
manifest, if He denied his blessed Mother the favor of
accompanying Her upon earth, while He remained seated
at the glory of the right hand of his Father. Besides, the
most ardent love of the blessed Mother, having been
accustomed and nourished in the presence of the Lord
her Son, would have inflicted upon Her insufferable violence, if for so many years She was to be deprived of
that kind of presence of Him, which was possible during
her stay in the Church.

From the understanding which has been given
me of the mystery of the love of Christ the Lord for his
most holy Mother and of the force with which He was
drawn toward Her, I would go so far as to say, that if
He had not found this way of remaining with Her in the
sacramental species, He would have come down from the
right hand of the Father to the world in order to render
companionship to his Mother while She sojourned with
his Church. And if it had been necessary that the heavenly mansions and the celestial courtiers should be deprived of the presence of the most sacred humanity from
that time, He would have considered that of less im-

portance than to be deprived of the company of his Mother. It is no exaggeration to say this, when we all must confess, that in the purest Mary the Lord found a correspondence and a degree of love more conformable to his will than in all the blessed combined; and consequently, his own love for Her exceeded his love for all others. If the Shepherd of the Gospel leaves the ninety-nine sheep in order to go in search of only one that is lost, and if we nevertheless dare not say of Him that He leaves the greater for the less; it should not cause wonder in us that this divine Shepherd should leave all the rest of the saints in order to be in the company of his most sincere Sheep, who clothed Him with her own nature and raised and nourished Him as a Mother. Without a doubt the eyes of his beloved Spouse and Mother would attract Him in swiftest flight from those heights (Cant. 6, 4) to that earth, where He had lived, whither He had before this come for the salvation of the children of Adam, toward whom He was less attracted, yea rather repelled by their sins and by the necessity of suffering for them. If now He descended to live with his beloved Mother, it would not be to suffer and die; but to enjoy the delights of her company. Fortunately it was not necessary to rob heaven of his presence; since by descending in sacramental form He could satisfy both his own love and that of his most blessed Mother, in whose heart, as in his couch, this true Solomon could take up his rest without leaving the right hand of his eternal Father (Cant. 3, 7).

WORDS OF THE QUEEN.

Consider attentively the common deception of mortals and the woeful damage they suffer. For in the decisions of their will they ordinarily are moved solely by what they perceive through the senses, and they immediately proceed to act upon their choice without further consideration or counsel. Since the sensible impressions immediately move the animal passions and inclinations, it is evident that men do not act according to right reason, but according to the impulse of passion, excited by the senses and their objects. Hence, he that considers only the injury and pain caused, is straightway moved to vengeance; he that follows only his hankering after strange property, as soon as he lays his eyes upon it, is impelled to injustice. In the same manner act so many unfortunates, who follow the concupiscence of the eyes, the movements of the flesh, and the pride of life, because these are the only things offered by the world and the devil. In their blind deception they follow darkness as their light, taste the bitter as sweet, take deadly poison for remedy of their souls, and hold that for wisdom which is nothing but diabolical and earthly ignorance. Do thou guard thyself against these pernicious errors, and never resolve on anything, or govern thyself by anything that is merely sensible or arising from sensible impressions, nor pursue the advantages held out through them. In thy actions take counsel first of all from the interior knowledge and light communicated to thee by God, in order that thou mayest not go blindly forward; and He shall always grant thee sufficient guidance. Immediately seek the advice of thy superiors and teachers, if thou canst do so before making thy choice. And if thy superior or teacher is not at hand, seek counsel of others, even inferiors; for this is more secure than to follow thy own will, which may be disturbed and blinded by passion. This is the rule to be followed especially in the exterior works, pursuing them with recollection, with secrecy, and according to the demands of circumstances and fraternal charity as they occur. In all of them it is necessary not to lose out of sight the north-star of interior light, while moving in the profound gulf of the intercourse with creatures, where there is continual danger of perishing.

CHAPTER IV.

SOLICITUDE OF MARY FOR THE APOSTLES AND THE FAITHFUL.

As the new law of grace continued to spread in Jerusalem so the number of the faithful increased and the new evangelical Church was augmented day by day (Acts 5, 14). In like manner did the solicitude and attention of its great Queen and Teacher, Mary, expand toward the new children engendered by the Apostles through their preaching. As they were the foundation-stones of the Church, on which the security of that building was to depend, the most prudent Lady lavished especial care upon the apostolic college. Her heavenly solicitude augmented in proportion to the wrath of Lucifer against the followers of Christ and especially against the Apostles, as the ministers of eternal salvation to the other faithful. It will never be possible to describe or to estimate in this life the blessings and favors conferred by Her upon the Church and upon each of its mystical members. This happened especially in regard to the Apostles and disciples; for as has been revealed to me not a day or hour passed, in which she did not work for them many wonders. I will relate in this chapter some of the events, which are very instructive on account of the secrets of divine Providence therein contained. From them we can form an estimate of the most vigilant charity and zeal of the blessed Mary for souls.

All the Apostles She loved and served with incredible affection and reverence, both on account of their great holiness and on account of their dignity as priests, as ministers, preachers and founders of the Gospel. During all their stay in Jerusalem She attended upon them, counseled and directed them in the manner noted above. With the increase of the Church they were obliged to go outside of Jerusalem in order to baptize and admit to the faith many of the inhabitants of the neighboring places; but they always returned to the city, because they had purposely delayed separating from each other, or leaving Jerusalem, until they should receive orders to do so. From the Acts we learn that saint Peter went to Lydda and Jaffa, where he raised Tabitha from the dead and performed other miracles, returning again to Jerusalem. Although saint Luke relates these excursions after speaking of the death of saint Stephen (of which I shall treat in the following chapter), yet during these events, many were converted throughout Palestine, and it was necessary, that the Apostles go forth to preach to them and to confirm them in the faith, always returning in order to give an account of their doings to their heavenly Mistress.

During all their journeys and preachings the common enemy of all sought to hinder the spread of the divine Word, or its fruit, by rousing the unbelievers to many contradictions and altercations with the Apostles and their listeners or converts; for it seemed to the infernal dragon more easy to assault them, when he saw them removed and far from the protection of their Mistress. So formidable the great Queen of the angels appeared to the hellish hosts, that in spite of the eminent holiness of the Apostles, Lucifer imagined them disarmed and at his mercy, easily approachable to his temptations, as soon as they left the presence of Mary. The furious pride of this dragon, as is written in Job (Job 41, 18), esteems the toughest steel as weak straw, and the hardest bronze as a stick of rotten wood. He fears not the dart nor the sling; but he dreaded the protection of the most blessed Mary, and in tempting the Apostles, he waited until they should have left her presence.

But her protection failed them not on that account; for the great Lady, from the watch-tower of her exalted knowledge, reached out in every direction. Like a most vigilant sentinel She discovered the assaults of Lucifer and hastened to the relief of her sons and ministers of her Lord. When in her absence She could not speak to the Apostles in any of their afflictions, She immediately sent her holy angels to their assistance in order to encourage, forewarn and console them; and sometimes also to drive away the assaulting demons. All this the celestial spirits executed promptly in compliance with the orders of their Queen. At times they would do it secretly by inspirations and interior consolations; at others, and more frequently, they manifested themselves visibly, assuming most beautiful and refulgent bodies and informing the Apostles of what was proper for the occasion, or what had been ordered by their Mistress. This happened very often on account of their purity and holiness and on account of the necessity of favoring them with such an abundance of consolation and encouragement. In all their difficulties and labors the most loving Mother thus assisted them, besides offering up for them her continual prayers and thanksgiving. She was the strong Woman, whose domestics were sheltered by double garments; the Mother of the family, who supplied all with nourishment and who by the labors of her hands planted the vineyard of the Lord.

With all the other faithful She proportionately exhibited the same care; and although there were many converts in Jerusalem and in Palestine, She remembered them all in their necessities and tribulations. And She thought not only of the needs of their souls, but of those of the body, and many She cured of most grave sicknesses. Others, whom She knew were not to be cured miraculously, She visited and assisted in person. Of the poor She took a still greater care, with her own hand administering to them food on their beds of sickness, and seeing to their being kept clean, as if She were the servant of all, infirm with the infirm. So great was the humility, the charity and solicitude of the great Queen of the world, that She refused no service or lowliest ministry to the faithful, no matter how humble and insignificant the condition of those applying for her assistance. She filled each one with joy and consolation and lightened all their labors. Those upon whom on account of their absence She could not personally attend, She assisted secretly through her holy angels or by her prayers and petitions.

In an especial manner her maternal kindness exhibited itself to those who were in the agony of death; for she attended many of the dying and would not leave them, until they had secured their eternal salvation. For those who went to purgatory She offered up most fervent prayers and performed some works of penance, such as prostrations in the form of a cross, genuflections and other exercises, by which She satisfied for their faults. Then She sent one of her angels in order to draw them from purgatory and present them to her Son in heaven as his own and as the fruits of his blood and Redemption. This happiness the Queen of heaven procured to many souls during her stay upon earth. And, as far as was made known to me, this favor is not denied in our days to those, who during their earthly life dispose themselves properly for meriting her presence, as I have written in another place. But, since it would be necessary to extend the scope of this history very much, if I were to describe how the most blessed Mary assisted many in the hour of death, I cannot dilate upon this matter. I will recount only one incident, in which She freed a girl from the jaws of the infernal dragon. It is one which is so extraordinary and worthy of the attention of us all, that it would not be right to omit it in this history, or deprive ourselves of the lesson it contains.

Among the five thousand who were first converted and who received Baptism in Jerusalem, there was also a young girl of poor and humble parentage. This young woman, busying herself with her household duties, took ill and for many days She dragged on in her sickness without improvement. As happens to many other souls, she on that account fell from her first fervor and in her neglect committed some sins endangering her baptismal grace. Lucifer, who never relaxed in his thirst for the ruin of souls, approached this woman and attacked her with fiercest cruelty, being thus permitted by God to do so for his greater glory and that of his most blessed Mother. The demon appeared to her in the form of another woman and with much cajolery told her to withdraw from those people, who were preaching the Crucified, and not to believe anything they said, because it was all falsehood; that, if she would not follow this advice, she would be punished by the priests and judges who had crucified the Teacher of that new and counterfeit religion; whereas, if she obeyed, she would live peacefully and free from danger. The girl answered: "I will do what thou sayest; but what shall I do in regard to that Lady, whom I have seen with these men and women and who appears to be so kind and peaceful? I desire her good will very much." The demon replied: "This One, whom thou mentionest, is worse than all the rest, and Her thou must shun before all. It is most important, that thou withdraw from her snares."

Infested with this deadly poison of the ancient serpent, the soul of this simple dove was brought near to eternal death and her body, instead of being relieved, dropped into more serious illness and was in danger of a premature end. One of the seventy-two disciples, who visited the faithful, was informed of the dangerous illness of the girl; for from her neighbors he heard that one of his sect living in that house, was on the point of expiring. The disciple entered in order to visit her and encourage her according to her necessities. But the sick girl was so ensnared by the demons, that she did not receive him or answer him one word, although he zealously sought to exhort and instruct her; she on the contrary sought to hide and stop her ears in order not to hear him. From these signs the Apostle saw the imminent peril of this soul, although he did not know the cause. Eagerly he hastened to report to the Apostle saint John, who without delay visited the patient, admonishing her and speaking to her words of eternal life, if she would only listen. But she treated him in the same way as the disciple, obstinately resisting the efforts of both. The Apostle saw many legions of devils surrounding the girl, and, though they retired at his approach, they failed not immediately afterward to renew the illusion with which they had filled the unhappy girl.

Seeing her obstinacy, the Apostle betook himself in great affliction to the most blessed Mary in order to ask for help. Immediately the great Queen turned her interior vision upon the sick one and She recognized the unhappy and dangerous condition, in which the enemy had drawn that soul. The kind Mother bewailed this simple sheep, thus deceived by the bloodthirsty infernal wolf; and prostrate upon the floor She prayed for her rescue.

The most blessed Mary continued for some time in this petition; but she received no answer from the Lord, in order that her invincible heart and her charity toward her neighbor might be put to the proof. The most prudent Virgin bethought Herself of what had happened to the prophet Eliseus (IV Kings 4, 34), who had vainly sent his staff with his servant Giezi to resuscitate the boy and had found that he himself must touch and stretch himself over his body in order to restore him to life. Neither the angel nor the Apostle were powerful enough to awaken from sin and from the stupor of satan that unfortunate girl; therefore the great Lady resolved to go and heal her in person. This resolve She recommended to the Lord in her prayer, and, although She received no answer, She considered that the work itself was a sufficient warranty to proceed. She arose therefore to leave her room and to walk with saint John to the dwelling of the sick woman, which was at some distance from the Cenacle. But no sooner had She taken the first steps than the holy angels, at the command of the Lord, approached to bear Her up on the way. As God had not manifested his intention, She asked them, why they thus detained Her; to which they answered: "There is no reason why we should consent to thy walking through the city, when we can bear Thee along with greater propriety." Immediately they placed her upon a throne of resplendent clouds, on which they bore Her along and placed Her in the sick-room. The dying girl, being poor and now speechless, had been forsaken by all and was surrounded only by the demons, who waited to snatch off her soul.

But as soon as the Queen of angels made her appearance all the evil spirits vanished like flashes of lightning and as if falling over each other in their dismay. The powerful Queen commanded them to descend into hell and remain there until She should permit them to come forth, and this they were forced to do without the least power of resistance. The kindest Mother then approached the sick woman and taking her by the hand and calling her by her name, spoke sweetest words of life. Instantly a complete change came over the girl, and she began to breathe more freely and recover herself. Then she said to the heavenly Mary: "My Lady, a woman came to me, who persuaded me to believe, that the disciples of Jesus were deceiving me and that I had better immediately separate myself from them and from Thee; otherwise, if I should accept their way of life, I should fall into great misfortune." The Queen answered: "My daughter, she, who seemed to thee a woman, was thy enemy, the devil. I come in the name of the Most High to give thee eternal life; return then to his true faith, which thou hast received, and confess Him with all thy heart as thy God and Redeemer, who, for thy salvation and that of all the world, has died upon the Cross. Adore and call upon Him, and ask Him for the pardon of thy sins."

"All this," the patient answered, "I have believed before; but they told me, it was very bad, and that they would punish me, if I should ever confess it." The heavenly Teacher replied: "My friend, do not fear this deceit; but remember that the chastisement and pains which are really to be feared are those of hell, to which the demons wish to bring thee. Thou art now very near death and thou canst avail thyself of the remedy I now offer thee, if thou wilt only believe me; and thou shalt thus free thyself of the eternal fire, which threatens thee on account of thy mistake." Through this exhortation and the graces procured for this poor woman by Mary, she was moved to abundant tears of compunction and implored the blessed Lady further to assist her in this danger, declaring herself ready to obey all her commands. Then the loving Mother made her openly profess her faith in Jesus Christ and elecit an act of contrition in preparation for confession. At the same time She sent for the Apostles to administer the Sacraments to her. The sick girl, repeating the acts of contrition and love, and invoking Jesus and Mary, who was directing her, happily expired in the arms of her Protectress.

WORDS OF THE QUEEN.

My daughter, since in this chapter thou hast particularly learnt of the matchless and bitter sorrow, with which I bewailed the perdition of souls, thou thyself must learn also what thou must do for the salvation of thy own and that of others in order to imitate me in the perfection which I require of thee. No torment, nor death itself, would I have refused, if such had been necessary to save any of the damned, and to save them, I would have esteemed all sufferings a sweet alleviation in my most ardent charity. Hence, if thou dost not die of this kind of sorrow, thou art at least not excused from willingness to suffer all that the Lord sends thee for advancing this cause, or from praying and laboring all in thy power to prevent any sin in thy neighbor; and when thou canst not all at once obtain thy object, or dost not know whether the Lord has heard thee, do not lose confidence, but enliven it and persevere in thy efforts; for such a solicitude can never displease Him, who desires the salvation of all his redeemed more than thou. If nevertheless thou art not heard in thy prayers, make use of the means, which prudence and charity require, and return anew to thy prayers. The Most High is always attracted by this sort of charity for the neighbor and by the love which seeks to hinder sin. He desires not the death of the sinner (Ezech. 33, 11) ; and, as thou hast written, He does not entertain an absolute and antecedent decree of damning his creatures, but seeks to save them all, if they do not pursue perdition of their own free will. Although He permits this in his justice as being inseparable from the free will of man, it is against his inclination. Do not restrict thyself in these petitions, and in those concerning temporal things, pray that his holy will be done in all that is proper.

If I desire that thou labor with such fervor of charity for the salvation of thy brethren, consider what thou must do to save thyself, and in what estimation thou must hold thy own soul, for which an infinite price was offered. I wish to admonish thee as a Mother, that when temptations and passions incline thee toward the commission of any sin, no matter how small, remember the sorrows and the tears which the knowledge of the sins of men and the desire to prevent them has caused me. Do not thou cause the like in me, my dearest; for although I am now incapable of that pain, yet thou deprivest me of the accidental joy of seeing thee, to whom I condescended to become a Mother and Teacher, really endowed with the perfection taught in my school. If thou art unfaithful in this, thou wilt frustrate my great desire of seeing thee please my divine Son and accomplish his holy will in all its plenitude. By the infused light which thou receivest, do thou ponder how great are any faults thou mayest commit after being so favored and bound in duty to the Lord and to myself. Dangers and temptations will not be wanting to thee during the rest of thy earthly life; but in all of them remember my teaching, my sorrows and my tears, and above all what thou owest to my divine Son, who is so liberal toward thee in applying to thee the fruit of his blood for the purpose of eliciting thy grateful correspondence.

CHAPTER V.

Among the saints who were especially fortunate in meriting the greater love of the Queen of heaven, there was one by the name of Stephen, who belonged to the seventy-two disciples; for from the very beginning of his following Christ our Savior, She looked upon him with an especial love, placing him first, or among the first, in her estimation.   She immediately saw, that this saint was chosen by the Master of life for the defense of his honor and his holy name, and that he was to give up his life for him.   Moreover this courageous saint was of a sweet and peaceful disposition; and he was rendered much more amiable and docile to all holiness by the workings of grace.   Such dispositions made him very pleasing to the sweetest Mother; and whenever She found any persons naturally of a peaceful and meek character, She was wont to say, that they resembled her divine Son. On this account and on account of many heroic virtues of saint Stephen She loved him tenderly, procured him many blessings, and thanked the Lord for having created, called and chosen such a one for the first-fruits of his martyrs.   In consideration of his coming martyrdom, revealed to Her by her divine Son, her heart was filled with additional affection for this great saint.

The blessed saint corresponded in most faithful attention and deepest reverence with the benefits conferred upon him by Christ our Savior and his heavenly

Mother; for he was not only of a peaceful, but of an humble heart, and those that are so disposed in truth, are thankful for all benefits, even though they may not be so great as those conferred on saint Stephen. He always entertained the highest conceptions concerning the Mother of mercy, and in his high esteem and fervent devotion he continued to seek her favor. He asked information on many mysterious matters; for he was very wise, full of the Holy Spirit and of faith, as is told us by saint Luke. The great Lady answered all his inquiries, encouraged and exhorted him zealously to work for the honor of Christ. In order to confirm him more in his strong faith, Mary forewarned him of his coming martyrdom and said: "Thou, Stephen, shalt be the first-born of the martyrs, engendered by my divine Son and Lord by the example of his death; thou shalt follow his footsteps, like a privileged disciple his master, and like a courageous soldier his captain; and at the head of the army of martyrs, thou shalt carry his banner of the Cross. Hence it is meet thou arm thyself with fortitude under the shield of faith, and be assured, that the strength of the Most High shall be with thee in the conflict."

This warning of the Queen of the angels inflamed the heart of saint Stephen with the desire of martyrdom. As is recorded in the Acts of the Apostles, he was filled with grace and fortitude and wrought great wonders in Jerusalem. Besides the Apostles saint Peter and saint John, no one except he dared to dispute with the Jews. His wisdom and spirit they could not resist, because he preached to them with an intrepid heart, refuted and accused them oftener and more courageously than the other disciples (Acts 68, 9). All this saint Stephen did with burning desire of attaining the martyrdom of which he had been assured by the great Lady. As if he were afraid of any one gaining this crown in advance of him, he offered himself before all others to engage in the disputes with the rabbis and teachers of the law of Moses, so eager was he to defend the honor of Christ, for whom he knew he would lay down his life. The infernal dragon, gradually becoming observant of the ambitions of saint Stephen, directed his malignant attention toward him and strove to hinder his attaining public martyrdom in testimony of the faith of Christ. In order to destroy him, he incited the most incredulous of the Jews to kill saint Stephen in secret.

But saint Stephen did not on that account neglect preaching or arguing with the unbelieving Jews. As these Jews could not murder him in secret, nor overcome his wisdom in public, they vented their mortal hatred in seeking false testimony against him (Acts 6, 1). They accused him of blasphemy against God and against Moses, of inveighing continually against the holy temple and the Law, and of asserting that Jesus would destroy as well the one, as the other. As the witnesses loudly proclaimed their slander and the people were being roused by their falsehoods, they brought him into the hall where the priests were gathered as the judges of these accusations. The presiding judge first took the deposition of saint Stephen before the court. The saint took occasion to prove with highest wisdom, that Christ was the true Messiah promised to them in the holy Scriptures; and in conclusion he reprehended them for their unbelief and hardness of heart so strongly, that they could find no answer and, gnashing their teeth, they stopped their ears, in order not to be obliged to hear his words.

The Queen of heaven knew of the seizure of saint Stephen; and, in order to animate him in her name for the approaching conflict, She immediately sent him one of her angels, even before He entered into dispute with the priests. Through the holy angel saint Stephen sent Her answer, that he went with joy to confess his Master and with unflinching heart to give his life for Him, as he had always desired. Through the same messenger, he begged Her, as his kindest Teacher and Mother, to assist him and, from her retirement, to send him her blessing, since his not having been able to obtain her parting benediction was the only regret he felt now, when he was about to lay down his life according to Her wishes. These last words of saint Stephen moved the maternal bosom of Mary to even greater love and esteem than hitherto; and She desired to attend upon him in person, at this hour, when her beloved disciple was to give up his life for the honor and defense of his God and Redeemer. But the blessed Mother hesitated at the difficulties, which would arise in her passing through the streets of Jerusalem at a time of popular excitement and also in finding an opportunity of speaking publicly to saint Stephen.

She prostrated Herself in prayer, begging the divine favor for her beloved disciple; and She presented to the Lord her desire of helping him in the last hour. The clemency of the Most High, which is always at the beck of his Spouse and Mother and which was anxious to enhance the death of his faithful disciple and servant Stephen, sent from heaven a multitude of angels, who, with those of her guard, should carry their Queen to the place where the saint then was. And immediately the mandate of the Lord was executed: the angels placed Her upon a refulgent cloud and bore Her to the tribunal, where the highpriest was examining into the charges against saint Stephen. The vision of the Queen of heaven was hidden from all except the saint. He however saw Her before him, supported in the air by the holy angels in a cloud of heavenly splendor and glory. This extraordinary favor inflamed anew the divine love and the ardent zeal of this champion of the honor of God. In addition to the joy of seeing Mary, the splendors of the Queen shone from the countenance of saint Stephen, so that it gleamed with wonderful beauty and light.

At the end of this discourse, through the intercession of the Queen and as a reward of the unconquered zeal of saint Stephen, the heavens opened and the Savior appeared to him standing at the right hand of the Father in the act of assisting him in the conflict. Saint Stephen raised his eyes and said: "Behold I see the heavens opened and its glory, and in it I see Jesus at the right hand of God himself" (Acts 7, 55). But the obdurate perfidy of the Jews esteemed these words as blasphemy and they stopped their ears in order not to hear them. As the punishment of blasphemers according to the law, was death by stoning, they passed upon him that sentence. Then they all surrounded him like wolves and dragged him from the city with great haste and noise. At this juncture the blessed Mother gave him her benediction; and speaking to him words of encouragement and endearment, She left him in charge of her angels, whom She ordered to accompany him and to remain with him until they should present his soul to the Most High. Only one of the guardian angels, in company with those that had descended from heaven as her escort to saint Stephen, now returned with Her to the Cenacle.

From her retirement the great Lady by an especial vision saw all that happened in the martyrdom of saint Stephen: how they led him forth from the city with great haste and violence, shouting that he was a blasphemer worthy of death; how Saul was among them, more zealous than the rest, guarding the vestments of those who had taken them off to stone saint Stephen; how the shower of stones fell upon the saint and wounded him, some of them remaining fixed in his head and stained by his blood. Great and tender was the compassion of our Queen at such cruel martyrdom; but still greater her joy in seeing saint Stephen meeting it so gloriously. The kindest Mother failed him not in her tearful prayers from her oratory. When the invincible martyr saw himself near to death, he prayed: "Lord receive my spirit!" Then, on his knees, he exclaimed with a loud voice: "Lord lay not this sin to their charge!" (Acts 6, 55). In these prayers he was supported by those of the blessed Mary, who was filled with incredible joy to see the faithful disciple imitating so closely his divine Master by praying for his enemies and persecutors and commending his spirit into the hands of his Creator and Redeemer.

Covered with wounds from the shower of stones thrown by the Jews, saint Stephen expired, while they became still more hardened in their perfidy. Immediately the angels of the Queen bore his pure soul to the presence of God in order to be crowned with eternal honor and glory.

Saint Luke says, that on the same day on which saint Stephen was stoned to death, a great persecution arose against the Church in Jerusalem. He mentions especially that Saul devastated it, searching through the whole city for the followers of Christ in order to seize and denounce them before the magistrates. This he did to many of the believers, who were arrested, illtreated, and killed in this persecution. Although it was very severe on account of the hatred, which the princes and priests had conceived against the Christians, and on account of the zealous efforts of Saul in his jealous defense of the law of Moses (of which he himself speaks in the letter to the Galatians 1, 13) ; yet there was another cause for this severity, the effects of which they felt, though they knew not its origin.

The most prudent Mother bore in mind, that the disciples, having dispersed to preach the name and faith of Christ the Savior, had as yet no formula or express creed to guide themselves uniformly and without differences, so that all the faithful might believe one and the same express truths. Moreover She knew that the Apostles would soon have to go forth over the whole world in order to spread and establish the Church through their preaching, and that it was proper that all should be united in their doctrine, upon which was to be founded all the perfection of a Christian life. Therefore the most prudent Mother of wisdom wished to see all the divine mysteries, which the Apostles were to preach and the faithful to believe, reduced to a short formula. For if those truths were moulded into a few articles, they could more conveniently be brought to the mind of all, the whole Church would be united in one belief without any essential difference, and the whole spiritual edifice of the Gospel would thus rest and be built up on the same firm columns of one foundation. In order to prepare for this work, the importance of which She recognized, She presented her wishes to the Lord, who had inspired them, and for more than forty days She persevered in this prayer with fasting, prostrations and other exercises.

In answer to her prayer for the Apostles, besides promising to assist them in preparing the symbol of the faith, the Lord informed his Mother of the very wording of the propositions or articles, of which the Creed was to be composed. Of all this the most prudent Lady was well capable, as was explained more fully in the second part of this history; but now, when the time had arrived for executing what had been intended so long before, He wished to renew it all in the purest heart of his virgin Mother, in order that the fundamental truths of the Church might flow from the lips of Christ himself. He inspired saint Peter his vicar and the rest with the desire of setting up a symbol of the universal faith of the Church. Accordingly they sought conference with the heavenly Mistress concerning its opportuneness and the measures to be taken for this purpose. They resolved to fast and persevere in prayer for ten continuous days, in order to receive the inspiration of the Holy Ghost in this arduous affair. Having completed these ten days, which were also the last ten of the forty, in which the Queen had treated with the Lord about this matter, the twelve Apostles met in the presence of Mary, and saint Peter spoke to them as follows:

"My dear brethren, the divine mercy, in its infinite goodness and through the merits of our Savior and Master Jesus, has favored his holy Church by gloriously multiplying its children, as we have seen and experienced in this short time. For this purpose the Almighty has multiplied miracles and prodigies and daily renews them through our ministry, having chosen us (though unworthy) as the instruments of his divine will in this work and for the glory and honor of his holy name. Together with these favors He has sent us tribulations and persecutions of the devil and of the world, in order that we may imitate our Savior and Captain, and in order that the Church, evenly ballasted, might reach more securely the port of rest and eternal felicity. The disciples have evaded the wrath of the chief priest and spread through the neighboring cities, preaching the faith of Christ our Redeemer and Lord. We must also soon depart and preach throughout the globe, according to the command of the Lord before ascending into heaven (Matth. 28, 19). Just as there is but one Baptism in which men are to receive this faith, so there must be but one doctrine, which the faithful are to believe. Hence it is meet that we, who are as yet gathered harmoniously in the Lord, define the truths and mysteries which we are to propound expressly to all the nations of the world, and thus, without difference of opinions, believe the same doctrines. It is the infallible promise of the Lord, that where two or three shall be gathered in his name, He shall be in their midst (Matth. 18, 20). Confiding in his word we firmly hope, that He will now assist us with his divine Spirit to understand and define, in his name and by an unchangeable decree, the articles to be established in his holy Church as long as it shall last, to the end of the world."

All the Apostles consented to this proposal of saint Peter. Then he celebrated a Mass, in which he gave Communion to the most holy Mary and the Apostles, whereupon they all, including the blessed Mother, prostrated themselves in prayer calling upon the Holy Ghost. After continuing their prayers for some time, they heard the rumbling of thunder, as on the first coming down of the Holy Ghost upon the gathering of the faithful; at the same time the Cenacle was filled with light and splendor and all were enlightened by the Holy Spirit. Then the most blessed Mary asked each of the Apostles to define a mystery, according as the divine Spirit should inspire them. Thereupon saint Peter began, and was followed by the rest in the following order:

1. Saint Peter: I believe in God, the Father almighty, Creator of heaven and earth.

2. Saint Andrew: And in Jesus Christ, his only Son, our Lord.

3 and 4. Saint James the Greater: Who was conceived through operation of the Holy Ghost, born of the Virgin Mary.

5. Saint John: Suffered under Pontius Pilate, was crucified, died and was buried.

6 and 7. Saint Thomas: Descended into hell, arose from the dead on the third day.

8. Saint James the Less: Ascended into heaven, is seated at the right hand of God the Father almighty.

9. Saint Philip: From thence He shall come to judge the living and the dead.

10. Saint Bartholomew: I believe in the Holy Ghost.

11. Saint Matthew: In the holy Catholic Church, the Communion of saints.

12. Saint Simon: Forgiveness of sins.

13. Saint Thaddeus: The resurrection of the flesh.

14. Saint Mathias: Life everlasting. Amen.

This symbol, which we ordinarily call the Creed, the Apostles established after the martyrdom of saint Stephen and before the end of the first year after the death of the Savior. Afterwards, in order to refute the Arian and other heresies, the Church, in the councils held on their account, explained more fully the mysteries contained in the Apostles' Creed and composed the one now chanted in the Mass. But in substance both are one and the same and contain the fourteen articles, which are the basis for the catechetical teaching of the Christian faith and which we are all bound to believe in order to be saved. As soon as the Apostles had finished pronouncing this Creed, the Holy Ghost approved of it by permitting a voice to be heard in their midst saying: "You have decided well." Then the great Queen and

Lady of heaven with all the Apostles gave thanks to the Most High; and She thanked also them for having merited the assistance of the divine Spirit, so as to be his apt instruments in promoting the glory of the Lord and the good of the Church. In confirmation of her faith and as an example to the faithful, the most prudent Mistress fell at the feet of saint Peter, loudly proclaimed her belief in the Catholic doctrine as contained in the symbol they had just now composed and formulated. This She did for Herself and in the name of all the faithful, saying to saint Peter: "My lord, whom I recognize as the vicar of my most holy Son, in thy hands, I, a vile wormlet, in my name and in the name of all the faithful of the Church, confess and proclaim all that thou hast set down as the divine and infallible truth of the Catholic Church; and in it I bless and exalt the Most High, from whom it proceeds." She kissed the hands of the vicar of Christ and of the rest of the Apostles. Thus She was the first one thus openly to profess the Catholic faith after it had been formulated into articles.

Already a full year had passed since the death of the Savior, and now the Apostles, by divine impulse, began to consider about going forth to preach the faith throughout the world; for it was time that the name of God be preached also to the heathens and that they be taught the way of eternal salvation. In order to consult the will of God in the assignment of the kingdoms and provinces in which each one was to preach, they, upon the advice of their Queen, resolved to fast and pray for ten successive days. This practice of fasting and praying for ten days, which they had observed immediately after the Ascension in disposing themselves for the coming of the Holy Ghost, they afterwards also retained in preparing themselves for the more important undertakings.

Having completed these exercises, the vicar of Christ celebrated Mass and communicated the most blessed Mary and the eleven Apostles, as they had done in preparing the Creed and as is mentioned in the last chapter. After Mass they all persevered with their Queen for some time in most exalted prayer, ardently invoking the assistance of the Holy Ghost for the manifestation of his will in this matter.

At the ending of this prayer a wonderful light descended upon the Cenacle surrounding them all and a voice was heard saying: "My vicar Peter shall point out the province, which falls to each one. I shall govern and direct him by my light and spirit." The appointments themselves the Holy Ghost left to saint Peter in order to confirm anew his power as head and universal pastor of the Church, and in order that the Apostles might understand, that it was to be founded throughout the world under the direction of saint Peter and his successors, to whom they were to be subject as the vicars of Christ. They were filled with a new light and knowledge concerning the peoples and provinces assigned to them by saint Peter, and each one recognized the conditions, nature and customs of the kingdoms singled out for him, being furnished interiorly with the most distinct and abundant information concerning each. The Most High gave them new fortitude to encounter labors; agility for overcoming distances, although in this regard they were afterwards to be frequently assisted by the holy angels; and the fire of divine love, so that they became inflamed like seraphim lifted far beyond the condition and sphere of mere human creatures.

The most blessed Queen was present at all these events, and the workings of the divine power in the Apostles and in Herself, were very clear to Her; for on this occasion, She experienced more of the divine influences than all of them together. As She was exalted supereminently above all creatures, so the increase of her gifts was in like proportion, transcending immeasurably those of others. The Most High renewed in the purest spirit of his Mother the infused knowledge concerning all creatures, and especially concerning the kingdoms and nations assigned to the Apostles. She knew all that each one knew, and more than they all together, because She received a personal and individual knowledge of each person to whom the faith of Christ was to be preached; and She was made relatively just as familiar with all the earth and its inhabitants, as She was with Her oratory and all those that entered therein.

As I have said above and shall often repeat farther on, the knowledge of Mary was the knowledge of a supreme Mistress, Mother, Governess and Sovereign of the Church, which the Almighty had placed in her hands. She was to take care of all, from the highest to the lowest of the saints, and also of the sinners as the children of Eve. As no one was to receive any blessing or favor from the hands of her Son except through that of his Mother, it was necessary that this most faithful Dispensatrix of grace should know all of her family, whom She was to guard as a Mother, and such a Mother! The great Lady therefore had not only infused images and knowledge of all this, but She actually experienced it according as the disciples and Apostles proceeded in their work of preaching. Before Her lay open all their labors and dangers, and the attacks of the demons against them; the petitions and prayers of these and of all the faithful, so that She might be able to support them with her own, or aid them through her angels or by Herself in person; for in all these different ways did She render her assistance, as we shall see in many events yet to be described.

I wish merely to state here, that besides the knowledge derived by our Queen from infused images She had also in God himself another knowledge of things through her abstractive vision, by which She continually saw the Divinity. But there was a difference between these two different kinds of knowledge: since, when she saw in God the labors of the Apostles and of all the faithful of the Church, enjoying at the same time through this vision a certain participation of the eternal beatitude, the most loving Mother was not affected with the sensible sorrow and compassion, which filled Her when perceiving these tribulations themselves through images. In this latter kind of vision She felt and bewailed them with maternal compassion. In order that this merit might not be wanting in Her, the Lord conferred this second kind of knowledge upon Her for all the time of her pilgrimage here below. Joined with this plenitude of infused species and knowledge, She held also absolute command of her faculties, as I said above, so that She admitted no images or ideas except those that were absolutely necessary for sustaining life, or for some work of charity or perfection. With this adornment and beauty, which was patent to the angels and saints, the heavenly Lady was an object of admiration, inducing them to praise and glorify the Most High for the worthy exercise of all his attributes in Mary, his most holy instrument.

A few days after the partition of the earth among the Apostles, they began to leave Jerusalem, especially those that were allotted the provinces of Palestine, and first among them was saint James the greater. Others stayed longer in Jerusalem, because the Lord wished the faith to be preached there more abundantly and the Jews to be called before all others, if they chose to come and accept the invitation to the marriage-feast of the Gospel; for in the blessing of the Redemption this people, although more ungrateful than the heathens, was especially favored. Afterwards all the Apostles gradually departed for the regions assigned to them, according as time and season demanded and as obedience to the divine Spirit, the counsel of the most holy Mary, and the order of saint Peter dictated. But before leaving Jerusalem each one visited the holy places, such as the garden, Calvary, the holy Sepulchre, the place of the Ascension, Bethany and the other memorable spots as far as possible. All of them showed their veneration, moved even to tears and regarding with loving wonder the very earth, which the Savior had touched. Then they visited the Cenacle, reverencing the spot where so many mysteries had taken place. There, again commending themselves to her protection, they took leave of the great Queen of heaven. The blessed Mother dismissed them with words full of sweetness and divine virtue.

But admirable was the solicitude and care of the most prudent Lady in showing Herself as the true Mother of the Apostles at their departure. For each of the twelve She made a woven tunic similar to that of Christ our Savior, of a color between brown and ash-gray; and in order to weave these garments She called to aid her holy angels. She furnished each of the Apostles garments of the same kind and like to that formerly worn by their Master Jesus: for She wished that they should imitate Him even in their garments and thereby be known exteriorly as his disciples. The great Lady procured also twelve crosses of the height and size of each of the Apostles and gave one to each, so that, as a witness of their doctrine and for their consolation, they might carry it along in their wanderings and their preaching. Each of the Apostles preserved and carried this cross with him to his death; and as they were so loud in praise of the Cross, some of the tyrants made use of this very instrument to torment them happily to death.

Moreover the devout Mother furnished each one of them with a small metal case, in which She placed three of the thorns from the crown of her divine Son, some pieces of the cloths in which She had wrapped the infant Savior, and of the linen with which She had wiped and caught the most precious blood of the Circumcision and Passion of the Lord. All these sacred pledges She had preserved with the greatest care and veneration, as the Mother and the Treasure-keeper of heaven. In order to consign them to the Apostles She called them together and, with the majesty of a Queen and the tenderness of a Mother, She told them that these remembrances, with which She would enrich them on their departure, were the greatest treasures in her possession; for in them they would carry with them vivid remembrances of her divine Son and the certain assurance, that the Lord loved them as his children and as ministers of the Most High. Then She handed them those relics, which they received with tears of consolation and joy. They thanked the great Queen for these favors and prostrated themselves in adoration of the sacred relics. Embracing they bade farewell to each other, saint James being the first to depart and commence his mission.

WORDS OF THE QUEEN.

My daughter, by the lessons contained in this chapter I wish to draw thee to deplore, with inmost groaning and sighing and, if possible, with tears of blood, the difference between the state of the holy Church in our times and that of those primitive times; how its purest gold of holiness has been obscured (Thren. 4, 1), and the ancient beauty in which the Apostles have founded it, is lost; how it has sought foreign and deceitful powders and paints to cover the horrid and distorted ugliness of vice. In order that thou mayest penetrate into this truth, thou must renew in thyself the consideration of the force and eagerness, with which the Divinity seeks to communicate his goodness and perfection to creatures. So great is the impetus of the river of God's goodness overflowing on mankind, that only the free will of man, which He has given to Him in order to receive its benefits, can raise a dam against it; and whenever, through this free will, man resists the influence and force of the divine Goodness, he (according to thy mode of understanding), violates and grieves this immense love in its very essence. But if creatures would place no obstacle and permit its operations, the whole soul would be inundated and satiated with participation in its divine essence and attributes. It would raise the fallen from the dust, enrich the indigent children of Adam, place them above all their miseries and seat them with the princes of his glory (I Kings 2, 8).

From this, my daughter, thou wilt understand two things unknown to human wisdom. First, how pleasing to the highest Goodness is the service of those who, with an ardent zeal for God's glory, devote their labor and solicitude toward removing the obstacles, which men place to their own justification and the communication of his favors. The satisfaction of the Most High, arising from this work in others, cannot be estimated in this mortal life. On this account the ministry of the Apostles, the prelates, the priests and preachers of the divine word are so highly exalted; for they succeed in office those, who founded the Church and who labored in its preservation and extension; all of them are to be co-operators and executors of the immense love of God for the souls created to be sharers in his Divinity. Secondly, thou must ponder the greatness and abundance of the gifts and favors, which the infinite power communicates to those souls, who do not hinder his most liberal bounty. The Lord manifested this truth immediately in the beginnings of the evangelical Church, when, to all those who were to enter into it, He showed his bounty by such great prodigies and wonders, frequently sending the Holy Ghost in a visible manner, working miracles in those who accepted the Creed, and showering forth other hidden favors on the faithful.

CHAPTER VI.

CONVERSION OF SAINT PAUL.

Saint Paul was distinguished in Judaism for two reasons. The one was his own character, and the other was the diligence of the demon in availing himself of his naturally good qualities. Saint Paul was of a disposition generous, magnanimous, most noble, kind, active, courageous and constant. He had acquired many of the moral virtues. He glorified in being a staunch professor of the law of Moses, and in being studious and learned in it; although in truth he was ignorant of its essence, as he himself confesses to Timothy, because all his learning was human and terrestrial; like many Jews, he knew the law merely from the outside, without its spirit and without the divine insight, which was necessary to understand it rightly and to penetrate its mysteries.

The disposition of Saul was most noble and generous, and therefore it appeared to him beneath his dignity and honor to stoop to such crimes and act the part of an assassin, when he could, as it seemed to him, destroy the law of Christ by the power of reasoning and open justice. He felt a still greater horror at the thought of killing the most blessed Mother, on account of the regard due to Her as a woman; and because he had seen Her so composed and constant in the labors and in the Passion of Christ. On this account She seemed to him a magnanimous Woman and worthy of veneration. She had indeed won his respect, together with some compassion for her sorrows and afflictions, the magnitude of which had become publicly known.   Hence he gave no admittance to the inhuman suggestions of the demon against the life of the most blessed Mary.   This compassion for Her hastened not a little the conversion of Saul.   Neither did he further entertain the treacherous designs against the apostles, although Lucifer sought to make their assassination appear as a deed worthy of his courageous spirit.   Rejecting all these wicked thoughts, he resolved to incite all the Jews to persecute the Church, until it should be destroyed together with the name of Christ.

As the dragon and his cohorts could not attain more, they contented themselves with having brought Saul at least to this resolve.   The dreadful wrath of these demons against God and his creatures can be estimated from the fact, that on that very day they held another meeting in order to consult how they could preserve the life of this man, whom they had found so well adapted to execute their malice.   These deadly enemies well know, that they have no jurisdiction over the lives of men, and that they can neither give nor take life, unless permitted by God on some particular occasion; nevertheless they wished to make themselves the guardians and the physicians of the life and health of Saul as far as their power extended, namely, by keeping active his forethought against whatever was harmful and suggesting the use of what was naturally beneficial to the welfare of life and limb.   Yet with all their efforts they were unable to hinder the work of grace, when God so wished it.   Far were they from suspecting, that Saul would ever accept the faith of Christ, and that the life, which they were trying to preserve and lengthen, was to redound to their own ruin and torment.   Such events are provided by the wisdom of the Most High, in order that the devil, being deceived by his evil counsels, may fall into his own pits and snares, and in order that all his machinations may serve for the fulfillment of the divine and irresistible will.

Such were the decrees of the highest Wisdom in order that the conversion of Saul might be more wonderful and glorious. With this intention God permitted Satan, after the death of saint Stephen, to instigate Saul to go to the chief priests with fierce threats against the disciples of Christ, who had left Jerusalem, and to solicit permission for bringing them as prisoners to Jerusalem from wherever he should find them (Acts 9, 1). For this enterprise Saul offered his person and possessions, and even his life; at his own cost and without salary he made this journey in order that the new Law, preached by the disciples of the Crucified, might not prevail against the Law of his ancestors. This offer was readily favored by the high-priest and his counselors; they immediately gave to Saul the commission he asked, especially to go to Damascus, whither, according to report, some of the disciples had retired after leaving Jerusalem. He prepared for the journey, hiring officers of justice and some soldiers to accompany him. But his by far most numerous escort were the many legions of demons, who in order to assist him in this enterprise, came forth from hell, hoping that with all this show of force and through Saul, they might be able to make an end of the Church and entirely devastate it with fire and blood. This was really the intention of Saul, and the one with which Lucifer and his demons sought to inspire him and his companions. But let us leave him for the present on his journey to Damascus, anxious to seize all the disciples of Christ, whom he should find in the synagogues of that city.

Nothing of all this was unknown to the Queen

of heaven; for in addition to her science and vision penetrating to the inmost thoughts of men and demons, the Apostles were solicitous in keeping Her informed of all that befell the followers of her Son. Long before this time She had known that Saul was to be an Apostle of Christ, a preacher to the gentiles, and a man distinguished and wonderful in the Church; for all of these things her Son informed Her, as I said in the second part of this history. But as She saw the persecution becoming more violent and the glorious fruits and results of the conversion of Saul delayed, and as She moreover saw how the disciples of Christ, who knew nothing of the secret intentions of the Most High, were afflicted and somewhat discouraged at the fury and persistence of his persecution, the kindest Mother was filled with great sorrow. Considering, in her heavenly prudence, how important was this affair, She roused Herself to new courage and confidence in her prayers for the welfare of the Church and the conversion of Saul.

He permitted his blessed Mother to suffer some sensible pain and, as it were, to fall into a kind of swoon, yet her Son, who according to our way of understanding, could not longer resist the love which wounded his heart, consoled and restored Her by yielding to her prayers. He said: "My Mother, chosen among all creatures, let thy will be done without delay. I will do with Saul as Thou askest, and will so change him, that from this moment he will be a defender of the Church which he persecutes, and a preacher of my name and glory. I shall now proceed to receive him immediately into my friendship and grace."

Thereupon Jesus Christ our Lord disappeared from the presence of his most blessed Mother leaving Her still engaged in prayer and furnished with a clear insight into what was to happen. Shortly afterward the Lord appeared to Saul on the road near Damascus, whither, in his ever increasing fury against Jesus, his accelerated journey had already brought him. The Lord showed himself to Saul in a resplendent cloud amid immense glory, and at the same time Saul was flooded with divine light without and within, and his heart and senses were overwhelmed beyond power of resistance (Acts 9, 4). He fell suddenly from his horse to the ground and at the same time he heard a voice from on high saying: "Saul, Saul, why dost thou persecute Me?" Full of fear and consternation he answered: "Who art Thou, Lord?" The voice replied: "I am Jesus whom thou persecutest; it is hard for thee to kick against the goad of my omnipotence." Again Saul answered with greater fear and trembling: "Lord, what dost Thou command and desire to do with me?" The companions of Saul heard these questions and answers, though they did not see the Savior. They saw the splendor surrounding him and all of them were filled with dread and astonishment at this sudden and unthought of event, and they were for some time dumbfounded.

This new wonder, surpassing all that had been seen in the world before, was greater and more far-reaching than what could be taken in by the senses. For Saul was not only prostrated in body, blinded and bereft of his strength so that, if the divine power had not sustained him, he would have immediately expired; but also as to his interior he suffered more of a change than when he passed from nothingness into existence at his conception, farther removed from what he was before than light from darkness, or the highest heaven from the lowest earth; for he was changed from an image of the demon to that of one of the highest and most ardent seraphim. This triumph over Lucifer and his demons had been especially reserved by God for his divine Wisdom and Omnipotence; so that, in virtue of the Passion and Death of Christ this dragon and his malice might be vanquished by the human nature of one man, in whom the effects of grace and Redemption were set in opposition to the sin of Lucifer and all its effects. Thus it happened that in the same short time, in which Lucifer through pride was changed from an angel to a devil, the power of Christ changed Saul from a demon into an angel in grace. In the angelic nature the highest beauty turned into the deepest ugliness; and in the human nature the greatest perversity into the highest moral perfection. Lucifer descended as the enemy of God from heaven to the deepest abyss of the earth, and a man ascended as a friend of God from the earth to the highest heaven.

And since this triumph would not have been sufficiently glorious, if the Lord had not given more than Lucifer had lost, the Omnipotent wished to add in saint Paul an additional triumph to his victory over the demon. For Lucifer, although he fell from that exceedingly high grace which he had received, had never possessed beatific vision, nor had he made himself worthy of it, and hence could not lose what he did not possess. But Paul, immediately on disposing himself for justification and on gaining grace, began to partake of glory and clearly saw the Divinity, though this vision was gradual. O invincible virtue of the divine power! O infinite efficacy of the merits of the life and death of Christ! It was certainly reasonable and just, that if the malice of sin in one instant changed the angel into a demon, that the grace of the Redeemer should be more powerful and abound more than sin (Rom. 5, 20), raising up from it a man, not only to place him into original grace, but into glory.

Greater is this wonder than the creation of heaven and earth with all the creatures; greater than to give sight to the blind, health to the sick, life to the dead. Let us congratulate the sinners on the hope inspired by this wonderful justification, since we have for our Restorer, for our Father, and for our Brother the same Lord, who justified Paul; and He is not less powerful nor less holy for us, than for saint Paul.

During the time in which Paul lay prostrate upon the earth, he was entirely renewed by sanctifying grace and other infused gifts, restored and illumined proportionately in all his interior faculties, and thus he was prepared to be elevated to the empyrean heaven, which is called the third heaven. He himself confesses, that he did not know whether he was thus elevated in body or only in spirit (I Cor. 12, 4). But there, by more than ordinary vision, though in a transient manner, he saw the Divinity clearly and intuitively. Besides the being of God and his attributes of infinite perfection, he recognized the mystery of the Incarnation and Redemption, and all the secrets of the law of grace and of the state of the Church. He saw the peerless blessing of his justification and of the prayer of saint Stephen for him; and still more clearly was he made aware of the prayers of the most holy Mary and how his conversion had been hastened through Her; and that, after Christ, her merits had made him acceptable in the sight of God. From that hour on he was filled with gratitude and with deepest veneration and devotion to the great Queen of heaven, whose dignity was now manifest to him and whom he thenceforth acknowledged as his Restorer. At the same time he recognized the office of Apostle to which he was called, and that in it he was to labor and suffer unto death. In conjunction with these mysteries were revealed to him many others, of which he himself says that they are not to be disclosed (II Cor. 7, 4). He offered himself in sacrifice to the will of God in all things, as he showed afterwards in the course of his life. The most blessed Trinity accepted this sacrifice and offering of his lips and in the presence of the whole court of heaven named and designated him as the preacher and teacher of the gentiles, and as a vase of election for carrying through the world the name of the Most High.

On the third day after the disablement and conversion of Saul the Lord spoke in a vision to one of the disciples, Ananias, living in Damascus (Acts 9, 10). Calling him by name as his servant and friend, the Lord told him to go to the house of a man named Judas in a certain district of the city and there to find Saul of Tarsus, whom he would find engaged in prayer. At the same time Saul had also a vision, in which he saw and recognized the disciple Ananias coming to him and restoring sight to him by the imposition of hands. But of this vision of Saul, Ananias at that time had no knowledge. Therefore he answered: "Lord, I have information of this man having persecuted thy saints in Jerusalem and caused a great slaughter of them in Jerusalem; and not satisfied with this, he has now come with warrants from the high-priests in order to seize whomever he can find invoking thy holy name. Dost thou then send a simple sheep like myself to go in search of the wolf, that desires to devour it?" The Lord replied: "Go, for the one thou judgest to be my enemy, is for Me a vase of election, in order that he may carry my name through all the nations and kingdoms, and to the children of Israel. And I can, as I shall, assign to him what he is to suffer for my name." And the disciple was at once informed of all that had happened.

Relying on this word of the Lord, Ananias obeyed and betook himself at once to the house, in which saint Paul then was. He found him in prayer and said to him: "Brother Saul, our Lord Jesus, who appeared to thee on thy journey, sends me in order that thou mayest receive thy sight and be filled with the Holy Ghost." He received holy Communion at the hands of Ananias and was strengthened and made whole, giving thanks to the Author of all these blessings. Then he partook of some corporal nourishment, of which he had not tasted for three days. He remained for some time in Damascus, conferring and conversing with the disciples in that city. He prostrated himself at their feet asking their pardon and begging them to receive him as their servant and brother, even as the least and most unworthy of them all. At their approval and counsel he went forth publicly to preach Christ as the Messias and Redeemer of the world and with such fervor, wisdom and zeal, that he brought confusion to the unbelieving Jews in the numerous synagogues of Damascus. All wondered at this unexpected change and, in great astonishment, said: Is not this the man, who in Jerusalem has persecuted with fire and sword all who invoke that name? And has he not come to bring them prisoners to the chief priests of that city? What change then is this, which we see in him?

Saint Paul grew stronger each day and with increasing force continued his preaching to the gathering of the Jews and gentiles. Accordingly they schemed to take away his life and then happened, what we shall touch upon later. The miraculous conversion of saint Paul took place one year and one month after the martyrdom of saint Stephen, on the twenty-fifth of January, the same day on which the Church celebrates that feast; and it was in the year thirty-six of the birth of our Lord; because saint Stephen, as is said in chapter the twelfth, died completing his thirty-fourth year and one day of his thirty-fifth; whereas the conversion of saint Paul took place after he had completed one month of the thirty-sixth; and then saint James departed on his missionary journey, as I will say in its place.

Let us return to our great Queen and Lady of the angels, who by means of her vision knew all that was happening to Saul; his first and most unhappy state of mind, his fury against the name of Christ, his sudden casting down and its cause, his conversion, and above all his extraordinary and miraculous elevation to the empyrean heaven and vision of God, besides all the rest, that happened to him in Damascus. This knowledge was not only proper and due to Her, because She was the Mother of the Lord and of his holy Church and the instrument of this great wonder; but also because She alone could properly estimate this miracle, even more so than saint Paul and more than the whole mystical body of the Church; for it was not just, that such an unheard of blessing and such a prodigious work of the Omnipotent should remain without recognition and gratitude among mortals. This the most blessed Mary rendered in all plenitude and She was the first One, who celebrated this solemn event with the acknowledgment due to it from the whole human race.

WORDS OF THE QUEEN.

My daughter, none of the faithful should be ignorant of the fact, that the Most High could have drawn and converted saint Paul without resorting to such miracles of his infinite power. But He made use of them in order to show men, how much his bounty is inclined to pardon them and raise them to his friendship and grace, and in order to teach them, by the example of this great Apostle, how they, on their part, should co-operate and respond to his calls. Many souls the Lord wakes up and urges on by his inspiration and help. Many do respond and justify themselves through the Sacraments of the Church; but not all persevere in their justification and still a fewer number follow it up or strive after perfection: beginning in spirit, they relax, and finish in the flesh. The cause of their want of perseverance in grace and relapse into their sins is their not imitating the spirit of saint Paul at his conversion, when he exclaimed: "Lord, what is it Thou wishest with me, and what shall I do for Thee?" If some of them proclaim this sentiment with their lips, it is not from their whole heart, and they always retain some love of themselves, of honor, of possessions, of sensual pleasure or of some occasion of sin, and thus they soon again stumble and fall.

But the Apostle was a true and living example of one converted by the light of grace, not only because he passed from an extreme of sin into that of wonderful grace and friendship of God; but also because he cooperated to his utmost with the call of God, departing at once and entirely from all his evil dispositions and self-seeking and placing himself entirely at the disposal of the divine will and pleasure. This total denegation of self and surrender to the will of God is contained in those words: "Lord, what dost Thou wish to do with me?" and in it consisted, as far as depended upon him, all his salvation. As he pronounced them with all the sincerity of a contrite and humbled heart, he renounced his own will and delivered himself over to that of the Lord, resolved from that moment forward to permit none of his faculties of mind or sense to serve the animal or sensual life into which he had strayed. He delivered himself over to the service of the Almighty in whatever manner or direction should become known to him as being the divine will, ready to execute it without delay or questioning. And this he immediately set about by entering the city and obeying the command of the Lord given through the disciple Ananias. As the Most High searches the secrets of the human heart, He saw the sincerity, with which saint Paul corresponded to his vocation and yielded to his divine will and disposition. He not only received him with great pleasure, but multiplied exceedingly his graces, gifts and wonderful favors, which even Paul would not have received or ever have merited without this entire submission to the wishes of the Lord.

Conformably to these truths, my daughter, I desire thee to execute fully my oft-repeated commands and exhortations, that thou forget the visible, the apparent and deceitful. Repeat very often, and more with the heart than with the lips those words of saint Paul: "Lord, what dost Thou wish to do with me?" For as soon as thou beginnest to do anything of thy own choice, it will not be true, that thou seekest solely the will of the Lord. The instrument has no motion or action except that imparted to it by the artisan; and if it had its own will, it would be able to resist and act contrary to the will of the one using it. The same holds true between God and the soul: for, if it entertains any desire of its own independently of God, it will militate against the pleasure of the Lord. As He keeps inviolate the liberty of action conceded to man, He will permit it to lead man astray, as soon as he decides for himself without reference to the direction of his Maker.

BOOK EIGHT

Describes the Journey of the Most Blessed Mary with Saint John to Ephesus; the Death and Chastisement of Herod; the Destruction of the Temple of Diana; the Return of the Most Blessed Mary from Ephesus to Jerusalem; the Instructions She gave to the Evangelists; the exalted State of Her purest Soul before Her death; Her most blessed Transition, Assumption and Coronation in heaven.

CHAPTER I.

THE PERSECUTION OF HEROD AND THE WILL OF GOD MADE KNOWN TO MARY OCCASION HER SOJOURN IN EPHESUS.

Saint John made preparations for the journey and embarkation for Ephesus, and on the fourth day, which was the fifth of January of the year forty, saint John notified Her that it was time to leave; for there would be a ship and all things had been arranged for the journey. The great Mistress of obedience, without answer or delay, knelt down and asked permission of the Lord to leave the Cenacle and Jerusalem; and then She proceeded to take leave of the owner of the house and its inhabitants. It can easily be imagined, how sorrowful they were at this leave-taking; for on account of her most sweet conversation, and because of the favors and blessings received at her liberal hands, all were held captives and prisoners in love and veneration of Her, whereas now all at once they were to be deprived of her consoling presence and of this rich Treasure, the well spring of so many blessings.

All of them offered to follow and accompany Her; but as this was not opportune, they asked Her to hasten her return and not to forsake forever this house, which was entirely at her disposal. The heavenly Mother thanked them for these pious and loving wishes by expressing her own humble love, and She somewhat allayed their grief by giving them hope of her return.

Then She asked permission of saint John to visit the holy places of our Redemption and there to worship and adore the Lord, who had consecrated them by his presence and his precious blood. With the Apostle She made these sacred stations, exhibiting incredible devotion and tears of reverent love, and saint John, deeply consoled at being permitted to accompany Her, exercised himself in heroic acts of virtue. The most blessed Mother saw at each of the holy places the angels, who had been deputed to guard and defend them; and anew She charged them to resist Lucifer and his demons, lest they destroy or profane by irreverence those sacred spots, as they desired and intended to do through the unbelieving Jews. She told the angels to drive away by holy inspirations the bad thoughts and diabolical suggestions, by which the infernal dragon sought to excite the Jews and other mortals to blot out the memory of Christ our Savior in those holy places, and She charged them with this duty for all the future times, since the wrath of the evil spirits against the places and the works of the Redemption endures through all the ages. The holy angels obeyed their Queen and Mistress in all that She ordained.

Having satisfied her piety, She asked saint John on her knees to bless Her for the journey, just as She had been wont to do with her divine Son; for She continued to exercise the same great virtues of obedience and humility toward the beloved disciple, his substitute. Many of the faithful of Jerusalem offered Her money, jewels, vehicles and all things necessary for her journey to the sea and to Ephesus. The most prudent Lady humbly showed her appreciation to all, but accepted nothing. For her journey to the sea She made use of an unpretentious beast of burden, on which She was carried along as the Queen of the virtues and of the poor. She recollected the journeys and pilgrimages She had made with her divine Son and with her spouse Joseph, and these recollections, together with the heavenly love, which had induced Her once more to travel, awakened in her dove-like heart tender and devout affections.

They came to the harbor and immediately embarked in the ship with other passengers. The great Queen of the world was now for the first time upon the sea. She saw and comprehended with clearness the vast Mediterranean and its communication with the great ocean. She beheld its height and depth, its length and breadth, its caverns and secret recesses, its sands and minerals, its ebb and tide, its animals, its whales and fishes of all sizes, and whatever other portentous animals it enclosed.

When this great panorama of creatures, in which were reflected, as from a most clear mirror, the greatness and omnipotence of the Creator, was presented to her faculties filled with heavenly wisdom, her spirit winged its ardent flight to the very being of God, so wonderfully reflected in those creatures, and for all of them, and in all of them, She gave praise and glory and magnificence to the Most High. With the compassion of a most loving Mother for those who trusted their lives to the indomitable fury of the sea in navigating over its waves, She most fervently besought the Almighty to protect from its dangers all who should call upon her name and ask for her intercession. The Lord immediately granted this petition and promised to favor whoever upon the sea should carry some image of Her and should sincerely look upon this Star of the sea, most blessed Mary, for help in its perils. Accordingly it will be understood, that, if the Catholics and the faithful encounter ill success and perish in navigation, it is because they ignore the favors to be obtained from the Queen of the angels, or because on account of their sins they fail to remember Her in the raging storms, or fail to seek her favors with sincere faith and devotion; for neither can the word of the Lord ever fail, nor will the great Mother ever deny assistance to those endangered by the perils of the sea.

When they landed the great Queen continued to work miracles equal to those wrought upon the sea. She cured the sick and the possessed, who, as soon as they came into her presence, were set free. I will not tarry to relate all these wonders; for many books would be necessary and much time to describe all the doings of the most blessed Mary and the favors of heaven, which She dispensed as the instrument and medium of the omnipotence of the Most High. I will record only those, which are necessary for this history and which shall suffice to manifest in some measure the unknown and wonderful works of our great Queen and Lady. In Ephesus lived some Christians, who had come from Jerusalem. There were not many, but on learning of the arrival of the Mother of Christ the Redeemer, they hastened to pay Her a visit and offer their dwellings and their possessions for her use. But the great Queen of virtues, who sought neither ostentation nor temporal commodities, chose for her dwelling the house of a few retired and poor women, who were living by themselves free from intercourse with men. By the intervention of the angels, they lovingly and generously placed their home at the disposition of the Lady. In it they selected a very retired room for the Queen and another for saint John, which these Two occupied during their stay in Ephesus.

The most blessed Mary thanked the owners, who were to live with Her. Then She retired to her room and, prostrate upon the ground as was usual in her prayers, She adored the immutable essence of God, offering to sacrifice Herself in his service in this city and saying: "Lord God omnipotent, by the immensity of thy Divinity Thou fillest all the heavens and the earth (Jer. 23, 34). I, thy humble handmaid, desire to fulfill entirely thy holy will, on all occasions, in all places, and at all times, in which thy Providence shall deign to place me; for Thou art my only Good, my being and my life, and toward thy pleasure and satisfaction tend all my thoughts, words and actions." The most prudent Mother perceived that the Lord accepted her prayer and her offering, and that He responded to her desires with divine power, ready to assist and govern Her always.

She continued her prayer for the holy Church and laid out her plans for the assistance of all the faithful. She called her angels and sent some of them to aid the Apostles and disciples, whom She knew to be much pressed in the persecutions, raised by the demons through infidel men. In those days saint Paul fled from Damascus before the attacks of the Jews, as he himself mentions in the second epistle to the Corinthians, where he says, that he was let down from the walls of the city in a basket (II Cor. 11, 23). To defend him from these perils and those with which Lucifer threatened him on his way to Jerusalem, the great Queen of angels sent her angels to be his guard and protection; for the wrath and fury of hell was roused against saint Paul more than against any of the other Apostles. This is the journey the Apostle himself refers to in his letter to the Galatians (Gal. 1, 18), where he says, that after three years he went to Jerusalem to visit saint Peter. These three years are not to be counted from the time of his conversion, but from the time he had returned from Arabia to Damascus. This is to be inferred from the text itself, for after stating that he returned from Arabia to Damascus, he immediately adds, that after three years, he went up to Jerusalem. If those three years are counted from the time before his sojourn in Arabia, the text would occasion much confusion.

376. With greater clearness this may be proved by computing the time of the death of saint Stephen and the journey of the most blessed Virgin to Ephesus. For counting from the day of his Nativity, saint Stephen died at the end of the thirty-fourth year of Christ, but counting them from the day of the Circumcision, as the Church does now, saint Stephen died seven days before the completion of the thirty-four years, being the seven days before the first of January. The conversion of saint Paul happened in the year thirty-six, on the twenty-fifth of January. If he had come to Jerusalem three years afterwards, he would have found there the most holy Mary and saint John, while he himself says, that he had not seen any one of the Apostles there, except saint Peter and saint James the less, who was called Alpheus. If the holy Queen and saint John had at that time been in Jerusalem saint Paul would certainly not have missed seeing them, and he would have mentioned at least saint John; yet he says, that he had not seen him. The explanation is, that saint Paul came to Jerusalem in the year forty, four years after his conversion, and a little less than a month after the most blessed Mary had departed for Ephesus. Saint Paul had entered the fifth year of his conversion

and the other Apostles, except the two he saw, had already left Jerusalem and were preaching the Gospel of Christ, each one in his appointed province.

Conformably with this reckoning we must assume, that saint Paul spent the first year after his conversion, or the greater part of it, in journeying to Arabia and preaching the Gospel there; then, the three following years, in Damascus. Hence the evangelist Luke, in the ninth chapter of his Acts of the Apostles, although he says nothing of Paul's journey to Arabia, nevertheless says that for many days after his conversion the Jews of Damascus plotted to take his life, these many days referring to the four years thus passed. Then he adds, that his disciples, aware of the plots of the Jews, on a certain night lowered him in a basket from the city walls and thus despatched him on his journey to Jerusalem. There, although knowing of his miraculous conversion, the Apostles and the new disciples, nevertheless retained a certain fear and suspicion of his not persevering, because he had been such a professed enemy of Christ, our Savior. Hence they at first held themselves aloof from saint Paul, until saint Barnaby spoke to them and introduced him to saint Peter, saint James and other disciples (Acts 26, 27). Saint Paul prostrated himself at the feet of the vicar of Christ, kissed them in acknowledgment of his errors and sins, and begging to be admitted as one of his subjects and as a follower of his Master, whose holy name and faith he desired to preach at the cost of his blood.

From the fear and suspicion of saint Peter and James concerning the perseverance of saint Paul we can likewise deduct that he arrived in Jerusalem in the absence of the most blessed Mary and saint John; for he would have presented himself first of all to Her to allay suspicion against him; and the two Apostles would likewise have first asked Her, whether they could trust saint Paul. All of them would have been set at ease by the most prudent Lady, as She was so solicitous and attentive in consoling and instructing the Apostles, especially saint Peter. But since the great Lady had already left for Ephesus, they had no one to assure them of the constancy of saint Paul, until saint Peter reassured himself of it at seeing him thus prostrate at his feet. Thereupon he was received with great joy of soul by saint Peter and the other disciples. All of them gave humble and fervent thanks to the Most High, and commissioned saint Paul to preach in Jerusalem. This he gladly did, to the astonishment of all the Jews who knew him. As his words were like burning arrows, that penetrated into the hearts of all that heard him, they were struck with terror; and in two days all Jerusalem was roused by the news of his arrival, flocking to see him with their own eyes.

Lucifer and his demons were not asleep on this occasion, for they were visited by the Almighty with an increase of torment at the arrival of saint Paul. The divine power, so evident in him, oppressed and paralyzed the infernal dragons. But as their pride and malice shall never be extinguished through all the eternity of their existence (Ps. 73, 23), they were roused to fury, as soon as they recognized this divine virtue as flowing from Paul. Lucifer, with incredible rage, called together many legions of the demons and exhorted them anew to rouse themselves and exert all the forces of their malice for the entire destruction of saint Paul, and not to leave any stone unturned in Jerusalem and in all the world for the attainment of this object. The demons without delay set about this work, exciting Herod and the Jews against the Apostle, and directing their attention to the burning zeal with which he began to preach in Jerusalem.

The great Mistress of heaven perceived all this from her retirement in Ephesus; for in addition to the knowledge of all things through her heavenly science, She received information of all that happened to saint Paul from the angels She had sent for his defense. As the most blessed Mother expected the disturbance about to be raised by the malice of Herod and the Jews, especially against saint Paul, and as, on the other hand, She knew the importance of preserving his life for the exaltation of God's name and the spread of the Gospel, the great Queen was filled with new solicitude and regret at being absent from Palestine, where She could have rendered more immediate assistance to the Apostles. Therefore She sought to furnish it so much the more abundantly from Ephesus by multiplying her prayers and petitions, her ceaseless tears and sighs, and by other measures through the hands of her holy angels. In order to allay her anxieties, the Lord, one day in her prayer, assured Her, that He would fulfill her petitions and protect the life of saint Paul in this danger and in these assaults of the devil. And so He did: for one day saint Paul, while praying in the temple, was raised to an ecstatic rapture and filled with most exalted enlightenment and understanding, wherein the Lord commanded him immediately to leave Jerusalem and save his life from the hatred of the unbelieving Jews.

Hence saint Paul sojourned in Jerusalem at that time not more than fifteen days, as he himself says in his epistle to Galatians (Gal. 1, 18). After some years he returned thither from Miletus and Ephesus and was taken prisoner, and he refers to this ecstasy in the temple and to the command of the Lord to leave Jerusalem in the twenty-second chapter of the Acts. Of this vision and command he informed saint Peter, as the head of the apostolic college; and after consultation concerning his mortal danger, he was secretly sent to Caesarea and Tarsus with orders to preach indiscriminately to the gentiles, which he did.   The most blessed Mary was the instrument and Mediatrix of all these miraculous favors.   It was through Her that her Divine Son operated them, and from Her, God received the proper thanks for the graces distributed to the whole Church.

Having thus been reassured in regard to the life of saint Paul, the most blessed Mother entertained the hope that through the assistance of divine Providence She might save the life of her cousin James, who was very dear to Her and who was still in Saragossa, protected by the hundred angels She had appointed for his guardians and companions at Granada. These holy angels frequently went back and forth, bringing the petitions of the Apostles to the most blessed Mary and her counsels back to him.   In this way saint James learned of the sojourn of the great Queen in Ephesus.   When he had brought the chapel or small temple of the Pillar in Saragossa to a sufficient state of completion, he consigned it to the care of the bishop and the disciples appointed by him here as in other cities in Spain.   Some months after the apparition of the Queen, he departed from Saragossa, continuing to preach through different provinces. Having come to Catalonia, he embarked for Italy, where without much delay, he pursued his journey overland always preaching until he again embarked for Asia, and ardently desiring to see there the most blessed Mary, his Mistress and Protectress.

Saint James happily attained his object and reached Ephesus.   There he prostrated himself at the feet of the Mother of his Creator, shedding copious tears of joy and veneration.   From his inmost heart he thanked Her for the peerless favors obtained at her hands from

the Most High during his travels and his preaching in
Spain, and especially for her having visited him and conferred such blessings upon him during her visits. The
heavenly Mother, as Mistress of humility, immediately
raised him from the ground and said to him: "My
Master, remember thou art the anointed of the Lord and
his minister, and that I am an humble wormlet." With
these words the great Lady fell on her knees and asked the
blessing of saint James as a priest of the Most High. He
remained for some days in Ephesus in the company of
the most blessed Mary and of his brother John, to whom
he gave an account of all that had happened to him in
Spain. With the most prudent Mother during those days
he held most exalted colloquies and conferences, of which
it will suffice to record the following.

When the Jews, through the conviction and conversion of Philetus and Hermogenes, saw their hopes
frustrated, they were filled with new anger against the
apostle saint James and they determined to put an end to
his life. For this purpose they bribed Democritus and
Lysias, centurions of the Roman militia, to furnish them
with soldiers for the arrest of the Apostle. In order to
hide their treachery they were to raise a feigned quarrel
or disturbance on a certain day during his preaching and
thus get him within their power. The execution of this
wicked design was left to Abiator, the high-priest of that
year, and to Josias, a scribe of the same mind as the highpriest. As they had planned, so they executed their
scheme; for, while the saint was preaching to the people
about the mystery of the Redemption, proving it to them
with admirable wisdom from the testimonies of the ancient writings and moving his audience to tears of compunction, the priest and the scribe were roused to diabolical fury. Giving the signal to the Roman soldiers,

the priest sent Josias to throw a rope around the neck
of saint James and fell upon him, proclaiming him a dis-
turber of the people and the author of a new religion in
opposition to the Roman empire.

Democritus and Lysias thereupon rushed up with
their soldiers and brought the Apostle bound to Herod,
the son of Archelaus, whose malice had been roused interiorly through the astuteness of Lucifer and exteriorly
by the evil-minded and hateful Jews. Thus doubly incited,
Herod began against the disciples of the Lord, whom he
abhorred, the persecution mentioned by saint Luke in
the twelfth chapter of the Acts and sent his soldiers to
afflict and imprison them. He instantly commanded saint
James to be beheaded, as the Jews had asked. Incredible
was the joy of the holy Apostle at being seized and bound
like his Master and at seeing himself conducted to the
place, where he was to pass from this mortal life to the
eternal through martyrdom, as he had been informed by
the Queen of heaven. He offered most humble thanks for
this benefit and publicly reiterated the open profession of
his faith in Christ our Lord. Remembering the petition
he had made in Ephesus, that She be present at his death,
he called upon Her from his inmost Soul.

The most holy Mary from her oratory heard
these prayers of her beloved Apostle and cousin; for
She was attentive to all that happened to him and She
helped and favored him with her own efficacious petitions. During this her prayer, She saw a great multitude of angels and heavenly spirits of all hierarchies
descending from heaven, part of them surrounding the
Apostle in Jerusalem as he was led to the place of execution, while numerous others approached their Queen at
Ephesus. Presently one of them addressed Her saying:
"Empress of heaven and our Lady, the most high Lord
and God bids you immediately to hasten to Jerusalem to

console his great servant James, to assist him in his death and to grant all his loving and holy desires." This favor the most blessed Mary joyfully and gratefully acknowledged. She praised the Most High for the protection granted to those who trust in his mercy and put their lives in his hands. In the meanwhile the Apostle was led to execution and on the way thereto he wrought great miracles upon the sick and ailing and on some possessed by the demons. There were a great number of them, because the rumor of his execution by Herod had spread about and many of the unfortunates hastened to receive his last ministrations and counsels. All that applied were healed by the great Apostle.

In the meanwhile the holy angels placed their Queen and Mistress upon a most refulgent throne, as they had done on other occasions, and on it bore Her to Jerusalem and to the place of the execution of saint James. The holy Apostle fell upon his knees in order to offer his life to the Most High in sacrifice, and when he raised his eyes toward heaven, he saw in the air near him the Queen of heaven, whom he had been invoking in his heart. He beheld Her clothed in divine splendors and great beauty, surrounded by multitudes of the angels. At this heavenly spectacle the soul of James was moved to new jubilee and his heart was seized with the ardors of a divine love. He wished to proclaim the most blessed Mary as the Mother of God and the Mistress of all creation. But one of the sovereign spirits restrained him in this fervent desire and said: "James, servant of our Creator, restrain within thy own bosom these precious sentiments and do not manifest to the Jews the presence and assistance of our Queen; for they are not worthy or capable of knowing Her, but instead of reverencing Her will only harden themselves in their hatred." Thus advised the Apostle forebore and moving his lips in silence, he spoke to the heavenly Queen as follows:

"Mother of my Lord Jesus Christ, my Mistress and Protectress, Thou consolation of the afflicted and refuge of the needy, in this hour bestow upon me, my Lady, thy so much desired blessing. Offer for me to thy Son and Redeemer of the world, the sacrifice of my life, since I am burning with desire to be a holocaust for the glory of his name. Let today thy most pure and spotless hands be the altar of my sacrifice, in order that it may become acceptable in the eyes of Him, who died for me upon the cross. Into thy hands, and through them into the hands of my Creator, I commend my spirit." Having said these words, and keeping his eyes fixed upon the most holy Mary, who spoke to his heart, the holy Apostle was beheaded by the executioner. The great Lady and Queen of the world (O wonderful condescension!) received the soul of her beloved Apostle and placing it at her side on the throne, ascended with it to the empyrean heavens and presented it to her divine Son. As the most blessed Mary entered the heavenly court with this offering, She caused new joy and accidental glory to all the heavenly inhabitants and was received with songs of praise. The Most High received the soul of James and placed it in eminent glory among the princes of his people. The most blessed Mary, prostrate before the throne of the Almighty, composed a song of praise and thanksgiving for the triumphal martyrdom first gained by one of his Apostles. On this occasion the great Lady did not see the Divinity by intuitive vision, but by an abstractive one, such as I have described before this. But the blessed Trinity filled Her with new blessings and favors for Herself and for the holy Church, for which She had made great preparations. All the saints likewise blessed her and then the holy angels brought Her back to her oratory in Ephesus, where in the meanwhile an angel had impersonated Her. On arriving the heavenly Mother of virtues prostrated Herself as usual in order to give thanks to the Most High for all that had happened.

The disciples of saint James during the following night secured his sacred body and secretly brought it to Jaffa, where by divine disposition they embarked with it for Galicia in Spain. The heavenly Lady sent an angel to guide and accompany them to the port, where according to the divine will they were to disembark. Although they did not see the angel, they felt his protection during the whole voyage and often in a miraculous manner. Thus Spain, just as it owed its first instruction in the faith so deeply rooted in the hearts of its people, to the protection lavished by most holy Mary upon the Apostle, now also owes to Her the possession of his sacred body for its consolation and defense. Saint James died in the year forty-one of our Lord, on the twenty-fifth of March, five years and seven months after his setting out to preach in Spain. According to this count and that which I gave above, the martyrdom of saint James happened seven full years after the death of our Savior Jesus Christ.

The death of saint James and the haste of Herod in inflicting it, greatly increased the most impious cruelty of the Jews; for in the savage brutality of the wicked king they saw a valuable means of pursuing their vengeance against the followers of Christ the Lord. Lucifer and his demons were of like opinion; they, by their suggestions, and the Jews, by their insistent flatteries, persuaded him to seize upon saint Peter, which he readily did in order to gain the good will of the Jews for his own temporal ends. The demons stood in great awe of the vicar of Christ on account of the power emanating from him against them; and therefore they secretly sought to hasten his imprisonment. Saint Peter, bound with many chains, lay in the dungeon awaiting his execution after the holidays of the Pasch. (Acts 12, 4).

The dangerous crisis impending over the Church was not unknown to the heavenly Mother, for, from her retreat in Ephesus, by her clearest interior vision of all things, She saw all things that passed in Jerusalem. She likewise increased her ardent requests, her sighs, prostrations and bloody tears, supplicating the Lord for the liberation of saint Peter and the protection of the holy Church. These prayers of the blessed Mother penetrated the heavens and wounded the heart of her Son Jesus, Savior. In response the Lord descended in person to her oratory, where She was lying prostrate with her virginal face upon the ground mingling with the dust. The sovereign King entered and raised Her lovingly from the ground, saying: "My Mother, moderate thy sorrow and ask whatever thou wishest; for I shall grant it all and thou shalt find grace in my eyes to obtain it. I desire that thou act according to thy wishes, using the powers I have given Thee: do or undo whatever is necessary for the welfare of my Church, and Thou mayest be sure, that all the fury of the demons will be turned toward Thee." She thanked him for this new favor and offered to undertake the battles of the Lord for his faithful, saying: "Most High Lord, hope and life of my soul, prepared is the heart and spirit of thy servant to labor for the souls bought with thy blood and life. Although I am but useless dust, I know Thee to be infinite in power and wisdom; with the favor of thy assistance I fear not the infernal dragon. As Thou wishest me to dispose and act in thy name for the welfare of the Church, I now command Lucifer and all his ministers of wickedness, who are disturbing the Church, to descend to the abyss and there be silenced until it shall please thy Providence to permit their return to the earth." This command of the Queen of the world in Ephesus was so powerful, that at the very moment of her issuing it, all the demons in Jerusalem were precipitated into hell, the whole multitude descending into the eternal caverns without power of resisting the divine force exerted through the most blessed Mary.

Lucifer and his companions knew that this chastisement proceeded from our Queen, whom they called their enemy because they dared not pronounce her name. They remained in hell, confounded and dismayed as on other occasions, until they were permitted to rise in order to battle against Mary, as will be related further on. During that time they consulted anew about the means of attaining this end. Having obtained this triumph over the demons the most blessed Mary bethought Herself of overcoming likewise the opposition of Herod and the Jews, and therefore She said to her divine Son: "Now, my Son and Lord, if it is thy will, let one of thy holy angels be sent to deliver thy servant Peter from prison." Christ our Lord approved of her wish and, at the orders of both these Sovereigns, one of the heavenly spirits there present hastened to liberate saint Peter from his prison in Jerusalem.

The angel executed these orders very swiftly. Coming to the dungeon, he found saint Peter fastened with two chains, guarded by two soldiers at his side and by a number of other soldiers at the entrance of the prison. The Pasch had already been celebrated and it was the night before he was to be executed according to the sentence passed upon him. But the Apostle was so little disturbed that he was sleeping with as much unconcern as his guards (Acts 12, 6). When the angel arrived, he was obliged to wake him by force and while saint Peter was still drowsy, said to him: "Arise quickly; put on thy girdle and thy shoes, take thy mantle and follow me." Saint Peter found himself free of the chains and, without understanding what was happening to him and ignorant of what this vision could mean, followed the angel. Having conducted him through some streets, the angel told him, that the Almighty had freed him from prison through the intercession of his most blessed Mother, and thereupon disappeared. Saint Peter, coming to himself understood the mystery and gave thanks to the Lord for this favor.

Saint Peter thought it best first to give an account of his liberation and consult with James the Less and others of the faithful, before seeking safety in flight. Hastening his steps he came to the house of Mary, the mother of John, who was also called Mark. This was the house of the Cenacle, where many of the disciples had gathered in their affliction. Saint Peter called to them from the street, and a servant-maid, by the name of Rhode, descended to see who was calling. As She recognized the voice of Peter, She left him standing at the door outside and fled excitedly to the disciples, telling them that it was Peter. They thought it some foolish misunderstanding of the servant; but she maintained, that it was Peter; so they, far from guessing the liberation of Peter, concluded that it might be his angel. During these questions and answers saint Peter was in the street clamoring at the door, until they opened it and with incredible joy and gladness saw the holy Apostle and head of the Church freed from the sorrows of prison and death. He gave them an account of all that had happened to him through aid of the angel, in order that they might in strict secrecy notify saint James and all his brethren. Foreseeing that Herod would search for him with great diligence, they unanimously decided that he leave Jerusalem that very night and not return, lest he should be taken in some future search. Saint Peter therefore fled, and Herod, having instituted a search in vain, chastised the guards, and was roused to new fury against the disciples. But on account of his pride and impious designs, God cut short his activity by a severe punishment, of which I shall speak in the following chapter.

In her anxieties and in her reliance upon the divine help our Queen labored incessantly in prayers and tears, travailing in her clamors as I have shown on other occasions. Ever governed by her most exalted prudence, She spoke to one of the highest angels of her guard, saying: "Minister of the Most High and creature of his hands, my solicitude for the holy Church strongly urges me to seek its welfare and progress. I beseech thee to ascend to the throne of the Most High, represent to Him my affliction; ask Him in my name, that I may be permitted to suffer instead of his faithful servants and that Herod be prevented from executing his designs for the destruction of the Church." Immediately the angel betook himself to the Lord with this message, while the Queen of heaven, like another Esther, remained in prayer for the liberty and salvation of her people and of Herself. (Esther 4, 16). The heavenly ambassador was sent back by the blessed Trinity with the answer: "Princess of heaven, the Lord of hosts says, that Thou art the Mother, the Mistress and the Governess of the Church, and that Thou holdest his power while Thou art upon earth; and He desires Thee, as the Queen and Mistress of the heaven and earth, to execute sentence upon Herod."

In her humility the most blessed Virgin was somewhat disturbed by this answer, and urged by her charity, She replied to the angel: "Am I then to pronounce sentence against a creature who is the image of the Lord? Since I came forth from his hands I have known many reprobates among men and I have never called for vengeance against them; but as far as I was concerned, always desired their salvation if possible, and never hastened their punishment. Return to the Lord, angel, and tell Him that my tribunal and power is inferior to and dependent upon his, and that I cannot sentence any one to death without consulting my Superior; and if it is possible to bring Herod to the way of Salvation, I am willing to suffer all the travails of the world according to the disposition of his divine Providence in order that this soul may not be lost." The angel hastened back with this second message of his Queen and having presented it before the throne of the most blessed Trinity, was sent back to Her with the following answer: "Our Mistress and Queen, the Most High says, that Herod is of the number of the foreknown, since he is so obstinate in his malice, that he will take no admonition or instruction; he will not co-operate with the helps given to him; nor will he avail himself of the fruits of the Redemption, nor of the intercession of the saints, nor of thy own efforts, O Queen and Lady, in his behalf."

For the third time the most holy Mary despatched the heavenly prince with still another message to the Most High, saying: "If it must be that Herod die in order to hinder him from persecuting the Church, do thou, O angel, represent to the Almighty, how in the infinite condescension of his charity, He has granted me in mortal life to be the Refuge of the children of Adam, the Advocate and Intercessor of sinners; that my tribunal should be that of kindness and clemency for the refuge and assistance of all that seek my intercession; and that all should leave it with the assurance of pardon in the name of my divine Son. If then I am to be a loving Mother to men, who are the creatures of his hands and the price of his life-blood, how can I now be a severe judge against one of them? Never was I charged with dealing out justice, always mercy, to which all my heart inclines; and now it is troubled by this conflict of love with obedience to rigorous justice. Present anew, O angel, this my anxiety to the Lord, and learn whether it is not his pleasure that Herod die without my condemning him."

The holy messenger ascended for the third time and the most blessed Trinity listened to his message with the plenitude of pleasure and complacency at the pitying love of his Spouse. Returning, the angel thus informed the loving Mistress: "Our Queen, Mother of our Creator and my Lady, the almighty Majesty says that thy mercy is for those mortals who wish to avail themselves of thy powerful intercession, not for those who despise and abhor it like Herod; that Thou art the Mistress of the Church invested with all the divine power, and that therefore it is meet Thou use it as is opportune: that Herod must die; but it shall be through thy sentence and according to thy order." The most blessed Mary answered: "Just is the Lord and equitable are his judgments (Ps. 118, 137). Many times would I suffer death to rescue this soul of Herod, if he himself would not by his own free will make himself unworthy of mercy and choose perdition. He is a work of the Most High (Job. 10, 8), formed according to his image and likeness (Gen. 1, 27); he was redeemed by the blood of the Lamb, which taketh away the sins of the world (Apoc. 1, 5). But I set aside all this and, considering only his having become an obstinate enemy of God, unworthy of his eternal friendship, by the most equitable justice of God, I condemn him to the death he has merited, in order that he may not incur greater torments by executing the evil he has planned."

This wonder the Lord wrought for the glory of his most blessed Mother and in witness of his having constituted Her as the Mistress of all creatures with supreme power to act as their Sovereign like her divine Son. I cannot explain this mystery better than in the words of the Lord in the fifth chapter of saint John, where He says of Himself: "The son cannot do anything that the Father does not; but He does the same, because the Father loves Him; and if the Father raises the dead, the son also raises whom he pleases, and the Father has given to the Son to judge all, in order that just as all honor the Father, they may also honor the Son; for no one can honor the Father without honoring the Son." And immediately He adds: that He has given Him the power of judging, because He is the Son of man, which He is through his most blessed mother. On account of the likeness of the heavenly Mother to her Son (of which I have often spoken) the relation or proportion of the Mother with the Son in this power of judgment must be transferred to the Mother in the same manner as that of the Son from the Father. Mary is the Mother of mercy and clemency to all the children of Adam that call upon Her; but in addition to this the Almighty wishes it to be understood that She possesses full power of judging all men and that all should honor Her, just as they honor her Son and true God. As his true Mother He has given Her the same power with him in the degree and proportion due to Her as his Mother and a mere creature.

Making use of this power the great Lady sent the angel to Cæsarea, where Herod then was, to take away his life as the minister of divine justice. The angel executed the sentence without delay. The evangelist saint Luke says, that the angel of the Lord struck Herod and, eaten up by worms, the unhappy man died the temporal and eternal death. The wound of this stroke was interior and from it sprang the corruption and the worms that so miserably finished him. From the same text it appears that, after having beheaded saint James and after saint Peter had escaped, Herod descended to Cæsarea in order to compose some differences that had arisen between him and the inhabitants of Sidon and Tyre (Acts 12, 23). Within a few days, vested in the royal purple and seated upon a throne, he harangued the people with great show of words. The people, full of vain flattery, proclaimed him as a victor and as a god; and Herod, in foolish vanity, was pleased with this adulation of the people. Because he had not given honor to God, but usurped to himself divine honor in vain pride, as saint Luke says, the angel of the Lord struck him. Although this was his last crime, which filled the measure of his iniquity, he merited the chastisement not only for this, but for so many other crimes committed by him in persecuting the Apostles, mocking the Lord our Savior (Luke 23, 11), beheading the Baptist (Mark 6, 27), committing adultery with his sister-in-law Herodias, and for many other abominations.

Immediately the angel returned to Ephesus and gave an account of the execution of the sentence against Herod. The merciful Mother wept over the loss of this soul; but praised the judgments of the Lord and gave him thanks for the benefit, which the Church would derive from his chastisement; for, as saint Luke says (Acts 12, 24), the Church grew and increased by the word of God. This was true not only in Galilee and Judea, where the persecutor Herod was removed, but, through saint John and the help of the most holy Mother, the Church was taking root in Ephesus. The science of the blessed Apostle was full as that of the cherubim, and the love of his heart was inflamed like that of the seraphim; and he had with him as his Mother and Teacher, the Mistress of wisdom and grace. On account of these precious advantages the Evangelist could undertake great and wonderful works for the foundation of the law of grace, not only in Ephesus, but in all neighboring regions of Asia and in the borderlands of Europe.

Arriving at Ephesus the Evangelist began to preach in the city, baptizing those whom he converted to the faith of Christ our Savior and confirming the faith by great miracles and prodigies, such as had never been witnessed by those gentiles. Since the Greek schools in those countries turned out many philosophers and men learned in what, notwithstanding the admixture of many errors, could be called human sciences, the blessed Apostle convincingly taught them the true science, making use not only of miracles and signs, but of argumentation for the credibility of the Christian faith. All his catechumens he immediately sent to the most holy Mary and She instructed many; as She knew the interior inclinations of all, She spoke to the heart of each one and filled it with heavenly light. She wrought prodigies and miracles for the benefit of the unfortunate, curing the possessed and the infirm, succored the poor and the needy and, by the labor of her own hands, gave assistance to the sick in the infirmaries, attending upon them in person. In her house the kindest Queen had a supply of clothes for the most poor and forsaken of her fellowmen. She helped many in the hour of their death, gaining these souls in their last agony and bringing them safely through all the assaults of the demon to their Creator. So many souls did She draw to the path of truth and life eternal, and so numerous were the wonders She wrought for this end, that they could not be recorded in many books; for no day passed in which She did not increase the possessions of the Lord by the copious and abundant fruit of souls.

WORDS OF THE QUEEN.

All are the children of the eternal Father who is in heaven (Matth 23, 9) and all are obliged to have a care of their brethren according to each one's condition.

This obligation rests more especially upon the children of the Church, who can live up to it by their prayers and supplications. But this duty lies still more directly upon those who have influence, upon those who are nourished by the Christian faith, and who enjoy more of the benefits of the liberal hand of the Almighty. Those who through the law of Christ are favored with temporal advantages and who make use of them for the service and the delights of the flesh, are they who, as the powerful, are to be more powerfully tormented (Matth 23, 9). If the pastors and the chiefs of the house of the Lord seek only a life of ease, without caring to engage in true earnest labor, they will make themselves accountable for the ruin of the flock of Christ and for the carnage brought on by the infernal wolves. O my daughter, into what a lamentable state has the Christian people been cast by the powerful, by the pastors, and by the wicked ministers, whom God has given them in his secret judgments! O what confusion and chastisements await them! Before the tribunal of the just Judge they will have no excuse; since the Catholic truth undeceives them, their conscience loudly protests, while they wilfully remain deaf to all warnings.

The cause of God remains neglected and without a champion; his possessions, which are the souls, are left without increase; all as it were look but to their own interest and preservation, each one according to his own diabolical cunning and according to his state of life. Truth is obscured, flattery raises its voice, avarice is unbridled, the blood of Christ is trodden under foot, the fruits of the Redemption are held in contempt; no one wishes to risk his own comfort or interest in order to save what has cost the Savior his blood and life. Even the friends of God are influenced by the evils; for they do not make use of their charity and its holy liberty as they ought; and most of them allow themselves to be overcome by their cowardice and content themselves with working for themselves alone, forsaking the common cause of the souls of others. Hence thou mayest understand, my daughter, that now, after the evangelical Church has been established by my divine Son and fertilized by his own blood, those unhappy times have come, of which the Lord himself complains through his holy Prophets, saying: what the palmerworm hath left the locust has eaten, and what the locust left the bruchus consumed, and the residue is destroyed by the mildew; (Joel 1, 4) and in order to gather some fruits from his vineyard, the Lord goes about like the gleaner after the vintage, who seeks some remaining grape, or some olive, which is not dried up, or carried away by the demons (Is. 24, 13).

Tell me now, my daughter, how is it possible, if thou still hast a true love for my divine Son and for me, that thou find consolation or rest in thy heart at the sight of the loss of souls, which He redeemed by his blood and I have sought with blood-mingled tears? Even today, if I could shed them, I would begin to do so with new weeping and compassion; and since it is not possible for me now to weep over the dangers threatening the Church, I wish that thou do it and that thou spurn consolation in a misfortune so calamitous and so worthy of lament. Weep bitterly then, and lose not the merit of such a sorrow; and let it be so deep, that thou findst no relief except in affliction for the sake of the Lord whom thou lovest. Think of what I did, in order to stave off the damnation of Herod and to prevent it for those who wish to avail themselves of my intercession. In the beatific vision I pray without ceasing for the salvation of my clients. Let not the labors and tribulations sent to thee by my divine Son intimidate thee from helping they brethren and acquiring them for the possession of Christ Amidst the injuries done to Him by the children of Adam, do thou labor to recompense them in some measure by the purity of thy soul, which I desire shall be rather that of an angel than of an earthborn woman. Fight the battles of the Lord against his enemies and in his name and mine, crush their head, reign over their pride and cast them into hell. Do thou also counsel the ministers of Christ with whom thou conversest, to use their power in doing the same, to defend the souls in lively faith and, in them, the honor and glory of the Lord; for thus shall they repress and vanquish them with divine power.

CHAPTER II.

COUNCIL OF THE APOSTLES.

After the death of the unhappy Herod the primitive Church of Jerusalem enjoyed some measure of quiet and tranquillity for a considerable time. The great Lady of the world merited this favor through her maternal solicitude and care. During this time saint Barnaby and saint Paul preached with wonderful success in the cities of Asia Minor, Antioch, Lystra, Perge and others, as is related by saint Luke in the thirteenth and fourteenth chapter of the Acts of the Apostles and in connection with the miracles and prodigies performed by saint Paul in those cities and provinces. The apostle saint Peter, after his liberation from prison, fled from Jerusalem and retired to another part of Asia not under the jurisdiction of Herod. From that place he governed the faithful accruing to the Church in Asia and those that were in Palestine. All of them acknowledged and obeyed him as the Vicar of Jesus Christ and head of the Church, believing that all he ordained and enacted upon earth was confirmed in heaven. With this firm faith they came to him with all their doubts and difficulties as to their supreme pontiff. Among other matters they asked him to decide the questions raised by some of the Jews concerning the doings and teachings of saint Paul and Barnaby as well in Jerusalem as in Antioch, in opposition to the circumcision and the law of Moses, as I will relate later on and as is recorded by saint Luke in the fifteenth chapter of the Acts of the Apostles.

On this occasion the Apostles and disciples of Jerusalem begged saint Peter to return to the holy city in order to settle these controversies and establish order, so that the preaching of the faith might not be hindered; for since the death of Herod the Jews had no one to assist them in their persecutions, and therefore the Church enjoyed greater peace and tranquillity in Jerusalem. On the same grounds they also asked him to request the holy Mother of Jesus to come to that city; for all the faithful longed for Her with loving hearts, expected to be consoled in the Lord and hoped for the prosperity of all the affairs of the Church through her presence. On account of these appeals saint Peter resolved to return at once to Jerusalem, and before setting out, he wrote the following letter to the most holy Queen.

Letter of Saint Peter to most holy Mary.

"To Mary, the Virgin, Mother of God:

Peter, the Apostle of Jesus Christ, thy servant and the servant of the servants of God."

"Lady, among the faithful some doubts and differences have arisen concerning the doctrine of thy Son and our Redeemer, whether the ancient law of Moses is to be observed in conjunction with his teachings. They wish to know from us what is proper, and that we state to them what we heard from the mouth of the divine Teacher. In order to consult with my brethren, the Apostles, I am now setting out for Jerusalem and, for the consolation of all and by thy love for the Church, we beseech Thee likewise to come to that city, where, since the death of Herod, the Jews are more peaceful and the faithful more at ease. The multitude of the followers of Christ desire to see Thee and console themselves in thy presence. When we shall have arrived at Jerusalem, we shall notify the other cities, and with thy assistance will be established what shall be conducive to the interests of the holy faith and to the excellence of the law of grace."

I cannot restrain my wonder and confusion at the humility and obedience of the most holy Mary in a matter of so small moment; for only her heavenly prudence could inspire Her, the Mother of God, with the thought, that it would be more humble and submissive not to read this letter of the Vicar of Christ except in the presence and under the obedience of the one to whose guidance She had submitted Herself as her superior. Her example reproves and stigmatizes the presumption of inferiors, who try to find excuses and pretenses for evading the humility and obedience due to their superiors. But the most holy Mary was a model and a teacher of holiness in all things, great or small. Having read the letter to Her, he asked Her, what She thought best to write to the Vicar of Christ. But also in this She did not wish to give any appearance of her being his equal or superior, preferring to obey; and therefore She answered: "My son and master, do thou arrange whatever shall be proper; for I, as thy servant, will obey." The Evangelist replied, that it seemed to him best to obey saint Peter and return immediately to Jerusalem. "It is right and proper to obey the head of the Church," answered the purest lady; "let us prepare even now for our departure."

Thus resolved, saint John went out to seek passage for Palestine and to prepare whatever was necessary for a speedy departure. In the meanwhile, at the request of the Evangelist, most blessed Mary called together the women who were her acquaintances and disciples in Ephesus, in order to take leave of them and instruct them in what they must do to persevere in their holy faith.

When the day of departure arrived, the Humblest of the humble asked saint John for his blessing and with it they betook themselves to the ship, having remained in Ephesus two years and a half. On leaving their dwelling all her thousand angels manifested themselves in visible human forms, but all of them were armed for battle and formed into squadrons. This unwonted sight gave Her to understand, that She was to be prepared to continue her conflict with the great dragon and his allies. Before reaching the sea She saw a great multitude of the infernal legions meeting Her in various dreadful and terrific shapes; in the midst of them came a dragon with seven heads, so horrible and huge as to exceed the size of a large ship, and so fierce and abominable as to cause torment by its mere presence. Against these formidable hosts the invincible Queen fortified Herself by the most firm faith and fervent love, repeating the words of Psalms and the sayings from the mouth of her most holy Son. She ordered her holy angels to assist Her, for those terrific shapes naturally inspired Her with some human dread and horror. The Evangelist knew nothing of this conflict until the heavenly Lady afterwards informed him and gave him an insight into it.

Our blessed Lady embarked with the saint, and the ship's sails were set. But it had proceeded only a short distance from the port, when those dragons of hell, making use of the permission given them, stirred up the sea by a tempest such as had not been seen before that time nor until now; for the Almighty wished to exalt the power of his arm and the holiness of Mary and therefore He permitted such liberty to the malice and powers of the demons in this battle. The waves rose with terrific roarings, piling themselves upon the winds and apparently even upon the very clouds, forming with them mountains of water and foam, as if they were preparing for an onset to break the bounds of the abysses that imprisoned the ocean (Ps. 13, 9). The ship was lashed and battered to and fro, and it seemed a miracle that it was not shattered to splinters at each shock. Sometimes it was hurled up into the clouds, at others sent to plow up the sand of the ocean's abysses; often its sails and masts were buried in the foaming waves. During some of the onsets of this unspeakably furious hurricane the ship was held in the air by the angels in order to save it from some of the vaster billows, which would inevitably have overhelmed and sent it to the bottom.

The mariners and passengers perceived the effects of this assistance, but remained ignorant of the cause; in their distress they were beside themselves, bewailing their ruin, which they deemed inevitable. The demons added to their terror; for, assuming human shapes, they loudly called upon the mariners as if from neighboring ships sent to their aid and urged them to forsake their ship and save themselves in the others. For though all the vessels suffered in this storm, yet the wrath of the demons and their power of doing harm was confined principally to the ship on which our Lady sailed and the distress and peril of the other vessels was not so great. The malicious designs of the demons were known only to the most blessed Virgin and not to the sailors, and therefore they believed these voices as of true passengers and sailors. Thus deceived they at times gave up caring for their own ship and left it to the fury of the sea, expecting to save themselves on one of the other ships. But the angels supplied their place directing and steering it when the sailors gave it up in despair to the destruction of the waves.

In the midst of this confusion and distress the most holy Mary preserved her tranquillity, serenely borne up by the ocean of her magnanimity and virtue, but at the same time practicing all the virtues by acts heroic in proportion to the exigencies of the occasion and the dictates of her wisdom. As during this tempestuous voyage She personally experienced the dangers of navigation, which She had understood on her former voyage by divine inspiration, She was moved to new compassion for all voyagers at sea and renewed her former prayers and petitions. The most prudent Virgin also admired the indomitable forces of the sea and was led to consider the wrath of divine justice, so well represented by this insensible creature. And passing from these considerations to that of the sins of mortals, who drew it upon themselves from the Almighty, She entered into the most ardent prayers for the conversion of the world and the increase of the Church. For this She offered up the hardships of this voyage; since notwithstanding the tranquillity of her soul, She suffered much bodily inconvenience and still greater affliction at the thought that all her fellow-voyagers were made to suffer this persecution and tribulation of the demons on her account.

A large share of this suffering fell to the evangelist saint John on account of his deep solicitude for his true Mother and Mistress of the world. To this was added his own actual suffering. All was so much the more dreadful to him, because at that time he did not know what was passing in the interior of the most blessed Virgin. He sought a few times to console Her and console himself by assisting and comforting Her. Although the voyage from Ephesus to Palestine usually lasted only about six days, this one lasted fifteen, of which fourteen were tempestuous. One day saint John was very much disheartened at the continuance of this measureless hardship and, no longer able to restrain himself, said "My

Lady, what is this? Are we to perish at sea? Beseech thy divine Son to look upon us with the eyes of a Father and to defend us in this tribulation." The blessed Mother answered him: "Do not be disturbed, my son; for we must now fight the battles of the Lord and overcome his enemies by fortitude and patience." I shall beg of Him that no one who is with us shall perish, and that He sleep not, who watches over Israel (Ps. 70, 4); the strong ones of his court assist us and defend us; let us suffer for Him who placed Himself upon the Cross for the salvation of all." At these words saint John recovered the necessary courage.

Lucifer and his demons with increasing fury threatened the powerful Queen by telling Her that She would perish in this sea and not escape alive. But these and other threats were but spent arrows and the most prudent Mother despised them, not even listening to them, or looking upon the demons, or speaking to them a single word. They themselves on the other hand could not bear even to glance at her face on account of the virtue of the Most High shining from it. And the more they strove to overcome this virtue, the weaker they became and the more were they tormented by those offensive weapons, with which the Lord had clothed his most holy Mother.

Saint Paul and saint Barnaby were aware of the return of the Queen of heaven when they came to Jerusalem. In his ardent desire of seeing Her saint Paul with saint Barnaby, at once sought her presence, and they cast themselves at her feet, shedding abundant tears of joy. Not less was the joy of the heavenly Mother at meeting these Apostles, toward whom She bore an especial love in the Lord on account of their zealous labors for the exaltation of God's name and the spread of the faith. The Mistress of the humble desired them to present themselves first to saint Peter and the rest, and last to Her, judging Herself to be the least of all creatures. But they, preserving the proper order in their reverence and love, thought that none should be preferred to Her who was the Mother of God, the Mistress of all creation and the beginning of all our happiness. The great Lady prostrated Herself before saint Paul and Barnaby, kissed their hands and asked for their blessing. On this occasion saint Paul was favored with a wonderful ecstatic abstraction, in which were revealed to him great mysteries and prerogatives of this mystical City of God, the Blessed Mary, and he saw Her as it were completely invested with the Divinity.

Saint Peter, as the head of the Church, had called upon the Apostles and disciples then in and around Jerusalem, and convoked them to a meeting in the presence of the Mistress of the world. In order that the most prudent Virgin, in her profound humility, might not absent Herself from this council, saint Peter had interposed his authority as Vicar of Christ. All of them being gathered, saint Peter said: "My brethren and children in Christ our Savior, it was necessary that we meet in order to solve the difficulties and decide upon the affairs, which our most beloved brethren Paul and Barnaby have brought to our notice, and to determine other matters touching the increase of the holy faith. For this it is proper that we engage in prayer to obtain the assistance of the Holy Ghost and we shall persevere therein for ten days as is our custom. On the first and on the last day we shall celebrate the sacrifice of the Mass, by which we shall dispose our hearts to receive the divine light." All of them approved of this arrangement. In order to celebrate the first Mass on the next day the

Queen prepared the hall of the Cenacle, cleaning and decorating it with her own hands and holding all things in readiness for the Communion of Herself together with the Apostles and disciples during those Masses. Saint Peter alone celebrated, observing all those rites and ceremonies which I have described, when speaking of the Masses on other occasions.

The other Apostles and disciples communicated at the hands of saint Peter; then the most blessed Mary, taking the last place. Many angels descended to the Cenacle. All those present saw them and at the time of the consecration the Cenacle was filled with a wonderful light and fragrance, through which the Lord wrought wonderful effects in their souls. Having celebrated the first Mass, they agreed upon certain hours, in which they were to persevere together in prayer, as far as they could without neglecting the necessary ministry of souls. The great Lady retired to a place, where She remained alone and motionless for those ten days without eating or speaking to any one. During that time She experienced such hidden mysteries as to move the angels to astonishment; and I find myself unable to describe what has been manifested to me concerning them. I will briefly indicate a small part of these mysteries, for to state all is impossible. The heavenly Mother having received holy Communion on the first of the ten days and retired to pray alone, at the command of the Lord, was immediately raised up by her angels and others there present to the empyrean heavens. Since She was taken up body and soul, one of the angels took her shape in order that the Apostles in the Cenacle might not become aware of her absence. They bore Her up with the splendor and magnificence described by me on other occasions. and on this occasion it was even greater on account of the designs of the Lord. When Mary arrived in a region of the air far removed from the earth, the almighty Lord commanded Lucifer and all his hellish hosts to come into the presence of the Queen into those higher regions. Immediately all of them came before Her and She saw them and knew them all just as they were and the condition they were in. The sight was somewhat painful to her, because the demons are so abominable and disgusting; but She was armed with divine virtue, so that She could not be harmed by this horrible and execrable sight. Not so the demons; for the Lord gave them to understand by an especial insight the greatness and superiority of that Woman, whom they were persecuting as their Enemy. They were made to perceive how foolishly presumptuous they had been in their attempts against Her. To their still greater terror they saw that She carried in her bosom the sacramental Christ and that the whole Divinity held Her as it were enveloped in its Omnipotence for their humiliation, overthrow and destruction.

The demons moreover heard a voice proceeding from the Deity itself, saying: "With this shield of my powerful arm, invincible and strong, I shall always defend my Church. This Woman shall crush the head of the ancient serpent (Gen. 3, 15), and shall forever triumph over its haughty pride for the glory of my holy name." All these and other mysteries of the most holy Mary the demons perceived and understood while they were gathered around Her in dismay. So great was the despair and crushing pain which they felt, that they, with loudest clamors, said: "May the power of the Almighty cast us immediately into hell, and let it not keep us in the presence of this Woman, who torments us more than the fire. O invincible and strong

46

Woman! Recede from us, since we ourselves cannot fly from thy presence, where we are bound by the chains of the Almighty. Why dost Thou also torment us before our time? (Matth. 8, 29). Thou alone of all human nature art the instrument of the Omnipotent against us; and through Thee men can acquire the eternal blessings we have lost. Those that have sunk into despair of ever seeing God eternally, are now rewarded for the accredited good works of their Redeemer by the vision of Thee, which in our hate is to us a torment and chastisement. Release us, almighty Lord and God; let this new punishment, in which Thou renewest that of our fall from heaven, cease; for in it Thou executest the punishment Thou hast threatened us with in this wonder of thy powerful arms."

During these and other lamentations of despair the demons were held spellbound in the presence of the Queen for a long time, and although thy made the most violent efforts to fly, they were not permitted to do it as fast as their fury urged them on. In order that the terror of the most holy Mary might strike them so much the deeper and become the more notorious, the Lord ordained, that She herself should use her authority as Mistress and Queen in permitting them to leave. At the instant in which She did this, all of them cast themselves, with all the swiftness in their power, from the upper regions into the abyss. They gave forth dreadful howls, terrorizing all the damned souls with new punishments, and, full of dismay and torments in not being able to deny their defeat, they proclaimed in their presence the power of the Almighty and of his holy Mother. Having won this triumph the most serene Empress proceeded on her way to the empyrean heaven, where She was received with new and admirable jubilee, remaining there for twenty-four hours.

She prostrated Herself before the throne of the most blessed Trinity and adored It in the unity of its undivided nature and majesty. She prayed for the Church, in order that the Apostles might understand and resolve what was proper for the establishment of the evangelical law and the termination of the law of Moses. In answer to these petitions She heard a voice from the throne, by which the three divine Persons, One after the Other and each One for Himself, promised to assist the Apostles and disciples in declaring and establishing the divine truth, assuring Her, that the Father would direct its establishment by his Omnipotence, the Son, as head of the Church, assist it by his Wisdom, and the Holy Ghost, as its Spouse, by his Love and his enlightening gifts. Then the heavenly Mother saw, that the most holy humanity of her Son presented to the Father the prayers and petitions, which She Herself had offered for the Church, and how, approving of them, He proposed the reasons why they should be fulfilled, in order that the faith of the Gospel and his entire holy law might be established in the world in accordance with the decrees of the divine will and mind.

Immediately, in execution of this will and proposal of Christ our Savior, the Lady saw issuing forth from the Divinity and immutable essence of God the form of a temple or Church, beautiful, clear and resplendent as if built of diamond or the sparkling crystal, adorned with many enamels and reliefs to enhance its beauty. The angels and saints saw it and in astonishment exclaimed: "Holy, holy, holy and powerful art Thou, Lord, in thy works" (Apoc. 4, 8). This Church or temple the most blessed Trinity placed in the hands of the most holy humanity of Christ, and, in a manner which cannot be described in words, He united it with

Himself.   Thereupon He turned it over to the most
holy Mother and as soon as Mary received it, She was
filled with new splendor.   She annihilated Herself within
Herself and then saw the Divinity, clearly and intuitively, by eminent and beatific vision.

The great Queen remained in this joy for many
hours, truly introduced into the cellar of fermented
wine spoken of in the Canticles (Canticle 8, 2).   Since
what She experienced and received there surpasses all
created thought or capacity, it suffices here to say, that
anew was ordered in Her love (Cant. 2, 4) and directed with new fervor toward the Church consigned
to Her under the above symbol.   Enriched by these favors, She was borne back by the angels to the Cenacle,
having in her hands the mystical temple She had received from her divine Son.   She remained in prayer
during the other nine days without motion and without
interrupting the acts, in which She had been left by the
beatific vision.   They fall not within human thought,
and can much less be indicated by human words.   Among
other things which She did, was to distribute the
treasures of the Redemption among the children of the
Church.   Commencing with the Apostles and going
through the different ages, She applied them separately
to the just and the saints, according to the secret disposition of eternal predestination.   The execution of these
decrees her divine Son had consigned to the most holy
Mary, giving Her dominion over the whole Church and
the dispensation of all the graces, that each one earns
through the merits of the Redemption.   Regarding a
mystery so exalted and hidden, I cannot say more than
this.

On the last of the ten days saint Peter celebrated
the other Mass and all received holy Communion as in the

first. Then, all being gathered in the name of the Lord, they invoked the Holy Ghost and began to consult about the solution of the difficulties that had arisen in the Church. Saint Peter, as the head and the highpriest, spoke first, then saint Paul and Barnaby, and saint James the Less, as is related by saint Luke in the fifteenth chapter of the Acts. The first decision of this council was, that the exact law of the circumcision and the law of Moses should not be imposed upon the baptized; since eternal salvation was given through Baptism and faith in Christ. Although saint Luke principally mentions only this decision, yet there were others, which defined certain matters concerning the government and the ceremonies of the Church, in order to stop some abuses introduced by the indiscreet piety of some of the faithful. This is held to be the first council of the Apostles, although they had also gathered to establish the Credo and other things as mentioned before. However, at that only the Apostles had convened, whereas now also those disciples took part, who could come. Also the manner of conferring and of resolving was different, being a formal decision, as is clear from the words of saint Luke: "It has seemed good to the Holy Ghost and to us," etc. (Luke 15, 28).

Couched in these terms the decision of the council was sent by letter to the faithful and to the churches of Antioch, Syria and Cilicia; and they remitted these letters through the hands of saint Paul and Barnaby and of other disciples. In order that the approbation of the Lord might not be wanting, it happened, that, both in the Cenacle at coming to their decision, and in Antioch when the letters were read before the faithful, the Holy Ghost descended in visible fire, so that all the faithful were consoled and confirmed in the Catholic truth.

The most holy Mary gave thanks to the Lord for the blessings thus bestowed upon the Church. She immediately despatched saint Paul and Barnaby with the rest and for their consolation She gave them as relics part of the clothes of Christ our Lord and some objects She had still left of the Passion. Offering them her protection and prayers, She sent them filled with new consolation and spiritual force upon the labors still awaiting them. During all these days of the council, on account of the terror with which most holy Mary had inspired him, Lucifer and his ministers could not come near the Cenacle; yet they prowled about in the distance, without being able to execute any of their malice against its members. Happy age, and fortunate congregation!

WORDS OF THE QUEEN.

My daughter, in the constancy and invincible fortitude with which I vanquished the demons, thou hast one of the most urgent motives for persevering in grace and acquiring great crowns. The human nature and that of the angels (even though they be devils) are subject to contrary and opposite conditions; for the spiritual nature is indefatigable, and that of mortals weak and so prone to fatigue, that it soon tires and succumbs in labor. As soon as it finds any difficulty in the practice of virtue it is discouraged and turns back; what it pursues with pleasure on one day, it contemns the next; what seemed agreeable today, it finds hard tomorrow; now it wishes, then again it does not wish; sometimes it is fervent, sometimes lukewarm. But the demon is never fatigued or weakened in his efforts at tempting souls. The Almighty, however, is not wanting in his providence; for He limits and restrains the power of the demons, so that they cannot pass the measure set for them, nor exert all their indefatigable powers for the persecution of souls. On the other hand He supports the weakness of men, giving them grace and strength to resist and overcome their enemies on the prescribed battleground.

Hence the inconstancy of souls in virtuously maintaining their position during temptation and in not bearing with fortitude and patience the inconveniences of doing good and fighting against the demons, is not excusable. The bent of passion, drawing man toward the sensible and pleasurable, suddenly presents itself across the path of duty and the demons, with diabolical astuteness, seek to exaggerate the hardship and disagreeableness of mortification, representing it as dangerous to health and life. Thus he deludes innumerable souls to precipitate themselves from one abyss to another. In this thou hast before thy eyes, my daughter, a very common aberration of the worldly-minded, but which is very abominable in the sight of the Lord and myself. Hence it is, that many men are weak, wavering and indisposed toward the practice of virtue or penitential mortification for their sins. And the very ones who are so weak in doing good, are strong in doing evil. In the service of the devil they are constant and are ready to undergo much more difficult and arduous tasks in sinning, than the law of God commands for the practice of virtue. They show themselves tardy and imbecile in the work of saving their souls, eager and strong to load upon themselves eternal damnation.

This damage also those who profess a life of perfection are wont in part to incur, if they unduly consider the hardships attached to such a life. Drawn into this deception, they either hinder their advance in perfection or afford the devil many victories in temptation. In order that thou, my daughter, mayest not incur this danger, thou shouldst consider the fortitude and constancy with which I resisted Lucifer and all hell, and the magnanimity with which I despised his illusions and temptations, not permitting myself to be disturbed, or to pay any attention to them; for this is the best way to overcome his haughty pride. Nor was I ever led by temptation to remissness in my labors or in my exercises; but I augmented them, together with my prayers, petitions and tears, as is necessary in the time of battle with those enemies. Hence I exhort thee to do the same in eager watchfulness; because thy temptations are not of the ordinary kind, but are directed against thee in highest malice and astuteness. Of this I have warned thee many times and this experience teaches thee.

Since thou hast noticed the great terror caused to the demons at perceiving the sacramental Lord resting in my bosom, I wish to call thy attention to two things. First, that for the overthrow of hell and for causing fear in the demons, all the holy Sacraments of the Church are most powerful means; but above all the holy sacrament of the Eucharist. This was one of the hidden purposes of the Lord my Son, in the institution of this sovereign mystery and of the other Sacraments. If in our time men do not ordinarily feel these powerful effects, it is because in the frequency of the reception of the Sacraments much of the veneration and estimation in receiving them has been lost. But do not doubt, that souls who frequent them with devotion and piety, are formidable to the demons and that they exercise great power and dominion over them in the same way as thou hast seen and described it of me. The explanation of this fact is: that this divine fire, in the pure souls, finds itself as it were in its own element. In me it was active to the limit of possibility in a mere creature, and therefore I inspired such terror to the demons.

CHAPTER III.

THE GOSPELS.

I have described, as far as I was permitted, the exalted state of the great Queen and Lady after the first council of the Apostles, and also her victories over the infernal dragon and his demons. Although the wonderful works which She accomplished during these times and at all times, cannot be recorded in a history, nor even summed up, I was nevertheless given special light for the purpose of describing the beginnings of the Gospels and the call of the Evangelists to undertake their writing, the part which Mary bore in their being written, her solicitous care for the absent Apostles, and the miracles She wrought for them. In the second part, and on many occasions I have stated, that the heavenly Mother had a positive knowledge of all the mysteries of grace, of the Gospels and other holy writings, which were to serve for the confirmation of the new Law. In this knowledge She was confirmed many times, especially on the day of her ascension with her divine Son into heaven. From that day on, without forgetting anything, She often prostrated Herself in prayer before the Lord, asking Him to send his divine light upon the Apostles and holy writers and to order them to write, when the opportune time should have come.

Afterwards, when the Queen returned from heaven and was put in charge of the Church (as related in the sixth chapter of this book), the Lord made known to Her that the time for beginning to write the holy Gos-

727

pels had arrived and that She should make her arrangements for this purpose as the Mistress and Instructress of the Church.   But in her profound humility and discretion She obtained the consent of the Lord, that this should be attended to by saint Peter, his vicar and the head of the Church; and that he should be specially assisted by divine enlightenment for a matter of such importance.   All this was granted by the Most High; and when the Apostles met in the council mentioned by saint Luke in the fifteenth chapter of the Acts, after they had settled the doubts about circumcision, as I described in the sixth chapter, saint Peter proposed to them all the necessity of recording in writing the mysteries of the life of Christ our Savior and Teacher, so that they might be preached to all the faithful in the Church without variation or difference, thus doing away with the old Law and establish the new.

Saint Peter had already consulted with the Mother of wisdom; and all the council having approved of his proposal, they called upon the Holy Ghost to point out the Apostles and disciples who should write the life of the Savior. Immediately a light was seen descending upon saint Peter and a voice was heard saying: "The highpriest and head of the Church shall assign four for recording the works and the teachings of the Savior of the world."   Saint Peter and all present prostrated themselves, giving thanks to the Lord for this favor.   When all of them had again risen, saint Peter spoke: "Matthew, our beloved brother, shall immediately begin to write his Gospel in the name of the Father, the Son and the Holy Ghost.   Mark shall be the second, who shall likewise write the Gospel in the name of the Father, the Son and the Holy Ghost. Luke shall write the third, in the name of the Father, the Son and the Holy Ghost.   Our most beloved brother John shall be the fourth and last to write the mysteries of our Savior and Teacher in the name of the Father, the Son and the Holy Ghost." This decision the Lord confirmed by permitting the heavenly light to remain until these words were repeated and formally accepted by all those appointed.

Within a few days saint Matthew set about writing the first Gospel. While praying in a retired room of the Cenacle and asking to be enlightened for the inception of his history, the most blessed Mary appeared to him seated on a throne of great majesty and splendor, the doors of the room still remaining closed. The great Lady told him to arise, which he did, asking for her benediction. Then She spoke to him and said: "Matthew, my servant, the Almighty sends me with his blessing, in order that with it thou begin the writing of the Gospel which thou hast the good fortune to be entrusted with. In this thou shalt have the assistance of the Holy Ghost and I shall beg it for thee with all my heart. But concerning myself it is not proper, that thou write anything except what is absolutely necessary for manifesting the Incarnation and other mysteries of the Word made man, and for establishing his faith in the world as the foundation of his Church. This faith being established, the Almighty will find other persons, who, when the times arrive in which it shall become necessary, shall reveal to the faithful the mysteries and blessings wrought by his powerful arm in me." Saint Matthew signified his willingness to obey the mandate of the Queen; and while he conferred with Her about composing his Gospel, the Holy Ghost came down upon him in visible form; and in the presence of the Lady He began to write the words as they are still extant in his Gospel. The blessed Mary then left him and saint Matthew proceeded in his history, finishing it in Judea. He wrote it in the Hebrew language in the year forty-two of our Lord.

The Evangelist Mark wrote his gospel four years later, in the forty-sixth year after the birth of Christ. He likewise wrote it in Hebrew and while in Palestine. Before commencing he asked his guardian angel to notify the Queen of heaven of his intention and to implore her assistance for obtaining the divine enlightenment for what he was about to write. The kind Mother heard his prayer and immediately the Lord commanded the angels to carry Her with the usual splendor and ceremony to the Evangelist, who was still in prayer. The great Queen appeared to him seated on a most beautiful and resplendent throne. Prostrating himself before Her, he said: "Mother of the Savior of the world and Mistress of all creation, I am unworthy of this favor, though I am a servant of thy divine Son and of Thyself." The heavenly Mother answered: "The Most High, whom thou servest and lovest, sends me to assure thee, that thy prayers are heard and that his holy Spirit shall direct thee in the writing of the Gospel, with which He has charged thee." Then She told him not to write of the mysteries pertaining to Her, just as She had asked of saint Matthew. Immediately the Holy Ghost, in visible and most refulgent shape, descended upon saint Mark, enveloping him in light and filling him with interior enlightenment; and in the presence of the Queen he began to write his Gospel. At that time the Princess of heaven was sixty-one years of age. Saint Jerome says, that saint Mark wrote his short Gospel in Rome, at the instance of the faithful residing there; but I wish to call attention to the fact, that this was a translation or copy of the one he had written in Palestine; for the Christians in Rome possessed neither his nor any other Gospel, and therefore he set about writing one in the Roman or Latin language.

Two years afterwards, in the year forty-eight and of the Virgin the sixty-third, saint Luke wrote his Gospel in the Greek language. To him also, as to the others, Mary appeared when he was about to begin it. Having represented to the heavenly Mother, that, in order to manifest the Incarnation and life of her divine Son, it was necessary to touch upon the manner of the actual conception of the Word made man and upon other things concerning her dignity as the natural Mother of Christ, and having received orders from Her to pass over in silence the other mysteries and wonders connected with her dignity as Mother of God, saint Luke obtained her permission to write somewhat more freely of the heavenly Mary in his Gospel. The Holy Ghost descended upon him and in the presence of the great Queen he began to write his Gospel, drawing his information principally from direct inspiration of her Majesty. Saint Luke continued a most devoted servant of the Lady and never permitted the image of the sweetest Mother seated on the throne of majesty, as he had seen Her on this occasion, to be effaced from his mind. Thenceforward he lived continually in her presence. Saint Luke was in Achaia, when this apparition happened to him, and there also he wrote his Gospel.

The last of the four Evangelists who wrote the Gospels, was the apostle saint John in the year fifty-eight of the Lord. He wrote his in the Greek language, during his stay in Asia Minor after the glorious transition and assumption of the most blessed Mary. His Gospel was directed against the heresies and errors, which, (as indicated above), the devil immediately after the transition of the Virgin Mother began to sow for undermining the faith in the Incarnation of the divine Word. For as Lucifer had been humiliated and vanquished by this mystery, he at once directed the onslaught of heresy against it. For this reason the evangelist saint John writes so sublimely and adduces so many arguments for the true and undoubted Divinity of Christ our Savior, far surpassing the other Evangelists in this regard.

Although when the Evangelist was about to begin his Gospel the most blessed Mary was already in heaven, She descended in person, resplendent with ineffable glory and majesty and surrounded by thousands of angels of all choirs and hierarchies. Appearing to saint John She said: "John, my son and servant of the Most High, now is the proper time for writing the life and mysteries of my divine Son, so that all mortals may know Him as the Son of the eternal Father, as true God and at the same time as true man. But it is not yet the opportune time for recording the mysteries and secrets which thou knowest of me; nor shall they as yet be manifested to a world so accustomed to idolatry, lest Lucifer abuse them for disturbing those who are to receive the faith in their Redeemer and in the blessed Trinity. The Holy Ghost will assist thee and I desire thee to begin writing in my presence." The Evangelist worshipped the great Queen of heaven and was filled with the divine Spirit as the others had been. Assisted by the kind Mother, he immediately set about writing his Gospel. Before She departed to the right hand of her divine Son, She gave him her benediction and promised him her protection for all the rest of his life. Such were the beginnings of the sacred Gospels, all of them having been commenced with the assistance and by the intervention of the most blessed Mary, giving the Church to understand, that all these benefits have been vouch-safed at her hands. After having thus anticipated the history of the Evangelists, in order to account for the beginnings of the Gospels, we shall now return to our narrative.

In proportion as the most blessed Lady after the council of the Apostles was exalted by her divine knowledge and the abstractive vision of God, so her care and solicitude for the welfare of the Church increased; for the faith was now spreading out over the earth day by day. As a true Mother and Teacher, She lavished her special attention upon the Apostles, whose names and whose welfare She bore written in her heart. All of them, except saint John and saint James the less, immediately after the termination of the council, left Jerusalem for the field of their labors, and the kindest Mother was deeply concerned at the thought of the hardships and difficulties connected with their preaching. She looked upon them with tender pity in their peregrinations, and held them in highest veneration on account of their holiness and dignity as priests, as Apostles of her divine Son, founders of the Church, preachers of his doctrine, and as the elect of the divine Wisdom chosen for such high ministries to the glory of the Most High. It was truly necessary that the most blessed Lady and Mistress, in order to attend to and take care of so many matters throughout the holy Church, should be raised to the state which She now held: for in any lower condition She could not have so easily and properly attended to so many duties and at the same time maintain that interior tranquillity and peace, which her soul enjoyed.

Besides her own knowledge and solicitude for the whole Church, the most holy Mother again charged her angels to take care of all the Apostles and disciples, to console them in all their tribulations and to haste to their aid in all their difficulties. For by the subtlety of their spiritual nature they could attend to all this without losing sight of the face of God and enjoying beatific vision. She thus charged them because it was so important to establish the Church and because they were the ministers of the Most High and the works of his hands. She told them also to inform Her of all that the Apostles and disciples were doing, and especially when they were in need of any clothing; for to this matter the watchful Mother wished to attend in particular, in order that they might go about clothed in a uniform manner, such as they wore when they departed from Jerusalem. By this prudent foresight, the Apostles showed no difference in their garments as long as the great Lady was alive; but all of them wore clothes of the same form and color, similar to that worn by her divine Son. Assisted by the holy angels, She wove with her own hand the tunics for this purpose and sent them through the angels to the Apostles on their journeys. In thus making it possible for them to wear vestments similar to those which had been worn by Christ our Savior, the great Mother provided that even in their exterior appearance the Apostles preached his doctrines and his most holy life. In regard to the other necessities of life, such as food, She left them to begging and to the labor of their hands, or to the alms which were offered to them.

At the orders of the Queen the angels frequently assisted the Apostles in their travels and tribulations and in the persecutions as well of the gentiles and the Jews, as of the demons, who continually excited evil-minded men against the preachers of the Gospel. The angels often visited them in visible shapes, conversing with them and consoling them in the name of the most blessed Mary. At other times they performed the same office interiorly without manifesting themselves; sometimes they freed them from prison; sometimes they warned them of dangers and snares; sometimes they accompanied them on their way or carried them from one place to another where they were to preach, or informed them of what they were to do according to the circumstances peculiar to certain places or peoples. Of all these things they also kept their blessed Lady informed; for She took care of all of them and labored with them more than all of them together. It is not possible to enumerate the cares, solicitudes and diligent doings of this kindest Mother; for not a day or a night passed, in which She did not perform many miracles for the Apostles and for the Church. Besides all this She wrote to them many times, animating them with heavenly exhortations and doctrines, and filling them with consolation and strength.

WORDS OF THE QUEEN.

My dearest daughter, at other times I have spoken to thee of a complaint, which I have against the children of the Church, and especially against the women, in whom the fault is greater. In my sight it is abominable, because it is so much opposed to my own conduct in life. I repeat it here, in order that thou mayest imitate me and keep away from what the foolish women and daughters of Belial are guilty of: namely, treating the priests of the Most High without reverence, esteem, or respect. This fault increases day by day in the Church, and therefore I renew this warning already several times recorded. Tell me, my daughter, what must be thought of the fact, that priests, the anointed of the Lord, appointed to represent Christ and to consecrate his body and blood, are serving vile, impure, and earthly

47

women? That they should stand uncovered and do reverence to a proud and miserable woman, only because she is rich and they are poor? I ask, has the poor priest less dignity than the rich? Or do riches confer a greater or equal dignity, power and excellence, than the one given to priests and ministers by my divine Son? The angels have no regard for the rich on account of their possessions, but they respect priests for their exalted dignity. Hence, how could such an abuse and perversity creep into the Church, that the anointed of the Lord should be outraged and despised by the faithful, who know and confess them to be sanctified by Christ himself?

It is true that the priests themselves are very guilty and reprehensible when they, disregarding their dignity, enslave themselves to the service of other men, and much more, of women. But if priests have some excuse in their poverty, the rich have none in their pride, that they should, on account of the poverty of the priests, oblige them to be servants, when in reality they are masters. This monstrosity is very abominable to the saints and very disagreeable in my eyes on account of the veneration I had for the priests. Great was my dignity as Mother of God; yet I often prostrated myself at their feet and considered it a great happiness to kiss the ground on which they trod. But the blindness of the world has obscured the sacerdotal dignity and confounded the precious with the vile (Jer. 15, 19); it has lowered the priests to the position of the common people by its laws and disorderly customs (Is. 25, 2), making use of the one as well as the other for their degradation; and the same minister who now at the altar offers the tremendous sacrifice of the sacred body and blood, afterwards leaves it to serve and subject himself to the service even of women, who by nature and by the condition are so inferior, and sometimes are made even more unworthy by their sins.

I wish then, my daughter, that thou seek to make up for this fault and abuse among the children of the Church as far as possible. I give thee to understand, that even from my throne in heaven I look with veneration and respect upon the priests who are on earth. Thou must always regard them with the same veneration, as if they were at the altar, or holding the most blessed Sacrament in their hands or at their breast; and even the ornaments and all their vestments thou shouldst hold in great veneration, just as I with reverence provided garments for the Apostles.

CHAPTER IV.

HER DEVOTION TO THE PASSION OF CHRIST AND TO THE
HOLY EUCHARIST—HOW SHE CELEBRATED THE
IMMACULATE CONCEPTION AND OTHER
FEASTS.

Without ever failing in her attention to the exterior government of the Church (as I have until now made plain), the most blessed Mary in secret practiced other exercises and good works, by which She merited innumerable gifts and blessings from the Most High, as well for the common benefit of all the faithful, as for myriads of particular souls in furtherance of their salvation. As far as I can in these last chapters, I shall, for our instruction and admiration and for the glory of the most blessed Mother, write of these hidden and unknown works. First of all I will state, that notwithstanding the many privileges which the great Queen of heaven enjoyed, She constantly kept present in her memory the doings and the mysteries of the life of her divine Son; for besides the abstractive vision, by which She in these last years continually saw the Divinity and knew all things, the Lord had from her Conception conceded to Her the privilege of never forgetting what once She had known or understood; for in this regard She enjoyed the privilege of an angel, as I have stated in the first part.

I also stated in the second part, in writing of the Passion, that the blessed Mother felt in her body and purest soul all the pains and torments of our Savior Jesus, so that none of them were hidden to Her or without the corresponding suffering in her own self. All the images or impressions of the Passion remained imprinted in her interior just as She had received them; for She had made this request of her Lord.

Hence She ordered all her occupations in such a manner, that She might at all times preserve in her heart the image of her divine Son, afflicted, outraged, wounded and disfigured by the torments of his Passion, and within Herself She beheld this image as in a most clear mirror. She heard the injuries, outrages, affronts and blasphemies against Him, with all the circumstances of time and place, and She beheld the whole Passion as in one living and penetrating vista. Throughout the day this sorrowful vision excited Her to most heroic acts of virtue and stirred her sorrow and compassion; but her most prudent love did not content itself with these exercises. During stated hours and times She engaged in other exercises with her holy angels, especially with those I have mentioned in the first part as bearing the tokens or the escutcheons of the instruments of the Passion. These in the first place, and then the other angels, She engaged as assistants in the following exercises.

For each kind of the wounds and sufferings of Christ our Savior She recited special prayers and salutations, in order to give them special adoration and worship. For each of the contemptuous and insulting words of the Jews and his other enemies, which had been spoken either in envy or in fury or vengeance, for each of the blasphemies uttered, She composed special hymns of veneration and honor to make up for their attempts at diminishing it. For the insulting gestures, mockeries and personal injuries, She practiced most profound humiliations, genuflections and prostrations, and in this manner She sought continually to make up for the affronts and injuries heaped upon her divine Son in his life and his passion; and thus She confessed his Divinity, his humanity, his holiness, his miracles, his works and his doctrines. For all She gave Him glory and magnificence; and in all the holy angels joined Her, and corresponded with Her full of admiration of such wisdom, fidelity and love united in a mere creature.

Even if the most blessed Mother during her whole life had engaged in no other occupation than these exercises, She would have accomplished and merited more than all the saints in all that they have done or suffered for God. By the force of love her sorrow in these exercises was equal to martyrdom many times over; and many times would She have died in them, if the divine power had not sustained her life for still greater merit and glory. And if, as is true, She in her immense charity offered all these works for the Church, let us consider how much we are in her debt as faithful children for thus increasing the treasures of help, which She left at the disposal of us unfortunate children of Eve. And in order that our meditation may not be half-hearted and lukewarm, I will say, that the effects of her contemplations were often astounding; many times She wept tears of blood, which covered her whole face; at other times in her agony She was not only bathed in perspiration, but in a bloody sweat, running from Her even to the ground. What is more, sometimes her heart was wrenched from its natural position by the violence of her grief; and when She was in such extremes, her divine Son came from heaven, furnishing Her with new strength and life to soothe her sorrow and heal the wounds caused by love of Him, and in order that by such assistance and comfort, She might continue the exercises of her compassion.

The Lord however wished Her to lay aside these sorrowful sentiments and affections on the days in which She commemorated the mystery of his Resurrection, as I will speak of later on, in order that there might be maintained the proper relation between cause and effect. For some of these sorrows were incompatible with the favors overflowing in their effects upon the body, yet excluding pain. But She never lost sight of his sufferings and therefore felt other effects of her compassion by uniting with her joys, the gratitude for what the Lord endured. Thus in the sweetness of all the favors of the Lord his Passion entered as a mixture of bitterness. She obtained also the consent of the evangelist saint John to remain retired in her oratory for celebrating the death and burial of her divine Son on the Friday of each week. On those days saint John remained in the Cenacle to receive those who called upon Her and allowed none to disturb Her; and whenever he could not attend to this duty, it was performed by some other disciple. The most blessed Mary retired for this exercise at five o'clock on Thursday and did not reappear until toward noon of Sunday. In order that during these three days no important matter pertaining to the government of the Church might be neglected, the great Lady appointed one of her angels to take her shape and briefly despatch what would suffer no delay, so provident and attentive was She in all affairs of charity touching her children and domestics.

To describe or comprehend what happened with our heavenly Mother during the exercises of these three days can never be within our capacity; the Lord alone, who was the Author of them, shall one day manifest it to us in the light of the saints. Also what I myself have come to know of it, I am unable to describe; I will only say that beginning with the washing of the feet, the most blessed Mary commemorated all the mysteries up to that of the Resurrection; and in each hour and moment She renewed in Herself all the movements, actions, works and sufferings as they had happened in her divine Son. She repeated the same prayers and petitions as He himself had made and as we have seen described in their place. Anew the most pure Mother felt in her virginal body all the pains endured by Christ our Savior. She carried the Cross and placed Herself upon it. In short, I will say, that as long as She lived, the whole passion of her divine Son was renewed in Her week for week. Through this exercise the great Queen gained great favors and blessings for those who devoutly bear in mind the Lord's passion; and hence the powerful Queen has promised to all such souls, especial assistance and participation in the treasures of the Passion; for She desired from her inmost heart, that the Church should continue and preserve its commemoration. In virtue of her wishes and prayers the Lord ordained, that afterwards many persons in the holy Church should follow these exercises of the Passion, imitating his most blessed Mother, who was the first one to teach and practice such an exalted profession.

In these exercises the great Queen sought especially to celebrate the institution of the most blessed Sacrament by new hymns of praise, of thanksgiving and fervent love. She was solicitous to invite for this purpose her own angels and many others from the empyrean heaven, in order to assist and accompany Her in these praises of the Lord. It was a wonder worthy of his Omnipotence, that the Most High should send from heaven multitudes of angels to view this prodigy of Christ's remaining sacramentally present in her heart from one Communion to the other and to incite them to give glory and praise for the wonderful effects of his sacramental presence in this Creature, whom they beheld more pure and more holy than the angels and seraphim and the like of which they had not seen or would ever see in all the rest of creation.

It was not less wonderful to them (just as it ought to be to us) to see, that though the great Queen was worthy of preserving within Herself the sacred species as in a tabernacle, She was so solicitous in preparing Herself anew by the most fervid exercises and devotions every time She was again to receive holy Communion; and this She did nearly every day except on those in which She remained in her oratory. She first offered up for this purpose her weekly exercises of the Passion; and besides this, whenever She retired at nightfall before the day of Communion, She began other exercises, such as prostrations in the form of a cross, genuflections, prayers, and adorations of the immutable essence of God. She asked permission of the Lord to speak to Him and to permit Her, in spite of her earthly lowliness, to partake of his Son in the holy Sacrament; She appealed to his infinite bounty and to his love toward the Church in thus remaining sacramentally present, as a reason that She should be favored with this blessing. She offered to Him his own Passion and Death, the worthiness with which He had communicated Himself, the union of his human nature with the divine, all his works from the moment of his conception in the virginal womb, all the virtue of the angelic nature and its works, of all the just in past, present and future times.

Then she made most intense acts of humility, professing Herself but dust and ashes in comparison with the infinite being of God, to which the highest creatures are so inferior and unequal. In the contemplation of what She was to receive sacramentally, She was so affected and so deeply moved, that it is impossible to describe it in words; for She raised Herself and transcended above the choirs of seraphim and cherubim; and as, in her own estimation, She considered Herself the lowest of all creatures, She called upon her guardian angels and upon all the other angels, asking them, with incomparable humility, to supplicate the Lord to dispose and prepare Her for receiving Him worthily, since She was but an inferior and earthly creature. The holy angels, obeying Her in joyful admiration, assisted and accompanied Her in these petitions, in which She persevered for the greater part of the night preceding her Communion.

As the wisdom of the great Queen, although in itself finite, is for us incomprehensible, we can never worthily understand to what height rose her virtues and works of love on these occasions. But they were often of such a kind as to oblige the Lord to respond by a personal visit, in which He gave Her to understand with what pleasure He came to dwell sacramentally in her heart and to renew in Her the pledges of his infinite love. When the hour of her Communion arrived, She first heard the Mass usually celebrated by the Evangelist. In these Masses, although the Epistles and Gospels, being not yet written, were not read, the consecration was always the same as now, and to it were added other rites and ceremonies with many psalms and orations. At the end of Mass the heavenly Mother approached, making three most profound genuflections; all inflamed with love She received her Son in the Sacrament, welcoming in her purest bosom and heart that same God, to whom She had given the most sacred humanity in her virginal womb. Having communicated, She retired, and, unless some very urgent need of her fellowmen demanded otherwise, remained alone for three hours. During these hours the Evangelist was often privileged to see rays of light darting forth from Her as from the sun.

The prudent Mother also provided that for the celebration of the unbloody sacrifice of the Mass the Apostles and priests be clothed in ornate and mysterious vestments, different from those they wore in ordinary life. Accordingly, with her own hands, She provided ornaments and sacerdotal vestments for its celebration, thus originating the ceremonious observances in the Church. Although these vestments were not quite of the same form as nowadays; yet they were not materially different in appearance from those which in the course of time came into use in the Roman Church. The material was more alike; for She made them of linen and rich silks, purchased with the alms and presents made to Her. Whenever She worked at these vestments, sewing or fitting them, She remained on her knees or on her feet, and She would not entrust them to other sacristans than the angels, who assisted and helped Her in all these things; likewise She kept these ornaments and all that pertained to the service of the altar in incredible order and cleanliness; and from such hands as hers, all came forth with a celestial fragrance, which enkindled the spirit of the ministers.

From many kingdoms and provinces, where the Apostles were preaching, numbers of converts came to Jerusalem in order to visit and converse with the Mother of the Redeemer of the world, at the same time offering rich gifts. Among others, four sovereign princes, who were royal governors of provinces, visited Her and brought many valuable presents, which they placed at her disposal for her own use and for the Apostles and disciples. The great Lady answered that She was poor like her Son, and that the Apostles likewise were poor in imitation of their Master; that hence these riches were not appropriate to the life they professed. They begged Her to console them by accepting their gifts for the poor or for the divine worship. On account of their persistent requests She received part of what they offered, and from the rich silks She made some ornaments for the altar; the rest She distributed among the indigent and the infirmaries. For She was accustomed to visit such places and often served and washed the poor with her own hands, performing such services, as well as distributing the alms, on her knees. Wherever it was possible She consoled the needy and assisted the sick in their last agony. Nor did She ever rest from works of charity, either actually engaging in them, or pleading and praying for others in her retirement.

During these last years the Queen ate or slept very little; and this little only, because saint John asked Her to rest for at least a small portion of the night. But this sleep was only a slight suspension of the senses, lasting no longer than a half hour, during which, in the manner above described, She lost not the vision of the Divinity. Her food was a few mouthfuls of ordinary bread and sometimes a little fish, taken at the instance of the Evangelist and in order to keep him company; for in this, as in other privileges, saint John was thus fortunate, not only eating with Her from the same table, but having the food prepared for him by the great Queen and administered to him as from a mother to her son, and moreover being obeyed by Her as a priest and a substitute of Christ. Very well could the great Queen get along without even this sleep or nourishment, which seemed more a ceremony than the sustenance of life; but She partook of them not from necessity, but in order to practice obedience and humility and thus pay some tribute to human nature; for in all things She was most prudent.

All the offices and titles of honor, which the most blessed Mary held in the Church, that of Queen, Mistress, Mother, Governess and Teacher, and all the rest, were given to her by the Omnipotent not as empty and fruitless names, but were accompanied by the superabundant plenitude of grace which is proper and which the Almighty can communicate to each. This plenitude consisted in this, that as Queen She knew all that concerned her reign and its extent; as Mistress She knew the measure of her power; as Mother She knew all the children and dependents of her household, without excepting anyone through all the ages of the Church until the end; as Governess She knew all that were subject to Her; and as Teacher, She possessed the wisdom and science through which the holy Church, by her intercession, was to be instructed and guided, while enjoying the presence and the influence of the Holy Ghost until the end of the world.

Hence our great Queen had a clear knowledge not only of all the saints that preceded or followed Her in the Church, of their lives, their works, their deaths, and rewards in heaven; but also of all the rites, ceremonies, decisions, and festivities of the Church in course of the ages, and of all the reasons, motives, necessities and opportunities, in and for which they were established with the assistance of the Holy Ghost. For He gives us our spiritual nourishment in proper time for the glory of the Lord and the increase of the holy Church. As I have spoken of this matter in the course of this history, especially in the second part, I need not repeat it here. From her full knowledge and her corresponding holiness, there arose within the heavenly Instructress a certain thankful eagerness, to introduce into the Church militant the worship, veneration and festivities observed by the holy angels in the triumphant Jerusalem, and thus imitate, as far as was possible, what She had so often seen done in heaven for the praise and glory of the Most High.

In this more than seraphic spirit She commenced to practice by Herself many of the ceremonies, rites and exercises, which were afterwards introduced in the Church; and these She also inculcated and impressed upon the Apostles, in order that they might introduce them as far as the circumstances then allowed. She not only invented the exercises of the Passion, of which I have spoken above, but many other customs and ceremonies, which were later on received in the churches, in the congregations and religions. For whatever She knew as pertaining to the worship of the Lord or the practice of virtue, She performed, and in her wisdom She was ignorant of nothing that ought to be known. Among these exercises and rites was the celebration of the feasts of the Lord and of Herself, in order to renew the memory of the benefits for which She stood indebted, as well the benefits relating in general to the human race, as those especially referring to Herself, striving thus to give thanks and adoration for all. Although She had spent her whole life in this pursuit without relaxation or forgetfulness, yet, when She entered upon this new mysterious phase of her life, She prepared to signalize these feast days by celebrating them with exercises founded on a deeper insight. As I will speak of the other festivals in the following chapters, I will describe here only how She celebrated her Immaculate Conception and Nativity, the first mysteries of her life. These commemorations or feasts She had begun to celebrate since the Incarnation of the Word; but She celebrated them more particularly after the Ascension, and especially in these last years of her life.

On the eighth day of December of each year She celebrated her Immaculate Conception with a jubilee and gratitude beyond all human words; for this privilege was for the great Queen of the highest importance and value. She imagined Herself altogether incapable of ever acknowledging it with sufficient gratitude. She commenced her exercises on the evening before and spent the whole night in admirable devotions, shedding tears of joy, humiliating Herself, prostrating Herself, and singing the praises of the Lord. She deeply reflected, that She was formed of the same earth and descended from Adam according to the common order of nature; that She was preserved and exempted from the weight of the same guilt and conceived with such a plenitude of graces and gifts only because She was set apart and snatched from the rest by the Almighty. She invited her own angels to help Her to return proper thanks, and in union with them She alternated new songs of praise. Then She asked the same favor of the rest of the angels and saints in heaven; but during all this time the divine love so inflamed Her, that the Lord was obliged to strengthen Her, lest all her natural forces be consumed and death ensue.

After She had spent the whole night in these exercises, Christ descended from heaven and the angels raised Her to his royal throne in heaven, where the celebration of the feast was continued with new glory and to the accidental joy of the courtiers of the heavenly Jerusalem. There the blessed Mother prostrated Herself and adored the most holy Trinity, again giving thanks for the benefit of her immunity from sin and her Immaculate Conception.   Then She again took her place at the right hand of Christ her Son and the Lord himself as it were acknowledged the goodness of the eternal Father in having given Him a Mother so worthy and so full of grace, exempt from the common guilt of Adam.   Anew the three divine Persons confirmed upon Her this privilege, as it were ratifying and approving it and pleasing Themselves in thus having distinguished Her among all the creatures.   In order to give repeated testimony to this truth, a voice proceeded from the throne in the name of the Father, saying: "Beautiful are thy footsteps, O prince's Daughter, conceived without sin."   Another in the name of the Son, said: "Altogether pure and without contact of guilt is my Mother, who gave Me human form to redeem men."   And in the name of the Spirit: "All fair art thou, my Spouse, all fair art thou and without stain of the universal guilt."

In between these voices were heard the choirs of all the angels and saints, singing in sweetest harmony: "Most holy Mary, conceived without original sin." To all these honors the most prudent Mother answered by thanksgiving, worship and praise of the Most High, rendered with such profound humility that it passed all angelic understanding.   In order to conclude the solemnity She was raised to the intuitive and beatific vision of the most holy Trinity; and after enjoying this glory for some hours, She was brought back by the angels to the Cenacle. This was the manner in which her Immaculate Conception was solemnized after the Ascension of her divine Son.

WORDS OF THE QUEEN.

My daughter, through the whole course of my life is evident how gratefully I kept in mind the works of the Redemption, the passion and death of my divine

Son, especially after I had actually seen Him sacrificed on the Cross for the salvation of men. But in this chapter particularly have I wished to draw thy attention to the care and the continual exercises, by which I renewed in me not only the remembrance, but the sufferings of the Passion. I desire that the knowledge of this cause men to feel reproach and confusion at their monstrous forgetfulness of the incomprehensible benefit of the Redemption. O what a shameful, what a horrible and dangerous ingratitude of men is this! Forgetfulness is a clear proof of contempt, for one does not forget so easily, what one holds dear. What reason or excuse then can there be, that men forget the eternal blessings they have received? That they should despise the love, with which the eternal Father has delivered over to death his only begotten Son? The charity and patience with which his and my Son accepted it for them (John 3, 16.) The insensible earth responds to the efforts of those that cultivate it; wild beasts become tame and domesticated in return for benefits. Men among themselves are beholden to their benefactors; and when such thankful feelings are not forthcoming, they resent it, condemn it, and call it a great offense.

What is the reason then, that only toward their God and Redeemer they should be ungrateful and forget what He suffered in order to rescue them from eternal damnation? And in view of this very evil return, they complain of not receiving his assistance as they desire. In order that they may understand what fearful guilt they load upon themselves by their ingratitude, I will remind thee, my daughter, that Lucifer and his demons, seeing so many souls oblivious of the sufferings of Christ, draw the following conclusions and say of such souls: "This soul does not remember or hold in esteem the benefit of God's Redemption and we are certain of gaining it over to our side; for the soul that is so foolish as not to remember such a blessing, will certainly not detect our wiles.   Let us proceed to tempt and destroy it, since it is deprived of its strongest defense."   Having in their large experience found their reasoning on this point to be almost infallible, they zealously seek to blot out the memory of the passion and death of Christ and to excite a contempt for the preaching or discoursing about it among men; and they have succeeded to a great extent, causing dreadful damage to souls.   On the other hand they are wary and fearful of tempting those who have accustomed themselves to the meditation and the remembrance of the sufferings of Christ; for from this source they feel issuing against them a force and influence, which often prevents them from approaching those who thus piously cherish the memory of the Passion.

In order to dispose thyself day by day for holy Communion thou shouldst apply whatever thou performest in these exercises; imitate also the other works and practices, which thou hast come to know of me.   If I, the Mother of Him whom I was to receive, deemed myself unworthy of Communion and by so many means sought the purity necessary for such a Sacrament, consider what thou must do, so poor and subject to so many miseries and imperfections!   Purify the temple of thy interior, scrutinizing it by the divine light and adorning it with great virtues, since it is the eternal God, whom thou art to receive; One, of whom nobody but Himself is worthy.   Invoke the intercession of the angels and saints to obtain grace from the Lord.   Above all I exhort thee to call upon me and ask me to help thee; for thou must know, that I am the special Advocate and Protectress of those, who desire to arrive at great purity for receiving holy Communion. Whenever they invoke me for this purpose, I present myself before the throne of the Most High, and, as one well knowing the disposition required for harboring God himself, I ask his favor and grace for those who are about to receive Him in the holy Sacrament. I have not lost in heaven the solicitude and zeal, which I exhibited upon earth. Having asked me, proceed to ask also the intercession of the angels, for they also are very anxious to see souls approach the holy Eucharist with great devotion and purity.

CHAPTER V.

In writing of what still remains of the history of our Lady, of our only and heavenly Phœnix, the most blessed Mary, it is no more than right that our hearts be filled with tenderness and our eyes with tears at the sweet and touching marvels of the last years of her life. I should wish to exhort the devout faithful not to read of them nor consider them as past and absent, since the powerful virtue of faith can make these truths present to the mind; and if we look upon them with the proper piety and Christian devotion, without a doubt we shall gather the sweetest fruit, and our hearts shall feel the effects and rejoice in the good, which our eyes cannot see.

The most holy Mary had arrived at the age of sixty-seven years without having tarried in her career, ceased in her flight, mitigated the flame of her love, or lessened the increase of her merits from the first instant of her Conception. As all this had continued to grow in each moment of her life, the ineffable gifts, benefits and favors of the Lord had made Her entirely godlike and spiritual; the affectionate ardors and desires of her most chaste heart did not allow Her any rest outside the centre of her love; the bounds of the flesh were most violently irksome; the overwhelming attraction of the Divinity to unite Itself with Her with eternal and most close bonds, (according to our mode of speaking) had attained the summit of power in Her; and the earth itself, made unworthy by the sins of mortals to contain the Treasure of heaven, could no longer bear the strain of withholding

Her from her true Lord. The eternal Father desired his only and true Daughter; the Son his beloved and most loving Mother; and the Holy Ghost the embraces of his most beautiful Spouse. The angels longed for their Queen, the saints for their great Lady; and all the heavens mutely awaited the presence of their Empress who should fill them with glory, with her beauty and delight. All that could be alleged in favor of Her still remaining in the world and in the Church, was the need of such a Mother and Mistress, and the love, which God himself had for the miserable children of Adam.

But as some term and end was to be placed to the earthly career of our Queen, the divine consistory (according to our mode of understanding), conferred upon the manner of glorifying the most blessed Mother and established the kind of loving reward due to Her for having so copiously fulfilled all the designs of the divine mercy among the children of Adam during the many years in which She had been the Foundress and Teacher of his holy Church. The Almighty therefore resolved to delight and console Her by giving Her definite notice of the term still remaining of her life and revealing to Her the day and hour of the longed for end of her earthly banishment. For this purpose the most blessed Trinity despatched the archangel Gabriel with many others of the celestial hierarchies, who should announce to the Queen when and how her mortal life should come to an end and pass over into the eternal.

The holy prince descended with the rest to the Cenacle in Jerusalem and entered the oratory of the great Lady, where they found Her prostrate on the ground in the form of a cross, asking mercy for sinners. But hearing the sound of their music and perceiving them present, She rose to her knees in order to hear the message and show respect to the ambassador of heaven and his companions, who in white and refulgent garments surrounded Her with wonderful delight and reverence. All of them had come with crowns and palms in their hands, each one with a different one; but all of them represented the diverse premiums and rewards of inestimable beauty and value to be conferred upon their great Queen and Lady. Gabriel saluted Her with the Ave Maria, and added thereto: "Our Empress and Lady, the Omnipotent and the Holy of the holy sends us from his heavenly court to announce to Thee in his name the most happy end of thy pilgrimage and banishment upon earth in mortal life. Soon, O Lady, is that day and hour approaching, in which, according to thy longing desires, Thou shalt pass through natural death to the possession of the eternal and immortal life, which awaits Thee in the glory and at the right hand of thy divine Son, our God. Exactly three years from today Thou shalt be taken up and received into the everlasting joy of the Lord, where all its inhabitants await Thee, longing for thy presence."

The most holy Mary heard this message with ineffable jubilee of her purest and most loving spirit, and, prostrating Herself again upon the earth, She answered in the same words as at the incarnation of the Word: "Ecce ancilla Domini, fiat mihi secundum verbum tuum." "Behold the handmaid of the Lord, be it done according to thy word" (Luke 1, 38). Then She asked the holy angels and ministers of the Most High to help Her give thanks for this welcome and joyful news. The blessed Mother alternately with the seraphim and other angels, sang the responses of a canticle that lasted for two hours. Although by their nature and supernatural gifts the angelic spirits are so subtle, wise and excellent, they were nevertheless excelled in all this by their Queen and Lady, as vassals are by their sovereign; for in Her, grace and wisdom abounded as in a Teacher, in them, only as in disciples. Having finished this canticle and humiliating Herself anew, She charged the supernal spirits to beseech the Lord to prepare Her for her passage from mortal to eternal life, and to ask all the other angels and saints in heaven to pray for the same favor. They offered to obey Her in all things, and therewith saint Gabriel took leave and returned with all his company to the empyrean heaven.

The great Queen and Lady of all the universe remained alone in her oratory, and amid tears of humble joy prostrated Herself upon the earth, embraced it as the common mother of us all, saying: "Earth, I give thee thanks as I ought, because without my merit thou hast sustained me sixty-seven years. Thou art a creature of the Most High and by his will thou hast sustained me until now. I ask thee now to help me during the rest of my dwelling upon thee, so that, just as I have been created of thee and upon thee, I may through thee and from thee be raised to the blessed vision of my Maker." She addressed also other creatures, saying: "Ye heavens, planets, stars and elements, created by the powerful hands of my Beloved, faithful witnesses and proclaimers of his greatness and beauty, you also I thank for the preservation of my life; help me then from today on, that, with the divine favor, I may begin anew to perfect my life during the time left of my career, in order that I may show myself thankful to my and your Creator."

The devout Queen resolved to take leave of the holy places before her departure into heaven, and having obtained the consent of saint John She left the house with him and with the thousand angels of her guard. Although these sovereign princes had always served and accompanied Her in all her errands, occupations and journeys, without having absented themselves for one moment since the instant of her birth; yet on this occasion they manifested themselves to Her with greater beauty and refulgence, as if they felt special joy in seeing themselves already at the beginning of her last journey into heaven. The heavenly Princess, setting aside human occupations in order to enter upon her journey to the real and true fatherland, visited all the memorable places of our Redemption, marking each with the sweet abundance of her tears, recalling the sorrowful memories of what her Son there suffered, and fervently renewing its effects by most fervent acts of love, clamors and petitions for all the faithful, who should devoutly and reverently visit these holy places during the future ages of the Church. On Calvary She remained a longer time, asking of her divine Son the full effects of his redeeming Death for all the multitudes of souls there snatched from destruction. The ardor of her ineffable charity during this prayer rose to such a pitch, that it would have destroyed her life, if it had not been sustained by divine power.

The Queen asked also the angels of the sanctuaries and the Evangelist to give Her their blessing in this last leave-taking; and therewith She returned to her oratory shedding tears of tenderest affection for what She loved so much upon earth. There She prostrated Herself with her face upon the earth and poured forth another long and most fervent prayer for the Church; and She persevered in it, until in an abstractive vision of the Divinity, the Lord had given Her assurance that He had heard and conceded her petitions at the throne of his mercy. In order to give the last touch of holiness to her works, She asked permission of the Lord to take leave of the holy Church, saying: "Exalted and most high God, Redeemer of the world, head of the saints and the predestined, Justifier and Glorifier of souls, I am a child of the holy Church, planted and acquired by thy blood. Give me, O Lord, permission to take leave of such a loving Mother, and of all my brethren, thy children, belonging to it." She was made aware of the consent of the Lord and therefore turned to the mystical body of the Church, addressing it in sweet tears as follows:

"Holy Catholic Church, which in the coming ages shall be called the Roman, my mother and Mistress, true treasure of my soul, thou hast been the only consolation of my banishment; the refuge and ease of my labors; my recreation, my joy and my hope; thou hast sustained me in my course; in thee have I lived as a pilgrim to the Fatherland; and thou hast nourished me after I had received in thee my existence in grace through thy head, Christ Jesus, my Son and my Lord. In thee are the treasures and the riches of his infinite merits; thou shalt be for his faithful children the secure way to the promised land, and thou shalt safeguard them on their dangerous and difficult pilgrimage. Thou shalt be the mistress of the nations to whom all owe reverence; in thee are the rich and inestimable jewels of the anxieties, labors, affronts, hardships, torments, of the cross and of death, which are all consecrated by those of my Lord, thy Progenitor, thy Master, thy Chief, and are reserved for his more distinguished servants and his dearest friends. Thou hast adorned and enriched me with thy jewels in order that I might enter in the nuptials of the Spouse; thou hast made me wealthy, prosperous and happy, and thou containest within thee thy Author in the most holy Sacrament. My happy Mother, Church militant, rich art thou and abundant in treasures! For thee have I always reserved my heart and my solicitude; but now is the time come to part from thee and leave thy sweet companionship, in order to reach the end of my course. Make me partaker of thy great goods; bathe me copiously in the sacred liquor of the blood of the Lamb, preserved in thee as a powerful means of sanctifying many worlds. At the cost of my life a thousand times would I bring to thee all the nations and tribes of mortals, that they might enjoy thy treasures. My beloved Church, my honor and my glory, I am about to leave thee in mortal life; but in the eternal life I will find thee joyful in an existence which includes all good. From that place I shall look upon thee with love, and pray always for thy increase, thy prosperity and thy progress."

This was the parting of the most blessed Mary from the mystical body of the holy Roman Catholic Church, the mother of the faithful, in order that all who should hear of Her, might know by her sweet tears and endearments, in what veneration, love and esteem She held that holy Church. After thus taking leave, the great Mistress, as the Mother of Wisdom, prepared to make her testament and last Will. When She manifested this most prudent wish to the Lord, He deigned to approve of it by his own royal presence. For this purpose, with myriads of attending angels, the three Persons of the most blessed Trinity descended to the oratory of their Daughter and Spouse, and when the Queen had adored the infinite Being of God, She heard a voice speaking to Her: "Our chosen Spouse, make thy last will as thou desirest, for We shall confirm it and execute it entirely by our infinite power." The most prudent Mother remained for some time lost in the profoundness of her humility, seeking to know first the will of the Most High before She should manifest her own. The Lord responded to her modest desires and the person of the Father said to Her: "My Daughter, thy will shall be pleasing and acceptable to Me; for thou art not wanting in the merits of good works in parting from this mortal life, that I should not satisfy thy desires." The same encouragement was given to Her by the Son and the Holy Ghost. Therewith the most blessed Mary made her will in this form:

"Highest Lord and eternal God, I, a vile wormlet of the earth, confess and adore Thee with all the reverence of my inmost soul as the Father, the Son and the Holy Ghost, three Persons distinct in one undivided and eternal essence, one substance, one in infinite majesty of attributes and perfection. I confess Thee as the one true Creator and Preserver of all that has being. In thy kingly presence I declare and say, that my last will is this: Of the goods of mortal life and of the world in which I live, I possess none that I can leave; for never have I possessed or loved anything beside Thee, who art my good and all my possession. To the heavens, the stars and planets, to the elements and all creatures in them I give thanks, because according to thy will they have sustained me without my merit, and lovingly I desire and ask them to serve and praise Thee in the offices and ministries assigned to them, and that they continue to sustain and benefit my brethren and fellowmen. In order that they may do it so much the better, I renounce and assign to mankind the possession, and as far as possible, the dominion of them, which thy Majesty has given me over these irrational creatures, so that they may now serve and sustain my fellowmen. Two tunics and a cloak, which served to cover me, I leave to John for his disposal, since I hold him as a son. My body I ask the earth to receive again for thy service, since it is the common mother and serves Thee as thy creature; my soul, despoiled of its body and of all visible things, O my God, I resign into thy hands, in order that it may love and magnify Thee through all thy eternities. My merits and all the treasures, which with thy grace through my works and exertions I have acquired, I leave to the holy Church, my mother and my mistress, as my residuary heiress, and with thy permission I there deposit them, wishing them to be much greater. And I desire that before all else they redound to the exaltation of thy holy name and procure the fulfillment of thy will on earth as it is done in heaven, and that all the nations come to the knowledge, love and veneration of Thee, the true God."

"In the second place I offer these merits for my masters the Apostles and priests, of the present and of the future ages, so that in view of them thy ineffable clemency may make them apt ministers, worthy of their office and state, filled with wisdom, virtue and holiness, by which they may edify and sanctify the souls redeemed by thy blood. In the third place I offer them for the spiritual good of my devoted servants, who invoke and call upon me, in order that they may receive thy protection and grace, and afterwards eternal life. In the fourth place I desire that my services and labors may move Thee to mercy toward all the sinning children of Adam, in order that they may withdraw from their sinful state. From this hour on I propose and desire to continue my prayers for them in thy divine presence, as long as the world shall last. This, Lord and my God, is my last will, always subject to thy own." At the conclusion of this testament of the Queen, the most blessed

Trinity approved and confirmed it; and Christ the Redeemer, as if authorizing it all, witnessed it by writing in the heart of his Mother these words: "Let it be done as thou wishest and ordainest."

If all we children of Adam, and especially we who are born in the law of grace, had no other obligation toward the most blessed Mary than this of having been constituted heirs of her immense merits and of all that is mentioned in this short and mysterious testament, we could never repay our debt, even if in return we should offer our lives and endure all the sufferings of the most courageous martyrs and saints.

WORDS OF THE QUEEN.

Among the absurd fallacies introduced by the demon into the world none is greater or more pernicious than the forgetfulness of the hour of death and of what is to happen at the court of the rigorous Judge. Consider, my daughter, that through this portal sin entered into the world; for the serpent sought to convince the first woman principally, that she would not die and need not think of that matter (Gen. 11, 4). Thus continually deceived, there are uncountable fools who live without thought of death and who die forgetful of the unhappy lot that awaits them. In order that thou mayest not be seized by this human perversity, begin to convince thyself now that thou must die irrevocably; that thou hast received much and paid little; that the account shall be so much the more rigorous, as the Judge has been more liberal in the gifts and talents lavished upon thee in thy sphere. I do not ask of thee more, and also not less, than what thou owest to thy Spouse and to thy Lord, which is always to operate the best in all places, times and occasions, without permitting any forgetfulness, intermission or carelessness.

CHAPTER VI.

THE GLORIOUS TRANSITION OF THE VIRGIN MARY.

And now, according to the decree of the divine will, the day was approaching in which the true and living Ark of the covenant was to be placed in the temple of the celestial Jerusalem, with a greater glory and higher jubilee than its prophetic figure was installed by Solomon in the sanctuary beneath the wings of the cherubim (III King 8, 8). Three days before the most happy Transition of the great Lady the Apostles and disciples were gathered in Jerusalem and in the Cenacle. The first one to arrive was saint Peter, who was transported from Rome by the hands of an angel. At that place the angel appeared to him and 'told him that the passing away of the most blessed Mary was imminent and that the Lord commanded him to go to Jerusalem in order to be present at that event. Thereupon the angel took him up and brought him from Italy to the Cenacle. Thither the Queen of the world had retired, somewhat weakened in body by the force of her divine love; for since She was so near to her end, She was subjected more completely to love's effects.

The great Lady came to the entrance of her oratory in order to receive the vicar of Christ our Savior. Kneeling at his feet She asked his blessing and said: "I give thanks and praise to the Almighty, that He has brought to me the holy Father for assisting me in the hour of my death." Then came saint Paul, to whom the Queen showed the same reverence with similar tokens of her pleasure at seeing him. The Apostles saluted Her as the Mother of God, as their Queen and as Mistress of all creation; but with a sorrow equal to their reverence, because they knew that they had come to witness her passing away. After these Apostles came the others and the disciples still living. Three days after, they were all assembled in the Cenacle. The heavenly Mother received them all with profound humility, reverence and love, asking each one to bless Her. All of them complied, and saluted Her with admirable reverence. By orders of the Lady given to saint John, and with the assistance of saint James the less, they were all hospitably entertained and accommodated.

Some of the Apostles who had been transported by the angels and informed by them of the purpose of their coming, were seized with tenderest grief and shed abundant tears at the thought of losing their only protection and consolation. Others were as yet ignorant of their approaching loss, especially the disciples, who had not been positively informed by the angels, but were moved by interior inspirations and a sweet and forcible intimation of God's will to come to Jerusalem. They immediately conferred with saint Peter, desirous of knowing the occasion of their meeting; for all of them were convinced, that if there had been no special occasion, the Lord would not have urged them so strongly to come. The apostle saint Peter, as the head of the Church, called them all together in order to tell them of the cause of their coming, and spoke to the assembly: "My dearest children and brethren, the Lord has called and brought us to Jerusalem from remote regions not without a cause most urgent and sorrowful to us. The Most High wishes now to raise up to the throne of eternal glory his most blessed Mother, our Mistress, our consolation and protection. His divine decree is that we all be present at her most happy and glorious Transition. When our Master and Redeemer ascended to the right hand of his Father, although He left us orphaned of his most delightful presence, we still retained his most blessed Mother and our light now leaves us what shall we do? What help or hope have we to encourage us on our pilgrimage? I find none except the hope that we all shall follow Her in due time."

Saint Peter could speak no farther, because uncontrollable tears and sighs interrupted him. Neither could the rest of the Apostles answer for a long time, during which, amid copious and tenderest tears, they gave vent to the groans of their inmost heart. After some time the vicar of Christ recovered himself and added: "My children, let us seek the presence of our Mother and Lady. Let us spend the time left of her life in her company and ask Her to bless us." They all betook themselves to the oratory of the great Queen and found Her kneeling upon a couch, on which She was wont to recline for a short rest. They saw Her full of beauty and celestial light, surrounded by the thousand angels of her guard.

The natural condition and appearance of her sacred and virginal body were the same as at her thirty-third year; for, as I have already stated, from that age onward it experienced no change. It was not affected by the passing years, showing no signs of age, no wrinkles in her face or body, nor giving signs of weakening or fading, as in other children of Adam, who gradually fall away and drop from the natural perfection of early man or womanhood. This unchangeableness was the privilege of the most blessed Mary alone, as well because it consorted with the stability of her purest soul, as because it was the natural consequence of her immunity from the sin of Adam, the effects of which in this regard touched neither her sacred body nor her purest soul. The Apostles and disciples, and some of the other faithful, occupied her chamber, all of them preserving the utmost order in her presence. Saint Peter and saint John placed themselves at the head of the couch. The great Lady looked upon them all with her accustomed modesty and reverence and spoke to them as follows: "My dearest children, give permission to your servant to speak in your presence and to disclose my humble desires." Saint Peter answered that all listened with attention and would obey Her in all things; and He begged Her to seat Herself upon the couch, while speaking to them. It seemed to saint Peter that She was exhausted from kneeling so long and that She had taken that position in order to pray to the Lord, and that in speaking to them, it was proper She should be seated as their Queen.

But She, who was the Teacher of humility and obedience unto death, practiced both these virtues in that hour. She answered that She would obey in asking of them their blessing, and besought them to afford Her this consolation. With the permission of saint Peter She left the couch and, kneeling before the Apostle, said to him: "My lord, I beseech thee, as the universal pastor and head of the holy Church, to give me thy blessing in thy own and in its name. Pardon me thy handmaid for the smallness of the service I have rendered in my life. Grant that John dispose of my vestments, the two tunics, giving them to the two poor maidens, who have always obliged me by their charity." She then prostrated Herself and kissed the feet of saint Peter as the vicar of Christ, by her abundant tears eliciting not less the admiration than the tears of the Apostle and of all the by-standers. From saint Peter She went to saint John, and kneeling likewise at his feet, said: "Pardon, my son and my master, my not having fulfilled toward thee the duties of a Mother as I ought and as the Lord had commanded me, when from the Cross He appointed thee as my son and me as thy mother (John 19, 27). I humbly and from my heart thank thee for the kindness which thou hast shown me as a son. Give me thy benediction for entering into the vision and company of Him who created me."

The sweetest Mother proceeded in her leave-taking, speaking to each of the Apostles in particular and to some of the disciples; and then to all the assembly together; for there were a great number. She rose to her feet and addressed them all, saying: "Dearest children and my masters, always have I kept you in my soul and written in my heart. I have loved you with that tender love and charity, which was given to me by my divine Son, whom I have seen in you, his chosen friends. In obedience to his holy and eternal will, I now go to the eternal mansions, where I promise you as a Mother I will look upon you by the clearest light of the Divinity, the vision of which my soul hopes and desires in security. I commend unto you my mother, the Church, the exaltation of the name of the Most High, the spread of the evangelical law, the honor and veneration for the words of my divine Son, the memory of his Passion and Death, the practice of his doctrine. My children, love the Church, and love one another with that bond of charity, which your Master has always inculcated upon you (John 13, 34). To thee, Peter, holy Pontiff, I commend my son John and all the rest."

The words of the most blessed Mary, like arrows of a divine fire, penetrated the hearts of all the Apostles and hearers, and as She ceased speaking, all of them were dissolved in streams of tears and, seized with irreparable sorrow, cast themselves upon the ground with sighs and groans sufficient to move to compassion the very earth. All of them wept, and with them wept also the sweetest Mary, who could not resist this bitter and well-founded sorrow of her children. After some time She spoke to them again, and asked them to pray with Her and for Her in silence, which they did. During this quietness the incarnate Word descended from heaven on a throne of ineffable glory, accompanied by all the saints and innumerable angels, and the house of the Cenacle was filled with glory. The most blessed Mary adored the Lord and kissed his feet. Prostrate before Him She made the last and most profound act of faith and humility in her mortal life. On this occasion the most pure Creature, the Queen of the heavens, shrank within Herself and lowered Herself to the earth more profoundly than all men together ever have or ever will humiliate themselves for all their sins. Her divine Son gave Her his blessing and in the presence of the courtiers of heaven spoke to Her these words: "My dearest Mother, whom I have chosen for my dwelling-place, the hour is come in which thou art to pass from the life of this death and of the world into the glory of my Father and mine, where thou shalt possess the throne prepared for thee at my right hand and enjoy it through all eternity. And since, by my power and as my Mother, I have caused thee to enter the world free and exempt from sin, therefore also death shall have no right or permission to touch thee at thy exit from this world. If thou wishest not to pass through it, come with Me now to partake of my glory, which thou hast merited."

The most prudent Mother prostrated Herself at the feet of her Son and with a joyous countenance answered: "My Son and my Lord, I beseech Thee let thy mother and thy servant enter into eternal life by the common portal of natural death, like the other children of Adam. Thou, who art my true God, hast suffered death without being obliged to do so; it is proper that, as I have followed Thee in life, so I follow Thee also in death." Christ the Savior approved of the decision and the sacrifice of his most blessed Mother, and consented to its fulfillment. Then all the angels began to sing in celestial harmony some of the verses of the Canticles of Solomon and other new ones. Although only saint John and some of the Apostles were enlightened as to the presence of Christ the Savior, yet the others felt in their interior its divine and powerful effects; but the music was heard as well by the Apostles and disciples, as by many others of the faithful there present. A divine fragrance also spread about, which penetrated even to the street. The house of the Cenacle was filled with a wonderful effulgence, visible to all, and the Lord ordained that multitudes of the people of Jerusalem gathered in the streets as witnesses to this new miracle.

When the angels began their music, the most blessed Mary reclined back upon her couch or bed. Her tunic was folded about her sacred body, her hands were joined and her eyes fixed upon her divine Son, and She was entirely inflamed with the fire of divine love. And as the angels intoned those verses of the second chapter of the Canticles: "Surge, propera, amica mea," that is to say: "Arise, haste, my beloved, my dove, my beautiful one, and come, the winter has passed," etc., She pronounced those words of her Son on the Cross: "Into thy hands, O Lord, I commend my spirit." Then She closed her virginal eyes and expired. The sickness which took away her life was love, without any other weakness or accidental intervention of whatever kind. She died at the moment when the divine power suspended the assistance, which until then had counteracted the sensible ardors of her burning love of God. As soon as this miraculous assistance was withdrawn, the fire of her love consumed the life-humors of her heart and thus caused the cessation of her earthly existence.

Then this most pure Soul passed from her virginal body to be placed in boundless glory, on the throne at the right hand of her divine Son. Immediately the music of the angels seemed to withdraw to the upper air; for that whole procession of angels and saints accompanied the King and Queen to the empyrean heavens. The sacred body of the most blessed Mary, which had been the temple and sanctuary of God in life, continued to shine with an effulgent light and breathed forth such a wonderful and unheard of fragrance, that all the bystanders were filled with interior and exterior sweetness. The thousand angels of her guard remained to watch over the inestimable treasure of her virginal body. The Apostles and disciples, amid the tears and the joy of the wonders they had seen, were absorbed in admiration for some time, and then sang many hymns and psalms in honor of the most blessed Mary now departed. This glorious Transition of the great Queen took place in the hour in which her divine Son had died, at three o'clock on a Friday, the thirteenth day of August, she being seventy years of age, less the twenty-six days intervening between the thirteenth of August, on which She died, and the eighth of September, the day of her birth. The heavenly Mother had survived the death of Christ the Savior twenty-one years, four months and

nineteen days; and his virginal birth, fifty-five years.
This reckoning can be easily made in the following manner: when Christ our Savior was born, his virginal
Mother was fifteen years, three months and seventeen
days of age. The Lord lived thirty-three years and three
months; so that at the time of his sacred Passion the
most blessed Lady was forty-eight years, six months and
seventeen days old; adding to these another twenty-one
years, four months and nineteen days, we ascertain her
age as seventy years, less twenty-five or twenty-six days.*

Great wonders and prodigies happened at the
precious death of the Queen; for the sun was eclipsed (as
I have mentioned above) and its light was hidden in sorrow for some hours. Many birds of different kinds gathered around the Cenacle, and by their sorrowful clamors
and groans for a while caused the bystanders themselves
to weep. All Jerusalem was in commotion, and many of
the inhabitants collected in astonished crowds, confessing
loudly the power of God and the greatness of his works.
Others were astounded and as if beside themselves. The
Apostles and disciples with others of the faithful broke
forth in tears and sighs. Many sick persons came who
all were cured. The souls in purgatory were released.
But the greatest miracle was that three persons, a man
in Jerusalem and two women living in the immediate
neighborhood of the Cenacle, died in sin and impenitent
in that same hour, subject to eternal damnation; but
when their cause came before the tribunal of Christ, his
sweetest Mother interceded for them and they were
restored to life. They so mended their conduct, that

---

*In figures as follows:

Birth of Christ,	15 years,	3 months, 17 days.
Death of Christ,	33 years,	3 months, .. days.
	48 years,	6 months, 17 days.
Death of Mary,	21 years,	4 months, 19 days.
Age at death,	69 years,	11 months, 5 or 6 days.

afterwards they died in grace and were saved. This privilege was not extended to others that died on that day in the world, but was restricted to those three who happened to die in that hour in Jerusalem. What festivities were celebrated on that occasion in heaven I will describe in another chapter, lest heavenly things be mixed up with the sacred things of earth.

WORDS OF THE QUEEN.

My daughter, besides what thou hast understood and written of my glorious Transition, I wish to inform thee of another privilege, which was conceded to me by my divine Son in that hour. Thou hast already recorded, that the Lord offered me the choice of entering into beatific vision either with or without passing through the portals of death. If I had preferred not to die, the Most High would have conceded this favor, because sin had no part in me, and hence also not its punishment, which is death. Thus it would also have been with my divine Son, and with a greater right, if He had not taken upon Himself the satisfaction of the divine justice for men through his Passion and Death. Hence I chose death freely in order to imitate and follow Him, as also I did during his grievous passion. Since I had seen my Son and true God die, I would not have satisfied the love I owe Him, if I had refused death, and I would have left a great gap in my conformity to and my imitation of my Lord the Godman, whereas He wished me to bear a great likeness to Him in his most sacred humanity. As I would thereafter never be able to make up for such a defect, my soul would not enjoy the plenitude of the delight of having died as did my Lord and God.

Hence my choosing to die was so pleasing to

Him, and my prudent love therein obliged Him to such an extent, that in return He immediately conceded to me a singular favor for the benefit of the children of the Church and conformable to my wishes. It was this, that all those devoted to me, who should call upon me at the hour of death, constituting me as their Advocate in memory of my happy Transition and of my desiring to imitate Him in death, shall be under my special protection in that hour, shall have me as a defense against the demons, as a help and protection, and shall be presented by me before the tribunal of his mercy and there experience my intercession. In consequence the lord gave me a new power and commission and He promised to confer great helps of his grace for a good death and for a purer life on all those who in veneration of this mystery of my precious death, should invoke my aid. Hence I desire thee, my beloved daughter, from this day on to keep in thy inmost heart a devout and loving memory of this mystery, and to bless, praise, and magnify the Omnipotent, because he wrought such sacred miracles for me and for the mortals. By this solicitude thou wilt oblige the Lord and me to come to thy aid in that last hour.

And since death follows upon life and ordinarily corresponds with it, therefore the surest pledge of a good death is a good life; a life in which the heart is freed and detached from earthly love. For this it is, which in that last hour afflicts and oppresses the soul and which is like a heavy chain restraining its liberty and preventing it from rising above the things loved in this world. O my daughter! How greatly do mortals misunderstand this truth, and how far they err from it in their actions! The Lord gives them life in order that they may free themselves from the effects of original sin, so as to be unhampered by them at the hour of their death;

and the ignorant and miserable children of Adam spend all their life in loading upon themselves new burdens and fetters, so that they die captives of their passions and in the tyranny of their hellish foes. I had no share in original sin and none of its effects had any power over my faculties; nevertheless I lived in the greatest constraint, in poverty and detached from earthly things, most perfect and holy; and this holy freedom I did indeed experience at the hour of my death. Consider then, my daughter, and be mindful of this living example; free thy heart more and more each day, so that with advancing years thou mayest find thyself more free, more detached and averted from visible things, and so that when the Spouse shall call thee to his nuptials, thou wilt not need to seek in vain the required freedom and prudence.

CHAPTER VII.

BURIAL AND ASSUMPTION OF THE VIRGIN.

In order that the Apostles, the disciples, and many others of the faithful might not be too deeply oppressed by sorrow, and in order that some of them might not die of grief caused by the passing away of the most blessed Mary, it was necessary that the divine power, by an especial providence, furnish them with consolation and dilate their heart for new influences in their incomparable affliction. For the feeling, that their loss was irretrievable in the present life, could not be repressed; the privation of such a Treasure could never find a recompense; and as the most sweet, loving and amiable intercourse and conversation of their great Queen had ravished the heart of each one, the ceasing of her protection and company left them as it were without the breath of life. But the Lord, who well knew how to estimate the just cause of their sorrow, secretly upheld them by his encouragements and so they set about the fitting burial of the sacred body and whatever the occasion demanded.

Accordingly the holy Apostles, on whom this duty specially devolved, held a conference concerning the burial of the most sacred body of their Queen and Lady. They selected for that purpose a new sepulchre, which had been prepared mysteriously by the providence of her divine Son. As they remembered, that, according to the custom of the Jews at burial, the deified body of their Master had been anointed with precious ointments and spices and wrapped in the sacred burial cloths; they thought not of doing otherwise with the virginal body of his most holy Mother. Accordingly they called the two maidens, who had assisted the Queen during her life and who had been designated as the heiresses of her tunics, and instructed them to anoint the body of the Mother of God with highest reverence and modesty and wrap it in the winding-sheets before it should be placed in the casket. With great reverence and fear the two maidens entered the room, where the body of the blessed Lady lay upon its couch; but the refulgence issuing from it barred and blinded them in such a manner that they could neither see nor touch the body, nor even ascertain in what particular place it rested.

In fear and reverence still greater than on their entrance, the maidens left the room; and in great excitement and wonder they told the Apostles what had happened. They, not without divine inspiration, came to the conclusion, that this sacred Ark of the covenant was not to be touched or handled in the common way. Then saint Peter and saint John entered the oratory and perceived the effulgence, and at the same time they heard the celestial music of the angels, who were singing: "Hail Mary, full of grace, the Lord is with thee." Others responded: "A Virgin before childbirth, in childbirth and after childbirth." From that time on many of the faithful expressed their devotion toward the most blessed Mary in these words of praise; and from them they were handed down to be repeated by us with the approbation of the holy Church. The two holy Apostles, saint Peter and saint John, were for a time lost in admiration at what they saw and heard of their Queen; and in order to decide what to do, they sank on their knees, beseeching the Lord to make it known. Then they heard a voice saying: "Let not the sacred body be either uncovered or touched."

Having thus been informed of the will of God, they brought a bier, and, the effulgence having diminished somewhat, they approached the couch and with their own hands reverently took hold of the tunic at the two ends. Thus, without changing its posture, they raised the sacred and virginal Treasure and placed it on the bier in the same position as it had occupied on the couch. They could easily do this, because they felt no more weight than that of the tunic. On this bier the former effulgence of the body moderated still more, and all of them, by disposition of the Lord and for the consolation of all those present, could now perceive and study the beauty of that virginal countenance and of her hands. As for the rest, the omnipotence of God protected this his heavenly dwelling, so that neither in life nor in death any one should behold any other part except what is common in ordinary conversation, namely, her most inspiring countenance, by which She had been known, and her hands, by which She had labored.

So great was the care and solicitude for his most blessed Mother, that in this particular He used not so much precaution in regard to his own body, as that of the most pure Virgin. In her Immaculate Conception He made Her like to Himself; likewise at her birth, in as far as it did not take place in the common and natural manner of other men. He preserved Her also from impure temptations and thoughts. But, as He was man and the Redeemer of the world through his Passion and Death, He permitted with his own body, what He would not allow with Hers, as that of a woman, and therefore He kept her virginal body entirely concealed; in fact the most pure Lady during her life had Herself asked that no one should be permitted to look upon it in death; which petition He fulfilled. Then the Apostles consulted further about her burial. Their decision becoming known among the multitudes of the faithful in Jerusalem, they brought many candles to be lighted at the bier, and it happened that all the lights burned through that day and the two following days without any of the candles being consumed or wasted in any shape or manner.

In order that this and many other miracles wrought by the power of God on this occasion might become better known to the world, the Lord himself inspired all the inhabitants of Jerusalem to be present at the burial of his most blessed Mother, so that there was scarcely any person in Jerusalem, even of the Jews or the gentiles, who were not attracted by the novelty of this spectacle. The Apostles took upon their shoulders the sacred body and the tabernacle of God and, as priests of the evangelical law, bore the Propitiatory of the divine oracles and blessings in orderly procession from the Cenacle in the city to the valley of Josaphat. This was the visible accompaniment of the dwellers of Jerusalem.

In the midst of this celestial and earthly accompaniment, visible and invisible, the Apostles bore along the sacred body, and on the way happened great miracles, which would take much time to relate. In particular all the sick, of which there were many of the different kinds, were entirely cured. Many of the possessed were freed from the demons; for the evil spirits did not dare to wait until the sacred body came near the persons thus afflicted. Greater still were the miracles of conversions wrought among many Jews and gentiles, for on this occasion were opened up the treasures of divine mercy, so that many souls came to the knowledge of Christ our

Savior and loudly confessed Him as the true God and Redeemer, demanding Baptism. Many days thereafter the Apostles and disciples labored hard in catechizing and baptising those, who on that day had been converted to the holy faith. The Apostles in carrying the sacred body felt wonderful effects of divine light and consolation, in which the disciples shared according to their measure. All the multitudes of the people were seized with astonishment at the fragrance diffused about, the sweet music and the other prodigies. They proclaimed God great and powerful in this Creature and in testimony of their acknowledgment, they struck their breasts in sorrow and compunction.

When the procession came to the holy sepulchre in the valley of Josaphat, the same two Apostles, saint Peter and saint John, who had laid the celestial Treasure from the couch onto the bier, with joyful reverence placed it in the sepulchre and covered it with a linen cloth, the hands of the angels performing more of these last rites than the hands of the Apostles. They closed up the sepulchre with a large stone, according to custom at other burials. The celestial courtiers returned to heaven, while the thousand angels of the Queen continued their watch, guarding the sacred body and keeping up the music as at her burial. The concourse of the people lessened and the holy Apostles and disciples, dissolved in tender tears, returned to the Cenacle. During a whole year the exquisite fragrance exhaled by the body of the Queen was noticeable throughout the Cenacle, and in her oratory, for many years. This sanctuary remained a place of refuge for all those that were burdened with labor and difficulties; all found miraculous assistance, as well in sickness as in hardships and necessities of other kind. After these miracles had continued for some years in Jerusalem, the sins of Jerusalem and of its inhabitants drew upon this city, among other punishments, that of being deprived of this inestimable blessing.

Having again gathered in the Cenacle, the Apostles came to the conclusion that some of them and of the disciples should watch at the sepulchre of their Queen as long as they should hear the celestial music, for all of them were wondering when the end of that miracle should be. Accordingly some of them attended to the affairs of the Church in catechizing and baptizing the new converts; and others immediately returned to the sepulchre, while all of them paid frequent visits to it during the next three days. Saint Peter and saint John, however, were more zealous in their attendance, coming only a few times to the Cenacle and immediately returning to where was laid the treasure of their heart.

If on this account the glory even of the least of the saints is eneffable, what shall we say of the glory of the most blessed Mary, since among the saints She is the most holy and She by Herself is more like to her Son than all the saints together, and since her grace and glory exceed those of all the rest, as those of an empress or sovereign over her vassals? This truth can and should be believed; but in mortal life it cannot be understood, or the least part of it be explained; for the inadequacy and deficiency of our words and expressions rather tend to obscure than to set forth its greatness. Let us in this life apply our labor, not in seeking to comprehend it, but in seeking to merit its manifestation in glory, where we shall experience more or less of this happiness according to our works.

Our Redeemer Jesus entered heaven conducting the purest soul of his Mother at his right hand. She alone of all the mortals deserved exemption from particular judgment; hence for Her there was none; no account was asked or demanded of Her for what She had received; for such was the promise that had been given to Her, when She was exempted from the common guilt and chosen as the Queen privileged above the laws of the children of Adam. For the same reason, instead of being judged with the rest, She shall be seated at the right hand of the Judge to judge with Him all the creatures. If in the first instant of her Conception She was the brightest Aurora, effulgent with the rays of the sun of the Divinity beyond all the brightness of the most exalted seraphim, and if afterwards She was still further illumined by the contact of the hypostatic Word, who derived his humanity from her purest substance, it necessarily follows that She should be his Companion for all eternity, possessing such a likeness to Him, that none greater can be possible between a Godman and a creature. In this light the Redeemer himself presented Her before the throne of the Divinity; and speaking to the eternal Father in the presence of all the blessed, who were ravished at this wonder, the most sacred humanity uttered these words: "Eternal Father, my most beloved Mother, thy beloved Daughter and the cherished Spouse of the Holy Ghost, now comes to take possession of the crown and glory, which We have prepared as a reward for her merit. She is the one who was born as the rose among thorns, untouched, pure and beautiful, worthy of being embraced by Us and of being placed upon a throne to which none of our creatures can ever attain, and to which those conceived in sin cannot aspire. This is our chosen and our only One, distinguished above all else, to whom We communicated our grace and our perfections beyond the measure accorded to other creatures; in whom We have deposited the treasure of our incomprehensible Divinity and its gifts;

who most faithfully preserved and made fruitful the talents, which We gave Her; who never swerved from our will, and who found grace and pleasure in our eyes. My Father, most equitous is the tribunal of our justice and mercy, and in it the services of our friends are repaid in the most superabundant manner. It is right that to my Mother be given the reward of a Mother; and if during her whole life and in all her works She was as like to Me as is possible for a creature to be, let Her also be as like to Me in glory and on the throne of our Majesty, so that where holiness is in essence, there it may also be found in its highest participation."

This decree of the incarnate Word was approved by the Father and the Holy Ghost. The most holy soul of Mary was immediately raised to the right hand of her Son and true God, and placed on the royal throne of the most holy Trinity, which neither men, nor angels nor the seraphim themselves attain, and will not attain for all eternity. This is the most exalted and supereminent privilege of our Queen and Lady, that She is seated on the throne with the three divine Persons and holds her place as Empress, while all the rest are set as servants and ministers to the highest King. To the eminence and majesty of that position, inaccessible to all other creatures, correspond her gifts of glory, comprehension, vision and fruition; because She enjoys, above all and more than all, that infinite Object, which the other blessed enjoy in an endless variety of degrees. She knows, penetrates and understands much deeper the eternal Being and its infinite attributes; She lovingly delights in its mysteries and most hidden secrets, more than all the rest of the blessed.

Just as little can be explained the extra joy, which the blessed experienced on that day in singing the new songs of praise to the Omnipotent and in celebrating the glory of his Daughter, Mother and Spouse; for in Her He had exalted all the works of his right hand. Although to the Lord himself could come no new or essential glory, because He possessed and possesses it immutably infinite through all eternity; yet the exterior manifestations of his pleasure and satisfaction at the fulfillment of his eternal decrees were greater on that day.

On the third day after the most pure soul of Mary had taken possession of this glory never to leave it, the Lord manifested to the saints his divine will, that She should return to the world, resuscitate her sacred body and unite Herself with it, so that She might in body and soul be again raised to the right hand of her divine Son without waiting for the general resurrection of the dead. The appropriateness of this favor, its accordance with the others received by the most blessed Queen and with her supereminent dignity, the saints could not but see; since even to mortals it is so credible, that even if the Church had not certified it, we would judge those impious and foolish, who would dare deny it. But the blessed saw it with greater clearness, together with the determined time and hour as manifested to them in God himself. When the time for this wonder had arrived, Christ our Savior himself descended from heaven bringing with Him at his right hand the soul of his most blessed Mother and accompanied by many legions of the Angels, the Patriarchs and ancient Prophets. They came to the sepulchre in the valley of Josaphat, and all being gathered in sight of the virginal temple, the Lord spoke the following words to the saints.

"My Mother was conceived without stain of sin, in order that from Her virginal substance I might stainlessly clothe Myself in the humanity in which I came to the world and redeemed it from sin. My flesh is her flesh; She co-operated with Me in the works of the Redemption; hence I must raise Her, just as I rose from the dead, and this shall be at the same time and hour. For I wish to make Her like Me in all things." All the ancient saints of the human race then gave thanks for this new favor in songs of praise and glory to the Lord. Those that especially distinguished themselves in their thanksgiving were our first parents Adam and Eve, saint Anne, saint Joachim and saint Joseph, as being the more close partakers in this miracle of his Omnipotence. Then the purest soul of the Queen, at the command of the Lord, entered the virginal body, reanimated it and raised it up, giving it a new life of immortality and glory and communicating to it the four gifts of clearness, impassibility, agility and subtlety, corresponding to those of the soul and overflowing from it into the body.

Endowed with these gifts the most blessed Mary issued from the tomb in body and soul, without raising the stone cover and without disturbing the position of the tunic and the mantle that had enveloped her sacred body. Since it is impossible to describe her beauty and refulgent glory, I will not make the attempt. It is sufficient to say, that just as the heavenly Mother had given to her divine Son in her womb the form of man, pure, unstained and sinless, for the Redemption of the world, so in return the Lord, in this resurrection and new regeneration, gave to Her a glory and beauty similar to his own. In this mysterious and divine interchange each One did what was possible: most holy Mary engendered Christ, assimilating Him as much as possible to Herself, and Christ resuscitated Her, communicating to Her of his glory as far as She was capable as a creature.

Then from the sepulchre was started a most solemn procession, moving with celestial music through the regions of the air and toward the empyrean heaven. This happened in the hour immediately after midnight, in which also the Lord had risen from the grave; and therefore not all of the Apostles were witness of this prodigy, but only some of them, who were present and watching at the sepulchre. The saints and angels entered heaven in the order in which they had started; and in the last place came Christ our Savior and at his right hand the Queen, clothed in the gold of variety (as David says Ps. 44, 10), and so beautiful that She was the admiration of the heavenly court. All of them turned toward Her to look upon Her and bless Her with new jubilee and songs of praise. Thus were heard those mysterious eulogies recorded by Solomon: Come, daughters of Sion, to see your Queen, who is praised by the morning stars and celebrated by the sons of the Most High. Who is She that comes from the desert, like a column of all the aromatic perfumes? Who is She, that rises like the aurora, more beautiful than the moon, elect as the sun, terrible as many serried armies? Who is She that comes up from the desert resting upon her Beloved and spreading forth abundant delights? (Cant. 3, 6-9; 8, 5). Who is She in whom the Deity itself finds so much pleasure and delight above all other creatures and whom He exalts above them all in the heavens! O novelty worthy of the infinite Wisdom! O prodigy of his Omnipotence, which so magnifies and exalts Her!

Amid this glory the most blessed Mary arrived body and soul at the throne of the most blessed Trinity. And the three divine Persons received Her on it with an embrace eternally undissoluble. The eternal Father said to Her: "Ascend higher, my Daughter and my Dove." The incarnate Word spoke: "My Mother, of whom I have received human being and full return of my work in thy perfect imitation, receive now from my hand the reward thou hast merited." The Holy Ghost said: "My most beloved Spouse, enter into the eternal joy, which corresponds to the most faithful love; do Thou now enjoy thy love without solicitude; for past is the winter of suffering for Thou hast arrived at our eternal embraces." There the most blessed Mary was absorbed in the contemplation of the three divine Persons and as it were overwhelmed in the boundless ocean and abyss of the Divinity, while the saints were filled with wonder and new accidental delight. Since, at the occasion of this work of the Omnipotent happened other wonders, I shall speak of them as far as possible in the following chapter.

WORDS OF THE QUEEN.

My daughter, lamentable and inexcusable is the ignorance of men in so knowingly forgetting the eternal glory, which God has prepared for those who dispose themselves to merit it. I wish that thou bitterly bewail and deplore this pernicious forgetfulness; for there is no doubt, that whoever wilfully forgets the eternal glory and happiness is in evident danger of losing it. No one is free from this guilt, not only because men do not apply much labor or effort in seeking and retaining the remembrance of this happiness; but they labor with all their powers in things that make them forget the end for which they were created. Undoubtedly this forgetfulness arises from their entangling themselves in the pride of life, the covetousness of the eyes, and the desires of the flesh (John 2, 16); for employing therein all the forces and faculties of their soul during the whole time of their life, they have no leisure, care or attention for the thoughts of eternal felicity. Let men acknowledge and confess, whether this recollection costs them more labor than to follow their blind passions, seeking after honors, possessions or the transitory pleasures, all of which have an end with this life, and which, after much striving and labor, many men do not, and can never attain.

This is a sorrow beyond all sorrows, and a misfortune without equal and without remedy. Afflict thyself, lament and grieve without consolation over this ruin of so many souls bought by the blood of my divine Son. I assure thee, my dearest, that, if men would not make themselves so unworthy of it, my charity would urge me, in the celestial glory where thou knowest me to be, to send forth a voice through the whole world exclaiming: "Mortal and deceived men, what are you doing? For what purpose are you living? Do you realize what it is to see God face to face, and to participate in his eternal glory and share his company? Of what are you thinking? Who has thus disturbed and fascinated your judgment? What will you seek, if once you have lost this true blessing and happiness, since there is no other? The labor is short, the reward is infinite glory, and the punishment is eternal."

CHAPTER VIII.

THE CORONATION OF THE MOTHER OF GOD.

We call that the throne of the Divinity, from which God manifests Himself to the saints as the principal cause of their glory and as the infinite, eternal God, independent of all things and on whose will all creatures depend, from which He manifests Himself as the Lord, as the King, as the Judge and Master of all that is in existence. This dignity Christ the Redeemer possesses, in as far as He is God, essentially, and as far as He is man, through the hypostatic union, by which He communicates his Godhead to the humanity. Hence in heaven He is the King, the Lord and supreme Judge; and the saints, though their glory exceeds all human calculation, are as servants and inferiors of this inaccessible Majesty. In this the most holy Mary participates in a degree next inferior and in a manner otherwise ineffable and proportionate to a mere creature so closely related to the God-man; and therefore She assists forever at the right hand of her Son as Queen (Ps. 44, 10), Lady and Mistress of all creation, her dominion extending as far as that of her divine Son, although in a different manner.

After placing the most blessed Mary on this exalted and supereminent throne, the Lord declared to the courtiers of heaven all the privileges She should enjoy in virtue of this participation in his majesty. The Person of the eternal Father, as the first principle of all things, speaking to the angels and saints, said to them: "Our Daughter Mary was chosen according to our pleasure from amongst all creatures, the first one to delight Us, and who never fell from the title and position of a true Daughter, such as We had given Her in our divine mind; She has a claim on our dominion, which We shall recognize by crowning Her as the legitimate and peerless Lady and Sovereign." The incarnate Word said: "To my true and natural Mother belong all the creatures which were created and redeemed my Me; and of all things over which I am King, She too shall be the legitimate and supreme Queen." The Holy Ghost said: "Since She is called my beloved and chosen Spouse, She deserves to be crowned as Queen for all eternity."

Having thus spoken the three divine Persons placed upon the head of the most blessed Mary a crown of such new splendor and value, that the like has been seen neither before nor after by any mere creature. At the same time a voice sounded from the throne saying: "My Beloved, chosen among the creatures, our kingdom is Thine; Thou shalt be the Lady and the Sovereign of the seraphim, of all the ministering spirits, the angels and of the entire universe of creatures. Attend, proceed and govern prosperously over them, for in our supreme consistory We give Thee power, majesty and sovereignty. Being filled with grace beyond all the rest, Thou hast humiliated Thyself in thy own estimation to the lowest place; receive now the supreme dignity deserved by Thee and, as a participation in our Divinity, the dominion over all the creatures of our Omnipotence. From thy royal throne to the centre of the earth Thou shalt reign; and by the power We now give Thee Thou shalt subject hell with all its demons and inhabitants. Let all of them fear Thee as the supreme Empress and Mistress of those caverns and dwelling-places of our enemies. In thy hands and at thy pleasure We place the influences and forces of the heavens, the moisture of the clouds, the growths of the earth; and of all of them do Thou distribute according to thy will, and our own will shall be at thy disposal for the execution of thy wishes. Thou shalt be the Empress and Mistress of the militant Church, its Protectress, its Advocate, its Mother and Teacher. Thou shalt be the special Patroness of the Catholic countries; and whenever they, or the faithful, or any of the children of Adam call upon Thee from their heart, serve or oblige Thee, Thou shalt relieve and help them in their labors and necessities. Thou shalt be the Friend, the Defender and the Chieftainess of all the just and of our friends; all of them Thou shalt comfort, console and fill with blessings according to their devotion to Thee. In view of all this We make Thee the Depositary of our riches, the Treasurer of our goods; we place into thy hands the helps and blessings of our grace for distribution; nothing do We wish to be given to the world, which does not pass through thy hands; and nothing do We deny, which Thou wishest to concede to men. Grace shall be diffused in thy lips for obtaining all that Thou wishest and ordainest in heaven and on earth, and everywhere shall angels and men obey Thee; because whatever is ours shall be thine, just as Thou hast always been ours; and Thou shalt reign with Us forever."

In the execution of this decree and privilege conceded to the Mistress of the world, the Almighty commanded all the courtiers of heaven, angels and men, to show Her obedience and recognize Her as their Queen and Lady. There was another mystery concealed in this wonder, namely, it was a recompense for the worship and veneration, which, as is clear from this history, the most blessed Mary, notwithstanding that She was the Mother of God, full of grace and holiness above the angels and saints, had bestowed upon the saints during her mortal pilgrimage. Although during the time when they were comprehensors and She yet a pilgrim, it was for her greater merit, that She should humble Herself beneath them all according to the ordainment of the Lord; yet now, when She was in possession of the kingdom, it was just, that She should be venerated, worshipped and extolled by them as her inferiors and vassals. This they also did in that most blessed state, in which all things are reduced to their proper proportion and order. Both the angelic spirits and the blessed souls, while rendering their adoration to the Lord with fear and worshipful reverence, rendered a like homage in its proportion to his most blessed Mother; and the saints who were there in their bodies prostrated themselves and gave bodily signs of their worship. All these demonstrations at the coronation of the Empress of heaven redounded wonderfully to her glory, to the new joy and jubilee of the saints and to the pleasure of the most blessed Trinity. Altogether festive was this day, and it produced new accidental glory in all the heavens. Those that partook more especially therein were her most fortunate spouse saint Joseph, saint Joachim and Anne and all the other relatives of the Queen, together with the thousand angels of her guard.

Within the glorious body of the Queen, over her heart, was visible to the saints a small globe or monstrance of singular beauty and splendor, which particularly roused and rouses their admiration and joy. It was there in testimony and reward of her having afforded to the sacramental Word an acceptable resting-place and sanctuary, and of her having received holy Communion so worthily, purely and holily, without any defect or imperfection, and with a devotion, love and reverence attained by none other of the saints. In regard to the other rewards and crowns corresponding to her peerless works and virtues, nothing that can be said could give any idea; and therefore I refer it to the beatific vision, where each one shall perceive them in proportion as his doings and his devotion shall have merited.

WORDS OF THE QUEEN.

My daughter, if anything could lessen the enjoyment of the highest felicity and glory which I possess, and if, in it, I could be capable of any sorrow, without a doubt I would be grieved to see the holy Church and the rest of the world in its present state of labor, notwithstanding that men know me to be their Mother, Advocate and Protectress in heaven, ready to guide and assist them to eternal life. In this state of affairs, when the Almighty has granted me so many privileges as his Mother and when there are so many sources of help placed in my hands solely for the benefit of mortals and belonging to me as the Mother of clemency, it is a great cause of sorrow to me to see mortals force me to remain idle, and that, for want of calling upon me, so many souls should be lost. But if I cannot experience grief now, I may justly complain of men, that they load themselves with eternal damnation and refuse me the glory of saving their souls.

How much my intercession and the power I have in heaven is worth has never been hidden in the Church, for I have demonstrated my ability to save all by so many thousands of miracles, prodigies and favors operated in behalf of those devoted to me. With those who have called upon me in their needs I have always shown myself liberal, and the Lord has shown himself liberal to them on my account. The Most High still wishes to give liberally of his infinite treasures and resolves to favor those who know how to gain my intercession before God. This is the secure way and the powerful means of advancing the Church, of improving the Catholic reigns, of spreading the faith, of furthering the welfare of families and of states, of bringing the souls to grace and to the friendship of God.

THE END.

OTHER TITLES AVAILABLE

Available wherever Catholic books are sold.

NOTES

NOTES